D0907053

MATTHEW 1-7

NCMC
BS
2575.3
.L8913
1992
v.1

ULRICH LUZ

MATTHEW 1–7

A Continental Commentary

Translated by
Wilhelm C. Linss

FORTRESS PRESS
MINNEAPOLIS

MATTHEW 1-7
A Continental Commentary

Original German edition published 1985 under the title *Das Evangelium nach Matthäus*, 1. Teilband, *Mt 1-7* in the Evangelisch-Katholischer Kommentar zum Neuen Testament series. Copyright © 1985 Benziger Verlag, Zurich, Einsiedeln, Cologne, and Neukirchener Verlag des Erziehungsvereins GmbH, Neukirchen-Vluyn.

English translation, including subsequent emendations by the author, © 1989 Augsburg Fortress, Minneapolis.

All rights reserved. Except for brief quotations in critical articles or reviews, no part of this book may be reproduced in any manner without prior permission from the publisher. Write to: Permissions, Augsburg Fortress, 426 S. Fifth St., Box 1209, Minneapolis, MN 55440.

Library of Congress Cataloging-in-Publication Data

Luz, Ulrich.
    [Evangelium nach Matthäus. English]
    Matthew : a continental commentary / translated by Wilhelm C.
Linss.—1st Fortress Press ed.
      p. cm.
    Originally published: Minneapolis : Augsburg, c1989.
    Includes bibliographical references and index.
    Contents: [1] 1-7
    ISBN 0-8006-9600-X (v. 1 : alk. paper)
    1. Bible N.T. Matthew—Commentaries. I. Title.
BS2575.3.L8913   1992
226.2'07—dc20
                                       92-23792
                                          CIP

The paper used in this publication meets the minimum requirements of American National Standard for Information Sciences—Permanence of Paper for Printed Library Materials, ANSI Z329.48-1984.

Manufactured in the U.S.A.   AF 1-9600

3   4   5   6   7   8   9

MATTHEW 1-7

To Salome

Contents

Preface

With relief and gratitude, I submit the first volume on "Matthew." A sympathetic colleague of another discipline once suggested that it probably is *the* penitential act par excellence today to write a voluminous commentary on a New Testament book. He was thinking of the flood of secondary literature which proves to be more a hindrance to scholarly communication and especially an obstacle to access to the text itself. I did not find it so. My own basic, recurring experience was that the text proved itself supportive and so fascinating that it kept me engaged without effort. On the contrary, the commentary is probably that genre of literature where it appears immediately that we exegetes owe everything we are to our texts and are obliged to serve them faithfully. Because of this, I am grateful I could write a commentary.

Its length poses a problem. It is not directly a result of the immensely swollen secondary literature but rather of the concept which stands behind this commentary: First, I am convinced that a commentary which not only explains biblical texts but aids in their understanding must not remain simply in the past but must draw lines into the present. Second, I am convinced that the history of the interpretation of a book can contribute greatly to this understanding. Second only to the text, I probably owe most to the church fathers and the Protestant and Catholic exegesis of the 16th to 18th centuries. Their exegesis is in a magnificent way an occupation not only with the words but with the subject matter of the texts. Third, behind this commentary stands the conviction (or the hope!) that an intensive interaction with the subject matter of their texts is a labor which will stimulate clergypersons and prevent them from premature burnout. I know too well that such labor on the part of the pastor with biblical texts is today rather the exception than the rule. It has fallen victim less to scholarly work in other areas than to the hectic life of the pastorate, and I believe that this has taken place to the detriment of our church. I have written this commentary particularly for priests, pastors, and teachers of religion. Will it help them to attain an intensive interchange with the text, or will it, because of its length, actually deter them from such a desired result? To learn something about this is more important to me than all the critical reviews.

There remains the pleasant duty of gratitude. Such a book cannot be accomplished without help. In the course of the years, Peter Lampe, Reinhard Gorski, Andreas Karrer, Ernst Lüthi, Christian Inäbnit, Andreas Dettwiler, but especially Wolf Dietrich Köhler and Andreas Ennulat have assisted as student coworkers with the history of interpretation. I owe thanks to the Land of Niedersachsen and to the Canton Berne for providing assistants, to the Swiss National Foundation for a temporary position of a half assistantship. Numerous colleagues, especially church historians in whose field I walked around as an amateur, have helped me willingly; as representative of this assistance I will mention only one in whose study I was enabled to glean so much, the late Old Master Hermann Dörries. Joachim Gnilka, Eduard Schweizer, and Hans Weder have read the manuscript and helped with critical questions. Numerous students in lectures, seminars, and seminar papers contributed to "Matthew." I wonder what this meant to them? "Matthew is groovy" was found once on a Göttingen poster. Ms. Karin Janecke and Ms. Beata Gerber have typed the manuscript. Publisher and printer had no little pain with the manuscript which was marred by only moderately successful attempts at shortening the manuscript. Thanks be to them all. The one to whom I owe the most gratitude, because she had to suffer the most when this commentary "devoured" me, is named in the dedication.

Ulrich Luz

Translator's Preface

This commentary on Matthew 1–7 is significant for various reasons. It was published in German in the series Evangelisch-Katholischer Kommentar zum Neuen Testament and thus contributes to the ecumenical rapprochement of these branches of the Christian church. Moreover, it breaks new ground in the interpretation of many passages. Not least, it includes references to the history of interpretation and the history of influence of each passage. The commentary is primarily intended for the practical work of the priest, pastor, and teacher and can furnish not only useful information but also hints for the use of these materials in preaching and teaching. It can serve as a bridge from the study of the scholar to the hearer of sermons and lessons.

The text of the Gospel of Matthew is translated from Luz's German translation in order to facilitate Luz's understanding of the text. Other biblical passages are cited from the Revised Standard Version of the Bible, copyright 1946, 1952, 1971, and 1973, by the Division of Christian Education of the National Council of the Churches of Christ in the U.S.A.

The sections labeled *Wirkungsgeschichte,* which I have translated "history of influence," are one of the main contributions of the commentary. According to Luz's own statement, the history of influence is the "history, reception, and actualizing of a text in media other than the commentary, e.g., in sermons, canonical law, hymnody, art, and in the actions and suffering of the church" (introduction, §6).

For this English-language edition I was able to incorporate several minor corrections which Professor Luz communicated to me. The index is planned for the third volume of this commentary, following the pattern of the German edition. Since the commentary is arranged according to the order of the Gospel itself, the reader will be able to locate most materials without much difficulty.

I wish to express my gratitude to the Lutheran School of Theology at Chicago for granting me a sabbatical leave so that the translation could proceed expeditiously, to the Aid Association for Lutherans for a grant for research assistance, to Mr. David Housholder for his assistance in tracking down often obscure references, to the Jesuit-Krauss-McCormick Library for its kind cooperation in making available references and research facilities, to the publishers, Augsburg Fortress, and especially the editor, Dr. Marshall D. Johnson, for his painstaking attention to the immense details involved in producing this volume, and to my family for their support during the many hours needed for this project.

I join Professor Luz in the hope that the commentary may assist a wide range of readers "to attain an intensive interchange with the text."

WILHELM C. LINSS

11

Abbreviations

Abbreviations of ancient Christian, Greek, Roman, and Jewish writings for the most part follow the style of the Society of Biblical Literature (*JBL* 107 [1988] 588-596) or of *TDNT*, 1:xvi-xl. Other abbreviations may be identified by consulting Siegfried Schwertner, *Internationales Abkürzungsverzeichnis für Theologie und Grenzgebiete* (Berlin and New York: Walter de Gruyter, 1974).

AASF	Annales academiae scientiarum Fennicae
AB	Anchor Bible
ABR	Australian Biblical Review
AbrN	*Abr-nahrain.* Leiden
AGJU	Arbeiten zur Geschichte des antiken Judentums und des Urchristentums
AGK	Arbeiten zur Geschichte des Kirchenkampfes
AnBib	Analecta Biblica
ANRW	*Aufstieg und Niedergang der römischen Welt*
AOT	*Altorientalische Texte zum Alten Testament*
ASNU	Acta seminarii neotestamentici Upsaliensis
ASTI	*Annual of the Swedish Theological Institute* (in Jerusalem)
ATLA	American Theological Library Association
AzTh	Arbeiten zur Theologie
b.	Babylonian Talmud
BAC	Biblioteca de autores christianos
BAGD	W. Bauer, W. Arndt, F. W. Gingrich, and Frederick W. Danker, *A Greek-English Lexicon of the New Testament* (1979)
BBB	Bonner biblische Beiträge
BbETh	Beiträge zur biblischen Exegese und Theologie (Frankfurt)
BDF	F. Blass, A. Debrunner, and R. W. Funk, *A Greek Grammar of the NT*
BensH	Bensheimer Hefte
BETL	Bibliotheca ephemeridum theologicarum lovaniensium
BEvTh	Beiträge zur evangelischen Theologie
BFCT	Beiträge zur Förderung christlicher Theologie
BGBE	Beiträge zur Geschichte der biblischen Exegese
BGLRK	Beiträge zur Geschichte und Lehre der reformierten Kirche
BHT	Beiträge zur historischen Theologie
Bib	*Biblica*
BibLeb	*Bibel und Leben*

BibS(F)	Biblische Studien (Freiburg, 1895—)
BJRL	*Bulletin of the John Rylands Library*
BK	Biblischer Kommentar
BKon	Biblische Konfrontationen (Stuttgart)
BKV	Bibliothek der Kirchenväter
BSac	*Bibliotheca Sacra*
BSKORK	Bekenntnisschriften und Kirchenordnungen der nach Gottes Wort reformierten Kirche
BSRK	*Bekenntnisschriften der reformierten Kirche*
BT	*The Bible Translator*
BTB	*Biblical Theology Bulletin*
BTS	Bible et terre sainte
BVC	*Bible et vie chrétienne*
BZ NF	Biblische Zeitschrift, neue Folge
BZNW	Beiheft zur *ZNW*

CBG	Collationes Brugenses et Gandavenses
CB.NT	Coniectanea biblica, New Testament series (Lund)
CBQ	*Catholic Biblical Quarterly*
CD	Karl Barth, *Church Dogmatics*
CIC	Codex Iuris Canonici (Washington, D.C.: Canon Law Society of America, 1983)
CNT	*Coniectanea neotestamentica*
CSEL	Corpus scriptorum ecclesiastociroum latinorum

DACL	*Dictionaire d'archéologie chrétienne et de liturgie*
Ditt. Syll.	W. Dittenberger, *Sylloge Inscriptionum Graecarum*, 4th ed.

EBib	Études bibliques
EHS	Einleitung in die Heilige Schrift
EHS.T	Europäische Hochschulschriften, Theologie
EK	Evangelische Kommentare
EKK	Evangelisch-katholischer Kommentar zum Neuen Testament
EstBib	*Estudios biblicos*
ÉtFr	*Études franciscaines*
ETL	*Ephemerides theologicae lovanienses*
EvT	*Evangelische Theologie*
EWNT	*Exegetisches Wörterbuch zum Neuen Testament* (Stuttgart, 1980–1983)

FBESG	Forschungen und Berichte der Evangelischen Studiengemein-schaft
FGLP	Forschungen zur Geschichte und Lehre des Protestantismus
FRLANT	Forschungen zur Religion und Literatur des Alten und Neuen Testaments
FsB	Franziskanische Studien, Beiheft

FS	Festschrift
GCS	Griechischen christlichen Schriftsteller der ersten drei Jahrhunderte
GPM	Göttinger Predigtmeditationen
HKNT	Handkommentar zum Neuen Testament
HM	Hallische Monographien
HNT	Handbuch zum Neuen Testament
HTKNT	Herders theologischer Kommentar zum Neuen Testament
HTR	*Harvard Theological Review*
IBSt	*Irish Biblical Studies*
JBL	*Journal of Biblical Literature*
JeC	Judaica et Christiana (Bern)
JR	*Journal of Religion*
JSNT	*Journal for the Study of the New Testament*
JTS	*Journal of Theological Studies*
Jus Ecc	Jus ecclesiasticum
KBANT	Kommentare und Beiträge zum Alten und Neuen Testament
KD	*Kerygma und Dogma*
KEK	Kritisch-exegetischer Kommentar über das Neue Testament (Meyer)
KlT	Kleine Texte für (theologische und philologische) Vorlesungen und Übungen
KP	Kleine Pauly
KThQ	Kirchen- und Theologiegeschichte in Quellen, I-IV/2 (Neukirchen, 1977–1981)
KVR	Kleine Vandenhoeck-Reihe
KW	Kirchen der Welt
LBW	*Lutheran Book of Worship*
LD	Lectio divina
LSJ	Lidell, Scott, and Jones, *Greek-English Lexicon*
LuJ	*Luther-Jahrbuch*
LW	*Luther's Works,* American edition
LXX	The Septuagint
Mar.	*Marianum*
MD	Maison-Dieu
MNTC	Moffatt New Testament Commentary
MPARA	Memorie della pontificia accademia romana di archeologia
MSS	Manuscripts

MTZ   *Münchener theologische Zeitschrift*

NCB   New Century Bible
NedTTS   *Nederlands(ch)e theologisch tijdschrift*
Neot   *Neotestamentica* (Pretoria)
NHL   *Nag Hammadi Library in English*, ed. J. Robinson
NorTT   *Norsk teologisk tidsskrift*
NovT   *Novum Testamentum*
NTA   Neutestamentliche Abhandlungen
NTD   Das Neue Testament Deutsch
NTS   *New Testament Studies*
NT.S   Novum Testamentum Supplements

OBO   Orbis biblicus et orientalis
OrChr   *Oriens Christianus*

p.   Palestinian Talmud
PCB   *Peake's Commentary on the Bible*, ed. Black and Rowley
PG   *Patrologia graeca*, J. Migne
PL   *Patrologia latina*, J. Migne

Q   Non-Markan material common to Matthew and Luke
QGT   *Quellen der Geschichte der Täufer*

RAC   *Reallexikon für Antike und Christentum*
RB   *Revue biblique*
RCB   *Revista de cultura bíblica*
RECA   *Real-Encyclopädie der classischen Alterthumswissenschaft*
Red.   Redactional
Ref.   *Reformatio*
RevQ   *Revue de Qumran*
RGG   *Religion im Geschichte und Gegenwart*
RHPR   *Revue d'histoire et de philosophie religieuses*
RSPT   *Revue des sciences philosophiques et théologiques*
RSR   *Recherches de science religieuse*
RVV   Religionsgeschichtliche Versuche und Vorarbeiten

SANT   Studien zum Alten und Neuen Testament
SBFLA   *Studii biblici franciscani liber annuus*
SBLDS   Society of Biblical Literature Dissertation Series
SBS   Suttgarter Bibelstudien
ScEs   *Science et esprit*
SE   *Studia Evangelica I, II, III* (= ´TU 73, 87, 88, etc.)
Semeia.S   Semeia Supplements
SGV   Sammlung gemeinverständlicher Vorträge und Schriften

SHCT	Studies in the History of Christian Thought
SIJB	*Schriften des Instituts Judaicum in Berlin*
SJ	Studia Judaica
SJT	*Scottish Journal of Theology*
SMGH	Schriften der Monumenta Germaniae historica
SNT	Schriften des Neuen Testaments
SNTSMS	Society for New Testament Studies Monograph Series
SNTU A	Studien zum Neuen Testament und seiner Umwelt, Reihe A (Linz)
SNTU B	Studien zum Neuen Testament und seiner Umwelt, Reihe B (Linz)
SO	*Symbolae Osloenses*
SPAW	Sitzungsberichte der preussischen Akademie der Wissenschaften
SPB	Studia patristica et Byzantina
SR	*Studies in Religion/Sciences religieuses*
Stö.T	Sammlung Töpelmann—Theologie im Abriss
StPatr	Studia patristica
Str-B	H. Strack and P. Billerbeck, *Kommentar zum Neuen Testament aus Talmud und Midrasch*
SUNT	Studien zur Umwelt des Neuen Testaments

t.	Tosephta
TB	Theologische Bücherei
TBl	*Theologische Blätter*
TDNT	*Theological Dictionary of the New Testament*, ed. Kittel
TEH	Theologische Existenz heute
TeTR	Texts and Translations (Scholars Press)
Tg or Targ	Targum or Targums
THAT	*Theologisches Handwörterbuch zum Alten Testament*
ThH	*Théologie historique*
ThV	*Theologische Versuche* (Berlin, GDR)
TM.FEST	Texte und Materialien der Forschungsstätte der Evangelischen Studiengemeinschaft (Heidelberg)
TP	*Theologie und Philosophie*
TQ	*Theologische Quartalschrift*
TRE	*Theologische Realenzyklopädie*
TRu	*Theologische Rundschau*
TS	*Theological Studies*
TSK	*Theologische Studien und Kritiken*
TTZ	*Trierer theologische Zeitschrift*
TU	Texte und Untersuchungen
TynBul	*Tyndale Bulletin*
TZ	*Theologische Zeitschrift*

UNT	Untersuchungen zum Neuen Testament

VC	*Vigilae christianae*

VD	*Verbum Domini*
VetChr	*Vetera Christianorum*
VT.S	Vetus Testamentum Supplements
WA	Weimar edition, Luther's works
WJ	*Wichmann-Jahrbuch für Kirchengeschichte im Bistum Berlin*
WuD	*Wort und Dienst*
WUNT	Wissenschaftliche Untersuchungen zum Neuen Testament
ZDPV	*Zeitschrift des deutschen Palästina-Vereins*
ZEE	*Zeitschrift für evangelische Ethik*
ZKT	*Zeitschrift für katholische Theologie*
ZNW	*Zeitschrift für die neutestamentliche Wissenschaft*
ZTK	*Zeitschrift für Theologie und Kirche*

Bibliography

Method of citation of literature in the notes (examples)

Collins 27—p. 27 of Collins's commentary on Matthew listed in the bibliography.
Collins, *Religion* 27—p. 27 of a writing by Collins listed in the bibliography, the writing identified by abbreviation of the title.
Collins* 27—p. 27 of a writing by Collins listed in literature at the beginning of the section in which the note occurs.
Collins**(*) 27—p. 27 of a writing by Collins that is mentioned in a different place in the commentary; the page on which publication data may be found is mentioned at the end of literature that is found at the beginning of the section in which the note occurs.

1. Commentaries prior to 1800

Albertus Magnus (ca. 1200–1280). *In Evangelium secundum Matthaeum luculenta expositio.* In *Opera Omnia,* ed. A. Borgnet, volumes 20-21. Paris: Ludoricum Vives, 1893–1894.
Anselm of Laon (Pseudo Anselm = Gottfried Babion, d. 1135?). *Enarationes in Matthaeum. PL* 162. Paris: Garnieri Fratres, 1844–1891.
Apollinaris of Laodicea, see Reuss.
Aretius (Marti), B. (ca. 1522–1574). *Commentarii in Domini nostri Jesu Christi Novum Testamentum.* Paris: Ioannem le Preux, 1607.
Augustine of Hippo (354–430). *De Consensu Evangelistarum libri 4.* CSEL 43. Vindobonae: F. Tempsky, 1904. English trans.: *The Harmony of the Gospels,* in *Nicene and Post-Nicene Fathers,* ed. P. Schaff, vol. 6, pp. 65-236. Grand Rapids: Eerdmans, 1956.

Bede, the Venerable (Pseudo Bede, prior to 820). *In Matthaei Evangelium exposito. PL* 92, pp. 9–132.
Bengel, J. A. (1687–1752). *Gnonom Novi Testamenti* (1742). English trans.: *Gnomon of the New Testament.* Edinburgh: T. & T. Clark, 1877.
Beza, Theodore de (1519–1605). *Jesu Christi Novum Testamentum.* Geneva: Stephanus, 1582.
Bousset, J. B. (1627–1704). *Méditations sur l'Évangile.* 2 volumes. Paris: Garnier Frères, 1922.
Brenz, J. (1499–1570). *In scriptum . . . Matthaei de rebus gestis . . . Jesu Christi commentarius.* Tübingen, 1566.
Bruno of Segni (ca. 1049–1123). *Commentaria in Matthaeum. PL* 165, pp. 63-314. Paris: Garnier Fratres, 1844–1891.
Bucer, M. (1491–1551). *Enarrationes perpetuae in Sacra quatuor Evangelia.* Argentoriati: I. Heruagium, 1530.
Bullinger, H. (1504–1575). *In Sacrosanctum . . . Evangelium secundum Matthaeum*

Commentariorum libri XII. Zurich: Froschoverum, 1554.

Cajetan, Thomas de Vio (1468–1534). *Commentarii in Evangelia* (folio). Venezia, 1530.

Calixtus, G. (1586–1656). *Quatuor Evangelicorum Scriptorum Concordia . . .* Helmstedt: Mullerus, 1663.

Calovius, A. (1612–1686). *Biblia Novi Testamenti illustrata,* vol. 1. Dresden-Leipzig: Zimmermann, 1719.

Calvin, J. (1509–1564). *A Harmony of the Gospels: Matthew, Mark, and Luke.* 3 volumes. Grand Rapids: Eerdmans, 1972.

Christian of Stavelot (= Christianus Druthmarus, d. 880). *Expositio in Matthaeum Evangelistam. PL* 106, pp. 1261-1504.

Chemnitz, M. (1522–1586). *Harmonia Chemnitio-Lysero-Gerhardina.* Volume 1, 2d edition. Hamburg: Hertel & Libernickel, 1704.

Chromatius of Aquileia (ca. 400). *Tractatus XVII in Evangelium S. Matthei. PL* 20, pp. 327-368.

Chrysologus. See Petrus Chrysologus.

Chrysostom, John (ca. 354–407). *Commentarius in sanctum Matthaeum Evangelistam. PG* 57–58. English trans.: *Homilies on the Gospel of Saint Matthew,* in *Nicene and Post-Nicene Fathers,* volume 10.

Cocceius, J. (1603–1669). *Commentarius sive notae breves in Matthei Evangelium.* In *Opera IV,* pp. 1–43. Frankfurt am Main, 1702.

Cramer, J. A., editor. *Catenae Graecorum Patrum in Novum Testamentum,* vol. 1: *Catenae in Ev. S. Matthei et S. Marci,* 1840. Reprinted, Hildesheim: G. Olms, 1967.

Crell, Johann (Crellius, 1590–1636). *Commentarii in Evangelium Matthei & Epistulam Pauli ad Romanos.* In *Opera Omnia.* Eleutheoplii: Philaletheii, 1656.

Cyril of Alexandria (d. 444). *Commentariorum in Matthaeum quae supersunt.* PG 72, pp. 365-474. (See also Reuss, J.)

Dickson, D. (1583–1663). *A Brief Exposition of the Evangel of Jesus Christ according to Matthew,* 1647. Reprinted: Edinburgh: Banner of Truth Trust, 1981.

Dionysius bar Salibi (d. 1171). *Commentarii in Evangelia,* ed. I. Sedlacek and A. Vaschalde. 3 vols. Louvain: L. Durbecq, 1953.

Dionysius the Carthusian (Denys van Leeuwen, d. 1471). *In quatuor Evangelistas enarrationes.* In *Opera,* vols. 1–14. Paris: Poncetum le Preux, 1552.

Ephraem Syrus (306–377). *Commentaire de l'Évangile Concordant ou Diatessaron.* SC 121. Translated into French by L. Leloir. Paris: Editions du Cerf, 1966.

Episcopius, Simon (1583–1643). *Notae breves in Matthaeum.* Amsterdam, 1665.

Erasmus of Rotterdam, D. (1469–1536). *Novum Testamentum, cui . . . subjectae sunt . . . Adnotationes.* In *Opera Omnia* VI. Abdruck Hildesheim, 1962, pp. 1–148 (cited: Erasmus, *Adnotationes).*

———. *In Evangelium Matthaei Paraphrasis.* In *Opera Omnia* VII, pp. 1–146.

Euthymius Zigabenus (12th century). *Commentarius in quatuor Evangelia. PG* 129, pp. 107–766.

Faber Stapulensis (Le Fèvre, Jacques [d'Étaples]) (ca. 1455–1536). *Commentarii initiatorii in quatuor Evangelia.* Basel, 1523.

Glossa Ordinaria. See Strabo.

Gregory the Great (d. 604). *Homiliarum in Evangelia libri 2. PL* 76, pp. 1075–1314.

Griesbach, J. J. (1745–1812). *Commentarius Criticus in textum Graecum Novi Testamenti.* Jena, 1792.

Grotius, H. (1583–1645). *Annotationes in Novum Testamentum.* Groningen: Zuidema, vol. 1: 1826, vol. 2: 1827.

Hieronymus. See Jerome.

Hilarius of Poitiers (ca. 315–367). *In Evangelium Matthaei Commentarius* PL 9, 917–1078. Translated into French by Jean Doignon, SC 254, 258. Paris: Editions du Cerf, 1978–1979.

Hugo of Saint Viktor (+ 1141). *Allegoriae in Novum Testamentum liber II: In Matthaeum.* PL 175, pp. 763–802.

Hunnius, Aegidius (1550–1603). *Commentarius in Evangelium S. Matthaei Apostoli & Evangelistae,* in *Operum Latinorum tomus tertius,* pp. 1–616. Wittenberg, 1608.

Isho'dad of Merv (d. 805). *The Commentaries.* Horae Semiticae 5. Edited by M. D. Gibson. Cambridge: At the University Press, 1911–1916.

Jansen, C. (1585–1638). *Tetrateuchus sive Commentarius in sancta Jesu Christi Evangelia.* Lugduni: Benedictum Bailly, 1676, and Bruxelles, 1737.

Jerome (ca. 340–420). *Commentariorum in Matthaeum libri IV,* 1959. CChr. SL 77.

Lapide (= van den Steen), Cornelius à (d. 1687). *Commentarius in quatuor Evangelia. Argumentum in S. Matthaeum.* Antwerp: Meurstum, 1660.

Lightfoot, J. (1602–1675). *A Commentary on the New Testament from the Talmud and Hebraica (= Horae Hebraicae et Talmudicae,* 1658–1674). Reprint, Grand Rapids, Mich.: Baker, 1979.

Luther, M. (1483–1546). *D. Martin Luthers Evangelien-Auslegung.* Edited by E. Mülhaupt. 5 volumes. Göttingen: Vandenhoeck & Ruprecht, 1964–1973.

Maldonado, J. (1533–1583). *Commentarii in quatuor Evangelistas.* Ed. J. Raich, vol. 1, pp. 1–679. Moguntiae/Kirchheim, 1874.

Melanchthon, P. (1497–1560). *Annotationes in Evangelium Matthaei iam recens in gratiam studiosorum editae.* (1523). In *Werke IV,* pp. 133–208. Edited by R. Stupperich. Gütersloh: Bertelsmann, 1963.

Musculus, W. (1497–1563). *In Evangelistam Matthaeum commentarii . . .* Basel: Heruagius, 1544.

Nicholas of Lyra (ca. 1270–1349). *Postilla super Novum Testamentum,* ca. 1480.

Opus Imperfectum (= Pseudo-Chrysostomus, 6th century, Arian). *Diatriba ad opus Imperfectum in Matthaeum.* PL 56, pp. 601–946. Paris: Garnieri Fratres, 1844–1891.

Origen (185–254). *Matthäuserklärung.* In *Die Griechischen Christlichen Schriftsteller der ersten Jahrhunderte.* 3 volumes. Leipzig: J. C. Heinrichs, 1935–1941. English trans.: *Commentary on the Gospel of Matthew,* in *The Ante-Nicene Fathers,* ed. Allan Menzies. Volume 10, pp. 411–512. Grand Rapids: Eerdmans, 1951.

Paschasius Radbertus (ca. 790–859). *Expositio in Evangelium Matthaei, PL* 120, pp. 31–994.

Petrus Chrysologus (ca. 380–450). *Sermones.* PL 52, pp. 183-680. Paris: Garnieri Fratres, 1844–1891. Quoted according to *Ausgewählte Predigten,* trans. G. Böhmer, part of series: Bibliothek der Kirchenväter, vol. 43, pp. 15–140. Munich: Kösee & Pustet, 1923.

Petrus of Laodicea (7th century). *Erklärung des Matthausevangeliums.* In Beiträge zur Geschichte und Erklärung des Neuen Testaments V. Leipzig, 1908.

Philoxenus (d. 523). *The Matthew-Luke Commentary of Philoxenos.* Edited by D. F. Fox. SBLDS 43. Missoula, Mont.: Scholars Press, 1979.

Photius of Constantiople. See Reuss.

Rabanus Maurus (780–856). *Commentariorum in Matthaeum libri VIII.* PL 107, pp.

727–1156. Paris: Garnieri Fratres, 1844–1891.
Reuss, J. *Matthäus-Kommentare aus der griechischen Kirche.* TU 61. Includes: Apollinaris of Laodicea (d. ca. 390), Theodore of Heraclea (d. ca. 355), Theodore of Mopsuestia (ca. 350–428), Theophilus of Alexandria (d. ca. 410), Cyril of Alexandria (d. 444), Photius of Constantinople (820–891). Berlin: Akademie-Verlag, 1957.
Rupert of Deutz (ca. 1070–1129). *In Opus de gloria et honore Filii Hominis super Matthaeum. PL* 168, pp. 1307–1634.

Salmeron, A. (1515–1585). *Commentarii in Evangelicam Historiam, Tom I-IX.* Coloniae Agrippinae: Antonium Hierat, 1612.
Smith, H. *Antenicene Exegesis of the Gospels.* 5 volumes. London: SPCK, 1925–1928.
Strabo, Walafrid (attributed, 12th century). *Glossa Ordinaria. PL* 114, pp. 63–178.

Theodore of Heraclea, see Reuss.
Theodore of Mopsuestia, see Reuss.
Theophilus of Alexandria, see Reuss.
Thomas Aquinas (1225–1274). *Catena Aurea.* Ed. I Nocolai. 3 volumes. English trans.: *Catena Aurea: Commentary on the Four Gospels Collected out of the Works of the Fathers.* 4 volumes. Oxford: Parker, 1864.
————. *Super Evangelium S. Matthaei Lectura.* 5th edition. Torino and Rome: Marietti, 1951.
Tostatus, A. (d. 1454). *Commentarii in Matthaeum, Opera 18–24.* Venezia: Balleoniana, 1728.

Valdes, J. de (d. 1541). *Commentary upon the Gospel of S. Matthew.* Translated into English by J. B. Betts. London: Trübner, 1882.
Valla, L. (1407–1457). *Annotationes in Novum Testamentum.* Paris, 1505.

Wettstein, J. (1693–1754). *Novum Testamentum Graecum.* Volume 1. Amsterdam, 1752. Reprint, Graz, 1962.
Wolzogen, J. L. (1633–1690). *Commentarius in Evangelium Matthei.* Irenopolis, 1656.

Zinzendorf, N. L. von (1700–1760). *Reden über die vier Evangelisten.* Edited by G. Clemens. 3 volumes. Barby: Theological Seminary, 1766–1769.
Zwingli, H. (1484–1531). *Annotationes in Evangelium Matthaei.* Opera VI. Volume 1, edited by M. Schuler and J. Schulthess, pp. 203–483. Zurich, 1836.

2. Commentaries on Matthew since 1800

Albright, W. F., and Mann, C. S. *Matthew.* AB. Garden City, N.Y.: Doubleday, 1971.
Allen, W. C. *A Critical and Exegetical Commentary on the Gospel according to St. Matthew.* ICC. Edinburgh: T. & T. Clark, 1907; 3d edition, 1912.
Argyle, A. W. *The Gospel according to Matthew.* Cambridge Bible Commentary. Cambridge: At the University Press, 1963.

Beare, F. W. *The Gospel according to Matthew: A Commentary.* Oxford: Blackwell, 1981.
Benoit, P., and Boismard, M. E. *Synopse des quatres Évangiles en français.* 2 volumes. Paris: Cerf, 1972.
Bisping, A. *Erklärung des Evangeliums nach Matthäus.* Münster: Aschendorf, 1867.
Billerbeck. See Strack.
Boismard. See Benoit.
Bonnard, P. *L'Évangile selon saint Matthieu.* CNT. Neuchâtel: Delachaux & Niestlé,

1963; 2d edition, 1970.

Ewald, H. *Die drei ersten Evangelien.* Göttingen: Dieterische Buchhandlung, 1850.

Fenton, J. C. *Saint Matthew.* Pelican Gospel Commentaries. Baltimore: Penguin, 1964. Provence: Faculté libre de théologie protestante, 1967–1970.

Filson, F. *A Commentary on the Gospel according to St. Matthew.* Black's New Testament Commentaries. London: A. & C. Black, 1960.

Gaechter, P. *Das Matthäus-Evangelium.* Innsbruck: Tyrolia, 1963.

Gander, G. *Évangile de l'Église. Commentaire de l'Évangile selon Matthieu.* Aix en Provence: Faculté libre de théologie protestante, 1967-1970.

Grundmann, W. *Das Evangelium nach Matthäus.* THKNT. Berlin: Evangelische Verlagsanstalt, 1968.

Gundry, R. H. *Matthew: A Commentary on His Literary and Theological Art.* Grand Rapids: Eerdmans, 1982.

Hendriksen, W. *The Gospel of Matthew.* Edinburgh: Banner of Truth Trust, 1974.

Hill, D. *The Gospel of Matthew.* NCB. London: Marshall, Morgan, and Scott, 1972.

Holtzmann, H. J. *Die Synoptiker.* HKNT I/1. Tübingen: Mohr, 1901; 3d edition, 1911.

Keil, C. F. *Commentar über das Evangelium des Matthäus.* Leipzig: Dörffling und Francke, 1877.

Klostermann, E. *Das Matthäusevangelium.* HNT 4. Tübingen: Mohr, 1909; 2d edition, 1927.

Knabenbauer, J. *Commentarius in Evangelium secundum Mattheum.* Paris: Lethielleeux, 1922.

Lagrange, M. J. *Évangile selon Saint Matthieu.* EBib. Paris: Gabala, 1923.

Lohmeyer, E. *Das Evangelium des Matthäus.* W. Schmauch, ed. 2d ed. Kritisch-exegetischer Kommentar über das Neue Testament (Sonderband). Göttingen: Vandenhoeck & Ruprecht, 1958.

Loisy, A. *Les Évangiles Synoptiques.* Volume 1. Ceffonds: Loisy, 1907.

McNeile, A. H. *The Gospel according to St. Matthew.* London: Macmillan, (1915) 1965.

Maier, G. *Matthäus-Evangelium.* Bibel-Kommentar, volumes 1 & 2. Neuhausen-Stuttgart: Hänssler, 1979.

Meier, J. P. *Matthew.* New Testament Message 3. Wilmington: Glazier, 1981.

Meyer, H. A. W. *Kritisch-exegetisches Handbuch über das Evangelium des Matthäus.* 2d edition. Kritisch-exegetischer Kommentar I/1. Göttingen: Vandenhoeck & Ruprecht, 1844.

Michaelis, W. *Das Evangelium nach Matthäus.* 2 volumes. Zurich: Zwingli, 1948–1949.

Minear, P. S. *Matthew: The Teacher's Gospel.* New York: Pilgrim, 1982.

Migne, J. P., editor. *Scripturae Sacrae Cursus Completus ex commentariis omnium . . . conflatus, vol. 21.* Paris: Migne, 1840.

Montefiore, C. G. *The Synoptic Gospels II.* 2d edition. London: Macmillan, 1927.

Nösgen, C. F. *Die Evangelien nach Matthäus, Markus, und Lukas.* 2d edition. Kurzgefasster Kommentar. Munich: C. H. Beck, 1897.

Olshausen, H. *Biblischer Kommentar über sämtliche Schriften des Neuen Testaments . . . .* 2d edition. Königsberg: A. W. Unzer, 1833. English trans. of 2d edition: *Biblical Commentary on the New Testament.* New York: Sheldon, Blakeman, 1857.

Paulus, H. E. G. *Kommentar über die drey ersten Evangelien.* 4 volumes. Lübeck: J. F. Bohn, 1800–1808.

Plummer, A. *An Exegetical Commentary on the Gospel according to St. Matthew.* London: Stock, 1910.

Radermakers, J. *Au fil de l'Évangile selon saint Matthieu.* 2 volumes. Heverlee-Louvain: Institut d'études théologiques, 1972.

Robinson, T. H. *The Gospel of Matthew.* MNTC 1. Garden City, N.Y.: Doubleday, 1928.

Sabourin, L. *L'Évangile selon saint Matthieu et ses principaux parallèles.* Rome: Biblical Institute Press, 1978.

Schanz, P. *Kommentar über das Evangelium des heiligen Matthäus.* Freiburg: Herder, 1879.

Schlatter, A. *Der Evangelist Matthäus.* 2d edition. Stuttgart: Calwer, 1933.

Schmid, J. *Das Evangelium nach Matthäus.* Regensburger NT 1. Regensburg: Pustet, 1965.

Schniewind, J. *Das Evangelium nach Matthäus.* 8th ed. NTD 2. Göttingen: Vandenhoeck & Ruprecht, 1956.

Schweizer, E. *The Good News according to Matthew.* Atlanta: John Knox, 1975.

Da Spinetoli, Ortensio. *Matteo. Commento al "Vangelo della Chiesa."* Assisi: Cittadella editrice, 1971.

Stendahl, K. "Matthew," in *PCB,* pp. 769–798. M. Black and H. Rowley, eds. New York: Nelson, 1962.

Strack, H. L., and Billerbeck, P. *Kommentar zum Neuen Testament aus Talmud und Midrasch.* 4 volumes. 3d edition. Munich: Beck, 1951–1956. (cited: Str-B)

Trilling, W. *The Gospel according to St. Matthew.* New York: Herder & Herder, 1969.

Wellhausen, J. *Das Evangelium Matthaei.* Berlin: Reimer, 1904.

De Wette, W. M. L. *Das Neue Testament, griechisch mit kurzem Kommentar.* Volume 1. Halle: Anton, 1887.

Weiss, B. *Das Matthäus-Evangelium.* 9th ed. Kritisch-exegetischer Kommentar I/1. Göttingen: Vandenhoeck & Ruprecht, 1898.

Weiss, J. *Das Matthäus-Evangelium.* 2d edition. SNT 1. Göttingen: Vandenhoeck & Ruprecht, 1907.

Zahn, T. *Das Evangelium des Matthäus.* Kommentar zum Neuen Testament 1. Leipzig: Deichert, 1903.

3. Monographs and Essays on Matthew

Bacon, B. W. *Studies in Matthew.* New York: Holt, 1930.

Barth, G. "Matthew's Understanding of the Law." In G. Bornkamm, G. Barth, and H. J. Held, *Tradition and Interpretation in Matthew.* London: SCM, 1972.

Blair, E. P. *Jesus in the Gospel of Matthew.* New York and Nashville: Abingdon, 1960.

Bornkamm, G. "Der Auferstandene und der Irdische. Mt 28, 16–20." In *Zeit und Geschichte* (FS R. Bultmann), pp. 171–191. E. Dinkler, editor. Tübingen: Mohr, 1964.

———. "Die Binde- und Lösegewalt in der Kirche des Matthäus." In G. Bornkamm, editor, *Geschichte und Glaube II* (Essays IV), pp. 37-50. BEvT 53. Munich: Kaiser, 1971.

———. "End-Expectation and Church in Matthew." In *Tradition and Interpretation in Matthew.*

Burnett, F. W. *The Testament of Jesus-Sophia: A Redaction-Critical Study of the Eschatological Discourse in Matthew.* Washington: University Press of America, 1979.

Butler, B. C. *The Originality of St. Matthew: A Critique of the Two Document Hypothesis.* Cambridge: At the University Press, 1951.

Cope, M. L. *Matthew: A Scribe Trained for the Kingdom of Heaven.* CBQMS 5. Washington: Catholic Biblical Association of America, 1976.

Davies, W. D. *The Setting of the Sermon on the Mount.* Cambridge: At the University Press, 1966.

Didier, M., editor. *L'Évangile selon Matthieu.* BETL 29. Gembloux: Duculot, 1972.

Von Dobschütz, E. "Matthäus als Rabbi und Katechet." *ZNW* 27 (1928): 338–348. Reprinted in Lange, *Das Matthäus-Evangelium* (see below), pp. 52–64.

Dupont, J. *Les Béatitudes. I Le problème littéraire,* 1958. *II La bonne nouvelle,* 1969. *III Les Évangelistes,* 1973. EBib. Paris: Gabalda.

Ellis, P. F. *Matthew: His Mind and His Message.* Collegeville, Minn.: Liturgical Press, 1974.

Farrer, A. *St. Matthew and St. Mark.* Westminster, Eng.: Dacre, 1954.

Fiedler, M. J. "Gerechtigkeit im Matthäus-Evangelium." *Theologische Versuche* 8 (1977): 63–75.

Frankemölle, H. "Amtskritik im Matthäus-Evangelium?" *Bib* 54 (1973): 247–262.

_____. *Jahwebund und Kirche Christi.* NTA, new series, 10. Münster: Aschendorf, 1974.

Gaechter, P. *Die literarische Kunst im Matthäusevangelium.* SBS 7. Stuttgart: Verlag Katholisches Bibelwerk, 1965.

Gaston, L. "The Messiah of Israel as Teacher of the Gentiles." *Int* 29 (1975): 25–40.

Gerhardsson, B. " 'An ihren Früchten sollt ihr sie erkennen.' Die Legitimitätsfrage in der matthäischen Christologie." *EvT* 42 (1982): 113–126.

_____. "Gottes Sohn als Diener Gottes. Agape und Himmelsherrschaft nach dem Matthäusevangelium." *ST* 27 (1973): 25–50.

Giesen, H. *Christliches Handeln. Eine redaktionskritische Untersuchung zum* δικαιοσύνη-*Begriff im Matthäus-Evangelium.* Europäische Hochschulschriften 23/181. Frankfurt am Main: Lang, 1982.

Goulder, M. D. *Midrash and Lection in Matthew.* London: SPCK, 1974.

Gundry, R. H. *The Use of the Old Testament in St. Matthew's Gospel.* NovTSup 18. Leiden: E. J. Brill, 1967.

Hare, D. *The Theme of Jewish Persecution of Christians in the Gospel according to St. Matthew.* SNTSMS 6. Cambridge: At the University Press, 1967.

Held, H. J. "Matthew as Interpreter of the Miracle Stories." In *Tradition and Interpretation in Matthew.* London: SCM, 1972.

Hirsch, E. *Frühgeschichte des Evangeliums II. Die Vorlagen des Lukas und das Sondergut des Matthäus.* Tübingen: Mohr, 1941.

Hummel, R. *Die Auseinandersetzung zwischen Kirche und Judentum im Matthäusevangelium.* BEvT 33. Munich: Kaiser, 1963.

Humphrey, H. M. *The Relationship of Structure and Christology in the Gospel of Matthew.* New York: Fordham, 1977.

Johnson, M. D. "Reflections on a Wisdom Approach to Matthew's Christology." *CBQ* 36 (1974): 44–64.

Jülicher, A. *Itala I. Matthäus-Evangelium.* Berlin: De Gruyter, 1938.

Kilpatrick, G. D. *The Origins of the Gospel according to St. Matthew.* Oxford: Clarendon, 1946, 1959.

Kingsbury, J. *Jesus Christ in Matthew, Mark, and Luke.* Proclamation Commentaries. Philadelphia: Fortress, 1981.

_____. *Matthew: Structure, Christology, Kingdom.* Philadelphia: Fortress, 1975.

_____. *The Parables of Jesus in Matthew 13.* Richmond: John Knox, 1969.

_____. "The Title 'Kyrios' in Matthew's Gospel." *JBL* 94 (1975): 246–255.

_____. "The Title 'Son of David' in Matthew's Gospel." *JBL* 95 (1976): 591–602.

_____. "The Title 'Son of God' in Matthew's Gospel." *BTB* 5 (1975): 3–31.

Knox, W. L. *The Sources of the Synoptic Gospels, II: St. Luke and St. Matthew.* Cambridge: At the University Press, 1957.

Kratz, R. *Auferweckung als Befreiung. Eine Studie zur Passions- und Auferstehungstheologie des Matthäus.* SBS 65. Stuttgart: KBW, 1973.

Kretzer, A. *Die Herrschaft der Himmel und die Söhne des Reiches.* SBM 10. Stuttgart: KBW, 1971.

De Kruijf, T. *Der Sohn des lebendigen Gottes.* AnBib 14. Chicago: Loyola, 1962.

Künzel, G. *Studien zum Gemeindeverständnis des Matthäus-Evangeliums.* Calwer theologische Monographien 10. Stuttgart: Calwer, 1978.

Lange, J. *Das Erscheinen des Auferstandenen im Evangelium nach Matthäus.* Forschung zur Bibel 11. Würzburg: Echter-Verlag, 1973.

Lange, J., editor. *Das Matthäus-Evangelium.* Wege der Forschung 525. Darmstadt: Wissenschaftliche Buchgesellschaft, 1980.

Luz, U. "Die Erfüllung des Gesetzes bei Matthäus (Mt 5.17–20)." *ZThK* 75 (1978): 398–435.

_____. "Die Jünger im Matthäusevangelium." *ZNW* 62 (1971): 141–171. Reprinted in Lange, *Matthäus-Evangelium*, pp. 377–414.

Marguerat, D. *Le Jugement dans l'Évangile de Matthieu.* Geneva: Éditions Labor et Fides, 1981.

Massaux, E. *Influence de l'Évangile de saint Matthieu sur la littérature chrétienne avant S. Irénée.* Louvain and Gembloux: University Press, 1950.

McConnell, R. S. *Law and Prophecy in Matthew's Gospel.* Theologische Dissertationen 2. Basel: Reinhardt, 1969.

Meier, J. P. *Law and History in Matthew's Gospel.* AnBib 71. Rome: Biblical Institute Press, 1976.

_____. *The Vision of Matthew: Christ, Church and Morality in the First Gospel.* New York: Paulist, 1979.

Merx, A. *Das Evangelium Matthäus.* Die vier kanonischen Evangelien nach ihrem ältesten bekannten Text II/1. Berlin: Reimer, 1902.

Mohrlang, R. *Matthew and Paul: A Comparison of Ethical Perspectives.* SNTSMS 48. Cambridge: At the University Press, 1984.

Nepper-Christensen, P. *Das Matthäusevangelium. Ein judenchristliches Evangelium?* Acta Theologica Danica 1. Aarhus: Universitetsforlaget, 1954.

Nolan, B. *The Royal Son of God: The Christology of Mt 1–2.* OBO 23. Göttingen: Vandenhoeck & Ruprecht, 1979.

Ogawa, A. *L'histoire de Jésus chez Matthieu. La signification de l'histoire pour la théologie matthéenne.* Europäische Hochschulschriften 23/116. Frankfurt am Main: Lang, 1979.

Pesch, W. *Matthäus der Seelsorger.* SBS 2. Stuttgart: Verlag Katholisches Bibelwerk, 1966.

Pregeant, R. *Christology beyond Dogma: Matthew's Christ in Process Hermeneutic.* Semeia 7. Philadelphia: Fortress, 1978.

Przybylski, B. *Righteousness in Matthew and His World of Thought.* SNTSMS 41. Cambridge: At the University Press, 1980.

Punge, M. "Endgeschehen und Heilsgeschichte im Matthäus-Evangelium." Dissertation, Greifswald, 1961.

Rigaux, B. *The Testimony of St. Matthew.* Chicago: Franciscan Herald Press, 1968.

Rothfuchs, W. *Die Erfüllungszitate des Matthäus-Evangeliums.* BWANT 88. Stuttgart: Kohlhammer, 1969.

Sand, A. *Das Gesetz und die Propheten. Untersuchungen zur Theologie des Evangeliums nach Matthäus.* Biblische Untersuchungen 11. Regensburg: Pustet, 1974.

———. "Propheten, Weise, und Schriftkundige in der Gemeinde des Matthäusevangeliums." In J. Hainz, editor, *Die Kirche im Werden,* pp. 167–185. Munich: Schöningh, 1976.

Schlatter, A. *Die Kirche des Matthäus.* BFCT 33/1. Gütersloh: Bertelsmann, 1929.

Schmid, J. *Matthäus und Lukas.* Biblische Studien (Freiburg) 23/2–4. Freiburg: Herder, 1930.

Schottroff, L. "Das geschundene Volk und die Arbeit in der Ernte. Gottes Volk nach dem Matthäusevangelium." In L. and W. Schottroff, editors, *Mitarbeiter der Schöpfung. Bibel und Arbeitswelt,* pp. 149–206. Munich: Kaiser, 1983.

Schweizer, E. "Christus und Gemeinde im Matthäusevangelium." In E. Schweizer, editor, *Matthäus und seine Gemeinde,* pp. 9–68. SBS 71. Stuttgart: KBW, 1974.

———. "Gesetz und Enthusiasmus bei Matthäus." In E. Schweizer, editor, *Beiträge zur Theologie des Neuen Testaments,* pp. 49–70. Zurich: Zwingli-Verlag, 1970.

———. "Die Kirche des Matthäus." In *Matthäus und seine Gemeinde,* pp. 138–170.

———. *Matthäus und seine Gemeinde.* See above.

Soares-Prabhu, G. M. *The Formula Quotations in the Infancy Narrative of Matthew.* AnBib 63. Rome: Biblical Institute Press, 1976.

De Solages, M. *La composition des Évangiles de Luc et de Matthieu et leurs sources.* Leiden: Brill, 1973.

Stendahl, K. *The School of St. Matthew.* 2d ed. Philadelphia: Fortress, 1968.

Strecker, G. "Das Geschichtsverständnis des Matthäus." EvT 26 (1966): 57–74. Reprinted in Lange, *Matthäus-Evangelium,* pp. 326–349.

———. *Der Weg der Gerechtigkeit. Untersuchung zur Theologie des Matthäus.* FRLANT 82. Göttingen: Vandenhoeck & Ruprecht, 1962.

Suggs, M. J. *Wisdom, Christology and Law in Matthew's Gospel.* Cambridge, Mass.: Harvard, 1970.

Suhl, A. "Der Davidssohn im Matthäus-Evangelium." ZNW 59 (1968): 36–72.

Thysman, R. *Communauté et directives éthiques: La catéchèse de Matthieu.* Recherches et Synthèses: Section d' exégèse: I. Gembloux: Duculot, 1974.

Van Tilborg, S. *The Jewish Leaders in Matthew.* Leiden: Brill, 1972.

Trilling, W. "Amt und Amtsverständnis bei Matthäus." In A. Descamps, editor, *Mélanges Bibliques* (FS B. Rigaux), pp. 29–44. Gembloux: Duculot, 1969.

———. *Das wahre Israel. Studien zur Theologie des Matthäusevangeliums.* 3d ed. Erfurter theol. Studien 7. Leipzig: St. Benno, 1975.

Walker, R. *Die Heilsgeschichte im ersten Evangelium.* FRLANT 91. Göttingen: Vandenhoeck & Ruprecht, 1967.

Walter, N. "Zum Kirchenverständnis des Matthäus." *Theologische Versuche* 12 (1981): 25–46.

27

Zumstein, J. *La condition du croyant dans l'Évangile selon Matthieu.* OBO 16. Göttingen: Vandenhoeck & Ruprecht, 1977.

4. Additional Literature

Abrahams, J. *Studies in Pharisaism and the Gospels.* New York: Ktav, 1967.

Albertz, M. *Die synoptischen Streitgespräche.* Berlin: Trowitsch, 1921.

Andresen, C., editor. *Handbuch der Dogmen- und Theologiegeschichte.* 2 volumes. Göttingen: Vandenhoeck & Ruprecht, 1980–1982. (Cited: author of the article, in Andresen [ed.], *Handbuch).*

Bacher, W. *Die exegetische Terminologie der jüdischen Traditionsliteratur.* (I) *Die bibelexegetische Terminologie der Tannaiten* (1899). (II) *Die bibel- und traditionsexegetische Terminologie der Amoräer* (1905). Darmstadt: Wissenschaftliche Buchgesellschaft, 1965.

Barth, K. *Church Dogmatics,* I,1–IV,4. Edinburgh: T. & T. Clark, 1975. (Cited: Barth, *CD . . .)*

Bauer, B. *Kritik der evangelischen Geschichte der Synoptiker I,II.* Reprint. Hildesheim: Olms, 1974.

Bauer, W. *Das Leben Jesu im Zeitalter der neutestamentlichen Apokryphen* (1909). Reprint. Darmstadt: Wissenschaftliche Buchgesellschaft, 1967.

Bauer, W., W. Arndt, F. Gingrich, F. Danker. *A Greek-English Lexicon of the New Testament and Other Early Christian Literature.* Chicago: University of Chicago Press, 1979. (Cited: *BAGD)*

Baumbach, G. *Das Verständnis des Bösen in den synoptischen Evangelien.* Theologische Arbeiten 19. Berlin: Evangelische Verlagsanstalt, 1963.

Ben-Chorin, Schalom. *Bruder Jesus.* 2d edition. Munich: Paul List, 1969.

Berger, K. *Die Amenworte Jesu.* BZNW 39. Berlin: De Gruyter, 1970.

──────. *Die Gesetzesauslegung Jesu I, Markus und Parallelen.* WMANT 40. Neukirchen-Vluyn: Neukirchener, 1972.

Beyer, K. *Semitische Syntax im Neuen Testament,* vol 1: *Satzlehre Teil 1.* 2d edition. SUNT 1. Göttingen: Vandenhoeck & Ruprecht, 1968.

Black, M. *An Aramaic Approach to the Gospels and Acts.* 3d ed. Oxford: Clarendon, 1967.

Blass, F., Debrunner, A., Funk, R. *A Greek Grammar of the New Testament and Other Early Christian Literature.* Chicago: University of Chicago Press, 1961. (Cited: BDF)

Bornkamm, G. *Jesus of Nazareth.* New York: Harper & Row, 1959.

Braun, H. *Jesus of Nazareth.* Philadelphia: Fortress, 1979.

──────. *Qumran und das Neue Testament I, II.* Tübingen: Mohr, 1966.

──────. *Spätjüdisch-häretischer und frühchristlicher Radikalismus I,II.* BHT 24. Tübingen: Mohr, 1957.

Bultmann, R. *Exegetica.* E. Dinkler, editor. Tübingen: Mohr, 1967.

──────. *History of the Synoptic Tradition.* New York: Harper & Row, 1976.

──────. *Jesus and the Word,* New York: Scribner's, 1958.

──────. *Theology of the New Testament.* 2 volumes. New York: Scribner's, 1951–1955.

Burger, C. *Jesus als Davidssohn.* FRLANT 98. Göttingen: Vandenhoeck & Ruprecht, 1970.

Calvin, J. *Institutes of the Christian Religion.* 2 volumes. Grand Rapids: Eerdmans, 1962.

The Cambridge History of the Bible. P. R. Ackroyd, S. L. Greenslade, G. W. H. Lampe, and others, editors. 3 volumes. Cambridge: At the University Press,

1963–1970. (Cited: Author + *Cambridge History of the Bible*).

Catechismus ex decreto Concilii Tridentini. Pope Pius V, editor. Leipzig edition, 1862. English translation: *Catechism of the Council of Trent.* Rockford, Ill.: Tan, 1982. (Cited: Catechismus Romanus)

Codex iuris canonici. Popes Pius X and Benedict XV, editors. Rome edition, 1918. English translation: *Codex Iuris Canonici (Code of Canon Law).* Washington, D.C.: *Canon Law Society of America,* 1983. (Cited: CIC).

Dalman, G. *Jesus-Jeshua: Studies in the Gospels.* New York: Ktav, 1971.

———. *Orte und Wege Jesu.* BFCT II 1. 2d edition. Gütersloh: Bertelsmann, 1921.

———. *The Words of Jesus.* Edinburgh: T. & T. Clark, 1909. (Cited: Dalman, *WJ*)

Daube, D. *The New Testament and Rabbinic Judaism.* London: Athlone, 1956.

Dibelius, M. *From Tradition to Gospel.* New York: Scribner, 1965.

Dodd, C. H. *The Parables of the Kingdom (1935).* London: Collins, 1961.

Farmer, W. R. *The Synoptic Problem.* Dillsboro, N.C.: Wester, 1976.

Fiebig, P. *Die Gleichnisreden Jesu.* Tübingen: Mohr, 1912.

Fiedler, P. *Jesus und die Sünder.* Beiträge zur biblischen Exegese und Theologie 3. Frankfurt am Main: Lang, 1976.

Fitzmyer, J. *A Wandering Aramean.* Missoula, Mont.: Scholars Press, 1979.

Flusser, D. *Die rabbinischen Gleichnisse und der Gleichniserzähler Jesus I.* Judaica et Christiana 4. Bern: Lang, 1981.

Gerhardsson, B. *Memory and Manuscript.* Uppsala: Acta Seminarii Neotestamentici Upsaliensis, 1961.

Ginzberg, L. *The Legends of the Jews.* 7 volumes. Reprint. Philadelphia: Jewish Publication Society of America, 1967–1969.

Gnilka, J. *Das Evangelium nach Markus.* 2 volumes. EKKNT II 1–2. Zürich: Benziger, 1978–1979.

Goppelt, L. *Theology of the New Testament.* Grand Rapids: Eerdmans, 1982.

Goulder, M. *The Evangelist's Calendar.* London: SPCK, 1978.

Grässer, E. *Das Problem der Parusieverzögerung in den synoptischen Evangelien und in der Apostelgeschichte.* BZNW 22. 2d ed. Berlin: Töpelmann, 1960.

Haenchen, E. *Der Weg Jesu.* Sammlung Töpelmann II 6. Berlin: Töpelmann, 1966.

Hahn, F. *The Titles of Jesus in Christology.* New York: World, 1969.

———. *Mission in the New Testament.* London: SCM, 1965.

Harnack, A. *Marcion. Das Evangelium vom fremden Gott* (2d ed.1924). Reprint Darmstadt: Wissenchaftliche Buchgesellschaft, 1960. English trans.:*Marcion: the Gospel of the Alien God.* Durham, N.C.: Labyrinth, not yet published.

———. *Sprüche und Reden Jesu. Beiträge zur Einleitung in das Neue Testament II.* Leipzig: Hinrichs, 1907.

Hasler, V. *Amen.* Zurich: Gotthelf, 1969.

Hawkins, J. C. *Horae Synopticae* (1909). Reprint. Oxford: Clarendon, 1968.

Hengel, M. *Judaism and Hellenism.* 2 volumes. Philadelphia: Fortress, 1981.

Hoffmann, P. *Studien zur Theologie der Logienquelle.* NTAbh, New Series 8. Münster: Aschendorf, 1972.

Hoffmann, P., und Eid, V. *Jesus von Nazareth und eine christliche Moral.* Quaestiones disputatae 66. 2d edition. Freiburg: Herder, 1975.

Holtzmann, H. J. *Lehrbuch der neutestamentlichen Theologie I.* 2d edition. Tübingen: Mohr, 1911.

Hübner, H. *Das Gesetz in der synoptischen Tradition.* Witten: Luther-Verlag, 1973.

Jeremias, J. *Abba.* Göttingen: Vandenhoeck & Ruprecht, 1966. Selections translated into English in: *The Prayers of Jesus.* Philadelphia: Fortress, 1978.

29

_____. *The Parables of Jesus*. New York: Scribner, 1972.

_____. *New Testament Theology*. New York: Scribner, 1972.

Jülicher, A. *Die Gleichnisreden Jesu I,II*. 2d edition. Tübingen: Mohr, 1911.

Jüngel, E. *Paulus und Jesus*. Hermeneutische Untersuchungen zur Theologie 2. Tübingen: Mohr, 1962.

Käsemann, E. *Exegetische Versuche und Besinnungen*. 2 volumes. Göttingen: Vandenhoeck & Ruprecht, 1960, 1964. English trans.: *Essays on New Testament Themes*. Philadelphia: Fortress, 1982.

Köster, H. *Synoptische Überlieferung bei den Apostolischen Vätern*. TU 65. Berlin: Akademie-Verlag, 1957.

Krauss, S. *Talmudische Archäologie* (1910-1912). 2 volumes. Reprint. Hildesheim: Olms, 1966.

Krumwiede, H. W., editor. *Neuzeit*. 2 volumes. Kirchen- und Theologiegeschichte in Quellen IV 1,2. Neukirchen-Vluyn: Neukirchner, 1979-1980.

Kümmel, W. G. *Introduction to the New Testament*. Nashville: Abingdon, 1986.

_____. *Heilsgeschehen und Geschichte*. Marburger theologische Studien III 16. 2 volumes. Marburg: Elwert, 1965–1978.

_____. *The New Testament: The History of the Investigation of Its Problems*. Nashville: Abingdon, 1972.

Laufen, R. *Die Doppelüberlieferungen der Logienquelle und des Markusevangeliums*. BBB 54. Bonn: Hanstein, 1980.

Von Loewenich, W. *Luther als Ausleger der Synoptiker*. Forschungen zur Geschichte und Lehre des Protestantismus-X,5. Munich: Kaiser, 1954.

De Lubac, H. *Exégèse médiévale*. Théologie [Paris] 41–42, 59. Paris: Aubier, 1959–1964.

Lührmann, D. *Die Redaktion der Logienquelle*. WMANT 33. Neukirchen-Vluyn: Neukirchener, 1969.

Machoveč, M. *A Marxist Looks at Jesus*. Philadelphia: Fortress, 1976.

Manson, T. W. *The Sayings of Jesus*. 2d edition. London: SCM, 1949.

Marquardt, J. *Das Privatleben der Römer* (1886). 2 volumes. Reprint. Darmstadt: Wissenschaftliche Buchgesellschaft, 1975.

Merklein, H. *Die Gottesherrschaft als Handlungsprinzip*. Forschung zur Bibel 34. 2d edition. Würzburg: Echter-Verlag, 1981.

Metzger, B. M. *A Textual Commentary on the Greek New Testament*. London: United Bible Societies, 1971.

Mokrosch, R., and Walz, H., editors. *Mittelalter*. Kirchen- und Theologiegeschichte in Quellen 2. Neukirchen-Vluyn: Neukirchener, 1980.

Montefiore, H. *Rabbinic Literature and Gospel Teachings* (1930). Reprint. New York: Ktav, 1970.

Moore, G. F. *Judaism in the First Centuries of the Christian Era*. 3 volumes. Cambridge, Mass.: Harvard University Press, 1927–1930.

Neirynck, F. *The Minor Agreements of Matthew and Luke against Mark*. BETL 37. Louvain: University Press, 1974.

Nissen, A. *Gott und der Nächste im antiken Judentum*. WUNT 15. Tübingen: Mohr, 1974.

Oberman, H. A., editor. *Die Kirche im Zeitalter der Reformation*. Kirchen- und Theologiegeschichte in Quellen 3. Neukirchen-Vluyn: Neukirchener, 1981.

Percy, E. *Die Botschaft Jesu*. Lund: Gleerup, 1953.

Pesch, R. *Das Markusevangelium*. HTKNT II 1–2. 2 volumes. Freiburg: Herder, 1976–1977.

Polag, A. *Die Christologie der Logienquelle.* WMANT 45. Neukirchen-Vluyn: Neukirchener, 1977.

————. *Fragmenta Q.* Neukirchen-Vluyn: Neukirchener, 1979.

Riesner, R. *Jesus als Lehrer.* WUNT II 7. Tübingen: Mohr, 1981.

Ritter, A. M., editor. *Alte Kirche.* Kirchen- und Theologiegeschichte in Quellen 1. 2d edition. Neukirchen-Vluyn: Neukirchener, 1982.

Roloff, J. *Das Kerygma und der irdische Jesus.* Göttingen: Vandenhoeck & Ruprecht, 1970.

Sato, M. "Q und Prophetie." Dissertation. Bern, 1984.

Schellong, D. *Calvins Auslegung der synoptischen Evangelien.* Forschung zur Geschichte und Lehre des Protestantismus X, 38, Munich: Kaiser, 1969.

Schleiermacher, F. *Predigten, 7 Sammlungen.* Reutlingen: Ensslin, 1835. English translation of a selection of these sermons: *Servant of the Word: Selected Sermons.* Philadelphia: Fortress, 1987.

Schlingensiepen, H. *Die Wunder des Neuen Testaments. Wege und Abwege ihrer Deutung in der alten Kirche bis zur Mitte des 5. Jhdt.s.* BFCT II 28. Gütersloh: Bertelsmann, 1933.

Schmidt, K. L. *Der Rahmen der Geschichte Jesu.* Berlin: Trowitsch, 1919.

Schoeps, H. J. *Theologie und Geschichte des Judenchristentums.* Tübingen: Mohr, 1949.

Schürmann, H. *Das Lukasevangelium.* HTKNT III 1. Freiburg: Herder, 1969.

————. *Traditionsgeschichtliche Untersuchungen zu den synoptischen Evangelien.* Kommentare und Beiträge zum Alten und Neuen Testament. Düsseldorf: Patmos, 1968.

Schulz, S. Q. *Die Spruchquelle der Evangelisten.* Zurich: Theologischer Verlag, 1972.

————. *Die Stunde der Botschaft. Einführung in die Theologie der vier Evangelisten.* Hamburg: Furche, 1967.

Schwyzer, E. *Griechische Grammatik.* Volume 1: 5th edition, 1977. Volume 2: revised by A. Debrunner, 1950. Volume 3: revised by D. Georgacas, 1953. Munich: Beck.

Smalley, B. *The Study of the Bible in the Middle Ages.* New York: Philosophical Library, 1952.

Smith, M. *Tannaitic Parallels to the Gospels.* JBL manuscript series 6. Philadelphia: SBL, 1951.

Spicq, C. *Ésquisse d' une histoire de l'exégèse latine au Moyen Age.* Bibliothèque Thomiste XXVI. Paris: Vrin, 1944.

————. *Notes de lexicographie Néo-Testamentaire.* OBO 22, 1–3. Fribourg, Switzerland: Vandenhoeck & Ruprecht, 1978–1982.

Stauffer, E. *Die Botschaft Jesu. Damals und heute.* Dalp-Taschenbücher 333. Bern: Francke, 1959.

————. *Jesus and His Story.* New York: Knopf, 1960.

Steck, O. H. *Israel und das gewaltsame Geschick der Propheten.* WMANT 23. Neukirchen-Vluyn: Neukirchener, 1967.

Stegmüller, *Repertorium Biblicum Medii Aevi.* 5 volumes. Madrid: Consejo Superior, 1940–1955.

Strauss, D. F. *The Life of Jesus Critically Examined.* 3d German edition, 1838–1839. Reprinted, Philadelphia: Fortress, 1973.

Strecker, G. *Eschaton und Historie.* Göttingen: Vandenhoeck & Ruprecht, 1979.

————. *Das Judenchristentum in den Pseudoclementinen.* TU 70. Berlin: Akademie-Verlag, 1958.

Streeter, B. H. *The Four Gospels.* London: Macmillan, 1924.

Theissen, G. *Studien zur Soziologie des Urchristentums.* WUNT 19. Tübingen: Mohr,

1979. Partial English trans.: *The Social Setting of Pauline Christianity.* Philadelphia: Fortress, 1982.

St. Thomas Aquinas. *Summa Theologica.* BAC. 5 volumes. English/Latin critical edition: *Summa Theologiae.* 60 volumes. New York: McGraw-Hill, 1963. (Cited: *STh*)

Torrey, C. C. *The Four Gospels.* 2d ed. New York: Harper, 1947.

Urbach, E. *The Sages: Their Concepts and Beliefs.* 2 volumes. Jerusalem: Magnes, 1975.

Vielhauer, P. *Geschichte der urchristlichen Literatur.* Berlin: DeGruyter, 1975.

Vögtle, A. *Das Evangelium und die Evangelien.* Kommentare und Beiträge zum Alten und Neuen Testament. Düsseldorf: Patmos, 1971.

————. *Das Neue Testament und die Zukunft des Kosmos.* Kommentare und Beiträge zum Alten und Neuen Testament. Düsseldorf: Patmos, 1970.

Wanke, J. *"Bezugs- und Kommentarworte" in den synoptischen Evangelien.* Erfurter theologische Studien 44. Leipzig: St. Benno, 1981.

Wesley, J. (1703–1791). *Sermons on Several Occasions.* London: Epworth, 1961.

Wünsche, A. *Aus Israels Lehrhallen.* 5 volumes. Hildesheim: Olms, 1967.

Zeller, D. *Die weisheitlichen Mahnsprüche bei den Synoptikern.* Forschung zur Bibel 17. Würzburg: Echter-Verlag, 1977.

Introduction

Research Surveys

Conzelmann, H. "Literaturbericht zu den synoptischen Evangelien," *ThR* 37 (1972) 220–72, especially 257–63; 43 (1978) 3–51, especially 35–43.

Harrington, D. *Light of All Nations*, pp. 83-109 (Wilmington: Glazier, 1982).

Hill, D. "Some Recent Trends in Matthean Studies," *IBSt* 1 (1979) 139–49.

Rohde, J. *Rediscovering the Teaching of the Evangelists* (Philadelphia: Westminster, 1968).

Senior, D. *What Are They Saying about Matthew?* (New York: Paulist, 1983).

Stanton, G. "The Origin and Purpose of Matthew's Gospel: Matthean Scholarship from 1945–1980," *ANRW* II 25/3, pp. 1889–1951 (1984).

Preliminary Remark. As in the analytical sections of the commentary, so in the introduction, problems of synchronous analysis will be discussed first and then diachronous analysis. Next, problems of style, of the situation of origin, and of reception will be discussed. It is not possible to cite references comprehensively. Almost everything which is offered is therefore exemplary. The reader is requested to use the index at the conclusion of the third volume. With its help, the material that pertains to the key terms which are designated by ◗ can be comprehended more fully.

The introduction neither contains a description of Matthean theology nor a summary of the history of influence nor a view to the present. This is planned for the theological summary at the conclusion of the third volume. In order that the reader may not be left completely in the dark, the concluding section of the introduction on pp. 00–00 will indicate the direction taken.

1. STRUCTURE AND GENRE

Literature

Bacon, B. W. "The 'Five Books' of Moses against the Jews," *Expositor* 15 (1918) 56–66.

_____. *Studies in Matthew*, pp. 80–90 (New York: Holt, 1930).

Combrink, B. "The Structure of the Gospel of Matthew as Narrative," *TynBul* 34 (1983) 661–90.

Fenton, J. "Inclusio and Chiasmus in Matthew," *SE* I 1959 (TU 73), 174–79.

Frankemölle, H. *Jahwebund und Kirche Christi*, pp. 331–47 (Münster: Aschendorf, 1974).

Gaechter, P. *Die literarische Kunst im Matthäusevangelium* (Stuttgart: Katholisches Bibelwerk, 1965).

Gooding, D. W. "Structure littéraire de Matthieu 13,53 à 18,35," *RB* 85 (1978) 227–52.

Green, H. B. "The Structure of St. Matthew's Gospel," *SE* IV, 1968 (TU 102), 47–59.

Humphrey, H. M. *The Relationship of Structure and Christology in the Gospel of*

Matthew, pp. 6–154 (New York: Fordham, 1977).

Kingsbury, J. *Matthew: Structure, Christology, Kingdom*, pp. 1–37 (Philadelphia: Fortress, 1975).

Krentz, E. "The Extent of Matthew's Prologue," *JBL* 83 (1964) 409–14.

Kürzinger, J. "Zur Komposition der Bergpredigt nach Matthäus," *Bib* 40 (1959) 549–89.

Léon–Dufour, X. "Vers l'annonce de L'Église. Matthieu 14,1–16,20," in *Études d'Évangile*, pp. 231–54 (Paris: Éditions du Seuil, 1965).

Lohr, C. H. "Oral Techniques in the Gospel of Matthew," *CBQ* 23 (1961) 403–35.

Murphy–O'Connor, J. "The Structure of Matthew 14–17," *RB* 82 (1975) 360–384.

Neirynck, F. "La rédaction matthéenne et la structure du premier Évangile," in *De Jésus aux Évangiles*, ed. J. de la Potterie, BETL 25 pp. 41–73 (1967).

The Structure of Matthew 1–13: An Exploration into Discourse Analysis. Neot 11 (1977) (with essays by K. Kotzé, M. van der Merwe, A. Snyman, A. B. du Toit, P. Maartens, W. Nicol, J. P. Louw, H. Combrink, B. Lategan, W. Vorster).

Structure and Meaning in Matthew 14–28. Neot 16 (1982) (with essays by H. Combrink, A. van Aarde, H. C. van Zyl, P. de Villiers, B. Lategan, P. Maartens, S. Riekert).

Ramaroson, L. "La structure du premier Évangile," *ScEs* 26 (1974) 69–112.

Riesner, R. "Der Aufbau der Reden im Matthäus-Evangelium," ThBeitr 9 (1978) 172–82.

Via, D. "Structure, Christology and Ethics in Matthew," in *Orientation by Disorientation* (FW W. A. Beardslee), pp. 199–217, ed. R. A Spencer (Pittsburgh: Pickwick, 1980).

Preliminary Remarks

Exegetes seem to be in broad agreement that our Gospel actually can be arranged in sections. But when it comes to carrying out such an arrangement concretely, the disagreement becomes widespread. The question is seldom asked: did Matthew plan an arrangement of his book at all?[1] Or was he bound too strongly by his sources? It may be seen already here that diachronous questions cannot be excluded from the analysis of the structure.[2] If we seek the thread of the narrative only synchronously—in terms of its structure and the function of individual elements in it—we would presuppose that Matthew wanted to create out of his material his *own* entity and thus to "dominate" it in a certain way.[3] But perhaps he rather wanted to serve his material and "only"

---

[1]Stanton* 1905 asks: "Did the Evangelist intend to provide a broad overall structure at all?" Senior* 25–27 rightly calls attention to the fact that a narrator normally does not have in mind a "rigid comprehensive plan" of the story when he or she begins to write and can be compared more with the composer of a symphony than with the architect of a house.

[2]Especially in narratives which are strongly oriented to tradition and whose content was already familiar to the first readers, a narrative analysis which remains on the level of the text runs the risk that the modern reader who also has some prior knowledge and brings along certain analytical categories hears the narrative differently from the reader originally intended by the author. The essay by Via*, e.g., shows that such attempts betray perhaps more about the categories and historical formation of their authors than about the text.

[3]The problem appears in H. Frankemölle who rightly criticizes atomizing source criticism which finds only fragments and who demands onesidedly that exegesis must first emphasize "the individuality and creative achievement of theologians and evangelists" (*Evangelist und Gemeinde. Eine*

interpret it. Then Matthew would not be so much master of his material, but his material would be master over him. Then a structure unique to Matthew could be discovered only partially.[4] Therefore, we put three methodological theses at the beginning:

1. Methodologically controllable questions can be raised solely with regard to the structure *consciously intended* by the evangelist, not about a structure independent of that, existing on the level of the text alone.

2. The thought of being able to discover a structure in the Gospel of Matthew is not "neutral" but contains already premises for a possible understanding of the Gospel.

3. If no continuous structure can be discovered, it would not necessarily mean that Matthew is a poor author; an intention of the evangelist might be hidden which would have to be interpreted.

Present State of Research

Research into this question presents a quite chaotic picture. There is no end to new proposals concerning the structure of the Gospel of Matthew. Roughly three basic types may be distinguished:

a. The first, which goes back to Bacon, is the *model of five books*. The starting point for this view is the five discourses, Matthew 5–7; 10; 13:1–53; 18; 23–25, which Matthew has lifted out by an almost identical formula. Bacon saw before each of them a narrative section, so that the whole Gospel consists of the five books 3–7; 8–10; 11:1–13:52; 13:53–18:35; 19–25, the introduction 1–2, and the conclusion 26–28.[5] It is possible but not necessary to contrast this fivefold structure with the five books of the Pentateuch so that the Gospel of Matthew would be the new Torah and Jesus the new Moses.[6] As to content, the narrative sections have varying relationships with the corresponding discourse, at times very minimal ones. Therefore the narrative portions

---

methodenkritische Besinnung mit Beispielen aus dem Matthäusevangelium, Bib. 60 [1979] 153–190, there 183–185).His book (*Jahwebund*) presents Matthew as an individual and creative theologian and author.

[4]This does not suggest a giving up of a total approach to the Matthean narrative. It is not a question of putting the historical fragments with which the evangelist works in the place of his own work but rather of the ability to understand the *manner and kind* of his work correctly: If an author serves the material with respect, if he or she suppresses literary freedom in favor of the tradition and puts away his or her own individuality in favor of the common language of the community, then this *also* is a literary achievement. I am concerned that we do not by such categories as "individuality" or by an ahistorical approach to narrative structures prevent the insight into the *peculiarity* of the literary achievement of Matthew. Therefore, synchronous and diachronous analysis, "literary criticism" and "*Literarkritik*" of European provenance, the inner world of the narrative and its historical place cannot challenge each other in the sense of a one-sided prominence of the one over the other.

[5]Bacon* 48–50.

[6]For Bacon*, the Gospel of Matthew is "the great apostolic refutation of the Jews." Davies, *Setting* represents the most basic exorcism of the "awe-inspiring ghost" of Bacon (107). But he denies only that the Matthean Jesus puts his torah as a new one over against the Jewish Torah. Bacon's thesis was taken over widely in Anglo–Saxon research; cf. Frankemölle, *Jahwebund* 339, n. 16.

might also be associated with the discourses in a different manner.[7]

b. I would like to call the second basic type the *center model*:[8] The Gospel is structured chiastically around a center. In most cases, the third discourse, ch. 13, is considered the center, and the other sections are chiastically related. Thus chs. 1–4 correspond to the concluding chs. 26–28, the Sermon on the Mount to the eschatological discourse, etc. There are indeed indications for such correspondences: chs. 5–7 and 23–25 are the longest discourses, chs. 10 and 18 the shortest. In addition the two disciples discourses are almost exactly of the same length. Interpreters have tried to see many other such corresponding chiastic features, but these have found less consensus.[9] Sometimes, the center was found in ch. 11 or between ch. 13 and ch. 14.[10] There are many variations to this basic type too.

A third basic type follows closely the Gospel of Mark. Therefore I want to call it the *Markan model*.[11] It sees a major break between 16:20 and 16:21, i.e., after the Confession of Peter at Caesarea Philippi. The new beginning in 16:21, ἀπὸ τότε ἤρξατο Ἰησοῦς Χριστὸς δεικνύειν τοῖς μαθηταῖς, is very similar to the new beginning in 4:17: ἀπὸ τότε ἤρξατο ὁ Ἰησοῦς κηρύσσειν. Thus, two main sections result: Jesus' ministry and proclamation in Galilee and his proceeding to the passion in Jerusalem, which somewhat correspond to the two large main parts of the Gospel of Mark. Matthew 1:1–4:16 is the introduction. In distinction from the two earlier basic types, there is here a clear dominance of the basic narrative pattern: the narrative, not the teachings of Jesus included in the five discourses, determines the structure. This is not without consequences for the determination of the genre and the interpretation of the Gospel of Matthew.

Difficulties in Assessing the Structure

A clear disposition is obviously not in hand. There are three basic reasons for this:

1. The Matthean language is highly formulaic. There are numerous phrases or individual words which are repeated. Therefore it is difficult to make full use of the similarities in vocabulary. The Gospel of Matthew overflows with possible inclusions. But which ones are consciously intended by the evangelist? Formulaic beginnings of sentences, as, e.g., 4:17 and 16:21, are by no means

---

[7] Chs. 8–10 belong better to chs. 5–7; cf. the inclusion 4:23/9:35. Ch. 18 is best connected with 16:13–20:34. Chs. 11f. have no close connection with either ch. 10 or ch. 13. Frankemölle, *Jahwebund* 342, reverses Bacon: Each discourse belongs together with the following narrative text. A mixed solution is proposed by Gaechter, *Kunst* 60–66.

[8] E.g., Fenton* 179; Lohr* 427; P. F. Ellis, *Matthew* 12; Combrink* 71.

[9] Lohr* 428–30 attempts, for the sake of his schema, to discover correspondences between the narrative parts of the first and second main parts. That fails: Matthean language is so formulaic that correspondences can easily be found between all parts. Sometimes, the center was found in ch. 11 or between ch. 13 and ch. 14.

[10] Green* puts the center into the 11th chapter; the second part of the Gospel deals with the rejection of Jesus. Léon–Dufour* has this part begin with 14:1.

[11] This basic type was developed by Kingsbury, *Structure* 7–25, in following Lohmeyer 7*–10*,64,264 and N. B. Stonehouse, *The Witness of Matthew and Mark to Christ* (London 1944) 129–131. It fits with the broadening of the prologue to 4:16 by Krentz*. The prologue deals with the person of the Messiah Jesus, the first main part with his proclamation, the second with his way to suffering (Kingsbury, 25).

rare.[12] Why should exactly these two be singled out?

2. Beginning with ch. 12, the Gospel of Matthew follows closely the structure of Mark. Leaving aside the discourses, only few texts are inserted. But in chs. 3–11 non–Markan texts predominate. The sequence of Mark 1:1–2:22 seems to be presupposed in Matthew 3–11, but it determines the structure only minimally. It seems as if the evangelist Matthew relaxed in his redactional activity.[13] This discrepancy between Matthew 1–12 and 13–28 must be explained.

3. Matthew does not seem to value delimitations. On the contrary, again and again we find transitional verses or pericopes which because of their relationships to what precedes and what follows can be considered only as transitional pericopes. Thus, only rarely can major parts be clearly delimited.

Examples of such ◗ *transitional verses* or ◗ *transitional pericopes* are the following: 4:17; 4:23–5:2; 5:20; 6:1; 10:16,26; the whole of ch. 11;[14] 24:1f. Certain phrases also are characteristic: the phrase at the end of discourses: καὶ ἐγένετο ὅτε ἐτέλεσεν etc. in 7:28; 11:11; 13:53; 19:1; 26:1 syntactically does not conclude a discourse but introduces a new stage in the narrative! Phrases such as ἐν ἐκείνῳ τῷ καιρῷ and the like appear exactly where there is a new beginning in content and have the function of a bridge and of establishing the impression of a seamless run of the narrative (e.g., 3:1; 12:1; 14:1). Also the Matthean favorite word τότε (e.g., 3:13; 4:1; 11:20; 15:1; 18:21; 19:13; 20:20; 21:1; 27:3 etc.) or the phrase ἀπὸ τότε (4:17; 16:21; 26:16) often function as a transition between two pericopes.[15]

Matthew obviously values a seamless course of narrative more than a clear distinction of major parts. That speaks in favor of assuming that the Gospel of Matthew, as far as genre is concerned, has to be understood as a connected *narrative* and not as a collection of individual texts which could be used liturgically as pericopes or catechetically as texts for instruction.[16]

Structuring of Shorter Sections

Generally it is much easier to recognize the evangelist's careful arrangement of shorter sections of text than to discern the disposition of the Gospel as a whole. Therefore, we will proceed in such a way that the literary means which Matthew uses for structuring will be discussed first. As examples we can point to the arrangement of individual sections. Only then can considerations concerning the

---

[12]E.g., nobody yet has had the idea to let the corresponding main parts begin with 5:17 and 10:34, although purely formally this would be just as cogent as with 4:17 and 16:21.

[13]Gundry 10: "Editorial fatigue set in." Neirynck's* essay is fruitful because he begins with just this observation (59–63) and uses redaction criticism for his analysis of the structure of the Gospel of Matthew.

[14]Matthew 11:5f. points back to chs. 8 and 9; 11:3,7 to 3:11,5; 11:22,24 to 10:15. Γενεά is a central word in ch. 12 (4 times), also κρίσις (5 times). Matthew 11:27 points ahead to 28:18–20.

[15]Neither at 4:17 nor at 16:21 does a new main part begin. This is especially clear in the case of 16:21: Matthew makes the effort to integrate his insertion of vv. 17–19 into Mark 8:27–33 so that *one* pericope, Matt. 16:13–23 is created: anticipation of υἱὸς τοῦ ἀνθρώπου v. 13; antithetical correspondence of v. 17 and v. 23.

[16]This confirms a basic concern of Kingsbury, independently from his suggestion of structure.

arrangement of the whole Gospel follow.

A. *Matthew puts together materials which are formally or materially similar.*

The following examples can be mentioned: the collections of miracle narratives in chs. 8f., the collection of parables in 21:28–22:14; the discourse against the Pharisees in ch. 23; and, of course, the discourses as such. This principle of arrangement is not new: already Q is constructed according to thematically related blocks; Mark also uses blocks which are due partly to pre–Markan sources. In Matthew it is new that in several cases he brackets a block solidly in the thread of the narrative to enable it to receive a clear function in its place, as, e.g., the collection of miracle narratives in chs. 8–9 between the Sermon on the Mount and the discourse at the sending out of the disciples. In the same way, the collection of parables in 21:28–22:14 has a clear function in the preparation of the great accounting with Israel.

B. *There is a noticeable ◆ correspondence in the length of materials.*

The first and the last Matthean discourses are the longest, the second and fourth—almost of equal length—are the shortest, and the middle one, ch. 13, is of medium length. Of approximately equal length are in each case 2:1–12 and 2:13–23; 5:21–32 and 5:33–48; 8:1–17; 8:18–9:1a; 9:1b–17 and 9:18–34; 18:1–14 and 18:21–35; 24:4–41 and 25:14–46, etc. Naturally one may be of different opinion concerning the delimitation of the pericopes, but it can hardly be contested that there are such formal symmetries.[17] This makes it obvious that Matthew has written his own manuscript and did not dictate it.

C. *Matthew composes according to certain ◆ number schemes.* The number *three* seems most important. But also *two, four,* and *seven* play a certain role.

There are three sections each in 1:18–2:23; 5:21–7:11; 5:21–32,33–48; 6:1–18; 6:19–7:11; 6:19–24; 7:1–11; 8:1–17; 9:1b–17; 13:1–52; 18:1–35; 23; 24:4–25:46. Examples can be increased at will. Often main sections and subsections are composed according to the number *three,* e.g., 1:18–2:23 and 2:13–23; 5:21–7:11; 5:21–33 and 5:21–26; 6:1–18; 6:7–15 and 6:9–13 (2 × 3 petitions!) etc. The number *three* is frequent in Jewish texts.[18] One has to beware of interpreting it as to content, e.g., as a number of perfection.[19] It is only a literary systematizing principle, one which is frequent in oral instruction.

The other numbers are less important. Matthew forms two series of four beatitudes (5:3–10). The complex of the miracle narratives in chs. 8–9 also is fourfold. The number *seven* plays a role in the genealogy, in the parable chapter 13, in 21:28–22:46 and in the chapter of the woes (23).[20] The number *two* is important especially in connection with the duplications which will be mentioned later.

---

[17]Cf. Kürzinger* 572f. The findings are difficult to interpret. Since such correspondences do not appear in all places, the possibility of coincidence cannot be completely excluded. So far I have not become aware of OT analogies. J. Smit Sibinga, "Eine literarische Technik im Matthäusevangelium," in Didier, *Évangile* 99–105, moves on similar paths: he counts syllables.

[18]G. Delling, "τρεῖς κτλ." TDNT VIII, 216ff. presents the evidence which is interesting primarily from a didactic point of view (3 in enumerations, memory verses, as rhetorical arrangement). Cf. also Goulder, *Midrash* 26.

[19]Ramaroson* 77 thinks that among Jews *seven* designates perfection, *three* the deity and *two* "l'insistance ou le superlatif" (without references).

[20]The number *seven* which often is mentioned as important for Matthew, seems to play a role in pre–Matthean series, e.g., 5:3–9; 23:13–36.

D. *Matthew often hints at his themes by the repetition of* ♦ key words.[21]

Examples: Ἄγγελος κυρίου (4× in 1:18–2:23; as pointing to God's guidance); δικαιοσύνη 5× in Matthew 5–7; ἀποστέλλω/ἀπόστολος 4× in 10:2–42; κρίσις 7× in 11:20–12:45; Φαρισαῖος 4× in 12:1–45; ὄχλος 16× in chs. 14f.; ἀδελφός 4×, μικρός 3× and ἀφίημι 4× in ch. 18; ἀκολουθέω 9× in chs. 8f. and 6× in chs. 19f., etc. This literary device is strengthened by the tendencies to formulaic language and to the combination of similar materials.

Naturally, one is here reminded of oral tradition which uses key-word connecting links as a mnemonic device. Key words have become in Matthew a literary means, for they are meant to clarify the theme of a section. Therefore, we speak of ♦ *key words* or *lead words*. They furnish an important hint at how the Gospel is to be read: Matthew wanted a sequential reading as well as a reading by pericopes; for only then can key words disclose the sense of larger sections. He wished for an intensive reading, with the possibility of reviewing; only in this way does the larger context become fruitful for the individual text, and only in this way do the key words reveal their fullness of meaning.

E. *Matthew hints at his themes by* ♦ central verses (kelalim).[22]

These central verses are, e.g., 5:17, 20, 48; 6:1; 7:12, 21; 10:16, 26 or 18:10, 14. In a figurative sense there are also "central texts,"[23] e.g., 5:17–20; 12:35–40; 22:34–40 or 28:16–20. Such verses or texts are distinguished by their position; they open up larger contexts. They are not simply titles but rather combinations of materials and generalizations at the beginning or end of a section, often with explicit transitional function. Matthew here comes close to the Hillel rule of the general and the specific (כלל ופרט) which was much more than an exegetical rule.

F. *Matthew creates* ♦ doublets,[24] *which clarify his intention.*

Doublets may serve various purposes. They create, e.g., a compositional frame around certain sections (e.g., 4:23/9:35; 19:30/20:16; 24:42/25:13 = inclusions!). They set off important situations (e.g., 9:13/12:7). Sometimes they help in treating the same materials under different aspects (e.g., 10:17–22/24:9–13; 7:16–19/12:33–35). Or they serve special intentions, e.g., the demonstration of the continuity of the proclamation

---

[21]Repetitions and the tendency to retain an expression are considered signs of a mediocre author. But in contrast to merely formulaic language, here it is a question of the repetition of key words which are relevant to the theme. Examples in Lohr* 422–24. The technique is found in the OT, cf. M. Buber, "Leitwortstil in der Erzählung des Pentateuch," in M. Buber, *Werke II* (Munich, 1964) 1131–49; also M. Buber, "Das Leitwort und der Formtypus der Rede," ibid., 1150–58; J. Muilenburg, "A Study in Hebrew Rhetoric: Repetition and Style," *VT.S* 1 (1953) 97–111.

[22]On the *kelal* see Bacher, *Terminologie* I 79–82; Gerhardsson, *Memory* 136–141; on the rule of the general and the specific, J. Bonsirven, *Exégèse rabbinique et exégèse paulinienne* (Paris 1938) 106–15.

[23]Grundmann speaks of "center point pericopes."

[24]This technique is already traditional; cf., e.g., the redactional formation of the third passion prediction, Mark 10:32–34. In evaluating it, one has to consider the fact that normally reading was done aloud so that duplications, particularly within a shorter section, entered the memory. Lists of Matthean duplications are given in Hawkins, *Horae* 170f.; Rigaux, *Témoignage* 43; Butler, *Originality* 138–147; Kilpatrick, *Origins* 84–93. Naturally, there also are doublets which permit a source critical explanation (variants of logia in Mark and Q). But since Matthew controls his sources very exactly (in distinction from Luke) and avoids doublets, at least with larger text sections, one must ask whether Matthew intentionally leaves doublets which can be explained source critically so that the logia may be committed to memory. This consideration has to be entertained at the following passages: 5:29f./18:8f.; 5:31f./19:7–9; 10:38f./16:24f.; 12:38f./16:1–4; 17:20/20:21; 20:26/23:11.

among John, Jesus, and the disciples (cf. 3:2 with 4:17 and 10:7). It is particularly striking that Matthew shows no qualms about relating one and the same miracle narrative twice, and even as different stories (9:27–31/20:29–34; 9:32–34/12:22–24). Here can be observed the formation of variants so to speak *in situ*. This feature fits rather poorly into the image of a tradition–bound Matthew. However, it is not without analogies in the Old Testament tradition, [25] where repetitions serve to center the thought. At the same time they are a help for the reader for the conscious acquisition of the main thoughts. Here also it becomes clear that Matthew presupposes a continuous reading of his book. Only then are such techniques meaningful.

G. *Matthew loves* ♦ inclusions[26] *in larger and smaller contexts.*

Repetitions of key words and doublets lead to the phenomenon that there are inclusions in large number which means that one must not construct every repeated word into an intended inclusion. [27] An impressive inclusion which spans the whole Gospel is the resumption of Immanuel, "God with us" (1:24f.), at the end in 28:20. Inclusions around smaller units of text are found, e.g., in the repeated nota bene 7:16, 20, the apodosis of the first and last beatitude 5:3, 10, the key words δικαιοσύνη and περισσός (5:20, 47f.) or the washing of hands in 15:2, 20. We are dealing here with a habitual Old Testament technique of composition. Inclusions in large contexts become evident only to continuous reading. Again it becomes obvious that Matthew wishes that his book be read and meditated upon as a whole again and again.

H. *Matthew loves* ♦ chiastic ring compositions. [28]

By chiastic ring composition I mean a series of several inclusions which surround a text in the form of a ring, i.e., the compositional scheme A B (C) . . . D . . . . (C′) B′ A′. Even if one cannot observe this compositional principle with the Gospel as a whole, as the "center model" assumes, nevertheless, it is present certainly in individual sections. An example is the Sermon on the Mount whose center is the Lord's Prayer. Examples of smaller text sections with chiastic structure are 9:1b–8; 13:13–18 and 18:10–14. A pre–Matthean example is 23:16–21 with the impressive climax in v. 22. Here again we are dealing with a customary technique, spread throughout the Old Testament, while it occurs in Greek literature more frequently only in the earliest period. [29]

---

[25] Especially with logia, the notice of Gerhardsson, *Memory* 163–170, of rabbinical techniques of repetition for mnemonic reasons is helpful.

[26] Cf. the material in Fenton* 174f.; Lohr* 408–410; Lagrange LXXXI.

[27] One should speak of inclusions only where a clearly discernible textual unit is stressed at the beginning and at the end by like formulations or contents. In other cases one should be cautious in light of the Matthean formulaic language.

[28] Since such constructions are being "discovered" in the Gospel of Matthew in large numbers, a caution is appropriate. One should speak of chiastic ring compositions (Rigaux, Témoignage 38; "enveloppement") only where the correspondending items are located within a clearly discernible textual unit. A rich palette of probable, possible, and impossible chiasms is presented by Gaechter, *Kunst* 26–44, and N. W. Lund, *Chiasmus in the New Testament* (Chapel Hill 1942), 233–319.

[29] W. A. van Otterlo, *Untersuchungen über Begriff, Anwendung und Entstehung der griechischen Ringkomposition* (Amsterdam 1944): The ring composition disappears in Greek literature in the 5th century B.C.E. In the Jewish area, it is widespread. On the Old Testament: L. Alonso–Schökel, *Das Alte Testament als literarisches Kunstwerk* (Cologne 1971) 364–406; N. W. Lund in various articles (see Schökel, 367–369, with examples primarily from the psalms and prophets); E. Galbiati, *La struttura letteraria dell'Esodo* (Alba 1956) 48ff.; J. R. Lundblom, *Jeremiah: A Study in Ancient He-*

I. A gift of Matthew consists in his working with ◗ "signals" and anticipations which forecast coming materials, hint at the meaning of the whole context, and sensitize the reader for that which is narrated later.[30]

This narrative technique has a certain but only relative parallel in the promises of Old Testament historical books. Its presupposition is that an individual event stands in the large context of a divine plan. Thus particularly the prologue 1:1–4:22, a christological, salvation historical, and ecclesiological prelude of grand style, is filled with "signals." Examples are the two Old Testament pointers to the "son" in 1:24; 2:15 which are emphasized by the key word κύριος or the history of Herod and the Gentile Magi (2:1–12) which is a prelude to the whole tragic fate of Israel. Matthew 4:8 contains a clear "signal" to 28:15–20, Matt. 2:23 together with 4:12–16 a "signal" to the Gentile mission, or 3:15 a signal to 5:17 and the Sermon on the Mount. Matthew took over from Mark the signal function of the passion of John, which is a prelude to the passion of Jesus, and the signals of the passion predictions. The "signal technique" also shows that the Gospel of Matthew was intended to be read as a whole, and as a narrative. In many a place it has a depth dimension which discloses itself only when the Gospel is viewed as a whole.

The survey brings the following *results*: (a) The Gospel of Matthew is fashioned intensively, noticeably in the smaller units. (b) It is not a collection of individual texts which would serve liturgical[31] or catechetical[32] purposes. Its *Sitz im Leben* is study, perusal, from beginning to end.[33] It is written for repeated reading. (c) A similarity of the Matthean method of composition with that of Old Testament and Jewish literature is apparent. Several aspects have their correspondence in the Old Testament, and some become more understandable through the rabbinical school usage.

---

brew Rhetoric, SBLDS 18 (1975) 23–112; M. Weiss, "Wege der neuen Dichtungswissenschaft in ihrer Anwendung auf die Psalmenforschung" *Bib.* 42 (1961) 255–302.

[30]Lohr* has pointed out this technique under the catchword "foreshadowing." Otherwise it was hardly ever described; an exception is Gundry (see index s.v. Anticipation). Perhaps one must distinguish three different situations: (a) In the prologue, 1:1–4:22, Matthew gives an inventory of themes of his Gospel, e.g., Son of God, Son of Abraham, righteousness, Gentiles; (b) There are narratives, not only in the prologue, which foreshadow later materials and thus assume, so to speak, a "typological" function, e.g., 2:1–12 (the "No" of Israel, Gentiles); 2:19–23 (the journey of Jesus into Gentile Galilee); (c) there are words of Jesus which are not directly predictions (as, e.g., 8:11f.; 21:43), but have, in opposition to their immediate context, an overreaching meaning which is not disclosed for the believing community except on the basis of the whole Gospel, e.g., 3:9 (to raise children for Abraham from stones); 9:8 (authority of humans to forgive sins); 11:27 (all things are given to me).

[31]That Matthew is a lectionary was advocated especially by Kilpatrick, *Origins* 59–100, and Goulder, *Midrash* 227–451. Goulder reconstructs for this purpose a lectionary schedule for the Jewish year, the hypothetical character of which has often been pointed out. Kilpatrick is much less speculative, but his observations suffer from a lack of clarity concerning liturgical language.

[32]G. Schille, "Bemerkungen zur Formgeschichte des Evangeliums II. Das Evangelium des Matthäus als Katechismus," *NTS* 4 (1957/58) 101–114. Stendahl, *School* 20–29, speaks more cautiously of a "handbook"; however, he also does not recognize the character of Matthew as a *narrative*. I do not wish to exclude the possibility that Matthew was used in Christian instruction. It is important: in instruction too, the narrative of Matthew was (we hope!) read and contemplated continuously.

[33]This applies to *all* the Gospels, as R. Guelich, "The Gospel Genre," in *Das Evangelium und die Evangelien*, ed. P. Stuhlmacher, 1983 (WUNT 28) 219, rightly says.

Overall Contours

Several signs indicate that the Gospel of Matthew was intended to be primarily a *narrative book*. Matthew made a decision to this effect by using the Gospel of Mark as the basis for his own presentation, even though in several points it was not close to him theologically.[34] This is evident beginning with Matthew 12; Matthew 12–28 has to be understood as an altered and enlarged new formulation of Mark 2:12–4:34; 6:1–16:8.

4:23–11:30

The situation appears to be different in chs. 1–11, where Matthew's structuring is most in evidence. In any case, it is noteworthy that the order of Mark 1:2–2:22 is preserved in principle, making apparent just how seriously Matthew takes the Markan narrative.

In general it is striking how conservatively he deals with his sources, even in chs. 1–11. Not only the sequence of Mark 1:4–2:22 but also that of Q are completely preserved in Matthew 3–9 and—apart from the reversal of two main blocks, the discourse concerning the Baptist and the sending discourse, which is easily explained in terms of Matthew's redaction—in Matthew 3–11.[35] The unique contribution of Matthew consists only in insertion of additional material from later sections (Mark 4:35–5:43). Nevertheless, the reader has the impression of a completely new creation. In view of his piety toward his sources, this is a splendid literary achievement of Matthew!

Decisive for the outline of the first half of the Gospel is the observation that 4:23 and 9:35 are arranged like a ring around the Sermon on the Mount and the two miracle chapters, 8 and 9. A ring-shaped composition within the section corresponds to this inclusion.[36] Thus there is a unity in the description of the Messiah of the word (chs. 5–7) and of the deed (chs. 8–9). The sending discourse, ch. 10, where the disciples take over Jesus' activity of healing and Jesus' mission of proclamation[37] also belongs to this complex. Thus ch. 10 inaugurates, in a manner of speaking, the ecclesiological continuation of the ministry of Jesus. It is difficult to evaluate ch. 11. From a literary-critical point of view, the evangelist adds here material from Q which he has left aside so far. In the composition, this chapter marks a transition:[38] the beginning points in vv. 5f. to the miracle activity of Jesus in chs. 8–9 while vv. 25–30 point forward to 28:16–20. The transitional character is visible also in the fact that 12:1 does not present a new beginning but, by ἐν ἐκείνῳ τῷ καιρῷ, connects the following narratives with ch. 11.

---

[34]Cf. below, pp. 75-76.

[35]Luke 3:2–9, 16–22; 4:1–13; 6:20–7:10 = Matt. 3:1–8:13 (with interruptions). Luke 7:18–34 were transposed by Matthew and inserted between Luke 9:57–10:12 and 10:13.

[36]Cf. the analysis of Matt. 4:23–25 and the introduction to Matthew 5–7 no. 1.

[37]Matthew 10:1 refers back to 4:23; 9:35; and 10:7 to 4:17.

[38]Cf. details above, n. 14, and the introduction to ch. 11.

1:1–4:22

The prologue accordingly should be considered as consisting of 1:1–4:22. It constitutes a Christological and salvation-historical prelude. Christologically, the title "Son of God" is decisive. It is introduced in chs. 1 and 2 and interpreted in 3:13–4:11. The salvation-historical motif stands behind the geographical statements, the path of the Jesus child from David's city of Bethlehem to the Galilee of the Gentiles. Similarly to ch. 10, the call of the disciples in 4:18–22 indicates the ecclesiological dimension of the story of the Son of God.

Chapters 12–28

In Matthew 12–28, the passion narrative, chs. 26–28, and the ministry of Jesus in Jerusalem (chs. 21–25), which in Matthew becomes a great rendering of accounts with Israel and an exhortation for the church, form a unit. The structure of chs. 12–20 is difficult. The second part of this section, 16:13–20:23, with ch. 18 as the center, is determined by questions of the church. It corresponds to the Markan instruction of the disciples and the instruction concerning the passion, 8:27–10:52. Matthew 12:1–16:12 describes in several thrusts the "withdrawal" of Jesus from the disputes with Israel and God's presence in the church of the disciples of which the following major section speaks. In the introductory chapter 12 the dispute with the enemies dominates. The central parable chapter 13 contains after the public instruction of Jesus a detailed instruction of the disciples (36–52). In the two following sections, beginning respectively with 13:53 and 14:34, the decisive word ἀναχωρέω each time marks the point where the disciple community emerges from the struggle over Israel (14:13; 15:21).[39] A last series of disputes (16:1–12) is the transition to the section on the disciples (16:13–20:23). One might speak in this major section of the "origin of the disciple community in the struggle over Israel."

It is certainly wrong to speak of a growing relaxing of the creative power of the evangelist in the second part of his Gospel. Rather, the beginning chapters 1–11 communicate to the reader the most important points of view from which the evangelist might have read the Gospel of Mark. Later on, i.e., in the light of chs. 1–11, the reader can understand the retold Gospel of Mark correctly. Once more, it becomes obvious that the Gospel was intended to be read from beginning to end; for without the introductory chapters 1–11 the second half hardly could be read "in a Matthean manner."

The Discourses

It seems to me that the structure of the Gospel is not disclosed on the basis of the five great discourses. A schematic division in five "books" is not possible. However, Matthew has clearly made the five discourses conspicuous through their concluding phrases.

---

[39]Léon–Dufour* arranges similarly. However, he sets the beginning of this part at 14:1 and distinguishes then three "withdrawals" (14:13; 15:21; 16:4). Murphy–O'Connor* 371–84 follows this in general. In contrast with them, A. van Aarde, "Structure," *Neot* 16 (1982) 21–34 (following Ellis, *Matthew* 66f.) wants to divide 13:53–17:27 into three sections, each of which has a climax in a Peter pericope (14:28–33; 16:13–20; 17:24–27).

One should not read anything mysterious into the number *five*. Not only the Pentateuch but also other Old Testament writings are divided into five books (*The Megillot*, the Psalms).[40] If the remembrance of Sinai stands behind the "Sermon on the Mount," then this remembrance cannot without tension be combined with the schema of five books.[41] Why did Matthew not mark other discourses of Jesus also by his particular concluding formula? The answer is simple: other discourses (e.g., 11:7–24) are much shorter and have not been composed and arranged by Matthew to the same extent as the five great discourses. The discourse concerning the Pharisees, ch. 23, and the eschatological discourse, chs. 24f., are considered as a single discourse because they belong intrinsically together but also, more importantly, because according to Mark no narratives are to be reported between them. Briefly, the arrangement of the logia material in five discourses is a splendid and—as the history of interpretation demonstrates—successful didactic achievement. It makes the overview and the appropriation of the proclamation of Jesus far easier. In my opinion, a theological mystery is not to be sought here. The arrangement of Matthew is determined by the Jesus *narrative*; the discourses fit into its course in suitable places.

Result

The Gospel of Matthew tells the story of Jesus the Son of God. The most important basic theological decision of Matthew was to take the Gospel of Mark as the basis from which alone Jesus' proclamation can be correctly illuminated. This means theologically: *He has tied the ethical proclamation of Jesus concerning the kingdom of God to the history of God's actions with Jesus. In this way, it becomes the proclamation of grace.* Here it becomes clear how inappropriate is the alternative between theological independence and dependence on the sources.[42]

Genre

What is the *genre* of the Gospel of Matthew? Certainly it had to remind the Jewish-Christian readers first of all of a *Hellenistic* βίος,[43] particularly if one considers

---

[40]Cf., moreover, five books by Jason of Cyrene and by Papias.

[41]According to the scheme of Bacon*, the Sermon on the Mount would stand in the second half of the new "Genesis," according to Frankemölle and Gaechter (cf. above, n. 7) one would have to put it at the beginning of the book of Genesis. According to Green* 50 (cf. above, n. 10), who subdivides the first section of the Gospel into five books, the Sermon on the Mount is "Matthew's Leviticus." On the Sinai typology in the Sermon on the Mount, cf. the interpretation of 5:1f. below.

[42]Since here a relatively close approximation to the approach of Frankemölle, *Jahwebund*, is obvious, I would like briefly to indicate where I differ from him. Matthew is, according to my opinion, not a "covenant theological view of history" (hinged text) but a narrative. The theologically decisive element is not the presentation of the story of Jesus for the sake of a *theology* of history with the help of Old Testament theologies of history but the ordering of the εὐαγγέλιον τῆς βασιλείας into the *story* of God with Jesus. Matthew is concerned neither with de-historicizing (e.g., 349) nor with historicizing (cf. the concept of Strecker, *Geschichtsverständnis*), but with putting the ethical "gospel of the kingdom of heaven" into the story of God's actions with his Son, Jesus. Thus Matthew has to be interpreted on the level of a *narrative*, not on the level of a theological plan.

[43]The relationship of the Gospels to "biography" is today very controversial. One has to distinguish a general concept of "biography," understood as the description of the life of a person, which begins with the birth and ends with the death of that person, from that which in the ancient world was meant by the "genre of biography" (= βίος).

the fact that a biography of a person from birth to death was something unusual in the milieu of Jewish literature.[44] For a Jewish reader the first impression had to be: This human being has a very special significance. But the Gospel of Matthew is not a biography in the technical sense of ancient literature;[45] in some features it indeed comes close to it, especially by its parenetic basic tone or by the systematic arrangement of its material.[46] There are more features which distinguish it: most importantly, Matthew does not tell the *typical* story of an exemplary human being but the *unique* story of God with the human Jesus. The reference to the Bible which is so basic to Matthew is alien to ancient biography.[47]

Rather, one must seriously consider that Matthew was oriented precisely on compository techniques of Old Testament and Jewish literature.[48] Aside from the "Jewish style" of the Gospel[49] two "Jewish" characteristics are noteworthy: *genealogies* at the beginning of a book are found only in the Jewish milieu (Genesis, 1–2 Chronicles, Libanius of Antioch). They serve the salvation-historical connection and must not be confused with notices of ancient biographies concerning the ancestry of a hero. And the *discourses* have nothing to do with the speeches in a Greek historical monograph or historical writing. As, e.g., the great speech of Moses in Deuteronomy (chs. 4–30), they have a direct application to the present, leaping over the interval of time. Matthew thus attempts something unique: *In a deliberate Jewish dress he does something very un-Jewish*—he narrates the story of Jesus from his birth until his resurrection in the light of the Bible.

So it is close to the truth when H. Frankemölle designates the Gospel of Matthew as a *kerygmatic work of history* of an Old Testament style, as a new sketch of a sacred foundational history which has a literary orientation to Deuteronomy and the

---

[44]The Λόγοι περὶ τοῦ βίου Μωϋσέως of Philo is intended not only for Jewish readers. Aside from Philo, there are only beginnings of something similar to a "biography": the "lives" of the prophets and the *Paralipomena of Jeremiah*, in addition from court circles the biography of Augustus by Nicolaus of Damascus, the ὑπομνήματα of Herod and the autobiographies of Nicolaus of Damascus and of Josephus, none of which is truly Jewish. It is striking that there are no biographical traditions of some great figures of religion, e.g., the teacher of righteousness and of the rabbis; cf. G. Stanton, *Jesus of Nazareth in New Testament Preaching*, SNTSMS 27 (1974), 126–29.

[45]On the genre of biography cf. over against the imprecision of C. H. Talbert, *What Is a Gospel?* (Philadelphia 1977) the cautious deliberations of A. Dihle, "Die Evangelien und die griechische Biographie," in *Evangelium*, ed. Stuhlmacher, op.cit. (above n. 33) 384f., 390–96: Biography is not one of the genres considered by ancient theories of literature. It becomes discernible as genre in the circle of Plutarch because he delimits his own intention over against historiography. Biographies contain essentially moral examples and betray an image of human beings, which is influenced by Aristotle.

[46]Stanton (above, n. 44), 119f. Matthew arranges systematically in individual units, in accordance with his sources, but as a whole he tells a continuing *story* of Jesus which is characterized by the opposition "Jesus and Israel." P. L. Shuler, *A Genre for the Gospels: The Biographical Character of Matthew* (Philadelphia, 1982) 34–87 postulates a genre of the "encomium biography" on the basis of Isocrates, *Helena;* Busiris; Euagoras; Xenophon, *Agesilaus;* Philo, *De Vita Mosis;* Tacitus, *Agricola;* Lucianus, *Demonax.* It seems questionable to me whether one may, on the basis of such scattered and varying examples, reconstruct a genre which existed in the consciousness of ancient people and not only in the consciousness of modern authors. Still more problematical is the transference of this model to Matthew: particularly the prologue and the passion narrative where Shuler sees the most analogies show that the specifically *Matthean* accents cannot be captured in this way. Cf. also the skepticism of Guelich, (above, n. 33) 190–92.

[47]Dihle (above, n. 45) 404f.

[48]Cf. above p. 38–41. under C (number schemes), D (key words), E (kelalim), G (inclusions), H (ring compositions) and the repetitive style of Matthew.

[49]Cf. below p. 50.

Chronicler's history.[50] But it should not stop here: our analysis of details will show that Frankemölle overestimates the originality of Matthew. Matthew is not consciously oriented on certain Old Testament books as literary or especially theological prototypes, but he thinks and writes in their sphere of influence. Rather he is oriented on the Gospel of Mark.

The early church saw this correctly when—under the influence of the Markan and Matthean linguistic use of εὐαγγέλιον—it entitled its Jesus books εὐαγγέλιον κατὰ. . . . With this the distinctiveness of the Gospel genre was established. From Matthew and on this was rightly seen: he shows clearly that the given model by which he allows himself to be guided is the Gospel of Mark alone.

2. THE SOURCES

The two-source hypothesis is the basis for this commentary. To question this hypothesis is to refute a large part of the post–1945 redaction-critical research in the Synoptics, a truly daring undertaking which seems to me to be neither necessary nor possible.[51]

The Sayings Source (Q)

We make the following assumptions concerning the Sayings Source: it was a written document: that seems to be certain, not so much because of the verbal agreement as because of the Q sequence of the individual pericopes which is often retained in Matthew.[52] But it circulated in different recensions,[53] whereby QMt is closer to the "common" form than the version of the Sayings Source used by Luke, which was most likely enlarged substantially. In my opinion, we observe with the Sayings Source a process of expansion which began with smaller collections, as, e.g., the Sermon on the Plain, and proceeded by way of different steps of redaction as far as the version of the Source which can be reconstructed from Matthew and Luke, and from there led on to the very much enlarged version, QLk. QMt is a version of Q which is altered and enlarged only minimally. The so-called "final redaction" of Q has to be distinguished fundamentally from the redaction of the Synoptics. In intensity and dignity it was not different from earlier redactions of the source. It did not make a literary document from the collection of Q material. Paleographically one might assume: the collection of Q material was a rather large notebook, bound together

---

[50]*Jahwebund* 331–400.

[51]J. M. Robinson, "On the Gattung of Mark and John," in *Jesus and Man's Hope* I, ed. D. Miller (Pittsburgh, 1970) 101f. The success of redaction criticism on the basis of the two-document hypothesis is the most important argument against the "new" hypotheses on the synoptic sources.

[52]Cf. above, n. 35, in the commentary the introduction to 5–7, and the analysis of 6:19–24; 10; 12:22–37; 13:31–33; 24.

[53]E.g. with Sato, *Q* 53–71. Against J. P. Brown, "Mark as Witness to an Edited Form of Q," *JBL* 80 (1961) 29–44, and others, I do not presuppose a literary relationship between Q and Mark.

with strings on the margin. It permitted an insertion of new leaves at any time.[54] The Gospel of Mark, however, was a solidly bound codex and therefore a literary work which for this reason continued to be handed down even after its expansion by Matthew.

Alternatives to the Two-Source Hypothesis

I will forgo a critical discussion of the counter proposals to the two-source hypothesis, since its verification is carried out implicitly through the whole commentary, and limit myself to brief information.

According to C. Butler, Mark wrote his Gospel with the aid of Matthew and of the notes of Peter.[55] W. R. Farmer, B. Orchard, D. Dungan, and some others are renewing the Griesbach-Owen hypothesis that Luke is dependent on Matthew and that Mark is an epitome of both.[56] A. Gaboury on the basis of the triple tradition reconstructs a basic gospel which lies as a foundation behind all Synoptics.[57] J. Rist thinks that Matthew and Mark are independent of each other but are based on a common oral tradition.[58] A. M. Farrer and M. Goulder accept the priority of Mark but reject Q and consider Matthew an expansion of Mark on the basis of the lessons of the Jewish-Christian order of pericopes.[59] M. E. Boismard[60] sees the origin of the Synoptics as very complicated: Our extant Matthew is independent of our extant Mark. The extant Matthew is based on an earlier form of Matthew and of Mark; the older Matthew on its part is dependent on Q and a still older basic text. This hypothesis probably is the most elaborate and most thought–through hypothesis of all the alternatives to the two-source hypothesis. It has the advantage and at the same time disadvantage that it seems to be able to explain all phenomena because it is so complicated that it integrates in itself more or less all other hypotheses.

"Minor Agreements"

In my opinion, there is only one problem that poses serious difficulties for the two-source

---

[54]In the framework of this commentary, a foundation for this hypothesis unfortunately cannot be laid. Its feasibility is presented by Sato, *Q*, 72–77.

[55]Butler, *Originality* (modified Augustinian hypothesis!). Other advocates of the classical hypothesis of the priority of an (original) Matthew: P. Parker, *The Gospel before Mark* (Chicago, 1953); L. Vaganay, *Le Problème Synoptique. Une hypothèse de travail* (Tournai, 1954); similarly X. Léon–Dufour, "The Synoptic Gospels" in A. Robert and A. Feuillet, *Introduction to the New Testament* (New York: Desclee, 1965), 266ff; Gaechter 19–21 (partial destruction of the original formal principles through the translator of the original Matthew).

[56]Farmer, *Synoptic Problem*; B. Orchard, *Matthew, Luke and Mark* (Manchester 1976); D. Dungan, "Mark—An Abridgement of Matthew and Luke," in *Jesus and Man's Hope* I (above, n. 51) 51–97. Critical analysis by C. M. Tuckett, *The Revival of the Griesbach Hypothesis*, SNTSMS 44 (1983).

[57]*La structure des Évangiles synoptiques NT.S* 22 (1970). It comprises mainly the second part from Matt. 14 on. The first part was transmitted to the Synoptics in various forms and without stable order. For a critical analysis cf. F. Neirynck, "The Gospel of Matthew and Literary Criticism: A Critical Analysis of A. Gaboury's Hypothesis," in Didier, *Évangile*, 37–69.

[58]J. Rist, *On the Independence of Matthew and Mark*, SNTSMS 32 (1978).

[59] A. Farrer, "On Dispensing with Q," in *Studies in the Gospels* (FS R. H. Lightfoot), ed. D. Nineham (Oxford 1955), 55–86; Goulder, *Midrash*, especially 137–52.

[60]Benoit and Boismard, *Synopse II: Commentaire* (by M. E. Boismard) passim.

hypothesis. It consists in the minor agreements[61] between Matthew and Luke. They are numerous and in many places not even "minor." But it is my view that the minor agreements do not necessitate a basic revision of the two-source hypothesis. Since they do not show a clear common linguistic and/or theological profile, it is not necessary to limit their explanation to one single hypothesis. Rather, depending on the passage, one may cite various hypotheses. Often one may assume corrections of the Markan text by Matthew and Luke which were done independently.[62] But we should also seriously consider that there could have been slightly differing versions of Mark. Why should that which is taken for granted for other semi-literary documents from a religious marginal culture or subculture, e.g., for the hortatory speeches of 1 Enoch, the Testaments of the Twelve Patriarchs, the Life of Adam and Eve, the Testament of Job, the Sayings Source, the Epistula Apostolorum, the Didascalia, the Apocryphon of John, the book of Acts,[63] etc., not apply to the Gospel of Mark?[64] It seems to me that Matthew and Luke made use of a recension of Mark which in a number of points is secondary to our Mark.

Special Sources

A final remark is necessary on the question of a *special source M* which would have contained the unique materials.[65] This hypothesis of Streeter had many adherents, especially in English scholarship.[66] In my opinion it may be filed away. The analysis of the Matthean language in the commentary will show that there is a clear distinction between texts in which Matthew was bound by a source and texts which were taken over by Matthew from oral tradition and formulated in writing for the first time. In the latter, the Matthean peculiarities of language are found in much greater density. Almost all individual stories which were inserted by Matthew as additions to the Markan text have been formulated in writing by him for the first time (e.g., Matt. 17:24–27; 27:3–10).[67] In

---

[61]Selected literature: Schmid, *Matthäus und Lukas*, 31–81; S. McLoughlin, "Les accords mineurs Mt–Lc contre Mc et le problème synoptique," *ETL* 43 (1967) 17–40; Neirynck, *Minor Agreements*; A. Fuchs, "Die Behandlung der mt/lk Übereinstimmungen gegen Mk durch S. McLoughlin," *SNTU A* 3(1978) 24–57 (literature there in note 2 and 3).

[62]That is the "normal solution" of Schmid 179, which he has to supplement in a few cases by the possibility of changes in the text. Without wanting to explain all minor agreements in this way, I would like to point to an experience in the writing of this commentary: the first version was checked by three different coworkers for possibilities of abbreviating and improving it. The number of passages where two of them improved my text was considerable, on an average two to four times per page. The number of places where they improved the text beyond this independently in the same manner was still considerable, on an average once per page. This is an experience which demonstrates that Schmid's hypothesis is basically possible but in view of the large number of the minor agreements is not sufficient as an explanation!

[63]Western text!

[64]The hypothesis (in my opinion, very difficult!) that Matthew was used by Luke as a subsidiary source so that in this way a number of minor agreements could be explained (e.g., R. Morgenthaler, *Statistische Synopse* [Zürich 1971], 279) is without direct consequences for the interpretation of Matthew.

[65]Streeter, *Gospels*, esp. 150, 232f., 249–61 (from Jerusalem, c. 65).

[66]E.g., Manson, *Sayings* 21-26 (with content overview of M); Kilpatrick, *Orgins*, esp. 35f.; Hirsch, *Frühgeschichte II* 332-38, 352, 354.

[67]Thus two phenomena supplement each other: (a) the linguistic demonstration that a text on the basis of the density of its linguistic peculiarities has been formulated by the evangelist for the first time in written form, and (b) the compositional demonstration that a narrative was inserted into the Markan order. Cf. e.g., on 17:24–27; 20:1–16; 21:28–32; 22:1–14; 25:1–11; 27:3–10; 27:62–66.

the same way, to my view, the infancy narratives Matt. 1:18–2:23 were formulated in writing for the first time by the evangelist himself, on the basis of oral traditions.[68] Even for the fulfillment quotations a written source is not to be assumed.[69] It is conceivable only that Matthew found some of his larger unique parables already in a written source.[70] It is almost certain that he used a (continuous?) written source for the primary antitheses of the Sermon on the Mount and for the text on almsgiving, prayer, and fasting (Matt. 5:21–24, 27f., 33–37; 6:1–6, 16–18).[71]

3. THE STYLE

Matthean linguistic peculiarities occur significantly more frequently than in the other texts in redactional fragments or in uniquely occurring narratives that are formulated by the evangelist for the first time in written form. Therefore, one has to begin with these parts of the Gospel; the two-source hypothesis stands the test also for the investigation of the style.

Basic Characteristics

The evangelist writes expressly *"synagogue Greek."*[72] It can be characterized more closely as follows:

1. It is more differentiated, polished and "elevated" than the popular, Semitic Greek of Mark or Q.

2. The Matthean style is *sparser* than that of Mark. The narratives are *tightened*. The Matthean abridgements try to bring out clearly what is essential. They have a didactic function.[73]

3. The Matthean style is *repetitive*. The evangelist knows a great many *formulas* which he repeats. Even in individual texts, he employs ♦ leading words, ♦ chiasms, or ♦ inclusions. The formulaic character of Matthean language has a positive sense: it is didactic and a means of interpretation. Formulaic character belongs also to the style of many basic Old Testament texts (e.g., the Priestly source, Chronicles) which influenced Matthew. This leads to the next point:

4. Matthew is strongly *influenced by the Septuagint*. While Luke in certain sections inserts ♦ Septuagintisms and avoids them in others, the language of Matthew is throughout stamped by biblical Greek; more than likely he does not *consciously* write in Septuagintal style. The finding is the same as with the Old Testament quotations, the wording of which in Matthew is sometimes, but

---

[68]Cf. the introduction to Matt. 1–2 and the analysis of 1:18–25; 2:1–12, 13–23, section 2 in each case.

[69]Cf. the excursus "Fulfillment Quotations" at 2:23.

[70]Cf. the excursus "Parable Source" at Matt. 13:24–30.

[71]Cf. the introduction to Matthew 5–7, section 2.

[72]Bacon, *Studies*, 497–99.

[73]They belong together with the arrangement of narratives or larger text complexes through catchwords, chiasms, or inclusions and are, in a manner of speaking, the "negative side" of the latter. Cf. Gerhardsson, *Memory*, esp. 141–48: The rabbis hand down traditions in a pregnant manner and as tersely as possible.

rarely consistently[74] closer to the Septuagint than in his sources: the Septuagint influences his language but is not his stylistic norm.

5. Matthew writes a *Greek which is influenced by Jewish, occasionally rabbinic features.* His language sometimes shows a clear relationship to the linguistic development in rabbinic Judaism of the time.[75]

Leaving aside the improvements in the Greek, all other stylistic peculiarities betray the fact that Matthew belongs to a community, even that he deliberately desired to incorporate himself into it. Many stylistic peculiarities are an expression of his adaptation to a certain tradition. The example of Matthew splendidly confirms what E. Norden pointed out as a general difference between classical Greek and early Christian literature: Christian authors are not primarily literary personalities who freely display themselves and do not attempt to be such. They understand themselves as representatives of a community.[76]

3.1. On Syntax

It is hardly possible any more to present an adequate morphology of the Matthean language, one that differentiates it from the other evangelists. Very fine observations are collected in older commentaries, by Allen, Lagrange, and Schlatter. Since today the Jewish and Hellenistic Jewish comparative materials are more readily available than in earlier times, it is urgently necessary to bring the older syntactical investigations up to date. We have chosen to include here only some details of striking syntactic phenomena that demonstrate the change of the Matthean language in comparison with Mark. We will attempt to integrate them into the above-mentioned basic characteristics.

Re 1. It belongs to the linguistic *improvements of Markan popular Greek* that Matthew indeed, like Mark, uses the *adjective* very sparingly but knows more incidents of the attributive adjective in prior position than Mark.[77] Semitic languages generally put the adjective after the noun; in Greek the word order is freer. Different from Mark, Matthew knows the *purpose infinitive* with τοῦ, a mark of "a higher stratum of Koine."[78] It is a sign of finer Greek that the number of *participles* is much larger than in Mark.[79] Often parataxis is replaced by a participial construction. The use of participles in

---

[74]Cf. the excursus "Fulfillment Quotations" at 2:23, section 3.

[75]Copious quantities of related insights are found in Schlatter's commentary. The splendid investigation by Przybylski, *Righteousness*, shows with the example of δικαιοσύνη how fruitful it is to present a Matthean key term within its Jewish linguistic history.

[76]E. Norden, *Antike Kunstprosa II*, reprint (Darmstadt 1981 [= 1909]) 453: "Christian literature lacks the freedom of ancient literature. . . . Christianity brought authority and with that eliminated individuality."

[77]Schlatter 105 gives a long list of such adjectives which is the more impressive if one considers that the adjective in Matthew (as in NT Greek in general) is used rather sparingly. Redactional instances adduced are: 13:23 and 15:34.

[78]Blass–Debrunner, §400. Examples in Moulton and Geden, *Concordance* s.v. ὁ (p. 679). Luke, the best stylist in the NT, has three times as many occurrences.

[79]Solages, *Composition* 111f., 114; Schmid, *Matthäus und Lukas* 39; Neirynck, *Agreements* 207–09 (51 occurrences of the participle instead of parataxis, of those 19 times in minor agreements).

such places is in many cases very stereotypical and formulaic.[80] It corresponds to good Greek that Matthew frequently substitutes *an aorist for the Markan imperfect*.[81] In many of these cases, Matthew shows a good sense for the differences among the Greek tenses. The improvement of the quality of Greek can be demonstrated finally in the Matthean avoidance of Markan awkwardnesses: he avoids the frequent Markan *asyndeta*.[82] He avoids *paratactic construction with* καί.[83] He tends to replace the Markan periphrastic conjugations by a finite verb.[84]

Re 4 and 5. *Matthean language is Semitizing*. This means first that the closeness of Semitic idioms generally becomes clear (bilingual milieu!) and, second, that Semitic texts—or their prior translations in poor Greek—have had an influence. A clear interpretation of the individual phenomena is often difficult. Matthew has a preference for *parallelisms*. The influence of Semitic poetry is here most likely decisive. The number of cases where he improves or even creates parallelisms in sayings of Jesus is quite large.[85] The fact that Matthew frequently chooses *direct discourse* instead of indirect discourse (which does not occur in Semitic languages) is not to be traced exclusively to the influence of Semitic literature but also to the bilingual milieu.[86] Or is he interested here in emphasizing for didactic reasons the address to the readers which might be found in the saying of Jesus or the disciples? A general proximity to the Semitic linguistic milieu is shown in the frequent genitive constructions which remind us of the Semitic *status constructus*.[87] It is striking that Matthew has difficulties with the *genitive absolute*. Several Markan occurrences are eliminated.[88] He often does not observe the rule that the subject of the participle in the genitive case must not occur in the main clause.[89] Although such errors are more frequent in Matthew than in any other New Testament author, they must not be overemphasized since similar errors occur in the

---

[80]Cf. section 3,2 below, s.v. ἀκούω, ἀπέρχομαι, ἀποκρίνομαι, γινώσκω, ἐγείρω, ἔρχομαι, λαμβάνω, λέγω, ὁράω, πίπτω, πορεύομαι.

[81]Solages, *Composition* 113; Schmid, *Matthäus und Lukas* 39, counts 30 cases whereby Matthew goes here beyond Luke. Cf. also Neirynck, *Agreements* 230–36.

[82]Neirynck, *Agreements* 211–13, counts 39 cases where Matthew substitutes usually a paratactical conjunction for a Markan asyndeton. Of the 22 inverse cases where Matthew has created an asyndeton, this was done in more than half of the cases in order to lift out the present tense use of λέγει.

[83]Neirynck, *Agreements* 203–11.

[84]Neirynck, *Agreements* 240–42.

[85]A Denaux, "Der Spruch von den zwei Wegen im Rahmen des Epilogs der Bergpredigt," in *Logia*, ed. J. Delobel, BETL (1972), 331–35 counts the following Matthean procedures with respect to the parallelisms of the Markan tradition (in parentheses the corresponding figures for Luke): retaining of the parallelism 20 times (11 times), strengthening of the parallelism 26 times (8 times), weakening of the parallelism 4 times (20 times), omission of the Markan passage 27 times (38 times). For the Q traditions the figures are the following: parallelisms in Matthew and Luke 22 times, stricter parallelism in Matthew 40 times, stricter parallelism in Luke 8 times; parallelism in Matthew alone 13 times; in Luke alone 10 times.

[86]Solages, *Composition* 119–21, counts 22 cases where Matthew has changed indirect discourse of Mark into direct discourse, as against 5 inverse cases (121f.) Cf. also section 3.2 below, s.v. λέγων.

[87]Cf. in section 3.2 γῆ + names of regions, ἡμέρα κρίσεως, γέεννα or κάμινος τοῦ πυρός and the list in Schlatter 27. The nominative case is, according to the Semitic manner, anarthrous.

[88]In the Markan source I count after Neirynck, *Agreements* 210, 244f., 20 omissions and 17 additions of genitive absolute.

[89]Incorrect are perhaps the redactional passages 5:1; 8:28; 9:10,18; 12:46; 22:41; 27:17.

paryri.[90] A favorite is the completely un-Greek construction genitive absolute + ἰδού + main clause.[91]

Finally it is striking that compound verbs are less frequent in Matthew than in Luke and not more frequent than in Mark. Here also possibly the proximity of the Semitic milieu is evident.[92]

The remaining basic characteristics of the Matthean language which were set forth above can be seen only poorly in syntactic peculiarities.

Re 2. Possibly, however, there are observations which betray the *didactic Matthew*. He is fond of the *casus pendens*. The evidence suggests less the bilingual writer who is tied to Semitic syntax than the "teacher" Matthew who uses the *casus pendens* for accenting.[93] The "teacher" Matthew shows himself perhaps in the use of the historical present. It is equally frequent in Mark. In Matthew it recedes,[94] but not uniformly. In most cases, a form of the past—often the aorist—is substituted. With λέγω, it usually is left standing or is even newly written by the evangelist. Since Matthew in his narratives likes to tighten the narrating and thus lets the dialogs become prominent, perhaps the historical present also is a means of directing the attention of the readers to the most important element in the narratives, namely, the sayings of Jesus.

There remain a few syntactical peculiarities which cannot be interpreted at all. Matthew has a predilection for *general relative clauses* with ὅστις, ὃς ἐάν, etc. In comparison with Mark, he has an increased inclination to passive forms of the verb.[95]

3.2. Vocabulary Preferred by Matthew[96]

Preliminary remarks: The alphabetical list contains all vocables which result in a significant redactional finding. The list of the "formulas" is therefore not complete because it contains only those with "redactional vocables."

Col. 1: The numbers refer to the basic characteristics above pp. 49-50 (1 = linguistic improvements, 3 = formulaic phrases and key words, 4 = LXX language, 5 = Hellenistic Jewish and rabbinical material).

Col. 2: The numbers behind the vocables indicate the total number of occurrences of a word in Matthew, Mark, and Luke, respectively (according to Aland).

Col. 3: The numbers indicate occurrences in Matthew that are probably redactional (red).

---

[90]BDF §423.

[91]Eleven times according to Soares–Prabhu, *Quotations* 180.

[92]Schmid, *Matthäus und Lukas* 49f.; Neirynck, *Agreements* 252–55. One may be even more precise: Matthew with his inclination to formulaic phrases replaces in 17 of 22 cases a Markan *verbum simplex* with προσέρχομαι or προσφέρω, of the remaining cases there are two instances of ἐπιζητέω and two compound forms of ἔρχομαι. Conversely, the cases where Matthew brings a simplex instead of a compound include Markan verbs with ἀπο–, ἀμφι–, ἀνα–, δια–, εἰσ–, ἐξ–, ἐπι–, κατα–, παρα–, συν– and ὑπο–. Matthew in fact reduces the Markan richness in compounds considerably, in contrast to Luke.

[93]J. Jeremias, "Die Deutung des Gleichnisses vom Unkraut unter dem Weizen," in J. Jeremias, *Abba* 262, n. 7, notes 14 Matthean examples (4 Mark, 10 Luke), 8 of these redactional. *Casus pendens* + resuming οὗτος is typically Matthean.

[94]Historical present tenses: Matthew 93 times, Mark 151 times, Luke 9 times (Schmid, *Matthäus und Lukas* 38; cf. Hawkins, *Horae* 144–49; Neirynck, *Agreements* 223–29).

[95]Cf. section 3.2 under ἐάν, ὃς ἄν, ὅστις.

[96]Cf. also the lists in Goulder, *Midrash* 477–85, and in Gundry 641–49. Both contain more than the truly significant vocables. My attempt (which naturally presupposes a circle) to state the number of redactional occurrences (column 3) and the "glosses" (column 4) is new.

ca.   relatively great uncertainty
+   or more than the number mentioned
−   or fewer than the number mentioned
Col. 4: Special remarks and references to the literature
◆   references to other vocables in this list

3	ἀγαθός 16,4,16	ca. 8×	
	ἀγαθός/πονηρός 4,0,0	4×	
	ἄγγελος 20,6,25	ca. 10×	
	ἄγγελος κυρίου	ca. 5×	ἄγγελος κυρίου LXX ca. 50× 4× in Matt. 1:20–2:19, 3×9 with φαίνεσθαι κατ' ὄναρ; Jewish expression, Schlatter 15
3,4	ἅγιος 10,7,20	ca. 5×	2× ἁγία πόλις red., LXX!
	ἀγρός 17,9,10	ca. 3×	often in unique material: 13:24–44; 27:3–10. Uncertain.
4	ἀδελφός 39,20,24	ca. 5×	2× with ἀθῷος, LXX!
	αἷμα 11, 3, 8,	ca. 4×	5× red. συντέλεια τοῦ αἰῶνος; rabb.; cf. Schlatter 445
3,5	αἰών 8, 4, 7	ca. 6×	
	ἀκολουθέω 25,18,17	ca. 10×	9× chs. 8–9, key word; 6× 19:2–20:34, key word; 4× red. with ὄχλοι
	ἀκούω 63,46,65	more than 18×	
1	ἀκούσα(ς) δέ 7,1,8	ca. 6×	Statements about redaction are difficult; always occurs at the beginning.
	ἄλλος 29,22,11	ca. 9×	
	ἀμήν 31,14,6		
	ἀμήν (γάρ) λέγω ὑμῖν 29,14,5	2×	
	ἀναγινώσκω 7,4,3	+2×	
	ἀνάκειμαι 5,2,2	–8×	
3	ἀναχωρέω 10,1,0	+21×	Key word, 2:12–22 R. Pesch, ZNW 59 (1968) 46
	ἄνθρωπος 116,56,95	2x	
	ἔμπροσθεν τῶν ἀνθρώπων 3,0,1		

3,4	ἄνθρωπος + participle 8,1,5	-6×	
	ἀνοίγω 11,1,7	3-5×	2× ἀνοίγω τὸ στόμα; LXX ca. 40×
	ἀνομία 4,0,0	3×	
	ἄξιος 9,0,8	-6×	6× 10:10-38, key word; 6× final position, never in Luke-Acts
1	ἀπέρχομαι 35,23,20	ca. 12×	
	ἀπελθών κτλ. 12,5,7	+4×	
	ἀπό 115,48,125		ἀπ' ἄρτι 3,0,0; ἀπὸ τότε 3,0,1 3×red.; ἀπό often instead of ἐκ; Neirynck, *Agreements* 282
	ἀπό—ἕως 12,4,2		Gundry 642
	ἀπό temporal 23,2,12	ca. 4×	Often in unique material: 6:2-18; 18:23-35
	ἀποδίδωμι 18,1,8		
	ἀποκρίνομαι 55,30,46		
1,3,4	ὁ δὲ ἀποκριθεὶς εἶπεν 18,2,0	17×	Gen. 18:9 LXX
1,3,4	ἀποκριθεὶς δὲ + subject 17,0,5	17×	LXX, often; Neirynck, *Agreements* 249-251
	ἀπόλλυμι 19,10,27	ca. 6×	
	ἅπτω 9,11,13	4×	
1	ἄρα 7,2,6	ca. 5×	ἄρα γε 2× red.; τί(ς) ἄρα 3,1,4 3× red.
	ἀργύριον 9,1,4	+5×	In Matthew, almost always plural
	ἄρτι 7,0,0		
3	ἀρχιερεῖς 25, 22, 15	+6×	ἀρχιερεῖς always occurs first
	ἀρχιερεῖς /πρεσβύτεροι 8,1,1	7×	
	ἀρχιερεῖς / Φαρισαῖοι 2,0,0	2×	
	ἀρχιερεῖς in a pair 11,6,8	ca. 7×	
3	ἀσθεν—7,2,6	1×	
3	ἀφίημι 47,34,31	ca. 5×	4× in 25:31-46
3	βάλλω 34,18,18	ca. 10×	Key word, 18:12-35 5×
3	βαπτιστής 7,2,3	ca. 3×	Matthew avoids ὁ βαπτίζων

	βασαν- 5,2,3	ca. 2×	
	βασιλεία 55,20,46	ca. 21×	Kretzer, *Herrschaft* 21–63 rabb.; cf. comm. on 3:2
5	βασιλεία τῶν οὐρανῶν 32,0,0	always red.	
3	εὐαγγέλιον τῆς βασιλείας 3,0,0	always red.	
	βασιλεία of Jesus, the Son of man 3,0,2		
	βλέπω 20,15,15	ca. 5×	
1	Γαλιλαία 16,12,13	ca. 8×	
1	γάρ 123,64,97		Red., e.g., 3:3; 5:20; 9:5, 13; 16:27; 24:28; 25:14; 26:28
	introductory γάρ		
	γάρ after prepositions 4,0,1	3×	
1	γε 4,0,9	4×	⁃ ἄρα; εἰ δὲ μή γε 2× red.
5	γέεννα 7,3,1	ca. 2×	2× red. addition τοῦ πυρός; cf. comm., note 18 to 5:21–26
	γῆ 43,19,25	+8×	
4,5	γῆ with a place-name 6,0,0	4×	2× Formula citation; LXX; Hellenistic Jewish
	γίνομαι 75,55,131	ca. 20×	
	γενηθήτω 5,0,0	ca. 4×	
	γινώσκω 20,12,28	ca. 8×	
1,3	γνούς 4,2,3	3×	3× γνοὺς δὲ ὁ Ἰησοῦς red.
	γραμματεύς 23,21,14	ca. 16×	
3	γραμματεῖς in a pair 15,6,10	ca. 12×	γραμματεῖς always occurs first; ⁃ ἀρχιερεύς
3	γραμματεῖς/Φαρισαῖοι 11,3,5	10×	
	δαιμονίζομαι 7,4,1	ca. 6×	

1	δέ 495,164,543		Cf. J. M. Heer, *Die Stammbäume Jesu nach Matthäus und Lukas* (Freiburg 1910), 220: If a sentence begins with the article, δέ occurs almost without exception.
	δεξιός 12,7,6	−4×	
	δεῦτε 6,3,0	+1×	
	διά 60,33,39		
3	διά with the genitive 26,11,14	ca. 15×	Used in formula citations
	διὰ τοῦτο 10,3,4	ca. 7×	
	διάβολος 6,0,5	ca. 1×	
4	διασαφέω 2,0,0	uncertain	4× in Matt. 4:1–11(Q) Hapax legomenon in the NT; LXX, esp. 2 Maccabees
	διδάσκαλος 12,12,17	ca. 4×	
	διδάσκω 14,17,17	ca. 6×	
3	with συναγωγή 3,2,3	2×	
	δίκαιος 17,2,11	ca. + 10×	rabb.; cf. Przybylski, *Righteousness* 39–76
5	δικαιοσύνη 7,0,1	ca. 7×	4×; key word, 5:10–44
3	διώκω 6,0,3	ca. 4×	
3	δοκέω 10,2,10	5–9×	τί + dative + δοκεῖ ca. 6×, red.
	δοξάζω 4,1,9	2×	
	δύναμις for miracle 7,2,2	3×	
	δύο 40,18,28	11×	
	ἐάν 64,36,31		
	ἐάν οὖν 3,0,0		
	ἐάν in relative clause with ὅς 22,11,8		Pronouncements on redaction are difficult. Textual variants ἐάν/ἄν. Luke often has the participle. Cf. also → ὅς.
	ἐάν in relative clause with ὅσος 5,1,0		

4,5	ἑαυτοῦ 32,24,57	+12×	ἐν ἑαυτοῖς 6,3,3;4× red.
3	ἐγείρω 36,19,18	always red.	
	ἐγερθείς 8,0,1	ca. 8×	
	ἐγώ nom. 29,16,22	+4×	
	κἀγώ 9,0,7	2–6×	
	ἔθνος 15,6,13	2–3×	Hellenistic Jewish = "Gentiles"
3	πάντα τὰ ἔθνη 4,1,2		
	εἰς 218,168,226		→ πρός
	εἰς τό with infinitive 3,1,1	3×	
	εἰς 66,44,45	+4×	
	εἰς postposition 9,1,1	2×	Q Luke 12:27; often in unique material
3	εἰς τούτων 8,1,1	ca. 10× (7× eschatological)	Red.; βασιλεία sayings: 5:20; 7:21; 18:3, cf. 7:13; 19:17
	εἰσέρχομαι 36,30,50	ca. 15–19×	
	ἐκεῖ 31,12,16	ca. 9×	After a participle, 6×, of which 5× red.
	ἐκεῖθεν 12,6,4	+25×	
3,4	ἐκεῖνος 56,27,37	3×	LXX frequently
3	ἐν ἐκείνῳ τῷ καιρῷ 3,0,0	7×	
3,5	ἐκείνη + ὥρα 7,1,0	3×	
3,4	ἀπὸ τῆς ὥρας ἐκείνης	8×	In healing narratives; rabb.; Schlatter 318
	ἐκείνη + ἡμέρα 11,9,9		5× red. in narratives; LXX very often
	ἐλάχιστος 5,0,4	3×	in unique material
4	ἐλεέω 8,3,4	ca. 7×	→ υἱός
3	ἔμπροσθεν 18,2,10	3×	LXX
	ἔμπροσθεν τῶν ἀνθρώπων 5,0,1		
	ἔνδυμα 7,0,1	1×	
4	ἐνθυμε- 4,0,0	4×	LXX word stem
4	ἐντέλλομαι 4,2,1	2×	LXX term

	ἐπάνω 8,1,5	ca. 4×	
	ἐπί 122,72,161		
	ἐπί with accusative 67,34,96	+ 20×	Gundry 644
	ἔργ-19,3,8	ca. 3×	
	ἔργον 6,2,2		
	ἔρχομαι 115,85,101		
	ἔρχομαι ἐπί 6,1,4	3×	
	ἐλθών 34,14,13	+ 17×	
	ἔρχομαι + infinitive of purpose 12,5,8	4×	
	ἔσται 37,7,33		
3	ἑταῖρος 3,0,0	-3×	Gundry 644 Always vocative singular - βασιλεία
	εὐαγγέλιον		
	εὐθέως 13,1,6	11×	
	εὑρίσκω 27,11,45	ca. 5×	
	ἕως preposition 28,10,13	-8×	LXX: ἕως predominates greatly over μέχρι
4	ἕως conjunction 20,5,15	ca. 9×	
	ἕως ἄν 10,3,3	ca. 4×	
	ἕως οὖ 7,0,7	3×	
4	ζάω 6,3,9	-2×	2× θεὸς ὁ ζῶν, cf. LXX
	ἤ 68,33,45	ca. 25×	Expansions with ἤ: 5:17; 10:11,14,37; 12:25,29; 18:8; 26:53; etc.
	ἡγεμών 10,1,2	ca. 7×	
	ἡμέρα 45,27,83	ca. 16×	
3,5	ἡμέρα κρίσεως 4,0,0	2-4×	- ἐκεῖνος; Hellenistic Jewish, Schlatter 335
	θαρσέω 3,2,0	2×	
	θαυμάζω 7,4,13	3×	
	θεάομαι 4,0,3	2×	Red. 2× πρός τὸ θεαθῆναι
3	θελ- 48,25,32	2×	

	Word	Count	Notes
3	θέλημα 6,1,4	3×	3× with ποιέω, 2× with γίνομαι; always the will of God (3× θ. πατρός, 2× θ. σου)
	θέλω 42,25,28	ca. 12×	
	εἰ + θέλω 6,2,1	4–5×	
	θεραπεύω 16,5,14	ca. 9×	
	θησαυρός 9,1,4	ca. 2×	
	ἴδιος 10,8,6	ca. 4×	
4,5	ἰδού 62,7,57	40–50×	LXX. A. Vargas–Machuca, *Bib.* 50 (1969) 233–244; P. Fiedler, *Die Formel »und siehe« im NT,* SANT 20 (1969), 23–29.
4,5	καὶ ἰδού 28,1,25	+25	
5	Ἱεροσόλυμα 11,10,4	ca. 5×	OT Apocrypha, Josephus, Ep. Aristeas, etc. With the article
	Ἰησοῦς 152,82,88		
	Ἰσραήλ 12,2,12	3–5×	
	ἵστημι 21,10,16	+7×	
	ἕστηκα 11,4,9	+5×	
3	καιρός 10,5,13	ca. 6×	→ ἐκεῖνος; cf. Strecker, *Weg* 86–89
	κακῶς 7,4,2	ca. 3×	
	καλέω 26,4,43	+2×	
3	κατά + genitive 16,7,6	2–6×	Often unique material 6× 12:14–32 key word
	καταδικάζω 2,0,2	2×	
	καταλείπω 4,4,4	3×	3 Markan occurrences left out
	καταποντίζομαι 2,0,0	2×	In the NT only in Matthew
3,4	κατοικέω 4,0,2	2×	Both times ἐλθών + κ. + εἰς; LXX
	κελεύω 7,0,1	+5×	
3	κηρύσσω 9,14,9	ca. 3×	3× along with διδάσκω
3	κλαυθμός 7,0,1	5×	6× ἐκεῖ ἔσται ὁ κλαυθμός καὶ ὁ βρυγμός τῶν ὀδόντων (1× from Q, Luke 13:28)
	κοσμ- 12,3,5		

3	κόσμος 9,3,3		
	κράζω 12,10,4	ca. 4×	
	κρίσις 12,0,4	ca. 5×	
	κρυπτ- 12,1,5	+4×	5× with → λέγων → ἡμέρα; Gundry 645, but hardly ever demonstrably red.
3	κύριος 80,18,104	ca. 16×	19× 24:42–25:44 key word; → ἄγγελος
3	κύριε 30,2,25	4×	LXX
3	κύριε + ἐλεέω		
	λαμβάνω 54,20,22	ca. 16×	5× 16:1–10 and 7× 25:1–24, key word, often in unique material red.
3	λαβών 20,7,8	+4×	
	συμβούλιον λ. 5,0,0	+4×	
	λαμπ-	2×	λαμπάς 5× 25:1–8, key word
	λάμπω		
4	λαός 14,2,36	ca. 8×	LXX, 4× in OT quotations, cf. ἀρχιερεῖς καὶ γραμματεῖς τοῦ λαοῦ 2:4
3	πρεσβύτεροι τοῦ λαοῦ 4,0,0	4×	
	λέγω altogether 505,291,534		
	λέγων before direct discourse 112,33,92	80–100×	Schlatter 16f.; Neirynck, *Agreements* 246f.; Hebr. אמר?
3	λεγόμενος before a name 4,0,0	4×	
	ὁ λεγόμενος before a name or surname 9,1,1	8×	
3	λέγω ὑμῖν 52,11,35		
	λέγω δὲ ὑμῖν 7,0,4	+5×	Cf. also → Tilborg, ἀμήν; *Leaders* 127
	λέγω with dative, ca. 160,100,75		Matthew and Mark; Luke with first or second person pronoun; otherwise he prefers πρός.
	πλὴν λέγω ὑμιν 3,0,0	3×	

3	λέγω in historical present 71,73,4		Gundry 645; mainly at the beginning. Cf. section 3.1 and → ἀποκρίνομαι
3	ἐρῶ 30,2,19	+17×	
	ῥηθείς 13,0,0	13×	10 formula quotations; always referring to Scripture. Cf. 6× ἐρρέθη Matt. 5:21–43
3	εἶπον 179,80,293		
	ὁ δὲ εἶπον (or plural) 16,13,29	13×	As above re λέγω with the dative
	εἶπον with dative 90,56,87		
	λίαν 4,4,1	2×	
3	λόγος 33,24,32	ca. 14×	→ τελέω
	λυπέω 6,2,0	3×	
	μαθητεύω 3,0,0	–3×	
3	μαθητής 72,46,37	ca. 34×	→ προσέρχομαι
3,4	μαλακία 3,0,0	3×	Always θεραπεύ . . . πᾶσαν νόσον καὶ πᾶσαν μαλακίαν; LXX word
3	μᾶλλον 9,5,5	1–4×	3× red.? After present imperative
3	μανθάνω 3,1,0	+1×	Always μάθετε
1	μέλλω 9,2,12	ca. 8×	3× μέλλει + subject + infinitive (LXX very seldom)
	μέν . . . δέ 20,3,8	+9×	
	μέρος 4,1,4	3×	
4	μέσος 7,5,14	+2×	4× ἐν μέσῳ (3× red.?, LXX); 1× ἐκ μέσου LXX
4	μετά with genitive 61,48,51	ca. 30×	LXX and the Gospels: strong preponderance of μετά instead of σύν
3	μεταβαίνω 6,0,1	+4×	3× with ἐκεῖθεν
	μεταμέλομαι 3,0,0	–3×	
3	μέχρι 2,1,1	–2×	2× μέχρι τῆς σήμερον 2:12; 5:(34,)39; 6:1
	μὴ with infinitive, as prohibition 5,0,2	3×?	

4	μήποτε 8,2,7	+1×	LXX word
4	μικροί for the community 4,1,1	+2×	Always εἰς with genitive, τῶν μ.
3	μιμνήσκομαι 3,0,6	−2×	LXX word
	μισθός 10,1,3	−2×	4× 6:1–16 key word
	μόνον 7,2,1	−7×	
	μωρός 6,0,0	+1×	
	ναί 9,0,4	+4×	
	νεκρός 12,7,14	+4×	
	νόμος 8,0,9	7×	
3,4	νόμος/προφῆται 4,0,1	3×	LXX; cf. Berger, *Gesetzesauslegung* I 212f.
3	νόσος 5,1,4	3×	- μαλακία
	νύξ 9,4,7	−4×	
	οἰκοδεσπότης 7,1,4	2×	
	ὀλιγοπιστία 1,0,0	1×	
5	ὀλιγόπιστος 4,0,1	3×	25:21, 23, Str-B I 438, Jewish, Luke 12:28, Q
	ὅλος 22,18,17	ca. 9×	
	ὅμοιος 9,0,9	1×	Introduces parables; cf. the excursus on 13:24–30
	ὁμοιόω 8,1,3	2×	
	ὅμοιος 3,1,11	ca. 2×	
	ὁμολογέω 4,0,2	6×	
3	ὄναρ 6,0,0	ca. 9×	6× 1:20–2:22 key word; 6× κατ' ὄναρ
3	ὅπως 17,1,7		- πληρόω
	ὁράω 72,50,81		
3	ὁρᾶτε μή 2,0,0	2×	
3	ἰδού 21,14,28	+15×	
3	ἰδὼν δέ 8,2,14	8×	

4	ὅριον 6,5,0	+2×	Always plural; LXX
	ὅρκος 4,1,1	2×	2× μετὰ ὅρκου
	ὅρος 16,11,12	+4×	
1	ὅς ἄν (ἐάν) 35,19,20	ca. 5×	
	ὅστις 29,5,18	ca. 18x	13:52; 20:1; 21:33,41; 22:2; 27:62 red.
	ὅστις = ὅς	3×	
	πᾶς ὅστις 3,0,0	ca. 13×	
	οὐδέ 27,11,21	–5×	
	οὐδέποτε 5,2,2	28–46×	
	οὖν 56,6,33	ca. 37×	
5	οὐρανοί 82,19,35	ca. 50×	– βασιλεία, Jewish; Schlatter 57f.
	οὐρανοί 55,5,4	2×	Always singular
	οὐρανός/γῆ 13,2,5	–7×	Always with πατήρ μου/ὑμῶν
	οὐράνιος 7,0,1		
	οὗτος 149,79,229		
3	ταῦτα πάντα 6,2,4	6×	Matthew changes the ταῦτα πάντα from tradition into π. τ.
3	οὗτός ἐστιν 13,2,3 (sing.)	10×	
	οὗτος 32,10,21	ca. 22×	
	ὀφθαλμός 24,7,17	5×	
	ὄχλος 50,38,41	ca. 30×	
3	ὄχλοι 28,0,17	29×	ὄχλοι πολλοί 5×; – ἀκολουθέω
3	παιδίον 18,12,13	4(+9)×	9× 2:8–21 key word; – παραλαμβάνω
	παῖς 8,0,9	ca. 4×	
	πάλιν 17,28,3	+5×	
3	πάλιν before finite verb 7,2,1	ca. 4×	G. Strecker, ZNW 69 (1978) 46
	παρά with dative 6,3,7	–5×	
3	παραβολή 17,13,18	ca. 6×	4× ἄλλη παραβολή red.

4	παραγίνομαι 3,1,8	−3×	LXX often
3	παραδίδωμι 31,10,17	ca. 9×	3× ὁ παρα(δι)δούς αὐτόν red.
3	παραλαμβάνω 16,6,7	+1(+6)×	2:13–21 4× π. τὸ παιδίον; 6× 1:20–2:21 key word
3	παρέρχομαι 9,5,9	3×	4× 24:3–39 key word; 3× οὗτος ἔσται ἡ
	παρουσία 4,0,0	4×	παρουσία τοῦ υἱοῦ τοῦ ἀνθρώπου
	πᾶς 129,68,157		
3,1	πᾶς οὖν 6,0,1	5×	- ὅστις
	πᾶς ὁ with participle 13,2,17	3×	3× πάντας τοὺς κακῶς ἔχοντας
	πᾶς ὅστις 3,0,0	3×	2× with οὖν
1	πᾶς γάρ 6,2,2	6×	
3	πᾶς re sick people		4:23f.; 8:16; 9:35; 10:1; 12:15; 14:35
	πᾶς + anarthrous singular 20,0,11	ca. 1×	2× with οὖν
	πάντα (οὖν) ὅσα 6,3,2	ca. 3×	14× 5:45–6:32 key word; 7× 10:20–37
	πατήρ 63,19,56	ca. 19×	- οὐράνιος; rabb.: Dalman, *WJ* I 152; Str-B
3,5	πατὴρ ὁ ἐν (τοῖς) οὐρανοῖς 12,1,0	ca. 11×	I 393–396
	πατήρ, of God 45,5,17	ca. 20×	- θέλημα
	πατήρ μου, ὑμῶν 34,2,7	+30×	
3	πείθω 3,0,4	−3×	
	πεινάω 9,2,5	+1×	with διψάω 5× (1× red., 4× in unique material)
1,3	πειράζω 6,4,2	ca. 2×	always πέμψας
	πέμπω 4,1,10	1–3×	
	περιάγω 3,1,0	2×	
	περιπατέω 7,9,5	3×	

3	περισσεύω 5,1,4	5×	2× περισσεῦον τῶν κλασμάτων; 2× δοθήσεται . . . καὶ περισσευθήσεται
1,3,4	πίπτω 19,8,17	+6×	Participle πεσών 5×; with προσκυνέω 3× red.; LXX
	πιστεύω 11,14,9	5×	
	πίστις 8,5,11	3×	
	πλανάω 8,4,1	3×	4× 24:4–24 key word
	πλεῖον 7,1,9	+2×	
	πλεῖστος 2,1,0	2×	
4	πληρόω 16,3,9	13×	LXX
3	πληρωθῇ τὸ ῥηθέν	10×	Formula citations 6× with ἵνα; 3× with ὅπως; 8× + διά; 2× + ὑπὸ κυρίου; LXX 2 Chr. 36:21f. and elsewhere
3	πληρωθῶσιν αἱ γραφαί 2,1,0	1×	
	ποιέω 86,47,88	+25×	
	ποιέω ὡς/καθώς 4,0,0	4×	see on 1:24
	πόλις 27,8,39	ca. 14×	→ ἅγιος
	πονηρός 26,2,13	ca. 12×	→ ἀγαθός
	ὁ πονηρός =the devil	15–26×	13:19 red.; 13:38 red.
3	πορεύομαι 29,3,51	6–8×	
3,4	πορευθείς 11,0,9	3×	
	πορευθέντες with imperative 4,0,4	1×	Semitism, cf. Schlatter 37
	πραΰς 3,0,0	4–6×	
3	πρεσβύτερος 12,7,5	4×	→ ἀρχιερεύς
	πρεσβύτερος τοῦ λαοῦ 4,0,0	3×	
	πρόβατον 11,2,2		
	πρός 41,65,166		
3	πρός with infinitive 5,1,1	3×	→ θεάομαι

3	προσέρχομαι 51,5,10	ca. 40×	Often at the beginning of the sentence; - προσκυνέω
3	προσέρχομαι + αὐτῷ 15,2,0	13×	
3	subject: μαθηταί 13,1,0	12×	
3	aorist participle 28,6,7	+20×	
3	προσέρχομαι after τότε 7,0,0	7×	
4	προσέχω 6,0,4	6×	5× before ἀπό; 5× imperative (LXX) προσέχετε
4	προσκυνέω 13,2,3	+7×	πεσὼν . . . π. 2× unique material (red.?); LXX
4?	προσκυνέω with dative 10,1,0	5×	+4× unique material; LXX?
3	προσκυνέω after προσέρχομαι 4,0,0	4×	
3	προσφέρω 15,3,4	ca. 9×	
	before αὐτῷ 9,2,1	8×	2× πίπτω ἐπί π. LXX
3	πρόσωπον 10,3,13	–5×	11× in formula quotations; - νόμος
	προφήτης 37,6,29	–20×	11× in formula quotations
3	προφήτης after διά 13,0,2	13×	
	πρῶτον 8,6,10	1–4×	
3	πῦρ 12,6,7	–5×	6× with βάλλω εἰς, 2× with κατακαύω;
3,4,5	πυρός as construct state 4,0,0	2×	2× with κάμινος (=LXX Dan.); 2× with γέεννα; red. adoption of traditional formulations 7:19 = 3:10; 13:40 = 3:12; 18:9 = 5:22
3	πῦρ αἰώνιον 2,0,0	2×	
	ῥῆμα 5,2,19	–2×	
3	Σαδδουκαῖοι 7,1,1	6×	5× red. Φαρισαῖοι καί Σ.
	σεισμός 4,1,1	1–3×	
	σείω 3,0,0	1–3×	

3,4	σεληνιάζομαι 2,0,0	2×	
	σημεῖον 13,7,11	2×	
	σήμερον 8,1,11	−5×	
	ἡ σήμερον (ἡμέρα)	−3×	LXX. 2× with μέχρι, 1× with ἕως
	σκάνδαλον 5,0,1	−2×	
3	σκανδαλ- 19,8,3		Gundry 648
	σκότος 7,1,4	−3×	3× ἐκβάλλω . . . εἰς τὸ σκότος τὸ ἐξώτερον
			12 13:3–39 key word
3	σπείρω 17,12,6	2×	
	σπλαγχνίζομαι 4,4,3	2×	
3,4	σταυρόω 10,8,6	4×	2× red. before the passion narrative - ἀνοίγω
	στόμα 11,0,9	+5×	
	στρέφω 6,0,7	+3×	
3,4	συμβούλιον 5,2,0	3×	5× with λαμβάνω; συμβουλεύω 1× red. (hapax legomenon in Matthew)
	συμφέρω 4,0,0	+1×	
3,4	συνάγω 24,5,6	ca. 10×	From 22:34 7× red. in the passive, of opponents of Jesus; LXX. Cf. A. Weiser, *Die Knechtsgleichnisse in den synoptischen Evangelien*, StANT 29 (1971), 246f.
3	συναγωγή 9,8,15	−2×	
3	συναγωγὴ αὐτῶν (ὑμῶν)	4(1)×	3× unique material, with λόγον
	συναίρω 3,0,0	+4×	
	συνίημι 9,5,4	+2×	
4	συντάσσω 3,0,0	5×	LXX
3	συντέλεια 5,0,0	−7×	Always συντέλεια τοῦ αἰῶνος
4	σφόδρα 7,1,1	4×	LXX. Always (LXX often) re emotions
	σῴζω 16,15,17		

4,5	τάλαντον 14,0,0	ca. 4×	Gundry 648; LXX language (= humble)
	ταπειν- 4,0,7	−3×	
	τάφος 6,0,0	3×	
	ταχύ 3,1,1		
	τέλειος 3,0,0	+2×	
3,4	τελευτάω 4,2,1	5×	
	τελέω 7,0,4		Cf. 2:15 τελευτή, hapax legomenon 5× ὅτε ἐτέλησεν ὁ Ἰησοῦς (. . .) (4×) τοὺς λόγους τούτους, cf. on 7:28 (LXX!)
	τέλος 6,3,4	2×	
	τηρέω 6,0,0	+4×	- ἄρα
	τίς 91,71,114		2× unique material
	τί ὑμῖν/σοι δοκεῖ 4,0,0	2×	
	διὰ τί 7,2,5	4×	
	τόπος 10,10,19	4×	
3,4	τότε 90,6,15	+80×	ἀπὸ τότε 3× (2× + ἤρξατο [ὁ] Ἰησοῦς . . .); almost exclusively at beginning of sentence; cf. LXX, Daniel
	τότε + finite verb 65,3,11		
3	τότε + historical present 20,0,3		12× + λέγει
1	τότε + participle 15,0,1		
	τροφή 4,0,1	−3×	
	τυφλός 17,5,8	+9×	
	υἱός 90,35,77		
3	υἱὸς Δαυίδ 9,3,4	6×	4× ἐλέησον . . . ὁ. Δ. (3× with κύριε)
	υἱὸς θεοῦ, μου, e.g. (sing.) 11,7,9	4×	
	υἱὸς τοῦ ἀνθρώπου 29,14,26	7×	
	ὑμεῖς nom. 30,10,10	+12×	Gundry 648
	ὑπάγω 19,15,5	ca. 4×	Imperative

3	ὑπαντα- 4,1,2	+2×	
	ὑποκριτής 14,1,3	ca. 9×	Ch. 23–7× οὐαὶ ὑμῖν γραμματεῖς καὶ Φαρισαῖοι ὑποκριταί
3	ὕστερον 7,0,1	3×	
	φαίνω 13,2,2	3(+4?)×	→ ἄγγελος
	Φαρισαῖος 30,12,27	ca. 18×	→ ἀρχιερεύς, → γραμματεύς, → ὑποκριτής, → Σαδδουκαῖος
3	φημί 16,6,8	ca. 12×	ἔφη + dative + subject 8×
	φοβέομαι 18,12,23	7–10×	
4	μὴ φοβ- 8,2,8	+4×	LXX often
	φόβος 3,1,7	3×	
	φονεύω 5,1,1	2×	
	φῶς 7,1,7	–3×	
	χαίρω 6,2,12	2×	2× χαρὰ μεγάλη
	χαρά 6,1,8	1×	3× Ἰησοῦς ὁ λεγόμενος Χριστός; 5×
3	Χριστός 16,7,12	+7×	1:1– 2:4 unique material
	χρυσός 5,0,0	+1×	
	χωρέω 4,1,0	+2×	
	ὧδε 18,10,15	+4×	→ ἐκεῖνος
	ὥρα 21,12,17	6×	
	ὅς 40,22,51	14–20×	
	ὡσεί 3,1,9	3×	
1	ὥσπερ 10,0,2	4×	4× ὥσπερ γάρ
1	ὥστε 15,13,4	10×	8× red. with infinitive, 2× with indicative in main clause

Preliminary remarks: In order to avoid uncertainties, this list is limited to those words that Matthew took over from the Gospel of Mark only haltingly, as far as a significant result can be determined.

The columns are the same as in the preceding table. "Mark" in the first column means that the vocable under consideration belongs to the preferred vocables of the Markan redaction. → indicates a reference to list 3.2.

1	ἀκάθαρτος 2,11,6 ἀλλά 37,45,35	Mark 11× with πνεῦμα; → δαιμονίζομαι Matt. avoids ἀλλά after preceding negatives (simplification) and at the beginning of a main clause; cf. Neirynck, *Agreements* 221f.
1, Mark	ἀνίστημι 4,17,17 ἄρχω 13,27,31	Matt. prefers ἐγείρω; when used theologically, it is community language. Matt. 20× omits ἄρχομαι with infinitive (retained 13×; red. 3×). Awkward because superfluous, perhaps Aramaism (Dalman, *WJ* I 21f.)? Cf. Neirynck, *Agreements* 242–244.
1	βαπτίζω 7,13,10 διαστέλλομαι 1,5,0 δύναμαι 27,33,26 ἑαυτοῦ	→ βαπτιστής. Matt. avoids the nontechnical usage. Community language. Vocable of the Markan messianic secret. Matt. omits ca. 7× red. passages from Mark, ca. 20× for other reasons.
1	πρὸς ἑαυτούς 0,7,6 εἰσπορεύομαι 1,8,5 ἐκπορεύομαι 6,11,3	Textually often uncertain. Schmid, *Matthäus und Lukas* 54: vulgar.
(1,2), Mark	εὐθύς 5,41,1	Neirynck, *Agreements* 274f. Mark εὐθύς is not unclassical but partially pleonastic; Matt. eliminates it and replaces it by → εὐθέως
2	θεωρέω 2,7,7 Ἰάκωβος 6,15,8 ἴδε 4,9,0 ἵνα 39,64,46	James, the son of Zebedee, omitted 5×. 5× omitted as pleonastic; 3× → ἰδού Where Mark has a nonpurposive ἵνα Matt. often uses direct discourse. Lampe, *EWNT* II 462, says that the linguistic use of Matt. and Mark is unclassical. For material cf. Neirynck, *Agreements* 217–219
	Ἰωάννης 26,26,31 καθώς 3,8,17	John, son of Zebedee, omitted 6×.
Mark	κηρύσσω 9,14,9 κοράσιον 3,5,0	In Mark almost always red., often in summaries. Matt. deals freely with it. Matt. eliminates popular diminutives, also ὠτάριον, θυγάτριον

1 Mark 1 2	κράβατος 0,5,0 μηδείς 5,9,9 ξηραίνω 3,6,1 ὅπου 13,17,5 οὐδείς 19,26,33 οὐκέτι 2,7,3 ὅτι 141,101,174	"The poor man's bed" (*BAGD*, s.v.), popular Greek. In part, a vocable of the Markan messianic secret. Avoided in reference to illnesses because it is popular Greek. Avoidance of superfluous parentheses. Matt. avoids double negatives. Neirynck, *Agreements* 213–217: ὅτι recitative before direct discourse is usually omitted by Matt. (ca. 40×), interrogative ὅτι always omitted (3×).
2, Mark Mark 2, Mark	πάλιν 17,28,3 παρίστημι 1,6,3 περιβλέπω 0,6,1 πολλά adv. 2,16,2 πρός 41,65,166	In Mark a red. embellishment; used by Matt. only with a clear reference. Markan red. participle, οἱ παρεστηκότες, is always paraphrased by Matt. Red. word in Mark, at times omitted, at times replaced. Neirynck, *Agreements* 278f.
1 2	σατανᾶς 4,6,5 συζητέω 0,6,2 τίθημι 5,11,16 τις 21,34,80	Matthew avoids Aramaisms, but not as consistently as Luke. Markan red. word. Usually tightened.
1 1 2	τρυμαλιά 0,1,0 φέρω 4,15,4 φονέω 5,10,10	Unusual word. Usually replaced by ἄγω or → προσφέρω; nonspecific word; Neirynck, *Agreements* 279 Usually tightened.

The list on pp. 54-72 permits us to draw some conclusions:

1. Matthew deals relatively freely with Markan redaction, but it is remarkable that, on the whole, he accepts the Markan redactional wording.

2. Matthew indeed improves Markan Greek in many points but rarely as consistently as Luke.[97]

3. Neither Aramaisms[98] nor Latinisms[99] are consistently eliminated.

4. THE RELATIONSHIP OF THE EVANGELIST TO HIS SOURCES

The more important question is not *what* sources the evangelist used but *how* he used them. The analysis of the structure has demonstrated that the evangelist was not a "free" author but *willingly* let himself be influenced to a large extent by his main source, Mark. The analysis of the individual texts· will show that Matthew knows the Gospel of Mark well, that he anticipates future material in his redaction, and that he reuses in other places sayings from omitted verses of Mark. It is as if the evangelist, despite his considerable condensations, wanted to use as much of the text of Mark as possible! We will attempt to intensify this picture of an evangelist who is oriented to the tradition in two directions.

4.1. Matthew as an Heir of Mark and of the Sayings Source

Linguistic Influences

Many vocables of Matthew's preferred vocabulary are not new creations of the evangelist but were suggested by his sources.

Examples of how the Sayings Source influenced Matthew are ὀλιγόπιστος (Q: Matt. 6:30), ἀνομία (Q: Matt. 7:23) or the threatening phrase about weeping and gnashing of teeth (Q: Matt 8:12). From Q come further ὁ νόμος καὶ οἱ προφῆται[100] (Matt. 11:13) and perhaps the preference for ἀμήν (λέγω ὑμῖν). From QMt comes πραΰς(Matt. 5:5). The *Gospel of Mark* influenced the language of Matthew almost more strongly. For example, the following vocables come from Mark: Ἀναχωρέω (Mark 3:7), ἀκολουθέω, the phrase πάντα τὰ ἔθνη (Mark 13:10), εἰσέρχομαι into life or into the kingdom of heaven, μαθητής,[101] μικρός (Mark 9:42), προσκυνέω. It is of

---

[97]Matthew has not consistently avoided popular formulations or formulations which for other reasons are stylistically poor. Lagrange CXVIf. gives a list of formulations which the Atticist Phrynichos censures, among others κερδαίνω, ἀπ' ἄρτι, ὀψία as a noun. Luke has a far better style than Matthew, also in the Gospel. Cf. Norden, *Kunstprosa* (above, n. 76) II 482–92.

[98]Aramaic words which are removed by Matthew: ἀββά, Βαρτιμαῖος, Βοανηργές, ῥαββουνί, ταλιθὰ κοῦμ. But he leaves standing, e.g., ῥαββί, Γεθσημανί, Ἰσκαριώτης (Mark Ἰσκαριωθ), Γολγοθά, μαμωνάς, σατανᾶς, Βεελζεβούλ. The two Hebrew passages 1:24 and 27:46 are translated.

[99]Avoided are Markan κεντυρίων, σπεκουλάτωρ, ξέστης; remaining from Mark are μόδιος, φραγελλόω, κῆνσος, κοδράντης, λεγιών, δηνάριον; newly added are μίλιον, ἀσσάριον, κουστωδία, συμβούλιον λαμβάνω. From the Latinisms of a Gospel it is best to conclude—nothing! In addition, Latin words are often also loanwords in Aramaic.

[100]In reverse formulation οἱ προφῆται καὶ ὁ νόμος?

[101]In his use of μαθητής and ἀκολουθέω Matthew naturally is not influenced *only* by Mark but also by Q and—as often—by the language of his community.

theological importance that Matthew was prompted by Mark to connect the title Son of David with the miracle narratives (Mark 10:47f. with ἐλεέω!) and perhaps to formulate his introductory phrase to the fulfillment quotations (πληροῦσθαι of the scripture, Mark 14:49).[102] Other important vocables of the redaction of Mark also are taken over redactionally by Matthew: scribes, elders, Pharisees, and Sadducees as opponents of Jesus; Γαλιλαία, διδάσκω, εὐαγγέλιον, κηρύσσω, ὄχλος, συνίημι, etc.[103]

Matthew owes the antithesis formula and the catchword ὑποκριτής (Matt. 6:2, 5, 16) to the written source of Matt. 5:21–6:18.

Theological Influences

These redactional vocables have also theological weight.[104] Thus the evangelist even theologically continues to a large extent thoughts of his two main sources. *Matthew is the disciple or, better, the heir of his theological fathers, Mark and Q.*

The Sayings Source

Matthew holds in common with the *Sayings Source* the central significance of *judgment*. Most of the individual "blocks" of the Sayings Source as well as the source as a whole culminate in the concept of judgment.[105] The composition of the discourses in the Gospel of Matthew corresponds to this: with the exception of the mission discourse they all end with the threat of judgment; and this is exactly the theme of the entire last discourse. For both, the *Son of man Christology* has central significance: in Q, sayings concerning the Son of man often are found in marked places at the beginning or at the end of individual blocks or at the beginning and at the end of the whole source.[106] The Son of man is in Q the future judge of the world, noticeably also in words of the "present" Son of man.[107] Matthew has formulated four new Son of man sayings which speak of the future judgment of the Son of man.[108] As in Q, so also in Matthew, the sayings of Jesus are at the same time those of the future judge of the world. Finally, both are marked by *conflict with Israel*. It is direct polemic which influences Q: beginning with the speech of the Baptist, the words against "this"

---

[102]Cf. the excursus "Fulfillment Quotations" at 2:23, section 2.

[103]Cf. result no. 1 of section 3.3 above.

[104]The following section is sketchy since it presupposes a certain view of Mark and Q. I will forgo a debate with the literature.

[105]Luke 3:16f. (first block concerning the Baptist); Luke 6:16–19 (Sermon on the Plain), Luke 7:31–35 (second block concerning the Baptist); Luke 10:12–16 (sending discourse); Luke 11:31f. (miracle block); Luke 11:49–51 (woes); Luke 12:39–46, 57–59; 13:28–35 (parenesis to the disciples), Luke 17:23–37 (whole Sayings Source).

[106]Cf. Luke 3:16 (ὁ ἰσχυρότερος; beginning of the source); Luke 6:22 (beginning of the Sermon on the Plain); Luke 7:34 (end of the second block concerning the Baptist); Luke 9:58 (beginning of the block discipleship—sending); Luke 12:8–10 (beginning of the parenesis to the disciples); Luke 17:24–30 (end of the Source).

[107]Luke 7:34, in my opinion, speaks of mockery against the Son of man, the judge of the world, Luke 9:58 of his homelessness. It is different only in (the difficult community formulation) Luke 12:10.

[108]Matt. 13:41; 16:28; 24:30; 25:31.

evil and perverse generation are repeated (Luke 7:31 etc.). The mission discourse leads to the sayings of judgment on the Galilean cities (Luke 10:13–15). The miracle cycle leads into a debate with those who are not with—and who are therefore against—Jesus (Luke 11:23–32). Especially the sevenfold woe against the Pharisees and scribes has to be pointed out (Luke 11:37–52). The section regarding the disciples which follows the woe sayings speaks of persecution in Israel (Luke 12:2–12; cf 6:22f.; 11:49–51) and culminates again in the accusation against Israel (Luke 13:25–35). On this background the collection of minatory words of the judgment of the Son of man (Luke 17:23–37) has to be read. For Matthew, the judgment on Israel is just as central, but he speaks about it differently. Many a Q minatory saying against Israel becomes with him a threat which is directed at the church.[109] In contrast, the judgment on Israel obtains decisive significance in the *story* of Jesus which is taken over from Mark. But this does not yet exhaust the basic contacts between Matthew and Q. They can be grasped not only on the theological but also on the sociological level.[110]

Mark

Between *Mark* and Matthew also there are very close theological contacts. Matthew, who has taken over the narrative structure of the Gospel of Mark, is literarily a new conception of the Gospel of Mark and not a new conception of Q. Several things depend on this: as for Mark, so for Matthew the *title Son of God* is decisive.[111] For both, the story of Jesus is transparent of the situation of their own community, i.e., it is *inclusive history*.[112] For both, μαθηταί and ἀκολουθέω are key terms which circumscribe not only the history of Jesus but also their own existence. For both, the *miracle narratives* express the experiences of their own existence with Jesus. For Mark also, the debate with Israel was important;[113] Matthew here follows Mark's story and intensifies it in a dramatic way with the help of the threatening words against Israel from Q and from his special material. At other points, however, Matthew seems to be farther removed from the basic attitude of the Second Gospel: the passion narrative is accented quite differently by the two. Therefore also the "messianic secret" no longer seems to play a key role in Matthew.

Differences between Mark and Q

Especially at two points are the differences between the Gospel of Mark and the Sayings Source substantial; Matthew here faced a choice. The one concerns *the*

---

[109]In Q, only Luke 6:47–49; 12:42–46, 57–59 (not formal minatory sayings!) are to be interpreted like this. In Matthew, also Luke 12:39f.; 17:23–37 (as a part of chs. 24/25) and indirectly the whole divine judgment on Israel is directed critically against the church.

[110]Cf. below pp. 82-87.

[111]"Son of God" is indeed understood differently by Matthew and Mark, cf. the commentary on 3:17; 4:1–11 (summary); 27:43, 54.

[112]Cf. U. Luz, "Geschichte" IV, *TRE* 12, 598, 600.

[113]Cf. on this aspect of the Gospel of Mark especially Z. Kato, "Die Völkermission im Markusevangelium," Diss. Bern, 1984.

relationship of Jesus to the Torah. Mark stresses the elements of the proclamation of Jesus which are critical of the law; especially Mark 7:1–23 with its detailed interpretation for the church, 7:18–23, which is attached to 7:15, shows that Mark evidently is basically free toward the ritual law.[114] In Q, almost all Jesus traditions critical of the law are missing; it seems that Jesus' proclamation was understood rather as a new accenting of the law which is always valid (cf. Matt. 23:23–26; Luke 11:39–42). Matthew decisively aligns himself on the side of those who affirm the validity of the whole law; in distinction from the Sayings Source, he even puts the question of the law into the forefront (Matt. 5:17–19). On the other point, however, he accepts the Markan position: while indeed the Q materials contain Jesus' pointed openness toward Gentiles in individual cases but nowhere presuppose the existence of a *Gentile mission,* in Mark it is affirmed implicitly (5:18–20; cf. 7:24–8:10) and explicitly (13:10; 14:9; 15:39). Matthew especially stresses it: his Gospel ends in 28:15–20 with the programmatic command of Jesus to make disciples of all Gentiles (πάντα τὰ ἔθνη).

Result: not only Matthean language but also Matthean theology is a continuation—distinctive but basically tradition-bound—of the heritage from his fathers. If we ask what is new in his theology, then the answer has to be nuanced: In comparison with Q, Matthew emphatically turns the conception of judgment "inward," i.e., the parenesis of judgment applies to the church. What is new in comparison with Mark is the accenting of the "gospel of Jesus Christ" (Mark 1:1) as a "gospel of the kingdom," i.e., as ethical proclamation of Jesus.[115] This accenting has become possible through the combination of the "doctrineless" Gospel of Mark with the Q materials. But new is also the integration of the Q materials into the story of God with his Son, Jesus, which discloses a new, deep dimension of grace for the hearers of the ethical gospel. The community which is confronted by the demand of Jesus knows itself directed first of all to the story of Jesus in which it experiences the "with us"—Immanuel—of God. New furthermore is the programmatic turning to the Bible of Israel which is claimed for the history and proclamation of Jesus in an equal manner. But just at this point probably it is not Matthew himself who is absolutely new; rather he is an exponent of his community who accepts and sharpens not only his theological "teachers," but also the language and the thinking of his community.

---

[114]R. Smend and U. Luz, *Gesetz*, BKon (1981), 116–119.

[115]Cf. the excursus after 4:25 below.

4.2. Matthew as an Exponent of His Community[116]

4.2.1. The Rooting in Worship

The Matthean version of the Lord's Prayer gives a clear indication. It has always been rightly emphasized that it is inconceivable that Matthew has redacted this quintessential community prayer as a free author. In my opinion it can still be observed in the wording that Matthew presents the version which was spoken in his church.[117] If this is correct, then the following consequences result: it is evident that the language of the Matthean Lord's Prayer and the language of the Matthean redaction are to a large extent identical: πατὴρ ὁ ἐν τοῖς οὐρανοῖς, θέλημα τοῦ πατρός, and πονηρός are central vocables of the evangelist and at the same time prayer language of his church. That means that in important points the redactional language of Matthew is rooted in worship.

This conclusion may be strengthened by reference to another text. When in Matt. 26:26–28 the words of institution of the Lord's Supper are formulated as an imperative, "Take, eat" and "drink of it, all of you," this reflects the liturgy just as does the addition "of this fruit of the vine" in the eschatological saying.[118] Also, εἰς ἄφεσιν ἁμαρτιῶν in the saying over the cup points to its use in the worship service. It is attested also by Matt. 9:8 that forgiveness of sins plays a large role for the community of Matthew. In Matthew 18, the whole second half of the community discourse is overshadowed by the theme of forgiveness, and the old community order of 18:15–17 is "framed" correspondingly.[119] The experience which the Matthean community makes with the eucharistic worship service determines the theology of the evangelist.

This thesis can be carried further but only as we approach the borders of speculations. From Matt. 28:19 we know that baptism was done in the name of the Father, the Son, and the Holy Spirit (cf. *Did.* 7:1f.). This agrees not only with the understanding of God as Father but also with the use of the title Son of God in the Gospel of Matthew. It probably agrees with the linguistic usage of the community when "Son of God" becomes the most important Matthean confessional title (14:33; 16:17; 27:54). It probably also is in connection with the experience of worship that the influence of the LXX in the Gospel of Matthew becomes visible again and again. Κύριε σῶσον (2 times) and κύριε ἐλέησον (3–4 times) is the language of the psalms.[120] Elsewhere phrases of the Septuagint flow from the pen of the evangelist. The terminology, formulation, and structure of his Gospel are influenced strongly by the LXX, although it was not the intention of Matthew to write in the LXX style. He is at home in his Greek Bible because the worship service plays a decisive role for him.

---

[116]Reflections in this direction are found in several authors. Already Schlatter (*Gemeinde* passim) recognizes in the Gospel of Matthew the way a community thinks. Tilborg, *Leaders*, by his very unassuming redaction-critical analyses, looks anew at the possibility that there could be stages of tradition and revisions between Mark or Q and Matthew. Most important are Kilpatrick and Stendahl. Kilpatrick, *Origins*, asked decidedly about the liturgical rooting of the Matthean use of language (doublets, 92; Old Testament quotations, 94f.; in general, 59–71); Stendahl, *School*, understands Matthew as a "handbook issued by a school" (20), which for him does not exclude the question of an individual author (30). We understand "Matthew" clearly as an individual author but as one who is rooted in his community.

[117]Cf. the analysis of Matt 6:9–14, no. 2 below.

[118]Does the liturgist point to the cup (τούτου)?

[119]Cf. the summary on Matthew 18.

[120]Cf., e.g., Ps. 11:1; 105:47; 117:25; 6:2; 30:9; 40:4, 10; 85:3; 122:3.

4.2.2. Matthew and the Scribes of His Community

Matthew speaks of Christian ♦ scribes (13:52; 23:34), and, in regard to Israel, of "their synagogues" (4 times) and "their scribes" (7:29)—but not of "their Pharisees." May we assume that this is done because there were besides "their" scribes and synagogues also "our" scribes and synagogues? The activity of these scribes becomes evident in the background of the Gospel of Matthew. I am anticipating here the excursus on the fulfillment quotations[121] and indicate some results: the "school" which is evident behind the fulfillment quotations is, as I believe, not identical with the evangelist. The evangelist, who is influenced by the LXX, is hardly himself responsible for their wording. Since most of the fulfillment quotations belong together with those traditions in which they are found today and since Matthew is not their author, it is to be assumed that in his community many traditions, especially also oral traditions of the uniquely Matthean material, were seen by scribes in the light of the Bible. Behind Matthew the work of scribes becomes visible which were an influence on him. It is not without preparation that he lays claim to the Old Testament programmatically.

The activity of these scribes is perceptible in other places as well: the pre-Matthean addition to the story of the plucking of heads of grain (Matt. 12:1–8) or the traditional "rabbinical" argument of the sheep which fell into the pit (Matt. 12:11f.) shows that the Gospel of Mark also was contemplated by scribes in the Matthean community. Or to whom could the Hebraization of the last cry of Jesus from the cross (Matt. 27:43) be traced if the evangelist supposedly did not know Hebrew? Other insertions in the Gospel of Mark also point to a Jewish-Christian milieu even if not to a specifically scribal milieu, namely, the narrative of the temple tax (Matt. 17:24–27) or additions to the passion narrative, 26:52f.; 27:52f., 62, etc. With most of these additions, the Matthean linguistic characteristics are so prolific that it can only be the evangelist who put them in writing. The inviolability of the Gospel of Mark obviously was felt to be so great that only rarely were additions made in writing. But it was different with the collection of Q material which, like a notebook, could easily be enlarged by additional little leaves.[122] This happened in the enlarged recension QMt, e.g., by the addition of Matt. 5:5, 7–9; 6:34; 7:6; 10:5f., 23(–25?); 18:15–20; 23:16–22. All these texts breathe a Jewish-Christian spirit, perhaps having been influenced by biblical language or by wisdom motifs or perhaps reflecting questions of community practice or the mission to Israel.

Thus, behind the Gospel of Matthew, Jewish-Christian, partly scribal circles become evident, circles which were interested in Q, the Gospel of Mark, other Jesus traditions, and the Bible. It is my opinion that such traditions must not be shunted aside and the evangelist must not be placed apart from them. Not only his own language, which repeatedly demonstrates contact with contemporary rabbinic Judaism, or his conservative attitude toward the law which is evident in 5:17–19 and multiple other texts, but also the whole contour of his Gospel, which resembles closely the Semitic world, point to the contrary. Result: Matthew is influenced in his language and his theology by his community; he does not write in a vacuum.

---

[121] At 2:23 below.

[122] Cf. above, p. 46-47.

5. THE SETTING OF THE GOSPEL OF MATTHEW

Literature

Bacon, *Studies* 3–49.
Dobschütz, *ZNW* 27 (1928) 338–48.
Kilpatrick, *Origins* 101–39.
Kürzinger, J., "Das Papiaszeugnis und die Erstgestalt des Matthäusevangeliums," *BZ* NF 4 (1960) 19–38, quoted from idem, *Papias von Hierapolis und die Evangelien des Neuen Testaments*, Eichstätter Materialien 4, pp. 9–32 (Regensburg: Pustet, 1983).
_____ , "Irenäus und sein Zeugnis zur Sprache des Matthäusevangeliums," *NTS* 10 (1963/64) 108–15, quoted from idem, *Papias von Hierapolis*, 33–42.
Nepper-Christensen, *Matthäusevangelium* 13–100, 180–207.
Schweizer, *Kirche* 138–70.

5.1. The Gospel of Matthew—A Jewish-Christian Gospel

Literature

Clark, K. W., "The Gentile Bias in Matthew," *JBL* 66 (1947) 165–72.
_____ . *Vision* 15–25.
Strecker, *Weg* 15–35.

Not infrequently, the thesis is advocated that the Gospel of Matthew in its final redaction comes from a Gentile-Christian community and from a Gentile-Christian author.[123] The Jewish-Christian elements then belong to the tradition. The most important reasons for this assumption are:

1. Matthew affirms the Gentile mission and condemns Israel severely.
2. Matthew avoids Aramaic words.[124] Both arguments are not sufficiently convincing, in my opinion. It is to be expected especially of Jewish Christians that they would carry on with great intensity the debate with the synagogue, which remained far from Jesus, and would arrive at a severe judgment on Israel.[125] The linguistic findings indicate nothing. Greek stylistic feeling commands Jews and Gentiles to reduce the use of foreign words. Moreover, in Syria Jews and Gentiles spoke Aramaic.
3. Therefore only the third reason might be decisive: Matthew writes of things which demonstrate an ignorance of Judaism impossible for a Jewish Christian. But on closer inspection, the passages blend quite seamlessly.[126]

---

[123]Clark*; Nepper-Christensen, *Matthäusevangelium* 202–208; Strecker, *Weg* 15–35; Trilling, *Israel* 215; Walker, *Heilsgeschichte* passim; Tilborg, *Leaders* 171f.; Frankemölle, *Jahwebund* 200; Gaston, *Messiah* 33–39; Meier, *Law* 14–21 (bibl.); idem, *Vision* 17–25.

[124]Cf. above n. 98.

[125]Cf. the Jewish-Christian book of Revelation (2:9; 3:9), the Jewish-Christian Gospel of John (8:44) and the Jewish-Christian Paul (1 Thess. 2:16; the later text Romans 9–11 indicates a change in the thinking of Paul!). The "protest exegesis" of the OT in Jewish Gnosis advocates a similar harsh anti-Jewishness.

[126]Untenable are the references to 16:12 (that Matthew presupposes a common teaching of the Pharisees and Sadducees) and 22:23 (from the lack of the article it could be concluded that according to Matthew only a few Sadducees denied the resurrection), contra Meier, *Vision* 20f. The riding on two animals 21:5–7 is not a misunderstanding of parallelism (contra Strecker, *Weg* 18f.); it would be obvious even to a Gentile Christian that one cannot ride on two animals at the same time. Instead, an—exegetical!—intention is to be seen here. Matthew 12:11 shows not a rabbinical but still the popular

I believe that the Gospel of Matthew comes from a Jewish-Christian community and from a Jewish-Christian author. The following reasons speak for this view:

1. The structure and composition of the Gospel demonstrate that the evangelist is influenced by Jewish literature.

In his famous "testimony," *Papias of Hierapolis* writes in the first half of the second century: Ματθαῖος μὲν οὖν Ἑβραῗδι διαλέκτῳ τὰ λόγια συνετάξατο. Our observations on the composition and structure of Matthew make it enticing to understand this sentence in the sense of the philologically well-grounded interpretation of Kürzinger: Matthew ordered[127] the traditions[128] in a Jewish manner of presentation.[129] The sentence was then misunderstood in the ancient church by interpreting Ἑβραῗς διάλεκτος as "Hebrew language."[130] The error of later ecclesiastical authors came about when there was mention of the existence of a Hebrew Gospel of "Matthew" (= Nazarenes), e.g., in the library of Pamphilus in Caesarea.[131] Papias was chronologically and geographically rather close to the Gospel of Matthew and was concerned about the Jesus tradition. It is pure prejudice to assume that he was completely uninformed. He deserves a better judgment than he is usually accorded in New Testament research.

2. The Matthean sources, Mark and Q, were handed down and worked over in a Jewish-Christian community shortly before the Gospel of Matthew was written.[132]

3. The numerous similarities of the language of the Gospel of Matthew with the Septuagint and with Jewish linguistic characteristics point to a Jewish-Christian author.[133]

---

conviction that an animal which falls into a pit on the sabbath should be rescued. The Greek word φυλακτήριον in 23:5 is most difficult; cf. the commentary on this passage.

[127]Kürzinger, *Papiaszeugnis* 13, 20. This means (as in the preceding text about Mark) the literary ordering of the material which speaks for the meaning διάλεκτος = manner of presentation. According to Kürzinger, Papias compares the unordered manner of presentation of Mark with the "Hebrew" manner of presentation of Matthew and concludes: "Each (i.e., Matthew and Mark) interpreted (ἡρμήνευσεν) them (i.e., the traditions) as he was able."

[128]Λόγια is in Papias's preceding text about Mark a summary of τὰ ὑπὸ τοῦ κυρίου λεχθέντα ἢ πραχθέντα. Cf. also the title of his main opus!

[129]Kürzinger, 20–23: Διάλεκτος as a "technical term of rhetorical technique" (21) means conversation, spoken language, way of expression, style; the meaning "language" does not become prominent until the time of the Alexandrians. The article is missing before Ἑβραῗς, which speaks against "language."

[130]Irenaeus, *Haer.* 3,1,1, formulates just as Papias; his testimony perhaps has to be understood in the same way, cf. Kürzinger, *Irenaeus**. Origen (in Eusebius, *Hist. Eccl.* 6,25,4: γράμμασιν Ἑβραϊκοῖς and Eusebius, *Hist. Eccl.* 3,24,6: πατρίῳ γλώττῃ) knows as the first one the Hebrew "original language" of Matthew. At the same time, according to Eusebius, *Hist. Eccl.* 5,10,3, since Pantaenus the existence of the Hebrew "Gospel of Matthew" (= Gospel of the Nazarenes) was known in the congregations in the east. Therefore one has to assume that the spurious tale of the Hebrew Matthew originated in the ancient church after the Aramaic Gospel of the Nazarenes was known and considered as the original text of Matthew. It is significant that this happened in the east, not in the west.

[131]Jerome, *Vir. ill.* 3 = Aland, *Synopsis* 545.

[132]Cf. above p. 78.

[133]Cf. above section 3.1–3.3, no. 3–5.

It is uncertain whether the evangelist knew Aramaic.[134] It is certain only that his mother tongue was Greek; not only his excellent Greek but also the fact that he was indirectly influenced by the LXX is in favor of this view. But why should a Syrian—whether Gentile or Jew—not know Aramaic? I see no convincing reason to exclude this possibility.

4. Matthean theology, especially his understanding of the law and his appeal to the Old Testament, seem to me to speak for a Jewish-Christian author.

5. The Gospel of Matthew became not only the most important Gospel in the Great Church, but beyond that it has had an interesting history in Jewish-Christian circles.

The special role of the Gospel of Matthew in comparison with other Gospels in several Jewish-Christian writings or writings influenced by Jewish-Christianity is striking. Among them is the Gospel of the Nazarenes in the 2d century which was used by the Jewish Christians of northern Syria in the 4th century and which can almost be designated as an amplified paraphrase of Matthew.[135] Belonging here also is the Gospel of the Ebionites, which was both taken to be the Gospel of Matthew and at the same time contains important Matthean theological statements.[136] The following Jewish-Christian writings are strongly influenced by Matthew: the Pseudo-Clementines,[137] in Gnostic circles the Apocalypse of Peter of Nag Hammadi,[138] perhaps the Gnostic Apocryphon of James[139] as well as the Syrian Didascalia, which belongs in a Jewish-Christian environment.[140] Fifth Ezra, which is strongly influenced by Matthew,[141] the Gospel of Peter,[142] and the Passover Homily of Melito of Sardes[143] could be designated as

---

[134]J. Jeremias, "Die Muttersprache des Evangelisten Matthäus," in *Abba* 252–60, from the fact that the liturgical text of the Shema in 22:37 does not follow the LXX but Mark, wants to draw the conclusion that the former Jew Matthew did not come from a Greek-speaking synagogue. The conclusion is not cogent: Why should Matthew here not follow Mark for his OT texts as he did usually? Besides, Deut. 6:5 LXX is difficult from a textual-critical point of view.

[135]Cf. Hennecke 1: 139–52.

[136]According to Epiphanius *Haer.* 30:3,7 (= Hennecke I 124), a Gospel of Matthew which the Ebionites themselves call the Gospel of the Hebrews. According to fragment 1 (ibid. 146) it is supposedly written by Matthew. Matthean theologoumena especially in fragment 4:5.

[137]According to W. D. Köhler.

[138]Schweizer, *Kirche* 167f.

[139]Cf. especially *NHL* 32f. (kingdom of the heavens, hypocrisy, Matthean parable materials). According to H. F. Weiss, "Das Gesetz in der Gnosis," in *Altes Testament—Frühjudentum—Gnosis*, ed. K. W. Tröger (Berlin, 1980), 84, the letter is addressed to Cerinthus, who on his part was influenced by Matthew; cf. below n. 159.

[140]G. Strecker, "Zum Problem des Judenchristentums," in W. Bauer, *Orthodoxy and Heresy in Earliest Christianity* (Philadelphia: Fortress, 1971), 252.

[141]Cf. G. N. Stanton, "5 Ezra and Matthean Christianity in the Second Century," *JTS* 28 (1977) 67–83. However, this writing is Jewish-Christian only in Danielou's broad sense.

[142]C. Maurer, "The Gospel of Peter," in Hennecke I 180: Matthew furnishes the basic material of the composition. The Gospel of Peter belongs to Syria, shows a certain closeness to the Didascalia, but is not itself Jewish-Christian.

[143]It combines a passion narrative, influenced by Matthew, with the Johannine *logos* Christology and so comes to the charge of deicide. On the "Jewish-Christian" character compare the passover celebration and the synagogue in Sardes.

Jewish-Christian in the broadest sense of the word. In these writings the Matthean debate with Israel, referred to earlier, had its effect. It is striking that Matthew plays a special role in the Jewish-Christian "Peter" literature more than in the "James" literature.[144] Thus the Gospel of Matthew has exercised an intensive effect in many sections of Jewish Christianity. It is in agreement with this phenomenon that the ancient church tradition understood Matthew as a missionary to Jews[145] and that the Gospel writings of the Ebionites and Nazarenes were considered to have been the Gospel of Matthew.

If Matthew has had an especially intensive influence in certain areas of Jewish Christianity, an influence which goes beyond the fact that it has become the most influential Gospel generally in the church, then this has to be explained. It is our thesis that the Gospel of Matthew was in a special way the central Gospel in *its own* narrower church area, namely, in (Petrine?) Syrian Jewish-Christianity.[146]

5.2. The Place of the Gospel of Matthew in the History of Jewish Christianity

Literature

Abel, E. L., "Who Wrote Matthew?" *NTS* 17 (1970/71) 138–52.
Brown, S., "The Matthean Community and the Gentile Mission," *NT* 22 (1980) 193–221.
Stanton, G., "The Gospel of Matthew and Judaism," *BJRL* 66 (1984) 264–84.
Tagawa, K., "People and Community in the Gospel of Matthew," *NTS* 16 (1969/70) 149–62.
Thompson, W. G., "A Historical Perspective in the Gospel of Matthew," *JBL* 93 (1974) 243–62.
Thompson, W. G., and Laverdière, E. G., "New Testament Communities in Transition: A Study of Matthew and Luke," *TS* 37 (1976) 567–97.
Further bibliography ** see above p. 79.

The Gospel of Matthew came into being when the Q tradition was integrated into the Markan material. It seems to me that this literary procedure has to be related back to the history of the Matthean community: the combination of these two sources reflects a piece of the history of the Matthean community. There is, to my mind, substantial evidence that the prehistory of the Matthean community is connected in a special way with the *Sayings Source*.

A look at the church offices[147] makes this point clear. In the Matthean community there are ♦ prophets. The exalted Lord says in 23:34 that he will send to

---

[144]Künzel, Studien 253–256. The thesis is correct only conditionally; evidences against it are, e.g., Apocryphon of James (*NHL* 29–36); Letter of Peter to Philip (*NHL* 394–98), hardly Matthean influences.

[145]Origen, in Eusebius, *Hist. Eccl.* 6,25,4; Eusebius *Hist. Eccl.* 3,24,6.

[146]Matthew was situated in church history at a point prior to the decision of Jewish Christianity—which became unavoidable after 70— whether it should integrate itself into the Great Church or should go its own way; thus it becomes understandable why he came to be honored in Jewish Christianity *and* in the Great Church. Matthew has decisively determined this decision of Jewish Christianity; cf. pp. below, 84–86.

[147]Cf. on this matter especially Frankemölle, *Amtskritik*; Sand, *Propheten*; Schweizer, *Kirche* 140–163; Trilling, *Amt*.

Israel prophets, sages and scribes.[148] Matthew 10:41 speaks of the acceptance of wandering prophets into the community; 5:12 and 23:37 also speak of Christian prophets. Certainly almost all these sayings come from Q. But the manner in which they are used by the evangelist makes obvious that his community also knows prophets, and particularly wandering prophets, as we know them from the Sayings Source and as they occur again in the Didache (11–13) alongside the community prophets (10:7, cf. 13:1–4; 15:1f.). The warning against pseudo–prophets (7:15–23; 24:10–12) also presupposes that there were prophets in the Matthean community. Similar statements may be made concerning the ♦ *scribes*. In contrast to the prophets they are mentioned by the evangelist in the redaction (13:52, cf. 8:19; 23:34). The Sayings Source spoke of the σοφοί who were sent to Israel with the prophets (23:34).[149] It is not the intention of Matthew to emphasize especilly the place of the scribes in the community. Quite the contrary! Since "one is your teacher" (23:8) and "all"—also the scribes—are "brothers" and since the whole community has the power of binding and loosing (18:18), the Matthean tendency moves more in the direction of integrating the scribes as members of the community. He also is not interested in stressing the inherent dignity of the wandering radicals, viz., of the prophets and righteous (10:41), but rather in strengthening the "little ones" of the community as disciples of Jesus in the full sense of the word (cf. 10:42!). It is my view that the evangelist presupposes the wandering prophets and sages of Q. But the perspective has shifted in comparison with Q: Matthew writes from the perspective of a resident community. Wandering charismatics are only transient visitors. The Matthean Jesus has a firm residence in Capernaum (4:13).

Therefore we argue that the Gospel of Matthew comes from a community which was founded by the wandering messengers and prophets of the Son of man of the Sayings Source and remains in close contact with them. The traditions of Q thus reflect, for the community, experiences from its own history. They are "its own" traditions.[150]

It fits into this thesis that the Gospel of Matthew is indeed influenced by Jewish Christians but that it mentions James, the brother of the Lord, who belongs to Jerusalem, only marginally (13:55). Matthew has contact rather with those parts of the church which look to Peter as the central figure.

It is much more difficult to determine the place of the Gospel of Mark in the history of the church. O. H. Steck has proposed the helpful hypothesis that after the Jewish War Jewish Christians who had been expelled from Palestine had "joined the Hellenistic Christian churches" in Syria.[151] The Gospel of Mark would then be essentially the tradition of the indigenous Hellenistic church. The Gospel of Matthew would be an ecumenical Gospel. Historical development and the findings of literary criticism are related to each other in this hypothesis. As helpful as this thesis is, it seems to me that critical scrutiny of details is necessary. Against this hypothesis stands the supposition, which is preferred again today, that the Gospel of Mark originated in Rome.

---

[148]Matthew formulates in the present tense (ἀποστέλλω) and thus refers the sending to his own present time.

[149]Schweizer, *Kirche* 148: Since Sir. the sage can be thought of only as a scribe.

[150]Hare, *Theme,* has demonstrated this convincingly for the topic of persecution by the Jews.

[151]Steck, *Israel* 310f.

If this is correct, it would be even from a purely geographical viewpoint a foreign book in Syria which had been introduced from the outside. The hypothesis of Steck is opposed further by our literary-critical observation that the Gospel of Mark before its utilization by Matthew was handed down in a Jewish-Christian scribal milieu which was foreign to the Gospel of Mark. Furthermore, the plea of Matthew for basic loyalty to the law (5:17–19) and the fact that Matthew, in distinction from Mark, does not hint at an anchoring of the Gentile mission in the life of the earthly Jesus speak against this thesis. All these features contradict the supposition that Mark was the primary Gospel of the Syrian community of Matthew and for the fact that it came from the outside into a Jewish-Christian community whose own traditions basically were represented by the Sayings Source. There it quickly became important.

Thesis

Thus it is our thesis that the Gospel of Matthew comes from a situation in which the Jewish-Christian community stood at a turning point.[152] Already the Sayings Source with its heightened proclamation of judgment on Israel demonstrated that the proclamation of Jesus in Israel had reached a crisis. The destruction of Jerusalem in the Jewish War was experienced by the community as the judgment of God on Israel. In this situation the community decided to carry its proclamation of Jesus to the Gentiles. This decision most likely was controversial in the community. Matthew elected himself its advocate. In my view, one of his most important concerns is to defend in his community the decision for the Gentile mission.

Gentile Mission

The fact that the Gentile mission is not simply taken for granted by the Matthean church but is a deliberate, new venture is shown, it seems to me, by the observation that the narrative of Matthew contains a fracture at this point—and only at this point: the commission of the risen Lord is antithetically contrasted with the command of the earthly Jesus (28:19f.; 10:5f.). The whole course of the story of Jesus lays the foundation for this fracture: Matthew relates it as the story of the activity of Messiah Jesus among his holy people, Israel. He describes the conflict which is emerging and the "withdrawal" of Jesus from his people into the circle of the disciples. This is followed by the last great dramatic conflict with Israel in Jerusalem. It culminates in the passion narrative where the holy people aligns itself with the leaders who lead it into error (27:24f.). The Gospel of Matthew thus describes how Israel becomes "the Jews" (cf. 28:11–15). The response consists in the command of the risen Lord to the disciples to make disciples of the Gentiles (28:16–20). This fracture also

---

[152]Something similar is advocated by Humphrey, *Relationship* 247–252 (Matthew decides for "catholic Jewish Christianity"), Brown* 217–21, and Thompson-Laverdière* 571–82. Meier, *Vision* 28, on the other hand, sees the "turning point" in such a way that a formerly Jewish-Christian community now is composed of a majority of Gentile Christians. Abel advocates a completely different route out of the difficulty that Matthew seems to be both pro- and anti-Jewish: there is not just one Matthew but two, a Jewish-Christian and a Gentile-Christian Matthew. With this thesis he destroys the linguistic and compositional unity of the Gospel. Tagawa* points to the rooting of Matthew in the church which is at the same time the true Israel. But in this way one cannot explain passages like 10:5f., for there it is not a question of the "true" Israel.

took place in the history of the community, which failed with its mission to Israel, experienced the divine judgment of the destruction of Jerusalem, and now is called by the evangelist to a new undertaking. The beginning of the Gentile mission may have been motivated in addition by the encounter with the Gospel of Mark, which already was advocating it in the name of Jesus himself. The Matthean community thus had to confront that decision which Torah-obedient Jewish Christianity as a whole faced after the separation from the synagogue and after the Jewish War—the decision between its own peculiar route, which ultimately led to its existence as an independent marginal phenomenon between the non-Christian Israel and the Great Church, and the possibility to open itself up to the Gentile mission and so to take a basic step in the direction which finally led to integration into the Great Church. Matthew stands at the beginning of this second course.[153]

This hypothesis, which naturally can be confirmed only by the interpretation in the commentary, invites some reflections related to early church history. It is not incomprehensible that a Jewish-Christian community decided for Gentile mission only after the destruction of Jerusalem; similar developments could have happened in those communities which stand behind the Pseudo-Clementines.[154] The problem of the law is a more difficult dilemma.[155] If Matthew with his advocacy of Gentile mission stands basically on the side of Paul, nevertheless his affirmation of the unlimited validity of the law seems un-Pauline or pre-Pauline. How did he visualize the Gentile mission? With circumcision and basic obedience to the law for the Gentiles who would come to believe in Christ? This question is problematic; and it is no wonder that it caused many an exegete to doubt the basic affirmation of the law by Matthew or to relegate it to the pre-Matthean tradition. Exaggerating the difficulties is not helpful: a Torah-obedient Jewish Christianity which carries on a Gentile mission is demonstrated frequently. Just think of the opponents of Paul in Galatia, of the Jewish Christians who are mentioned by Justin, *Dial.* 47:2f., who want to "persuade" other Christians to be circumcised and to celebrate the sabbath, and perhaps of the Jewish Christians with whom the Syriac *Didascalia* is in disagreement.[156] It may be wise to mention at this place the opponents of the letter to the Colossians and the Jewish-Christian Gnostics in the Pastoral Epistles (cf. 1 Tim. 1:7). Quite numerous are the occurrences, if we take into consideration the Jewish Christians who do not demand full, but a limited obedience to the law (limited, e.g., by the thesis of "falsified" pericopes), e.g., the Elkesaites, the Jewish Christians standing behind the Pseudo-Clementines, the Cerinthians, etc. Thus a combination of Gentile mission with affirmation of the law is widely evidenced. But one must not harbor the

---

[153]Thus I see Matthew not primarily as a connecting link on the way "from Jesus to the monastic movement of the catholic church," cf. Schweizer, *Kirche* 163, following G. Kretschmar, "Ein Beitrag zur Frage nach dem Ursprung frühchristlicher Askese," *ZTK* 61 (1964) 27–67. In contrast to early Christian itinerant radicalism, the wandering ascetics of the Pseudo-Clementine letters, *Ad virgines*, and the *perfecti* of the *Liber Graduum*, Matthew is a perfectionist for the entire community (see Schweizer 168f). A two-stage ethic is found in his Gospel only in the margin (19:12).

[154]*PsClem Rec* 1:64: The time of sacrifices will be ended, the abomination of desolation will stand at the holy place; "et tunc gentibus evangelium praedicabitur" (and then the gospel will be preached to the Gentiles), cf. 1:41f.

[155]Cf. the interpretation of 5:17–19.

[156]Cf. especially *Didascalia* 26. The situation is murky. Is it a Jewish-Christian group outside of the community of the *Didascalia* (so Strecker [above n. 140] 258), or does the writer address a Torah-obedient group within the community with his thesis of the "repetition" of the law?

suspicion that this question had been decided by the Apostolic Council. The earlier, intensifying discussion in the church concerning Paul already shows that the reality was quite different.[157]

The question of the validity of the law for the Gentiles who were to receive the gospel was not yet solved in Matthew. It would be wrong, in my opinion, to consider as impossible on the basis of Matt. 5:17–19 a later solution in the sense of a complete or partial liberation of the Gentiles from the law. Matthew affirmed the validity of the whole law, but in his understanding of the law he was a ''Jesus person'' and not a Pharisee. Even though the ritual law and the law of circumcision was valid for him, this is not where the stress lay. The distinction between the βαρύτερα τοῦ νόμου, i.e., the commandment of love, the Decalogue and the moral law (Matt. 23:23), and the rather peripheral ceremonial laws, including purity commandments, sabbath, and circumcision, makes it understandable how it was possible for later successors of Matthew to waive them entirely for the Gentiles.

''Post-Matthean'' Jewish Christians solved this problem in diverent ways. The Judaists of the letters of Ignatius are notably interesting to us. We do not know whether they appealed to Matthew, just as ''their'' bishop did. They appealed to the OT (cf. Ignatius, *Philadelphians* 8:2), kept the sabbath and other ''old things''(cf. *Magnesians* 9:1) and did not hold to the bishop. Already the fraternal church order of Matthew left no room for an episcopacy understood in the sense of Ignatius! These Jewish Christians did not demand circumcision.[158] In the Pseudo-Clementines, which also show strong Matthean influence, circumcision was replaced by baptism, but many purity commands remain intact. Conversely, in Cerinthus we have the example of a Christian influenced by Matthew who probably demanded circumcision.[159] In other cases of Jewish Christians who also insisted on circumcision, Matthean influences can be felt at least indirectly.[160]

Result

This attempt to place the Gospel of Matthew into the history of Jewish Christianity naturally is a hypothesis. It is based on the assumption that behind the origin of the Gospel of Matthew there is not simply some kind of ''literary-critical operation'' but that an author who is obligated to his community works with its own normative traditions and contemplates them anew in the light of the Gospel of Mark. Thus our hypothesis presupposes that, in reference to texts like ours which are related to communities, one can draw

---

[157]Cf. G. Lüdemann, *Paulus, der Heidenapostel: Antipaulinismus im frühen Christentum*, FRLANT 130 (1983), 167–263 (Eng. trans.,) *Anti-Paulinism in Jewish Christianity*, Fortress, 1989).

[158]*Phld*. 6:1 (παρὰ ἀκροβύστου Ἰουδαϊσμόν) permits this conclusion. I presuppose here that Ignatius speaks of the same people in *Magnesians* and *Philadelphians*.

[159]According to Epiphanius, *Haer*. 28:5, Cerinthus used the Gospel of Matthew and at the same time rejected Paul because he insisted on circumcision.

[160]Irenaeus, *Haer*. 1,26,2 says of the Ebionites: They affirm creation, circumcision, temple and the other prescriptions of the law. They reject Paul and keep only Matthew as valid; cf. also *Haer*. 3,11,7. Probably ''Ebionites'' means the Gospel of the Ebionites which circulated under the name of Matthew (cf. above n. 136), and which Irenaeus took to be the canonical Gospel of Matthew.

inferences for church istory from a *unique* "literary-critical" process. This is similar to the way form critics draw sociological conclusions from the *general* characteristics of a micro genre to its *Sitz im Leben*. I am satisfied to have demonstrated the *possibility* of this procedure and, with this, the *possibility* of a self-consistent setting of the Gospel of Matthew within church history.

If this conclusion is correct, then it permits a clearer understanding of the Gospel of Matthew within the whole of the New Testament. In a certain light, the Galatian heretics are the closest relatives of the Gospel of Matthew. Matthew in any case is quite distant from the Epistle of James,[161] not only because the latter understands under the "perfect law of liberty"(1:25) only the moral law,[162] but also because Matthew contemplated the grace of God in a depth completely in contrast to the letter of James. Matthew obviously does not know Paul and his theology;[163] but it is basically the case that he would belong to the side of the opponents of Paul. In my opinion he advocates a theological basic type which thinks of law and grace together. We will still have to consider the question of what this means for the unity of the New Testament.[164]

Because Matthew encouraged his Jewish-Christian community to the Gentile mission, his Gospel was received by the Great Church, which consisted of a majority of Gentile Christians and became very early—in my opinion, already with Justin—its chief Gospel.[165] It is obvious that there must be a development between Matthew and the Gentile-Christian church which received him. The Matthean integral affirmation of the law was not accepted, and his "ethical" Gospel was accepted at most as to structure. Only in a limited sense, therefore, can the Great Church claim the Matthean heritage for itself. It can do so because Matthew himself in the name of the exalted Christ has opened his community to the Gentile mission, and because in his understanding of the law he preserved the Jesuanic priority of love over the ritual law—a perspective in which the freedom of the Gentile Christians from the law could become conceivable.

5.3. Matthew and Judaism

Literature

Davies, *Setting* 208–315.
Hummel, *Auseinandersetzung* 26–33, 159–61.
Further literature ** see above p. 79.

---

[161]Between Matthew and James there are contacts in traditional subjects: Τέλειος (1:4; Matt. 5:48; 19:21); faith in prayer (1:5–7; general topic); ταπεινός (1:9f.; general topic); doing of the word (1:23, cf. Matt. 5:19; 7:24–27; general topic); keeping of the entire law (2:10, cf. Matt. 5:18; in James related only to the Decalogue); works of love (2:15, cf. 25:35f.; general topic); judging (4:11; general topic); oath (5:12 = Matt. 5:37; the same logion; closest similarity to Matthew!).

[162]Cf. Luz (above, n. 114) 134f.

[163]Cf. the commentary on 5:19 and 13:25.

[164]Cf. the section "Matthew and Paul" at the end of vol. 3.

[165]On the reception of Matthew in the Great Church cf. below pp. 92-93.

The Matthean community, whose mission in Israel has come to an end, no longer belongs to the Jewish synagogue system. The fissure between community and synagogue is final. Any attempt to situate the Matthean community within the Jewish synagogue system must be considered a failure.[166] The evangelist speaks emphatically of "their" or "your" synagogues and scribes (4:23; 9:35; 12:9; 13:54; 23:34; 7:29). Even if in Matthew no direct trace of the "blessing of the heretics"[167] can be found, relations with the synagogue apparently have broken off. There is no hint of discussions held between the community and the synagogue. Matthew does not expect to find non-Christian Jewish readers of his Gospel. Only so is it understandable that the Jewish leaders and the role of the Jewish people are so extensively typecast. Matthew accepts even historical incongruities in order to describe the salvation-historical drama which led to the split of the community from the rest of Israel.[168] The commentary will attempt to show that the evangelist no longer makes an appeal to the nation of Israel to believe in Christ. Rather he describes for his readers, who believe in Christ, how it came about that this appeal is no longer being made. The debate with Israel has lost its direct addressee and has the function of strengthening the self-understanding of the community, the community which has to cope with the break with Israel, and at the same time to question a false security through pointing to the destiny of Israel. The judgment on Israel which Matthew describes thus becomes an indirect address to the community. The manner in which this is done by Matthew is possible only outside of the synagogue.

Thus it has become clear that the Gospel of Matthew is not a Christian answer to "Jamnia."[169] Rather it is a Christian answer to Israel's no to Jesus or the attempt to cope with this no in a fundamental definition of a position. The internal Jewish definition of a position after the destruction of Jerusalem no

---

[166]Bornkamm, *Enderwartung* 17; Hummel, *Auseinandersetzung* 28–33, 159–161; Davies, *Setting* 332 (on his thesis cf. nn. 167, 169); Cope, *Scribe* 126f.; and Brown* (above. p. 82) 216. In later publications, Bornkamm (*Der Auferstandene* 180: Matthew as a "Hellenistic Jewish-Christian") and Hummel (Supplementary ch. 6 to the 2d edition of his *Auseinandersetzung* 166: "Jewish Christianity, oriented toward universality") formulate much more cautiously. Numerous other authors assume a Jewish-Christian origin of Matthew without seeing the Matthean community within the synagogue association, e.g., Kilpatrick, *Origins* 111 (after the "Birkat ha-Minim"); Hare, *Theme* 164f. (shortly after the separation from the synagogue); Schweizer, *Christus* 12f. ("synagogue across the street"); Stendahl, *School* XIIIf.

[167]Cf. especially Davies, *Setting* 275–282. More recent research on the "Birkat ha-Minim" has shown, however, that this was not directed especially against the Jewish Christians; cf. D. Flusser, "Das Schisma zwischen Judentum und Christentum," *EvT* 40 (1980) 229–33; R. Kimelman "Birkat Ha-Minim and the Lack of Evidence for an Antichristian Jewish Prayer in Late Antiquity," in *Jewish and Christian Self-Definition* II, ed. E. P. Sanders (Philadelphia: Fortress, 1981), 226–44; P. Schäfer, "Die sogenannte Synode von Jabne," in his *Studien zur Geschichte und Theologie des rabbinischen Judentums*, AGJU 15 (1978), 46–52. Therefore, one should not overestimate its importance.

[168]Examples: the appearance of Pharisees and Sadducees at the same time; the common fear of Herod and all Jerusalem of the Messiah (2:3); the self-cursing of the holy people (27:4f.) etc.

[169]Davies, *Setting*, advocates this for the Sermon on the Mount. The review by G. Strecker, *NTS* 13 (1966/67) 105–12 is critical of this opinion. I can fully agree with the critical questions of Strecker: Not only are the contacts of Matthew with "Jamnia" which are construed by Davies rather weak, but, especially, "Jamnia" itself needs some demythologizing. In reality, Davies with this word condenses a complex development in Judaism which took several decades.

longer concerned Matthew. For him the destruction of Jerusalem was not a foundational event[170] which would necessitate some new perspective but the confirmation of God's judgment on "Judaism" which Jesus had announced.

The Jewish-Christian Matthew doubtlessly is closer to the *Pharisaic scribes* than to any other Jewish groups. The contacts between Matthew and Yohanan ben Zakkai have always been pointed out.[171] They are indeed astonishing. Just as Matthew, so also Yohanan—in this he is un-Pharisaic—has decisively put mercy and benevolence before sacrifice and purity commands.[172] If the tradition is correct, then Hos. 6:6 ("I desire steadfast love and not sacrifice") was a central text for both. Like Matthew, so Yohanan was open to the Gentiles.[173] Both let the ritual law stand, although it is not a central theme.[174] Both ask for the norm of norms.[175] Both most likely belonged to the peace party in the Jewish War. For both, the future judgment was central.[176] A certain parable also is very similar in both.[177] As Matthew, so also Yohanan interprets faith ethically, as a practicable commandment for everyday life.

In my view, the similarities are not anywhere due to a direct relationship between the two.[178] The fact remains that Matthew and the leading representative of the Jewish consolidation after 70 were in accordance in so many things as it was not again the case between Christians and Jews for long centuries. But the chasm between the community and the synagogue was already too deep for a dialogue to take place.

5.4. The Situation Within the Community

The Gospel of Matthew is characterized not only by the break with Israel; a series of internal problems of the community also becomes visible. They are similar to those we know from other New Testament writings and thus are typical problems of the second and third generations.

1. It is of exceeding importance that Matthew has to admonish his community again and again to action. The key word "little faith" which is

---

[170]Jerusalem is for him, based on the Markan theological geography and also on Q (Luke 13:34f), the city which is guilty (of the death of Jesus).

[171]V. Dobschütz, *ZNW* 27 (1928) 339, 344. On Yohanan, cf. J. Neusner, *A Life of Yohanan ben Zakkai*, 2d ed., SPB 6 (1970).

[172]*b. B. Bat.* 10b = Str–B. 204f.: sacrifices secure expiation for the Israelites, benevolence for the nations (in explicit contradiction to the predominant interpretation of Prov. 14:34); *Abot R. Nat.* 4 = Str–B I 500, works of love as a means of expiation for Israel after the destruction of the temple, citing Hos. 6:6.

[173]Cf. above *b. B. Bat.* 10b and *b. Ber.*17a = Str–B I 198 (Yohanan greeted everybody first, even Gentiles—cf. on Matt. 5:47).

[174]*Num. R.* 19.8; *Pesiq.* 40b = Str–B I 719: It is not so that that which is dead makes someone unclean or that water cleanses, but the Holy One has commanded it! Cf. also *Ed.* 8:7 = Str–B IV 793: Elijah will not have a priestly function; t. Para 3:8 (6,32) = Str–B IV 347: conflict with the high priest.

[175]Cf. *Abot* 2:9 = Str–B II 15.

[176] Cf. the discussion at the death-bed, *b. Ber.* 28b = Str–B I 581.

[177]*b. Sabb.* 153a = Str–B I 878: banquet of the king. Further similarity: *Gen.R.* 42 (25c) = Str–B III 255; striking call of Eliezer to discipleship.

[178]Instead, the Galilean background (distance from the temple, contacts between Yohanan ben Zakkai and Hanina ben Dosa) which is important for Yohanan and for early Christianity will have to be considered; cf. *b. Ber.* 34b = Str–B II 441 and n. 174 above.

important to him may throw light on its situation. The community is exhorted to perseverance, to faithfulness, to practice, to courageous faith. It is the basic problem of how a Christian or a community *remains* constant to that which it is, without becoming paralyzed.[179] In this situation, parenesis and the prospect of judgment gain increased significance. But Matthew has given a new dimension to the proclamation of grace by narrating anew to his community the history of Jesus as the history of God's being-with-us and by anchoring God's will in it.[180]

2. It is of only secondary importance that the Matthean community needed to come to terms with false prophecy and heresy (7:15–23; 24:10–12). As far as the content is concerned, these heretics are not quite palpable.[181] We know only that they were pneumatics (prophets, miracle workers) (7:22). Possibly it is in regard to the heretics that Matthew so consistently understands his proclamation as the command of the *earthly* Jesus ($=$ εὐαγγέλιον τῆς βασιλείας!) and ties the community to the earthly Jesus. The Spirit plays a relatively subordinate role, since not the Spirit but Jesus himself will remain with his church all the days until the end of the age (28:20). Prophecy and miracles are evaluated on the basis of Jesus and his demands.

5.5. The Place of Origin

Literature

Kraeling, C., "The Jewish Community at Antioch," *JBL* 51 (1932) 130–60.
Meier, J., "Antioch," in R. Brown and J. Meier, *Antioch and Rome*, pp. 11-86 (New York: Paulist Press, 1983).
Osborne, R., "The Provenance of St. Matthew's Gospel," *SR* 3 (1973) 220–35.
Slingerland, H., "The Transjordanian Origin of St. Matthew's Gospel," *JSNT* 3 (1979) 18–28.
Viviano, B., "Where Was the Gospel according to St. Matthew Written?" *CBQ* 41 (1979) 533–46.
Zumstein, J., "Antioche sur l'Oronte et l'Évangile selon Matthieu," *SNTU* A 5 (1980) 122–38.
Further literature ** see above p. 79.

The question of the place of origin cannot be answered conclusively; the available information is too sketchy. The numerous hypotheses all have something in common: they are based on very insubstantial indications. It is, however, the consensus that Matthew comes from the Syrian area.[182] A more exact determination is disputed.

---

[179]Kingsbury, *Parables* 135, speaks of "materialism . . . spiritual slothfulness . . . hatred among Christians . . . lovelessness . . . lack of generosity . . . unwillingness to forgive the brother . . . cases of apostasy . . . lawlessness . . . disobedience of all kinds."

[180]The Epistle to the Hebrews faces a situation similar to that of Matthew. It also intensifies proclamation of grace and paraenesis.

[181]Cf. the commentary on Matt. 7:15–23, analysis no. 3.

[182]Only Tilborg, *Leaders* 172, puts Matthew in Alexandria—however, without stating reasons.

The primary suggestions: *Antioch* has the most supporters.[183] The reasons for this view are:[184]

1. The Gospel of Matthew must have originated in a large city with excellent traffic routes, otherwise it would not have become known so fast. But this could apply to many Syrian cities!

2. In Antioch there was a large Jewish population.[185] But this could be said of other cities. In the time of the Mishna and Talmud scribes are known to have lived in a number of Syrian cities.[186]

3. The Petrine traditions of Matt. 16:17–19 could point to Antioch. But the Peter/rock tradition is also known in the Gospel of John. It does not play a role in the Matthean redaction. It is indeed correct that there is a certain relationship between Matthew and "Petrine" Christianity,[187] but that does not have to point to Antioch.

However, the reasons against Antioch are no more convincing:

1. Matthew does not know the episcopacy. But this does not mean much: He writes approximately 30 years before Ignatius. Besides, not a single Gospel speaks of a bishop; the interest there centers in the story of Jesus!

2. The Antiochene community was intrinsically Hellenistic and receptive to the Gentile mission (Acts 11:19–26). That in Antioch Matthew would have had to know Paul is the more weighty argument, but one must not forget that Antioch was a large city in which there were several Jewish quarters.[188] Almost certainly there were several Christian house churches.[189] After 70 the composition of many communities changed through the immigration of dispersed Palestinians.

What other possibilities are there? The following have been proposed: Phoenicia,[190] Caesarea Maritima,[191] Caesarea Philippi,[192] East Jordan,[193] or East Syria

---

[183]Recently advocated by Meier* and Zumstein*.

[184]A precise reason was given by Streeter, *Gospels* 504: Only in Antioch and Damascus was the official shekel the exact equivalent of two double-drachmas (cf. Matt. 17:24–27). No! Στατήρ could be used as a designation for a silver coin of various values and was then four drachmas each, e.g., of Attic or Ptolemaic coinage (LSJ s.v.).

[185]According to Kraeling* 136 between 45,000 and 65,000 Jews in a total population of c. 300,000 inhabitants. For all of Syria Kraeling assumes c. 7 million inhabitants, among them 1 million Jews. If this assumption is correct, then the use of Josephus, *War* 2.479, is illegitimate, according to which Jews had survived the massacres at the beginning of the Jewish War only in Antioch, Apamea, and Sidon.

[186]Rabbis are documented for Tyre, Sidon, Damascus, Tripolis (= Trablus), Arkath Lebanah, Emesa (= Homs), and Antioch, according to A. Neubauer, *La géographie du Talmud* (Paris, 1868), 294f., 297–300, 306, 312.

[187]Cf. above, p. 81.

[188]Kraeling* 140–145.

[189]There were also several synagogues. However, G. Theissen pointed out to me that the Antiochene Jews had an ἄρχων, similar to the ethnarch of Alexandria and probably (but cf. Flavius Josephus, *De bello Judaico*, ed. O. Michel and O Bauernfeind, II/2 [Darmstadt 1969], 229, note 29!) different from Rome. A Jewish counterpart to the Christian bishop Ignatius?

[190]Kilpatrick, *Origins* 131–34.

[191]Viviano*.

[192]Künzel, *Studien*, as a possibility.

[193]Slingerland*.

(Edessa).[194] The arguments are so specious that the individual suggestions are not worthy of discussion. Generally it can be said: The smaller and the more remote the community of Matthew is, the more difficult it is to explain the swiftness of spreading of the Gospel of Matthew.

Can anything at all be said? In my opinion, Antioch is not the worst of the hypotheses. At least, the Gospel of Matthew was most definitely used there shortly after 100 by Ignatius. The possible similarities with 1 Peter[195] could also be understood in the setting of Antioch. Thus the Gospel of Matthew could be attributed to a (!) congregation in Antioch. But this is merely a hypothesis.

The indications contained in the Gospel itself are very sparse. Ναζωραῖος (2:23) was a Syrian designation for Christians. In 4:24 Syria is mentioned. These two facts speak decisively for Syria. The strong influence of the Sayings Source and the contacts with itinerant radicalism which belong to it also indicate Syria. It speaks for Syria that Matthew has had a decisive history of influence precisely in Syrian Jewish Christianity.[196] Where else except in Syria would a largely Torah-observant Gospel be conceivable at all? It is plausible that the Gospel comes from a city.[197] It is less plausible that the Matthean community must have been rich, as has been concluded on the basis of a certain preference of the evangelist for large sums of money.[198] Poor people also can speak of large sums! Briefly put: the Gospel of Matthew does not betray its place of origin. Certainly it was a large Syrian city whose *lingua franca* was Greek.

5.6. The Time of Origin

The terminus a quo is the origin of the Gospel of Mark and the destruction of Jerusalem (22:7).[199] The terminus ad quem is more difficult to determine. It depends on our answers to the questions of where and by whom the Gospel of Matthew was used.

So much is disputed that I must limit myself to presenting my view as a thesis,

---

[194]Bacon, *Studies* 18–23; Osborne*.

[195]Cf. below p. 93.

[196]Cf. above pp. 81f. The north Syrian Gospel of the Nazarenes is more important in this regard than the south Syrian Gospel of the Ebionites, because it is much closer to Matthew.

[197]Kilpatrick, *Origins* 124, on the basis of the Matthean usage of πόλις. But this does not prove anything, because the LXX usage was taken over (cf. the commentary on 9:1). Decisive alone is the reference to the quick spread of the Gospel of Matthew which therefore most likely comes from a city with good traffic routes.

[198]Kilpatrick speaks of a "well–to–do city church" and points to the occurrence of στατήρ, τάλαντον, χρυσός, ἀργυ- (cf. the list above at 3.2). Against this speaks, however, the probable lack of a complete Old Testament in the Matthean congregational library; cf. the excursus on 2:23, section 2.

[199]Early dating is only rarely advocated, e.g., by J. A. T. Robinson, *Redating the New Testament* (London 1976), 102–107 (between 50 and 64; according to Irenaeus, *Haer.* 3.1.1, during the lifetime of Peter and Paul) and by Gundry, 599–609. Cf. the commentary on the two passages important for dating: 17:24–27 and 22:7.

which on the whole is closer to Massaux than to Koester.[200] In the Didache[201] the Matthew redaction is presupposed without doubt. Passages such as ch. 8 or—less certain—10:5 or ch. 16 permit an almost certain hypothesis: the Didache has come into existence in a community influenced by Matthew. Unfortunately, the Didache cannot be dated precisely.

While Ignatius[202] is not primarily influenced by the Gospel of Matthew, there are indications that he knew it, for there are passages which presuppose the Matthean redaction (*Smyrn.* 1:1 = Matt. 3:15, cf. *Phld.* 3:1 = Matt. 15:13). Polycarp certainly knew Matthew in his (2d) letter (Pol. 2:3 = Matt. 7:1f.; 5:3,6,10; Pol. 7:2 = Matt. 6:13; 26:41). But since the date is uncertain, we can only say that Matthew was perhaps known in Smyrna c. 115. It is conceivable to me that there are contacts between Barnabas and Matthew (cf. especially Barn. 5:8–12 with Matt. 5:1–7:8f.; 7:23f.), but there is no possibility of proof. The same applies to 1 Clement (cf. especially 1 Clem. 24:5 with Matt. 13:3–9 and 1 Clem. 46:6–8 with Matt. 18:6f.). Thus it is possible that Matthew was known in Rome before 100 and in Egypt a little later. Finally, Justin, it seems to me, presupposes the Gospels, using the Gospel of Matthew the most.

A special problem is posed by *1 Peter*. The contacts with the Synoptic tradition are extremely dense (1 Pet. 2:7– Matt. 21:42par; 1 Pet. 2:20 – Luke 6:46?; 1 Pet. 2:25 – Matt. 9:36?; 1 Pet. 3:8f. – Matt. 5:39, 44; 1 Pet. 4:13 – Matt. 5:11f. par, etc.). There are notably two places where contacts with Matthean redaction are more than just possible (1 Pet. 2:12 – Matt. 5:16: καλὰ ἔργα, δοξάζω; 1 Pet. 3:14 – Matt. 5:10: εἰ καὶ πάσχοιτε, διὰ δικαιοσύνην μακάριοι). Certainly these similarities are not compelling in themselves, but in view of their large number they are striking. I believe one must seriously consider the possibility that 1 Peter presupposes Matthew.[203] If 1 Peter was written before the zenith of the Domitian persecution in Syria (Babylon = Rome [5:13] does not contradict this, for Rome belongs to the Petrine fiction) this would constitute the first testimony to Matthew.

The question arises from the Gospel itself whether it reflects the painful experience of the break with Israel in the immediate past or whether it reviews it after a larger time interval. The commentary will attempt to lay the foundation for the first alternative. It speaks in favor of a relatively early time of composition. If this is taken together with the early certain and possible references, then the indications are even more numerous. To be sure, one has to allow for a certain amount of time for the Gospel of Mark to come into the Jewish-Christian Matthean community; nevertheless, one should not put the date for the Gospel of Matthew long after 80.

5.7. The Author

We do not know who the author is. The ascription to Matthew is quite

---

[200]Massaux, *Influence* 664–77, counts in very many cases on "contact littéraire certain" while Koester, *Überlieferung*, considers Jewish tradition and oral traditions among the apostolic fathers far more important than the Gospels (cf. the overview on pp. 259f.). The difficulty consists in the fact that most authors of the 2d century indeed know the Gospels but do not cite them directly.

[201]For the following sections I owe much to the draft of the dissertation of W. D. Köhler.

[202]J. Smit–Sibinga, "Ignatius and Matthew," *NovT* 8 (1966) 263–83 rejects direct usage, in my opinion unjustifiedly.

[203]E. Best reaches a negative result, "1 Peter and the Gospel Tradition," *NTS* 16 (1969/70) 95–113.

ancient;[204] probably it originated on the basis of Matt 9:9; 10:3. It is an attractive supposition that the author had a function in his community, e.g., was a teacher,[205] but it cannot be proved. He possessed a Jewish-influenced feeling for style, good Greek linguistic feeling, and a synagogue education. He probably was not a scribe in the sense of a rabbinically trained exegete; the characteristics for this are lacking.

Thus I presuppose that the Apostle Matthew was not the author of the First Gospel.[206] In that case one who himself was an eyewitness would have used the book of someone who was not an eyewitness as his main source. This difficulty seems insurmountable. Even Matt. 9:9, the transfer of the tradition of the call of Levi to the "original disciple" Matthew, speaks, in my opinion, very clearly *against* Matthew as author.[207]

In all honesty, however, one has to point out that even this assumption, which has been prevalent for a long time, has its difficulties. They are of a double nature:

1. The title εὐαγγέλιον κατὰ Μαθθαῖον is ancient. It is prior to Papias who presupposes it, for he cites in his testimony the Elder (Eusebius, *Hist. Eccl.* 3.39.15 beginning). Depending on the dating of Papias, the testimony of the Elder points to the time shortly before or after 100.

2. The Elder was of the opinion that Matthew, who arranged his Gospel in the Hebrew manner of presentation, was its author, just as Mark, the interpreter of Peter, was the author of his Gospel. With the Gospel of Mark this is in any event the most likely explanation, for εὐαγγέλιον κατά can hardly be understood differently with a relatively unknown person who is not an apostolic authority and is not mentioned in the Gospel.[208] The prevailing hypothesis therefore involves assuming either that Matthew at one time had a different title, or that the title at one time was understood differently from later times and presumably also differently from the title of the Gospel of Mark, or that it at one time was without a title.

All these assumptions are difficult. Titles are necessary when several codices were lying together in the cabinet of a community's synagogue or room.[209] This was the case at an early time, for Matthew did not want to suppress Mark, and their works were probably preserved together. The possibility that an unknown Christian by the name of

---

[204]The presbyter quoted by Papias; the Gospel of the Ebionites, fragment 1 = Epiphanius, *Haer.* 30.13.2f.(Hennecke I 156) c. 100 or in the first half of the 2d century.

[205]Cf. the commentary on 13:52. V. Dobschütz, *ZNW* 27 (1928) 338 calls the author "rabbi and catechist," H. Schwarck, "Matthäus der Schriftgelehrte und Josephus der Priester," in *Theokratia* (FS K. H. Rengstorf), ed. W. Dietrich (Leiden 1973) 145, somewhat cavalierly "teacher of religion"; C. F. D. Moule, "St. Matthew's Gospel: Some Neglected Features," *SE II* (= TU 87 [1964]) 98, a "γραμματεύς . . . in its secular, not rabbinic sense."

[206]Differently, e.g., Gundry 609–22.

[207]Cf. the commentary on 9:9.

[208]Since the genitive with εὐαγγέλιον had already found a place in tradition (θεοῦ, Χριστοῦ κτλ.), only the preposition κατά remained to express the author, analogous perhaps to ἡ παλαιὰ διαθήκη κατὰ τοὺς ἑβδομήκοντα; κατὰ Νεεμίαν (2 Macc. 2:13); καθ' αὐτόν (Josephus, *Apion* 1.18; further evidence in *BAGD s.v.* κατά 6c). The ancient church always has understood (rightly!) the superscriptions of the Gospels as designations of the authors; cf. Th. Zahn, *Einleitung in das Neue Testament* II (Leipzig 1899), 172f., 179 n. 3.

[209]Suggestion by M. Hengel, *Die Evangelienüberschriften* (Heidelberg, 1984).

Matthew has composed the Gospel and was secondarily identified with the apostle[210] is improbable because of the relative rarity of the name Mattai—and the possibility is excluded by 9:9 and 10:3. That the title might have been different at one time is difficult to believe, because "Gospel" in the sense of a book of Jesus' proclamation and deeds follows more closely the Matthean linguistic use of εὐαγγέλιον than the Markan one;[211] it is thus more likely that a "Matthean" title would be transferred to Mark than vice versa. On the other hand, εὐαγγέλιον in the sense of a book is a possible linguistic usage on the basis of Matthew but it is not in itself Matthean. This points to the fact that the title εὐαγγέλιον κατὰ Μαθθαῖον is more recent than the Gospel of Matthew.

The difficulties are considerable. I would not want to avoid them by postulating the apostle Matthew as the author. But I mention them because they are often treated with gratuitous silence.

6. ON THE HISTORY OF INFLUENCE AND ON THE INTENTION OF THIS COMMENTARY

The history of the influence of the Matthean text has great weight in this commentary. It often will be placed in the midst of the interpretation, not at its end. A brief explanation follows.

First a definition. By "history of interpretation," I mean the history of the interpretations of a text in commentaries and other theological writings. Under "history of influence" (*Wirkungsgeschichte*) I understand the history, reception, and actualizing of a text in media other than the commentary, thus, e.g., in sermons, canonical law, hymnody, art, and in the actions and sufferings of the church.[212] The history of influence and the history of interpretation are related to each other like two concentric circles so that "history of influence" is inclusive of "history of interpretation."

Naturally a selection was necessary in this area. This meant (a) a *selection of pericopes*. Because Matthew is the chief Gospel of the church, the history of influence of the Synoptic material is predominantly that of the Gospel of Matthew. In distinction from other writings of the New Testament where it is more easily possible to speak of a history of influence of basic ideas, the history of influence of Matthew is one of individual pericopes, even of individual verses and half verses.[213] A selection was unavoidable. The following considerations were important: (1) a relative preference for Q and the Matthean special materials over the Markan materials;[214] (2) a preference for pericopes and verses which were especially effective, the history of whose influence illuminates the present situation of churches and Christians paradigmatically.

Still more difficult was (b) the *selection of material*. Here we must first acknowledge the role of chance: the history of the influence of biblical texts is infinite; the knowledge of every commentator is finite. Especially when the frame of the history of interpretation was crossed, it necessarily played a role. But it was also necessary to

---

[210]With the very common name of Mark a secondary identification of an unkown author Mark with the famous John Mark is conceivable.

[211]Cf. the excursus on 4:25.

[212]Cf. G. Ebeling, "Church History Is the History of the Exposition of Scripture," in *The Word of God and Tradition* (Philadelphia: Fortress, 1968), esp. 28: "in doing and suffering . . . in ritual and prayer, in theological work and in personal decisions, in church organization and ecclesiastical politics . . . in wars . . . and in works of compassionate love."

[213]Cf. K. Beyschlag, "Zur Geschichte der Bergpredigt in der alten Kirche," *ZTK* 74 (1977) 299.

[214]The references by Gnilka, *Markusevangelium*, to the history of Mark's influence are important also for Matthew.

select materials as examples. The aim was never to write an unbroken overview of the history of influence in chronological sequence. Rather the history of influence should aid in leading the interpretation of a text to our present time. From this point of view, rather "typological" representations suggested themselves. The following criteria of selection were determinative:

    1. Interpretations which determine our own preunderstanding of the texts were preferred.

    2. Interpretations which had an impact on the Protestant and the Catholic churches as confessional traditions were preferred in the framework of a "Protestant-Catholic Commentary" (Evangelisch-Katholischer Kommentar).

    3. Interpretations which came close to the original meaning of the text in a changed situation and can have corrective functions for us were preferred.

    4. Among various possible examples, the earliest and the most effective ones were preferred (e.g., Irenaeus or the *Glossa Ordinaria*).

Despite all criteria, to presume to undertake a commentary which is accented by the history of influence remains hopelessly dilettantish. But this dilettantism seemed to me to be necessary. If I see it correctly, a major problem of historical-critical exegesis today lies in isolating a text in its own time and its own situation of origin and thus preventing it from speaking to the present time.[215] Attempts to avoid this which skip over the historical dimension, as, e.g., a retreat from history into the narrated or construed world of the text or a fundamentalist elimination of history by a hypostasizing of the text as a word of God above history, do not seem feasible to me, even if they are signals of alarm. Historical-critical exegesis must have a double function: (1) It has the purpose of distancing the texts from the interpreter and of alienating them by transferring them back into their own time. And (2) it is a tool for making the interpreters conscious of their own preunderstanding in the confrontation with the now-alienated texts and to teach them something about themselves. The combination of these two should prevent the historical-critical interpretation from distancing a text *only* from the present time. For manifold reasons, historical-critical interpretation until recently has fulfilled the second aspect of its double task only insufficiently. Even on this point, the history of influence is meant to intrude in a reinforcing way and to clarify for the interpreter (1) who he or she is in confrontation with the texts and (2) who he or she could be in confrontation with them. This now needs to be developed.

    1. The history of interpretation and the history of influence clarify what we have become on the basis of the texts. Here the interpretive traditions of one's own church and cultural environment are most interesting.

    1.1 The history of interpretation and the history of influence teach us to understand what the interpreter owes to the texts. One never encounters them in an abstract space which would permit one without further ado to make them into an objectively confronted entity which can be scientifically investigated. Rather, the interpreter is like a person who must investigate the water of a river while sitting in a little boat which is carried and driven by this same river. Thus the interpreter is carried by the texts. To keep historical-critical distance is from this

---

[215]H. G. Gadamer, *Truth and Method* (New York: Seabury, 1975), 270, thinks that a historically understood text "is forced to abandon its claim that it is uttering something true."

point of view an attempt at avoiding a reality of life. The history of influence is to point to the power of the texts which precedes our interpretation.

1.2 The history of interpretation and the history of influence are meant to help us understand *how* each interpreter is influenced by the texts. It illuminates the prehistory of one's preunderstanding. For example, it shows the interpreter what this Catholicism or this Protestantism is which has defined itself again and again in interaction with biblical texts. It is here not primarily a question of Protestant or Catholic "misunderstandings." Rather, more fundamentally it is a question of discovering the distinctiveness which we, e.g., as Protestants or Catholics have obtained. But our distinctiveness—what we are— makes necessary a distinctive, situational listening to the original meaning of the text. The history of interpretation and the history of influence are intended to help us in this endeavor.

1.3 The history of interpretation and the history of influence have also a negative function: they tend to prevent us from making the text naively contemporary by passing over the centuries. By calling attention to the distinctiveness of each historical situation, including that of the interpreter, they unburden the present from premature biblical demands, the obverse of which in the history of interpretation every time has been the neutralization of the text by reinterpretation, internalization, etc. At the same time they call attention to the *singular* power of the texts to become alive *anew* in each new situation. They call attention to the uniqueness of each historical situation in narrating how—among other ways, through the texts—this uniqueness was arrived at. Thus they do not invite us, figuratively speaking, to leap over the "ugly wide ditch,"[216] but to climb down in it and up again on the other side.

2. But the history of interpretation and the history of influence also furnish correctives; they show by example what we can be on the basis of the texts. In seeking exemplary corrections, the interpreter is interested mainly in models from the history of influence from other ecclesiastical or cultural environments. To that extent, the history of influence also aids ecumenical understanding—a by-product. They provide correctives (a) in a basic hermeneutical aspect (= 2.1–3) and (b) for dealing with individual texts (= 2.4–5).

2.1 The interpretations of the early church, of the Middle Ages and of the subsequent era up to the Enlightenment are of permanent importance because of their understanding of an individual biblical text from the wholeness of the faith, whether this might be the *regula fidei*, Gnostic illumination, church doctrine, or the Reformation faith. In contrast with this, historical-critical interpretation distances the text which is to be interpreted not only from the interpreter and his or her faith but intentionally also from the entirety of the biblical testimony, by pointing out its distinctiveness. The classical church interpretation can constantly confront the interpreter of today with that which,

---

[216]I mean here not the ugly wide ditch which Lessing saw between historical truths of fact and eternal truths of reason; the exegesis of the ancient church with its offer of eternal truths of revelation offered a direct alternative to the bridging of this ditch. Rather it is here the question of the ugly wide ditch between what was historical truth then and what is historical truth today and of the difficulty of discovering present validity in unique, past truths—a difficulty which is due to historicism.

mutatis mutandi, is even now his or her proper task, namely, to interpret the meaning of an individual text from the wholeness of the faith.

This does not mean that the christological, dogmatic interpretation of the early church should be a model for today in a direct sense. It is fascinating because it does not splinter the biblical testimony into infinitely many individual statements among which the interpreter has to make a decision and because it does not know of a ditch between past and present but states the meaning of a text in and for the present of the interpreter.[217] It reminds the interpreter of the true meaning of biblical interpretation, i.e., a responsible and compelling new expression of that which motivated the author of a text.[218] The understanding of a biblical text can happen only in the present and the interpretation only for the present because only in the present can the concern of the text become the concern of the interpreter. The interpretation of the early church reminds us that biblical texts would be interpreted *thus*. It cannot release us from this task because it is not the same in the modern period as in former times. But it reminds the interpreter that his or her task is not yet completed with the historical-critical exegesis because one does not yet understand what the subject matter of the text *means* if one understands what it *has meant*. It is an aid to "dealing with the subject matter itself"[219] and helps to break through from interpreting to understanding.

2.2 Especially the history of influence, which goes beyond the history of interpretation, reminds us of the fact that the understanding of a biblical text happens not only through the elucidation of its statements but beyond that by practicing and suffering, by singing and poetry, by praying and hoping. It reminds us of the fact that the understanding of biblical texts is the task of the *whole* human being.

2.3 The history of interpretation and the history of influence remind us of the fullness of the potential of meaning which is inherent in biblical texts. It reminds us of the fact that biblical texts do not have simply a set, closed meaning but are full of possibilities.

The juxtaposition of different interpretations in the early church and in medieval and subsequent exegesis up to the 17th century is important. It is not simply the expression of a traditionalism which hands down everything without distinction but much

---

[217]One experience which constantly accompanied the work was repeated over and over, namely, that "the church fathers . . . treated themselves to an exegesis at which every philologist's hair would bristle. And yet, who would deny that they knew better than we what was at stake?" (G. Picht, "Theologie in der Krise der Wissenschaft," *EK* 3 [1970] 202).

[218]Cf. K. Barth's basic distinction between the riddle of "the original record" and the riddle of the "subject matter" (*Romans*, Preface to the second edition [Oxford: Oxford University Press, 1933, 1968], 7). Barth describes understanding of the subject matter of a text as driving on "till I have almost forgotten that I am not its author; till I know the author so well that I allow him to speak in my name and am even able to speak in his name myself" (p. 8). Again and again in classical church exegesis it has happened that the statement of the text merged with the statement of the interpreter. In this process of melding, the distancing interpretation of historical criticism can be a helpful controlling element—but not if it prevents the melding as such.

[219]E. Fuchs, *Marburger Hermeneutik* (Tübingen: Mohr, 1968), 18, in the context of a distinction between interpreting and understanding which takes up Dilthey and goes beyond him. One might say in picking up on Fuchs: in exegesis it is a question of deepening and enlarging the understanding by interpreting. The history of influence prevents us from the danger of the distancing interpretation destroying the understanding instead of deepening it; it does this by showing how the distanced text is always already present with the interpreter.

rather of the fundamental insight that the texts are full of possibilities of application which do not exclude each other. In the same way, I believe, the juxtaposition of various senses of Scripture in the Middle Ages has fundamental significance. All this belongs to the recollection of the freedom which is inherent in biblical texts.

2.4 The history of influence of biblical texts broadens our horizon by mediating a great treasury of experiences which other Christians have found. Experiences of Christians in other situations and contexts are particularly important as correctives.

2.5 The history of influence also aids us in learning from successful and unsuccessful realizations of biblical texts. It shows where historical experiences call attention to open passages and unsolved problems. It poses the question of the consequences of biblical texts. Matthew teaches that prophets can be recognized by their fruits (7:15–23). The history of influence asks for the fruits of biblical texts. Thus it assists not only in avoiding "bad fruit" but, on the basis of the fruit, perhaps asks questions of the texts themselves.[220]

These reflections attempt to make clear that the history of interpretation and the history of influence should not accumulate additional historical materials alongside of the exegetical material. Instead, they should overcome a deficiency of historical-critical interpretation. Their purpose is to introduce the biblical texts into the present. Therefore in the commentary, wherever possible, the history of interpretation and the history of influence are not an appendix but integrative parts of the interpretation.

Thus it is a special characteristic of this commentary that it—occasionally and perhaps still too infrequently—puts the biblical texts "of then" into the present and makes also judgments on the present. I believe that I can only in this way do justice to the claim of the texts. Thus the commentary speaks, e.g., of the significance of the Matthean "Christianity of praxis" in a situation where a culturally dominant church becomes the church of the minority. Or it attempts to speak of the Sermon on the Mount in the situation of the nuclear threat and of the Son of man/judge of the world/Christ in relation to Christian guilt over against Judaism. It attempts not to exclude some perplexity on the part of the interpreter. It contains thereby also an element of personal engagement and an element of subjective limitation. Such attempts are at the same time made possible and mediated by the history of influence. In my opinion they are not something which is subsequent to the understanding of the texts, but they belong to the text itself.

---

[220]Elsewhere I proposed on the basis of Matthew to understand love as one(!) truth criterion for the interpretation of biblical texts ("Erwägungen zur sachgemässen Interpretation neutestamentlicher Texte," *EvT* 42 [1982] 512–14).

I. Prelude[1]

Matthew endeavors at the beginning to point out the chief theological concerns of his Gospel. Christology and the way of salvation from Israel to the Gentiles are in the foreground. He works in a manner that lets motifs and themes resound, picking them up again later and intensifying them. Thus he speaks of the Messiah of Israel, the Son of David (1:1,6,16f.,18–25), the rejection by Israel which is foreshadowed (2:1–12,16–18), the threat of judgment over Israel (3:7–12), the coming of the Messiah to the Gentiles (1:1,13–15,22f.; 4:12–17), Jesus as the Son of God (1:21; 2:15; 3:15–17; 4:1–11) and the founding of the disciple group in the Galilee of the Gentiles (4:18–22). Thus one may designate Matt. 1:1–4:22 as a theological prelude to the Gospel. The thematic inclusiveness is emphasized by the numerous geographically accented Old Testament quotations (2:5,15,18,23; 3:3; 4:15f.).

From this overview the impression may arise that the beginning of the Gospel of Matthew has a strongly doctrinal character. This impression is correct. Nevertheless, an interpretation which asks primarily for the doctrinal content of the Matthean texts and is satisfied with its identification misses the point. The Gospel of Matthew is primarily a *narrative*. It has fundamental significance that Christological statements are *narrated* as history. The reader learns that the deed of God who acts in the history of Jesus and whose actions the narrative of Matthew pursues is the foundation of any explicative Christology. The same is true for the way of salvation beyond Israel to the Gentiles, which Matthew—for good reason—sees foreshadowed in the prologue in the path of Jesus from Bethlehem by way of Egypt to Galilee. A commentary always runs the risk of inquiring about the doctrinal content of texts and of

---

[1]Krentz* (see bibliography at Matthew 1–2, below) 409–14, following Lohmeyer, lets the prologue end at 4:16, most exegetes already at 2:23. Krentz points out correctly that 3:1 follows loosely and does not indicate a break (412); furthermore, there are key word connections between 2:1 and 3:1. Cf. the introduction. pp. 42ff., on the enlarging of the prologue to 4:22, which is here proposed.

seeing their proper meaning in that. It can never take the place of the narrative but only intensify and make it more profiled. Whoever wants to do justice to Matthew—in preaching or teaching—has to take him seriously as a *narrator* and to understand the linguistic form of narrative as a part of the matter with which he is concerned.

A. THE INFANCY NARRATIVES (CHS. 1–2)

Literature

Binder, G., *Die Aussetzung des Königskindes Kyros und Romulus*, Beiträge zur klassichen Philologie 10 (Meisenheim: Hain, 1964).

Bloch, R., "Die Gestalt des Moses in der rabbinischen Tradition," in *Moses in Schrift und Überlieferung*, ed. F. Stier and E. Beck, pp. 95–171 (Düsseldorf: Patmos, 1963).

Bourke, M., "The Literary Genus of Matthew 1–2," *CBQ* 22 (1960) 160–75.

Brown, R. *The Birth of the Messiah* (New York: Doubleday, 1977).

Cave, C. H., "St. Matthew's Infancy Narrative," *NTS* 9 (1962/63) 382–90.

Crossan, J. D., "Structure & Theology of Mt 1,18–2,23," *Cahiers de Joséphologie* 16 (1968) 119–35.

Daniélou, J., *The Infancy Narratives* (London: Burns & Oates, 1968).

Davis, C. T., "Tradition and Redaction in Matthew 1,18–2,23," *JBL* 90 (1971) 404–21.

Dibelius, M., "Jungfrauensohn und Krippenkind," in idem, *Botschaft und Geschichte* I, pp. 1–78 (Tübingen: Mohr, 1953).

Erdmann, G., *Die Vorgeschichte des Lukas– und Matthäusevangeliums*, FRLANT 48, pp. 53–70 (1932).

Globe, A. "Some Doctrinal Variants in Matthew 1 and Luke 2 and the Authority of the Neutral Text," *CBQ* 42 (1980) 52–57.

Krentz, E., "The Extent of Matthew's Prologue," *JBL* 83 (1964) 409–14.

Laurentin, R., "Approche structurale de Matthieu 1–2," in *De la Tôrah au Messie* (FS H. Cazelles), ed. M. Carrez et al., pp. 383–416 (Paris: Desclée, 1981).

Muñoz–Iglesias, S., "Midráš y Evangelios de la Infancia," *Estudios Eclesiásticos* 47 (1972) 331–59.

Nellessen, E., *Das Kind und seine Mutter*, SBS 39 (1969).

Nolan, *Son*, passim.

Paul, A., *L'Évangile de l'enfance selon Saint Matthieu* (Paris: Éditions du Cerf, 1968).

Peretto, E., "Ricerche su Mt 1–2," *Marianum* 31 (1969) 140–247.

Pesch, R., "Der Gottessohn im matthäischen Evangelienprolog (Mt 1–2). Beobachtungen zu den Zitationsformeln der Reflexionszitate," *Bib* 14 (1967) 395–420.

——— , (ed.), *Zur Theologie der Kindheitsgeschichten. Der heutige Stand der Exegese*, Schriftenreihe der kath. Akademie Freiburg (Munich, 1981).

Räisänen, H., *Die Mutter Jesu im Neuen Testament*, Suomalaisen tiedeakatemian toimituksia Series B 158, pp. 52–76 (1969).

Saintyves, P., "Le massacre des innocents ou la persécution de l'enfant prédestiné," in *Congrès d'histoire du Christianisme* I (FS A. Loisy), ed. P. L. Couchoud, pp. 229–72 (Paris/Amsterdam: Les Éditions Rieder, 1928).

Schubert, K., "Die Kindheitsgeschichten Jesu im Lichte der Religionsgeschichte des Judentums," *BiLi* 45 (1972) 224–40.

Schwarzenau, P., *Das göttliche Kind. Der Mythos vom Neubeginn* (Stuttgart 1984).

Soares-Prabhu, *Formula Quotations*, passim.

Stendahl, K., "Quis et unde? An Analysis of Mt 1–2," in *Judentum—Urchristentum—Kirche* (FS J. Jeremias), ed. W. Eltester, BZNW 26, pp. 94–105 (1964).

Tatum, W. B., " 'The Origins of Jesus Messiah' (Mt 1,1.18a): Matthew's Use of the

Infancy Traditions," *JBL* 96 (1977) 523–35.

Vögtle, A., "Die Genealogie Mt 1,2–16 und die matthäische Kindheitsgeschichte," in idem, *Evangelium*, 57–102.

――――― , "Die matthäische Kindheitsgeschichte," in Didier, *Évangile*, 153–83.

――――― , *Messias und Gottessohn. Herkunft und Sinn der matthäischen Geburts- und Kindheitsgeschichte* (Düsseldorf: Patmos, 1971).

Zinniker, F., *Probleme der sogenannten Kindheitsgeschichte bei Mattäus* (Freiburg/ Schweiz: Paulusverlag, 1972).

    1. *Structure.* The first two chapters of our Gospel are almost of equal length and are divided each into two sections. The first section, 1:2–17, is longer than all the others and is in this way distinguished from them. In form, the genealogy is unique. The following three narratives, 1:18–25; 2:1–12, 13–23, belong together. Not only does a common motif grid undergird them, but there are also numerous vocables which occur only or primarily in 1:18–2:23.[1] But 1:2–17 also is fully integrated into the context: The leading word γένεσις forms an inclusion (1:1,18). It is intensified as to content by the concept of Davidic sonship (1:1,20). The leading verb γεννάω is taken up again in 2:1. The genealogy follows closely the title of 1:1 in unfolding Jesus as a child of Abraham and, at the same time, giving David a prominent place. Thus chapters 1–2 form a unit within which 1:18–2:23 once again have a special place.[2]

    2. In the *tradition* the narratives of Matt. 1:18–2:23 seem already to have formed a unit before Matthew, which perhaps was handed down orally. Although there is a "gap" between 1:25 and 2:1—the birth of Jesus is not narrated—the common background of all narratives shows that they belong together: they belong to the narrative type that recounts the announcement, persecution and rescue of the "royal child," which was widespread in ancient times (cf. the chart on pp. 152-155, below). In particular, the contacts of the whole section 1:18–2:23 with the Haggadah of the child Moses are striking —without suggesting the idea that it is transferred to the child Jesus. The thesis of the pre-Matthean combination of 1:18–2:23[3] is preferable, in my opinion, to the other thesis, also frequently advocated, that only 2:1–23 are a pre-Matthean combination of narratives while 1:18–25 is due to the evangelist.[4]

    3. The *contacts with the Lukan birth narrative* are minimal and concentrated almost exclusively in 1:18–25.[5] On many points, both traditions

---

[1]The relationships are especially clear between 1:18–25 and 2:13–23 (ἄγγελος κυρίου. . . κατ' ὄναρ. . . φαίνειν); 1:20; 2:13,19, cf. 23 (the role of Joseph); 1:20,24; 2:13,19 (παραλαμβάνω); 1:24; 2:13,21 (ἐγερθείς). Cf. also 1:20 with 2:1,4; 1:21,25 with 2:2; 2:7 with 2:16; 2:11 (mother!) with 2:13f., 20f.; 2:12 with 13:22.

[2]The attempt of Stendahl to apply Matthew 1 to the question of *Quis?* and Matthew 2 to the question of *Unde?* is interesting. But it seems to me that he overlooks the complexity of ch. 2 and especially the fact that the (theological!) question of the provenance of the Messiah is maintained until ch. 4 (3:3; 4:15f.).

[3]E.g., Strecker, *Weg* 51f. On the attempts to isolate the story of the Magi out of the pre-Matthean context of 1:18–2:23, cf. analysis 3 on 2:1–12.

[4]Strongly advocated by Vögtle, *Kindheitsgeschichte*.

[5]Cf. n. 26 on 1:18–25.

are not only different but irreconcilable.[6] The fact that neither of the evangelists makes an attempt at reconciliation must serve as an indication that the classical assumption of the literary independence of Matthew and Luke is still correct. The two evangelists have in common the tendency to put the birth narratives in the service of Christology. Both also have certain basic assertions in common, as, e.g., the knowledge of the birth of Jesus in Bethlehem and the virgin birth, the temporal connection of the birth of Jesus with the time of Herod (Luke 1:5, despite 2:1!) and the knowledge of the betrothal of Mary and Joseph, the descendant of David. This demonstrates that there must have been certain basic convictions and data which are very ancient and existed before the Matthean and Lukan narratives. But with that nothing is yet said about their historicity.

1. THE "REGISTER OF THE ORIGIN" (1:1–25)

1.1. The Superscription (1:1)

Literature

Eissfeldt, O., "Biblos Geneseos," in idem, *Kleine Schriften* III, pp.458-70 (Tübingen: Mohr, 1966).
Frankemölle, *Jahwebund*, 360–65.
Further literature ** at Matthew 1–2, above pp. 101-102.

Text

1 "Register of the Origin" of Jesus Christ, the son of David, the son of Abraham.

The superscription is influenced on the one hand by Mark 1:1, on the other hand by Gen. 2:4; 5:1. It is disputed whether it refers to the whole Gospel of Matthew, only to the genealogy, or to the prologue.[1] Βίβλος in Greek and Jewish [2] occurrences means "book," but in translation of the Hebrew סֵפֶר it also may mean "piece of writing," "document," or "register." Probably this is meant in the two basic OT occurrences.[3] Γένεσις occurs only here and 1:18; 1:18–25 makes the "origin" of Jesus hinted at in 1:15 more explicit. Therefore, one should neither understand γένεσις as "story"[4] and interpret the title as

---

[6]In Luke, Nazareth is the place of residence of Joseph and Mary (2:4), in Matthew, it is Bethlehem; Nazareth is a place of escape from Archelaus. Matt. 2:1–15 can be combined with Luke 2:21–40 only if one assumes with parts of the ancient tradition that the Magi did not come to Bethlehem until two years later, cf. below, n. 74 on 2:1–12.

[1]Following Jerome, many Latin interpreters refer the title to the whole Gospel. But, e.g., Calvin I 63, Jansen the younger 1 ("catalogus genealogiae" [= catalog of the genealogy]) and Grotius I 12 ("descriptio originis" [= description of the origin]) refer it only to the genealogy.

[2]In book titles Tob. 1:1, cf. Nah. 1:1; Bar. 1:1, 3; Sir. Prol. 31; Hebr 1QS 1.1; 1QM 1.1.

[3]Cf. Eissfeldt; in addition Deut. 24:1,3 (bill of divorce); 2 Sam. 11:14f.; 1 Kings 20:8f.; 2 Kings 5:5–7; and often (letter); 2 Εσδρ. 17:5 (= Neh. 7:5)(family register); Jer. 39:10–16, 44 (bill of sale).

[4]Zahn 40 with many successors. But γένεσις cannot mean "history": of the two references for it, Gen. 6:9 does not become understandable without the "genealogy" of v.10; in Gen. 37:2 the story of Joseph(!) and his brothers significantly is introduced as the γένεσις Ἰακωβ(!)

referring to the entire Gospel, nor in the narrow sense as "birth," for birth is the theme neither in the genealogy nor in the appendix to it, vv. 18–25. The "register of origin"[5] comprises most likely the genealogy with appendix, i.e., Matthew 1. The evangelist, at home in the Greek Bible, wants to provide with this title a loose association to the Old Testament, in which one must not seek a deeper theological meaning.[6]

"Jesus Christ" is probably, as in 1:18; Mark 1:1; and frequently in Greek-speaking Christianity, a double name. When the evangelist uses Χριστός as a title, he generally uses the article. The two attributes "son of David" and "son of Abraham" correspond to the content statements of the two texts 1:18–25 and 1:2–17 which are here joined in titular fashion. "Son of David" means the Messiah of Israel from royal blood. Υἱὸς ’Αβραάμ is more striking because, of course, each Jew is a son of Abraham, and the expression does not appear to make a special statement about Jesus. The meaning of the expression is explained by the genealogy.

1.2. The Genealogy (1:2-17)

Literature

Bloch, R., "Juda engendra Pharès et Zara, de Thamar," in *Mélanges Bibliques* (FS A. Robert), pp. 381–89 (Paris: Bloud et Gay, 1966).

Frankemölle, H., *Jahwebund* 311-18.

Hood, R. T., "The Genealogies of Jesus," in *Early Christian Origins* (FS R. Willoughby), pp. 1–15 (Chicago: Quadrangle Books, 1961).

Jeremias, J., *Jerusalem in the Time of Jesus*, pp. 308–31 (Philadelphia: Fortress, 1969).

Johnson, Marshall D., *The Purpose of the Biblical Genealogies*, SNTSMS 8 (Cambridge: At the University Press, 1988²).

Kaplan, C., "The Generation Schemes in Matthew 1,1-17. Luke 3,24ff," *BSac* 87 (1930) 465-71.

Lambertz, M., "Die Toledoth in Mt 1,1-17 und Lc 3,23bff," in *FS F. Dornseiff*, ed. H. Kusch, pp. 201-25 (Leipzig: Bibliographisches Institut, 1953).

Metzger, B. M., "The Text of Matthew 1,16," in *Studies in New Testament and Early Christian Literature* (FS A. Wikgren), ed. D. Aune, pp. 16–24 (Leiden: Brill, 1972).

Nineham, D., "The Genealogy in St. Matthew's Gospel and Its Significance for the Study of the Gospel," *BJRL* 58 (1975/76) 421-44.

Pascual, E., "La Genealogia de Jesús según S. Mateo," *EstBib* 23 (1964) 109-49.

Ramlot, L., "Les généalogies bibliques," *BVC* no. 60 (1964), 53-70.

Schnider, F. and Stenger, W., "Die Frauen im Stammbaum Jesu nach Mattäus," *BZ* NF 23 (1979) 187-96.

Schöllig, H., "Die Zählung der Generationen im matthäischen Stammbaum," *ZNW* 59 (1968) 262-68.

---

[5]Βίβλος γενέσεως ’Ιησοῦ Χριστοῦ in this respect does not correspond to the linguistic usage of the LXX (e.g., γενέσεις τῶν υἱῶν Νῶε, Gen. 10:1), since the γένεσις reported is not that of the begetter but of the one who is begotten. This corresponds to common Greek usage. The Hebrew word תּוֹלְדוֹת (cf. יָלַד) is used differently so that the literal translation by γένεσις in LXX becomes un-Greek and was even avoided in the most important place, Num. 1:20–42.

[6]The reference to Gen. 5:1 is not carried out further; the genealogy begins with Abraham. The thesis of Frankemölle that Matthew consciously draws a parallel to the beginning of the work of history of the Chronicler is tempting, but βίβλος γενέσεως just does not point to Chronicles.

Speyer, W., art. "Genealogie," *RAC* 9 (1976), 1145-1268.

Stegemann, H., "Die des Uria," in *Tradition und Glaube* (FS K. G. Kuhn), ed. G. Jeremias et al., pp. 246–76 (Göttingen: Vandenhoeck & Ruprecht, 1971).

Vögtle, A., " 'Josias zeugte den Jechonias und seine Brüder' (Mt 1,11)," in *Lex tua Veritas* (FS H. Junker), ed. H. Gross et al., pp. 307–13 (Trier: Paulinus, 1961).

Vogt, P., *Der Stammbaum bei den heiligen Evangelisten Matthäus und Lukas*, BibS(F) 13/3 (Freiburg, 1907).

Waetjen, H., "The Genealogy as the Key to the Gospel according to Matthew," *JBL* 95 (1976) 205-30.

Zakowitch, Y., "Rahab als Mutter des Boas in der Jesus-Genealogie (Matt. 1,5)," *NovT* 17 (1975) 1-5.

Further literature ** at Matthew 1-2 above pp. 101-102.

Text

2 Abraham brought forth Isaac,
   Isaac brought forth Jacob,
   Jacob brought forth Judah and his brothers,
3 Judah brought forth Perez and Zerah[1] by Tamar,
   Perez brought forth Hezron,[2]
   Hezron brought forth Ram,[3]
4 Aram brought forth Amminadab,
   Amminadab brought forth Nahshon,[4]
   Nahshon brought forth Salmon,
5 Salmon brought forth Boaz by Rahab,[5]
   Boaz brought forth Obed[6] by Ruth,
   Obed brought forth Jesse,[7]
6 Jesse brought forth David the king.
   David brought forth Solomon[8] by the (wife) of Uriah,
7 Solomon brought forth Rehoboam,[9]
   Rehoboam brought forth Abijah,
   Abijah brought forth Asaph,[10]
8 Asaph brought forth Jehoshaphat,
   Jehoshaphat brought forth Joram,

---

[1] Φάρες, as LXX; Ζάρα, as LXX.

[2] Ἐσρώμ: LXX A 2 Chr. 2:5; Ruth 4:18; this form of the name is used only in LXX A. Otherwise in LXX: Ἐσρών, Ἀσρών.

[3] Ἀράμ: = LXX 1 Chr. 2:9f., also in LXX Ἀρράν, Ῥάμ.

[4] Ναασσών = LXX.

[5] Βόες: LXX usually Βόος; Hebr. בֹּעַז. Ῥαχάβ: Hebr. רָחָב; Josh. et al. Ῥα(χ)άβη; LXX Ῥαάβ.

[6] Ἰωβήδ: as LXX A 1 Chr. 2:12, otherwise LXX Ὠβήδ. Luke 3:32 has Ἰωβήδ.

[7] Ἰεσσαί: as LXX, Hebr. יִשַׁי.

[8] Σολομών; thus occasionally in LXX, primarily A, next to the majority reading, Σαλωμών.

[9] Ῥοβοάμ: as LXX.

[10] Confusion of king Asa with the psalmsinger Asaph.

      Joram brought forth Uzziah,[11]
 9 Uzziah brought forth Jotham,[12]
   Jotham brought forth Ahaz,
   Ahaz brought forth Hezekiah,[13]
10 Hezekiah brought forth Manasseh,
   Manasseh brought forth Amos,[14]
   Amos brought forth Josiah,
11 Josiah brought forth Jechoniah[15] and his brothers at the time of the
   deportation to Babylon.
12 After the deportation to Babylon Jechoniah brought forth Shealtiel,[16]
   Shealtiel brought forth Zerubbabel,[17]
13 Zerubbabel brought forth Abiud,[18]
   Abiud brought forth Eliakim,
   Eliakim brought forth Azor,
14 Azor brought forth Zadok,
   Zadok brought forth Achim.
   Achim brought forth Eliud,
15 Eliud brought forth Eleazar,
   Eleazar brought forth Matthan,
   Matthan brought forth Jacob,
16 Jacob brought forth Joseph, the husband of Mary, of whom Jesus who is
   called Christ was begotten.[19]
17 Thus all generations from Abraham to David are fourteen generations;
   from David to the deportation to Babylon fourteen generations; and from
   the deportation to Babylon to Christ fourteen generations.

---

[11] 'Οζίας: LXX as supplementary form next to 'Οχοζίας, e.g., 1 Chr. 3:11 LXX A B for Ahaziah. At the same time 'Οζίας is the rendering of Uzziah who, however, in most manuscripts appears by the name of Azariah. The kings between Ahaziah and Uzziah (Joash, Amaziah) are missing in the Matthean genealogy.

[12] 'Ιωαθάμ: LXX alongside of 'Ιωαθάν.

[13] 'Εζεκίας, as LXX.

[14] Confusion of king Amon with the prophet Amos.

[15] 'Ιεχονίας corresponds to Hebr. יְכָנְיָה, another form of יְהוֹיָכִין. But Jechoniah had no brothers. Was the author inspired by the (erroneous?) passages 2 Chr. 3:16; 36:20 in the Hebrew text? Jechoniah was the son of Jehoiakim (LXX: 'Ιωακ(ε)ίμ) and grandson of Josiah. Confusion between the two occurs variously in LXX, mostly so that 'Ιωακείμ takes the place of 'Ιεχονίας (e.g., 2 Kings 24:6-15, four times; Jer. 52:31, twice), vice versa only Jer. 22:24 A.

[16] Σαλαθιήλ, as LXX.

[17] Ζοροβαβέλ, as LXX. The author followed here 1 Chr. 3:19 LXX, Hag. 1:1 and often, Ezra 3:2 and often, but not 1 Chr. 3:19 Hebrew text, where Zerubbabel is the son of Pedaiah.

[18] In 1 Chr. 3:19, Abiud is not mentioned among the sons of Zerubbabel. From here on the genealogy no longer follows the LXX.

[19] Γεννάω may mean both "beget" (so in 1:20) and "bear" (so in 2:1). When here, despite the passive voice and the preposition ἐκ, preference is given to the meaning "beget," it is done for the sake of the consistency of the genealogy, cf. vv. 3, 5, 6.

Analysis

1. *Structure.* The genealogy consists of a long series of monotonous, short main clauses. Its organization is decoded by v. 17: it consists of 3 × 14 generations. However, these cannot be found exactly like this in the text: If one follows v. 17 literally, then David must be counted twice, and the second series of 14 goes from him until Josiah.[20] If one counts Josiah also twice, then one gets a second series of 14 until Jesus. Verse 17, however, accentuates the exile as a break, which is clearly marked also in the genealogy. If one does not begin the third series until v. 12, then one has only 13 generations for it. The structure given in v. 17 is not patently clear. It can only be explained by literary criticism.

Additional comments are inserted into the monotonous genealogy. They mention women (3, 5ab, 6b, cf. 16), brothers (2c, 11), David as king (6a) and, twice, the exile (11f.). Most striking is the mention of Mary in v. 16, because here the sentence structure is broken; γεννάω suddenly is constructed in the passive voice. Besides, Jesus receives the addition of Χριστός. Here lies a crucial point.

2. *Redaction and tradition.* Many interpreters consider the evangelist Matthew to have been the author of this genealogy.[21] But more likely it was already at his disposal. The following reasons speak for this: (1) The names are not always in agreement with the Bible of the evangelist, the LXX.[22] (2) An omission of the three kings by Matthew in the middle part could not be convincingly substantiated in view of the remaining "errors" in the schema of 14. It is most likely that the three kings at some time were excluded by mistake, i.e., because of the similarity of two names.[23] Matthew then determined that the genealogy as he found it contained for all intents and purposes 3 × 14 members and stated this in v. 17. The concluding v. 17 and with this the schema of the 3 × 14 generations probably is due to the evangelist Matthew.[24] Are the various additions in the genealogy due to his hand? The mention of the brothers of Joseph and Jechoniah can just as little be explained by the Matthean interpretation as the mention of Zerah next to Perez.[25] The—one time—naming of the royal title with David and the emphatic mention of the Babylonian exile twice could be related to the Matthean schema of periods of v. 17.[26] At most, the naming of the four ancestral women Tamar, Rahab, Ruth, and Bathsheba could be due to Matthew, although this thesis can be substantiated only by reference to the *possibility* of a suggestive interpretation on the basis of his theology. In the much discussed verse 16, at most the addition ὁ λεγόμενος Χριστός

---

[20]So the proposal of Schöllig*. In any case, "Matthew's reputation as a mathematician" (Brown** 84) cannot be salvaged.

[21]Frankemölle, *Jahwebund*, esp. 314 (prototype: 1 Chronicles!); Johnson* 210 and passim (Matthew 1 a "Midrash" on Mark 1:1); Lambertz* 218 (haggadic composition); Vögtle, *Genealogie* 102 (unitary conception, artificial construction).

[22]Disagreement: above nn. 5, 8, 18; agreement only with LXX A: nn. 2, 6, 11.

[23]Cf. above, n. 11. A similar copying mistake probably happened in Ezra 7:2f.; cf. 1 Chr. 5:34-38 and n. 46. The Latin tradition of interpretation explains profoundly: The evangelist punishes the descendants of Joram [Ahaziah, Joash, Amaziah] until the third generation by *damnatio memoriae* (condemnation of memory) because Jehoram married the daughter of the godless Jezebel (e.g., Jerome in commenting on this passage; *Opus Imperfectum* 1 = 623f.).

[24]Matthean language is: Οὖν; πᾶς οὖν; ἀπό . . . ἕως; cf. introduction 3.2.

[25]Lagrange 3 points correctly to the custom of mentioning both together.

[26]There are no linguistic indications: ἐπί in the meaning of "at the time" is non-Matthean, μετοικεσία is a usual word in the LXX.

can be demonstrated as Matthean.[27] The passive ἐγεννήθη remains uncertain; it is due to the belief in the virgin birth.[28] Whether at any time in an early stage of the history of the tradition the genealogy had counted on a physical paternity of Joseph is also uncertain.[29]

3. *Historicity.* Most likely the genealogy comes from Greek-speaking Jewish Christianity, influenced by the LXX, although it was not used directly in the writing.[30] One may not on principle be skeptical about the historicity of such genealogies in view of the fine genealogical traditions of the Jewish priests[31] and in view of the fact that descent from the Davidic family was claimed on occasion.[32] There is too much evidence against the historicity of our genealogy for it to be taken seriously into consideration: the broad disagreement with the Lukan genealogy (Luke 3:23-38), which has been the object of much contemplation since the earliest of times, especially the fact that the name of the grandfather of Jesus does not seem to be solidly established, as well as the much too small number of the generations for the time between the exile and Joseph.

The genealogy belongs to the type of the so-called "linear" genealogies (without branches)[33] which in the ancient period very often served the function of legitimation.[34] Its *original function* in the community before Matthew may have been this: Jesus has descended from the father Abraham by way of the royal dynasty of Israel. He is not only a true Jew but even a Davidite. What significance does the genealogy gain in its Matthean interpretation as an introit to the Gospel?

There are different accents which the evangelist puts on the traditional genealogy. Two of them are illuminated by the title (1:1): Jesus is son of David and son of Abraham. The significance of his *descent from David* is easier to understand. The genealogy interprets it through the royal line. Jesus is put into

---

[27]Χριστός is a favorite title in Matthew (16 times, only 6 times from the tradition). On λεγόμενος cf. 17:17,22 and the introduction 3.2.

[28] Ἐκ corresponds to vv. 3,5,6, the introduction of Joseph as the husband of Mary to v. 19.

[29]The text translated above, supported by most witnesses, is probably the oldest text. The different, mostly Western variants which supplant "husband of Mary" by a statement that Joseph was betrothed to the virgin Mary (Θ; several Old Latin manuscripts; sy^{cur}, arm), attempt a balancing with 1:18-25 and Luke 2:5 and stress the virgin birth. The—unique—text of sy^{sin} ("Joseph to whom was betrothed the virgin [!] Mary begat Jesus") remains noteworthy. In v. 21 sy^{sin} reads: "she will bear *you* a son"; in v. 25 it substitutes for the whole first half of the verse the statement: "she bore him a son." Not only v. 16 ("virgin") but also the entire text vv. 18-25 shows that sy^{sin} knows of the virgin birth and affirms it. Does it want to emphasize the legal paternity of Joseph? Or does it offer a formal improvement of the Western text? Only the fact is clear that sy^{sin} in no case represents the original text of Matt. 1:16. Cf. on the textual critical problem Metzger* and Globe** 64-66.

[30]Whether the genealogy can be traced back beyond Jewish Christianity to Jewish circles ("a popular genealogy of the royal lineage . . . as part of . . . speculations about the coming of the Messiah," Brown 88) and then was brought into connection with the name of Joseph in Christian congregations has to remain open.

[31]Jeremias* 308-24; Johnson* 99-108. Both authors are skeptical about the reliability of nonpriestly genealogies; but on the basis of Josephus, *Ap* 1,31-35; *Vit* 3-6; *m.Qid.* 4:5f. it is probable that at least in upper classes and pious circles people knew about their genealogy.

[32]Persecutions of Davidites by Vespasian, Domitian, Trajan: Eusebius *Hist. Eccl.* 3,12,19; 20,1-6; 32,3f. In Judaism perhaps the family of the messianic pretender Menahem has claimed Davidic descent (Jeremias* 310); it was also ascribed to Hillel (Jeremias* 318) and Hiyya the Elder (*b. Ketub.* 62b).

[33]Only in the case of Judah and of Jechoniah are the brothers mentioned. Is this supposed to underline the beginning and the end of the history of Israel as a people? Cf. Schnider-Stenger* 192.

[34]On the different functions of genealogies cf. Hood* 1-9; for the OT: Johnson* 77-82; Ramlet* 59- 63; for antiquity: Speyer* passim.

the continuity of the history of Israel as the Messiah of Israel. He is highlighted as king of Israel. Just for this reason v. 6 sets David apart as king. Jesus becomes then in 2:1-12 the counterpoint of King Herod. In 21:5 he will enter Jerusalem as the other, "meek" king. Matthew in this way provides a prelude for this important theme of his Gospel: Jesus is the Messiah of Israel.

The interpretation of his *descent from Abraham* is much more difficult. The genealogy would be easier to understand if it commenced with David. Does Jesus' descent from Abraham say more than the obvious truth that Jesus is a Jew? Perhaps there is a hint at the interpretation in the *four ancestral mothers* of vv. 3, 5, 6. Their selection is noteworthy. The great Jewish female personalities are missing: Sarah, Rebekah, Rachel. What is the common denominator of just these four women?

There are essentially three contrasting suggestions for interpretation:

1. A *divine "irregularity"* is a common denominator among the four women.[35] God's salvific action sometimes chooses unexpected ways. On the basis of this interpretation a relation could be drawn to the virgin Mary, with whom the irregularity had its peak. This interpretation cannot be refuted as long as it stops at the general thought of God's providential acting. But it would make it more difficult to determine the "irregularity" more precisely. It may lie (a) in the special relationship of the women to their partners. But are the marriage of Ruth, the adultery of Bathsheba, and the betrothal of Mary really comparable? Other interpreters want to understand all these women as instruments of the Holy Spirit. But part of the Jewish evidence is late, part not extant.[36]

2. Are the women placed in the genealogy as *sinners* in order that the grace of God may become visible with them?[37] This thought is attractive in the case of Bathsheba, to whose adultery the formulation "the one of Uriah" would point. But it is impossible with Ruth, on whom there is no blemish according to the OT and Jewish tradition. Even for Rahab this interpretation would be difficult according to Jewish testimonies; she is celebrated as a prototype of a proselyte and as a tool of the divine Spirit.[38] Tamar also is

---

[35]Stendahl** 101. Similarly, e.g., Brown** 73f.; Paul** 5; a little differently Räisänen** 59f. (the extension of the royal genealogy to Abraham and the mention of the women underscores the thought of election); Schweizer 8f. (the "strange justice of God . . . which does not choose that which is great before humans"). But against this speaks the positive evaluation of these women in Jewish tradition; cf. below nn. 38-40.

[36]Cf. Brown** 73f. There is evidence for *Tamar*: *GenR* 85,9 on Gen. 38:15 (R. Huna, c. 350; Str-B I 17); *b. Mak.* 23b (R. Eleazar, c. 270; Str-B ibid.); *GenR* 85,12 on Gen. 38:26 (R. Samuel b. Isaac, c. 300): "It was the Holy Spirit who proclaimed: These things came about through me." *Rahab: Midr. Ruth* 2,1 (126a) = Str-B I 21. These occurrences refer to special episodes, e.g., the voice which intervenes in the trial of Tamar or the "prophecy" of Rahab (Josh. 2:16). I do not know any evidence for Ruth or Bathsheba.

[37]Examples: Jerome on 1:3 ("ut . . . de peccatoribus nascens [sc. Christus] omnium peccata deleret" [that Christ, being descended from sinners, might destroy the sins of all]); John Chrysostom 3,2 = 47 (one must not hide the wickedness of the ancestors, seek one's own virtue, and not boast of others' merits). Often the idea is suggested that the sinful women are Gentiles, but according to most interpreters this applies only to Tamar, Rahab, and Ruth. Modern advocates of this type of interpretation are listed in Johnson* 77-82.

[38]Rabbinical evidence in Str-B I 20-23, also Heb. 11:31; 1 Clem. 12:1 (faith of Rahab); James 2:25 (works of Rahab). Rahab nowhere, not even in Jewish tradition, is included in the Davidic genealogy; rather she is considered as the spouse of Joshua and mother of prophets. Occasionally she is combined with Ruth, cf. *Pesiq. R.* 9,167b = Str-B I 21 and the occurrences in Zakowitch*.

exonerated and becomes in Philo even a symbol of virtue.[39] With Bathsheba the Jewish texts are more interested in the sin of David than in the sin of Bathsheba.[40] This interpretation must be discarded.

    3. A third suggestion is: All four women are *non-Jews*.[41] Tamar is considered an Aramaean,[42] Ruth is a Moabitess, Rahab an inhabitant of Canaanite Jericho. We know nothing concerning Bathsheba; yet, precisely for this reason, she is not mentioned by name but introduced as wife of Uriah who, as is well known, was a Hittite (2 Sam. 11:3). However, with this view the connection to Mary is minimal.[43]

        Thus the genealogy contains a universalistic overtone: it is indicated in a hidden way that the son of David, the Messiah of Israel, brings salvation for the Gentiles. This provides a clue for the interpretation of "son of Abraham" in 1:1, which is seemingly so taken for granted and yet so striking: it reminds us of the broad Jewish tradition which sees Abraham as the father of the proselytes.[44] The shifting of the salvation of Israel to the Gentiles, a predominant theme in the Gospel of Matthew, is addressed in its opening text.

1:17

The third accent which has been imposed on the genealogy by Matthew finds expression in v. 17: The evangelist divides the genealogy into 3 × 14 generations. This division is for him probably an expression of the divine plan that encompasses the history of Israel, which leads to Jesus.

        It is not unusual that the *number of generations in genealogies* is a round figure or is carefully stated,[45] but the material yields no definite schema of interpretation. Only uncertain conjectures can be made on the significance of the number *14*: a rabbinical parallel suggests that Matthew might have been inspired by the half of a lunar month and perhaps brought the 14 generations from Abraham to David into correlation with the time of the waxing of the moon, the 14 from David to the exile with the time of its waning and

---

[39]*Deus Imm* 137; *Congr* 124-26; *Mut Nom* 136; *Fug* 149. In the rabbinical testimonies the divine guidance and the messianic perspective are strongly emphasized, cf. the evidence in Bloch*.

[40]Johnson* 170-75 and Str-B I 28f.

[41]Stegemann* 260-66; Zakowitch*; Schnider-Stenger* 195; Nolan** 62f; Schweizer 9. The ancient exegesis has accepted this interpretation often for some of the women, rarely for all of them (so Luther, *Lectures on Genesis*, LW 7:35-36).

[42]Jub. 41:1; T. Jud. 10:1 (Aramaean); Philo, *Virt* 221 (Syrian Palestinian); rabbinical passages: Str-B I 16 (Canaanite daughter of a priest, Semite).

[43]R. Seeberg, "Die Herkunft der Mutter Jesu" in *Theologische FS G. N. Bonwetsch* (Leipzig, 1918) 13-24, concluded from this interpretation that Mary was a Gentile. That had its effects in church history: Hirsch, *Frühgeschichte* II 324, saw his thesis of Gentile descent of the family of Jesus, which was postulated already for the grandfather of Jesus (on the basis of the forced Judaizing of the population of Galilee, ibid. 193), "supplemented on the side of the mother in the most radical way possible," similarly W. Grundmann, *Jesus der Galiläer und das Judentum* (Leipzig: Wigand, 1940), 196.

[44]Str-B III 211, cf. 195.

[45]The genealogies in Gen. 5:3-32 and in 11:10-26 comprise 10 generations. *M. Aboth* 5:2 names 10 generations from Adam to Noah or from Noah to Abraham. *Num. Rab.* 13,14 on 7:15: 10 generations from Perez to David, 15 generations from Rehoboam to Zedekiah. *Midr. Pss.* on 105:3: 26 generations from Adam to Moses. See similar passages in Str-B I 45.

the 14 until Jesus again with the waxing.[46] But this is very hypothetical. The apocalyptic parallels on the division of world history into 10 weeks (1 Enoch 93; 91), into 12 times (2 Baruch 53-74) or the rabbinic tradition concerning the great world week of 7×1000 years are only in a general way relevant for the understanding of our text.[47] These conceptions also presuppose the thought of a divine plan in history.

1:16

Matthew probably accepted for his own use v. 16 from the tradition. The passive ἐγεννήθη and the mention of Mary show that the virgin birth is presupposed. The idea of the adoption of Jesus by Joseph is missing; the genealogy leaves it open how the son of Mary is a Davidite. Here an additional explanation is necessary, which Matthew supplies with the following text.

History of Influence

1. The church interpretation[48] was occupied mainly with the *difficulties*, posed by the Matthean and the Lukan genealogy. Two problems were in the forefront: (a) Why or in what way is the genealogy of Jesus, the son of the virgin, also that of Joseph? (b) How is the difference between the two NT genealogies of Jesus to be explained?

a. Since Justin[49] the *Davidic descent* of Jesus was safeguarded by the assertion that Mary also was a Davidite. Generally, the virgin birth by Mary was taken for granted; therefore one had to find reasons why the genealogy of Joseph, not that of Mary, is presented in the Gospels.[50] It was not until the 15th century that Alphonsus Tostatus admitted that the genealogy perhaps at the time of Matthew asserted something about the Davidic descent of Jesus; "nunc autem non procedit probatio" (but now the proof is not successful).[51] The thought that the "genealogy of Joseph" would serve as proof of the Davidic descent of Jesus through the fact that Joseph in any case was the legal father of Jesus is foreign to the interpretation of the ancient church.

b. The *difference between the two genealogies* was explained in various ways in the exegesis of the ancient church. The proposal of Julius Africanus, as reported by Eusebius (*Hist. Eccl.* 1,7), gained acceptance. According to him, Matthew offers the "natural," Luke the "legal" genealogy of Jesus. The differences originated when in the case of childlessness a levirate marriage was contracted. Opposing this thesis, other attempts, e.g., the allusion of Augustine to adoption as another possible form of legal

---

[46]*Ex. Rab.* 15,26 = 8d (Str-B I 43f.), cf. Kaplan* 466f.: Israel will rule from Abraham to Zedekiah during 30 generations, 15 (to Solomon) correspond to the waxing, 15 to the waning moon. The decreasing series counts 16(!) generations (a counting error, as in Matthew!) and omits Jehoiachin. In view of the Jewish lunar calendar it is not unthinkable that similar associations are in the background of the Matthean genealogy.

[47]2 Enoch 33,1-2; *b. Sanh.* 97a; *b. Abod. Zar.* 9a, etc. (Texts in Str-B IV 990-92). A direct relationship between Matthew and these speculations cannot exist, (a) because Matthew does not count 6 periods of 7 but 3 periods of 14 and (b) because according to the Jewish texts the Messiah comes already after the end of the fourth world week (*pace* Pascual* 146-48).

[48]This section owes much to the assistance of W. D. Koehler.

[49]*Dial.* 43,1; 100,3.

[50]Eusebius, *Quaest. ad Steph.* 1 = *PG* 22, 880-92. The information that Mary and Joseph (according to Num. 36:6!) were tribally related (ibid. 1,9 = *PG* 22,892) is here popular.

[51]Vol. 18,151; similarly Calvin I 60f.

paternity,[52] have not prevailed. In the 16th century, the Protestant side advocated the view that—inversely to Julius Africanus—Luke offers the natural and Matthew the legal genealogy.[53] But, in looking at the whole, one cannot discover a significant confessional difference on this point.

2. The *modern historical criticism* of the genealogies has its predecessors in ancient anti-Christian polemic.[54]

Celsus already rejected the genealogies as fiction.[55] Carrying weight until today is the assertion of the apostate emperor Julian that not even the name of the grandfather of Jesus is known without question.[56] The criticism of the genealogies by Porphyry had a substantial effect.[57] From modern times comes the use of the genealogies as an argument against the virgin birth.[58] Although the argument is widespread, it nevertheless stands on uncertain ground: it cannot appeal to the evangelist Matthew or to the Sinaitic Syriac and only possibly to a pre-Matthean stage of tradition which can no longer be demonstrated by means of tradition history.

Summary

The history of interpretation illustrates the difficulties which the genealogies present—and not only for today. The abundance of names and the contrived character misled the interpreters to constructions and apologies which led away from the concern of the text. The difficulties which especially the nontheologian always had with the large number of unknown names are illustrated by Luther: ''Da sihet sichs an, quasi sit unnutz, vergeblich schrifft, quod recensuit nomina der lieben veter, cum nos de illis nihil omnino sciamus und uns nichts damit geholffen.''[59] (It looks as if this was a useless and futile writing, that he has recited the names of the dear fathers, because we know nothing at all about them, so that this profits us nothing.) The distance between the lively genealogical thinking of the Jews and the earliest Jewish Christians is impressively illustrated by a poem by Friedrich von Sallet in which one almost too readily finds oneself:

> He was a son, he was a son, he was a son—
> He begat him, he begat him, he begat him—

---

[52] Augustine later revised this opinion in favor of the view of Julius Africanus; cf. Vogt* 60-66.

[53] Luther I 8; Calvin I 61. On Calvin's view, Maldonat 26, ''. . .absurdam . . . sententiam absurdioribus probat argumentis'' (he proves an absurd thesis with more absurd arguments).

[54] Maldonat 21: ''Premebant olim hoc loco Christianos non tantum Iudaei, verum etiam Gentiles'' (Not only the Jews but even the Gentiles pressured the Christians on this point formerly). Eusebius, *Hist. Eccl.* 1.7.1: most people believe that the Gospels contradict each other in the genealogies.

[55] Origen, *Cels.* 2.32.

[56] Jerome on 1:16.

[57] Jerome, in Dan. 1:1 = PL 25,495.

[58] F. Schleiermacher, *The Christian Faith* (Edinburgh: T & T Clark, 1928), 2:403 (= § 97,2): ''. . . the genealogies of Christ, which . . . go back to Joseph in a simple and straightforward way.''

[59] First Sermon on the Gospel of Matthew, December 18, 1533, WA 37,211.

Thus it continues in lazy monotone,
Until dead names turn around in my brain.

Genealogies, plumply inserted
By the limited sense of morons, if not by a base hand,
For squires, for the gain of vain women,
That they do not believe beneath their station—

I tear you out. What is this dry leaf doing
In the Holy Book full of fresh splendor of palms?
What is it whether John begat Joe,
Down to him who made the world free?[60]

It is not by accident that this text is rarely used for preaching nowadays. The history of interpretation demonstrates how it almost always led to difficulties, because the attempt was made to deal with its historical statements. In any case it confronts us with the necessity of distinguishing between its linguistic form and its theological concern. Jesus is the son of David, i.e., sent by God to Israel as its anointed one, and at the same time the son of Abraham, because God wants to address the whole world of the Gentiles through him. That is the message of this text. Today we must do without its linguistic expression, i.e., the genealogy, because research—in this case probably conclusively—has recognized it as contrived. Nevertheless we have to consider the seriousness with which the ecclesiastical interpretation of all ages has attempted to understand it as a piece of *history*. Here is found a fundamental statement of the Christian faith, namely, the knowledge of the fact that Jesus is a human, historical figure. For this reason, says Irenaeus, Matthew begins his Gospel with the human ancestry of Jesus, and for this reason, he continues, interpreting the human being as the symbol of the evangelist Matthew, in the whole course of the Gospel of Matthew "the meek and humble human being was preserved."[61]

1.3. Immanuel (1:18-25)

Literature

Bratcher, R. G., "A Study of Isaiah 7:14," *BT* 9 (1958) 97-126.
Broer, I., "Die Bedeutung der 'Jungfrauengeburt' im Matthäusevangelium," *BibLeb* 12 (1971) 248-60.
Brown, R., et al., eds., *Mary in the New Testament*, pp. 83–97 (Philadelphia: Fortress, 1978).
Campenhausen, H. v., "Die Jungfrauengeburt in der Theologie der alten Kirche," in idem, *Urchristliches und Altkirchliches*, pp. 63–161 (Tübingen: Mohr, 1979).
Ford, J. M., "Mary's Virginitas Post-Partum and Jewish Law," *Bib.* 54 (1973) 269-72.
Frankemölle, *Jahwebund* 12-21.
Germano, I., "Nova et Vetera in pericopa de sancto Ioseph (Mt 1,18-25)," *VD* 46 (1968) 351-60.

---

[60]Quoted according to G. Pfannmüller, *Jesus im Urteil der Jahrhunderte* (Leipzig 1908), 478.

[61]Irenaeus, *Haer.* 3.11.8 = *BKV* I/3 243f., in the context of his interpretation of the symbols of the evangelists.

————, "Et non cognoscebat eam donec . . .," *Mar.* 35 (1973) 184-240.

Krämer, M., "Die Menschwerdung Jesu Christi nach Matthäus (Mt 1)," *Bib* 45 (1964) 1-50..

Lachs, T., "Studies in the Semitic Background to the Gospel of Matthew," *NovT* 17 (1977) 195-217.

Léon-Dufour, X., "L'annonce à Joseph," in idem, *Études d'Évangile*, pp. 69-86 (Paris: Éditions du Seuil, 1965).

Pesch, R., "Eine alttestamentliche Ausführungsformel im Matthäus-Evangelium," *BZ* NF 10 (1966) 220-45; NF 11 (1967) 79-95.

Raatschen, J. R., "Empfangen durch den Heiligen Geist. Überlegungen zu Mt 1,18-25," *Theologische Beiträge* 11 (1980) 262-77.

Sicari, A., " 'Ioseph iustus' (Matteo 1,19): La storia dell'interpretazione e le nuove prospettive," *Cahiers de Joséphologie* 19 (1971) 62-83.

Sottocornola, F., "Tradition and the Doubt of St. Joseph concerning Mary's Virginity," *Marianum* 19 (1957) 127-41.

Spicq, C., " 'Joseph, son mari, étant juste . . .' (Mt 1,19)," *RB* 71 (1964) 206-14.

Suhl, "Der Davidssohn im Matthäus-Evangelium," *ZNW* 59 (1968) 62-68.

Tosato, A., "Joseph Being a Just Man (Mt 1,19)," *CBQ* 41 (1979) 547-51.

Trilling, W., *Die Christusverkündigung in den synoptischen Evangelien*, pp. 13-39 (Munich: Kösel, 1969).

Vögtle, A., "Mt 1,25 und die virginitas B. M. Virginis post partum," *TQ* 147 (1967) 28-39.

Wright, A., "The Literary Genre Midrash," *CBQ* 28 (1966) 105-38, 417-57.

Zeller, D., "Die Ankündigung der Geburt—Wandlungen einer Gattung," in R. Pesch, ed., *Theologie*** 27-48.

Further literature** at Matthew 1-2 above pp. 101-102.

Text

18 The origin of Jesus Christ[1] happened as follows: When his mother Mary was betrothed to Joseph, before they came together, it was found that she was pregnant by the Holy Spirit.

19 But her husband Joseph, who was just and did not want to cause a commotion about her, decided to dismiss her silently.

20 But after he had deliberated about this, behold, an angel of the Lord appeared to him in a dream and said, "Joseph, son of David! Have no fear to take your wife Mariam[2] to yourself. That which is begotten in her is of the Holy Spirit.

21 But she will bear a son, and you are to give him the name Jesus, for he will save his people from their sins."

22 But all this happened in order that the saying of the Lord by the prophet might be fulfilled,

23 "Behold, the virgin will be pregnant and bear a son, and he will be given the name 'Immanuel,' " which is translated, "God is with us."

24 When Joseph rose from sleep, he did what the angel of the Lord had commanded him and took his wife to himself.

---

[1] With the majority of witnesses, Ἰησοῦ Χριστοῦ is to be read (as in 1:1). The article with Ἰησοῦς Χριστός is extremely rare (BDF §260. 1, *lectio difficilior!*).

[2] Matthew more frequently than Mark and Luke has the Semitizing form of the name Μαριάμ (13:55; 27:61; 28:1). Proximity of Semitic sphere of language.

25 And he did not know her until she bore a son, and he gave him the name Jesus.[3]

Analysis

1. *Structure and Form*. This story is unique because it speaks as prosaically and soberly as possible. The stylistic difference from the beautiful Lukan legend 2:1-20 is striking. After the title sentence in v. 18a, which connects this pericope with 1:1, v. 18b speaks of the presupposition of the wondrous pregnancy of Mary. The participial style indicates that Matthew is not yet telling a story but mentioning only presuppositions. Verse 19 in the nominative case introduces the chief person of the story, Joseph the just one. Now the story takes over. In v. 20, the angel appears as a decisive person (ἰδού!), announces the birth of Jesus, and interprets his name. The angel's rather long announcement, after the brevity used thus far, leads smoothly into the formula quotation. This is noteworthy because it speaks a second time of pregnancy, the birth of the son and his name—but a different name. In v. 24, not only Joseph but also the narrator Matthew seem to revive: he brings his story to a conclusion with a few stereotypical brief sentences: the obedience of Joseph is described in narrating how he—with almost the same words—experiences and does exactly what the angel has commanded him (vv. 20f.//24f.).

The story is not a description of the birth, although it deals with the virgin birth, nor is it a legend.[4] With how minimal tension the story is narrated is visible in the fact that the real point, the word of the angel, is already anticipated in v. 18. The story concentrates completely on the person of Joseph, as in 2:13-23, but still differently from 2:1-12. Three times it is pointed out by the phrases τίκτω—υἱόν and καλέω—ὄνομα that the birth announcement of Jesus and the naming and interpretation of the name is the central theme. The angel's word and the scripture citation lead to a heavy amount of christological instruction. Our text thus, on the basis of material which is only hinted at and which is presupposed as familiar in the community, sets certain doctrinal accents. In this respect, all interpreters who designate our text as a "christological midrash"[5] are seeing something correctly. But our narrative is not a midrash in the sense of the genre "midrash."[6]

2. *Redaction*. In present research there is an increasing tendency to consider the whole pericope as redactional; Matthew thus would have used only traditional motifs.[7] The counterthesis is that Matthew has more or less thoroughly redacted a traditional narrative. The decision is not easy.

2.1 The vocabulary points to continuous but not complete Matthean editing of

---

[3]On textual criticism, cf. above at Matt. 1:2-17, n. 29.

[4]Bultmann, *Tradition* 291.

[5]Pesch, *BZ* 11 (1967)*, 87, cf. Trilling* 27: "didactic text like a midrash."

[6]מִדְרָשׁ, in the Jewish sense, designates not only a certain literary genre but especially the activity of studying the scriptures. On this basis, Munoz-Iglesias** 338-44, following R. le Déaut, "A propos d'une définition du midrash," *Bib* 50 (1969) 395-413, understands midrash not only as a term that designates a genre but also as a designation of a hermeneutical method. If one understands midrash as genre, then it is constitutive that it proceeds from a scripture passage on the basis of which an interpretation or a narrative is unfolded. According to Wright* 137, midrash in this sense is "a literature about a literature." Seen in such a way, the stories in Matt. 1:18–2:23 are not midrashim, because the formula quotations are not in the center and are not that which is to be explained but that which explains. Cf. Wright* 455; similarly Peretto*, esp. 245; Brown** 557-63.

[7]E.g., Dibelius, *From Tradition to Gospel* (New York: Scribners, 1965), 128; Pesch, *BZ NF* 11 (1967)* 88; Vögtle, "Kindheitsgeschichte"** 155f.; Broer* 255; Frankemölle, *Jahwebund* 310.

the pericope.[8] As in Matthew 2, so here also the number of clear Mattheanisms is larger than the average in the Gospel.

2.2 Verse 18a contains a reference to 1:1 and follows 1:16 in content; therefore it is most likely redactional.

2.3 The formula quotation from Isa. 7:14, a verse which is not quoted elsewhere in the NT,[9] in distinction from most other formula quotations in Matthew, corresponds almost literally to the LXX. Καλέσουσιν (instead of καλέσεις) could be occasioned by the context: "Someone," i.e., the community, will call Jesus *Immanuel*. Thus, we have to conclude that not only the introductory phrase v. 22 but also the quotation itself could be due to Matthew who generally quotes the OT according to the LXX text if he is not following sources.

2.4 Pesch[10] points to the close parallels between our text and 21:1-7. Both texts are determined by the so-called "formula of fulfillment,"[11] a Matthean expression which describes, in language influenced by the Old Testament, the precise carrying out of a divine command (vv. 24f.; cf. 21:6f. and 26:19; 28:15).

2.5 The formula quotation, vv. 22f., can easily be removed from its context. There still remain numerous contacts between the quotation and the text of the remaining pericope (ἐν γαστρὶ ἔχειν, vv. 18, 23; τέξεται υἱόν, vv. 21, 23, cf. 25; καλεῖν τὸ ὄνομα, vv. 21,23,25).

2.6 The linguistic and material contacts with the "dream narratives" of Matt. 2:13-15,19-23 are substantial.

2.7 The form of the text of vv. 20f. follows a text schema of "birth announcement," already shaped in the Old Testament.[12] Luke also is familiar with it.[13] But the similarities show only that the present form of the text is influenced by the LXX and do not permit a cogent conclusion about the author.

---

[8]The following are Matthean features (cf. introduction 3.2): in v. 18: γένεσις (referring back to v. 1), οὕτως + εἶναι; v.19: δίκαιος, θέλω, λάθρα (2:7!); v. 20: ἐνθυμέομαι, ἰδού, ἄγγελος κυρίου, φαίνω, κατ' ὄναρ, λέγων, υἱός Δαυίδ placed after the name as apposition, cf. also 15:22; 20:30f.; φοβέω, παραλαμβάνω, γεννάω (1:2-16; 2:1,4!). On the introduction to the formula quotation cf. excursus at 2:23; v. 24: ἐγείρω (in connection with παραλαμβάνω cf. 2:13,14,20,21); on the formula of fulfillment cf. 21:6 and below no. 2.4; v. 25: ἕως οὗ. In addition, there are the similarities to the (redactional?) quotation, cf. below 2.5. The incorrect genitive absolute v. 18 (the subject Mary is introduced as genitive absolute!) also is Matthean. Hapax legomena are συνέρχομαι, δειγματίζω, μεθερμηνεύω. Non-Matthean are βούλομαι and the Semitizing passive εὑρέθη (cf. אצמנ). The vocabulary of v. 21 comes almost completely from the LXX, cf. below no. 2.7.

[9]Luke 1:31 is not a quotation of Isa. 7:14 but is influenced by the Old Testament "birth announcement" (cf. below at no. 2.7).

[10]Pesch, *BZ* NF 11 (1967) 79f.

[11]ποιέω + (ὡς or something similar) + προσέταξεν or something similar. Pesch, *BZ* NF (1966) 225, cites about 30 OT passages.

[12]The most important OT texts are: announcement to Hagar (Gen. 16:7-12), to Abraham (Gen. 17:19), to Samson's mother (Judg. 13:3-5), to Ahaz (Isa. 7:14). The following are elements of the "birth announcement": appearance of an angel, message, naming (with prediction or explanation). Literal agreements: ἄγγελος κυρίου Gen. 16:7f.,11; Judg. 13:3; ἰδού Gen. 16:11; Judg. 13:3,5; Isa. 7:14; ἐν γαστρὶ ἔχειν Gen. 16:11; Judg. 13:5; Isa. 7:14; καλεῖν τὸ ὄνομα αὐτοῦ Gen. 16:11; 17:19; Isa. 7:14, cf. Judg. 13:6; τίκτειν υἱόν Gen. 16:11; 17:19; Judg. 13:5; Isa. 7:14. All similarities between the quotation Isa. 7:14 and the remaining verses of the pericope (cf. above no. 2.5) are also similarities with the type "birth announcement." Bibliography: S. Muñoz-Iglesias, "El Evangelio de la Infancia en San Lucas y las infancias de los héroes biblical," *EstBib* 16 [1957] 329-82; Léon-Dufour* 76-78; Peretto** 183-86; Brown** 155-59; Zeller*.

[13]Luke 1:13,30f.

Result: Matthew has formulated the pericope largely afresh and perhaps put it in writing for the first time. From him comes the formula quotation, vv. 22f., and the connection to the genealogy in v. 18a. Particularly the double scope of the double naming (no. 2.5), but also the material similarities with Matthew 2 (no. 2.6) and the scattered non-Matthean formulations (no. 8) speak in favor of the thesis that not only individual motifs but a story of the naming of the child Jesus were already at hand. It is probable that the story belonged to a pre-Matthean cycle of oral narratives in which Joseph played a central role.

3. *Development of the tradition*. Secure statements hardly can be made. The interpretation of the name of Jesus, which suggests the formulation of Ps. 129:8, is not exact; יְהוֹשֻׁעַ means: "Yahweh is help."[14] Probably in a Greek-speaking milieu it was known that the name Jesus is indicative in some manner of God's help.[15] Related statements are found occasionally at the announcements of births of important figures in the history of Israel.[16] In the present text-form the virgin birth is not the main concern but a relatively unemphasized presupposition of the narrative. Therefore it is improbable that it was added at a later stage of tradition to an older narrative which originally told only of the announcement of the birth of the Messiah to his father Joseph.[17] In that case, the virgin birth would probably be more strongly highlighted. It is not likely that the narrative originally was formulated in Aramaic.[18]

4. The *motifs* point in various directions. The combination of sonship with God and the Spirit (v. 18!) is ancient Christian thinking (Rom. 1:4; Mark 1:9-11); the special element in our text, however, is the relation with the virgin birth. Birth without action of a human father is found frequently in Hellenistic and Egyptian reports which speak of the divine begetting of kings, heroes, philosophers, etc. It occurred in a Jewish environment in Philo as a mystery in his interpretation of the history of the wives of the patriarchs whom he allegorically interprets as the virtues (*Cher.* 40-52). The idea of a sexual begetting by God is as foreign to him as to any Jew.[19]

Statements concerning the birth of Moses are also in content close to our pericope: Amram, the exemplary just man,[20] according to Josephus is instructed by God in a dream about the future of Moses.[21] According to another tradition, he rejects his wife but, on the basis of a reproach by Miriam, is induced to receive her again;[22] it is said of Moses in this connection that he will save Israel.[23] These parallels are more important

---

[14]Str-B I 64.

[15]Cf. Philo (who hardly new Hebrew), *Mut. Nom.* 121: σωτηρία κυρίου.

[16]Judg. 13:5 ("birth announcement"): αὐτὸς ἄρξεται τοῦ σῶσαι τὸν 'Ισραήλ; in the Moses haggadah, Pseud-Philo, *Lib. Ant.* 9.10; MekhEx on 15:20, *b. Meg.* 14a, further texts in Bloch** 111f.

[17]Bultmann, *Tradition* 291.

[18]Krämer*; M. Herranz-Marco, "Substrato arameo en el relato de la Anunciación a José," *EstBib* 38 (1979/80) 35-55, 237-68. Assuming an Aramaic "original text," dogmatic difficulties which are posed especially by v. 20 and v. 25 are alleviated. At such attempts one must not ask for the intentions of the present Matthew, i.e., of the translator into Greek!

[19]Gen. 6:1-4 had a prohibitive effect. The only questionable statement, "God begets (יוֹלִיד) the Messiah" (1QSa 2:11), probably has to be explained on the basis of Ps. 2:7.

[20]Texts in Bloch** 112-14.

[21]Josephus, *Ant.* 2.210-16.

[22]The haggadic tradition concerned with Amram's divorce is found frequently: ExR 1:13 on Ex. 1:15; further passages in Bloch 114, n. 40.

[23]Cf. above, n. 16.

because Matthew 2 shows throughout a close relationship with the Moses haggadah. In this context nothing is said about a divine begetting or virginal birth of Moses.[24]

Result: Our narrative is nourished by various traditions: next to the Old Testament "birth announcement," the different variants of the Moses haggadah are the most important, although they can only partially be harmonized with our text; we cannot rely on a direct transfer of a birth legend of Moses to Jesus. The connection with the idea of the virgin birth (not found in Palestinian Judaism) rather points to a Hellenistic Jewish-Christian community as the milieu of tradition.

5. In view of the numerous parallels, the question of *historicity* is hopeless: for *this* narrative which follows so closely along traditional lines, no information is needed from the circle of the family of Jesus. The prospects also are not favorable for the historicity of the virgin birth, which is transmitted in the New Testament only by Matthew and Luke.[25] To be sure, it belongs to the numerous agreements of our pericope with the Lukan birth narratives.[26] However, it is very rarely indicated in the whole New Testament. Probably it is a part of the attempt of Jewish-Christian communities to witness to the faith in Jesus, who was appointed as son by God according to his Spirit (Rom. 1:4) in analogy to other ancient narratives in the form of an infancy narrative. The virgin birth then belongs to the means for witnessing to the faith and has no direct historical background.

Interpretation

1:18

The short title-sentence v. 18a connects this pericope with v. 1 and explains v. 16. To this extent the evangelist attaches our pericope as an "enlarged footnote to the crucial point in the genealogy"[27] of 1:2-17. But our pericope is not only a footnote! Verse 18b is the statement of the situation. The evangelist gives only the crucial information. The early reference to the testimony of the Spirit, which removes the tension, presupposes knowledge of the reader. *He or she* knows already what Joseph does not learn until v. 20. Joseph and Mary are betrothed,[28] i.e., from a legal point of view they are bound to each other. A betrothal can be

[24]For the connection of the motifs of the casting out of the wife with a virgin birth, the only evidence is the birth legend of Melchizedek, difficult to date, which N. Bonwetsch, *Die Bücher der Geheimnisse Henochs* (Leipzig 1922) prints as an appendix to 2 Enoch (ibid., 3:1-23). The legend was often considered as Christian; Schubert 230-34 recently defends its Jewish origin.

[25]Who would be ready to consider the report of the supernatural begetting of Plato by Apollo as historical although it appeals, among other things, to news from the family of Plato (Diogenes Laertius 3.2; Speusippos, nephew and successor of Plato, in the *Encomion,* a speech given in the year after Plato's death)? The source situation here is better than with Jesus.

[26](1) Joseph and Mary are betrothed, not married; (2) Joseph is Davidic (Luke 1:27); (3) the angelic announcement (Luke 1:30-35); (4) the virginity of Mary (Luke 1:34); (5) the begetting by the Spirit (Luke 1:35); (6) the command to name him (Luke 1:31); (7) Jesus as Savior (Luke 2:11); (8) Jesus as the Son of God (Luke 1:32,35); (9) the righteousness of the parents (Luke 1:6). These agreements are due to community tradition. Items 1 and 2 *possibly* could be evaluated historically.

[27]Stendahl** 102.

[28]The history of interpretation in general consistently distinguishes between the status of betrothal and the later marriage and states the reasons why Mary was betrothed: in order that she not be stoned by the Jews, in order that she have a comfort on the flight into Egypt. Luther I 17 equates the betrothal with the marriage: "It is a great honor for this estate that Christ did not want to be born outside of marriage. Otherwise, how many sects would have arisen!"

dissolved only by a bill of divorce. The betrothed woman lives in the house of her parents and does not yet have sexual intercourse with her bridegroom.[29] Συνελθεῖν most likely means the moving into the house of the bridegroom which takes place at the wedding.[30]

1:19

With v. 19, Joseph steps into the center of the events. The interpretation is very controverted. The main question is whether Joseph knew of Mary's pregnancy by the Spirit before the announcement of the angel. If he did not know, then it is most likely that he suspected his fiancée of adultery and therefore wanted to dismiss her.[31] But if he knew already about the special character of Mary's pregnancy, then one has to assume that he did not want to take her to himself from reluctance to touch Mary, who had been made sacred by God.[32] For the exegetical deliberations on this question, religious sensitivities often play a decisive part.[33] The frontlines—with noteworthy exceptions[34]—still coincide even today with the border between the Catholic and the Protestant interpretations, while the interpretation of the ancient church is divided.[35]

Verse 20 is the most important reason for the second, "Catholic," hypothesis: *"Do not be afraid* to take Mary to yourself . . .''*: Joseph was afraid to touch Mary, who belonged to God. Δειγματίζω is not an insurmountable obstacle. Indeed, the widespread meaning, "embarrass," "expose to contempt,"[36] fits the first interpretation better, but δειγματίζω could also mean "investigate"[37] or, neutrally, "make public."[38] The

---

[29]Str-B II 393-98. In view of the legal situation it is not surprising that Joseph is designated as ἀνήρ of Mary and she as γυνή (1:20f.). Str-B II 394: *t. Ketub.* 8,1 (270) gives a Jewish example where a betrothed woman is explicitly called "wife."

[30]For many predominantly Eastern church fathers, συνέρχεσθαι designates sexual intercourse, so that Mary is regarded as already living with Joseph (e.g., John Chrysostom 4.2 = 62; *Opus imperfectum* 1 = 631; Dionysiu bar Salibi 53, "For it was the custom among the betrothed to live with the men for three years and not have sexual intercourse during this time [*convenire*], in order to show in this manner that they came not to this union conquered by lust but in order to bring forth children. . .'').

[31]According to Deut. 22:23f., stoning was obligatory punishment for the adultery of betrothed persons. However, it was no longer practiced at that time, cf. Str-B I 51f.

[32]E.g., Léon-Dufour* 79-81.

[33]Krämer* 42 says of the so called "fear hypothesis" that "it is based more on religious feeling than on grammar." Maldonat 33: ". . . etsi loco non convenit, . . . tamen auctorum pietati maxime convenit" (even if it does not suit the passage, . . . nevertheless, it suits the piety of the authors very well).

[34]Among these are Schlatter 13; Suhl, *ZNW* 59 (1968) 64-67, et al., on the Protestant side; Broer* 251-53; Nolan, *Son* 73, et al., on the Catholic side.

[35]Detailed history of interpretation in Sottocornola*; Sicari* 63-71. Important representatives of the first type of interpretation are: Justin, *Dial.* 78,3; Augustine, *Ep ad Macedonium* (no. 153) 4,9 = *PL* 33,657; John Chrysostom 4,4 = 65; Luther I 19f. Important representatives of the second interpretation are: Eusebius, *Quaest. ad Steph.* 1.3 = *PG* 31, 1464D; Strabo 700. A further possibility: Joseph believed in the chastity of Mary but did not know the secret of her pregnancy and was waiting for a revelation: Jerome on 1:19; *Opus imperfectum* 1 = 633; Strabo on 1:19.

[36]BAGD, s.v., mentions it as the only one.

[37]Germano, *VD* 46[1968]* 353-55.

[38]X. Léon-Dufour, "L'annonce à Joseph," in *Mélanges Bibliques* (FS A. Robert) (Paris: Bloud et Gay, 1957), 397.

decisive difficulty for this thesis consists in the fact that it has the angel tell things to Joseph in v. 20 which he already knows—and especially in those parts of v. 20 which are not influenced by the Old Testament "birth announcement." Thus the first, "Protestant" hypothesis is more probable.[39] Joseph has a choice between the legally prescribed process in the case of adultery[40] and the writing of a bill of divorce. This also can indeed not be done "secretly," since two witnesses are required for the bill of divorce, it does, however, attract less attention. Besides, Matthew does not describe the scene with the interest of a realistic presentation. The question of whether the dismissed Mary would not be exposed to contempt at least when she gives birth to her child is of no concern to him, just as he does not worry about the question often asked by interpreters—whether the two betrothed people did not talk with each other.

The "righteousness" of Joseph thus consists in the fact that he does not expose Mary who is suspected of adultery to shame by the procedure which is indicated in the case of adultery. The alternative whether "righteousness" means the fulfillment of the Old Testament law[41] or simply kindness and leniency[42] is not faced by Matthew: Joseph interprets the law in the sense of the commandment of love and so aligns himself with the series of the righteous ones which extends from Abel (23:35) and the Old Testament righteous men (13:17) via Jesus (27:19,24) up to the doers of the commandments of Jesus who are affirmed in the final judgment (13:43; 25:46).

1:20

The appearance of the angel is not described; all the emphasis falls on the message. Joseph is addressed as son of David: as is already indicated in v. 18a, Matthew is concerned with explaining the engrafting of the son of the virgin into the descendancy of David. Παραλαμβάνειν means actually the wedding.[43] The reference to the Holy Spirit, already familiar from v. 18, is repeated. This refers to the creative intervention of God through the Spirit and not to the (Greek: neuter, Hebrew: female) Spirit as a sexual partner of Mary.[44]

---

[39]Léon-Dufour, ibid., 393f. interprets γὰρ . . . δέ as "indeed . . . but" and understands as follows: "(Take Mary to yourself), for indeed (as you know) that which is bogotten in her is from the Holy Spirit, but she will bear a son (to you)." But the adversative δέ comes too early, for the statement that 31would bear a son cannot overcome the religious reluctance of Joseph. Besides, γὰρ . . . δέ is understood quite differently in the neighboring passages 1:21f.; 2:2f., 13f., 20f.

[40]Deut. 22:23-27; 11QTemple 66.4f.; Philo, *Spec. Leg* 3,72-78; cf. on the legal situation Tosato*.

[41]So Brown* 84f. Since the law of Deut. 22:20f. demands a penalty at the adultery of the betrothed woman, the plan of Joseph cannot be considered as conforming to the law in the strict sense.

[42]Examples in Spicq* 207-14. In the history of interpretation, attempts at a broadening of the concept "righteousness" are numerous. Examples: Rabanus 749 (righteousness is related to pity); Paschasius Radbertus 108 (righteousness without *pietas* [piety, kindness] would be *crudelitas* [cruelty]); Wolzogen 45 applies the text parenetically and pleads for remission of punishment toward delinquent people.

[43]Examples for the same use of παραλαμβάνω in Josephus are offered by Schlatter 18.

[44]OT and Jewish examples for the creative activity of the Spirit are given by Paul** 81-88. The history of interpretation grasps this appropriately, cf. nn. 75f.

1:21

The naming, v. 21, is the goal of the traditional narrative. It is a widespread Jewish conception that the Messiah will be the savior of his people.[45] Matthew is especially interested in the forgiveness of sins occurring through Jesus and its further effectiveness in the community.[46] Λαός means, as throughout the Gospel of Matthew, the Old Testament people of God, Israel; the evangelist thus indicates, as through the genealogy and again in 2:2, that Jesus is the Messiah of Israel.

1:22

The introductory formula to the first Matthean formula quotation[47] does not completely correspond to the usual schema. The striking ὅλον[48] indicates that Matthew adduces the quotation not only for the sake of the name Immanuel but because the *entire* story of the birth announcement is important to him.[49] The Lord, as in 2:15, is the speaker of the biblical word, because both quotations speak of the son; the reader is prepared for the statement that the son of the virgin is the Son of God.[50] Thus our text is for Matthew not only an explanatory footnote to the genealogy; it indicates new christological themes to be unfolded further in the Gospel.

1:23

In the Isaiah quotation itself, the primary concern is the christological theme.[51] Jesus will be called Immanuel. Since Immanuel is not a name of Jesus and also not a usual title, the formulation has to attract attention. Immanuel is additionally emphasized by the translation. Allusions to God's being-with-us permeate the whole Gospel (17:17; 18:20; 26:29).[52] But Matthew has especially

---

[45]Jewish texts speak of the idea that the Messiah removes the sinners (Pss. Sol. 17:22-25), that he judges (1 Enoch 62:2; 69:27-29), but not of the idea that he forgives sins. The messianic age can be, but does not have to be, thought of as sinless (Str-B I 73f.).

[46]Cf. Matt. 9:8; 26:28.

[47]Cf. the excursus "Formula Quotations" at Matt. 2:23.

[48]Cf. only Matt. 26:56; 21:4, variant reading.

[49]The thesis of Strecker, *Weg* 56f., according to which the formula quotation is fulfilled "in the 'historical' fact of the miraculous birth of Jesus" (57) is thus relatively justified.

[50]Pesch, *Bib* 48 [1967]* 397. The connection of υἱός with κύριος is striking and on the one hand, is conditioned by the context (ἄγγελος κυρίου 1:20; 2:13); on the other hand, it is prefigured by the OT examples (ῥῆμα κυρίου in the fulfillment formulas of 1 Kings 2:27; 2 Chr. 36:22; cf. 2 Chr. 36:21; 2 Εσδρ 1:1).

[51]The striking position of the quotation in the middle of the pericope, before the birth of Jesus is mentioned, is also in favor of this view.

[52]Frankemölle, *Jahwebund* 7-83. He thinks primarily of influences of the Deuteronomist and the Chronicler's history. But the distribution of statements in the OT is broader, cf. H. D. Preuss, ". . . Ich will mit dir sein!" *ZAW* 80 (1968) 139-73; W. C. van Unnik, "Dominus vobiscum; the Background of a Liturgical Formula," in *New Testament Essays* (FS T. W. Manson), ed. A. J. B. Higgins (Manchester: Manchester University Press, 1959), 270-305. The fact that the interest of the evangelist already here

through the last verse of his Gospel ("I am with you always, to the close of the age," 28:20) created an inclusion which marks a basic theme: the presence of the exalted Lord with his community shows him as Immanuel, God with us.

It was already indicated by the use of ὅλον in v. 22 that the christological theme is indeed the most important but not the only motif in the quotation of Isa. 7:14. The prophetic word is fulfilled in the entire birth narrative. The virgin birth is also a part of the whole. Παρθένος is certainly to be understood as "virgin" from the context, although this is not necessary from the meaning of the word. The masoretic text reads עַלְמָה = young woman. Although the interpretation of Isa. 7:14 is still controversial, as always, Isaiah indubitably thought neither of a virgin birth nor of a Messiah to be born many centuries later. Thus the quotation is reinterpreted on the basis of the Septuagint text which, in distinction from Aquila and Thedotion (νεᾶνις!), reads παρθένος. The meaning of this unusual[53] LXX translation is unclear.

1:24–25

The concluding verses 24–25 describe the fulfillment of the heavenly command by Joseph. In v. 24 Matthew uses the "fulfillment formula," prefigured by the Old Testament, in order to present Joseph as an exemplary righteous person. It corresponds to an element which occurs often in Hellenism in connection with the birth of divine men that Joseph does not have sexual intercourse with Mary until the birth of Jesus.[54] The basic idea there is that intercourse with a woman who was considered worthy of sexual union with higher beings is not seemly. But in Matthew there is no hint at such thinking. Instead, Matthew is concerned with the idea of obedience:[55] The righteous Joseph fulfills the prediction of Isa. 7:14 also in the fact that Mary as a virgin will bear a son.

Summary

Matthew has added a new element to the traditional narrative of the naming of Jesus. It is most important for him that Jesus is Immanuel. With that he points from the beginning to the living reality of the community, "with" which Jesus will be always, to the close of the age (28:20). With this, a purely historical dimension of his story of Jesus is fractured from the beginning. Jesus is not a figure of the past, but the one who accompanies and bears his community. Our pericope and the final pericope, 28:16-20, stand in reciprocal relationship: If 28:16-20 is concerned with showing that the risen one is no other than the earthly one and that being a Christian means to keep the commandments of the *earthly* Jesus, then 1:18-25 make clear that the earthly one is no other than the

---

lies primarily on the "God with us" expression speaks, in my opinion, against making the idea of Jesus as the son of David the dominant motif of the whole prologue (against Tatum*).

[53]Hebr. עַלְמָה most of the time is translated νεᾶνις; παρθένος corresponds most of the time to בְּתוּלָה.

[54]Plutarch, *Quaest. Conv.* 8,1 = 717E (Dream of the father of Plato with the divine command not to touch his wife during the pregnancy), similarly Diogenes Laertius 3,2; Plutarch, *Alex.* 2,4f. = 665 (Alexander's father sees a snake next to the bed of Olympia); Hyginus, Fab. 29, ed. H. I. Rose (Leiden, 3rd ed. 1933) (Amphitryon no longer touches Alcmena). Cf. also Josephus, *Ant.* 20.18 (the father of Izates is prevented by a dream from intercourse with his wife).

[55]Vögtle, *TQ* 147 (1967)* 36.

exalted one who is "with" his community. At the same time, the Gospel of Matthew—and that is important in this Gospel of the law and the commandments—contains at the beginning a clear indication of the grace which occurs through Jesus Christ.

But this main goal of the Matthean narrative does not exclude subsidiary goals. It contains an ethical subsidiary goal: the figure of righteous Joseph and his obedience.[56] It is furthermore important as a narrative because in it an Old Testament prediction is fulfilled. To that extent, but only to that extent, the virgin birth also is important. It further explicates the "engrafting of Jesus into the tribe of David" which was left open in 1:16:[57] Jesus is a Davidite—to speak exaggeratedly—*despite* the virgin birth which is familiar to the community. All these are subsidiary elements which, while not in the center, were yet important to the evangelist. They show how multi-leveled such a story can be.

History of influence

The history of interpretation and the history of influence of our section are examples of how a text has had effects that do not correspond to its intention. Subsidiary points came to have an influence in history. Completely different situations caused the proper statement of a text to move into the background. The history of interpretation can here show only to a limited extent how a text gains new life in a new context. But it is nevertheless important, because its questions concern us too.

1. The quotation from Isa. 7:14 became a central point in the Christian-Jewish dialogue or in the *Christian polemic against Judaism*,[58] against which the Jews for centuries could hardly defend themselves.

Calvin, from whom one would not expect such inimical tones, is an example of the controversy concerning Isa. 7:14 : "For any sake, what kind of urge to falsehood drives them to reverse the natural order . . . .. Deservedly they are Christ's foes, whom God maddens with the spirit of giddiness, and strikes down in a stupor . . . .. We may see how the Jews, by their intemperate attitude have exposed, not themselves only, but the sacred mysteries of God to mockery."[59] The quotation, one example of many, is not to be considered only as boorish polemic in line with the spirit of the period, but is also to be evaluated in regard to the fact that such dealing with the Jews on a theological level has had destructive results in history. Luther declared his willingness to pay the "stubborn, condemned Jews" a hundred guilders if Isa. 7:14 really means "young

---

[56]It is striking that the parenetic interpretation of the figure of Joseph has great weight especially in the Protestant history of interpretation, e.g., with Melanchthon 142 ("fidei exemplum" [an example of faith]); Brenz 49 (forgiving).

[57]Schlatter 7.

[58]Justin, *Dial* 43,5-8; 84,1-4; Origen, *Cels* 1,34f. For the later time, cf. the overview in B. Blumenkranz, *Juifs et Chrétiens dans le Monde Occidental* (Paris 1960), 260-62.

[59]Calvin I 65-68 (on 1:22). On the position of Calvin toward the Jews—which as a whole is quite positive—cf. G. Locher, "Calvin spricht zu den Juden" *TZ* 23 (1967) 180-96. Cf. furthermore Brenz 61: "Pluris . . . nobis est interpretatio Angelica et Apostolica, quam onmium impiorum et excaecatorum Judaeorum somnia" (Of more value is for us the angelic and apostolic interpretation than the dreams of all the impious and blinded Jews).

woman" and not "virgin."[60] He owes them. The synagogue has interpreted Isa. 7:14 most of the time as referring to Hezekiah,[61] an interpretation which is still under discussion today and, in any case, in principle is on the right track in thinking of a contemporary figure. The traditional Christian interpretation of the Messiah Jesus, as an exegesis of Isa. 7:14, is untenable, and can be discussed at most as pneumatic exegesis. Matthew 1:22f. poses to the church in a paradigmatic way the problem of the hermeneutic of the Old Testament.

Thus one can at this passage no longer speak of the fulfillment of Old Testament predictions by God but only of the early Christian faith in this fulfillment. In place of God's action in history that leads up to Jesus there is—to say it exaggeratedly—faith in it. In place of Bible passages which the church triumphantly puts in opposition to Judaism, there is embarrassment. The traditional church interpretation of Matthew 1:22f. turns out to be evidence of Christian sin and is relevant exactly as such. The faithfulness of God to himself, to which Matthew 1:22f. wanted to point in the last analysis, is covered by a mystery—a mystery which cannot be deciphered superficially with individual proofs of predictions.

2. A second point in the history of interpretation especially concerns the Catholic exegesis: Matthew 1:25 plays a role still today in the discussion concerning the *perpetual virginity of Mary* even after the birth of Jesus.

Does v. 25 presuppose that Joseph after the birth of Jesus no longer had sexual intercourse with Mary? The vehement discussion of this point was already carried on in the ancient church.[62] The perpetual virginity of Mary was rejected by the Arians Eunomius and Eudoxius[63] and especially by Helvidius. Jerome debated against him in a brilliant polemical writing. Not only a Mariological interest but also the interest of the monk in virginity stands behind his polemic (cf. 18-22). The best argument for the *possibility* of a *virginitas post partum* is philological: Ἕως does not necessarily include the idea that after the indicated point of time something changes. This can be demonstrated convincingly, also from Matthew.[64] By contrast, the two other arguments are hardly tenable, viz., that γινώσκειν refers not to sexual intercourse but to the knowledge of the mystery of Mary,[65] or that from the imperfect tense ἐγίνωσκεν the

---

[60]M. Luther, *Vom Schem Hamphoras*, Munich ed. of Luther's works, suppl. vol. 3 (Munich, 1936), 290f. (WA 53, 579-648).

[61]Str-B I 75.

[62]Survey of the history of interpretation in Campenhausen* and Germano, *Mar.* 35 (1973)* 186-218. Zwingli 205f., Brenz 65, and Protestant Orthodoxy (e.g., Chemnitz, *Harmonia* VII 86) also interpret the verse of the *virginitas post partum* (virginity after the birth) while according to Bucer 37, Calvin I 73, or Grotius I 40f. the text does not permit a statement about Mary *post partum*.

[63]Philostorgius, *Hist. Eccl.* 6,2 = *GCS* 21,71.

[64]Jerome, *Adv. Helvidium* 4-7 = PL 23,185-191. Cf., e.g., Matt. 5:25; 16:28; 28:20. Differently, e.g., Matt. 2:9,13; 5:26, etc.

[65]In patristic interpretation both the sexual and the spiritual interpretation of γινώσκειν are widespread, cf. Germano, Mar. 35 (1973)* 200. Both the personal object αὐτήν and the course of the narrative argue against the spiritual interpretation.

perpetual virginity of Mary must be concluded.[66] Just as with the question of the "brothers" of Jesus,[67] the Catholic thesis of the perpetual virginity of Mary cannot be cogently refuted even here by means of exegesis. Overwhelming probability, however, suggests that such a thought was alien to Matthew. Since the perpetual virginity of Mary would have been considered very unusual by his readers, Matthew would have had to express it explicitly.[68]

Result: It is incontrovertible that ἕως οὗ ἔτεκεν υἱόν does not exclude the *possibility* of the perpetual virginity of Mary, but Matthew did not have to exclude this possibility at all because it was in any case foreign to him.

3. Especially the *virgin birth* itself has occupied the history of interpretation. The difficulties were in various times quite different. While (a) the early church[69] was concerned in placing the virgin birth into a superimposed Christological scheme, (b) in modern times the fundamental critique of the virgin birth arose mainly in Protestant, but also recently in Catholic discussion.[70]

a. That which is nowhere the case in the New Testament came to be taken for granted in the early church: The virgin birth *was connected with the idea of preexistence and incarnation.*[71] In Eastern tradition, the virgin birth, associated with the preexistence theology, has first of all a predominantly antidocetic aim. Later it becomes an honorific statement not about Jesus but about Mary: Mary is distinguished by becoming the vehicle of the birth of the preexistent Son of God—θεοτόκος! The accents lie differently in the Western tradition since the 4th century when questions of sin, concupiscence, and the sinlessness of the Savior become the context of statements about the virgin birth[72]—cf. *immaculata conceptio!*[73]

---

[66]E. Hofmans, "Maria altijd maagd," *CBG* 5 (1963) 53-78 (quoted according to *NTA* 8 [1963/4] 199), on the refutation Vögtle, *TQ* 147 (1967)* 38, n. 21. In my opinion, the suggestion of Ford* also is impossible: Joseph had to consider Mary as forbidden for all times on the basis of the purity laws. Has Mary been made unclean by God or the Spirit?

[67]Cf. Gnilka, *Markusevangelium* I 234f.; Brown* 86f.

[68]B. Weiss 43.

[69]Detailed discussion in Campenhausen*.

[70]On this see J. Fitzmyer, "The Virginal Conception of Jesus in the New Testament," in his *To Advance the Gospel* (New York 1981), 41-78.

[71]Ignatius, *Eph.* 7,2 (ἐν σαρκὶ γενόμενος θεός . . . ἐκ Μαρίας καὶ ἐκ θεοῦ), cf. 18,2; 19,1. The Syrian Ignatius, by the way, is the only one of the Apostolic Fathers who is cognizant of the virgin birth. The next example is probably Melito of Sardis, *Passover* 104 = SC 123,124.

[72]Since Pseud-Justin, *Res* (in Campenhausen* 43) it is considered as the destruction of "unlawful lust." In the context of this "ascetic" interpretation, the perpetual virginity of Mary naturally plays a role. This interpretation is advocated in the West noticeably by Jerome and Ambrose; it is sharpened by Augustine against Pelagius Christologically. Since then it has characterized occidental theology as articulated, e.g., by Olshausen 50: "A savior, conceived in sinful lust, proceeding from sinful humanity, is a self-contradictory concept."

[73]For Protestants it is perhaps not unnecessay to point out that Luther and Zwingli also understood the virgin birth in this way: Luther, Large Catechism. *Book of Concord,* ed. T. G. Tappert (Philadelphia: Fortress, 1959), 414 ("conceived and born without sin that he might become Lord over sin"); Zwingli, *Fidei Ratio* BSRK 80 ("totum hominem . . . ex immaculata perpetuaque virgine Maria adsumpserit" [he assumed total humanity . . . out of the immaculate and perpetual virgin Mary]).

A special problem was the connection of the virgin birth with the *doctrine of the Trinity*. Often the juxtaposition of virgin birth and preexistence was interpreted on the basis of the doctrine of two natures: Matthew 1 then describes the birth of the human being, John 1 that of the God Jesus. The virgin birth points more particularly to the human nature of Christ.[74]

On the basis of the doctrine of the Trinity, it is difficult to determine how the *participation of the Holy Spirit at the begetting of Jesus* is to be understood. The Holy Spirit cannot and must not be the father of Jesus; so it is then also emphasized that Christ was not "created" by the *substantia* (substance), but by the *virtus* (power) of the Holy Spirit. Christ is *creatura* (creature) of the Spirit.[75] The Holy Spirit can later be designated even as *causa efficiens* (efficient cause).[76] The birth of Christ is seen in the framework of the "works of the Trinity" in a special way as the work of the Holy Spirit because it is the greatest gift and benefaction for humans. For it is the work of the Spirit to endow humans and make them alive. And that happens through the birth of Christ.[77] It also was known that the reference to the creative agency of the Holy Spirit does not "explain" the birth of Christ: "Faith believes strongly, does not investigate; neither Gabriel nor Matthew was able to say *how* this happened."[78]

b. Except for a few Jewish-Christian and Gnostic groups of the first centuries,[79] the virgin birth as such has been *under widespread attack only since the early 19th century*. Even the rationalist H. E. G. Paulus still grants full confidence to the "Nazarethan family essay," available to Matthew,[80] because it supplements the Lukan birth narrative well from another perspective. But half a century later, the unsolvable contradictions between the two birth narratives were established for B. Bauer as fact, and he set himself the task "of restoring the marriage, of which Jesus is a result, to its true state as a marriage which has already been contracted in reality."[81] Schleiermacher's "critical treatment" of the "ecclesiastical formulae of the person of Christ" was influential: He rejected the virgin birth both with reference to the genealogies and in view of the fact that it is not a solid basis for the sinlessness of Jesus: to be consistent, one would have to assert not only the sinlessness of Mary, but also "the same of the mother of Mary and so on up."[82] Since then, the virgin birth is emphasized as a fact, evaded as difficult,[83] interpreted as a sign,[84] or rejected as a pseudo-explanation of the miracle of

---

[74]The interpretation of the virgin birth in the framework of a biblical theology, submitted by H. Gese, "Natus ex virgine," in *Vom Sinai zum Zion*, 1974 (*BEvT* 64), 145f., ("Indwelling of God in the world . . . in a final way not to be surpassed") corresponds to the antignostic and antidocetic interpretation of the virgin birth since Ignatius.

[75]Thus, e.g., Thomas, *Lectura* No. 111; Dionysius bar Salibi 59.

[76]Wolzogen 42.

[77]E.g., Maldonat 32, *Catechismus Romanus*, *Caput* 4, *quaestio* 3.

[78]Dionysius bar Salibi 55.

[79]Examples in W. Bauer, *Leben* 30-35.

[80]H. E. G. Paulus I 64f.

[81]B. Bauer, *Kritik* I 90f.

[82]F. Schleiermacher, *The Christian Faith* 405; quotations § 95 *Leitsatz* and § 97,2 (Berlin edition, 1836, II 46,67).

[83]So in the Dutch Catechism of 1966 (Catholic) according to Fitzmyer (above n. 70) 44f.

[84]Barth, *CD* I/2, 172-202 (as pointing to the mystery of the revelation. But Jesus is not God's Son *propter conceptionem sanctam* (on account of the holy conception) but is born as God's Son from the virgin, cf. 221).

the incarnation.[85]

Those who, like the author of this commentary, consider the virgin birth, in view of the rich Hellenistic parallel material and in view of its weak New Testament testimony, as rather improbable have to reflect on the question of how far the truth of the message of the text Matt. 1:18-25 is dependent on the factuality of the virgin birth. Matthew makes this task at the same time easier and more difficult. He himself naturally believed in the virgin birth, which had been handed down to him; but the main emphasis of our text is not the virgin birth. Closely connected with the virgin birth are only the subsidiary elements of the text, the obedience of Joseph and especially the proof from prophecy of Isa. 7:14.

The question of how the motif of the virgin birth, which is originally pagan, was transferred to Jesus must be directed to the pre-Matthean tradition. But there we are no longer able to reconstruct precisely the reasons and experiences which have led to this transfer, and so we also cannot discuss the legitimacy of this transfer in the context *of that time.*[86] It is clear only that it is hardly the connection of sexuality and sin, a connection which influenced the interpretation in the Western churches so strongly, which led to this transfer. In this point, the tension between the text and its history of interpretation admonishes us to think critically about our own tradition.

For Matthew, the virgin birth is not a central content of his faith but rather a conceptual basis which helps him to understand that Jesus is "Immanuel." But this basis is important because it aids in thinking very concretely of "God with us," to consider it as a *real* acting of God with Jesus *in* history and not simply as an abstract conviction. From this point of view, the virgin birth is not simply a secondary idea.

2. THE CHRIST COMES TO GALILEE (2:1–23)

2.1. Preview: The Gentiles before the King of the Jews (2:1-12)

Literature

Boll, F., "Der Stern der Weisen," *ZNW* 18 (1917/18) 40-48.
Broer, I., "Jesusflucht und Kindermord. Exegetische Anmerkungen zum zweiten Kapitel des Matthäusevangeliums," in Pesch, *Theologie*** 74-96
Derrett, J. D., "Further Light on the Narratives of the Nativity," *NovT* 127 (1975) 81-108, there 95-105.
Dieterich, A., "Die Weisen aus dem Morgenlande," *ZNW* 3 (1902) 1-14.
Ferrari-d'Ochieppo, K., *Der Stern der Weisen,* 2d ed. (Vienna: Herold, 1977).
France, R. T., "The Formula Quotations of Matthew 2 and the Problem of

---

[85]E. Brunner, *The Mediator* (1934), 322-27.

[86]Two critical questions must not be ignored: Is not Jesus as son of a virgin at least for Hellenistic readers and hearers coordinated with a relatively large group of heroes, kings, philosophers (θεῖοι ἄνδρες) instead of being distinguished from them? Can dualistic motifs, hostile to sexuality which, e.g., in Philo are connected with the virginity of the wives of the patriarchs, really be excluded completely?

Communication,'' *NTS* 27 (1980/81) 233-51.

Gaechter, P., "Die Magierperikope (Mt 2,1-12)," *ZKT* 90 (1968) 257-94.

Hengel, M., and Merkel, H., "Die Magier aus dem Osten und die Flucht nach Ägypten (Mt 2) im Rahmen der antiken Religionsgeschichte und der Theologie des Matthäus," in *Orientierung an Jesus* (FS J. Schmid), ed. P. Hoffmann, pp. 139-69 (Freiburg: Herder, 1973).

Hughes, D., *The Star of Bethlehem Mystery* (London: Dent & Sons, 1979).

Kehrer, H., *Die "heiligen drei Könige" in der Legende und in der deutschen bildenden Kunst bis Albrecht Dürer*, Studien zu deutschen Kunstgeschichte 53 (cited: Kehrer I*) (1904).

―――. *Die heiligen drei Könige in Literatur und Kunst*, 2 vols. (Hildesheim: Olms, 1976) (cited: Kehrer II*).

Leclercq, H., "Mages," *DACL* X 980-1067.

Marsh-Edwards, J. C., "The Magi in Tradition and Art," *IER* 85 (1956) 1-9.

Meisen, K., *Die heiligen drei Könige und ihr Festtag im volkstümlichen Glauben und Brauch* (Cologne, 1949).

Metzger, B., "Names for the Nameless in the New Testament," *Kyriakon* (FS J. Quasten) I, ed. P. Granfield and J. Jungmann (Münster: Aschendorf, 1970), 79-99, there 79-85.

Montefiore, H., "Josephus and the New Testament," *NovT* 4 (1960) 139-60, there 140-46.

Nestle, E., "Einiges über Zahl und Namen der Weisen aus dem Morgenland," in *Marginalien und Materialien* 2 (Tübingen: Heckenhauer, 1893), 67-83.

Nock, A. D., "Paul and the Magus," in Jackson-Lake V 165-88.

Riedinger, U. *Die Heilige Schrift im Kampf der griechischen Kirche gegen die Astrologie* (Innsbruck: Wagner, 1956), 130-46.

Schulze, A., "Zur Geschichte der Auslegung von Mt 2,1-12," *TZ* 31 (1975) 150-60.

Stuhlmacher, P., "Epiphanias. Matthäus 2,1-12," *GPM* 27 (1972) 63-70.

Vögtle, A., "Das Schicksal des Messiaskindes," *BibLeb* 6 (1965) 246-79.

Zani, L., "Abbiamo visto la sua stella," Diss. Padova, 1973.

Further literature** at Matthew 1-2, above pp. 101-102.

Text

1 But when Jesus was born in Bethlehem in Judea in the days of King Herod, behold, Magi from the east came to Jerusalem

2 and said, "Where is the newborn king of the Jews? For we have seen his star at its rising[1] and came to worship him."

3 When King Herod heard this, he was perplexed, and all Jerusalem with him.

4 And he assembled all the high priests and scribes of the people and inquired from them where the Messiah was to be born.

5 But they said to him, "In Bethlehem in Judea; for thus it is written by the prophet,

6 'And you, Bethlehem, land of Judah,

---

[1]Although it is awkward to assume a different meaning for the two occurrences of ἀνατολή in vv. 1f., and although the singular ἀνατολή in the meaning of "East" can be documented (cf. BDF, § 141, 2; frequently in Josephus), the astronomical meaning of ἀνατολή = "rising" is more probable. Only in this way can the singular in distinction from v. 1 be explained; besides, preposition + article is indeed not impossible with compass directions (thus BDF § 253, 5), but still rare (cf. Hermas, *Vis.* 1. 4. 1, 3, with πρός).

you are by no means the smallest among the princes of Judah.
For out of you a leader will rise,
who will pasture my people Israel.' "

7 Then Herod called the Magi secretly to himself and inquired from them the precise time of the appearance of the star,

8 sent them to Bethlehem, and said, "Go and search diligently for the child. But when you have found him, report it to me so that I also can come and worship him."

9 After they had heard this from the king, they went away. And behold, the star which they had seen in its rising preceded them until it arrived and stayed over the place where the child was.

10 But when they saw the star, they rejoiced greatly.

11 And when they came into the house, they saw the child with Mary, his mother. And they fell down, worshiped him and opened their treasure boxes and brought him gifts, gold, frankincense and myrrh.

12 And because they received in a dream the divine direction not to return to Herod, they went to their country on a different route.

Analysis

1. *Structure.* Our section is linked with the following one (2:13-23) by numerous common catchwords. Without 2:1-12, the section 2:13-23 would not be understandable. This applies to the whole section 2:13-23 and not only to the episode of the infanticide, vv. 16-18:[2] The rescue of the "royal child" and the massacre of the innocents are motifs which belong together and belong to the basic type of the ancient narrative of the persecution and rescue of the royal child. The connection with 1:18-25 is not as close. The transitional verse 2:1 must bridge a "gap" in the narrative, namely, the missing story of the birth. It abruptly introduces the place-name Bethlehem. The evangelist wanted to emphasize the close connection between 1:18-25 and ch. 2 (dream motif, angel of the Lord, dominating role of Joseph, idea of the people of God, fulfillment quotations, numerous common catchwords).

The narrative is divided, after the introductory question of the Magi (vv. 1f.), into two main parts, namely, the encounter with the "false" king of the Jews, Herod (vv. 3-9a) and that with the "genuine" royal child in Bethlehem (vv. 9b-12). The two parts correspond to the two "programmes narratifs conflictuels"[3] which also will govern vv. 13-23. On the one side, there is the strategy of Herod in Jerusalem, on the other side the strategy of God. But not only the kings Herod and Jesus but also the Magi and Herod are contrasted with each other: The narrator Matthew quite deliberately parallels the two direct discourses in vv. 2 and 8: Both begin with the question about the new king and end with the desire to worship him (προσκυνέω). The opposition between the king of the Jews, Herod, and the royal child, Jesus, is underscored by the star: it is not mentioned in Jerusalem but leads the Magi again after they have departed from Jerusalem.

2. *Redaction.* Our pericope also is shaped greatly by Matthew.[4] Non-Matthean

---

[2]Paul** 145-47 postulates a source which comprised only 2:1-12 and 16-18. Davis** 420, Zinniker** 24-29 and Brown** 109,117 assume that the story of the Magi (2:1-12) was inserted secondarily into a "Joseph block." Soares-Prabhu, *Formula Quotations* 269-98, distinguishes a "source of the Magi" 2:(1f.)9b-12 from a "source of Herod" 2:(1f.)3-9a,16-18 while he attributes 2:13-15,19-21 as the continuation of 1:18-25 to a "source of dream narratives."

[3]Laurentin** 405, cf. 410 (Opposition of the two places, Bethlehem or Nazareth and Jerusalem).

[4]The following are Matthean (cf. the introduction 3.1 and 3.2) in v. 1: genitive absolute + ἰδού, ἐν ἡμέραις Ἡρῴδου (LXX phrase), παραγίνομαι (points to 3:1,13); v. 2: λέγων, προσκυνέω, γάρ; v. 3: ἀκούσας δέ, perhaps πᾶσα Ἱεροσόλυμα (feminine perhaps also 3:5; cf. also 8:34; 21:10; 27:25); v.

language is found only rarely.[5] Unless one is of the opinion that Matthew has simply invented the pericope,[6] it has to be assumed that he has written down for the first time a traditional piece received by him.

2:5–6

The *formula quotation* in vv. 5b–6 can theoretically be lifted out of the pericope; because of its wording it is not probable that it was brought to light by Matthew. Only the introductory phrase is Matthean.[7] It does not contain the word πληρόω, which is typical of the formula quotations. Obviously Matthew was unwilling to attribute the fulfillment formula to the hostile high priests and scribes. The *wording* of the quotation deviates from all known text forms of Mic. 5:1. It is a mixed quotation; the little closing sentence comes almost literally from 2 Sam. 5:2, LXX (perhaps inserted because of its closeness to Mic. 5:3). It could be due to Matthew, because of his closeness to LXX and because it contains the idea of the people of God, which is so important for Matthew. All other peculiarities of the quotation[8] are hardly due to the evangelist, for they are not connected with the story of the Magi. Perhaps it was handed down independently from the story in the tradition.[9]

    3. *History of the Tradition.* If the evangelist was the first one to put a tradition into writing, then our chances of saying anything with certainty about the history of the tradition are minimal from the outset. That applies to our pericope too. One can hardly reconstruct a plausible original form of the tradition. It seems to me that it is not possible to arrive at an originally independent narrative of the Magi which was not already told in connection with the persecution and rescue of the Jesus child (2:13-23).

    However, this contradicts the theses usually advocated in scholarship. They either assume that the motif of Herod which led to the "superfluous" stay of the Magi in Jerusalem was added to an original Magi narrative or that a narrative of Herod which was originally the foundation for ch. 2 was secondarily enriched by the motif of the Magi. Or were two originally independent narratives connected with each other by Matthew or before him? Such theses, it seems to me, have little cogency. A Herod narrative without

---

4: συνάγω (of Jewish leaders 6 times!), ἀρχιερεῖς καὶ γραμματεῖς, τοῦ λαοῦ after opponents of Jesus; v. 5: οἱ δέ, εἶπον w. dative; οὕτως γάρ, cf. also n. 7; v. 7: τότε, λάθρα (pointing back to 1:19), καλέω, φαίνω; v. 78 is almost identical to v. 16; v. 8: πέμψας, πορευθείς, παιδίον (in ch. 1 nine times), ὅπως, κἀγώ, ἐλθών with verb following immediately, προσκυνέω; v. 9: οἱ δέ, ἀκούω (part. aor.), πορεύομαι, ἰδού, ἐλθών, ἐπάνω; v. 10: σφόδρα, χαρὰ μεγάλη (cf. 28:8); v. 11: ἐλθών, παιδίον, μήτηρ (in ch. 2 five times), πίπτω with προσκυνέω, ἀνοίγω, προσφέρω; v. 12: χρηματισθέντες κατ' ὄναρ (cf. 2:22; also 1:20; 2:13,19), ἀναχωρέω (cf. 2:13f.,22).

⁵The following are hapax legomena: πυνθάνομαι v. 4, ἐπάν v. 8, ἀνακάμπτω v. 12.

⁶Frankemölle, *Jahwebund* 310, considers our pericope with the whole prologue as redactional.

⁷Cf. 3:3; 24:15. Διὰ τοῦ προφήτου, without a name 1:22; 2:15; 13:35; 21:4, cf. 2:23. The missing name is perhaps connected with the fact that Micah is less a favorite with Matthew than are Isaiah or Jeremiah. Or did Matthew not know where the quotation comes from (as at 2:23; 27:9f.)? Cf. the excursus on 2:23 n. 2.

⁸1. The emphatically put οὐδαμῶς (*hapax legomenon* in the N T) changes Mic. 5:1 into its contrary. 2. Ἡγεμόσιν instead of LXX χιλιάσιν is probably due to a different pointing of the Hebrew text: אַלְפֵי (groups of a thousand), אַלֻּפֵי (leaders). 3. Ἐκ σοῦ is a mistake in hearing of LXX ἐξ οὗ or correspondence to the Hebrew text (מִמְּךָ). 4. Μοι is missing before ἐξελεύσεται. 5. Γῆ Ἰούδα is a geographical addition (perhaps of the evangelist?) in the style of the LXX, cf. Ruth 1:7 and elsewhere. Differently Gundry, *Use* 172 ("Mt was his own targumist"); Rothfuchs, *Erfüllungszitate* 60f.; France* 241-43.

⁹The interpretation Mic. 5:1 as referring to the coming of the Messiah from Bethlehem—an expectation which is known among Jews but not at all self-evident—corresponds to TgMic 5,1 (text in Str-B I 83).

the Magi would be incomplete; one would not know from where Herod received his information about the royal child. Conversely, the Magi narrative is designed with a view toward the Herod episode: The Magi are Gentiles; that required some form of confrontation with Israel. Besides, Magi or astrologers play a role in numerous parallels of the endangering of a royal child so that the appearance of Magi is not an alien element.

4. *Motifs and Analogies in the History of Religions.* Among kindred stories of the royal child, the Moses haggadah is closest to our story and to 2:13-23. Magi (TgJ on Exod. 1:15; ExR 1:18 on Exod. 1:22)[10] or scribes (Josephus, *Ant.* 2.205) predict for Pharaoh the birth of Moses; he is perplexed (Josephus, *Ant.* 2.206) and conceives the plan of infanticide. The Moses traditions probably have fructified our story. At the same time, it proves itself independent of them—especially in the use of the motif of the Magi—that it can in no way be understood as a mere copy of the Moses haggadah.

This does not explain the *motif of the star.* A star occurs in the story of the Abraham child who is pursued by Nimrod.[11] However, the examples are from a late period. In non-Jewish parallels there are reports of a comet at the birth of Mithridates and in the Nero episode in Suetonius.[12] A "great sign in the sky" is mentioned in Rev. 12:1. Comets or other phenomena of light at the birth of great men are widespread in antiquity.[13] The question is difficult whether there is a reminiscence of *Balaam's prophecy of the star out of Jacob* (Num. 24:17). The messianic interpretation of this passage was widespread;[14] the history of interpretation shows that Christian readers were aware of it.[15] But the star is not identified with the Messiah, as in the interpretation of Num. 24:17. Literal reminiscences of the story of Balaam in Numbers 22-24 are almost completely missing in 2:1-12.[16] In Jewish tradition, relationships are drawn between the Magi who appear in the Moses haggadah and Balaam, but the examples are late.[17] Thus caution is indicated.[18]

Noticeably in older literature, references are made again and again to the episode of *Tiridates, the king of the Armenians* who traveled to Rome with Magi in his retinue and with great pomp in order to do homage to Nero.[19] For time reasons it is improbable that this clever political maneuver from the year 66 C.E. has influenced our pericope; besides, the Magi do not play a large role there.

---

[10]Later parallels in Bloch** 109 and n. 22.

[11]Texts in Str-B I 77f.

[12]Justinus M. Junianus, *Epitome aus Pompeius Trogus* 1,37,2 (ed. O. Seel, 1935); Suetonius, *Nero* 36.

[13]Cicero, *Divin.* 1.23.47 (Alexander); Pausanias, 2.26.5 (Asclepios); light phenomena at the birth of Mithras in the rock cave (M. J. Vermaseren, *Mithras* [Stuttgart 1965], 59f.). A comet, according to Tacitus, *Annals* 14.22, is the omen of a *mutatio regis* (change of king).

[14]Examples in Str-B I 76f., furthermore CD 7 18-21; 4QTest 11-13; 1QM 11 6f.; *T. Levi* 18:3 (Christian?); *T. Judah* 24:1 (Christian?); Rev. 22:16.

[15]According to Justin, *Dial.* 106.4 and Origen *Cels.* 1.60 the Magi knew the predictions of Balaam (frequently since then, cf. Riedinger* 139-42).

[16]Most striking is the occurrence of θυμόω and ἐμπαίζω, Matt. 2:16 and Num. 22:27,29.

[17]Jannes and Jambres, the two chief Magi of Pharaoh, according to a later source (Yalkut Shimoni on Ex. 2:15) are considered as sons of Balaam. According to the *Sefer ha-Jashar* 239, Balaam himself has interpreted the dream for Pharaoh (according to Bourke** 162, n. 15). Cf. also Ginzberg, *Legends* II 254-56.

[18]Against Brown** 1193-96; Paul** 100-15; Stuhlmacher* 66.

[19]Dio Cassius Cocceianus 63,1-7; Pliny *Hist Nat* 30,16; Suetonius *Nero* 13, Josephus *Ant* 20,74. Especially Dieterich* 9-14 points to this.

5. *Historicity*. Our story is a legend told briefly and soberly which does not conform to the laws of historical probability. The desperate questions of the interpreters demonstrate this: Why did Herod not at least send a spy along with the Magi?[20] How could the whole population of Jerusalem, the scribes, and the unpopular King Herod be perplexed by the coming of the Messiah? The star also is not described realistically, i.e., as astronomically plausible.

In the rich *astronomical literature* on our text,[21] three possibilities of explanation are in the forefront: (1) A *supernova* which, however, is not documented for that time. (2) A *comet*. But the often-mentioned Halley's comet of the year 12/11 B.C.E.[22] came too early for the birth of Jesus. The comet attested by Chinese astronomers for the year 5/4 B.C.E. (or a nova?) is to be taken more seriously.[23] (3) The *conjunction of Jupiter and Saturn*, which appeared three times in the year 7/6 B.C.E.[24] It fit the situation not badly insofar as Jupiter is the royal star and Saturn, as the star of the Sabbath, sometimes was considered the star of the Jews.[25]

Of all these attempts it may be said that they rarely are a help for the explanation of our narrative. Matthew intended to describe a miraculous star which appeared in the East, preceded the Magi on the way from Jerusalem to Bethlehem (thus from north to south!), and then remained standing above the house where the child was to be found. Philologically, ἀστήρ means an individual star, not a group of stars (= ἄστρον).[26] At the conjunctions of Jupiter and Saturn in 7/6 B.C.E. both planets never stood so close to each other that they could have been seen as *one* star.[27] With all this I do not mean to exclude the possibility that the reminiscence of some striking astronomical phenomenon around the time of the birth of Jesus could have continued to live in the memory of the communities.[28]

Finally, the fact that Luke does not report a similar event argues against a historical nucleus; besides, the episode of the Magi could not be integrated into the Lukan birth narrative.[29] The parents of Jesus too seem not to know anything of the

---

[20]Montefiore, *Gospels* II 457: "Herod's action is charmingly naive!"

[21]Ferrari d'Ochieppo* 124-30 (lit.); Hughes* 93-194.

[22]Lagrange 23 reports how he himself observed this comet in Palestine in 1910.

[23]Montefiore* 143; Hughes* 148-52.

[24]On the so-called star calendar of Sippar and the Berlin table of planets, cf. Stauffer, *Jesus* 33, and Ferrari d'Ochieppo* 55-58.

[25]Albius Tibullus 1.3.18; Tacitus *Hist*. 5.4; Frontinus, *Strategemata* 2.1.17 (ed. G. Gundermann, 1888) and Dio Cassius Cocceianus 37.17f. could point to this fact.

[26]Cf. Boll*.

[27]Information from my Göttingen colleague H. H. Voigt.

[28]Almost all conservative research—quite numerous until today—pays homage to a peculiar neo-rationalism in the endeavor to save the historicity of the narrative. E.g., P. Gaechter, who reports, among other things, "The Magi knew where Bethlehem was located . . . , they knew the direction and condition of the way, first southward on the route to Hebron, then turning left." When they saw the star on their way, "not much was left for guidance, it was superfluous. . . . Its preceding therefore happened so to speak in a general way" (Gaechter 290). Whoever attempts to save the story historically by reducing its miracles destroys its message.

[29]The Matthean year of Jesus' birth cannot be brought in harmony with Luke 2:1f., the Lukan presentation of Jesus in Jerusalem 40 days after his birth (Luke 2:22) and the return to Galilee (Luke 2:39) cannot be brought in harmony with the Matthean visit of the Magi in Bethlehem. The Matthean οἰκία (v. 11) fits the stable which is to be assumed for Luke just as little as the birth cave of the church fathers (since Justin, *Dial*. 78.5 and Origen *Cels*. 1.51). The suggestion repeated again and again since

miraculous events at his birth (Mark 3:31-35)! In short, a historical nucleus is no longer comprehensible; however, the numerous parallel traditions in the history of religions make the embellishment of the narrative more understandable. But the narrative relays information about the Christian community in which it was fashioned. It is a community which is familiar with Jewish traditions but can now see Judaism only as the enemy. It differs from Luke by furnishing the royal child Jesus with gold and spices at his birth. Gentile Magi occur in its field of vision, and, as is shown especially also in 2:22, it is equipped with a certain historical sophistication. Perhaps an urban community in an area which is not purely Jewish?

Interpretation

Once more the interpreter confronts the problem how he or she is to deal with a narrative whose historicity is improbable. Since one of its most essential concerns is the proclamation of God's preserving guidance, the problem is sharpened: A guidance which is only narrated is close to an illusion. Where then does the act of God remain of which the story wants to speak? No easy answer is to be attempted here. For the community, the turning of God to the Gentiles, the experience of (its own?) preservation from the attacks of (Jewish?) enemies, the knowledge of the victory of Jesus over secular power, and thus faith in the power of the risen Lord Jesus was the presupposition for this narrative. The interpretation therefore must give attention to that which this "story" wants to attest; the proclaimer who uses it is asked for his or her own experiences which correspond to this testimony.

The history of interpretation shows that one can distinguish four basic types of the interpretation of our text, namely, the Christological interpretation, the interpretation for the Gentile mission, the paraenetic interpretation and the understanding of the story on the basis of the plan of God, which supplemented each other mutually. (a) The *Christologically centered interpretation* interpreted the coming of Christ as the dissolution of all magic[30] and antigodly knowledge through the true light of knowledge.[31] With the homage of the Magi the wisdom of the world gains a new orientation. (b) The interpretation in regard to the *Gentile mission* sees in the Magi the *primitiae gentium* (the firstfruits of the Gentiles)[32] and has the text take up again a concern of the genealogy. Often the accent is anti-Jewish: The adoration of the child Jesus by the Gentiles includes the *damnatio Iudaeorum* (the condemnation of the Jews)[33] portrayed with the

---

Eusebius, *Quaest. ad Steph.* 16.3 (= *PG* 22,936), that after the conclusion of the census the living conditions in Bethlehem had improved is hardly helpful for the reconciliation of the contradictions. However, the stable fits the shepherds just as well as the house fits the Magi.

[30]Ignatius, *Eph.* 19:3 who presupposes that our passage says: ἐλύετο πᾶσα μαγεία . . . , . . . ἄγνοια καθῃρεῖτο. Cf. later Justin, *Dial.* 78.9 (conversion of the Magi from the demons); Tertullian, *Idol* 9,7 = *BKV* I/7 149f; Clement of Alexandria, *Exc. Theod.* 74 (dissolution of astrology, granting of a new way). Further material in Riedinger* 142-46.

[31]*T. Levi* 18:3: Καὶ ἀνατελεῖ ἄστρον αὐτοῦ ἐν οὐρανῷ ὡς βασιλέως φωτίζων φῶς γνώσεως . . .

[32]This formulation, which governs the interpretations since that time, is found, to my knowledge, for the first time in Augustine, *Serm.* 200.1 and 202.1 = *PL* 38,1028.1033.

[33]Cf. Bede 13. The anti-Jewish elements of the text are brought out especially by John Chrysostom 6.3 = 102 (dissolution of the old covenant); 6.4 = 105 (the Magi followed the star, the Jews did not even

figure of Herod, his scribes, and his people. (c) For the *parenetic interpretation* naturally the behavior of the Magi is important, primarily their gifts,[34] but also their piety.[35] (d) Our story is an *expression of guidance by God,* especially in the legends which lay hold of it and embellish it. It constitutes an essential part of the history of interpretation. The detailed interpretation will have to pass judgment on these basic tendencies.

2:1

Verse 1 contains the statement of the situation and provides a link with 1:18-25. Matthew has to state that Bethlehem is in Judea not only because there is in the Old Testament also a Bethlehem in Zebulun;[36] rather, with the deliberately repeated expression (v. 5, cf. γῆ 'Ιούδα, v. 6) a theme of Matthew is struck: Jesus, the king of the Jews (v. 2) comes from Judea, and it will be in Judea that he is killed. The birthplace of the Messiah, Bethlehem—which already in Judaism was derived from the Scripture—is so definite for Matthew that Jesus' move to Nazareth needs special proof from Scripture (2:22f.). The action begins with a brief statement: Magi appear. The place of action is Jerusalem from the beginning. The journey of the Magi is not of interest to Matthew; his interest lies with the confrontation with Herod. Only one single statement is made concerning the Magi: they came from the East, the place of origin of magic, astrology, and religious wisdom, a place which is not defined further.

2:2

The reader knows that Magi are Gentiles; the evangelist underscores this fact through the remark in v. 2 that they ask for the birthplace not of the king of Israel but of the king of the Jews.[37]

Μάγος first means one who belongs to the Persian caste of priests, but is broadened since the Hellenistic age to designate other representatives of Eastern theology, philosophy, and natural science. The border between Magi, astrologers, and theurgists becomes fluid. Μάγος also is used negatively since the time of Sophocles and Euripides: Magi are sorcerers and charlatans. But in general the evaluation of the Magi is positive, understandably so in view of the high esteem which Eastern wisdom enjoyed at that time.[38] Judaism, which, on the basis of the Old Testament, is allergic to any form of sorcery, mostly evaluates negatively but can neither fully escape the influence of

---

believe their own prophets); 7.5 = 127 ("so you too . . . leave the Jewish people, the city full of confusion") and Peter Chrysologus 158 (the high priests and scribes as the prototypes of unbelief).

[34]Cf. below, p. 138.

[35]Some examples: Tertullian, *Idol.* 9.5, above n. 30 (conversion of the Magi, who return to their home by a different route); John Chrysostom 7.5 = 128 ("They brought gold; you hardly give a piece of bread"); Luther, *Predigten des Jahres 1532* no. 3 = WA 36,48: "Summary: Do away with Jerusalem, church, the law of the prince, but adhere alone to the word."

[36]Josh. 19:15.

[37] 'Ιουδαῖος is used by Matthew only in the mouth of Gentiles: 27:11,29,37. Exception: 28:15 where Matthew deliberately alienates.

[38]Nock* 164-82 gives a brief survey of the Magi in antiquity. On the role of astrology in the imperial courts, cf. J. Gage, *"Basileia." Les Césars, les rois d'Orient et les "Mages"* (Paris 1968).

astrology nor the Hellenistic high esteem of the Magi.[39] Christianity takes over the Jewish negative evaluation,[40] but has more and more difficulty propounding it in the Hellenistic culture of late antiquity, with its increasing irrationalism and obscurantism. From here our pericope obtains its polemic function in church history: Christ as the end of magic.

In our text the Magi are not sketched negatively. They are not converted by the child Jesus from their godless arts but they are wise and pious Gentiles who from the beginning seek that which is right, namely, to worship the child Jesus (v. 2). The star is the prime reason that associations with astrology cannot be completely excluded; but Matthew represses it indirectly by not indicating how the Magi recognized the significance of the star.[41] God's guidance alone is decisive. Matthew does not state directly that they are "the intellectual elite of the Gentile world";[42] many of his contemporary readers in Syria and Asia Minor probably thought so.

Much ink has been used on the *star*. The formulation αὐτοῦ τὸν ἀστέρα suggests that Matthew is thinking of the widespread idea that each person has his or her star, the important and rich people a bright one, the others an insignificant one which appears at birth and is extinguished at death.[43] The popular astrology of that time is based on this idea. Matthew, however, thinks of the star as a miraculous star. He is not concerned about a star of just any person but about a special phenomenon in the sky that happened often, according to ancient tradition, at the birth of a great person.[44]

2:3

Now Herod and "all Jerusalem with him" are contrasted with the Magi. Their reaction of dismay is a proof that they have understood the seriousness of the situation. Herod and the whole people of Jerusalem belong together in the front which rejects the new royal child. Every one who was even superficially familiar with the historical situation must have been surprised by the Matthean depiction: Herod was so unpopular with the Jerusalem inhabitants—aside from the upper class which was loyal to the king—that news of the birth of a royal child or especially a messianic child would have caused great joy. But Matthew is not concerned about historical realities. Jerusalem is for him the city of the

---

[39]M. Hengel, *Judaism and Hellenism,* 2 vols. (Philadelphia: Fortress, 1974), I 89f., II 60, n. 243. or the interesting remark in Pliny, *Hist. Nat.* 30.11: "est et alia magices factio, a Mose et Janne et Jotape ac Judaeis pendens" (there is also another group of Magi, deriving from Moses and Jannes and Jambres and the Jews).

[40]Acts 8:9,11; 13:5,8; *Did.* 2:2; 5:1. Magic as reproach against the Christians: *Acts of Thomas* 20.89.96.

[41]Scholarship, abounding in knowledge, could readily report on this: The expectation of a savior of the world from Judea was widespread (on the basis of Josephus, *War* 6.312!); from the conjunction of Jupiter and the (star of the Jews) Saturn a conclusion was easily to be drawn. Contact with Babylonian Jews have mediated to the Magi the necessary knowledge.

[42]Hengel-Merkel* 165.

[43]Plato, *Tim.* 41E (there are as many stars as people); Horace, *Ep.* 2.2.187 (the genius directs the birth star of each person); Pliny, *Hist. Nat.* 2.28 (he fights against this idea of popular astrology which *existimat vulgus* [the people esteems highly]); further examples in H. Usener, *Das Weihnachtsfest,* (Bonn, 3rd ed., 1969), 79f. n. 26. A Jewish example is MidrPs 148 n. 1 (trans. A. Wünsche II, 248).

[44]Cf. above nn. 11-13.

crucifixion of Jesus; its people are those who will say at the end of his gospel, "His blood be on us and our children" (27:25). Not until the passion narrative does he speak again of the "king of the Jews," about whom Herod and his people are so confounded (27:11,29,37,42). Thus Matthew gives a "signal" to that which is to take place in the passion narrative. Verse 4 confirms this: Herod assembles[45] the members of the high priestly clan[46] and the scribes, who emphatically are called scribes of the people (of God).[47] Again this beautiful harmony of Herod with the scribes—historically highly improbable—points the more clearly to the intention of the narrator. Herod asks the scribes for the birthplace of the Χριστός. The title[48] betrays that Herod fears more than a rival, namely, the Messiah of Israel.

2:5–6

The scribes answer the question of the king with Mic. 5:1. Matthew, who here—in the mouth of the scribes—avoids his fulfillment formula, sees in the quotation not in the first place an "Old Testament foundation of the beginning of the life of Jesus which can be fixed historically and biographically."[49] Rather he is interested, as is shown by the double Ἰούδα and the added piece from 2 Sam. 5:21 with the catchword λαός, in an anti-Jewish point: the Jewish scribes recognize that it is the matter of the expected messianic shepherd of God's people Israel but do not draw the consequences;[50] instead, they become indirectly the accomplices of Herod.

2:7

Verse 7 points ahead to the similarly formulated v. 16. Later the reader will comprehend the abysmal brutality of Herod; he or she receives the impression that the infanticide was calculated already at this time.

2:8

Verse 8 also serves the same intention; the reader perceives Herod to be a hypocrite. At the same time, the basis for v. 12 is laid: Herod attempts to

---

[45]Συνάγω is redactionally preferred and is often used redactionally of the Jewish leaders (22:34,41; 26:3,57; 27:62; 28:12). The suggestions of Brown** 183, n. 14, that this might indicate an association with συναγωγή is not without reason.

[46] Ἀρχιερεῖς means the members of the families from whom Herod at any given time appointed the high priest, and who as incumbents of the most important temple offices, as officiating or former high priests, exercised considerable power. The same usage in Josephus (Schlatter 33).

[47]Cf. on Matt. 1:21.

[48]He makes it here precise: βασιλεὺς τῶν Ἰουδαίων, similarly 27:17,22.

[49]Strecker, *Weg* 57.

[50]Ogawa, *Histoire* 57: While for the Gentile Magi the star was sufficient for the adoration of Jesus, the Jewish scribes who possess the Scripture and interpret it correctly are not even thereby brought to obedience. Calvin (Eerdmans, 1949), p. 133, gives a wrong interpretation of great theological power: "And so all ungodly persons find no difficulty in giving their assent to God on general principles; but when the truth of God begins to press them more closely, they throw out the venom of their rebellion."

involve the Magi in his game; but his evil intention will be destroyed by God's intervention.

2:9–10

The Magi travel by night, not because this was generally customary in the Orient, but because this gives the narrator the opportunity to speak anew of the star. As in kindred reports,[51] here also the reader is led to feel God's guidance which is at work in the entire event and is to share in the overwhelming joy which the Magi experience.

2:11

Verse 11 is the high point of the legend: The Magi find the child and his mother in the house. The formulation, which reminds the reader of 2:13f.,19,21, and the omission of Joseph indicate the special position of the virgin Mary in the sense of 1:18-25. The catchword προσκυνέω appears for the third time after vv. 2, 8.

προσκυνέω

This term denotes worshiping by throwing oneself on the floor which, according to Greek understanding, is appropriate before gods, according to Oriental custom also before people of higher position, as, e.g., kings.[52] Although the word in New Testament times could already be used in a less precise manner,[53] in Matthew a deliberate and pointed usage is present: proskynesis is used almost exclusively before Jesus, and that by supplicants (8:2; 9:18; 15:25; cf. 20:20) and disciples (14:33, in connection with the confession in the Son of God), especially to the risen one (28:9,17). In contrast to doubt, προσκυνέω designates in 28:17 the appropriate attitude before the risen Lord.

The proskynesis of the Magi directs the reader to the majesty of the Christ, son of David (1:1), Son of God (cf. 1:21; 2:15) and Immanuel Jesus. Thus our pericope fits itself into the Christological interest of the entire prologue of Matthew.

The Magi open their treasure chests and bring their presents to the child. The formulation is reminiscent of Isa. 60:6, secondarily of Song of Sol. 3:6.[54] Isaiah 60 speaks of the eschatological pilgrimage of the Gentiles and their kings to Zion. Does Matthew see in the worship of the Magi a symbolic fulfillment of this widespread promise? Since the Old Testament reminiscence is by no means so unambiguous, and since no reference is made to the context of Isaiah 60:6, it

---

[51]Clement of Alexandria, *Strom.* 1.24.163.1f. (Thrasybulus sees a wandering fire); Plutarch, *Timoleon* 8 (239D) and Diodorus Siculus 16,66,3 (to Timoleon προηγεῖτο λαμπὰς καιομένη κατὰ τὸν οὐρανόν on his sea journey to Italy); Virgil, *Aen.* 2.6692-97 (a star leads Anchises out of the burning Troy).

[52]On Oriental proskynesis before kings, cf. W. Fauth, "Proskynesis," *KP* IV 1189; on proskynesis before humans in the OT, H. Greeven, προσκυνέω κτλ. *TDNT* VI 758, nn. 38-40.

[53]As an expression of honor in letters: Greeven, op.cit., 761,2-10.

[54]Isa. 60:6: χρυσίον/λίβανος; Song of Sol. 3:6: σμύρνα/λίβανος. Χρυσίον and λίβανος are found also in Sir. 50:8f., χρυσίον and σμύρνα Song of Sol. 5:11,13, σμύρνα and λίβανος Exod. 23:34 relatively close together. Never in the OT are all three gifts mentioned together.

is not certain. Not until later has Isaiah 60 played a great role next to other Old Testament passages for the later legendary embellishment of the narrative of the Magi.[55] The gifts themselves cannot be clearly interpreted. Incense, rosin of the incense trees growing in Arabia,[56] India, and Somalia, and myrrh, rosin of the balsamlike myrrh trees, also growing in Arabia and Ethiopia, were used especially in the cult but also for magical practices, at wedding ceremonies, for cosmetic purposes, and as spice or medicine.[57] Both were considered very expensive (imported!) luxury items. The most likely meaning would be that, including the gift of gold, the Magi offer the child the most precious of presents.

The *gifts of the Magi* play a large role in the history of interpretation. In the framework of *Christological interpretation*, since Irenaeus, *Haer.* 3.9.2 and Origen, *Cels.* 1.60, myrrh is understood as pointing to the death of Jesus (Mark 15:23; John 19:39). Gold is fitting for Jesus as king, incense as God, myrrh as human.[58] Sometimes incense is also used to refer to the high priestly office of Jesus.[59] This interpretation of the gifts is an example of the interpretation by the ancient church of individual passages on the basis of the wholeness of the biblical message and thus is hermeneutically, not exegetically important. Greater variety exists in the frame of the *parenetical interpretation* which since the early Middle Ages stands beside the Christological one: Gold, incense, and myrrh are *fides rationabilis, munda ratio, bona opera* (reasonable faith, pure reason, good works) for the *Opus imperfectum*; they are pure works, prayer, and the mortification of passions for Euthymius Zigabenus; they are wisdom, prayer, and the *mortificatio carnis* (mortification of the flesh) for Gregory the Great; they are the confession or faith, love, hope ("these gifts anyone can bring to Christ, the poor no less than the rich") for Luther; they are *misericordia, preces, puritas* (mercy, prayer, purity) for Grotius; they are a believing heart, devoted prayer, and mortification of the flesh for Bengel.[60] Next to this broad palette of interpretations, the suggestion which can be found since the high Middle Ages that gold was given with respect to the poverty of the parents of Jesus, incense with a view to the odor in the stable, and myrrh for the health of the child seems almost sentimental.[61]

After the high point in v. 11 our narrative breaks off. Again the narrator through the means of a dream shows God's guidance; the evil plans of Herod are thwarted. It may be mentioned as a fine nuance that only Joseph is held worthy

---

[55]Cf. below pp. 139-140.

[56]Theophrastus, *Hist. Plant.* 9.4.2-4 (known to the Greeks only from Arabia). Nevertheless, this does not permit us to conclude that the Magi came from Arabia (cf. below n. 65), for through the trade with the Orient, incense was widespread everywhere as a luxury.

[57]K. Ziegler, "Myrrha," *KP* III 1524; C. J. Classen, "Weihrauch," *KP* V 1354f.

[58]The interpretation of gold already in Clement of Alexandria, *Paed.* 1.63.4. Characteristic formulations from later times: Juvencus in Jerome on this passage as a hexameter: *Thus aurum murram regique hominique Deoquel dona ferunt* (they bring incense, gold, myrrh as gifts for the king and for the human being and for God).

[59]Maximus of Turin, *Hom.* 21 = *PL* 57,270.

[60]*Opus imperfectum* 2 = 642; Euthymius Zigabenus 145; Gregory the Great 10 = 1113; Luther I 23f.; Grotius I 51; Bengel 24.

[61]Thomas, *Lectura* no. 201; cf. Erasmus, *Paraphrasis* 10.

of the appearance of an angel (1:20; 2:13,19). The Magi go back to their country; the narrator is not interested in their further fate.

Summary

Let us look back to the four types of interpretation sketched at the beginning: For Matthew the adoration of Jesus by Gentiles and his rejection by the Jerusalemites is in the foreground. With this he propagates a thought which was already hinted at in 1:1 and in the genealogy and shows as a prelude a main theme of his Gospel: the coming of the Gentiles to the Messiah of Israel and his rejection by Jerusalem, which culminates in the passion narrative.[62] The Christological theme is indicated only indirectly. It appears so to speak mirrored in the reaction of the people to Immanuel—in the rejection of the Christ by the Jews and in the proskynesis of the Gentile Magi which anticipates the worship of the disciples. With that, a parenetical side-motif also is given: the legend is edifying because the hearer can identify with the piety of the Magi. The point of contact in the text for this thought lies, however, in the proskynesis and not in the gifts of the Magi. Finally, the thought of God's guidance and plan is important for the traditional narrative of the preservation of the royal child Jesus and for Matthew, who describes God's intervention with almost stereotypical regularity.

History of Influence

Our narrative has had a strong influence on Christian piety.

    a. Above all, we must mention the continuing *formation of legends*,[63] which was done to a great extent with the help of Old Testament passages.[64]

    On the *origin of the Magi* there were already two contradictory opinions in the early period. Justin takes it for granted that they came from Arabia, obviously on the basis of Ps. 72:10 and Isa. 60:6.[65] But origin in Persia and corresponding Persian clothing has asserted itself, notably in the artists' representations.[66] Mesopotamia and Ethiopia as the homeland of the Magi are less frequently advocated.[67] In medieval times the conception occurs that the three Magi represent the descendants or the continents of Shem, Japheth, and Ham and thus the universal world church.[68] The *number of the Magi* was undetermined for a long time: while in the Western church the number three asserted

---

[62]Brown** 183: "a gospel in miniature."

[63]An excellent survey on the history of interpretation up to the Reformation is given by Schulze*.

[64]The post–New Testament embellishment is a prime example for the fruitfulness of the thesis of D. F. Strauss on the productive power of the OT for the formation of NT legends, but it applies only to the post-NT period.

[65]*Dial.* 77.4; 78.1; 106.4 (according to the "memorabilia of the apostles"); Tertullian, *Marc.* 3:13. Interestingly, Luther again assumes their coming from Arabia (*Festpostille* 1527, WA 17/II,360).

[66]Since Clement of Alexandria, *Strom* 1.15.71.4, in most interpreters. Ancient Christian art portrays the Magi throughout as Persians (Leclercq* 992).

[67]Cf. Knabenbauer I 128.

[68]Bede 13; Strabo, *Glossa* 73.

itself soon,[69] in the Syrian church often 12 Magi, with their large retinue, were believed to have gone to Jerusalem.[70]

The Magi became *kings* on the basis of the Old Testament; Isa. 60:3 and Ps. 72:10f. were decisive for this opinion. This thought was asserted from the Middle Ages on.[71] Since the Reformation, there was polemic against this view;[72] Catholic exegesis took over the skepticism of the Reformation relatively early.[73] However, this development shows how little influence exegesis had on popular piety: the Epiphany festival is still the festival of the three kings.

The *time* of their arrival and meeting with the child Jesus also is defined: while in the earliest period frequently a point in time up to two years after the birth was assumed on the basis of Matt. 2:16,[74] the 13th day after the birth asserted itself, especially under the influence of Augustine.[75] With this, the presupposition was given that the festival of the Epiphany, which, first in the West, had lost its particular character as Christmas festival in favor of December 25, became the festival of the three kings. The date of the Epiphany festival on its part has then made the date of arrival of the Magi certain.

The *names* of the Magi were not determined for a long time, neither in Syria nor in the West. Caspar, Melchior, and Balthasar appear first in the early Middle Ages[76] and predominated from that time on. The legend was embellished further and further. Sources for this ornamentation are not so much the commentaries and sermons as rather books of legends first found in the Middle Ages.[77] The appearance of the Magi is described: Caspar is the beardless young man, Melchior a bearded old man, Balthasar dark,[78] later a black man.[79] The return of the Magi by ship is reported,[80] and also their

---

[69]On the number of the Magi cf. Kehrer I* 22-25. The number three seems to have been stated for the first time by Origen, *Hom.* in Gen. 26:23ff. = *PG* 12,238. Except for very few representations in the catacombs, in the West only Abelard is an exception.

[70]Cf. the report of Dionysius bar Salibi 67f. on the various views in the Syrian church. The Reformers decisively argue against the number three for the Magi (Calvin I 82: "It is really a childish error that led the Papists to make the figure three according to the number of gifts"), but, as is shown by the history of piety also of the reformation churches, without success.

[71]Caesarius of Arles, *Sermo* 139 - *PL* 39, 2018. Especially the legends are here unambiguous. Johannes v. Hildesheim, *Die Legende von den Heiligen drei Königen* (Cologne 1960), 59, as an example, has to ask the other way around why the kings are Magi: because of their wonderfully rapid journey to Jerusalem!

[72]Luther, Sermon of 1524, WA 15,409; Calvin I 82 ("dubious").

[73]Maldonat 25 ("minus . . . certum" [less . . . certain]).

[74]E.g., in Eusebius, *Quaest. ad Steph.* 16.2 (= *PG* 22, 933).

[75]*Sermo* 203,1 = *PL* 38,1035f.

[76]In the so-called *Excerpta Latina Barbari* (6th century, presumably of Eastern origin). On the problem of the names cf. Kehrer II/1* 64-75; Leclercq* 161-67; Metzger* 79-85.

[77]Examples: Johannes of Hildesheim (above, n. 71); Jacobus a Voragine, *Legenda Aurea*, ed. R. Benz (Heidelberg, 9th ed., 1979), 103-11. From the Eastern area the apocryphal *Book of Seth* which is handed down in the *Opus imperfectum* 637f., was influential, as was the Syrian *Cave of Treasures*, which comes from the school of Ephraem (on the Magi ch. 46 = Riessler 998-1000).

[78]Pseudo-Bede, *Excerpta et Collectanea*,. *PL* 94,541 (date uncertain).

[79]For the first time in Elisabeth of Schönau (12th century), cf. Schulze* 156. Later Caspar often is the black man.

[80]*Hist. Schol. PL* 198,1542.

later conversion by the Apostle Thomas[81] and their death.

> b. The three kings played a considerable role in *popular piety*.

In early *catacomb painting* the motif of the Magi was the most frequent and important one in the framework of the presentations of the birth of Christ.[82] In the Middle Ages, the story of the Magi played a large role in several countries as the content of *mystery plays* and *plays of the three kings*.[83] That was important especially because the Magi became figures with whom the believers identified; the parenetical interpretation of the legend was furthered thereby. Since the late Middle Ages, more exactly since 1164, in the German area the *cult of relics* of the Magi became important: Friedrich Barbarossa had transferred the relics of the Magi to Cologne after the conquest of Milan.[84] The Magi in the Middle Ages had various *protective functions*: As kings they prevented misfortune, protected stable, house, and harvest against fire and bad weather. As Magi they helped to tame stubborn beasts and warded off illnesses, especially epilepsy.[85] Many of these customs have survived until today.

The discrepancy between the biblical text and popular piety is especially thought-provoking. The history of the influence of our text is also an example of its lack of influence. The exegesis therefore aids in critical examination of popular piety to find the way back from the abuses to the message of the text, without destroying the inherent important positive element, namely, the possibility for Christians to identify themselves with the Magi. On the basis of the text, the accent, however, must fall not so much on the parenetic element (gifts), but rather on the possibility, given by God's guidance, that Gentiles worship the Christ of Israel.

2.2. Flight to Egypt and Return to Nazareth (2:13-23)

Literature

Albright, W. F., "The Names 'Nazareth' and 'Nazoraean,' " *JBL* 65 (1946) 397-401.
France, R. T., "Herod and the Children of Bethlehem," *NovT* 21 (1979) 98-120.
Gärtner, B., *Die rätselhaften Termini Nazoräer und Iskariot*, Horae Soederblomianae 4, pp. 5-36 (Uppsala: Appelberg, 1957).
Lindars, B., *New Testament Apologetic*, pp. 194-99 (Philadelphia: Westminster, 1961).
Lyonnet, S., " 'Quoniam Nazaraeus vocabitur' (Mt 2,23).L'interprétation de S. Jérome," *Bib* 25 (1944) 196-206.
Medebielle, A., " 'Quoniam Nazaraeus vocabitur' (Mt 2,23)," *Miscellanea Biblica et Orientalia* (FS A. Miller), ed. A. Metzinger, StAns 27-28, pp. 301-26 (Rome: Herder, 1951).

---

[81]*Book of Seth, Opus Imperfectum* 638.

[82]Literature on the problem of the Magi in art: Kehrer II/2*; Leclercq*; G. Schiller, *Ikonographie der christlichen Kunst* I (Gütersloh, 2nd ed. 1969), 105-24; cf. also F. Cumont, *L'adoration des mages et l'art triomphal de Rome*, MPARA 3 (1932/33) 81-105.

[83]Kehrer II/1* 55-64; W. Flemming, "Weihnachtsspiele," *RGG* VI 1569-71.

[84]Kehrer II/1* 81f. Prior to this, the relics were in Constantinople; for a long time they had been missing in Milan.

[85]Kehrer II/1* 75-80; Meisen* 8-27.

Moore, G. F., "Appendix B. Nazarene and Nazareth," in Jackson-Lake I 426-32.
Rembry, J. G., " 'Quoniam Nazaraeus vocabitur' (Mt 2/23)," *SBFLA* 12 (1961/62) 46-65.
Schaeder, H., "Ναζαρηνός, Ναζωραῖος," *TDNT* IV 874-79.
Schweizer, E., "Er wird Nazoräer heissen," in idem, *Neot* (Zurich, 1963), 51-55.
Zolli, F. "Nazarenus vocabitur," *ZNW* 49 (1958) 135f.
Zuckschwerdt, E., "Nazoraios in Matth. 2,23," *TZ* 31 (1975) 65-77.
Further literature** at Matthew 1-2 above pp. 101-102.

Text

13 After they [i.e., the Magi] had returned, behold, an angel of the Lord appears to Joseph in a dream and says, "Rise, take the child and his mother, flee to Egypt and remain there until I tell you, for Herod intends to seek the child to kill him."

14 Then he rose, took the child and his mother at night and went away to Egypt

15 and remained there until the death of Herod in order that the word of the Lord through the prophet might be fulfilled, "Out of Egypt have I called my son."

16 Then when Herod saw that he had been deceived by the Magi, he became very angry, sent and caused all the boys in Bethlehem and its whole environment to be removed, from two years old and under, corresponding to the time which he had ascertained exactly from the Magi.

17 There was fulfilled the word spoken through the prophet Jeremiah,,

18 "A voice was heard in Rama,
    Weeping and much mourning,
  Rachel weeps for her children
    and could not be comforted
    because they are no more."

19 When Herod had died, behold, an angel of the Lord appears to Joseph in Egypt in a dream

20 and says, "Rise, take the child and his mother and go to the land of Israel, for those who sought the life of the child are dead."

21 Then he [Joseph] rose, took the child and his mother and went into the land of Israel.

22 But when he heard that Archelaus was king of Judea instead of his father, he was afraid to go there; since he received direction in a dream, he went away into the area of Galilee.

23 He came and settled in a city called Nazareth, so that the word through the prophet was fulfilled, namely, "He will be called a Nazorean."

Analysis

1. *Structure and Shape.* Our text is connected by numerous key words both with 1:18-25 and 2:1-12.[1] It is divided into three subsections (vv. 13-15, 16-18 and 19-23), which through the formula quotation that concludes each show a certain symmetry.[2] The

---

[1] Cf. above, p. 102, n. 1; n. 4 on 2:1-12.

[2] Postpositioned formula quotations occur also in 4:15f.; 8:17; 12:18-21; 13:35; 27:9.

first and the third sections are formulated in parallels (13a,b//19,20a; 14//21). In both sections, the command of the angel and the description of its execution by Joseph are almost identical. This makes the digressing elements of the narrative the more striking: vv. 13c,14 (καὶ ἴσθι . . . ἀπολέσαι αὐτό) bracket the first section with vv. 19-21 or 16-18. Verse 20 (τεθνήκασιν . . . παιδίου) has no corresponding element in 13-15; the 3rd person plural is also noteworthy. The evangelist alludes here to Exod. 4:19f. and thus underscores the Old Testament reminiscence. Verses 22f. also have no correspondence in that which precedes, even though some formulations are familiar to the reader. The two-stage return of the family of Jesus to Israel is curious; the move to Nazareth gains special attention. A distinctive position is taken by the midsection 16-18. As in 2:1-12, in the middle of the narrative the enemy of God, Herod, is active. The reference back to 2:7 cannot be missed. The malice of Herod which the reader already knows from 2:3-8 comes here to its fruition. The fact that even the action of Herod is concluded by a formula quotation points to the theological significance even of this central section. In form, the section—as already 1:18-25—is very sparse. There is not a word too many; the evangelist forgoes any legendary or novellistic embellishment. This sparseness itself needs interpretation.

2. *Redaction.* Already the close connections with 1:18–2:12 suggest that here also the share of the evangelist in the formulation is very large. Linguistic details[3] speak in favor of the assumption that the evangelist himself has largely formulated the material. Presumably he has here formulated in writing for the first time an orally transmitted cycle of narratives. Possibly the traditional narrative had spoken only of the return into the land of Israel and not, in the present awkward manner, first of a return into the land of Israel and then, after another divine revelation, to Galilee.[4] Verses 22f. contain numerous Matthean linguistic peculiarities and have a close correspondence in vv. 4:12f.[5] Perhaps the evangelist himself has formulated vv. 22f. according to the example of 4:12f.

3. Each of the three *fulfillment quotations* poses its own problems:
Verse 15 (= Hos. 11:1) follows the Hebrew text; the wording of LXX would not usable for Matthew.[6] Moreover, the quotation speaks of the calling of the son *out of* Egypt; this does not fit the context.
Verse 18 (= Jer. 31:15) follows the Hebrew text in its first sentence, which here corresponds exactly to LXX B; in its fourth sentence LXX A; in its third the Hebrew

---

[3]Cf. introduction 3,2. Matthean elements in v. 13: ἀναχωρέω, ἰδού after genitive absolute, ἄγγελος κυρίου, φαίνομαι κατ᾽ ὄναρ, λέγων, ἐγερθείς, παραλαμβάνω τὸ παιδίον καὶ τὴν μητέρα αὐτοῦ (as vv. 14, 20f.), ἕως ἄν, ἐκεῖ with εἶναι, μέλλει γάρ + subject + infinitive, infinitive of purpose with τοῦ; v. 14: largely repetition of v. 13, νυκτός; v. 15: ἐκεῖ with εἶναι as v. 13, ἕως with gen.; on the introductory phrase of the fulfillment quotation cf. excursus at 2:23 no. 2; v. 16: τότε, ἰδών, λίαν, ὅριον, cf. 4:13; v. 16, end: largely repetition of v. 7; v. 17: cf. above on v. 15; v.19: τελευτάω, ἰδού after genitive absolute; the remainder repeats v. 13; v. 20: v. 20a repeats v. 13, πορεύομαι?, γῆ with name (cf. also 2:6; 4:15); the remainder of the verse corresponds largely to Exod. 4:19 LXX; v. 21: corresponds largely to v. 14, cf. v. 20; v. 22: ἀκούσας, φοβέομαι, ἐκεῖ, ἀπέρχομαι, χρηματισθείς κατ᾽ ὄναρ = resumption of v. 12; ἀναχωρέω, μέρη with geographical statement; v. 23: ἐλθών, κατοικέω, πόλις, λεγόμενος before a name, ὅπως; on the introductory phrase to the fulfillment quotation cf. excursus at 2:23. Since the hapax legomenon τελευτή (v. 15) is connected with the verb τελευτάω, a larger accumulation of non-Matthean linguistic elements is found only in v. 16.

[4]Dibelius, *From Tradition to Gospel* 129, n. 1; Brown** 106-08; Soares-Prabhu, *Formula Quotations* 209-12; Davis** 420f.

[5]The following correspond: ἀκούσας δὲ ὅτι . . . ἀνεχώρησεν εἰς . . . Γαλιλαία(ν) καὶ . . . ἐλθὼν κατῴκησεν εἰς. . . . On the question of the sources for 4:12f. cf. the comments there.

[6]LXX, similarly Targum and Theodotion, read τέκνα instead of υἱόν, as to the sense completely correct, for the passage refers to Israel. For Jerome, *Ep.* 57.7 *ad Pammachium* = BKV II/18 276, this passage is an example of the necessity to return to the *Hebraica veritas* (Hebrew truth).

text; while the second is an independent abbreviation of all known variants. The quotation would be usable in each textual form for its present purpose; the textual form at hand thus is not to be explained as an adaptation to the present context.[7] The greatest difficulty consists in the place statement "in Rama," since this village is north of Jerusalem. It could have been corrected if Matthew had followed LXX A in the first sentence also where the Hebrew place statement is translated ἐν τῇ ὑψελῃ.[8] Presumably the quotation was already at the disposal of the evangelist in this wording, which is only relatively suitable.

Verse 23 is completely puzzling. The exegesis[9] will show that this quotation also is traditional.

As far as content is concerned, all three quotations are very specific; they can be properly applied only in connection with a story of Jesus' childhood which is similar to the Matthean one. In my opinion, they show that the Matthean birth narrative was known in his community and was reflected on by scribes.[10] Matthew has not created his materials freely.

4. *Motifs.* Our text also has numerous parallels in the ancient tales of the persecution and preservation of the royal child.[11] Naturally the Jewish-Christian narrators of our story were especially familiar with the tradition of the rescue of the Moses child in Egypt and the murder of the Israelite boys by Pharaoh,[12] although this did not lead to a unilineal dependence.[13] Matthew also is aware of the contacts of his traditions with the narrative of Moses since he describes the return of Joseph from Egypt in vv. 19f. with the Old Testament words which tell the return of Moses with his family from Midian to(!) Egypt (Exod. 4:19f.).[14]

This imbalanced doubleness of the relationship on the one hand to the childhood story of Moses, on the other hand to the flight of the adult Moses speaks against a unilinear fixation of the relationships of our narrative with Old Testament materials to *one* complex. Thus one may ask whether the reminiscence of the *journey of Jacob to Egypt* (Gen. 46:2-7) could have furnished a further point of contact. An ancient midrash on Deut. 26:5-8 which, however, cannot be dated with certainty and which interprets the

---

[7]The word "sons," attested to in the Hebrew text and in LXX, would have been much more suitable, since only boys were killed.

[8]This translation, which was not taken over, plays an essential role in the framework of the allegorical explanation in the Middle Ages. Jerome on the passage: "vox in excelso audita est" (the voice is heard in the highest place); Strabo on the passage: the voice of the mourning church ascends to the throne of the highest judge.

[9]Cf. below pp. 148ff.

[10]Cf. the excursus "Formula Quotations" at 2:23 below.

[11]Cf. below the table on pp. 152-155. For the flight of the threatened child, cf. especially Cyrus (Justin), Mithridates (Justin), Gilgamesh, Abraham, Leto, Isis; for the motif of the death of other children, Moses, Cyrus, Abraham, Augustus, Nero, Romulus.

[12]Material in Bloch** 117-20.

[13]The differences between Matt. 2:13-23 and the Moses haggadah are quite great and are brought out rightfully by Crossan** 130f.; Nolan, *Son* 88f.: Not only the cleverness of the mother or the father but God's intervention saves the child Jesus; Jesus flees to Egypt, (the adult) Moses flees from Egypt. In the passage deliberately adduced by Matthew, Exod. 4:19f., Moses has his correspondence in the father of Jesus, not in Jesus. Thus it is not so that in Matt. 2:13-23, as the late passage *Pesiq* 49b = Midr Ruth on 2:14 = 5:6 (Str-B I 86f.) says, the last deliverer is like the first one. If a correspondence is maintained, it is that between Herod and the Pharaoh, not that between Jesus and Moses.

[14]The allusion becomes clear through the plural τεθνήκασιν, which is otherwise unmotivated in Matthew.

journey of Jacob to Egypt as a flight from Laban would be particularly interesting.[15] However, there are no linguistic similarities between Matt. 2:13f. and Genesis 46. There are also a series of important differences from the Laban midrash,[16] so that a relation remains unprovable.

5. *Historicity.* Neither the sufficiently well-known cruelty of Herod[17] nor the fact that Egypt has always been a refuge for persecuted ones in Israel[18] is of help: Each saga or legend is connected with historical data. It is inexplicable why the devious fox Herod would wait so long until only a politically unwise mass murder was feasible. Our narrative is connected with the almost certainly unhistorical Bethlehem tradition[19] and has no analogy at all in Luke. Only one point must be taken seriously: One has to ask whether there is perhaps a kernel of truth behind the tradition of Jesus' stay in Egypt: Judaism is aware of this tradition, and that in a form which, it seems to me, in its oldest shape excludes dependence on Matthew.[20] If the pericope is unhistorical in its essential parts, then its theological profile and the situation of the Matthean community, separated from Judaism, as the historical background gains increased significance.

Explanation

This section too, as a part of the Matthean prologue, includes essential basic statements as a prelude to the whole Gospel. In a certain way it also is a didactic text, not in the sense of instruction about certain theological subjects, but in the sense of a foundational story which indicates the coming salvation history in an anticipatory way. But this can be known only by the Christian who from the Gospel as a whole again meditates on the material in the prologue.

---

[15]Discussed by L. Finkelstein, "The Oldest Midrash: Prerabbinic Ideals and Teachings in the Passover Haggadah," *HTR* 31 (1938) 291-317, adduced especially by Daube, *New Testament* 189-92; Bourke** 167-72; Cave** 387f. Daube points especially to the "half foreign" character of Laban and Herod, to God's command, mediated by a dream, to flee to Egypt, and to Rachel, Jacob's wife.

[16]Cf. the detailed critique of Daube's thesis by Vögtle, *Gottessohn* 43-53: textual references to Genesis 46 are missing; Laban is not a ruler; the child for whose sake the persecution occurs is missing in the Laban-Jacob midrash.

[17]A. Schalit, *König Herodes* (Berlin 1969), 648f., n. 11, and France* consider the infanticide as possible for this reason. *As. Mos.* 6:4, cf. 2, says of the "insolent king" that "he will murder the old and the young."

[18]First Kings 11:17 (Hadad); 1 Kings 11:40 (Jeroboam); 2 Kings 25:26; Jer. 41:17 (the people); Jer. 26:21 (Uriah); 43:7 (people); Josephus, *Ant.* 14. 21 (period of Hyrcanus I); 15:42-49 (time of Herod); *War* 7.410 (sicarii), 423 (Onias).

[19]Only the Bethlehem tradition is rooted in the pre-Matthean traditional material; the connection to the πατρίς Nazareth was not there until the evangelist (2:22f.).

[20]It is known to us from various rabbinical testimonies that Jesus was supposed to have been in Egypt and learned magic there. Basic types: the Joshua-ben-Perachiah tradition, *b. Sanh.* 107b and parallels; the Ben-Stada tradition, *b. Sabb.* 104b and parallels (text in Str-B I 84f.). J. Maier, *Jesus in der talmudischen Überlieferung* (Darmstadt: Wissenschaftliche Buchgesellschaft, 1978), 127-29, 203-10, 255f., proves its secondary character in comparison with the NT. But the statement handed down by Celsus (Origen, *Cels.* 1, 28.38) and others remains, that the adult Jesus had worked in Egypt as a day laborer. Celsus also states that Jesus as a child had fled to Egypt (ibid. 1.66). The duplication of the stay of Jesus in Egypt could be in connection with the fact that only an adult person can learn magic. But from where comes the report that Jesus had worked as a day laborer? Here a piece of information is glimpsed which becomes understandable neither as a further development of the traditions of Matthew 2 nor as an anti-Christian polemic.

2:13-15

The first episode, vv. 13-15, deals with the flight to Egypt. Its extreme conciseness makes clear what is essential: God's plan and God's hand stand over the destiny of Jesus. It is God's guidance alone which saves the child. The child and his mother are in the center; Joseph does not appear anywhere as the father. As indicated by the literal repetition of the angel's command in vv. 14f. (and 21) he is the obedient one.[21] The introductory formula to the quotation expresses through the verb πληρόω the direction of the divine plan. As in 1:22, God himself is the speaker of his word. It becomes clearer here than in 1:22f. that this is connected with the title υἱός: God himself speaks here of his *Son*.[22] This title, so extraordinarily important for Matthew, remains in this passage still undeveloped as to its content. Its mention has a compository function in the Gospel: it points ahead to the important section 3:13–4:11 where the Matthean conception of sonship of God is developed. The importance of this preannouncement is strengthened by the fact that υἱός is the only Christological title in the whole of chap. 2.[23] In our quotation an element of the Israel typology is connected with the title *Son*.[4] In Jesus the exodus from Egypt is repeated and completed. The catchword "Egypt" is thus for Matthew just as decisive as the catchword "Son."[25] This probably is the Matthean thought: Salvation happens once more anew. The reader well versed in the Bible senses that the action of God with his Son has fundamental character, that it is at the same time connected with Israel's basic experiences and carries them out anew.

It is questionable whether the evangelist, in mentioning "Egypt," has in his mind the idea of a Gentile country.[26] Although such a thought would be completely possible, nothing in the text indicates it. It is more likely that the theme of salvation for the Gentiles does not appear again until v. 23.

---

[21]Cf. above on 1:19,24f. In 2:1-12, where Joseph does not play a role, the Magi are the obedient ones.

[22]Pesch, *Bib.* 14 (1967)** 411-13. Cf. on 1:18-25 n. 50.

[23]Kingsbury, *Structure* 46.

[24]Naturally, Matthew understands the Hosea quotation as a prediction; Matthew does not recognize what has been widely perceived since Zwingli (208, on 2:18: "detorquet haec verba ad Christum" [he twists these words to Christ]) and Calvin I 201, that his interpretation does not correspond to the original meaning. "Israel typology" is not to be understood as meaning that Matthew sets Israel and Jesus over against each other but that, through the wording of the quotation which speaks of Jesus, the reader who is acquainted with the Bible is unavoidably reminded of Israel which also was called out of Egypt.

[25]Stendahl** 97 and Strecker, *Weg* 58, emphasize that the insertion of the quotation takes place under the catchword "Egypt." But it is not a matter of merely biographical interest to prove the individual stations of the *vita Jesu* from the Old Testament (so Strecker) but of the Christological statement which is indicated with geographical statements.

[26]Photius of Constantinople (in Reuss 272) and Theophylact 168 connect 2:1-12 and 2:13-23: Jesus has sanctified Babylonia and Egypt. The legend elaborates this aspect further, cf. below pp. 150f. In John Chrysostom 8:2 = 137, Babylonia and Egypt are considered as especially godless; in Melanchthon 144 the sanctification of Egypt, which is considered extremely sinful, becomes the representation of justification *sola gratia*.

2:16-17

The brief episode of the infanticide at Bethlehem furnishes an effective contrast: it shows the greatness of the danger which the child avoided. The malice of the tyrant becomes visible in the fact that the action of Herod is extended to the whole area around Bethlehem and includes all boys under two years of age. The introduction to the formula quotation is again deliberately varied: the infanticide does not happen *in order that* the scripture is fulfilled. It does not speak of the direct responsibility of God for the death of the children.

2:18

The quotation from Jer. 31:15 once more portrays for the reader the concept of God's plan: even this terrible event is predicted by the prophets. At the same time new light is shed on the infanticide and on Herod: the infanticide is not a harmless matter if the ancestral mother Rachel weeps for her children in Rama.[27] Herod cannot be a true king of the Jews if he kills Israel's children because of Jesus. It is indicated here in a veiled way that the rejection of Jesus by the king of the Jews is a contradiction vis-à-vis Israel itself. In a similar way Matthew later will interpret Israel's rejection of Jesus as a contradiction of that essence which made it Israel. Thus the mourning of the ancestral mother gains a proleptic depth dimension in the context of the Gospel of Matthew.

The modern reader notices that Matthew does not raise the question of theodicy in view of the suffering of the innocent children. The evangelist is concerned with the struggle between God and the enemy of Jesus, Herod; the innocent children appear so to speak only on the reverse side of this conflict. It does not disturb Matthew that God saves his Son at the expense of innocent children. The history of interpretation is only hesitantly concerned with this point. Herod, as was known from Josephus (*War* I.. 656-58), had received his merited punishment by his gruesome death. John Chrysostom, who explicitly dealt with the innocent children, contends that nothing good would have come of them because there *can be* no such thing as innocent human suffering.[28] Most interpreters do not agree with him on this matter; for them, these children were innocent. They were permitted to die for Christ; that is better than to live in sin.[29] From here the thought is not far away of understanding the suffering of the innocent children as martyrdom and of interpreting these children parenetically as an example for all

---

[27]The *statement of place* ἐν Ῥαμά confronts us with many difficulties. Since Gen. 35:19 and 48:7 there is a tradition which locates the tomb of Rachel near Bethlehem, in distinction from 1 Sam. 10:2. Cf. for the Bethlehem tradition *Jub.* 32:34; Justin, *Dial.* 78,8; *t. Sota* 11.11; Jerome on 2:18; John Chrysostom 9.3 = 152 (in the "hippodrome" near Bethlehem); J. Jeremias, *Heiligengräber in Jesu Umwelt* (Göttingen: Vandenhoeck & Ruprecht, 1958), 75 n. 2. In the Madaba mosaic, Rama also is located near Bethlehem (with quotation of Matt. 2:18). Presumably Matthew did not know that Rama in Benjamin is located north of Jerusalem.

[28]9.2 = 149f.

[29]Leo the Great, *Sermo* 37,4 = *BKV* I/54 134: The innocent children share in the suffering of Christ; *Legenda Aurea* I (ed. R. Benz, Jena 1917) 96: liberation from original sin through baptism of blood. Luther, *Hauspostille* 1544 = *WA* 52,603: A future death would be unavoidable, therefore it is better to die for Christ and in blessedness.

martyrs.[30] The Feast of the Holy Innocents, celebrated on December 28, was dedicated to this idea.

2:19-21

The return from Egypt takes place in two stages. Again the thought of divine guidance and the obedience of Joseph stands in the foreground. Matthew alludes to the reminiscence of the time of Israel in Egypt (Exod. 4:19f.). The formulation "to the land of Israel," corresponding to rabbinical expression,[31] has been chosen deliberately: Jesus the son of David and of Abraham returns into the land of the people for whom he is sent.

2:22

The more precise statement in v. 22, added by Matthew, stands in peculiar tension with this first statement: the family of Joseph, by divine command, turned not to Judea but to Nazareth in Galilee.

Matthew proves himself historically well informed: Archelaus, the son of Herod, who ascended to the rule of Judea and Samaria after his father's death in 4 C.E. had the most reprehensible reputation of all his brothers. Because of his character he had difficulties even at his ascent to government (Josephus, *War* 2.1-13). He was removed from power by Augustus after 10 years because of malfeasance. The designation βασιλεύει is popular but inexact since Archelaus was ethnarch and had never received the title of king (but cf. Mark 6:14-27). But Matthew shows himself inadequately informed when he designates Nazareth—rarely mentioned in Jewish sources[32] and evidently a village of little significance—as πόλις. With this designation he indicates not only that he does not know Palestine but perhaps also that he himself lives in a city and therefore assumes that Jesus also lived in a city.[33]

One is tempted at first to understand the two verses 22–23 as a mere geographical transition: since Jesus in the Gospel of Mark from the beginning (Mark 1:9) comes from Nazareth, somehow Matthew has to place him there.

2:23

However, the formula quotation in v. 23 shows that Nazareth has a more basic significance for Matthew. This quotation is a *crux interpretum*[34] since it cannot be identified in the Old Testament and since the meaning of Ναζωραῖος is unclear.

It is necessary to distinguish the following questions:

---

[30]Cyprian, *Ep.* 58.6 = *BKV* I/60 210; Rabanus 765: "Haec mors Innocentium praefigurat passionem omnium martyrum" (this death of the innocent prefigures the suffering of all martyrs); the littleness of the children indicates the humility of the martyrs.

[31]Str-B I 90f.

[32]Nazareth is missing in the OT and is mentioned in Jewish literature only in two songs of lamentation from the 9th century C.E. as the seat of a priestly division (texts in Dalman, *Orte* 52f.). According to the translation by Jerome of Eusebius's *Onomasticon*, Nazareth is a *viculus* (little village)(*GCS* 11/1 141,1f.), according to Epiphanius *Haer.* 29,6 = *PG* 41,401, a village.

[33]Cf. Kilpatrick,*Origins* 123f., but also introduction p. 92.

[34]Literature in Zuckschwerdt* 69 n. 19.

1. *How did Matthew understand the word* Ναζωραῖος? The answer is unambiguous: Ναζωραῖος is synonymous with Ναζαρηνός, which is used only by Mark and is taken over by Matthew.[35]

2. *What was the meaning of* Ναζωραῖος *originally?* Is the Matthean understanding correct? Is Ναζωραῖος a *nomen gentilicium* corresponding to an Aramaic נְצוֹרִי or נַצְרִי? The following three difficulties exist: (a) The vocalization Α-Ω cannot be understood either on the basis of the Hebrew נֵצֶרֶת,[36] documented not until the 9th century, or from the Syriac *naṣrath*.[37] (b) The transcription of צ in ζ and not σ is rare. (c) The feminine ending *-ath* would be eliminated in this *nomen gentilicium*. But analogies to the last two points can be found; the difficulty in the first point can be overcome by assuming a metathesis or by the transcription of a *šewâ* as ω.[38] Thus a *nomen gentilicium* Ναζωραῖος is not usual but entirely possible. This explanation is better than the derivation from the Jewish, Torah-observant sect of the Νασαραῖοι, mentioned by Epiphanius,[39] whose name would have been preserved also in the Mandean self-designation נאצוראייא.[40]

3. *What was the Old Testament passage of which Matthew was thinking?* The answer depends on whether Matthew (a) himself discovered the quotation or (b) found it in his tradition.

a. In the first case he must have thought of a specific passage of scripture. The only one possible would be Judg. 13:5,7; 16:17 where LXX A translates נָזִיר by Ναζιραῖος.[41] The vowel switch to Ναζωραῖος could have been done by Matthew himself, in an exegetical procedure which corresponds to the rabbinical 'Al-Tiqri interpretation.[42] All other texts which were suggested[43] would have to be eliminated for Matthew, because they are based on the Hebrew text and not on the LXX. Even if one could attribute the knowledge of Hebrew to Matthew, it remains inconceivable that his Greek-speaking readers would be able to comprehend this new evidence from Scripture.

---

[35]Matthew 26:71, Ναζωραῖος redactional; the four Markan occurrences of Ναζαρηνός do not have a corresponding occurrence in Matthew.

[36]The corresponding *nomen gentilicium* is נוֹצְרִי; cf. Shemoneh Esreh, Pal. rec.; *Ber* 12; *b. Abod. Zar.* 17a; and frequently in the Talmud as a designation for Jesus.

[37]The *nomen gentilicium nāṣrāyā* is a common Syriac designation for Christians.

[38]Cf. Moore,* Albright,* and Schaeder* 882f. The corresponding form of the place-name *nasorath* is documented in Christian-Palestinian Aramaic (F. Schulthess, *Lexicon Syropalaestinum* [Berlin 1903], 121b).

[39]*Haer.* 29.6.1 = *PG* 41,400. Epiphanius distinguishes these Jewish Nasareans from the OT Nazirites and the Christian Nazoreans. His information is very dubious.

[40]This view is advocated by Lidzbarski, *Liturg* XVI-XIX; Black, *Muttersprache* 197-202; K. Rudolph, *Die Mandäer* I, FRLANT 74 (1950), 112-18. The derivation of the Mandean self-designation from the Syriac designation of the Christians as *nāṣrāyā*, however, remains just as probable in my opinion as the one from the quite dubious sect of Epiphanius.

[41]The interpretation of Matt. 2:23 as to the OT Nazirites (mostly in reference to Judges 13) is ancient and is advocated, among others, by Tertullian, *Marc.* 4,8; Eusebius, *Dem. Ev.* 7.2(5) = *PG* 22,550; Jerome, *In. Isa.* 11.1 = *PL* 24,144 (on this Lyonnet*; Luther I 41 = *Tischreden* 464 and 2975; Bucer (according to Calvin I 106f.); Grotius I 56; Schweizer*; Zuckschwerdt* (the Hebrew original of Matthew read נזיר according to the Qere קָדוֹשׁ).

[42]Minor changes of vocalization of the text by the exegetes, cf. Str-B I 93f.; J. Bonsirven, *Exégèse rabbinique et exégèse paulinienne* (Paris: Beauchesne et ses fils, 1939), 120-28.

[43]Examples: Jer. 31:6 (Zolli); Isa. 40:3 (Rembry); Isa. 49:6 (Lindars).

b. If Matthew had already encountered this quotation,[44] one can think of many scripture passages because in this case the Hebrew original text may have been the basis of the quotation. Then Isa. 11:1, concerning the shoot from Jesse's stem, a passage that was explained messianically even in Judaism, clearly stands in the foreground.[45] Matthew needs the plural διὰ τῶν προφητῶν because, being unable to identify the quotation handed down to him, he preferred to use an indefinite statement. Ὅτι could, as in to 26:54, introduce an indirect quotation.[46] This second thesis, it seems to me, is on the whole to be preferred.

It was predicted in Scripture that Jesus would be called a Nazarene. What this means is not developed by the evangelist until later: Nazareth for him is located in "Galilee of the Gentiles"(4:15). The geographical statements of 2:19-23 anticipate the way of the Messiah of Israel to the Gentiles.[47] This thesis is supported from another side: exactly in the Syrian area in which the Matthean community is living, "Nazarean" is the designation for a Christian.[48] Thus in Ναζωραῖος an ecclesiological note is sounded: since Jesus comes to Nazareth in the Galilee of the Gentiles, he becomes a Ναζωραῖος, i.e., a "Christian," the teacher and Lord of the community which calls on him and which preaches to the Gentiles.

History of Influence

In comparison with the narrative of the Magi, the history of influence of our pericope is more limited. Naturally the *formation of legends* has taken hold of it and has described the events during the stay in Egypt, which is reputed variously to be a stay of between one and eight years.[49] In later times, seven years becomes usual (Strabo 76). The locations of the holy family in Egypt are given variously.[50] Legends, dealing in detail with the events on the flight itself, describe the adulation of the child Jesus by the wild beasts and the palm tree which bends low in order to present its fruit to the child.[51] The material has repeatedly been treated in literature up to the present and is therefore

---

[44]It is not unthinkable, in view of the Jewish skepticism regarding such an origin of the Messiah, as it is documented in John 1:46; 7:41f., that even before Matthew a basis for Nazareth should be sought in Scripture.

[45]This interpretation is found, e.g., in early Jerome, *Ep.* 57.7 *ad Pamm.* = *BKV* II/18 276f; today it is advocated, among others, by Gärtner* 10-18, Medebielle,* and Hengel-Merkel* (bibl. at 2:1-12) 163f.

[46] Ὅτι, therefore, does not belong to the quotation as is usually assumed in the Latin tradition of interpretation: *Quoniam Nazaraeus vocabitur* (because he will be called a Nazarean).

[47]In the interpretation of the ancient church, this was seen often, e.g., Cyril of Alexandria, in Reuss 158.

[48]In Syriac texts throughout, similarly also in Persian, Armenian, and Arabic writings. In Western texts there are only small traces: Acts 24:5; Tertullian, *Marc.* 4.8 (as a Jewish designation for Christians), cf. the Christian group of the Nazareans in the area of Beroea in Jerome, *Vir. ill.* 3 (cited in Aland, *Synopsis* on 2:23).

[49]Hippolytus on Matt. 24:22 = *GCS* I/2,201: 3 1/2 years (according to Rev. 12:14?). The statements of the infancy gospels may be found in A. Resch, *Das Kindheitsevangelium* 1897 (TU 10/5), 167. Subsequently 7 years predominates (Strabo 76).

[50]Cairo (Church Abu Sergis); Hermopolis (Gospel of Pseudo-Matthew 22-24 = Hennecke I 412f.); Matarea near Cairo, Memphis (Arabic Infancy Gospel 24,25 = Hennecke I 409).

[51]Gospel of Pseudo-Matthew 18-21 = Hennecke I 410-13 (8/9th century).

familiar.[52] The "scholarly" church literature in general has been noticeably immune to it. [53]

Summary

In distinction from the later legends, Matthew avoids any glorification of Jesus by miracles and describes briefly and soberly the preservation of the child by God, with a minimum of supernatural intervention. The child in the Matthean narrative is almost only "object," and God himself the center. The soberness of the narrative centers the attention on the theological main lines: the readers are made aware of how God, in correspondence with his plan, protects his Son and is "with him" on his journey. They sense that God will fulfill his work of salvation. They experience the failure of the malevolent plan instigated by Herod, the king of the Jews, against Jesus so that the children of Israel are annihilated by their own king. And they hear how the persecution by the Jewish kings brings the child Jesus to Nazareth so that he will be called Nazorean, just like the readers' own community in Syria. Thus the readers are presented with a foreshadowing of the coming of Israel's Messiah to the Christian community, in fulfillment of Israel's Scripture. Everything which this final text of the birth narrative indicates with almost formulaic conciseness will be unfolded in the Gospel.

---

[52]E.g., S. Lagerlöf, *Christ Legends* (Edinburgh: Floris Classics, 1984), 37-71.

[53]Eusebius, *Dem. Ev.* 6.20; 9.2 knows the tradition of the fall of the Egyptian idols, Sozomenos, *Hist. Eccl.* 5.21 = *PG* 67,1280f. the story of the palm tree of Hermopolis.

Excursus: The story of the persecuted and rescued royal child as background of Matthew 1:18–2:23

	Moses	Abraham	Revelation 12	Cypselus
	Josephus, *Ant.* 2; Ps. Philo; Targ Exod.; Exod. Rab. Mek. Exod.; Wünsche, *Lehrhallen* I 61–80; Ginzberg, *Legends* II 245–269	Str-B I 77f. Wünsche, *Lehrhallen* I 14 – 45; Ginzberg, *Legends* I 186–189		Herodotus 5.92; Binder* 150f.
1.	Dream of Pharaoh (Targ. Exod. 1:15); dream of Amram (Josephus); prophecy of Miriam (= revelation)	Star vision	Signs in the heaven	Pythian oracle
2.	Interpreted by scribes (Josephus), by the Magi Jannes and Jambres (Targ Exod.), by astrologers (Exod. Rab. 1:22)	Interpreted by sages, astrologers		
3.	Pharaoh is "alarmed"	Nimrod's anxiety		
4.	Reaction: children are killed	Reaction: Nimrod seeks to kill Terah's son	Reaction: the dragon casts the woman to earth	Reaction: the destruction of the child
5.	Rescue: Amram's dream, hiding of the small basket in stream, Pharaoh's daughter	Rescue: concealment of Abraham	Rescue: the child is transported to heaven	Rescue: the child smiles, is returned, is hidden in a chest (*kypselos*)
6.	Substitute sacrifice: slaying of the children	Substitute sacrifice: the killing of several boys	Persecution of the woman instead of the child	

	Mithridates	Romulus and Remus	Augustus	Nero
	Justin, *Epitome* (ed. O. Seel, 1935) 1.37.2	Livius 1.3–6 Binder* 78–115	Suetonius, *Aug.* 94.3; Dio Cassius 45.1f.	Suetonius, *Nero* 36
1.	Comet	Rhea conceives by Mars; dream of Rhea	Dream of the mother and father (Dio Cassius); lightning (Suetonius); dream of Atia (virgin birth?)	Comet
2.			The astrologer Nigidius Figulus interprets	The astrologer Balbilus
3.			The senate is alarmed	
4.	Persecution	Destruction of the descendants of Numitor: boys are thrown into the Tiber	Reaction: the senate decrees that no child is to be raised (Suetonius)	Reaction: the killing of prominent Romans and of children
5.	Rescue: flight to the mountains	Rescue by a female wolf	Rescue: abrogation of the decree	
6.				

	Gilgamesh	Sargon I	Cyrus	Zoroaster legend
	Claudius Ae-lianus, *Varia Historia* 12.21	J. B. Pritchard, *The Ancient Near East* (London, 1958), 85f.	Herodotus I 107–122; Justin, *Epitome* 1.4; Binder* 17–28	Zardusht-Nama 4f., 8f.; Binder* 193–195; Saintyves* 257f.
1.	(Virgin birth?)		Dream of Man-dane, dream of Astyages	Dream of the mother, Dugeda; miraculous birth
2.	The Chaldeans warn Socharos		The Magi inter-pret	The Magi and their king Du-ranserum are dis-turbed
3.			Astyages is alarmed	
4.	Reaction: the child is thrown from a tower	Reaction: set out in small container on the Euphrates	Reaction: Asty-ages would kill the child	Reaction: attempt to kill
5.	Rescue by an eagle; a peasant raises Gilgamesh	Rescue by Akki as he draws wa-ter.	Rescue: noncom-pliance, rescue by shepherds (from exposure)	Rescue: Duranse-rum's hand goes numb
6.			Substitute sacri-fice: exposure of a dead child	

	Frêdun	Krishna
	Firdausi, *Shah-Nama* 5.6; Binder* 176–179	Harivansa, *Mahabharata* 56–59; *Baghavata Purana* 10.3; Binder* 207f.
1.	Dream of the dragon king Sohak	
2.	Interpretation by the sages	Kansa is warned by Narada
3.	Impotence of Sohak	Unrest
4.	Reaction: persecution of Fredun	Reaction: killing of all descendants of Devagnis
5.	Rescue by shepherds and the cow Birmaye	Rescue: exchange of childen; divine insignia of Krishna disappear
6.		Substitute sacrifice: death of the false child

More remote parallels

Perseus (Binder* 132f.; Saintyves* 239f.)

Heracles (R. von Ranke-Graves, *Griechische Mythologie* II [Reinbek, 1960] 81-90).

Apollo (Ranke-Graves I 46f.)

Neleus/Peleus (Saintyves* 236f.; Binder* 46f.)

Agathocles (Diodorus Siculus 19.2.2-7)

Dionysos (Schwarzenau* 81-100)

Dorcetus' daughter (Saintyves* 236)

Arabian Nimrod legend (Binder* 260f.)

Seth-Horus (Plutarch, *Is. et Os.* 13)

John the Baptist (*Protev. of James* 22f.)

Ardashir (Binder* 184-189)

Shapur (Binder* 189-191)

Hormizd (Binder* 191-193)

Genghis Khan (Saintyves* 242)

Buddha legend (Saintyves* 256; Schwarzenau* 42–50)

Aghata (Binder* 196)

Candrahâsa (Binder* 199–201)

Elakamara Jataka (Binder* 203f.)

Trakan of Gilgit (Binder* 211-213)

Vanaraja (Binder* 213)

Emporer Henry III (Binder* 228f.)

Constantine legend (Binder* 246f.)

Excursus: The Formula Quotations

Literature

Cangh, J. M. van, "La Bible de Matthieu: Les citations d'accomplissement," *ETL* 6 (1975) 205-11.
Gärtner, B., "The Habakkuk Commentary (DSH) and the Gospel of Matthew," *ST* 8 (1955) 1-24.
Gundry, *Use*.
Hawkins, *Horae* 154-58.
McConnell, *Law and Prophecy* 101-41.
Rothfuchs, *Erfüllungszitate*.
Segbroeck, F. van, "Les citations d'accomplissement dans l'Évangile selon Matthieu . . .," in Didier, *Évangile* 107-30.
Soares-Prabhu, *Formula Quotations*.
Strecker, *Weg* 49-85.

    1. *Definition, Occurrence, Problems*. By the term "formula quotations" [1] is meant a series of quotations from Old Testament prophets which are introduced by a certain formulaic phrase, namely, (ἵνα) πληρωθῇ τὸ ῥηθὲν διὰ . . . τοῦ προφήτου λέγοντος. They are: Matt. 1:22f.; 2:15,17f.,23; 4:14-16; 8:17; 12:18-21; 13:35; 21:4f.; 27:9. Their distribution in the Gospel of Matthew is very unbalanced; the concentration in the prologue is striking. As far as sources are concerned, 8:17; 12:18-21; 13:35 and 21:4f. are inserted in Markan passages; the rest are found in stories from the special material of Matthew. In the majority of cases they have the character of a commentary, i.e., they are appended to the end of a narrative section and comment on it.
    The distinction of the formula quotations from the remaining Old Testament quotations is not unambiguous: 1:23f. and 2:15 are special cases because here the introductory formula mentions the κύριος who speaks through the prophet as the "author." Because of their introductory formula several other quotations are very similar to the formula quotations: Among them are 2:5 (οὕτως γὰρ γέγραπται διὰ τοῦ προφήτου),[2] 3:3 (οὗτος γάρ ἐστιν ὁ ῥηθεὶς διὰ Ἡσαίου τοῦ προφήτου), 13:14 (καὶ ἀναπληροῦται αὐτοῖς ἡ προφητεία Ἡσαίου ἡ λέγουσα) and to a certain extent 24:15 (the abomination of desolation = τὸ ῥηθὲν διὰ Δανιὴλ τοῦ προφήτου, not an explicit quotation). The formula quotations thus are not an absolutely special case within the Matthean Old Testament quotations; there are gradations to the "normal" quotations.

---

[1] Rothfuchs* uses the expression "fulfillment quotations"; he grasps what is the most important point in these quotations according to Matthew himself. It is customary, although unfortunate, to speak of "reflection quotations," in contrast to "context quotations"; on the basis of the formulaic introductory phrases, the term "formula quotations" is preferred in English.

[2] At 2:5 the problems of the wording are just as complicated as with many formula quotations; cf. the analysis on 2:1-12 no. 2.

Why did not all the other Bible quotations become "formula quotations"? Most of the time, external reasons were a factor. Their introductory phrase was already determined in the sources Mark and Q; the conservative evangelist did not want to alter radically their wording. Or/and: a quotation did not refer directly to Jesus and his story and therefore was less suitable for an introduction with πληρόω. Or/and: Matthew knew that a quotation did not come from a prophetic book. All this means that one may not consider the formula quotations as a unique theological problem; they have to be interpreted in connection with the other quotations. Consider the following problems:

a. Is the *introductory phrase* (cf. 2) redactional? What is its meaning?

b. The *wording* (cf. 3) of the quotations often (but not always) constitutes a special problem. Frequently it is a mixed text. Who is responsible for it?

c. What is the *theological significance* (cf. 4) of the formula quotations in the Gospel of Matthew?

2. The introductory phrase (=*fulfillment formula*). There is a broad consensus that the fulfillment formula comes from the evangelist. It clearly shows Matthean linguistic peculiarities.[3] Also, the variations of the introductory phrase can be explained in each case on the basis of the Matthean context.[4] In 1:23 and 2:15 the introduction of the Lord as "speaker" is connected with the Son of God being mentioned in the quotation. The plural διὰ τῶν προφητῶν (2:23) points to the fact that the evangelist was unable to identify the quotation which was received by him. It is similar with 13:35: either Matthew knew that the quotation comes from a psalm or he omitted the name of the prophet because he did not know it. In 21:14f. and 27:9, Matthew quotes Zechariah, one time without name, the other time incorrectly naming Jeremiah instead of Zechariah. One may draw the conclusion that no copy of the *Minor Prophets* was in the library of the Matthean community for consultation. Obviously, the synagogue library was no longer accessible to the evangelist. This has several results: for one, it is confirmed that the Matthean community no longer lived within the synagogue union.[5] In its library, there was a scroll of Isaiah; Isaiah plays the most important role of all prophets—in Matthew, as elsewhere in early Christianity. Of the Isaiah quotations the evangelist has compared at least some with the text of his Bible, the Septuagint.[6] No other prophetic scroll can be assumed to have been in the Matthean community library, not even a

---

[3]Cf. Soares-Prabhu, *Formula Quotations* 59-63, and introduction 3.1 (passive verb forms), 3:2 (ὅπως, τότε, πληρόω, λέγω [ἐρρέθη], διά, προφήτης, λέγων).

[4]So also the deviations at the "almost formula quotations": In 2:5, Micah 5 is quoted by the high priests and scribes; the fulfillment formula therefore is impossible. In 3:3 Matthew wants to put the quotation which is important to him in the first place; but the introductory formula, beginning with ἵνα or ὅπως, presupposes that that which is fulfilled was already reported. In 13:14, the quotation refers not to Christ but to the "non-hearing" Israel, therefore Matthew avoids (as in 2:17 and 27:9) ἵνα and substitutes the compound ἀναπληρόω for the Christologically characterized simple verb πληρόω.

[5]Cf. introduction 5.3.

[6]Among the explicit quotations from prophetical books, Isaiah usually (among others in Paul, Luke-Acts, and John) ranks before the other prophets; in Matthew he is cited frequently, as are Exodus, Deuteronomy, and Psalms, which occur the most. Among the Matthean Isaiah quotations, there are several restatements of considerable length of the LXX, i.e., 1:23; 3:13; 13:14f.; 15:8f. From no other OT author are there in Matthew so many virtually verbatim quotations. The difference from other Isaiah quotations (4:15f; 8:17; 12:18-21!) is considerable. It is a possibility (!) that Matthew had access to an Isaiah scroll.

Jeremiah scroll.[7] From this finding one may conclude with caution: If a Jewish-Christian community as interested in the Bible as was Matthew—its representative and evangelist—presumably did not possess the larger part of the Bible,[8] then the wealth of this so-called "well-to-do city church"[9] was meager. Finally, it can perhaps be concluded that the evangelist often quotes Old Testament citations from Christian sources and from memory even where he could have checked the biblical text. This is the case with almost all early Christian writers; for the so-called "rabbi" Matthew[10] it has to be underlined.

There remains the question of the point in the history of tradition where the fulfillment formula was fixed. The evangelist, who is bound to tradition, has not "invented" it. There are no direct models in the Old Testament and in Jewish texts: Πληρόω is rarely found in Old Testament texts for the fulfillment of prophecies; among the few examples, 2 Chr. 36:21 comes closest to the fulfillment formula.[11] I am not familiar with any corresponding statements from Jewish texts. It is noteworthy that the interpretations of the prophets in the Qumran community which refer to the present time are introduced by the catchword פֵּשֶׁר (interpretation)[12] which is missing from Matthew. That is probably not by accident; between these two basic words there is an essential difference.[13] פֵּשֶׁר begins with the text and interprets it; πληρόω begins with the historical event and understands it as the fulfillment of predictions. פֵּשֶׁר starts with the Bible and tries to understand it; πληρόω begins with the present and reflects on it in light of the Bible.[14] In brief, when one asks for the roots of the fulfillment statement in the history of tradition, there can be only one answer: Matthew is rooted in early Christian linguistic usage which speaks of the fulfillment of the Scripture.[15] He has found this expression, among others, in his Gospel of Mark (Mark 14:49). It is especially worth

---

[7]This probability follows, it seems to me, from the wrong attribution by Matthew of 27:9 to Jeremiah. Moreover, the finding corresponds to that in many early Jewish writings: C. Wolff, *Jeremia im Frühjudentum und Urchristentum*, TU 118 (1976), 191, ascertains that Jeremiah often was used indirectly.

[8]Did it possess a Genesis scroll? With other OT writings, there are no indications, in my opinion (this, however, does also not exclude anything). W. Bauer, *Orthodoxy and Heresy* (Philadelphia: Fortress, 1971), 156, no. 1, concludes from Eusebius, *Hist. Eccl.* 4.26.14, according to whom Melito of Sardis copied the complete series of OT books in Palestine, that Melito did not find an entire OT elsewhere (E.Sch.).

[9]Kilpatrick, *Origins* 124.

[10]V. Dobschütz, *ZNW* 27 (1928) 338. Cf. introduction 5.7.

[11]LXX: τοῦ πληρωθῆναι λόγον κυρίου διὰ στόματος Ἰερεμίου. The passage is all the more noteworthy because it is followed by an important OT parallel to Matt. 28:15-20, cf. on this the analysis of Matt. 28:15-20 and Frankemölle, *Jahwebund* 393. Nevertheless, the missing στόμα and the formulation ῥηθέν (instead of ῥῆμα) shows, in my opinion, that Matthew did not make a deliberate literary reference to 2 Chr. 36:21. Much further removed are 1 Kings 2:27; 8:15,24; 2 Chr. 6:4,15; 36:22; Ezra 1:1.

[12]H. J. Klauck, *Allegorie und Allegorese in synoptischen Gleichnistexten*, NTA NF 13 (1978), 57-91, puts the פֵּשֶׁר interpretation of Qumran's exegesis of the prophets in the larger context of Judaism: the line goes from the dream interpretation of the narrative (interpret = פָּתַר) by way of Daniel and the Qumran writings up to the "*pitra* exegesis" among the Palestinian Amoraim (cf. on this Bacher, *Terminologie* II 178-80).

[13]Klauck loc. cit. 82f. points to the fact that the Greek corresponding term for פֵּשֶׁר probably is ἐπίλυσις which is missing in Matthew, cf. 2 Pet. 1:20.

[14]Cf. Gärtner* 6-16.

[15]Mark, Luke-Acts, John, James, but not Paul.

noting that in the Gospel of John, which could also come from Syria, prolific fulfillment statements are found.[16]

The other parts of the fulfillment formula are theologically less central. There are analogies in rabbinical usage for designating the word of Scripture as τὸ ῥηθέν.[17] The formulation that God speaks "through" the prophet is perhaps exemplified in early Christianity.[18] Matthew adopts it with a certain consistency since it is important to him that God is the true "author" of the Scriptures; the prophet, on the other hand, is only God's tool. This is valid for all scripture passages, not only for those where he explicitly calls attention to it through κύριος (1:23; 2:15: cf. 15:4; 19:5; 22:31).

The evangelist himself, therefore, has created the fulfillment formula. He has distinguished by it certain Old Testament quotations, primarily those for which this was possible for external reasons. These emphases are frequent in the prologue. Before we seek their meaning, we have to pursue the question of the origin of the quotations.

3. *Wording and Origin of the Quotations.* The text form of most of the formula quotations is striking. Some[19] are closer to the Masoretic text than to the LXX; some show contacts with other Greek translations and targums as well.[20] There seems to be a considerable difference with those taken over from Mark and—few—from Q.[21] There Matthew transfers the text of his sources without change or he alters it only slightly, usually to resemble the LXX which is probably familiar to him from worship. There are two hypotheses to explain this:

a. According to one hypothesis, the fact that most formula quotations have a text strongly at variance with the LXX requires the conclusion that their wording is due not to the evangelist but to a source. Different sources were proposed: an Aramaic targum of Mark,[22] a Christian collection of testimonies,[23] or possibly an oral tradition.[24]

b. According to the other hypothesis, the evangelist himself is responsible for the mixed text. P. Kahle's hypothesis—that at the time of the New Testament there was not yet a fixed LXX text but rather a number of recensions and variants—was often

---

[16]Rothfuchs* 151-177. However, there are no direct contacts.

[17]Bacher, *Terminologie* 16: נֶאֱמַר "is the most frequent form of quotation of Biblical passages."

[18]Cf. Rom. 1:2; Luke 18:31; Acts 2:16 (τὸ εἰρημένον διὰ τοῦ προφήτου Ἰωήλ); 28:15. This usage could be rooted in Greek-speaking Judaism, cf. Sir. Prol. 1; Philo, *Decal.* 175. The formulation "through the hand" (בְּיַד) "of the prophets" (Zech. 7:7; Jer. 37:2; CDC 3:21; 4:13; Rabbinic sources in Bacher, *Terminologie* I 68; II 74) is Old Testament or rabbinic. This point shows that Matthew is not rooted directly in Hebrew exegetical terminology and is not a converted Jewish rabbi.

[19]The helpful table in Hawkins, *Horae* 52, shows how more or less close the individual formula quotations are to the LXX.

[20]The best survey of the text forms is found in Stendahl, *School* 39-142.

[21]This is contested by Gundry, *Use* 9-150, followed by van Cangh*. For Gundry only the explicit quotations which Matthew took over from Mark follow the LXX, but no other quotations do. Therefore, the quotations taken from Mark are the "exceptions" which need explanation. I cannot follow him here: one reason for Gundry's results lies in the fact that he includes all allusions to the OT, also the many cases where the character of the allusion makes a reflection on the text form illusory. On this question, those quotations (apart from the formula quotations) which Matthew, according to most exegetes, has redactionally interpolated into the text of Mark or Q are of special importance: 4:4b; 5:38,43; 9:13 = 12:7; 13:14f.; 21:16. They all follow the LXX.

[22]Bacon, *Studies* 475. Cf. also Baumstark's hypothesis below, n. 25.

[23]Following earlier English-language research, this is advocated especially by Strecker, *Weg*, esp. 49f., 82-84.

[24]Kilpatrick, *Origins* 56-58.

indirectly fruitful.[25] The question arises whether there were also Greek targums. Since this is completely improvable (and improbable!), it is assumed that Matthew himself is responsible for the text form of the quotations. Matthew then would have produced for his own purposes a sort of targum on the Old Testament text; he would be "his own targumist."[26] Research oriented in redaction criticism asserts that Matthew has edited redactionally the wording of the quotations available to him in view of his own intentions.[27] Stendahl, on the other hand, assumes that a "school" stands behind the Gospel of Matthew, the procedure of which was similar to that of the author of the exegesis of the prophets at Qumran, thus, e.g., of 1QpHab. Starting with the basic conviction that the fulfillment of the predictions will take place in their own time, Matthew and the author of the Habakkuk commentary, on the basis of several recensions of the biblical text, carefully produced their own and interpreted it for their own time. The school of Matthew would have exercised פֶּשֶׁר exegesis in the style of Qumran.[28]

In my opinion, one has to start with the first hypothesis. The Old Testament quotations from Mark and Q show that the evangelist Matthew changes very little in them. Thus, he quotes the Bible according to Mark or Q. At most, a slight assimilation to the LXX wording can sometimes be observed.[29] All this does not fit the picture of a scribe who would deliberately have produced *only* in his formula quotations a new form of the text which was familiar to him in different versions. The procedure of Matthew with the quotations from Mark and Q, in my opinion, speaks for the view that the formula quotations come from pre-Matthean Christian tradition.

Contrarily, it seems to me that the hypothesis of a testimony book is of little help. One cannot really imagine a collection of proof passages which would contain our formula quotations. What else should quotations like Hos. 11:1 (= 2:15), Jer. 31:15 (= 2:18), Zech. 9:9 (= 21:5) or 11:13 (= 27:9) prove than precisely the stories in which they now appear? The great majority of the formula quotations, especially in the realm of the special material, can, in my opinion, have been handed down only in connection with those narratives in which they are found today. But since the evangelist is not responsible for their wording, they ostensibly have already been handed down in the oral tradition

---

[25]P. Kahle, *The Kairo Geniza*, 1947 (Schweich Lectures, 1941). Kahle's assumption is that the terms which occur in the NT are exact quotations of "LXX" versions (238, cf. 250f.). A. Baumstark, "Die Zitate des Matthäus-Evangeliums aus dem Zwölfprophetenbuch," *Bib* 37 (1956) 296-313, supposes that Matthew took his quotations from a lost targum.

[26]Gundry, *Use* 172; similarly Rothfuchs, *Erfüllungszitate* 89,107; Soares-Prabhu, *Formula Quotations* 84-106. In my opinion, this thesis fails as a total explanation already because of the very small share of the redaction which is demonstrable in the fulfillment quotations.

[27]McConnell, *Law and Prophecy* 136, and Rothfuchs, *Erfüllungszitate* 57-89, count on intensive redactional activity; cf. also Segbroeck* 129. Our own detailed analysis led, as with Soares-Prabhu, *Formula Quotations*, e.g., 189, to the conclusion that redactional activity in the text of the formula quotations is probably throughout less than Rothfuchs assumes.

[28]Stendahl, *School*, especially 183-206. The relationship of the "school" to the author of the Gospel of Matthew (who belonged to it?) did not thereby become fully clear to me. The discussion of the exegesis of the prophets in 1QpHab has shown that one has to count on the occurrence of alterations of the biblical text, occasionally conditioned by the interpretation, both in Qumran and with the rabbis. However, they are relatively rare, and it hardly occurs that a new text recension is produced from several ones, as Stendahl seemed to suggest when he wrote his book. Cf. on this Gärtner* 2-6.

[29]Stendahl, *School* 148, asserts on the whole, but not with all individual texts, "a slight, but obvious tendency to greater fidelity to the LXX." Soares-Prabhu, *Formula Quotations* 77-84,105f. disagrees with the view that the LXX is the Bible of Matthew and considers the slight assimilations to it as pre-redactional. But cf. the passages in n. 21.

along with "their" stories.[30] Therefore, such special materials have been meditated on in scribal circles before Matthew on the basis of the Bible.[31] The formula quotations which stand in Markan contexts are sometimes (e.g., at 21:5) closely related to their context, sometimes (e.g., at 4:15f. and 12:18-21) loosely appended to it. In both cases, the Gospel of Mark was presumably reflected on and commented on by Jewish-Christian scribes before Matthew.[32]

It seems to me that one should not assume that the contribution of the evangelist Matthew to the wording of the formula quotations is higher than to the wording of the remaining quotations. A large number of recensions out of which he could have made his own was not available to him. Redactional intrusions in the wording of all (!) Old Testament quotations are relatively few.

The result of this investigation into the wording of the quotations for the understanding of the theology of Matthew is minimal, in my opinion. Nevertheless, it yields an insight into the milieu of Christian scribes in the Matthean community. Once again we see the evangelist as a conservative tradent and interpreter who is obligated to the tradition. He treated the wording of the quotations available to him with the same care as he treated the text of the Gospel of Mark or of Q..

4. *The theological problems of the formula quotations.* Why has Matthew distinguished by the fulfillment formula a series of quotations which were for the most part handed down to him? According to Strecker, Matthew was primarily concerned with demonstrating "the historical biographical facticity"[33] of the Gospel tradition with the aid of the formula quotations. Thus the interest of the evangelist would be a biographical, even a "historical understanding of the life of Jesus."[34] According to him, it is significant how often details of the life of Jesus are verified by a formula quotation, e.g., the stations of the journey of the child Jesus (2:6,15,18,23; 4:15f.), the riding on two mounts (21:5), or the purchase price of 30 pieces of silver (27:9). For other authors the apologetical motive is decisive: the formula quotations are a contribution to the Christian "vindication" over against Judaism.[35] Other authors refuse to see a unified significance behind the formula quotations. For E. Schweizer, e.g., the quotations of the prologue might be concerned with underscoring the itinerant life of Jesus as a "comforting and strengthening example for all itinerant prophets,"[36] while the quotations in the central part of the Gospel represent Jesus as the Messiah of word and deed, i.e., as the "prophetic revealer of the mysteries of God (13:13-16 and 35) and as the charismatic

---

[30] I am pleased to note my agreement with C. Wolff, (above, n. 7) 158.

[31] This does not mean that the formula quotations of the special materials are equally original as the narratives belonging to them or the nucleus from which the stories developed. In the case of 2:15,18, it seems to me it is still apparent that the quotations were added before Matthew, but secondarily to "their" narratives. This may be different in the case of 2:6; 27:9.

[32] Does perhaps the difference between Matt. 12:5f. (a traditional argument from the OT stands *before* the redactional addition 12:7) and 8:17; 12:18-21 (the traditional quotation is appended by Matthew himself with the redactional fulfillment formula) show that these "commentaries" (in distinction from 12:5) had not yet become a part of the text of Mark lying before Matthew?

[33] Strecker, *Weg* 85.

[34] Ibid. 72.

[35] This view is found already in the classical work of E. Massebieau, *Examen des citations de l'Ancien Testament dans l'Évangile selon saint Matthieu* (Paris, 1885); today, e.g., in B. Lindars, *New Testament Apologetic* (London 1961).

[36] Schweizer, *Kirche* 147.

healer (8:17 and 12:17-21)."[37]

Two considerations suggest themselves:

a. According to all of our foregoing considerations, Matthew is not concerned with distinguishing certain Old Testament quotations from others by the fulfillment formula and to make them into a special kind of quotations. Rather, he places the fulfillment formula first where it does not require radical altering of his source and where it fits the content of the quotation. The formula is inserted by him not to emphasize a special quality in certain quotations but in order to make clear with their use something which *mutatis mutandis* is important for all his Old Testament references. The formula quotations are notably frequent in the prologue,[38] because here the evangelist introduces those viewpoints and accents which are important for the whole Gospel and which the reader must keep in mind while perusing the entire Gospel. The formula quotations which are scattered in the rest of the Gospel are then reminders.

b. The second deliberation converges with the first. In my opinion, the formula quotations have no unique content but point to basic themes of the Matthean understanding of the Christ. The "way" of Jesus in Matt. 1:18–4:16 is told by Matthew not for the sake of historical facticity but because in it the progress of the gospel from Israel to the Gentiles is indicated proleptically. In many quotations, basic statements of Matthean Christology stand in the foreground, e.g., in 1:23 (Immanuel), 2:15 (Son), 8:17 (Jesus' healing as healing by the Messiah of Israel), 12:18-21 (the silent servant of God as hope for the Gentiles) and 21:5 (the powerless king). It is important for several quotations (2:5; 4:15f.; 12:18-21, cf. 2:15 [Egypt], 18 [mourning of the ancestral mother of Israel], 23 [Nazoreans as a designation for the Christians]; 13:14f. [hardening of Israel]; 21:16 [children and babes]) that Jesus as the Messiah of Israel brings salvation for the Gentiles. The historical viewpoint plays a role, not in the sense that the life of Jesus as past history is to be described with great precision and reliability,[39] but in the sense that the life of Jesus corresponds from the beginning to the plan of God to which Jesus is completely obedient (21:5; cf. 13:35; 21:9; of the remaining quotations, e.g., 2:5; 3:3; 4:4,6,8,10). The formula quotations thus lift out basic themes of Matthean theology. The center of the fulfillment formula with which Matthew underlines them is the word πληρόω. It is a "Christological" word. Aside from the history of Jesus there is no "fulfillment" of Scripture in the entire New Testament.[40] For the evangelist, πληρόω is important as well outside of our quotations: As Jesus has "fulfilled" by his life the prophetic predictions, so Matthew has also emphasized comprehensively and *programmatically*, particularly through Jesus' complete obedience, the demands of law and prophets through Jesus.

This programmatic emphasis on the fulfillment of law and prophets by Jesus became necessary, in my opinion, in the situation after the break of the Christian community with Israel. The Jewish-Christian Matthew, for whose community the separation from Israel was intensely traumatic, emphasizes the claim of the community to the Bible.[41] But also in the Lukan writings and in the

---

[37]Ibid. 146.

[38]Five (with 2:6 and 3:3, seven) formula quotations in the prologue.

[39]Example: in the formula quotations of 2:15 and 18 the primary concern cannot be the securing of the stations of the way of Jesus: Hos. 11:1 does not prove the flight *into* Egypt. And Jesus never was in Rama, where the ancestress Rachel mourns.

[40]The only exception is James 2:23. Luke therefore uses πίμπλημι in 21:22.

[41]Frankemölle, *Jahwebund* 389, formulates correctly: "The formula quotations [show themselves] as an unfolding of the θέλημα τοῦ πατροῦ under the aspect of theology of history."

Gospel of John[42] a similar programmatic is found in the same situation. Paul—in the situation before the definitive separation between Israel and the body of Christ—could demonstrate *exemplarily* with individual texts how the Bible testified to faith in Christ; he knew with certainty that the same Bible testified also that one "who practices the righteousness which is based on the law shall live by it" (Rom. 10:5 = Lev. 18:5). For Matthew and other Christian authors who wrote after the break between church and Israel this statement was no longer a possibility. They had to claim the *entire* Old Testament programmatically. Frankemölle has formulated this pointedly: "The common cloth with Israel has been torn asunder; now it is a struggle for the inheritance."[43] In the situation in which Israel and the Christian community are in confrontation as two definitively separated hostile brothers, each brother *was determined to* claim the whole heritage of the fathers explicitly and fundamentally for himself.

Our excursus demands two *concluding remarks,* which tend to lead the reader of this commentary into a dilemma:

1. There is an *indirect history of influence* of the Matthean and the early Christian programmatic claim to the Old Testament, which came to be fateful. The history of anti-Jewish polemic in Christian theology demonstrates that Old Testament words—noticeably of the prophets—during the struggle of the church against the Jews were used as cudgels—much more so than New Testament words. Particularly coarse anti-Jewish writings as, e.g., the sermons opposing the Jews by John Chrysostom and the late anti-Jewish writings of Luther, expressly demonstrate this. *The Christian programmatic and exclusive claim to the Old Testament which we find, e.g., in Matthew has laid the foundation for this.* To this extent, there is an indirect history of influence of the Matthean formula quotations which supersedes their direct influence. The consequences it entailed should have become clear in the second half of the 20th century.

2. The formula quotations of the Gospel of Matthew are not completely new in the history of early Christian theology. They are only the expression, intensified and made foundational, of a conviction which all of early Christianity shares: the Christ event is the fulfillment of Scripture. For Matthew also, Christological statements are the central concern of the Old Testament quotations. Beyond that, his Christology—still more emphatically than with his predecessors—is a reflection on the person and history of Jesus which is conditioned by the Old Testament. It is true of Matthew as of early Christianity as a whole: Only the Old Testament makes it possible that the risen Jesus can be proclaimed and understood. *To that extent it is not only understandable but even necessary that Matthew in conflict with Israel programmatically makes a claim to the Bible.* The Christian faith cannot easily forgo this dimension—which has become so fateful in its influence.

These two deliberations must for the present stand side by side. They are to prepare for the interpretation of the individual passages, especially of the

---

[42]Luke knows πληρόω in this sense too (4 times) but he emphasizes the foundational character of his claim to the Scriptures by formulations with πᾶς (all scriptures, etc.): 18:31; 21:22; 24:44; Acts 13:29; 24:14. In John, formulations with πληρόω are very frequent (6 times).

[43]*Jahwebund* 306.

central Israel sections, chaps. 21-24 and 27, and they call attention to the problem with which this material confronts us.

B. THE BEGINNING OF THE MINISTRY OF JESUS (3:1–4:22)

The identically formulated proclamation of the Baptist and of Jesus ("Repent, for the kingdom of heaven is at hand" 3:2; 4:17) is an inclusion which states the main theme of the section. The two "inner" pericopes of the section, 3:13-17 and 4:1-11, have again a common theme, Jesus' sonship with God. The "frame pericopes" 3:1-12 and 4:12-17 are also related to each other: they both contain a scripture quotation with a geographical statement. The notice on the great achievement of the Baptist (3:5) points ahead to the corresponding notice about the great achievement of Jesus in the next section, 4:23-25. We have here an indication of the fact that Matthew does not separate the main sections clearly from each other but connects them by "bracketing pericopes." Finally, 4:18-22 appears as a transitional passage, related to what precedes and to what follows. The fact that the length of 4:12-22 corresponds almost exactly to that of 4:1-11 might indicate that Matthew regarded the whole section 4:12-22 as part of the prologue.

1. JOHN THE BAPTIST (3:1-17)

1.1. The Baptist's Call to Israel to Repent (3:1-12)

Literature

Andersen, F. J., "The Diet of John the Baptist," *AbrN* 3 (1961/62) 60-74.
Brock, S., "The Baptist's Diet in Syrian Sources," *OrChr* 54 (1970) 113-24.
Laufen, *Doppelüberlieferungen* 93-125.
Marconcini, B., "Tradizione e redazione in Mt 3,1-12,"*RivB* 19 (1971) 165-86.
Meier, J., "John the Baptist in Matthew's Gospel," *JBL* 99 (1980) 383-405.
Vielhauer, P., "Tracht und Speise Johannes des Täufers," in idem, *Aufsätze zum Neuen Testament*, TBl 31, pp. 47-54 (1965).

Text

1 But in those days John the Baptist comes and preaches in the wilderness of Judea
2 and says: "Repent, for the reign of heaven has come near."
3 For he is the one of whom it was said by the prophet Isaiah:
"Voice of one who calls in the wilderness:
Prepare the way of the Lord.
Make his paths straight."
4 But he, John, had his clothing of camel's hair and a girdle around his waist; his nourishment consisted of locusts and wild honey.

5 At that time, Jerusalem went out to him and all of Judea and the entire surrounding region of the Jordan
6 and had themselves baptized by him in the Jordan river as they confessed their sins.
7 But when he saw that many Pharisees and Sadducees came to his baptism, he said to them,
"Brood of vipers,
who has warned you to flee the coming wrath?
8 Therefore bring fruit which corresponds to repentance.
9 And do not think you could say to yourselves,
'We have Abraham as father!'
For I say to you
that God can raise up children for Abraham from these stones.
10 But now the axe is laid to the root of the trees;
now every tree which does not bring useful fruit is cut down and thrown into the fire!
11 I baptize you with water for repentance;
the one who comes after me is stronger than I;
I am not sufficient to carry his shoes for him;
he will baptize you with Holy Spirit and fire.
12 In his hand is the winnowing fork,
and he will clean his threshing floor;
and he will gather his wheat into the granary,
but he will burn the chaff with unquenchable fire!"

Analysis

The evangelist used as a source Mark 1:2-8 and a piece of the Sayings Source which presumably consisted of a short report of the appearance of the Baptist with a scripture quotation from Isa. 40:3,[1] the preaching of repentance of the Baptist (v. 7-10), the announcement of the stronger one and his baptism by fire (v. 11) and the judgment word of the winnowing fork (v. 12). Matthew has combined these two reports. In distinction from Luke, who lets the preaching of repentance immediately follow the Isaiah quotation, Matthew alters the order of the Markan report and thus gains a compelling arrangement.

After the description of the appearance of the Baptist come those items which are most important for Matthew, namely, his announcement of the reign of God (v. 2) and the scripture quotation (v. 3). The more precise circumstances of his appearance (v. 4) and the reaction of the Jewish population (vv. 5f.) are described only subsequently. The preaching of repentance to the Pharisees and Sadducees follows this admirably. The whole second part of the text, vv. 7b-12, is a continuous sermon of the Baptist. Since Matthew already began with the preaching of the Baptist (v. 2), it is clear that the emphasis lies here. The main catchword of this sermon of the Baptist is πῦρ, the fire of judgment (vv. 10,11,12). In addition, the stem μετανο- is striking (v. 2 = the first word of the Baptist!; v. 11). The Baptist's sermon begins with an invective, then takes up again μὴ δόξητε λέγειν ἐν ἑαυτοῖς which is, in the threatening word of the Baptist, in sharp contrast to λέγω γὰρ ὑμῖν (v. 8a,c). This culminates in a series of brief statements about the judgment of the stronger one (vv.11b-12). Although the pericope takes a different bearing from that in the sources, the interventions of the evangelist are only

[1]Πᾶσα ἡ περίχωρος τοῦ Ἰορδάνου v.5 //Luke 3:5 seems to belong to the report of the Sayings Source about the Baptist. Whether the Isaiah quotation comes from Q must remain an open question.

minimal: with a few changes he has created a compelling text.[2]

Explanation

Matthew describes the appearance of John only in one brief scene.

3:1, 5

Παραγίνεται simultaneously points back to 2:1 and forward to v. 13, where the appearance of Jesus is described in the same phrase. The time statement "in those days" also indicates that the evangelist does not see a break between the infancy narratives and the appearance of the Baptist, which is to be thought of as coming about a generation later, but that he wishes to connect the two events. In harmony with this thinking, Matthew is concerned in this main section with creating a prelude to the basic theological themes of the Gospel. Presumably, "in those days" anticipates the time statement of Mark 1:9; this demonstrates how closely Matthew sees the relationship of John and Jesus.[3] The Baptist[4] appears in the wilderness of Judah.[5] With this, the evangelist gives a theological hint, not just a historical fact: The Baptist is sent to Israel;[6] all Jerusalem, Judea, and the area of the Jordan flock to him in the wilderness.[7]

3:2

Verse 2 makes the Matthean concern obvious: It is primarily a matter of the prophet John and not so much of the Baptist;[8] therefore Matthew puts John's proclamation at the beginning. But John is a prophet who is fundamentally different from his predecessors: his proclamation is that of the nearness of the

---

[2]Cf. introduction 3.2. Clearly redactional are in v. 1 δέ, βαπτιστής; in v. 3 γάρ, ῥηθείς διά as in the introductory phrase to the formula quotations; in v. 4 τροφή; in v. 5 τότε; in v. 7 ἰδών δέ, Φαρισαῖοι καὶ Σαδδουκαῖοι.

[3]The phrase must not be theologically overextended, as, e.g., in Strecker, *Weg* 91 ("time of revelation"); Kretzer, *Herrschaft* 66 ("time of judgment"); Kingsbury, *Matthew* 28-31 ("period of the 'last times,' " 31).

[4]Βαπτιστής is a new word which did not exist in Greek before, but which is used of the Baptist also by Josephus, *Ant.* 18.116.

[5]This localization is not completely correct: the place of baptism at the Jordan River is not located in the wilderness of Judah, as it must be understood on the basis of the OT (Ps. 63:1, cf. Judg. 1:16 LXX B), since the Jordan nowhere touches the tribal area of Judah. Either Matthew does not know the geography of Palestine exactly (cf. on 19:1 and Strecker, *Weg* 29, n. 4), or he is thinking of the territory of the procuraturship of Judea of that time, to which the lower part of the Jordan River belonged.

[6]The reader remembers 2:1,5f.

[7]The church interpretation often saw—incorrectly—in the geographical statement "wilderness of Judea" directly an anti-Jewish point; Hippolytus, *Dem. Christ. Antichr.* 45 = *PG* 10,763 (an indication of the salvation of the Gentiles who live in the "wilderness of the world'); Eusebius, *Dem. Ev.* 9.5 = *PG* 22,674 (not in Jerusalem; indication of the elimination of the Jewish law and cult); Bengel 28 ("non in templo aut in synagogis" [not in the temple or in synagogues]). Also the widespread "ascetic" interpretation of the wilderness (e.g., Gregory the Great 7 = 1100 [desertedness, solitude]; Strabo 79 [wilderness = renunciation of the enticements of the world]) does not fit the Matthean intention.

[8]Lohmeyer 45.

kingdom of heaven. It corresponds literally to that of Jesus (Matt. 4:17) and is later extended by the disciples, i.e., by the church (10:7). John and Jesus thus belong together.[9] With them the Christian proclamation begins. The coming kingdom of heaven determines the action already at this point. Matthew therefore has put the call to repentance ahead and thus he stresses for the first time the orientation of life to the coming kingdom—which is so important to him.[10]

βασιλεία τῶν οὐρανῶν

The expression βασιλεία τῶν οὐρανῶν is Matthean special material. The evangelist uses βασιλεία τοῦ θεοῦ only rarely and for clearly recognizable reasons. The Matthean usage corresponds to that of the synagogue, which can be found since Yohanan ben Zakkai alongside "reign of God."[11] In this regard, the articular Aramaic expression (מַלְכוּתָא דִשְׁמַיָּא). is closer to the Greek βασιλεία τῶν οὐρανῶν than the anarthrous Hebrew (מַלְכוּת שָׁמַיִם). Also in terms of content the Matthean use of "reign of heaven" with its strongly ethical accent fits admirably to the rabbinical use: just as the rabbis admonish people to carry already now the yoke of the reign of God,[12] it is decisive for Matthew to live in the present in agreement with the βασιλεία τῶν οὐρανῶν so that the community will be granted at the end the entrance into the reign of heaven. The meaning of the two expressions "reign of God" and "reign of heaven" is the same. Since no reason for a change of τοῦ θεοῦ into τῶν οὐρανῶν is recognizable from the Matthean theology, the simplest assumption is that the usage of his community has guided the evangelist. His Jewish-Christian background becomes the clearer if one recognizes that relatively few in the ancient church share this special usage of the main Gospel of the church.[13]

3:3
The coming of the Baptist is predicted in the Old Testament—so Matthew states the matter with an introductory formula, which reminds the reader of that of the formula quotations and additionally brings the Baptist to the side of Jesus, to whom all the formula quotations apply. The catchword "wilderness" is specifically stressed by the context. It is to be understood in the sense of the "wilderness of Judea" of v. 1 as a reference to the sending of the Baptist to Israel.

3:4
The description of the nourishment and clothing of the Baptist was taken by

---

[9]This corresponds to the tendency of Mark, who assimilates the Baptist to Jesus by the term κηρύσσω; cf. Gnilka, *Markusevangelium* I on Mark 1:4.

[10]Cf. U. Luz, βασιλεία, *EWNT* I 488, on the ethical aspect of the βασιλεία in Matthew. Μετάνοια is added by the evangelist also in v. 11.

[11]P.Qid 1,59d,29 = Str-B I 176 seems to be the earliest documentation; the situation is similar with "Father in heaven," cf. on 6:9-14.

[12]Cf. the examples in Str-B I, especially 176-78.

[13]Only in the Syrian area, in the Apostolic Constitutions and in the Pseudo-Clementines, does βασιλεία τῶν οὐρανῶν appear alongside βασιλεία τοῦ θεοῦ somewhat frequently (perhaps in the proportion of 1:2).

Matthew almost unchanged from Mark. Since he explicitly identifies John with Elijah (11:14; 17:12), he probably understood the leather girdle in the first place as an allusion to the clothing of Elijah (2 Kings 1:8).[14] Naturally the verse describes John also as ascetic.[15] Even if nothing else was originally thought of but the food and clothing of Bedouins,[16] the description of John must have been seen as ascetic in the Syrian city where Matthew was living. John, in stark contrast to Jesus, is an ascetic (11:18)—and thereby a unique figure. The description hardly has a parenetic undertone.

History of Influence

Nevertheless, the passage was *interpreted parenetically* in the explanation of the church and thereby was drawn into the maelstrom of church disputes. A "moderately ascetic" parenetic interpretation came to predominate, as John Chrysostom, for example, represents it: "We want to imitate him, strip ourselves of excess and drunkenness and live simply and modestly."[17] The Reformers also subscribed to this type of interpretation.[18] Although monasticism in its food and clothing was not influenced by John and although monasticism did not base poverty and celibacy on the practice of John, the Reformers nevertheless felt compelled to avert a "monkish" interpretation of the ascetic John.[19] The Catholics, on the other hand, polemicize against this interpretation.[20]

3:5–6

Like Mark, so Matthew also emphasizes the success of the Baptist. Verse 5

---

[14]The allusion would be even clearer if the short text which D *it* represents for Mark 1:5 would be original as a Western noninterpolation, and Matthew would have supplemented the text according to 2 Kings 1:8 LXX.

[15]In order to make John a vegetarian, the Gospel of the Ebionites reads ἐγκρίδες (honey cakes) instead of ἀκρίδες. The Diatessaron of Tatian read "milk and mountain honey" (Brock 115). Ishodad 23f., Dionysius bar Salibi 108 and Theophylact 173 list a whole series of substitutions for locusts: a plant melagron, tree fruits (ἀκρόδρυα), forest fruits; the honey obviously (and perhaps rightfully!) cf. Diodorus Siculus 19.94.10; Pliny *Hist. Nat.* 11.15.41; Josephus, *War* 4.468) was plant honey. Particularly the Syrian interpreters furnish a rich palette of "vegetarian" interpretations (cf. Brock). It is striking that "the" interpreter (Theodore of Mopsuestia) emphasizes explicitly that locusts have wings and that the honey is natural (in Ishodad of Merv 24). Our "St. John's bread tree" (carob tree) is still even today reminiscent of the vegetarian interpretations (Andersen 64f.). The clothing of John was interpreted ascetically: *Pili cameli* (camel's hairs) are coarse (as compared with *lana* [wool]), "ut ipsa asperitas ad virtutem patientiae animum exerceret" (in order that the roughness itself should train the spirit for the virtue of patience)(*Opus imperfectum* 3 = 648); John wears a fur girdle in distinction from a wool girdle as "mortificationis σύμβολον" (symbol of mortification) (Jerome on 3:14). Since Tertullian, *Monog* 8, it is said explicitly that the Baptist is unmarried. The connections between these interpretations and the ascetic and monastic movements are as clear as day.

[16]Thus recently Vielhauer* 53.

[17]John Chrysostom 10.5 = 173. Similarly, e.g., Rabanus 767f. (to live simply and modestly).

[18]E.g., Calvin I 118; John is a mountain resident, satisfied with countrylike, indigenous food.

[19]Calvin, op.cit.; Brenz 144: One ought not to wear clothes like John, "nec ut significaretur Christianismum debere esse Monachismum et secessionem hominum a politica seu civili vita" (and not that Christianity be interpreted as if it should be monasticism and separation of people from the political or civil life).

[20]Maldonat 64f.; further examples in Knabenbauer I 174.

gives the reader an important hint: in distinction from the identification of all Jerusalem with the evil Herod (2:3) here a differentiation is made between the people who come to John in droves, confess their sins, and are baptized, on the one hand, and the hardened leaders of the people, the Pharisees and Sadducees (v. 7), on the other. The meaning of this differentiation remains in the dark for now;[21] but the context and the formulation make it clear that it is Jews who repent.

According to v. 6, the confession of sins is tied to the *baptism of John*. But in Matthew the expression of John's baptism as "baptism . . . for the forgiveness of sins" (Mark 1:4) is missing. This designation has fallen victim to the new formulation of the proclamation of the Baptist in v. 2. The question is whether Matthew wants to distinguish between the baptism of John as a mere sign of repentance and Christian baptism, which grants forgiveness of sins. The ancient church has attributed to the baptism of John only rarely the character of an effective baptism of forgiveness.[22] The opposite opinion finally prevailed.[23] Modern exegesis has Matthew in general make a clear distinction between the baptism of John and Christian baptism.[24] Since the mention of the confession of sins at the baptism of John in v. 6 does suggest that forgiveness is also conveyed by this baptism and since Matthew nowhere else connects the forgiveness of sins explicitly with Christian baptism, it appears to me that this distinction is not justified.

3:7–10

With v. 7 Matthew picks up the Q text which he follows almost exclusively to v. 12. Through this, the preaching of judgment by the Baptist is in the foreground. The proclamation of the reign of heaven by the Baptist is thus understood first of all as a preaching of judgment.

The preaching of judgment by the Baptist is taken by Matthew almost literally from Q. It is a prophetic invective and threat (vv. 8f., 10) which perhaps goes back to John the Baptist himself and whose scope is the radical questioning of the visible people of God, Israel (cf. Rom. 9:6-13!). The Sayings Source probably has handed down this piece as a part of its own preaching of judgment to Israel.

Matthew can pass down this preaching of judgment as the first piece of John's proclamation because he himself is vitally concerned about the proclamation of judgment. The criterion in the judgment is human deeds (cf. 7:21-23; 12:50). Therefore the key word "fruit" plays a great role in his Gospel (cf. 7:16-20; 12:33; 21:43). As for Q, so also for Matthew the preaching of the Baptist is not a past matter but becomes his own preaching of judgment; the evangelist has Jesus take up in his vituperation against the Pharisees again the key word "brood of vipers" (12:34; 23:33).

---

[21]Cf. on 9:27-34; 12:23f.).

[22]Cyril of Jerusalem, *Cat. Myst.* 3.7 = *PG* 33,437; further examples in Knabenbauer I 177.

[23]Especially Tertullian, *Bapt.* 10 (the baptism of John is divine only in its commission, not in its effect), but also Greek fathers as, e.g., Cyril of Alexandria = Reuss 159; John Chrysostom 10.1 = 164, etc. The question is decided negatively also by Thomas (*Summa Theologica* III q. 38 art. 3); the Council of Trent anathematizes the opinion that the baptism of John and the baptism of Christ have the same power (Denzinger no. 857).

[24]Trilling, *Israel* 18; Kilpatrick, *Origins* 107 ("merely a preacher of repentance"); H. Thyen, *Studien zur Sündenvergebung*, FRLANT 96 (1970) 139f.

The distinction between Matthew and Q lies merely with the addressees. In his redactional introduction, v. 7a, the evangelist limits the judgment call to the Pharisees and Sadducees, whom he distinguishes from those who repent (vv. 5f.).

History of Influence

How often this was to be overlooked in the history of interpretation is puzzling. The *glossa ordinaria* (79), e.g., interprets the wilderness of Judea (v. 1) as referring to the "Godforsaken Jews" and the stones in v. 9 with a wide tradition of interpretation as referring to the Gentiles. Schlatter reports, "With the opposition of Judaism to the baptism . . . Jesus' way to the cross and the separation of Christianity from Judaism took its beginning"; the "Jewish calamity" consists in "repentance which is only play-acted, . . . religion which is only portrayed."[25] According to Lohmeyer, John "indicates that this people chosen by God is a devilish brood" (38f.).

On the contrary, one must ask for the meaning of the differentiation between people and leaders. It is the more striking since it is removed in the passion narrative (27:25!). The Matthean Jesus will find a surprisingly positive echo among the ὄχλοι of Israel, just as the Baptist did. Of course, it is important that the people do not simply reject the Baptist and Jesus. Rather, out of the people arises the community. On the other hand, in Matthew's portrayal the holy people, which identifies with its leaders in the passion, will lose its character as Israel; it will become the "Jews" (cf. on 28:15).

Jewish Leaders

According to his usual style of placing the opponents of Jesus together in groups of two, Matthew has here combined the Pharisees and Sadducees. The Pharisees and Sadducees, who are mutual enemies, fit together like "squires and clerics."[26] For Matthew (and the community of his time) the Pharisees, as the most important opponents of Jesus, are mentioned first. During his period there were relatively few Sadducees as a special group. One only can hazard a guess why they (instead of the otherwise preferred "scribes") appear here (perhaps because of the proximity of Jerusalem?). It is important for Matthew that the Jewish leaders whom the two groups represent act in harmony with each other against the Baptist (and Jesus): The Baptist and Jesus face a united front of Jewish leaders, but not a rejecting people.

Thus for Matthew, the salvation-historical interest of setting Jesus over against a united front of Jewish opponents is primary.[27] However, this excludes neither historicizing elements nor transparency for his own time. The relative preponderance of Pharisees and scribes in the rejecting front opposing Jesus reflects the conditions of the time of Matthew himself. The essentially different composition of the groups of opponents in the passion narrative—the elders are important, and the Pharisees recede—reflects the historical situation.

---

[25]Quotations on pp. 52,73, but cf. 69.

[26]Holtzmann 43.

[27]Walker, *Heilsgeschichte* 12-33.

3:11

The two following sayings also are given by Matthew essentially in the form of the Sayings Source.[28] As in v. 2, he emphasizes the importance of repentance. Because this key word is theologically significant only in connection with John's baptism, one can—in contrast to Luke—assume that he is thinking of a one-time repentance at the beginning of the Christian life.[29] Probably through the combination of the texts of Mark and Q in v. 11d, the baptism by Spirit has been added to the *baptism by fire.*

History of Influence

A brief survey of the history of interpretation[30] results in the following picture: Until the Middle Ages the two most important alternatives, sketched by Jerome on this passage, stand side by side: (1) "Ignis est Spiritus sanctus" (the fire is the Holy Spirit); baptism by Spirit and by fire thus mean the same thing.[31] (2) "In praesenti spiritu baptizamur et in futuro igni" (in the present we are being baptized by the spirit and in the future by fire) whereby fire can mean judgment,[32] purgatory,[33] or the future sufferings and temptations of the believers.[34] Later this eschatological interpretation recedes, and the first interpretation predominates. The emphasis may lie on the churchly sacrament of baptism or on the Pentecost event of Acts 2. In a third phase of the history of interpretation in modern times, the eschatological interpretation advances again into the foreground, whereby a distinction is often made between the eschatological sense of the baptism by fire in Q, or the Baptist himself and the new interpretation by the evangelist, in which baptism by fire is no longer understood eschatologically.

Since Matthew does not hand down the tradition of the fiery Spirit of Acts 2 and frequently speaks redactionally of fire as devastating judgment (7:19; 13:40, 42, 50; 18:9), he probably has related the baptism by fire to the destructive judgment. The context (vv. 10, 12) also suggests the same.[35] Then

---

[28]The chiastically constructed logion in v. 11 in Q probably contrasted John's baptism by water with the fire, i.e., the judgment "baptism" of the Son of man. In contrast to Luke, Matthew is hardly influenced by the parallel Mark 1:7f. which as a whole is secondary in the history of tradition. Matthew only makes use of πνεύματι ἁγίῳ from Mark. Therefore it can only be postulated, not proved, that in Q only πυρί was found; cf. Hoffmann, *Studien* 28-31.

[29]Strecker, *Weg* 227.

[30]Cf. Marconcini* 169-73.

[31]There are the following variations: (1) fire points to the power and irresistibility of the Spirit which is bestowed in Christian baptism (John Chrysostom 11.4 = 187); (2) fire points to the tongues of fire of Acts 2 (e.g., Theodore of Heraclea, fragment 18 = Reuss 62).

[32]This opinion, widespread today, is very rare in the ancient church; only Hilarius 926 ("ignis iudicii" [the fire of judgment]).

[33]E.g., Origen, *Hom. in Jer* 2:3 = *PG* 13,282; *Hom. in Ez.* 1:13 = *PG* 13,679.

[34]E.g. Strabo 82 ("probatione tribulationis" [the test of tribulation]).

[35]Luke, differently from Matthew, probably interprets it in the sense of Acts 2:1-4 as referring to the Spirit of Pentecost.

baptism by the Spirit does not mean the same as baptism by fire.[36] Rather, Matthew probabaly thought of the fact that Jesus himself was the bearer of the Spirit (12:18,28) and that baptism was commanded by him with the triadic baptismal formula (28:19). But already in v.16 the prediction of baptism by the Spirit is fulfilled with Jesus. If one remembers that the stronger one, as in Q, refers to the Son of man, then the statement concerning the Spirit and fire baptism of the stronger one corresponds closely with the Matthean theology of the Son of man. The Son of man is the earthly Jesus who is present in his community and at the same time the coming lord of judgment.

3:12

The images of the winnowing fork and the burning of the chaff from Q fit comfortably into Matthean theology: in v. 11, through the reference to the baptism of the stronger one, the community[37] was already unnoticeably taken into consideration. The word of judgment was meant for the community. The separation of chaff and wheat on the threshing floor corresponds to the conception of the Christian community as *corpus permixtum* (a mixed body)(13:40-43; 22:11-14). The accent lies on the warning of eternal destruction, completely in the sense of Matthean judgment parenesis. The whole pericope receives through v. 12 indirectly a parenetical point.

Summary

Matthew in our pericope has not only set the key word βασιλεία as a decisive signal, and not only differentiated the confrontation with Israel, which was important already in ch. 2, and not only prepared the pericope 3:13-17 which is foundational for him, but also especially given us a preview of his understanding of the judgment of the Son of man: he is the one who comes in judgment of fire. The proclamation in the Gospel of Matthew begins with the judgment of the Son of man; it will end with the judgment of the Son of man (chs. 24f.). "Fire" is a central key word of the first and the last proclamation in the Gospel of Matthew (25:41). The coming judgment of destruction is a key to the theology of Matthew; whoever finds fault with this, finds fault with Matthean theology.[38]

---

[36]The two most important counterarguments against this interpretation are: (1) the close connection of water and Spirit (without repetition of ἐν); (2) "baptism" and "baptize" are nowhere else in Matthew used metaphorically. It seems to me that they do not prevail against the weight of the context.

[37]Origen, *Hom. in Ez.* 1:11 = *PG* 13,676f.; Rabanus 774 (reference to 13:36-43).

[38]Cf. Marguerat, *Jugement* 563: The theme of judgment occurs in 60 out of 148 Matthean pericopes and provides a focus for "l'ensemble de la théologie mt." Basically, criticism may come from two possible sides: the conception of the judgment by the Son of man according to works may be considered meaningless for contemporary persons, or the conception of judgment, standing in the center of Matthean theology, may be considered destructive of grace and leading to works-righteousness. An answer can be given to this only on the basis of the whole of the Gospel of Matthew (according to my opinion, to the credit of Matthew); here the question shall remain open. Cf. the theological recapitulation at the conclusion of vol. 3.

1.2. The Revelation of the Righteous Son of God (3:13-17)

Literature

Beasley-Murray, G. R., *Baptism in the New Testament*, p. 62 (Grand Rapids: Eerdmans, 1981).
Bertrand, D. A., *Le baptême de Jésus. Histoire de l'exégèse aux deux premiers siècles*, BGBE 14 (Tübingen: Mohr, 1973).
Bornemann, J., *Die Taufe Christi durch Johannes in der dogmatischen Beurteilung der christlichen Theologen der ersten vier Jahrhunderte* (Leipzig: Hinrichs, 1896).
Dupont, *Béatitudes* III 225-45 (further bibliography there, 226 n. 4).
Feuillet, A., "La personnalité de Jésus entrevue à partir de sa soumission au rite de repentance du Précurseur," *RB* 77 (1970) 30-49.
Fridrichsen, A., "Accomplir toute justice," in *Congrès d'histoire du Christianisme* I (FS A. Loisy), ed. P. L. Couchoud, pp. 167-77 (Paris: Les Éditions Rieder, 1928).
Giesen, *Handeln* 21-41.
Lindijer, C. H., "Jezus doop in de Jordaan," *NedTTs* 18 (1963/64) 177-92.
Ljungman, H., "Das Gesetz erfüllen," *Lunds Universitets Årsskift* N.F. 1, 50/6 (Lund: Gleerup, 1954), 97-126.
Sabbe, M., "Le baptême de Jésus," in *De Jésus aux Évangiles*, ed. I de la Potterie, BETL 25, pp. 184-211 (1967).
Strecker, *Weg* 178-81.
Vögtle, A., "Die sogenannte Taufperikope Mk 1,9-11," in EKK 4, pp. 105-39 (Zurich: Benziger, 1972)

Text

13 Then Jesus comes from Galilee to the Jordan to John in order to allow himself to be baptized by him.
14 But John attempted to prevent him and said, "I have need to be baptized by you, and you are coming to me?"
15 But Jesus answered and said to him, "Let it be now; thus it is fitting for us to fulfill all righteousness." Then he let him.
16 But after his baptism, Jesus rose immediately out of the water; and behold, the heavens opened to him, and he saw the Spirit of God descend like a dove and come on him.
17 And behold, a voice from the heavens said, "This is my beloved Son, in whom I have found pleasure."

Analysis

This narrative is only the continuation of the preceding scene. Or, still more sharply phrased: after Matthew in 3:1-12 has described the circumstances in detail—John, his baptism and his proclamation—only now the story really begins. With παραγίνεται Matthew deliberately turns back to 3:1 and introduces the second figure important to him: the stronger one of whom John had already spoken. Thus our narrative has a close association with the preceding scene; indeed it actually is its climax. This means Christologically: the evangelist comes to his characteristic Christological expression with the presentation of Jesus as "Son of God."

   In comparison with the Markan source, vv. 14f. are new. Whether they are the creation of the evangelist or go back to oral traditions is disputed and cannot be decided convincingly on linguistic grounds.[1] The literary-critical situation is complicated in addition by the fact that Q in all likelihood contained a notice about the baptism of Jesus between the report about the Baptist and the temptation narrative. The minor agreements between Matthew and Luke and the relationships between the baptism pericope and the temptation narrative—in this case—point in this direction.[2] But the Mattheisms—too numerous for a written prototype—and the lack of the verses in Luke speak against the view that vv. 14f. come from the Sayings Source. Since the problem why the stronger one had to be baptized by the forerunner occupied the community elsewhere,[3] it is possible that the evangelist took up a question which was familiar to him from the community tradition.[4] Jesus' answer in v. 15 comes directly from the evangelist.

Interpretation

In Mark 1:9-11, the report of the baptism was transmitted to the evangelist as a "Christological foundational narrative."[5] Possibly it was important for the oldest Christian communities, precisely in view of the baptism of John, to underscore the uniqueness of Jesus: he is Son of God in a unique way,[6] despite the baptism by John which he underwent in common with all the people. In Matthew, the direction of the argumentation is reversed: It was certain for the believing community that Jesus was the chosen Son of God. Why did he then undergo the baptism by John? This means: While in the text of Mark the heavenly voice, the Christological predication alone, stood in the center of the interest of the narrator, now the act of baptism becomes a problem on the basis of the Christology.[7] Thus the question is: What sort of a Son of God is he who accepts baptism by the lesser one?

History of Influence

The history of interpretation shows that Jesus' submission to John's baptism was

---

[1]The following are Matthean (cf. introduction 3.1; 3.2): v. 14: ὁ δέ λέγων; τοῦ with inf.; v. 15: ἀποκριθεὶς δέ (. . . εἶπεν), ἄρτι, οὕτως, ἀφίημι (?), πληρόω, δικαιοσύνη, τότε. Composites with δια- may be Matthean, cf. introduction 3.1 (compound verbs).

[2]Cf. v. 16//Luke 3:21f.: Βαπτισθείς . . . Ἰησοῦς . . . ἠνεῴχθησαν . . . ἐπ᾽ αὐτόν. Jesus' sonship with God and πνεῦμα in Matt. 4:1, the wilderness setting, and the parallel pre-Markan connection in Mark 1:4-13 speak in favor of a baptismal notice in Q which, however, in content hardly went beyond Mark 1:9-11.

[3]In Luke, the baptism is told only marginally (3:21), in John not at all.

[4]Strecker, *Weg* 150, 178f., considers v. 14 as tradition. However, this verse demands an answer by Jesus which is found only in the almost certainly redactional verse 15.

[5]Gnilka, *Markusevangelium* I 54.

[6]Vögtle 134-39.

[7]In distinction from Luke (3:15), John (1:6-8,24,34), and the Pseudo-Clementines (Rec. 1.54.8; 60. 1-3) Matthew does not seem to have to argue with baptist groups who considered the Baptist to be the Messiah—a situation which made Jesus' baptism an especially delicate problem. Rather, the problem is more general: the "stronger one," the Son of God, by his baptism seems to be on the same level as "Jerusalem and all Judea" (3:5) and as the Christian community which also is baptized. Why did he allow himself to be baptized? These debates are reflected from the obverse side in M. Lidzbarski, *Das Johannesbuch der Mandäer* (1915) II, §§ 30,108: a heavenly letter commands Yahya to baptize the deceiver Jesus Christ.

a burning question.[8] Our pericope often has caused embarrassment to the church[9] and therefore has had only a limited influence. Despite some initial attempts,[10] it has not become a part of the creed. The reason lay in the altered Christology of the church: The Gnostics, for whom the Spirit-Christ, coming from beyond, combined himself in the baptism externally with the body-Jesus, which was actually alien to him, indeed could avail themselves of this pericope (docetism),[11] and the Adoptionists, for whom the human Jesus was adopted at baptism as Son of God, also could use this pericope.[12] But the orthodox could not use it; for them, Jesus was the eternal Logos whose real incarnation had taken place long before his baptism and who therefore did not need another bestowal of the Spirit. Our pericope also provided difficulties to a Trinitarian Christology which understood Jesus as the second person of the Trinity from all eternity. The history of interpretation therefore is widely a history of attempts to integrate our pericope into Christologies of another kind, "more divine."

a. In a very formal way the pericope could become a *testimony to the Trinity*. The Trinity appeared in our pericope as the voice of the Father, the obedience of the Son, and the anointing by the Spirit.[13] The difficulty that the Son is the Son of God from eternity is solved by the "hypothesis of manifestation" which Matthew more or less prepares in v. 17: the proclamation of sonship with God in the baptism of Jesus happens "not so much for his own sake, as for others."[14]

b. A Christological "surmounting" of our pericope is found also when it is understood as *material foundation of Christian baptism*.[15] In the ancient church, the thought is predominant that Jesus through his baptism has purified the element of water.[16] The baptism of Jesus is a type of Christian baptism,[17] e.g., because it shows the

---

[8]A survey of the history of interpretation, arranged by types of interpretation, is found in Lindijer*. The monograph by Bornemann* is most important for the ancient church. Bertrand* treats only the first two centuries.

[9] Ἄνθρωπος χρίεται, ὁ λόγος οὐ χρίεται (a human being is anointed, the Logos is not anointed; Paul of Samosata, in Harnack, *Dg*. I 725, n. 1, concerning a basic monarchian position); "ignoro mysterium" [I do not know the mystery] (Chromatius 329). Calvin asks, "Why did the Spirit *then* descend upon Christ, when it had *earlier* rested upon him?" (I 131).

[10]Ignatius, *Smyrn*. 1:1f., where the redactional form of Matt. 3:15 is presupposed, is a confessional text. Cf. A. Hahn, *Bibliothek der Symbole und Glaubensregeln der Alten Kirche*, reprint (Hildesheim: Olms, 1962), 126f., 136, 205, 211, 215-17, 224. Cf. also Acts 10:38.

[11]Cf. Cerinthus (Irenaeus, *Haer*. 1.26.1); Ophites (*Haer*. 1.30.12, with virgin birth); Valentinians (*Haer*. 1.7.2, with virgin birth; 3,11,3). Further examples in Bertrand* 56-82.

[12]Theodotus the Tanner and Theodotus the Money-Changer were put by Hippolytus, *Ref*. 7.35f., not incorrectly immediately behind Cerinthus and the Ebionites. Indeed, the Ebionites think of baptism in adoptionist terms (Justin, *Dial*. 49.1; Epiphanius, *Haer*. 30.16.2-4; 18,5 = *PG* 41,452.456, cf. Ps. Clem. Rec. 1.48 and Schoeps, *Jewish Christianity* [Philadelphia: Fortress, 1969], 61-73).

[13]Classically Theodore of Mopsuestia, fragment 166 = Reuss 102: "The testifier was the Father, the testified the Son, the Holy Spirit was the one who designates the testified one."

[14]Calvin I 131; the idea as such is widespread.

[15]Cf. Barth, *CD* IV/4,86. According to E. Schlink, *The Doctrine of Baptism* (St. Louis: Concordia, 1972), 21, Jesus has changed the baptism of John into Christian baptism.

[16]Since Ignatius, *Eph*. 13:2; Clement of Alexandria, *Ecl. Proph*. 7 = *PG* 9,701; Tertullian, *Adv. Iud*. 8 = *PL* 2,615.

[17]Theodore of Mopsuestia, *Fragm. Dogm*. VIII = *PG* 66,980: προετυποῦτο . . . τὸ ἡμέτερον βάπτισμα.

connection of water and word as it is decisive for baptism,[18] or because the bestowal of the Spirit on Jesus can be seen in the light of Christian baptism.[19] In Eastern tradition, the relation of the baptism of Jesus to Christian baptism is especially strong, because the baptism of Jesus was not only the chief content of the Epiphany festival but January 6 was also the most important time for baptism next to Easter.[20] The Matthean version, which directs the attention to Jesus and his motivation for being baptized, was then later connected with Christian baptism by the Baptists in a new way: it shows the voluntary character of baptism.[21]

  c. Already in the early church there are numerous attempts to bring our baptismal narrative in *connection with the expiatory death or the incarnation of Jesus* and to understand it on that basis. Then the baptism of Jesus can be understood directly as a baptism of expiation.[22] Or the interpretation takes its starting point at the catchword δικαιοσύνη: The righteousness of Jesus consists in becoming one with the sinners in his mercy.[23] In this case, the death of Jesus is less highlighted as a sign than his incarnation through accepting the baptism by John.

  d. Extraordinarily widespread is a form of explanation which sees the baptismal narrative within the *history of salvation*: Adam through his sins closed heaven, Christ opened it again.[24] Since Christ, and through him, heaven is open to us.[25]

  These interpretations are attempts out of embarrassment to set the text into a "high" Christology of the church. But in reality it seems to resist any "high" Christology. Jesus comes from Galilee to John, as one among many, and is baptized by him: What does this mean for Christology? And why is the proclamation of his sonship with God tied precisely to this event through the heavenly voice?

Interpretation

Jesus comes from Galilee—the reader of the Gospel knows already that it is Nazareth—to the Jordan.

---

[18]Augustine, *In Joh. Ev. Tract.* 15.4 = *PL* 24,1512: The baptism of Jesus is "lavacrum aquae in verbo. Tolle aquam, non est baptismus, tolle verbum, non est baptismus" (washing of water in the word. Take away the water, it is not a baptism; take away the word, it is not a baptism).

[19]Irenaeus, *Haer.* 3.9.3.

[20]K. Holl, "Der Ursprung des Epiphanienfestes," in *Gesammelte Aufsätze zur Kirchengeschichte* II (Tübingen: Mohr, 1928), especially 124-33.

[21]Beasley-Murray* 66f.

[22]Ephraem, *Nat.* 3.19 = CSCO 187,22 (he sank our sin into the depth); Chromatius 329 ("unus mersit . . . lavit omnes" [one has immersed himself, . . . he has washed all]); in more recent times, cf., e.g., Cullmann, *Baptism in the New Testament* (London: SCM, 1950), 16-21 (with reference to Mark 10:38 and John 1:29-34).

[23]Cf. John Chrysostom 12.1 = 197 (μετὰ τῶν δούλων ὁ δεσπότης [the master with the slaves]), today similarly perhaps Beasley- Murray* 57-66 ("solidarity," not "substitution"); Feuillet* 42-46.

[24]E.g., Rabanus 777; Euthymius Zigabenus 172; Thomas Aquinas, *Lecture* no. 298.

[25]Luther II 23 (= Sermon of 1544): "Still today heaven is open over the whole world. Note that this story does not have an end."

3:13

Matthew stresses Jesus' intention to be baptized and prepares in this way the following discussion.

3:14

John attempts[26] to prevent him:[27] John cannot baptize the one who is stronger, who bears the Spirit and who will in the future baptize with fire.

The idea of the *sinlessness of Jesus*, which has always played a decisive role for the church interpretation of our passage, is not at all expressed by Matthew or the Synoptics, although it does not contradict the Gospels. It does not appear until later, in the Gospel of the Nazarenes.[28]

3:15

Jesus answers the objection of the Baptist with a sentence that contains a central concern of Matthean theology: v. 15 is important for the reader of the Gospel in two ways: (1) here the first word of Jesus in the Gospel is reported and (2) the readers or hearers of the Gospel knew the story of the baptism until now without this sentence and therefore it jumped out at them. In this short saying of Jesus, every word is controversial.

δικαιοσύνη

Δικαιοσύνη is a key Matthean term (seven times, without exception redactional). The basic question is whether "righteousness" in Matthew means in all places a requirement which is addressed to a person and to be fulfilled by him or her, or whether the Old Testament–Jewish thought of a comprehensive order of law and salvation which God establishes is hinted at in a few passages. According to almost all interpreters,[29] the thought here, as in 5:10,20 and 6:1, is of a human deed. This corresponds to the Qumran writings and especially the Tannaitic literature, where, different from the Old Testament, צֶדֶק ever more clearly becomes an ethical and religious norm and refers to human conduct.[30] We will have to ask whether this clear Jewish usage is maintained in all Matthean occurrences of δικαιοσύνη .[31]

---

[26]Conative imperfect.

[27]Διακωλύω, as a compound verb and hapax legomenon, speaks against the thesis of a relationship between v. 14 and the ritual question of impediments to baptism, cf. Acts 8:36; 10:47; 11:17; Ps. Clem. Hom. 13.5.1; 13.11.2; Cullmann (above n. 22) 65-73.

[28]Jerome, *Pelag* 3,2 (in Aland, *Synopsis* 27). It is misguided to read the sinlessness of Jesus out of the fact that in v. 16 he rose from the water εὐθύς so that he would not have had time to confess his sins in the river (Gundry 51). As if the confession of sins had taken place at the baptism in the river!

[29]Exception: Ljungman* 124f.: Righteousness is God's action with his chosen people whose measure Jesus "makes full."

[30]The important investigations of Przybylski, *Righteousness*, cf. especially 75f., have shown this. A further peculiarity of Jewish usage of the time which is reflected in the Gospel of Matthew is the beginning of a distinction between צֶדֶק and צְדָקָה which corresponds to the Matthean δικαιοσύνη and ἐλεημοσύνη.

[31]Cf. especially below on 5:4 and 6:33.

Thus, δικαιοσύνη is first of all identical with δικαίωμα and means a requirement of law which is to be fulfilled. As far as the content is concerned, this refers probably not only to the Old Testament law,[32] in which the baptism by John obviously is not commanded, but in a more comprehensive sense to the entirety of the divine will as the Matthean Jesus interprets it. Πᾶσα δικαιοσύνη also points in this direction: "All righteousness" is not a special righteousness of the Son of God to be fulfilled only by Jesus[33] but "all that is righteous."[34] "All righteousness" thus does not isolate Jesus from the Christians, to whom the "higher" righteousness is assigned (5:20) and who are commanded (28:20) to observe "all that I have commanded you," but binds him with them, just as he is bound also with John (ἡμῖν).[35] Through πᾶσα the situation of the baptism is burst open. "All righteousness" does not *consist* in the baptism by John, but the latter only belongs to it. The sentence receives a programmatic character: Jesus, obedient to the will of God, becomes the prototype and example of the Christians.

This means agreement with the intention of all older and more recent interpretations which stress the exemplarity of Jesus. Jesus "came to John to teach *us* humility," Dionysius bar Salibi rightly says concerning our passage.[36] Πραΰς and ταπεινός are Christological and ethical key terms for Matthew (e.g. 11:29). Jesus is presented as the exemplary obedient and humble one. His first saying in the Gospel of Matthew refers to this. The behavior of Jesus has foundational significance.[37]

A Christological point of view is indicated only indirectly through πληρόω. One has to begin with the meaning "fulfill" in the sense of

---

[32]The interpretation of δικαιοσύνη as referring the Old Testament law is often connected by the church fathers with deliberations on the history of salvation. John Chrysostom 12.1 = 199: Jesus fulfills the Old Testament law entirely in order to be able to eliminate it; Theodore of Heraclea, *fragment* 21 = Reuss 63: Jesus who is perfect according to the law came through the baptism of John εἰς τὸ τοῦ νόμου τέλος (to be the end of the law). Theophylact 177: Jesus fulfills the law and liberates humans from its curse.

[33]Fiedler, *Gerechtigkeit* 66 ("the *one* demand to fulfill which Jesus knows himself obligated").

[34]BDF §275, n. 3; Mayser II/2.1 § 70 Ia (96f.). Dupont, *Béatitudes* III 240: "L'adjectif πᾶσαν nous oriente . . . vers une conception quantitative de la δικαιοσύνη" (with reference to 5:20).

[35]Cf. 21:32. Ἡμῖν refers only to Jesus and John, not directly to the Christians (so Giesen, *Handeln* 32).

[36]117; similarly already Ambrose, *In Luc.* 2:90 = *PL* 15,1586 (the righteousness of Jesus was shown in his doing first that which he demanded of others); Augustine, *Enchiridon* 49 = *BKV* I/49 438 (example of great humility), and many others. Theodotus the Tanner emphasizes Jesus' fear of God (Hippolytus, *Ref.* 7.35); in an "adoptionist" Christology, the exemplarity of Jesus can be used to better advantage than in the classical Logos Christology.

[37]That Jesus permits himself to be baptized, is therefore an exemplary expression of his obedience and of his righteousness. Therefore it presumably is not the intention "that the believers would learn that no one exists without baptism as a perfectly righteous person" (Bede 18, similarly Cyril of Jerusalem, *Cat. Myst.* 3.11 = *PG* 33,441; Grotius I 67 ["quantus honos instituta a Deo ritibus debeatur" (what great honor is due to the rites instituted by God)]). Cf. also the interpretations in regard to the rite of baptism, above nn. 16-20.

"actualize."[38] This choice of words must have been astonishing to a hearer or reader of that time.[39] For the actions of the disciples, Matthew uses, e.g., ποιέω (+ τὸ θέλημα) or τηρέω (+ τὰς ἐντολάς); πληρόω he reserves for Jesus alone. Certainly the nuance is implied that Jesus has done the will of God completely (cf. 23:32);[40] besides, the reader will discover at 5:17 what Christological dimension the statement of 3:15 has had. Thus, our verse has "signal character" and points ahead to 5:17.

Other Christological explanations of the fulfilling of all righteousness go beyond the intention of the text or miss it entirely. Notably the interpretation of our passage in reference to the passion is a widespread eisegesis into the text: it does not speak of the coming suffering of the righteous one[41] or of the suffering servant of the Lord.[42]

3:16

Matthew places even less weight on the act of baptism than Mark; not until the post-Matthean tradition is it embellished miraculously.[43] Did Matthew, by taking over the formulation "were opened" of the heavens (from Q?), deliberately want to recall Ezek. 1:1-4?[44] As in Luke, he also tends to represent the events at the baptism not as a vision but as a visible event; yet the manuscript tradition is not unambiguous.[45]

3:17

The high point of the Matthean baptismal narrative is, just as in Mark, the proclamation through the heavenly voice in v. 17. Matthew has "objectified" here: Out of the "formula of predication" in the second person he made a

---

[38]BAGD, s.v. πληρόω 4b.

[39]Cf. on πληρόω the interpretation of 5:17. On the basis of the LXX this usage is rather unusual, cf. only 1 Macc. 2:55 and 4 Macc. 12:14; classical examples in Luz, *ZThK* 75 (1978) 415 n. 84.

[40]Πληρόω thus also contains a statement of majesty. This is brought out in an especially impressive manner by Ephraem, *Carm. Sogyata* 5 = *CSCO* 187,202 in a long dialogue between Jesus and the Baptist: "Come near and baptize me in order that my will (!) be done."

[41]E. Schweizer, υἱός κτλ. *TDNT* VIII 379ff.; similarly G. Bornkamm, "Die neutestamentliche Lehre von der Taufe," in *TBl* 17 (1938) 45 ("With his baptism, Jesus begins the way of the passion . . .").

[42]Cullmann (above n. 22) 13-17.

[43]Some Latin manuscripts add that a great light had shone over the water. This tradition is found also in Justin, *Dial.* 88.1, in the Gospel of the Ebionites (Epiphanius, *Haer.* 30.13.7f. = Aland, *Synopsis* 27), in the Diatessaron of Tatian (Bauer, *Leben* 135), and in other, especially Jewish-Christian writings. E. Bammel, "Die Täufertraditionen bei Justin," in *StPatr* 8/2, 1966 (*TU* 93), 60, considers the motif a very old Jewish-Christian tradition.

[44]Ezek. 1:1: ἠνοίχθησαν οἱ οὐρανοί, καὶ εἶδον, cf. 3: ἐγένετο λόγος κυρίου, 4: καὶ εἶδον καὶ ἰδοὺ πνεῦμα.

[45]The majority of the MSS and numerous church fathers read after ἠνεῴχθησαν an αὐτῷ. Origen *Cels.* 1.48, and Theodore of Mopsuestia, *In Joh.* 1:32 = *PG* 66,736 designate the occurrences at the baptism explicitly as a vision.

"formula of identification" in the third person.[46] In Matthew, Jesus was already from the beginning, from his birth, the Son of God and did not become such through baptism. So the heavenly voice is no longer directed to Jesus, who knows his own identity, but rather to John the Baptist and particularly to the crowds who have to be considered as present since 3:5, i.e., to the Christian community.

The choice of the third person has the effect that the heavenly voice more so than in Mark corresponds to the *wording of Isa. 42:1*. But the completely different wording of the formula quotation in 12:18 shows that Matthew here did not want to quote Isa. 42:1,[47] but the heavenly voice of Mark 1:11. However, he has adapted the formula quotation of 12:18a to the heavenly voice and thus related Isa. 42:1—with v. 1b, which is important to the story of the baptism—perhaps for the first time to the baptism of Jesus.

Son of God

The most important observation is that *Jesus' sonship with God* gains from vv. 14f. a new accent that is determinative for Matthew. The Son of God is for him not only the one who was revealed from heaven (cf. 2:15; 16:16f.; 17:5) but especially the obedient one who subjects himself to God's will. This thought is so important to him that he repeats it as the main idea in the following story of the temptation. Indeed, at the end of the passion narrative he presents once more the same interpretation of Jesus' sonship with God (27:43; cf. 27:54). We encounter here the second basic Christological inclusion of the Gospel of Matthew: Next to "God with us" (1:23; 28:20) it is the obedient Son of God who gives to the whole Gospel the Christological frame. Now it also becomes understandable why Matthew indeed in the first two chapters let the title Son of God sound again and again but still did this allusively and with restraint: only in our pericope does it become clear what this "signal" really meant.

Quite deliberately Matthew refers to the conduct of Jesus at the beginning of his Gospel. Jesus is the obedient and humble one. It is precisely to this obedience of Jesus that God responds with his proclamation: "This is my beloved Son." The uniqueness of Jesus in our text consists not so much in the preexistence, also not in the miraculous conception—which is not central for the evangelist—but in his unique obedience. That does not mean that Jesus' sonship with God consists in a special human quality, namely, perfect obedience, but that God gives *his* answer to this perfect obedience. How foundational this Christological structure is for the evangelist can be seen in the fact that it is repeated with humans: Humans also "will be called sons of God," e.g., if they are peacemakers (5:9, cf. 5:45). The promise of 5:9 lies in the future, while with Paul or John humans are already children of God through baptism (Rom. 8:14-17; Gal. 4:5-7; John 1:12). The structure is the same with Jesus as with the disciples: God's promise pertains to obedience.

The way of the Christian in the Gospel of Matthew is the way to

---

[46]Frankemölle, *Jahwebund* 92f. n. 44; cf. E. Norden, *Agnostos Theos*, reprint (Darmstadt: Wissenschaftliche Buchgesellschaft, 1966), 177-201.

[47]Pace Sabbe* 206.

perfection in the conduct of one's life (5:48). It stands under the demand of higher righteousness (5:20). To it is promised entrance into the kingdom of heaven. Jesus goes this way ahead of his disciples. He enters as the obedient one into the Gospel; he fulfills all righteousness. God answers him as he will answer the disciples who do the will of the Father. For me, there is profound depth in the fact that Matthew does not wish to advocate a "high" Christology and that he brings Jesus' sonship with God, which is believed in by his community, to a climax in his obedience. The way of the disciples also is defined as the way of concrete, earthly obedience. There is in Matthew no room for looking past that which is earthly into heavenly dimensions, as in the Johannine Christology of the Son; there is only the way of obedience. The Son of God takes this way first.

History of Influence and Summary

The history of influence showed manifold attempts to deal with the difficulties of the text. It was important to bring it into harmony with the given church doctrine of the Trinity, to relate it to the "salvific event" of baptism or to put it into a larger context of the history of salvation. A concluding remark has to be made: it would be wrong if we would see in such interpretations only examples of Christian misinterpretations and unjustified dogmatic exaggerations. They also are more than a negative foil on the basis of which it becomes possible for us to free ourselves from our tradition and to encounter the text directly. In my opinion, they have a very important positive function: they furnish examples for the attempt to understand the text on the basis of the entirety of the faith of the church at a given time. They show how the text was integrated into the whole of faith and spoke on this basis. Certainly, they are not identical with the original sense of the text. The historical-critical interpreter of today knows this, as the church fathers did not. But they indicate the direction in which our own understanding also has to go. We too must understand an individual biblical text on the basis of the whole of our faith—which lives from the Bible. Only when the thought of an individual biblical text becomes *our* thought, which an interpreter cannot merely elicit but also affirm, proclaim, and live—only then has that understanding been reached which the biblical texts themselves intend. The church interpretations document this understanding for their particular time.[48]

Perhaps it is easier for us to discover in Matthean Christology "our" meaning than it was for the ancient church. The connection of the promise "Immanuel" with the concretion in the earthly obedience of Jesus makes it possible that God can be claimed and believed in the midst of actual human life. This was valid for Jesus and also for his successors. The foundational Matthean narrative of the obedient Son of God is a "narrative of God for life." If we discover it again behind the "high" church Christology, then we discover also that it speaks of God no less centrally than the classic Christology. It is its uniqueness that it ties the promise of the experiencing of God to practical, "simple" obedience in everyday life. Thus God showed himself in his Son. And at the same time, it becomes clear from here that the Matthean "Gospel of the deed" is throughout Christological.

---

[48]Cf. on the hermeneutical significance of the history of influence the introduction, pp. 97f.

2. THE AUTHENTICATION OF THE SON OF GOD IN THE TEMPTATION (4:1-11)

Literature

Dupont, J. *Die Versuchungen Jesu in der Wüste*, SBS 37 (Stuttgart: Katholisches Bibelwerk, 1969).

Eitrem, S., *Die Versuchung Christi*, NorTT Beiheft 3 (1924) 3-23.

Fascher, E., *Jesus und der Satan*, HM 11 (Halle: Niemeyer, 1949).

Gerhardsson, B., *The Testing of God's Son*, CB. NT 2 (Lund: Gleerup, 1966).

Harsch, H., "Psychologische Interpretation biblischer Texte?" in *Psychoanalytische Interpretationen biblischer Texte*, ed. Y. Spiegel (Munich: Kaiser, 1972), 49-59.

Hoffmann, P., "Die Versuchungsgeschichte in der Logienquelle," *BZ* NF 13 (1969) 207-23.

Jeremias, J., "Die Zinne des Tempels (Mt 4,5; Lk 4,9)," *ZDPV* 59 (1936) 195-208.

———, *Theology* 73-80.

Kesich, V., "Hypostatic and Prosopic Union in the Exegesis of Christ's Temptation," *St. Vladimir's Seminary Quarterly* (Crestwood 1965), 118-37.

———, "The Antiocheans and the Temptation Story," *StPatr* 7, 1966 (TU 92), 496-502.

Köppen, K. P., *Die Auslegung der Versuchungsgeschichte unter besonderer Berücksichtigung der Alten Kirche*, BGBE 4 (Tübingen: Mohr, 1961).

Mahnke, H., *Die Versuchungsgeschichte im Rahmen der synoptischen Evangelien*, BBET 9 (Bern: Lang, 1978).

Meyer, A., "Die evangelischen Berichte über die Versuchung Christi," *Festgabe H. Blümner*, pp. 434-68 (Zurich 1914).

Steiner, M., *La tentation de Jésus dans l'interprétation patristique de Saint Justin à Origène*, EBib (Paris: Gabala, 1962).

Wilkens, W., "Die Versuchung Jesu nach Matthäus," *NTS* 28 (1982) 479-89.

Zeller, D., "Die Versuchungen Jesu in der Logienquelle," *TTZ* 89 (1980) 61-73.

Text

1 Then Jesus was led by the Spirit up into the wilderness in order to be tempted by the devil.
2 And he fasted forty days and forty nights; afterwards he was hungry.
3 And the tempter approached and said to him, "If you are the Son of God, say that these stones shall become bread."
4 But he answered and said, "It is written, 'The human being will live not by bread alone but by each word which comes from God's mouth.'"
5 Then the devil takes him into the holy city, placed him on the pinnacle[1] of the temple

---

[1]Jeremias, *ZDPV* 59 (1936) on the basis of *p.Pes.* 7.35, 28ff. and *Test. Sol.* 22:8; 23,3 (= ἄκρα τῆς εἰσόδου τοῦ ναοῦ) interprets this in reference to the top part of a temple gate. The interpretation of πτερύγιον τοῦ ἱεροῦ as of the temple *gate* however, is not cogent, in my opinion: Πτερύγιον in the figurative sense corresponds to ἀκρωτήριον (Hesychius no. 4210) and means "top," "outermost part," e.g., of a rudder, of the nose, of the ear (in distinction from the "lower" ear lobe), of a net (= seam), cf. Julius Pollux, *Onom.* 1.78f.; 2.80.85; 5.29. Therefore, it is simplest to understand πτερύγιον τοῦ ἱεροῦ in a non-technical sense as the outermost or highest point in the temple. A local tradition does not have to be assumed; the author hardly thought of a specific point.

6 and says to him, "If you are the Son of God, throw yourself down. For it is written,
'He will command his angels for your sake,
and they will carry you on their hands,
in order that you do not strike your foot against a stone.' "
7 Jesus said to him, "It also is written, 'You shall not tempt the Lord, your God.' "
8 Again the devil takes him to a very high mountain and shows him all the kingdoms of the world and their splendor
9 and says to him, "All this I will give you if you fall down and worship me."
10 Then Jesus says to him, "Away with you, Satan! For it is written, 'You shall worship the Lord, your God, and serve him only.' "
11 Then the devil leaves him, and behold, angels approached and served him.

Analysis

1. *Structure.* Matthew has transmitted this pericope from Q pretty much without change, even in the sequence of the temptations. For the introduction (vv. 1f.) and the conclusion (v. 11) he used the form of Mark 1:12f., which probably was older in the history of tradition. The clear structure of the entire text was available to him. In the midst of a narrative frame (vv. 1f.,11) we have a three-part narrative. Πνεῦμα (v. 1) links the passage with the preceding pericope. The three temptations make do with a minimum of narrative requisites; thus, the weight falls on the central quotations of Scripture. Here there is strict symmetry: three times Jesus answers the devil with a quotation (three times γέγραπται) from Deuteronomy. The temptations of the devil become more intense: from the wilderness Jesus is led to the temple; finally on the high mountain it involves rule over the whole world.[2] Twice the devil refers to Jesus' sonship with God (εἰ υἱὸς εἶ τοῦ θεοῦ); thus, it involves confirming the proclamation of the Son of God of 3:17. The third temptation finally demands—completely without disguise—the worship of the devil. It ends with his banishment. The few redactional additions make this structure clearer: The introduction, vv. 1-3aα, corresponds to the conclusion, v. 11 (two times τότε, προσελθὼν ὁ πειράζων/ἄγγελοι προσῆλθον); the connections among the temptations are intensified (παραλαμβάνει/πάλιν παραλαμβάνει,[3] vv. 5, 8). In addition, Matthew puts in "signals" which recall reminiscences of our text for the reader of later pericopes. Among these are ὕπαγε Σατανᾶ (v. 10, cf. 16:23) and ὄρος ὑψηλὸν λίαν (v. 8, cf. 5:1; 17:1; 28:16).[4] Of the remaining redactional additions,[5] the supplement of the quotation from Deut. 8:3 in v. 4, literally according to LXX A, is the most important one.[6]

2. *Origin.*[7] The pericope belongs to the younger formations in the Sayings

---

[2]Πάσας τὰς βασιλείας τοῦ κόσμου stands over against the βασιλεία τῶν οὐρανῶν which Jesus and the Baptist proclaim (4:17; 3:2).

[3]Cf. introduction 3.2 on τότε, προσέρχομαι, παραλαμβάνω.

[4]Matthew, who himself prefers διάβολος, lets σατανᾶς stand in words of Jesus. Matt. 4:8 also corresponds, I think, essentially to the Q text while in 5:1; 28:16 the mountain is redactional.

[5]The following are also linguistically Matthean: ὕστερον (v. 3); ὁ δέ (v. 4); ἁγία πόλις (v. 5); φημί (v. 7); λίαν (v. 8); ταῦτα πάντα (v. 9); πεσών (v. 9); γάρ (v. 10); ἰδού (v. 11); cf. introduction 3.2.

[6]Schürmann, *Lukasevangelium* 210, n. 14, and Mahnke* 60f. advocate the view that the longer Matthean text of the quotation stood in Q. Luke 4:22 contains a reminiscence of the long text, according to them. But the wording of Luke 4:22 is completely different.

[7]I will only indicate my view and forgo offering detailed evidence. Cf. Zeller 61f.

Source. In my opinion it originated at a relatively late point in time without direct dependence on the Markan story of the temptation. Thus the pericope is a formation of the community. Jesus himself has spoken of his victory over Satan in a quite different context (Luke 10:18; 11:21f.). Our text is not a pictorial presentation of Jesus' own experiences, also not the report of a vision; instead, it intends to represent real occurrences in mythical language. One presupposition of its origin is the widespread motif of the temptation of significant religious figures (e.g., Buddha, Zarathustra, Heracles). Another is the community's looking back to Jesus; decisive in this respect were the faith that already the earthly Jesus was the Son of God, Jesus' refusal of heavenly signs, and his conviction that Satan was already dethroned by his ministry (Luke 10:18; 11:21f.). The formal self-enclosed nature of the text suggests that it was conceived in one stroke. The twice-repeated title Son of God[8] may demonstrate that from the beginning our pericope stood in juxtaposition with the baptismal narrative and interpreted Jesus' sonship with God which is proclaimed there on the basis of the memory of the life of Jesus and the faith of the community.

Interpretation

Since the evangelist interfered so little with the text redactionally, it is not easy to grasp *his* special interpretation of the temptation narrative. It probably is essentially identical with that of the Sayings Source to which the evangelist knows himself indebted theologically. At most the references to other parts of the Gospel can shed light on the evangelist's own accents. But this text is a good example of how problematical it is with a tradition-related Gospel to isolate the theology of the evangelist and to attempt to interpret it by itself. Thus we have to ask first of all for the meaning of our text in the pre-Matthean tradition; only later can we attempt to determine whether there are any special Matthean accents at all.

A brief sketch has to suffice. One important question of interpretation is whether the temptations are to be understood as universally human or as specifically "messianic."

1. From the first possibility there emerges what we might call the *parenetic interpretation* of the temptation narrative. It attempts to show how Jesus withstood the human temptations of gluttony, of vainglory, and of greed[9] and thus to admonish the community. A variant of this interpretation is the *psychological interpretation*: the temptations of Jesus show how a true human being overcomes the temptations of materialism, of thrill-seeking, and of power over the world.[10]

---

[8]The fact that it is missing in the third temptation does not speak against the view that it is basic for the whole story of the temptation. It is missing only because it is here not a question of a demonstrative miracle of the Son of God. "Satan can hardly say, 'If you are the Son of God, then fall on your knees and worship me' " (Gerhardsson, *EvT* 42 [1982] 121).

[9]This interpretation is widespread in the ancient church and in the Reformation; cf., e.g., Gregory the Great 16.2 = 1493: warning of *gula, vana gloria, avaritia* (gluttony, vainglory, avarice). It was, in my opinion, never understood as an alternative to the Christological interpretation. In more recent interpretation, the parenetical explanation is advocated, among others, by A. Meyer* 465f.; Bultmann, *Tradition* 256 ("temptations such as . . . every believer knows"); L. Schottroff and W. Stegemann, *Jesus von Nazaret, Hoffnung der Armen* (Stuttgart 1978), 72-77 (the temptations are illusionary desires of the Jesus followers of Q); Zeller* 69-71 (what applies to the Son of God applies much more to humans).

[10]Harsch* 54-59.

2. From the second possibility the *Christological interpretation* arises. It exists principally in two variations, namely, (a) our text could be directed primarily against an understanding of Jesus as θεῖος ἀνήρ or as a magician:[11] Jesus refuses to perform miracles of display. Or (b) our text could be directed primarily against a political misunderstanding of sonship with God:[12] Jesus rejects—in an anti-Zealot manner—political rule. The first interpretation receives its arguments particularly from the first two temptations, the second primarily from the third.

3. A third type of interpretation understands Jesus as the Son of God typologically as the *representative of the true people of God* who in the wilderness overcomes precisely those temptations to which the "son" Israel succumbed before the conquest.[13] The typology may have Christological or parenetical meaning.

4. A fourth interpretation, advocated again today, sees in the narrative of the temptation the *representation of the three basic dimensions of the messiahship of Jesus,* which Judaism already knew, viz., the prophetic, priestly, and royal dimension.[14]

I can only indicate my view here. It is certainly incorrect to claim such a mythical pictorial text for one single interpretation exclusively. Rather, it leaves great freedom for the associations of the readers. Nevertheless there is a clear main accent: if the text originated in one single throw and if in all temptations it is a matter of the temptation of the Son of God—even in the last one the offer of world rule involves the debate concerning Jesus' sonship with God— then one has to begin in any case with a *Christological interpretation.* With this, in all three temptations the main point is a *positive* statement: Jesus affirms his sonship with God which was attributed to him in the baptismal narrative, in *obedience to the word of God in the Old Testament,* and thus he overcomes Satan. In all three temptations the Son of God proves his relationship to God in his obedience vis-à-vis the Bible.

That means that the rejection of false hopes or conceptions, Jewish or Christian, is in my opinion not the main concern of the pericope. It is not possible to construct a unitary background against which our story polemicizes. Not the rejection of world rule by Jesus,[15] but the worship of God is the *theme* of the third temptation. This does not exclude the possibility that, in the time before the Jewish revolt, it took on a critical function against zealotism. In the first and second temptations it is a matter of a merely *tangential* rejection of miracles of display, not of special messianic miracles which Jesus

---

[11]Particularly for the first two temptations, e.g., Eitrem* 9-15, 19-23 (Jesus is not a magician); Schulz, *Q* 186f. (polemic against a Hellenistic miracle-worker Christology).

[12]E.g., Hoffmann*.

[13]Dupont 10-21 advocates this type of interpretation most convincingly and thinks of the manna in Exodus 16 and the water miracle of Massah in Exodus 17 as the substance of a temptation by God, and of the worship of the Canaanite gods (Exodus 23 and 34) as Old Testament background which would make the three temptations correspond to the series of occurrences in the book of Exodus. The third Old Testament type is the most uncertain one because it is the most general; one might just as well think, e.g., of the golden calf (Exodus 32).

[14]G. Friedrich, "Beobachtungen zur messianischen Hohepriestererwartung in den Synoptikern," *ZTK* 53 (1956) 300f.; Baumbach, *Verständnis* 108-10, in detail Mahnke*, expecially 122-24. The Achilles heel of this interpretation is the second temptation: Although it is striking that here the temple becomes the scene, it is true that neither the fall which is suggested to Jesus by Satan nor the temple as the scene of the appearance of the Messiah points to a priestly Messiah, cf. 4 Ezra 13:35 (*Son of man* on the pinnacle of Zion); Rev. 11:3-13; PesiqR 36 (162a) = Str-B I 151 (Messiah on the roof of the sanctuary).

[15]A widespread motif! Cf. Buddha Gautama, *Samyutta-Nikaya* 2.10 (text in J. Aufhauser, *Buddha und Jesus in ihren Paralleltexten* [Bonn: A. Marcus and E. Weber, 1926], 27f.), and Isaiah (*Mart. Isa.* 5). With Zarathustra (Vendidad 19.1) it is a question of abjuring the true religion.

refuses.[16] The connecting thought among all three temptations is not polemic against a certain (mis)understanding of Jesus' sonship with God but the obedience of Jesus to the word of God.

Our pericope lends itself only indirectly to a *parenetic interpretation*. It is not based on the need of Christians for an example in their own temptations, for Christians are tempted in a different way. But indeed it has an indirect parenetic character, because the obedience of the Son of God toward God's word is basically also demanded of Christians. All three sentences from Deuteronomy with which Jesus answers the devil have a fundamental significance for the life of Christians which goes beyond the concrete situation of the individual temptations. But what obedience means for the Christian community in regard to content they do not learn from the content of the individual temptations of Jesus but from the proclamation of Jesus which is transmitted by the Sayings Source.

4:1-2

The Matthean introductory comment ties this to the baptismal narrative. The Spirit, which was given to Jesus there, now leads him up into the wilderness; perhaps the evangelist is thinking of the mountainous wilderness above the Jordan. The divine Spirit is the true initiator of the occurrence; the devil is here—as also elsewhere in the New Testament and in Judaism—not simply the dualistic, equal opponent of God. Matthew emphasizes specifically the fasting of Jesus: Jesus fasts not only 40 days but also nights, as Moses (Exod. 34:28; Deut. 9:9,18), but not in life-sustaining closeness to God on Horeb, or as Elijah (1 Kings 19:1-8), but not miraculously fed with divine food. The recalling of Moses and Elijah makes clear that Jesus' fasting is extraordinary;[17] but the circumstances are too different to interpret Jesus typologically as the new Moses.[18]

---

[16]The flight miracle does not have messianic character, cf. the references in n. 27 below. The reference to the bitter water of Massah (cf. Dupont* above n. 12) is contained in Deut. 6:16b, a part of the verse which is not quoted. Why did Matthew not supply it as v. 4? Why does the second temptation of Jesus have such a different character from that in Exodus 17? It is more difficult to say whether the first temptation is meant to allude to the manna miracle as does Deut. 8:3. It seems to me certain that the original author of the three temptations who also put together the three quotations from Deut. 8:3; 6:16; and 6:13—must have been aware of the context of the quotations. It is the more striking that the context seems to play no role even in the first temptation: In Deuteronomy 8 nothing is said about a transformation of stones; the quotation in Deuteronomy 8 refers exactly to the miracle which *has* happened. In my opinion, only a few key words and the basic situation of the temptation of Israel have had an influence from the context.

[17]There is an example from antiquity that Pythagoras fasted before his death (!) 40 days (Diogenes Laertius 840; Porphyry, *Vit. Pyth.* 57; Themistius, *Or.* 23,285b [ed. W. Dindorf, reprint, Hildesheim: Olms, 1961]). In Judaism we hear, aside from Moses and Elijah, only with respect to Abraham of an uninterrupted fasting of 40 days (*Apoc. Abr.* 12:1 in imitation of 1 Kings 19:8). The remaining Jewish examples of a fasting of forty days (in H. Bals, τεσσεράκοντα, *TDNT* VIII 137ff.) do not mean complete fasting.

[18]A Moses typology is put into the foreground especially by Gundry 53-59. He points to the "being led up" (v. 1, as Moses to the Sinai), the fasting during 40 days and nights, and the survey of the land from Nebo (Deuteronomy 34). Matthew draws Jesus as the new Moses, in the album for all Christian antinomians, according to Gundry. I am skeptical. Only the second correspondence is truly clear, it seems to me, but it applies not only to Moses (cf. above n. 16). Elsewhere also, the Gospel of Matthew does not emphasize, I think, any personal correspondence between Jesus and Moses (T. Saito, *Die Mosevorstellungen im NT*, EHS. T 100 (1977), 78f.

Because Jesus' fasting is sketched by Matthew as an extraordinary fasting which distinguishes alone the Son of God, it is not legitimate to use our text as the foundation of Christian *quadragesimal fasting*, as has happened often since Augustine.[19] This association was intensified further by the assignment of pericopes which made our text the Gospel for the First Sunday in Lent.[20] The interpretation of the Reformers, which for familiar reasons polemicizes against the therapeutic value of fasting, had a good feel for the uniqueness of the fasting of Jesus.[21]

4:3-4

The hunger of Jesus becomes the occasion for the first temptation. Jesus renounces the miracle, which is not commanded by God. By expanding the quotation from Deut. 8:3, Matthew makes us understand that he is familiar with the Old Testament context, even if Jesus' proclamation is different: Deut. 8:2-5 was concerned with the way on which God led (ἤγαγεν) the people of Israel during 40 years (!) in the wilderness, by testing (ἐκπειράσῃ) to see whether they would keep his commandment, in order to train them like (!) a *son*.[22] Jesus, in contrast with Israel, resists his temptation and thus is the Son of God who "lives from each word which comes out of God's mouth," i.e., he is obedient.

Further possibilities of association are imaginable but not provable. Is there a special reason that Matthew in v. 3a says ὁ πειράζων instead of διάβολος? Does he want to make the temptation of Jesus by Satan in this way a possible introduction to all other later temptations of Jesus, e.g., by the Pharisees?[23] More plausible than this apparent overinterpretation is the deliberation that it is important for the Torah-observant Matthew that Jesus answer Satan three times with a word from the law.[24] One also can ask whether the evangelist thought of the feeding narrative where Jesus does create bread, even if not from stones. He does this, as is stated in 14:14 and 15:32, out of pity for the hungering people. The God-pleasing, not satanic, miracle then would be the one that is done from love.[25] But perhaps this also is an overinterpretation.

4:5-7

The thought which the evangelist has combined with the second temptation cannot be elicited from the Matthean redaction but only from contacts with other texts of the Gospel. Several items will become clear to the reader only at a

---

[19]Köppen* 19f. Tertullian uses our pericope for the legitimation of Christian fasting *after* baptism (*Bapt.* 20).

[20]Cf. the Invocavit sermon of Leo the Great, *Sermo* 39,3 - *BKV* I/55 3f.

[21]"Nobody can achieve such an example" (Luther, *Fastenpostille* 1525, WA 17,II 186), cf. Calvin I 134; Brenz 181; Chemnitz 187.

[22]In reference to the context Deut. 8:2-5, Haenchen *Weg* 67 is correct, "Not the sense of the words, but only the wording itself" has been used by the New Testament narrator.

[23]Cf. especially Wilkens* 481-83.

[24]Gerhardsson, *EvT* 42 (1982) 121f.

[25]Cf. Bornkamm, *"End-expectation,"* 37: "The miracles are . . . manifestation . . . of his mercy and lowliness."

"re-reading" of the Gospel.[26] The key word (ἐκ)πειράζω (v. 7) appears again in 16:1; there also it is the matter of a refusal of a verifying miraculous sign from heaven. Jesus does not authenticate himself by throwing himself from a mountain or by flying through the air as later, e.g., Simon Magus.[27] He will enter the temple the next time in 21:11-17 as a powerless king, without demonstration of his might. Two other associations are probably still more important: At his arrest Jesus forgoes calling God's angels to his aid (v. 6), and remains obedient to the scripture (26:53f.). A little later there is another significant scene: he refuses to follow the scribes who say to the crucified, "If you are the Son of God" (27:40, cf. v. 6), and admonish him to come down from the cross. What is happening here in the second temptation points forward to the obedience of the Son of God in his life and especially (during) his passion.

4:8-11

In a similar way we gain knowledge of the meaning of the last temptation. "Go away, . . . Satan" occurs again in 16:23: Peter, who wants to keep the Son of God from suffering, is rejected with these words. Jesus then speaks about suffering and self-sacrifice, which are involved in following him. Immediately afterwards, accompanied by some of his disciples, he again ascends a "high mountain" (17:1); there the second divine proclamation of the Son of God takes place. Matthew 16:23–17:9 thus recalls baptism and temptation, but in reverse order. The same understanding of sonship with God is the foundation. Most important, however, is the multiple intonation of the final pericope of the Gospel: After Jesus as the obedient Son of God has renounced divine demonstrations of power, has suffered and died on the cross, finally—and again on a mountain (28:16)—the proclamation of his power not only over all kingdoms of the world but over heaven and earth takes place (28:18). The renunciation of power by the earthly Jesus points ahead to the authority of the risen Lord. Through the concluding note that the devil left him and the angels served him, this perspective is already hinted at.

History of Influence and Summary

The difficulties presented by the temptation narrative were not always the same. To put it briefly: (a) In the ancient church it was repeatedly the human features of the temptation narrative, i.e., the fact that the Son of God was tempted at all, which made access to it difficult. (b) In more recent times, is seems that exactly the superhuman features, its mythological dimension, make it difficult to understand.

    a. The temptation narrative was thought through on the basis of the doctrine of two natures. The temptations and the hunger of Jesus refer rather to his humanity; but in

---

[26]Matthew has written his Gospel for this, cf. introduction p. 41.

[27]Ps. Clem. Rec. 2.9.3; 2.37.1, cf. Acts of Peter 31f., non-Christian parallels in Eitrem* 7-10. The fact that the public which would belong to a demonstrative miracle is not mentioned here is not a sufficient counterargument against this interpretation; in a temptation scene the public is not appropriate, for stylistic reasons.

the 40-day fasting of the Son of God, his divinity shows itself.[28] Jesus conquers Satan as God.[29] Monophysite Christology had great difficulty in taking the temptations of Jesus seriously. There was no problem for it to understand how Jesus conquered the tempter, but how the temptation could take place at all was quite another matter. Here the widespread explanation gained ground that the devil wanted to find out through the temptations whether Jesus was truly the Son of God.[30] The temptation of Jesus is an *exploratio Divinae unitionis* (an exploration of the divine union).[31] The human nature is the veil which deceives Satan.[32] His hunger is a pious ruse.[33]

On the other hand, Antiochene Christology was able to find real meaning in the temptation narrative. The Antiochenes agreed with Matthew insofar as they emphasized the willing obedience of Jesus.[34] For example, our story was understood as a test of Jesus' faith: the devil wanted to persuade Jesus that God did not care for his Son.[35] Very common are the interpretations which understand the temptations of Jesus as temptations of the second "man" and contrast them with the temptation of Adam: The devil observes the order of the first deception, but Christ conquers him through his renunciation (hunger), through his humility (pinnacle of the temple) and through his obedience to God's command.[36] The contrast between the temptations of Adam and of Christ stresses the humanity of Christ. This interpretation leads immediately into parenesis.[37]

This part of the history of interpretation makes clear the great distance between Matthew and any kind of Christology which speaks primarily of the divinity of Jesus. It is not by accident that Antiochene theology comes so close to our story. Matthew wants to say that Jesus is the Son of God by being obedient. Jesus is the Son of God by keeping the basic commandment of the

---

[28]Cf. especially Köppen* 85-89. Interesting is the idea of Origen, *Hom. in Luc* 29 = *GCS* 35,180f.: John does not know a story of temptation because he writes a Gospel about the God Jesus.

[29]Cyril of Alexandria, *Comm. in Luc* 4 = *PG* 72,533 (the Logos is οἰκονομικῶς πειραζόμενος); for him, the Almighty, it is a small matter (σμικρὸν . . . κομιδῇ) to overcome Satan (ibid., *Oratio altera* 36 = *PG* 76,1384).

[30]It is probably found for the first time in Clement of Alexandria, *Strom.* 1.9.44.4. The idea usually is that Christ outwitted the devil by an ambiguous use of the Scripture in order that the Sonship with God was hidden from him. Cf. M. Luther in the hymn "Dear Christians, one and all, rejoice" (*LBW* 299), stanza 6: "His royal pow'r disguised he bore/A servant's form, like mine he wore, /to lead the devil captive" (WA 35,424).

[31]Gregory of Nazianzus, *Poem Mor.* 2 = *PG* 37,959.

[32]Gregory of Nyssa, *Orat. Cat. M.* 26,1 = *BKV* I/56 52 ("a kind of deception and dissimulation"), but for Gregory, the (good) end sanctifies the means.

[33]Ambrose, *In Luc* 4:16 = *BKV* I/21 168 (apparent hunger of Jesus, *pia fraus* [pious fraud]). Hilary seeks to make something positive from it: "Dominus . . . salutem hominum esuriens" (the Lord hungering for the salvation of humankind)(929).

[34]Cf. the two articles by Kesich*, especially *Union* 133.

[35]Theodore of Mopsuestia, *Fragm. Dogm.* 13 = *PG* 66,989; similarly Calvin I 137: Satan attacks Jesus' faith: "When you see yourself abandoned by God. . . ."

[36]Especially impresssive is the interpretation for the history of salvation in Irenaeus, *Haer.* 5.21; further material in Köppen* 85-89.

[37]Cf. John Chrysostom 13 = 209-26.

love of God.[38] This understanding of sonship with God opens up a perspective for human existence: The Son of God lives in an exemplary way from God's word alone[39] and obeys God alone. One might say that the entire Gospel of Matthew unfolds what this sentence means for the disciples. Then it also is not by accident that Jesus quotes the scripture three times before he begins at all with his own proclamation.

     b. In modern times[40] our pericope came uniquely into the cross fire of criticism. It seemed mythological, therefore not only unhistorical but also untrue. A main point of offense was again and again the "anthropomorphic" personal appearance of the devil, which is a difficulty for modern persons.[41] Our text became suspect, for it was not from Jesus and was only a haggadic invention of the community in the service of Christology. On the other hand, there were naturally numerous attempts to save what could perhaps be saved. It is perhaps provocative to note that the still remaining saving anchors are exactly those of early rationalism. The most important one is the saving anchor of the vision hypothesis.[42] Conservative interpreters sought their refuge in "deception of the senses," "purely imaginary" changes of place or "hunger phantasms . . . in which the basic striving of human nature for self-preservation . . . makes itself felt."[43] Maldonat already has stated quite correctly that the evangelists could have said it if the temptation of Jesus had been a matter of visions or hallucinations.[44] Historical apologetic led to an emptying of the witness of the text. But the text also was robbed of its meaning when it was interpreted only parenetically and when not only its possibly historical statements but particularly its mythical expressions were no longer taken seriously.[45]

---

[38]I consider the exegetical exposition of this hypothesis, whose systematic basic concern I affirm, in Gerhardsson, *Testing*, to be exaggerated: According to Gerhardsson, the first episode shows that one must love God with one's whole heart, the second, with one's whole life, and the third, with all strength (with all possessions). Why so?

[39]The exegesis of the Reformers has emphasized this especially: It is the Scripture which Christ "held as a shield before him: . . . He had Scripture's testimony at hand with which to repel him" (Calvin I 137). "Christ fights with Satan with no other weapon and no other sword than the holy scripture" (Brenz 195). However, already Luther becomes conscious, on the basis of the second temptation, of his own experience: The devil also quotes Scripture, as did the enthusiasts in his time. Thus our pericope also points to the problematic of the scripture principle (cf. Köppen* 108).

[40]Cf. especially Fascher* 7-25.

[41]"But the personal appearance of the devil . . . is the great stumbling block" (Strauss, *The Life of Jesus*, reprint (St. Clair Shores: Scholarly Press, 1970), I 466); his own classical mythical explanation is developed on pp. 268-73.

[42]It goes back to the early church and was used there for the explanation of the second and third temptation, e.g., in Origen, *Hom. in Luc* 30 = *GCS* 35,184f.; Theodore of Mopsuestia, *fragment* 22 = Reuss 104). In the Middle Ages it is found only rarely (cf. Köppen 100), more frequent again since the Reformation and especially since the Enlightenment (e.g., Paulus I 245-51).

[43]Gaechter 117. Also for Sabourin 44 it is "sans doute" a matter of a "vision mentale."

[44]Maldonat 86: "At Evangelistae non solum non declarant Christi tentationes per visionem accidisse, sed etiam indicant accidisse re vera" (But the evangelists not only do not declare that Christ's temptations happened through a vision, they also indicate that they happened in reality). More indeed need not be said.

[45]An example for such a devaluation of the text as a result of a simple elimination (instead of interpretation) of the figure of the devil is provided by the "Proclamation of the Faith for Adults" (*A New*

Obviously it is not sufficient for the evangelist Matthew, who takes Jesus' humanity, i.e., his fulfillment of God's will, so seriously, to relate at the beginning of Jesus' ministry a purely human story of withstood temptation. Rather he is telling a mythological story. With this it is not our concern to delineate anew the form of mythology in vogue at that time, of which, it seems to me, the personification of the devil is a part. Rather it is our concern not to lose the basic dimension of the obedience of the Son of God which is presented in mythical categories. To the "devil" belongs the experience that the evil is not simply at the free disposal of the human being but can have power over him or her. It also belongs to the mythological dimension of our text that the angels served Jesus (v. 11). They fill the place which the devil has left. They are the mythical expression of the presence and aid of God. And finally it belongs to the mythological dimension that the story does not speak of everyday temptations but of temptations of the Son of God which are intensified into that which is fundamental. Human everyday experiences are not dealt with in our narrative, but it is the question of who has power in the world, the devil whom Jesus does not serve and who has to quit the field, or God who sends his angels. In short, without its mythical dimensions, our narrative would degenerate into an example of everyday experiences which anyone might encounter in various ways. Instead, through its mythical dimensions it becomes a ray of hope and an expression of confidence in the Son of God who through his obedience has overcome the devil and in God whose angels assisted the obedient one. Understood in this way, our story is meaningful at the beginning of a Gospel which unfolds what obedience to God means. Thus it anticipates, so to speak, *in nuce* the path on which the Son of God in the whole Gospel has gone before his disciples, the way which finally leads to resurrection and to authority over heaven and earth (28:18).[46]

3. THE BEGINNING OF THE COMMUNITY IN GALILEE (4:12-22)

3.1. Jesus in the Galilee of the Gentiles (4:12-17)

Literature

See the literature listed at the excursus on the formula quotations at 2:23 above.

Catechism [from *De Niewe Katechismus*, Nijmegen] [New York: Herder & Herder, 1967], 92-93). Here Jesus avoids "three ways . . . obviously desirable for anyone who aims at success." The scope of Matt. 4:1-11 is: "Not success but service."

[46]Dostoyevski's Grand Inquisitor in *The Brothers Karamazov* deepens the perspective in a splendid way: The Son of God who has rejected the devil's offer of rule is judged by his own church, which had to enter the pact with the devil for the sake of the people of whom the way of the Son of God demands too much. Thus the way of the Son of God leads to suffering for humans, through the church.

Text

12 But when he heard that John had been handed over, he returned to Galilee.

13 And he left Nazareth,[1] came and settled in Capernaum at the sea, in the area of Zebulun and Naphtali,

14 in order that that which was said by the prophet Isaiah would be fulfilled:

15 "The land of Zebulun and the land of Naphtali,
   toward the sea, beyond the Jordan,
   Galilee of the Gentiles,

16 the people who were sitting in darkness
      saw a great light,
   and for those who were sitting in the land and shadow of death,
      a light has shined."

17 From that time, Jesus began to preach and to say, "Repent, for the kingdom of heaven has come near."

Analysis

1. *Structure*. A clear delimitation is difficult. Verse 17 is considered by many authors as a new beginning, namely, as the beginning of the first main part of the Gospel. But ἀπὸ τότε is intended precisely to establish the connection with vv. 12-16.[2] It seems to me decisive that our section corresponds to the Markan summary 1:14f. Mark 1:14 has its correspondence in Matt. 4:12, Mark 1:15 in Matt. 4:17. In between, Matthew has inserted v. 13, the move of Jesus from Nazareth to Capernaum, and vv. 14-16 the formula quotation which belongs to it. Not until the move of Jesus to Capernaum, through which the prediction of Isaiah is fulfilled, can the Galilean proclamation of Jesus take place. Thus the text has three parts: v. 12 is the transition and prepares the following. Verse 17 contains the main statement, the beginning of Jesus' proclamation with his first word of proclamation, underscored by two verbs: κηρύσσειν καὶ λέγειν. Verses 13-16 mention the decisive presupposition for the Jesus proclamation which begins in v. 17.

2. *Redaction*. In the frame verses 12 and 17, the evangelist is responsible for the alteration of the Markan pattern.[3] The stereotypical formulations are striking. Verses 12f. correspond exactly to 2:22f. (inclusive formula quotation). In addition, v. 12 recalls 14:13: there Jesus hears of the fate of John and withdraws. The message of Jesus, v. 17, is formulated verbatim identical to the preaching of John in 3:2, and is very similar to the preaching of the disciples in 10:7. The introduction to v. 17 occurs similarly again in 16:21, there also more as a concluding resumption and summing up of earlier statements than as a new beginning. The striking Ναζαρά in v. 13 could be a reminiscence of a lost sentence in the Sayings Source, a trace of which is found also in Luke 4:16. The remainder of v. 13 is redactional: Matthew combines an old report concerning the move of Jesus to Capernaum (cf. below) with words from Isa. 8:23f. (Ζαβουλών, Νεφθαλίμ, παραθαλάσσιος). Perhaps the formulation is also determined already by Mark 1:16 (παρὰ τὴν θάλασσαν). Verse 13 thus is redactional but nevertheless throughout

---

[1]The (text-critically disputed) original text reads: Ναζαρά.

[2]Krentz, Kingsbury et al.; cf. introduction no. 11, concerning the criticism of this thesis, especially nn. 12, 15 there. Also in 16:21, the phrase ἀπὸ τότε ἤρξατο . . . has a connecting function; cf. the analysis of 16:13-20.

[3]Cf. introduction 3.2. Matthean in v. 12: ἀκούσας δέ, ἀναχωρέω, Γαλιλαία; in v. 17: (ἀπὸ) τότε, βασιλεία τῶν οὐρανῶν.

influenced by the tradition.[4]

3. The wording of the *formula quotation*[5] corresponds neither to the Hebrew text nor to the LXX nor to the Targum. It is closest to the Masoretic text.[6] In its first part the quotation is abbreviated in comparison with all known Old Testament texts, e.g., by omitting all verbal statements. This shifts the weight to the second part of the quotation from Isa. 9:2 (MT, 9:1); 9:1 (MT, 8:23) furnishes only a series of subjects for the aorist εἶδεν, subjects which are more closely determined by adverbial statements. Furthermore the second verb ἀνέτειλεν, is extraordinary because this translation of the Hebrew נָגַהּ (λάμπειν) is not at all close and also not documented elsewhere. One may ask whether here a recollection of Num. 24:17 is implied.[7] Then the wording of the quotation presumably presupposes a messianic interpretation of Isa. 9:1-2 and indeed a Christian interpretation, because the passage was not interpreted messianically in Judaism[8] and because the aorists also speak in favor of this. Does this suggest a Christian translation of our passage *ad hoc*? This translation cannot be due to Matthew,[9] for he runs into considerable difficulties in his context through the wording of the quotation. The lesser one consists in the fact that πέραν τοῦ Ἰορδάνου is completely superfluous, for the concern is exclusively with "Galilee of the Gentiles." Why did he not abbreviate here, especially since such large parts of Isa. 9:1 (MT, 8:23) already had been omitted? But the greater difficulty consists in the fact that γῆ Ζαβουλών does not fit into the Matthean context. Jesus moves from Nazareth, which lies in the area of Zebulun, to Capernaum, in the area of Naphtali. What, then, is the meaning of the proclamation of salvation for Zebulun, which Jesus has just left? It is clear that a tension exists here and that Matthew has taken over the quotation only because of "Galilee of the Gentiles" and not at all because of the geographical statements. Thus it was given to him by Christian tradition and has in this case—differently from several quotations from Matthew 1-2—not been "discovered" in connection with its immediate context, v. 13.

4. *Origin.* Leaving aside Mark 1:14f., Matthew obviously uses a tradition according to which Jesus had his established residence in Capernaum.[10] From the Gospel of Mark[11] and from other sources[12] such a tradition can be surmised only indirectly.

---

[4]Cf. introduction 3.1 (participle) and 3.2: Matthean are καταλείπω, ἐλθών, κατοικέω, ὅρια. The introduction to the formula quotation in v. 14 is completely Matthean, cf. excursus at 2:23, section 2.

[5]Cf. especially Stendahl, *School* 104-06, and Soares-Prabhu, *Formula Quotations* 84-105.

[6]In agreement with it alone is: γῆ, twice, connected with καί, the aorists εἶδεν and ἀνέτειλεν, καθήμενος. In agreement with the LXX only is: the form Νεφθαλίμ, σκιὰ θανάτου; the complete omission of the verbs in v. 15 follows the LXX; in addition, there is agreement with LXX A: Ὁδὸν θαλάσσης, ὁ καθήμενος. Ὁδὸν θαλάσσης agrees also with Aquila and Theodotion. One has to ask whether perhaps Ps. 106:10 (καθημένους ἐν σκότει καὶ σκιᾷ θανάτου) and Isa. 58:10 (ἀνατελεῖ ἐν τῷ σκότει τὸ φῶς σου) have influenced Matthew.

[7]Cf. Soares-Prabhu, *Formula Quotations* 100.

[8]Isaiah 9:2 was interpreted in Judaism of the enlightenment by the oral Torah, cf. Str-B. I 162; IV 961. However, "Light" is a name for the Messiah, cf. Luke 1:79 and Str-B I 67.151 (PesiqR 36 = 161a) and 161f.

[9]Pace Stendahl, *School* 106; Rothfuchs, *Erfüllungszitate* 67-70; McConnell, *Law* 119; Soares-Prabhu, *Formula Quotations* 103 (translation from the Hebrew "made in function of the role of the quotation in Mt's Gospel").

[10]Cf. Strecker, *Weg* 95f.

[11]Cf. Mark 2:1; 9:33.

[12]Cf. John 2:12: Here it speaks of a journey of the whole family of Jesus to Capernaum, with an addition (of the evangelist?): "not many days."

Only in Matthew does it gain clearer features: According to Matt. 13:55f. only the (married?) sisters of Jesus all live in Nazareth, but not his brothers and Mary who probably lived with the sons. Matthew 17:24f. also points to this: The temple tax is collected from Jesus in Capernaum (in his residence?). Whose house is the one mentioned in 17:25 remains just as unclear as in 9:10,28.[13] This tradition obviously has led to the formulation in v. 13. Another stumbling block may have been the verse Mark 1:21, which is omitted by Matthew. This detail is interesting in a double way: It shows first how faithfully Matthew paid attention to traditional materials even where he formulated redactionally, and even where he gets into difficulties (as here with the geographical statements of the quotation). Second, it shows that Matthew bears in mind his Gospel of Mark as a whole in advance and works "according to plan," i.e., he already knows at this time that he will omit Mark 1:21-28 and therefore can use v. 21 here.

Interpretation

4:12

After the arrest of the Baptist, Jesus goes to Galilee. The verb παραδίδωμι, familiar to the listener from the passion narrative, is used here in order to make clear the parallel between Jesus and John in proclamation and destiny. Matthew does not provide information about the subjective motives of Jesus for his return.[14] Jesus goes to Galilee for the sole and uncomplicated reason that it corresponds to the divine plan that he minister in the "Galilee of the Gentiles."

4:13

This applies precisely to the move to Capernaum also. Matthew underscores through the allusions to the following quotation that the move corresponds to the divine plan. Why Jesus (biographically) left Nazareth and chose Capernaum as residence[15] is of no interest to him.[16]

4:14-16

In the quotation, the phrase "Galilee of the Gentiles," which summarizes the four preceding geographical statements, is most important to Matthew. With

---

[13]Through Matthew's conception of Capernaum as the residence of Jesus, the thesis of Schweizer that Jesus was for Matthew the prototype of the wandering ascetics (29, cf. 68) becomes very improbable.

[14]Beginning with the early church, the return to Galilee has been interpreted as flight from the enemies of the Baptist, e.g., by John Chrysostom 14,1 = 226f. (Jesus flees from the hatred of the Jews to the Gentiles), Lohmeyer 63 ("secrecy of a human flight"). Linguistically, ἀναχωρέω *can* be understood in this way. But one is enmeshed in the difficulty that Matthew would in this case not have known that Herod, the Galilean tetrarch, who had John executed, ruled over Nazareth and Capernaum as well. Even if this could be accepted, another deliberation excludes the hypothesis of a flight: Matthew puts 4:12f. into parallel with 2:22f. There he speaks of a flight; but in 4:12f. he omits exactly those hints from 2:22f. which would point to a flight.

[15]Κατοικέω = "settle in" (Liddell-Scott s.v.).

[16]"Knowledge" about this we owe to the commentators. The usual information is that Capernaum lies at the lake and offers a favorable opportunity for fleeing. Another suggestion is offered by Meyer 116: Jesus prefers Capernaum because it is more free-thinking by virtue of its dealings with foreigners!

that it is clear that he does not mean that Galilee is settled by Gentiles[17] or that Jesus' ministry had taken place entirely or partly among Gentiles. Matthew in his Gospel makes it clear that Jesus was the Messiah of Israel, ministered in Israel's synagogues, and forbade his disciples to work outside of Israel (10:5f.). Historically also, Galilee was after 70 the heartland of Israel. Thus the designation "Galilee of the Gentiles" has a fictive character. With this Old Testament designation Matthew intends to point on a second level to that which the sending of Jesus has started in the history of salvation: the way of salvation to the Gentiles. In Galilee, the risen Lord will give the disciples the command to make disciples of all Gentiles (28:16-20). Under the future perspective of salvation which is to come to the Gentiles and precisely in agreement with God's plan, Jesus in v. 17 begins his proclamation to Israel.[18] Matthew thus wants to point to a perspective which applies to the entire ministry of Jesus in Israelite Galilee.[19] The formula quotations in 2:23 and 12:18-21 also indicate this hidden perspective. It is important for Matthew that salvation for the Gentiles is a biblical, prophetic perspective. The Gentiles come to salvation when the βασιλεία is taken away from Israel (21:43). Our quotation thus becomes an expression for the basically polemic claim to the Bible of Israel that the evangelist makes after the separation of church and synagogue and after the destruction of Jerusalem.

A theological discussion of this claim cannot be offered until after the exegesis of the decisive sections in Matt. 21–24 and 27.[20] Let me here merely refer to the fact that in the history of interpretation the church exegesis did not generally recognize the basic polemic function of our quotation. Therefore it only rarely had an anti-Jewish effect. The reason for this lies in the exegesis of "Galilee" which was customary since Eusebius:[21] Galilee consists of the "Galilee of the Jews" and the "Galilee of the Gentiles." Therefore our text concerns the sending of Jesus to the Jews, the people sitting in darkness, *and* to the Gentiles who are sitting in the land and shadow of death.[22] Interestingly, it was particularly the allegorical interpretation which came closer to the Matthean scope: "Jesus moves away from Judea to the Gentiles . . . Christ and the

---

[17]Pace Kretzer, *Herrschaft* 79. On the history of Galilee cf. the excursus in Gnilka, *Markusevangelium* I 69-71; on the understanding of Matthew, Ogawa, *Histoire* 60f. The interpretation of the early church often accepts Eusebius's explanation (*Onom.* = *GCS* 11,72): "There are two Galilees, of which one is called 'Galilee of the Gentiles' (namely, the area, probably in upper Galilee, of the tribe of Naphtali which according to 1 Kings 9:11 was granted by Solomon to Hiram) . . ., but the other is in the area of Tiberias and its lake," in the area of Zebulun. "Galilee of the Gentiles" then is a part of Galilee, namely, that situated toward the north and toward the desert area of Phoenicia, in distinction from the "Galilee of the Jews" in the south and on the lake of Tiberias.

[18]That Galilee "of the Gentiles" remains a region of Israel becomes clear at the latest in 4:23,25.

[19]Therefore v. 17 belongs to our text not only on the basis of the Markan source but also as far as its content is concerned. Matthew marks clearly the connection with vv. 13-16: ἀπὸ τότε, and here lays a theological foundation for the whole ministry of Jesus in Galilee which is described in 4:23–19:1.

[20]Cf. the concluding theological remarks at the end of vol. 3.

[21]Cf. above n. 17.

[22]Examples: *Didascalia* 21 (= Achelis-Flemming 109f.); Albertus Magnus 132f. ("uterque populus" [both peoples]).

splendor of the Gospel, no longer the law, is the 'great light.' "[23]

It is very difficult to judge how far the evangelist has interpreted the other statements of the quotation aside from "Galilee of the Gentiles."

Are the "people that sit in darkness" (v. 16) the Gentiles? Since λαός elswhere throughout Matthew means Israel, this is doubtful.[24] It cannot be decided alternatively whether φῶς refers to the person or to the teaching of Jesus. With the area "beyond the Jordan" the evangelist may have thought of the Transjordan, in which Jesus occasionally is active (8:28-34; 14:22-33; 16:5-20; 19:1). It as well as the mention of Zebulun can be understood only in the sense that for the evangelist the Isaiah quotation was fulfilled not specifically in the move of Jesus to Capernaum but in his entire Galilean ministry. "Toward the sea"[25] he understands on the basis of v. 13 not in reference to the Mediterranean Sea but—contrary to the Old Testament passage—of the Sea of Galilee.

Originally, Isa. 9:1-2 (MT, 8:23-9:1) probably dealt with the birth of a Davidite as a sign for the imminent liberation of the three provinces of Dor, Meggido, and Gilead, which had been occupied by the Assyrians.[26] The Matthean interpretation of the quotation does not and cannot agree with the original meaning. As with all of early Christianity and also the interpretation of the prophets by the Qumran sect, the meaning of an Old Testament prophecy opened itself to the evangelist on the basis of the present, which was understood as a special time of God's salvific action.[27] Only we are able to distinguish between the original meaning of a scripture passage and its later actualization.

In this case, there are "bridges" between the original meaning of the Isaiah quotation and its New Testament interpretation. In Isa. 9:5 the eschatological character of the throne names, which "transcended by far the historical significance of every individual Davidite,"[28] is striking. Therefore, there is in our prediction from the beginning an openness which is never historically closed.

In the church's interpretation of this passage, there is to a higher degree than with other Old Testament predictions an inkling of the tension between the original meaning and the New Testament application. Again and again there are deliberations on the fact that the Matthean text does not correspond to the wording of Isaiah. "Primo tempore" (in the first time) (Isa. 8:23 Vg) therefore was meant to refer to the time of

---

[23]Origen, fragment 70 = 44, cf. perhaps also Rabanus 733; Capernaum is interpreted as *villa pulcherrima* (most beautiful village) and *villa consolationis* (village of comfort) which means nothing else but the Gospel. John Chrysostom 14.1 = 226f. refers the quotation back to v. 12 and to the flight of Jesus before the Jews who pursue him "always and everywhere" into the Gentile Galilee.

[24]Cf. on 1:21. Jesus according to Matthew has crossed the borders of Israel only as an exception, cf. on 4:25 and especially 15:29 in difference from Mark 7:31.

[25] Ὁδόν is to be interpreted, as in LXX, as a preposition, cf. LXX Deut. 1:19; 11:30; 1 Kings 8:48; 18:43; etc.

[26]A. Alt, "Jesaja 8,23-9,6" in *Kleine Schriften zur Geschichte des Volkes Israel* II (Munich 1953), especially 210-12; on the total interpretation, H. Wildberger, *Jesaja* I, BK 10/1 (1972), especially 373f.,377,386-89.

[27]Cf. U. Luz, *Das Geschichtsverständnis des Paulus*, BEvTh 49 (1968), 89-94,103-07.

[28]Wildberger (above n. 26), 387.

Tiglath-Pileser.[29] Jerome transmits a Jewish-Christian exegesis which relates the time of the Assyrians and the time of Jesus typologically with each other: Because the tribes of Zebulun and Naphtali were led first into exile, they also were liberated from their errors by Jesus first.[30] Particularly interesting are the thoughts of Calvin, to whom it becomes clear "that Matthew seems to have misused the Prophet's testimony by altering its sense." But he points out that the claim of the Isaianic prediction is not fulfilled by the fact that "King Sennacherib was put to flight" before Jerusalem. The prophet "took a longer view" and predicts "the general restoration of the whole Church." The return of the people from the exile was perhaps the beginning of the light, "At length the fullness of its splendour emerged with Christ the Sun of righteousness."[31]

This interpretation of Calvin is interesting because he does not simply take the word of Isaiah away from Israel and transfer it to a new people, the church. Instead, the fate of Israel is like a "mirror" which furnishes "a portrayal of the state of the human race, previous to its deliverance by the grace of Christ."[32] Fulfillment of Old Testament predictions is found according to this interpretation of Calvin only when Israel participates in it. The idea seems systematically fruitful, but, it must be said clearly, it is not Matthean.

"From that time on"—with this the evangelist picks up everything that was connected with Jesus' residing in Capernaum—Jesus begins his proclamation of the coming kingdom of heaven. He takes up verbatim the proclamation of John the Baptist (3:2). In comparison with Mark 1:15, the reference to the fulfillment of the time,[33] and thus the present element in Jesus' proclamation, is missing. The kingdom of heaven becomes in Matthew clearly an entity which is still in the future (not until and only in 11:12 and 12:28 does the reader learn that it begins already now!).[34] It is the hour of truth which has come close when God reveals himself in his judgment. In view of this understanding of βασιλεία, it becomes comprehensible why Matthew can see the proclamation of the Baptist and of Jesus so closely related. Furthermore, the call to believe in the gospel is missing: Εὐαγγέλιον is for the evangelist nothing else than the βασιλεία proclamation of the earthly Jesus (cf. the excursus at 4:25) and not a Christological kerygma which can be separated from it. Thus this little Markan sentence is superfluous. "Repent, for the kingdom of heaven has come near" interprets in the sense of Matthew decisively and exhaustively what faith in the gospel means. The fact that μετανοεῖτε, the imperative, is put first is significant. If by that is meant the conversion which precedes the

---

[29]Thomas, *Lectura* no. 355 (as a possibility).

[30]Transmitted by Thomas, *Kette* I 147.

[31]Calvin I 153f.

[32]Ibid. 154.

[33]Καιρός is used by Matthew only once eschatologically, in the sense of the eschaton which is still in the future (8:29).

[34]Kingsbury, *Structure* 128-49, submits a completely different interpretation of βασιλεία: for him the present and the future aspect are of equal value; the kingdom is growing in the time of Jesus, which Kingsbury counts from the birth to the parousia (28:20!). This interpretation, it seems to me, overlooks the future eschatological accents of Matthean linguistic usage (cf. εἰσέρχεσθαι words, parables, etc.). Cf. above at 3:2.

Christian life and baptism,[35] then this imperative stands as the entry gate before the soon-to-come teaching concerning the higher righteousness which is to be realized in the life of the Christian.[36] It becomes clear in an exemplary way *that in Jesus' proclamation according to Matthew the imperative precedes and dominates it.* According to God's plan, the righteous Son of God, Jesus, who is victorious over Satan, proclaimed in Galilee God's demand in the light of the approaching kingdom of God, for the future salvation of the Gentiles. The nearness of the kingdom of heaven thus is for Matthew not a second ("indicative") content of the proclamation which would follow after the call to repentance, but is its foundational, intensifying, and sharpening underpinning.

For delineating the Matthean meaning, the completely different interpretation of the early *Luther,* which is based on Paul, is extraordinarily helpful. He sees in the proclamation of Jesus of v. 17 two kinds of speaking of the gospel which interprets the law: "In saying to all 'Repent,' it makes . . . all people sinners and . . . thus brings a *Kakangelium* . . . and exercises a strange office. But in speaking, 'the kingdom of heaven has come near,' it is a good sweet message . . ., and that is its true office, the office of the gospel."[37] Matthew could not distinguish in this manner. For him, the "gospel of the βασιλεία" is the only and indivisible gospel, God's call in the light of the approaching kingdom. His imperative would neither discourage people nor humiliate the proud and convict them of their sin; instead, it is a gift, the chance of salvation granted to the Gentiles.

3.2. The Call of the Disciples at the Sea of Galilee (4:18-22)

Bibliography

Bartina, S., "La red esparavel del Evangelio (Mt 4,18; Mc 1,16)," *EstBib* 19 (1960) 215-27.
Wuellner, W. H., *The Meaning of "Fishers of Men"* (Philadelphia: Westminster, 1967).

Text

18 But when he was walking beside the Sea of Galilee, he saw two brothers, Simon who is called Peter and his brother Andrew, throwing the casting net into the sea; for they were fishermen.
19 And he says to them, "Come here, follow me. I will make you fishers of people."
20 But they immediately left their nets lying and followed him.
21 And when he went on from there, he saw two other brothers, James the

---

[35]Cf. on 3:11.

[36]The *Opus imperfectum* 6 = 674 says in a noteworthy manner on the theme of repentance: "For God who at the beginning did not proclaim righteousness but repentance shows in this way that the guilt of sinners lies not in their ignorant nature but in their will. For repentance is a correction of the will, not an improvement of an evil nature."

[37]II 45f. = WA 1,113f. (Sermon of 1516).

son of Zebedee and his brother John, mending the nets with their father Zebedee; and he called them.
22 But they immediately left the boat and their father and followed him.

Analysis

With Γαλιλαία (v. 18) our text makes a connection with the preceding section, with ἀκολουθέω (vv. 20,22) it points ahead to the following one. The small Matthean emendation of the source Mark 1:16-20[1] increases the symmetry between the two call episodes. The reader is made to feel that this is exactly the way it is when one is called by Jesus.

Interpretation

The call of the two pairs of brothers is described with few words, as in Mark. Simon is introduced, in a different way than in Mark 3:16, from the beginning as Peter, as he is known to the community. As the first apostle (10:2), he is called first in the Synoptics, in contrast to John 1:40-42. Peter is a surname, not the name of an office.[2] Jesus meets the two fishermen as they cast out the casting net or round net.[3]

4:19

He calls them away from their work and wants to make them fishers of people. By means of the parable of the net, this expression is in the Gospel of Matthew clearly defined as missionary activity (cf. 13:47).

4:20

The two leave their nets immediately and follow Jesus. The word ἀκολουθέω, which is important for Matthew, occurs here for the first time. The little word εὐθέως and the leaving of the nets, which are not even pulled up on land, show the complete obedience of the two.

4:21–22

In the second episode, the reference to the day-laborers of Zebedee is omitted, certainly not because the evangelist wanted to conceal the relative wealth of the family and not because he wanted to underscore the harshness of the break with the father who is left alone after this, but because it is superfluous for the

---

[1] Cf. introduction 3.1 and 3.2. The following are Matthean: v. 18: περιπατέω (?, avoidance of the double pronominal παράγων παρά Mark 1:16); putting the apposition "two brothers" ahead at the introduction of new persons (cf. v. 21; 9:9); ὁ λεγόμενος after proper names; βάλλω; v.19: historical present with λέγει; omission of the superfluous ὁ Ἰησοῦς; ποιέω with double accusative (omission of γενέσθαι; v. 20: οἱ δέ, εὐθέως; v. 21: καί + participle + ἐκεῖθεν; the mention of the father in Mark 1:20 appears to be appended and is moved forward by Matthew; v. 22: cf. on v. 20.

[2] All apostles whose names could give rise to confusion have a surname or addition in Matt. 10:2-4. While Mark (almost) consistently avoids the name Simon, after 3:16 (change of name), in Matthew Simon appears in pericopes where this name is anchored in the tradition and in addresses (16:17; 17:25, as already in Mark 14:37).

[3] The ἀμφίβληστρον is cast out, sinks low, and is pulled together again, in distinction from the pull net (σαγήνη, cf. 13:47), cf. Krauss, *Archäologie* II 143,145f.; Dalman *Arbeit* VI 346f.; Bartina* 217-22.

narrative and disturbs the symmetry of the two call narratives. However, he has deliberately shifted the little word "immediately" in order to emphasize as in v. 20 that the two called persons were radically obedient to Jesus. The exactly parallel concluding words of the two episodes in v. 20 and v. 22 (οἱ δὲ εὐθέως ἀφέντες . . . ἠκολούθησαν αὐτῷ show what is important for the evangelist.

Summary

Since "disciples" is an ecclesiological term[4] in the Gospel of Matthew, and the community, on the basis of 4:15f., recognizes its own spiritual place in the "Galilee of the Gentiles," it knows that our text speaks of its own origin. Besides, Simon's call is put first and, by means of τὸν λεγόμενον Πέτρον, is emphasized; Peter has distinctive significance in the area of Syria.[5] But Matthew is not concerned with tracing the beginnings of the community back to Jesus historically. Nor is he primarily concerned in securing through eyewitnesses the reliability of the tradition, particularly of the immediately following Sermon on the Mount.[6] Neither are the beginnings of the circle of the twelve apostles (cf. 10:2), so important for the early period of the church, the object of his interest. How little he thinks "historically" is demonstrated by the fact that the circle of the twelve is never truly constituted; after the call of the four disciples and of Matthew (9:9) its existence is simply taken for granted in 10:1f.[7]

Rather, Matthew sees the earthly Jesus and the exalted Lord, active in the present, together. Thus this narrative of the origin of the community has at the same time "typical" significance for him. Where Jesus' gospel of the kingdom of heaven is proclaimed (4:17), there people are called to radical obedience. This is the way in which community arose and arises. In the summary of 4:23-25, the succession of v. 23 and v. 25 expresses the same thought. And finally this thought is determinative also for the structure of the following chapters: Matthew describes Jesus' ministry through word (chs. 5-7) and deed (chs. 8-9); but this description leads immediately to the activity of the disciples and to the community (ch. 10). For Matthew the ecclesiological dimension evidently belongs to the history of the proclamation and of the ministry of Jesus. Exactly for this reason it has to become clear in the prologue also that result and goal of the arrival of Jesus, the Son of God, in Galilee is the origin of the community. "Galilee of the Gentiles" is the place of origin (*Ur-Ort*) of the community.

In what way does the episode have "typical" significance? Since v. 19 speaks of the task of proclamation and the eleven disciples are entrusted with it also in 28:16-20, one might see in our text a call of the commissioned preachers

---

[4]Luz, *ZNW* 62 (1971) 141-60.

[5]Cf. introduction 5.1 and 5.5.

[6]*Opus imperfectum* 7 = 674.

[7]Matthew avoids the word ἀπόστολος (only 10:2) and calls the twelve also usually μαθηταί. Μαθητής is a term which permits the identification of the community with the twelve disciples, ἀπόστολος does not (cf. Luz [n. 4] 157).

of the church. But the resumption of the central key word ἀκολουθέω in v. 25 makes this impossible: There the concern is—typical for Matthew[8]—the discipleship of the ὄχλοι. The fact that Matthew uses the central verb ἀκολουθέω, which he applies so often to the disciples, immediately also for the relationship of the populace to Jesus gives a clear indication for the interpretation: following on the part of the disciples does not distinguish them from the people who are sympathetic to Jesus, but the people, by following, belong together with the disciples. We have here a first indication of the structure of the Matthean community, in which there is neither a special group of followers nor a constitutive structure of office.[9] For the Matthean understanding of discipleship, it is characteristic that it exists after Easter as well, and that it constitutes no less than the true essence of the church.[10]

It suits Matthew that he more or less radicalizes the demand of following Jesus. This is seen not only in the emphatic "immediately" in the description of the leaving of nets and father but also in the significance which the leaving of the physical father in favor of obedience to the heavenly Father has in the Gospel of Matthew as a whole (cf. 8:21; 10:35-37; 19:29; and especially 23:9, where earthly fatherhood seems generally excluded!). Possibly here the painful break with the synagogue is in view, which in the diaspora situation had still more importance and included also the division of families. However, it is important that such radical obedience, which entails the break with the family, is demanded in Matthew of *all* members of the community.

History of Influence

The history of interpretation[11] offers many deliberations which were remote from the evangelist. The concern of our narrative is not that uneducated people are to be called into the ministry of proclamation.[12] Contrary to many interpretations, it must be emphasized that Matthew depicts the four who are called as seeing Jesus for the first time. It belongs to the style of such call narratives that nothing is said about preceding encounters of the four with Jesus. These features try to bring out the authority of the command and the completeness of obedience. Contrary asseverations of earlier times were especially intended to harmonize our text with John 1:35-51 (and Luke 5:1-11).[13] In more recent times conservative rationalists (!) are concerned more with saving the psychological plausibility,[14] and therefore the historicity, of the "ideal" scene[15] with

---

[8]Cf. 8:1; 12:15; 19:2; 20:29 (always in the redaction).

[9]The expositions of Trilling, *Amt*, show how few occasions Matthew offers for this.

[10]Even Mark no longer understood "following" literally, but as the relationship of all Christians to Jesus, a relationship that has its center in suffering.

[11]On the later history of the motif of the fishers of people in the early church and in iconography, cf. Wuellner* 239-46.

[12]Since Jerome on this passage ("Uneducated people are sent to preach in order that one does not think that faith . . . arises through the art of rhetoric and teaching"). Calvin I 157-58 has to argue against the view that one belittles the education of pastors on the basis of this passage.

[13]Augustine 2,17 (37,41).

[14]Gaechter 133: Jesus earlier at the Jordan River made an appointment with the brothers. John 1:40-42!

[15]This designation does not imply a judgment on the historical content of the scene.

such assertions.

The history of influence is strongly determined by the name of one of the four who were called and concerning whom we know the least: Andrew. Precisely because we have no other information concerning Andrew, our text became the gospel for St. Andrew's day (November 30). Since so little about Andrew is known from the Bible, many originally Gentile customs could be connected with this day.[16] Numerous interpretations and sermons on the text therefore are influenced by the legends of Andrew,[17] particularly through the idea that he followed Jesus into death on the cross, a theme in the story of his martyrdom.[18]

---

[16]Andrew as a patron against gout and the so called "Andrew illnesses" (among others, anthrax); magic and spook on the night of St. Andrew; the night of Andrew as a night of coitus, etc.; cf. P. Sartori, "Andreas" II, *HWDA* I 398-405.

[17]P. M. Peterson, *Andrew, Brother of Simon Peter: His History and His Legends*, NT.S 1 (1958).

[18]Cf. Luther's impressive sermon of 1516 (!) = WA 1,101-04.

II. The Activity of Jesus in Israel in Word and Deed

INTRODUCTORY SUMMARY (4:23-25)

Literature

Lohfink, G., "Wem gilt die Bergpredigt? Eine redaktionskritische Untersuchung von Mt 4,23f and 7,28f," *TQ* 163 (1983) 264-84.
Neirynck, F., "The Gospel of Matthew and Literary Criticism," in Didier, *Évangile* 37-69.

Text

23 And he went about in all of Galilee, taught in their synagogues, proclaimed the gospel of the kingdom, and healed every sickness and every weakness among the people.
24 And his fame spread throughout all of Syria. And they brought to him all the sick who were suffering from various diseases and pains, those possessed and epileptics and paralytics, and he healed them.
25 Large crowds followed him, from Galilee, from the Decapolis, from Jerusalem, from Judea, and from the land beyond the Jordan.

Analysis

1. *Composition.* Verse 23 is repeated almost word for word in 9:35. Thereby, Matthew creates a clear inclusion for chapters 5-9. Particularly Schniewind has shown that v. 23 anticipates even the structure of these chapters: "The Messiah of the word, the preaching one, is described in chs. 5-7, the Messiah of the deed, the healing one, in chs. 8–9."[1] With the catchwords Γαλιλαία, κηρύσσω and βασιλεία, v. 23 connects with 4:12,15,17. The catchword διδάσκω points ahead to 5:1f. Our section, although a superscription for chapters 5-9, has a clearly connective character and illustrates the Matthean tendency to combine main sections with transitional pericopes instead of

---

[1] P.36.

separating them by caesuras. Verses 24f. also are carefully formulated from the point of view of composition and constitute with 5:1f. and 7:28–8:1; 8:16 a frame around the Sermon on the Mount:[2]

4:23 Καὶ περιῆγεν . . . διδάσκων – – – μαλακίαν	9:35
4:24 προσήνεγκαν αὐτῷ πάντας τοὺς κακῶς	
ἔχοντας/δαιμονιζομένους/ἐθεράπευσεν	8:16
4:25 ἠκολούθησαν αὐτῷ ὄχλοι πολλοί	8:1
5:1 (ἀναβαίνειν) ὄρος (καταβαίνειν)	8:1
5:2 (διδάσκω)	7:29

In form, our text is a summary statement. The healing activity of Jesus is the central theme, not, as in the following chapters 5-7, the teaching. Miracles of healing are handed down as the main content of the summary statements from Mark; Matthew follows his source here closely. The structure is awkward: After a titlelike sentence concerning Jesus' proclamation and healing in Galilee (v. 23), another remark concerning Jesus' healing follows in v. 24b; v. 24a hangs somewhat in the air and would be better suited as a preparation for v. 25 where he speaks of the crowds who follow Jesus.

2. *Redaction.* The awkward structure is explained on the basis of the sources. Although the summary as such has no parallel in Mark, Matthew, faithful to his tradition, formulates freely only in very few points:[3] The decisive title sentence v. 23 is indeed his creation, but formulated by closely following Mark 1:29, cf. 1:14,21,34; 6:6. Mark 1:28,32,34 is the basis of v. 24, Mark 3:7f. of v. 25. Thus the evangelist took an overview of broad parts of his Markan source and excerpted it. He knows in advance precisely which texts of Mark he will omit. He proceeds according to a well-deliberated plan.

Interpretation

Matthew composes a comprehensive summary statement before reporting any details of the teaching and healing activity of Jesus. The many passages which take up this summary (besides 9:35 also 8:1,16; 12:15f.; 14:35; 19:2), give the impression of something typical. The units from the proclamation and healing activity of Jesus which follow in chapters 5-9 are individual examples. Thus Matthew does not intend to present the historical biographical course of the ministry of Jesus. Rather he commences with a total picture which he makes concrete with individual examples in that which follows.

4:23

In accordance with the tradition (cf. Mark 6:6) Matthew has Jesus travel about in Galilee. The evangelist refers the little introductory sentence v. 23a ("he went about in all of Galilee") to everything which follows, up to the new approach in 19:1 which is emphasized just as much ("he went away from

---

[2]Neirynck* 67, Lohfink* 168-71. One really should take 4:23–5:2 as *one* pericope. It is not only the introduction to the Sermon on the Mount, however, but in its first part to the whole of chapters 5-9.

[3]The following are Matthean (cf. introduction 3.2): v. 23: εὐαγγέλιον τῆς βασιλείας, νόσος, μαλακία, λαός; v. 24: ἀπέρχομαι, σεληνιάζομαι, βασαν-, παραλυτικός (cf. 8:6; 9:2,6); v. 25: ἀκολουθέω with ὄχλοι. The place-names correspond partly to 3:5. Συρία and Δεκάπολις are hapax legomena.

Galilee"). The composition shows that he imagines Jesus at first in the environment of his place of residence, Capernaum (8:5,14; 9:1). The teaching of Jesus "in their synagogues" indicates two things: Jesus turns to Israel and teaches as a teacher of Israel in the synagogue just as his miracles are meant for the chosen people.[4] But at the same time the emphasis[5] *"their* synagogues" makes clear that the evangelist and his community have their own place outside these synagogues. It becomes perceptible only on the basis of the whole of the Gospel of Matthew that "preaching" and "teaching" do not mean two different things.[6] Matthew had indicated the content of the proclamation already in 3:2 and 4:17: It concerns repentance in view of the approaching kingdom. Chapters 5-7 will unfold what Matthew understands by "teaching."

Alongside of the teaching, there is the healing of Jesus. The evangelist emphasizes that all the sick were brought to Jesus and that he healed *every* illness.[7] He makes the healing miracles of Jesus practically his "normal" activity.[8] Important for him is probably not so much the embellishment of the miraculous power of Jesus as his obedience vis-à-vis the mission of the servant of God (cf. 8:14-17) and the basic turning to human beings. The Septuagintal word μαλακία[9] is used in the New Testament only by Matthew and means perhaps "weakness" in distinction from the stronger expression "illness."[10] The biblical coloring fits well the statement that Jesus heals the illnesses "among the people," i.e., in Israel, the people of God.

4:24

In v. 24, Matthew indicates with the three catchwords "demon possessed," "epileptics," and "paralytics" healings which he will relate later (8:28-34; 9:1-8; 17:14-21) as examples. In view of the Sermon on the Mount it is important that a summary portrayal of the teaching ministry of Jesus has already preceded it. Indeed Matthew is concerned in the first place with the *teaching* of Jesus, and therefore he puts chapters 5-7 before chapters 8-9. But the teacher Jesus is none other than the Son of God who accompanies the people—also the community—with his helping power so that the crowds can follow him. Verses 23f. thus point to a dimension of the "indicative" of salvation, which is so often missed in Matthew.

4:25

It belongs to the picture of Jesus' activity that the crowds follow him. From 4:21

---

[4]On λαός cf. on 1:21.

[5]Cf. 9:35; 10:17; 12:9; 13:54; 23:34 and introduction 5.2 and 5.3.

[6]Cf. the excursus at 4:25.

[7]Cf. 8:16; 9:35; 10:1; 12:115; 14:35.

[8]Jesus heals all illnesses also according to Justin *Apol.* 1.31,48,54; Pseudo-Clementine *Hom.* 1.6.4.

[9]Deut. 7:15 (πᾶσαν μαλακίαν/πάσας νόσους) and introduction 3.2. Μαλακία is also a loan-word in rabbinical language, cf. Kraus, *Lehnw.* II 340.

[10]Cyril of Alexandria, fragment 37 = Reuss 164: Μαλακία = πρόσκαιρος ἀνωμαλία τοῦ σώματος; νόσος = ἀσυμμετρία τῶν ἐν τῷ σώματι στοιχείων.

the reader knows what "following" means: Matthew indicates by mentioning the following of the crowds[11] that he understands the narrative of "following" (4:18-22) as paradigmatic. The crowds and the disciples who follow in vv. 18–22 must not be understood as two circles which have to be completely distinguished;[12] rather Matthew indicates by this method that discipleship will expand into the church. He also needs the crowds from a compositional point of view in order to secure his understanding of the Sermon on the Mount where the crowds along with the disciples will be the hearers (cf. on 5:1f.), for what is said there to the disciples applies also to the people who are called to follow him.

It is not easy to determine the meaning of the geographical data. In comparison with the source, Mark 3:8, Matthew omits (Gentile, 15:21f.) Tyre and Sidon, also Idumea.[13] Whether the regional terms describe the holy land Israel[14] depends on the understanding of the statement concerning the Decapolis. Strong Jewish minorities[15] were living in all cities of the Decapolis. But it is especially important that for the greatest part the area of the Decapolis belonged to the "biblical Israel." Presumably, the evangelist wanted to speak of the ministry and the success of Jesus in Israel. It is different only with v. 24a: The report about Jesus—and only that—already spreads beyond Israel and reaches probably the whole Roman province of Syria.[16]

Excursus: Preaching, Teaching, and Gospel in Matthew

The juxtaposition of *preaching* and *teaching* in Matthew is striking (4:23; 9:35; 11:1). Do we have to differentiate between the two?[1] The evidence seems ambivalent: Matthew more strongly than Mark combines with διδάσκω the interpretation of the law and

---

[11]Frequently redactional, cf. 8:1; 12:15; 14:13; 19:2; 20:29.

[12]Luke offers a completely different picture with the distinction of the δώδεκα, the μαθηταί, and the πλῆθος τοῦ λαοῦ, cf. Luke 6:12-17.

[13]In 4:25 and 5:1 he speaks of ὄχλοι, not as in 4:23 of the λαός. Naturally Matthew means de facto large crowds from Israel. But he formulates this very carefully: Jesus carries out his healings in and for the holy people (λαός). Not the holy people follow him, however, but the ὄχλοι. The evangelist was able thereby to accomplish different things: he could emphasize the great success of Jesus with large numbers of people from Israel (plural!). At the same time the term ὄχλος is more neutral than λαός and better suited for understanding the people who "follow" as the potential church.

[14]Trilling, *Israel* 111; Lohfink* 275f.

[15]Schürer II 121ff. passim.

[16]Matthew cannot simply designate the περίχωρος τῆς Γαλιλαίας (Mark 1:28), i.e., southern Syria, as Συρία; the expression ὅλην τὴν Συρίαν speaks unambiguously against this understanding (*pace* Maier I 96; Lohfink* 274). But he also does not mean Syria as the whole Levantine area of which Palestine is a part; this linguistic usage is, according to W. Röllig, "Syria," *KP* V (1975) 469, relatively rare and is missing in the NT; cf. also Zahn 172, n. 24. If the Roman province of Syria is meant, then it is a conspicuous change in comparison with Mark, which must have a reason. Is the evangelist thinking of his own home?

[1]The differentiation of *kerygma* and *didache* is fundamental in all of early Christianity, according to C. H. Dodd, *The Apostolic Preaching and Its Developments* (New York: Harper, 1964), 7-35. A differentiation for Matthew is advocated, e.g., by Bornkamm, "End-Expectation," 38, n.1; Hahn, *Mission* 120f. Schweizer 43f.; Ogawa, *Histoire* 75f.

ethical proclamation of Jesus in terms of content (5:2,19; 7:29; 15:9; 22:16; 28:20) and
with the synagogue or the temple, in terms of geography (4:23; 9:24; 13:54; 21:23;
22:16; 26:55). The addressees of the teaching are the disciples (5:2; 7:29) and the people
of Israel (5:2; 7:29; 9:35; 11:1; 13:54; 21:23; 26:55), only once the Gentiles (28:20). A
comparison with Mark reveals the deliberate changes Matthew made so as to combine
"teaching" with law and ethics.[2] A distinguishing nuance in comparison with Mark lies
in the fact that the command to "teach" is quite deliberately also given to the disciples
(28:20); in this way they continue also the work of Jesus.[3] The linguistic usage of
Matthew thus is not entirely original, even though it is more pointed than Mark's.

Matthew connects κηρύσσω with εὐαγγέλιον and with βασιλεία, thereby
taking up a widespread early Christian usage.[4] The addressees of κηρύσσειν for him are
the people of Israel and the Gentiles (24:14; 26:13), never the disciples, for κηρύσσειν
means the missionary proclamation. In distinction from Mark, the content of the
proclamation is nearly always[5] stated. Just as the content of the "gospel" in Matthew
must be determined by βασιλείας, he usually specifies the content of the proclamation
by the phrase "gospel of the kingdom" or by a brief sentence (3:1f.; 4:17; 10:7). Can we
say therefore that Matthew deliberately distinguishes the preaching and the teaching of
Jesus?

The summarizing of the Sermon on the Mount by the double expression
"preach" and "teach" in 4:23; 9:35; 11:1 contradicts this conclusion.[6] The mission
command also, which speaks only of "teaching" (28:20), contradicts this opinion,
although Matthew elsewhere can speak of the "proclamation" of the gospel to the
Gentiles (24:14). Is there then in Matthew beside the *didache*, or before it, still a special
kerygma? The question of the relationship of κηρύσσειν and διδάσκειν thus becomes a
basic question of Matthean theology.

The expression εὐαγγέλιον τῆς βασιλείας which Matthew in 4:23;
9:35; and 24:14 combines with κηρύσσειν could give a hint. He has subjected
the expression εὐαγγέλιον, so important to Mark, to a thoroughgoing revision.
He has eliminated all passages which could be understood as if the gospel, i.e.,
the proclamation of the church, would go beyond the earthly Jesus or stand
alongside him.[7] Quite consistently he has determined εὐαγγέλιον by an
attribute.[8] He emphasizes through the addition of τῆς βασιλείας that he
understands by εὐαγγέλιον the proclamation of the earthly Jesus. But in 26:13

---

[2]Διδάσκω is missing in the Matthean parallels to Mark 2:13; 6:30,34; 10:1; 11:17 (absolute statements); 4:1f. (parables); 8:31; 9:31 (passion predictions).

[3]H. Flender, "Lehren und Verkündigen in den synoptischen Evangelien," *EvT* 25 (1965) 705.

[4]Cf. Mark 1:14; 13:10; 14:9; Rom. 10:15f.; 1 Cor. 9:23,27; 15:1,11; 2 Cor. 11:4; Gal. 2:2; Phil. 1:15f.;
1 Thess. 2:9; Col. 1:23; with βασιλεία Luke 8:1; 9:2; Acts 20:25; 28:31.

[5]Exception (aside from 10:27): 11:1.

[6]The thesis of Schniewind, stated above on 4:23-25, n. 1, would be falsified if one would have to
distinguish between *kerygma* and *didache* in Matthew.

[7]Mark 1:1 (the book of Mark as the beginning of the proclamation); 8:35; 10:29 (εὐαγγέλιον next to
Jesus as his "extension" into the present time).

[8]According to P. Stuhlmacher, *Das paulinische Evangelium* I, FRLANT 95 (1966), 241, and G.
Strecker, "Das Evangelium Jesu Christi," in *Jesus Christus in Historie und Theologie* (FS H.
Conzelmann), ed. G. Strecker (Tübingen: Mohr, 1975), 541, Matthew is based on an open, not yet
Christologically fixed usage of εὐαγγέλιον, i.e., probably (so Stuhlmacher) on the Old Testament-
Jewish usage which permits a new determination.

he makes clear that this means not only the words of Jesus[9] but also his deeds. *It is decisive for Matthew that all church proclamation* (εὐαγγέλιον) *is oriented on the earthly Jesus and has no other content than his words and deeds.* The expression εὐαγγέλιον τῆς βασιλείας is "Matthew's own capsule-summary of his work."[10] Proclamation and ministry of the earthly Jesus become the only standard and content of the church's proclamation.

The formulation τοῦτο τὸ εὐαγγέλιον τῆς βασιλείας (24:14) is most difficult. Since τοῦτο is not made precise by the context, τοῦτο τὸ εὐαγγέλιον can mean only the gospel of Jesus contained in the whole Gospel of Matthew. The identification of εὐαγγέλιον with the Matthean writing has not yet been made directly but it is foreshadowed.[11] It is not by accident that the identification of εὐαγγέλιον with a book appears for the first time in the environs and in the sphere of influence of the Matthean community, namely, in the Didache.[12] The Matthean identification of εὐαγγέλιον with the proclamation and the ministry of the earthly Jesus is the Didache's presupposition.

All this means that *proclamation* of the kingdom and *teaching* about conduct that is desired by God cannot be separated from the totality of the Gospel of Matthew. Whoever reads the Gospel continuously will remember, in determining the content of the proclamation, the basic statements of 3:1f. and 4:17. But this proclamation of the kingdom has its zenith from the beginning in the call to action. We observe something similar in the Sermon on the Mount: it is διδαχή (5:2), and yet it is addressed not only to the disciples but also to the people. Here we find the commandments of Jesus which he has ordered to be kept (28:20). The Sermon on the Mount begins with a reference to the kingdom of heaven (5:3,10), which is the content of the proclaimed gospel (4:23). *The Sermon on the Mount thus does not presuppose the gospel of the kingdom but is this gospel.* From this it follows: preaching and teaching are related in Matthew not as announcement of salvation and imperative, for the proclamation also aims at the imperative,[13] and the teaching also points to the kingdom. The proclamation of the kingdom places the demand into the horizon which is set and promised by God while, on the other hand, the teaching makes concrete the demand of the gospel.[14] The accents are—on the basis of the linguistic usage of the tradition—a little different; the matter is the same.

---

[9]W. Marxsen, *Mark the Evangelist* (Nashville: Abingdon, 1969), 140ff., considers the five discourses of the Gospel of Matthew as *evangelia*.

[10]Kingsbury, *Matthew* 131.

[11]Cf. Schniewind 241 (on 24:14); Dibelius, *From Tradition to Gospel* 264, n. 1 ("this gospel which I proffer in my book," on 24:14); O. Michel, "Evangelium," *RAC* 6,1107-60, there 1114.

[12]Didache 8:2; 11:3; 15:3f.; cf. 2 Clem. 8:5. In Ignatius, εὐαγγέλιον also refers to the earthly Jesus (cf. *Phld.* 5:1; 9:2). It seems to me quite possible that Ignatius also can understand by εὐαγγέλιον a written Gospel, cf. *Phld.* 9:2; *Smyrn.* 7:2; *Phld.* 8:2 (alongside the OT).

[13]Cf. Strecker, *Weg* 127: Proclamation is "address through which a new condition is created, a call to decision which is answered by repentance or refusal and which is followed in the final judgment by preservation or rejection."

[14]Flender (above n. 3) 706: "With regard to form, . . . in Matthew the gospel has the form of teaching and the law the form of proclamation."

A. THE SERMON ON THE MOUNT (CHS. 5-7)

Literature

A. *Exegetical Literature:*
Barth, G., "Bergpredigt," *TRE* 5 (1980) 601-18.
Betz, H. D., "The Sermon on the Mount: Its Literary Genre and Function," *JR* 559 (1979) 285-97.
Bischoff, E., *Jesus und die Rabbinen*, SIJB 33 (Leipzig: Heinrichs, 1905).
Bligh, J., *The Sermon on the Mount. A Discussion on Mt 5-7* (Slough: St. Paul Publications, 1975).
Böcher, O. "Die Bergpredigt—Lebensgesetz der Urchristenheit," in O. Böcher, et al. *Die Bergpredigt im Leben der Christenheit*, BensH 56, pp 7-16 (Göttingen: Vandenhoeck & Ruprecht, 1981).
Bornhäuser, K., *Die Bergpredigt. Versuch einer zeitgenössischen Auslegung*, BFCT 2,7 (Gütersloh: Bertelsmann, 1923).
Bornkamm, G., "Der Aufbau der Bergpredigt," *NTS* 24 (1977/8) 419-32.
Burchard, C., "Versuch, das Thema der Bergpredigt zu finden," in *Jesus Christus in Historie und Theologie* (FS H. Conzelmann), ed. G. Strecker, pp 409-32 (Tübingen: Mohr, 1975).
Davies, *Setting.*
Dibelius, M. "Die Bergpredigt," in idem, *Botschaft und Geschichte* I, pp. 79-174 (Tübingen: Mohr, 1953).
Dupont, *Béatitudes* I-III.
Eichholz,. G., *Auslegung der Bergpredigt*, 6th ed. (Neukirchen-Vluyn: Neukirchner, 1984).
Fiebig, P., *Jesu Bergpredigt*, FRLANT 37 (Göttingen: Vandenhoeck & Ruprecht, 1924).
Friedlander, G., *The Jewish Sources of the Sermon on the Mount* (1911), reprint (New York: Ktav, 1969).
Goppelt, L., "Das Problem der Bergpredigt," in idem, *Christologie und Ethik*, pp. 27-43 (Göttingen: Vandenhoeck & Ruprecht, 1968).
Guelich, R. A., *The Sermon on the Mount. A Foundation for Understanding* (Waco: Word, 1982).
Heinrici, G., "Die Bergpredigt," in idem, *Beiträge zur Geschichte und Erklärung des NT* III, pp. 1-98 (Leipzig: Edelmann, 1905).
Hoffmann, P., "Auslegung der Bergpredit I-V," *BibLeb* 10 (1969) 57-65, 111-122, 175-89, 264-75; 11 (1970) 89-104.
Jeremias, J., *The Sermon on the Mount* (London: Athlone, 1961).
Kürzinger, J., "Zur Komposition der Bergpredigt nach Matthäus," *Bib* 40 (1959) 569-89.
Lapide, P., *The Sermon on the Mount: Utopia or Program for Action?* (Maryknoll: Orbis, 1986).
Lohfink, G., "Wem gilt die Bergpredigt? Eine redaktionskritische Untersuchung von Mt 4,23-5,2 und 7,28f." *TQ* 163 (1983) 264-84.
Miegge, G., *Il Sermone sul Monte* (Torino: Editrice Claudiana, 1970).
Pokorný, P., *Der Kern der Bergpredigt* (Hamburg: Reich, 1969).
Reuter, R., "Die Bergpredigt als Orientierung unseres Menschseins heute," *ZEE* 223 (1979) 84-105.
———, "Bergpredigt und politische Vernunft," in *Die Bergpredigt: Utopische Vision oder Handlungsanweisung?* ed. R. Schnackenburg, pp. 60-80 (Düsseldorf: Patmos, 1982).
Schnackenburg, R., "Die Bergpredigt," ibid. 13-59.
Schneider, G. *Botschaft der Bergpredigt* (Aschaffenburg: Pattloch, 1969).

Schweizer, E., *Die Bergpredigt*, KVB 1481 (Göttingen: Vandenhoeck & Ruprecht, 1982).

Soiron, T., *Die Bergpredigt Jesu* (Freiburg: Herder, 1941).

Strecker, G., *Die Bergpredigt. Ein exegetischer Kommentar* (Göttingen: Vandenhoeck & Ruprecht, 1984).

Stuhlmacher, P., "Jesu vollkommenes Gesetz der Freiheit. Zum Verständnis der Bergpredigt," *ZTK* 79 (1982) 249-82.

Tholuck, A., *Exposition, Doctrinal and Philological, of Christ's Sermon on the Mount, according to the Gospel of Matthew* (Edinburgh: T. & T. Clark, 1834-53).

Windisch, H., *Der Sinn der Bergpredigt*, 2d ed., UNT 16 (Leipzig: Hinrichs, 1937).

Wrege, H. T., *Die Überlieferungsgeschichte der Bergpredigt*, WUNT 9 (Tübingen: Mohr, 1968).

B. *Literature on the history of interpretation and influence:*

Althaus, P., "Luther und die Bergpredigt," *Luther* 27 (1956) 1-16.

Barth, G., "Bergpredigt" (loc. cit. sub A) 611-18 (good survey; bibliography).

Berner, U., *Die Bergpredigt. Rezeption und Auslegung im 20. Jhdt.*, GTA 12 (Göttingen: Vandenhoeck & Ruprecht, 1979).

Beyer, H. W., "Der Christ und die Bergpredigt nach Luthers Deutung," *LuJ* 14 (1932) 33-60.

Beyschlag, K., *Die Bergpredigt und Franz von Assisi*, BFCT 57 (Gütersloh: Bertelsmann, 1955).

Idem, "Zur Geschichte der Bergpredigt in der Alten Kirche," *ZTK* 74 (1977) 291-322.

Diem, Harald, *Luthers Lehre von den zwei Reichen, untersucht von seinem Verständnis der Bergpredigt aus*, reprint BEvT 5 (Munich: Kaiser, 1973).

Duchrow, U., *Christenheit und Weltverantwortung. Traditionsgeschichte und systematische Struktur der Zweireichelehre*, FBESG 25 (Stuttgart: Klett, 1970).

Fascher, E., "Bergpredigt II Auslegungsgeschichtlich," *RGG* 3d ed. I (1957) 1050-53.

Geyer, H.-G., "Luthers Auslegung der Bergpredigt," in *"Wenn nicht jetzt, wann dann?"* (FS H.-J. Kraus), ed. H.-G. Geyer et al., pp. 283-93 (Neukirchen-Vluyn: Neukirchner, 1983).

Heintze, G., *Luthers Predigt von Gesetz und Evangelium*, esp. pp. 147-211, FGLP 10/11 (Munich: Kaiser, 1958).

Jacobs, M., "Die Bergpredigt in der Geschichte der Kirche," in O. Böcher, *Bergpredigt* (loc.cit. sub A) 17-40.

Kantzenbach, F. W., *Die Bergpredigt* (Stuttgart: Kohlhammer, 1982).

Kissinger, W. S., *The Sermon on the Mount: A History of Interpretation and Bibliography*, ATLAMS 3 (Metuchen: Scarecrow, 1975) (bibliography).

Laurila, K. S., *Leo Tolstoi und Martin Luther als Ausleger der Bergpredigt*, AASF B 55 (Helsinki: Suomalainen Tideakatemie, 1944).

Luz, U., "Die Bergpredigt im Spiegel ihrer Wirkungsgeschichte," in *Nachfolge und Bergpredigt*, ed. J. Moltmann, KT 65, pp. 37-72 (Munich: Kaiser, 1981).

Scharffenorth, G., "Die Bergpredigt in Luthers Beiträgen zur Wirtschaftsethik," in *Schöpferische Nachfolge* (FS H. E. Tödt) ed. C. Frey and W. Huber, pp. 177-204, TM.FEST A 5 (Heidelberg: Forschungsstätte d. Evang. Studiengemeinschaft, 1978).

Schellong, D., *Das evangelische Gesetz in der Auslegung Calvins*, TEH 152 (Munich: Kaiser, 1968).

Schlingensiepen, H., "Die Auslegung der Bergpredigt bei Calvin," diss. Bonn 1927 (partial print, Berlin: Eberling, 1927).

Schnackenburg, R., *Bergpredigt* (loc. cit. sub A) 36-55.

Stadtland-Neumann, H., *Evangelische Radikalismen in der Sicht Calvins. Sein Verständnis der Bergpredigt und der Aussendungsrede (Mt 10)*, BGLRK 24 (Neukirchen-Vluyn: Neukirchner, 1966).

210

Stoll, B., "De Virtute in Virtutem," diss. Bern (typescript, 1986).

Stuhlmacher, P., *Gesetz* (loc. cit. sub A) 294-306.

Tholuck, A., *Auslegung* (loc. cit. sub A) passim (fundamental commentary on the history of interpretation).

Troeltsch, E., "Die Soziallehren der christlichen Kirchen und Gruppen," *Ges. Schr.* 1, 3d ed. (Tübingen: Mohr, 1923), passim.

Wünsch, G., *Die Bergpredigt bei Luther* (Tübingen: Mohr, 1920).

C. *Important Sources:*

Augustinus, *De Sermone Domini in Monte,* PS 34, 1230-1308; Engl.: *The Sermon on the Mount Expounded* (Edinburgh: T. & T. Clark, 1973).

Barth, K., *CD* II/2 (1957), 686-700.

Baumgarten, O. *Bergpredigt und Kultur der Gegenwart,* RV 6, 10-21 (Tübingen: Mohr, 1921).

Bonhoeffer, D., *Discipleship*, pp. 95-198 (New York: Macmillan, 1959).

Luther, M., "Wochenpredigten über Matth 5-7. Das fünffte, sechste und siebend Capitel S. Matthei gepredigt und ausgelegt (1532)," WA 32,299-555.

Ragaz, L., *Die Bergpredigt Jesu* (1945) (Hamburg: Furche, 1971).

Socinus, F., *Concionis Christi quae habetur capite 5-7 apud Matthaeum Evangelistam Explicatio* (Irenopolis 1656).

Thurneysen, E., *The Sermon on the Mount* (London: SPCK, 1965).

Tolstoy, L., *My Confession, My Religion, The Gospel in Brief* (New York: Scribners, 1929).

Wyclif, I., *Opus Evangelicum,* ed. I. Loserth (London: Wyclif Society, 1895).

Structure

1. *Structure of the Sermon on the Mount.* The analysis of 4:23-25 demonstrated that the evangelist has encased the Sermon on the Mount with ringlike inclusions.[1] This "ring shaped" conception seems to be continued in the inner parts of the Sermon on the Mount. It is built symmetrically around a center, namely, the Lord's Prayer (6:9-13). The sections before and after the Lord's Prayer correspond to each other. This results in the schema on p. 212.

---

[1]Cf. the analysis of 4:23-25.

5:1f. Situation	Framework	7:28–8:1a Reaction of the hearers

I: ὄχλοι, διδάσκω, ἀνα(κατα)βαίνω . . . ὄρος

Leading in/Leading out

5:3–16 Introduction		7:13–27 Conclusion

I: βασιλεία τῶν οὐρανῶν
twice: 5:3,10; 7:21
F: 5:3–10 3d person 7:21–27
5:11–16 2d person 7:13–20

5:17–20	Introit/Conclusion of the main section	7:12

I: νόμος καὶ προφῆται

Main section

5:21–48 Antitheses	6:19–7:11 Possessions, judging, and prayer

L: 59 lines in Nestle for each

6:1–6	6:16–18

Righteousness
before God

6:7–15

The Lord's Prayer
with frame

Correspondences: I = inclusions
L = correspondence in the length of the sections*
F = other formal correspondences
Cf. also the frame 4:23–9:35 at Matt. 4:23–25, above p. 203.

Correspondence in length is found elsewhere in Matthew, cf. introduction p. 38. Particularly the observations of Kürzinger are important here. The length of the sections which correspond to each other is unequal in each case and thus cannot be traced to a "normal size of paper." With the antitheses, the length of the antitheses 1-3 and 4-6 correspond exactly, cf. introduction to 5:21–48, n. 1.

Since Matthew largely uses traditional material, following closely his sources in wording and order, the architectonic symmetry is much the more astonishing. It is apparent only when the Sermon on the Mount is read in context, and even then it does not reveal itself in the first reading[2] but only to repeated perusal and, in a manner of speaking, in an "optical" view. The structure of the Sermon on the Mount already clearly gives indications as to how it should be understood: The Lord's Prayer is its central text. The kingdom of heaven, promised for the future, governs the whole Sermon on the Mount. The true sense of "law and prophets," opened up by Jesus is the leitmotif of the main part.[3]

Within the individual main sections, frequently but not always a three-part division can be seen as the principle of order: the introduction and conclusion are tripartite (5:3-10,11f.,13-16; 7:13f.,15-23,24-27); 2 times 3 antitheses are next, then the tripartite teaching on piety (6:1-18) with the insertion of the Lord's Prayer which is framed by one saying in each case and again tripartite. Matthew 6:19-24 and 7:1-11 have three parts as well. Naturally, such findings are partly questions of exegetical judgment. It remains striking, however, how often the judgment of the exegete is pointed in a certain direction. In addition to the inclusions, there are repetitions of catchwords, as, e.g., πατήρ . . . spread throughout the whole Sermon on the Mount, or μεριμνάω, προσεύχομαι, etc., in shorter sections. The frequency of repetitions, formulaic expressions, and parallelisms correspond to the Semitic manner of arrangement. However, the ring composition of the Sermon on the Mount, which stretches into the wider context, and the correspondence of individual sections in length in Matthew are without analogy, in my thinking.

Sources

2. *Sources.* The Sermon on the Mount is a composition shaped by the evangelist Matthew. We presuppose that the Sayings Source lies at the basis of the Sermon on the Mount. The evangelist is following the structure of the Sermon on the Plain (Luke 6:20-49). But it must be conceded to the critics[4] that precisely here

---

[2] Again an indication of the fact that the Gospel of Matthew was intended in the first place for reading and not for hearing (not a book of pericopes for worship!).

[3] The proposed arrangement follows especially Kürzinger* and R. Riesner, "Der Aufbau der Reden im Matthäus-Evangelium," *Theologische Beiträge* 9 (1978) 173-76, without being completely identical with them. As far as possible, formal viewpoints serve as the orientation in order to avoid the circle between interpretation and arrangement. Other proposals for the arrangement: Bornkamm* divides into three main sections: 5:1-48; 6:1-7:12; 7:13-27; the Lord's Prayer is central for the arrangement of 6:19-7:11 (cf. introduction to 6:19–7:11). At times the Beatitudes were understood as the table of contents of the entire Sermon on the Mount, and that in inverted order, cf. Dupont, *Béatitudes* III 316-20.

[4] Wrege* attempts to show that there was no Q and that the Sermon on the Mount throughout is based on reliable oral tradition. Peculiarly, he only discusses the question of the wording but not that of the common sequence of material in the Sermon on the Mount and Luke 6:20-49. Too one-sidedly he also excludes the influence of the texts of the Gospels on the Christian tradition of the 2d century. There is not only the alternative, influence of a Gospel text *or* influence of oral tradition, but as a rule, these two overlap; written texts can be passed on again in oral tradition or be cited by memory, etc. H. D. Betz presupposes in various publications on 5:3ff.; 5:17ff.; 6:1ff.; 6:22f.; 7:21ff. (cf. the bibliography on each passage) that the evangelist has used a Jewish-Christian Sermon on the Mount as source without changing it during the integration into the Gospel. The thesis, which never was substantiated in detail, fails, it seems to me, (a) because of the compositional integration of the Sermon on the Mount in the context (ring composition even beyond the Sermon on the Mount proper!) and (b) generally because of the impossibility of detecting any manner of difference between the author or redactor of the source and that of the Gospel of Matthew.

in the Sermon on the Plain it is not possible to reconstruct a Q text from Matthew and Luke which is identical in detail. There are several variants between the texts of "QMt" and "QLk," which is to be expected with a text that is used so frequently.

Matthew has supplemented the Sermon on the Plain with other material. This material comes from:
(a) other parts of Q, of which sometimes the texts lie adjacent and/or appear in the same order;[5] or
(b) special material. In the case of Matt. 5:21–6:18 it can be shown as probable that the special material was handed down in writing: Matthew has used as the foundation of this section a written source of 3 antitheses and 3 rules of piety and has added the Q material subsequently to this basic text.[6] Other verses (e.g., 5:5,7-9,14b,41; 6:34) Matthew probably has found in written form in his copy of Q. There are very few verses for which we cannot comment on the origin (e.g., 6:7f.; 7:6).

The Matthean redaction is very careful and at the same time very conservative. It is especially intensive in key passages (e.g., 5:17-20,48; 6:1; 7:12-14,21-23). In many cases it can be shown that Matthew has not edited the material simply as a free author but was influenced in his redaction by the language and the life of his community (e.g., 6:9-13; 7:13f.) or in an indirect way by his sources (e.g., 5:10,31,38,43; 7:15,19f.).

Meaning

3. *The meaning of the Sermon on the Mount in Matthew.* The Sermon on the Mount is the first detailed proclamation of Jesus in the Gospel of Matthew. For this reason, it has foundational character. It is the only discourse of Jesus which contains almost exclusively commandments of Jesus. When in 28:20—again on a mountain—Jesus commands the eleven disciples to teach the nations all "that I have commanded you," it is probably a recalling of the Sermon on the Mount. It is thus the central content also of the Christian mission proclamation. One might call its theme "the righteousness of the kingdom of heaven," using two catchwords which permeate the whole sermon. A few fundamental accents of the Matthean Sermon on the Mount are to be indicated before the interpretation:
a. *Matthew aims at Christian practice.* A Christian is one who acts according to the commands of Jesus. Therefore Matthew emphasizes the unity of teaching or hearing and acting (5:19; 7:21-23). The Sermon on the Mount thus is not "theology,"[7] but "command" of Jesus, fulfilled νόμος (5:17). Therefore, we are not at all confronted with the question of the true

---

[5]Luke 11:33-36 = Matt. 5:15; 6:22f.; Luke 12:22-34 = Matt. 6:25-33,19f.; Luke 13:23-29 = Matt. 7:13f.,22f.; 8:11f.; less certain: Luke 11:2-4,9-13 = Matt. 6:9-14; 7:7-11; completely uncertain or improbable: Luke 16:13,17f. = Matt. 6:24; 5:32,19.

[6]Cf. the introduction to 5:21-48 and to 6:1-18. A special source M which goes beyond this is improbable, contra Kilpatrick, *Origins* 14-26.

[7]For this reason already it is not an epitome in the ancient sense, contra Betz* 296f. Besides, it (1) does not summarize more detailed materials as, e.g., the κυρίαι δόξαι of Epicurus or the Enchiridion of Epictetus, and (2) is not a general summary of the teachings of Jesus but underlines a certain sphere, namely, ethics.

"understanding," but only with the more comprehensive question of the true practice of the Sermon on the Mount.[8]

Again and again in the recent history of interpretation the question of the *"practicability"* of the Sermon on the Mount is raised. It was clear for Matthew and the whole church until the post-Reformation period that the Sermon on the Mount is practicable. It not only must be done but also can be done. But Matthew has only in a small measure in his redaction made the Sermon on the Mount "practicable" by mediation of the "ideal" and "absolute" demands of Jesus with reality. There are a few such "adaptations" (e.g., [pre-Matthean?] 5:32,42), but they stand next to redactional additions which underscore the radicality of the demands all the more, e.g., 5:25f.,29f. Neither Matthew nor the community before him understood "practicability" in such a way that the minimum or the "more" of the commands of Jesus, which the community is necessarily obliged to keep, is defined. The commands of Jesus' Sermon on the Mount were not interpreted as Christian halakah.[9]

b. *The gospel of action is an expression of grace.* The Sermon on the Mount is demand, "imperative." Even the Beatitudes are not a proclamation of grace preceding the demands. Yet for Matthew grace happens in the proclamation of the demands of Jesus, and that in a double way: For one, the Sermon on the Mount is embedded in the history of God's action with Jesus. The one who forgets that the Sermon on the Mount does not come until after Matt. 1-4 and, in the meaning of Matthew *can* not come any earlier, has misunderstood it. The Sermon on the Mount is *Jesus'* sermon: in it Jesus the Son of God speaks, through whom God guarantees the truth of his claim. An interpretation which does not proceed from Christology but wants to be true, intelligible, or "rational" in itself is a misunderstanding according to Matthew. Furthermore, the Sermon on the Mount in its center (6:9-13) intends to lead the acting person in prayer to the Father. According to Matthew, an interpretation of the Sermon on the Mount is a misunderstanding if it overlooks the fact that the center of its practice is prayer.[10]

c. *The Sermon on the Mount puts the central command of love with other exemplary demands of Jesus.* Matthew has lifted out the command of love as the central command (first and last antithesis; golden rule). However, the will of God is not reduced by him to love; next to it there are the other commands. Matthew insists on the fruits (7:15-20). Therefore it is not sufficient that the person does something out of love. Matthew asks *what* the person does out of love. The individual commands of Jesus and of the Bible are for him valid

---

[8]While writing and reading a "scholarly" commentary on Matthew one should think about this discrepancy between the "fruit" which was desired by the evangelist and that which is present in the commentary: in 7:24-27 the evangelist speaks of hearing and doing; in 13:23 the evangelist redactionally adds "understanding" and "doing" to "hearing" and "bearing fruit." *For Matthew, the understanding and the practice of the Sermon on the Mount are indissolubly connected.*

[9]Only in 5:32 can one speak of halakah.

[10]Stuhlmacher* 291-93 brings this out beautifully. But I differ from him (a) through my "imperatival" interpretation of the Beatitudes and (b) by differentiating between the law of Moses in Matthew, which is fulfilled in Christ, and the Pauline "law of Christ" (Gal. 6:2), which includes the abrogation of a considerable part of the law of Moses.

commands of God up to the iota and dot.[11] But they are not laws which prescribe accurately how a Christian must act in every situation. They are not sentences of law but exemplary demands which portray in examples the manner and radicality in which God demands obedience. The freedom to invent new examples is always a part of exemplarity. Therefore, it is for Matthew neither an unambiguous definition of Christian action nor a complete freedom in the sense of "dilige et fac quod vis" (love and do what you wish)! He thinks of the Christian life most easily as a way which has the goal of perfection (5:20,48) and whose direction and radicality are clearly marked by the individual commands, like tracers which are lighted by their goal. Matthew does not define what the definitive way is for the situation of each community and every Christian and especially not how far one is supposed to go on that way. He only says: as far as possible, in any case further than the scribes and Pharisees (5:20).

d. *The Sermon on the Mount is ethics for disciples.*[12] It presupposes the calling of the disciples (4:18-22). Jesus teaches (5:1f.) the disciples. The higher righteousness of the Sermon on the Mount is a characteristic of the disciples which precisely distinguishes them from the Pharisees and scribes (5:20). Individual commands presuppose the proclamation of Christ (5:10-12) or the existence of the community (6:9-15,25-34; 7:15-20). The praxis of the Sermon on the Mount is conducive to the people praising the Father in heaven (5:16). Thus it is that the word of proclamation aims at deeds (Matt. 28:20!), and deeds, in turn, become proclamation. This entails that for Matthew the ethics for the disciples is not the unique ethics of a circle of followers of Jesus who live in isolation. Rather it is true that:

e. *The Sermon on the Mount makes a demand of the whole world through the proclamation of the disciples.* Not only the disciples but also the crowds are addressed by the Sermon on the Mount (4:25f.; 7:28f.). In the proclamation by word (28:20) and deed (5:16) the entire world is confronted. Many of the demands of Jesus clearly point beyond the limits of the community (cf. 5:25f.,39-41,44f.). The Sermon on the Mount as ethics for the people of God is at the same time God's will for the whole world to which it is proclaimed (28:19f.).

f. *The Sermon on the Mount gives instruction for the fulfillment of the law and prophets.* The Matthean Jesus programmatically appeals to the Old Testament, which he himself "fulfills" by his deeds and his proclamation as a permanently valid word of God (5:17). The Old Testament thus remains the basis and center (7:12; cf. 22:40) of the will of God and is deepened and intensified by Jesus' proclamation of the will of God. In the situation where the

---

[11]Thus, Matthew does not understand the ethics of Jesus in such a way that the human being, if he or she "really 'loves,' really 'knows' what he or she has to do" (Bultmann, *Jesus and the Word,* 94). The "formal, external authority of the scripture" is exactly not "surrendered" by Jesus (ibid., 67) according to Matthew. Nevertheless, obedience of the whole person is demanded. Thus the Bultmannian contrast between "formal," external "authority of law" with a "neutral attitude of the ego," on the one hand, and "total obedience," "insightful demand," and "absolute character of the demand of God," on the other hand (ibid.), does not at all paradigmatically agree with the Matthean understanding of Jesus.

[12]Lohfink* has brought out this and the following aspect in an especially fine way. It also stands in the center for Bornhäuser* and Jeremias* (particularly 183-89), however, without sufficient distinction between Jesus and the Matthean community.

community and the synagogue go separate ways, this programmatic reference back to law and prophets means a no toward Israel, for whom Jesus is not the key to the Bible.

g. *The Sermon on the Mount formulates the entrance demands for the kingdom of heaven.* The glance at the kingdom of heaven is laid like a bracket around the Sermon on the Mount (5:3,10; 7:21). Already 4:17 and 4:23 indicate that it is εὐαγγέλιον τῆς βασιλείας. Obviously the kingdom is future: the community *will* enter it if it walks on the way of righteousness (5:20). The petition of the Lord's Prayer for its coming is in the center. The practice of the disciples is for Matthew not an "ethical" sign of the new world already dawning,[13] but neither is it only "interim ethics," understood as the very *special* ethos of the last, brief time before the end.[14] Rather, the Sermon on the Mount is the pure uncorrupted expression of the will of God as it agrees with law and prophets, i.e., as it always was. In this sense, it defines the conditions of entry into the kingdom of God.[15] The peculiar situation of the Christian community consists in that God through his Son Jesus has given it an example, a teacher, and a helper, and that through him a community of brothers and sisters has been founded which practices the will of the Father.

Here, *differences of emphasis between Matthew and the proclamation of Jesus* become apparent: In the proclamation of Jesus, the hidden *presence* of the kingdom of God is emphasized more strongly. Jesus has understood his demands as an *ethics of contrast*, as a symbolic realization of the *coming* kingdom of God in the midst of the old world. In Matthew, the community only progresses toward the kingdom of heaven. The continuity with law and prophets was not lifted out programmatically by Jesus, as is done in Matt. 5:17-19 and 7:12, even if he obviously understood himself to be a messenger of God to his people. The Matthean community, naturally, looking back to Easter, accents the priority of grace in a different way than did Jesus himself.

But, on the whole, for me the *preserved continuity* is significant, rather than the newness of the Matthean conception. The basic elements of the proclamation of Jesus, the unity of word and deed, the combination of his proclamation with his mission, the radicality of his demands—and even the language of Jesus—have been preserved by Matthew to a high degree. Therefore it follows that in the Sermon on the Mount we have to do with a presumably very high proportion of genuine words of Jesus.

The differences for the most part are new accents which became necessary through the changed kerygmatic and historical situation. The relationship of Jesus to the βασιλεία breaking in in his ministry needed a new interpretation after Easter. The

---

[13]Dibelius* thinks along these lines, e.g., 134 (Jesus' sayings are "signs of the kingdom of God"). After Easter, the communities have adapted the sayings of Jesus to their own everyday life in the short time before the coming of the end (141f.). In a way, they are now in this period, where "they cannot be completely fulfilled" (146), signs of hope for the *coming* kingdom. Akin to Dibelius is also the basic approach of K. Barth* to the interpretation of the Sermon on the Mount as the "order of life proper to the Sabbath day" of the kingdom of God (CD II/2,686).

[14]A. Schweitzer, *The Quest of the Historical Jesus* (London: Black, 1936), 400. J. Weiss, *Jesus' Proclamation of the Kingdom of God* (Philadelphia: Fortress, 1971), 112, compares the commands of the Sermon on the Mount with "martial law," arising from the mood of battle, which is not suitable for peacetime. But Matthew does not understand his ethics specifically for the community prior to "entering into the kingdom of heaven" like this; these are not special prescriptions, but the true and always valid will of God.

[15]Windisch's basic thesis thus recognizes the *Matthean* conception (for which he was not highly concerned!); the difference consists only in the Christology which is presupposed in Matthew.

intensified parenesis corresponds to the situation of the community, which after approximately 50 years of Christian proclamation of grace obviously had to combat a flagging obedience and "little faith." The emphasis on the continuity with law and prophets became internally and externally necessary when the Christian communities found themselves no longer in but alongside of the synagogal mainstream of Israel.

History of Influence

4. *On the history of the interpretation of the Sermon on the Mount.* I would not want to present here the whole history of influence of the Sermon on the Mount,[16] but only to point to an aspect which is important to me, namely, the connection between the interpretation of the Sermon on the Mount and the church situation at any given time. Biblical interpretations cannot be freely chosen, particularly in the period before the Enlightenment, as if one might always make the choice for "the" correct interpretation. Rather they are to a high degree expressions of the church's understanding of itself and of the proper church reality at a given time. Thus they demonstrate how an author in his or her time has understood the commission of the church. The (relative) possibility of the separation of the interpretation of the Sermon on the Mount and the situation came about only through the historical-critical method, which permitted a basic distinction between that which was meant by the Sermon on the Mount and one's own position. Friedrich Naumann is a good example. A journey to Palestine led him to the insight that the Sermon on the Mount, in his words "the Protestant-Franciscan" form of Christianity, "has arisen in a completely different spiritual temperature from our own"[17] and therefore cannot be transferred to politics. Johannes Weiss and Albert Schweitzer, who recognized in Jesus an "interim ethic," did not at all think of accepting *it* as their own ethics. This possibility of differentiating, which is available through the historical method, means for us, on the one hand, a—relative—chance of knowledge; on the other hand, it has the result that the recognized text is principally without significance for the present, i.e., significant only insofar as the exegete, from his or her perspective, individuality, and competence, attributes significance to it.[18] Interpretations of the Sermon on the Mount from the time before the Enlightenment were always an expression of the relevance of the Sermon on the Mount for its interpreter, i.e., they reflected always his or her church situation and his or her own approach to interpretation. Therefore it is important to ask for the basic relationships between the interpretation of the

---

[16]For a short orientation, cf. Schnackenburg* 36-55, Stuhlmacher* 295-306 and the lexicon articles by Barth* and Fascher*. There is no detailed monograph on the interpretation of the Sermon on the Mount. Beyschlag, *ZTK* 1977, correctly deals mainly with individual texts for the ancient church, Berner* only with the 20th century. In particular, the Catholic realm lies completely fallow; the monograph by Soiron,* in the section on the history of interpretation, deals almost exclusively with Protestant scholars!

[17]F. Naumann, *Werke* I (*Religiöse Schriften*), ed. W. Uhsadel (Cologne-Opladen: Westdeutscher Verlag, 1964), 828 (in a debate).

[18]The final chapter in Windisch's book, entitled "Theological Exegesis of the Sermon on the Mount" (126-86), is an impressive documentation of how an exegete who is influenced by Lutheranism, i.e., by ethics of intention and the *usus elenchticus* of the law, struggles for the value of the Sermon on the Mount which he is not able to accept in the way in which he has interpreted it.

Sermon on the Mount and the ecclesiastical reality.

In this, the most helpful debate partner was for me Ernst Troeltsch, despite some corrections in individual matters. He distinguishes sociologically between the church and the sect. Certain types of piety and theology correspond to them. While a piety of salvation and religion of grace corresponds to the "church" as an institution of salvation and grace, the "sect," as a "free congregation of strong and conscious Christians," emphasizes "the law instead of grace" and establishes "in its circle with greater or lesser radicalism the Christian life-principle of love." In the sect, Christ is "the Lord, the example and the law-giver of divine majesty and authority," not primarily the Savior. The realization of holiness is central for the sect; "actual redemption" will take place only in the future, through judgment and "establishing the kingdom of God."[19] The piety of the sect is often the piety of Jesus while Paul is decisive for the church type.

Individual features of this conception need not be discussed here. The most fruitful thought is that the Matthean theology can be understood frankly as a classical example of "sect theology," i.e., as a theological draft of a minority group which was led by Jesus to *its* life-principle of obedience and love. Matthean theology is basically perfectionistic. It understands grace centrally as help in praxis. In a "sect" like the Matthean community, the piety of the Sermon on the Mount is brought to bear. The examples from the history of interpretation which will be given with the comments on the individual texts will show that it was again and again such small groups for which the Sermon on the Mount was central and which came very close to its meaning. Examples are the early church in the time before Constantine, early monasticism and church fathers close to it, such as John Chrysostom, medieval marginal groups like the Waldensians, Franciscans, or also Cathari, the marginal groups of the Reformation period, particularly the Anabaptists, also the Quakers and early Methodists. They all advocate a "perfectionist" type of interpretation. For all of them the command of God was a basic and immovable element in their piety and their life. It is astonishing in what measure one can find in these groups analogies to the Matthean design.

In comparison to this, it is amazing how distant the main churches are from the Sermon on the Mount. In the *Catholic tradition of interpretation*, the two-level ethic which is emphasized by the Reformation polemic is not the dominant model of interpretation. Rather, since Augustine and under constant appeal to him, the Sermon on the Mount is interpreted in a perfectionist manner: The "perfect . . . sermon" "shapes" through its commandments the "Christian life."[20] In the Sermon on the Mount "the whole perfection of our life is contained."[21] The two-level ethic appears only at the interpretation of individual passages and also only relatively late. It is true that since an early time individual commands of the Sermon on the Mount were related in a special way to individual groups, e.g., the clergy, but it was not until Rupert of Deutz (c. 1100) that the concept of *consilium* (counsel) was introduced in the exegesis

---

[19]Troeltsch* 967f.

[20]Augustine* 1 (1).

[21]Thomas, *Lectura* no. 403 ("in isto sermone Domini tota perfectio vitae nostrae continetur").

of the Sermon on the Mount.[22] Here monastic examples which up to then were connected rather with Matt. 19 (and Matt. 10) intrude into the interpretation of the Sermon on the Mount. Thomas Aquinas, whose interpretation represents an important attempt at systematizing the commandments of the Sermon on the Mount in light of *praecepta* (precepts) and *consilia* (counsels), shows that they apply now and always to every Christian and are only peripherally the basis for special *consilia*.[23] The polemic of the Reformers is directed against an interpretation which even in the medieval church hardly determined the interpretation of the whole Sermon on the Mount. Sociologically one may say, in a simplified way, that the dominant church of the Middle Ages preserved the type of interpretation of the time when it was still a minority church. It preserved—to use Troeltsch's language—the type of interpretation of its "past as a sect." The distinction between *praecepta* and *consilia*, which was added later, was an additional attempt at integrating rigorist, monastic traditions into the church's interpretation of the Sermon on the Mount which, despite its perfectionist understanding, went farther and farther away from the basic meaning of the Sermon on the Mount. But the opinion that the Sermon on the Mount did not apply to the "ordinary" Christian never existed. Rather, as in the past, it was supposed to lead *all* Christians on the way of Christian perfection and to preserve, so to speak, a grain of the salt of the minority church in the dominant church.

On the *Reformation interpretation* I deliberately would like to formulate only a few probably very subjective impressions. Luther's as well as Calvin's interpretations of the Sermon on the Mount are decisively influenced by discussions with Anabaptists. As an interpreter who himself stands in the Reformation tradition, I am at first impressed by the Anabaptists who not only understood but also practiced the Sermon on the Mount in an exemplary manner. The interpretation of the individual texts will repeatedly turn back to the Anabaptists. In the protocols of investigations and disputations with largely quite simple, theologically uneducated Anabaptists, one discovers over and over the basic elements of Matthean theology: the priority of practice before teaching, the will to obedience, the fact that the individual command is taken seriously, that it does not simply dissolve in the commandment of love, the will to the formation of brotherly and sisterly community. With the Reformers, on the contrary, one is impressed by the possibility for the Christian to engage in the world and the attempt to think of dealings in both kingdoms under the guideline of love.[24] Its central concern is to understand the activity of the Christian on the basis of justification as actions of a *person* who is beloved by God, and whose deeds are exactly for that reason free because they are not works.

---

[22]Stoll* 63f.

[23]Thomas, *ST* I/II, q. 108, art. 4 speaks of the three *consilia* of poverty (Matt. 19:21), chastity (Matt. 19:12) and obedience. It is interesting that he bases their integration into the *lex nova* (new law) on the freedom which belongs to the new law and which obviously was no longer contained in the Latin concepts of *lex* and *praeceptum*.

[24]Althaus* 2f.,11f.; Duchrow* 542-52.

However, from the viewpoint of Matthew, who asks so intensively for the *fruits* of the Christian (7:15-23!), the *consequences* of the Reformation approach to interpretation have to be thought through completely. Here I am confronted by weighty questions:

a. With the Reformers, for the first time the tones which emphasize the *unfulfillability of the Sermon on the Mount* gain the upper hand.[25] In the prior history of interpretation the basic tendency had been different.[26] This turn presumably came about with the Reformers' deepened understanding of sin and their central Pauline starting point. It had the result that in post-Reformation theology the Sermon on the Mount, which, it was now believed, nobody can completely keep anyway, became more and more the law in the Pauline sense—the accuser before the tribunal of God where the acquittal takes place alone on the basis of the expiatory death of Christ.[27] It is understandable that his interpretation in the long run did not lead to the insistence on the practice of the Sermon on the Mount but to its internalizing.

b. When can a Christian act independently of his or her secular relationships? Luther distinguishes between a Christian and his or her acting "in relatione" (Christian-in-relation), i.e., as man, woman, child, neighbor, or officeholder.[28] At the time of the Reformers it is already difficult to recognize where the Christian can act as a Christian. Theoretically, the approach of Luther is clear: Where the interests of the neighbor are involved, the behavior of the Christian has to be different than when only his or her own interests are concerned. But where is it *not* a matter of the interests of the neighbor? Renunciation of possessions, e.g., touches not only the owner but also, e.g., his or her family. Thus it is not surprising that the Reformers in contrast to their theological starting point give often very guarded advice for praxis. To obey Christ literally would also mean "to give room to that which is unjust," something which one

---

[25]Luther, "On the Councils and the Church," *LW* 41:71; "The Bondage of the Will," *LW* 33:140ff.; Zwingli, "Divine and Human Righteousness, July 1523," *Huldrych Zwingli Writings*, vol. 2, trans. and ed. H. W. Pipkin (Allison Park: Pickwick, 1984), 1-42; Calvin, *Institutes* 2,7,5.

[26]The fundamental unfulfillability of the Sermon on the Mount was stated only by the Jew Trypho in Justin, *Dial.* 10.2. For the ancient church, on the other hand, this question "actually did not exist" (Beyschlag, ZTK 1977*, 297, cf. the individual examples, ibid. 298f.). For individual commands, notably for the second, fourth, and fifth antithesis, the question of fulfillability is indeed discussed, but, e.g., the concept of the step-by-step progress of the Beatitudes presupposes the fundamental fulfillability of the Sermon on the Mount. But Beyschlag's judgment must be limited: the thesis of the possibility of Christian perfection is primarily a Pelagian thesis (E. Mühlenberg, in Andresen [ed.], *Handbuch* 1, 448), where Pelagius actually stands for large parts of the church of the time (which was ascetically oriented). Christ brings to the Christian who makes an effort "the grace which overcomes, in teaching and example" (ibid. 450). Pelagius's opponent Jerome hedges: It is impossible that a human being can remain without sin (*Pelagius* 1,6-9). God indeed has given commandments which can be fulfilled, otherwise he would become the originator of sin (ibid. 1,10). But no human being has completely fulfilled that which is possible, which God has commanded, because no one possesses all virtues at the same time (ibid. 1,23 = BKV I/15 345-49,375). The Matthean understanding of grace and human action obviously has a certain affinity to the Pelagian understanding of *sola gratia*.

[27]Formula of Concord, Epit. 5,7f. = *BSLK* 791f. Particularly impressive is the conclusion of the interpretation of the Sermon on the Mount by J. Brenz: "Who, you will ask, will be saved (*salvus*)?" This is followed by the Pauline thesis of universal sin. Then as the conclusion of the interpretation of the Sermon on the Mount (conceived in the Reformers' way on the basis of the decalog): Therefore the accusation of the decalog has no more authority toward those who have converted to Christ, . . . "nam qui in Christum credunt, omnia habent in Christo" (for those who believe in Christ have all things in Christ) (370f.).

[28]Luther*, *LW* 21, 109.

should not do "out of true love of justice."[29] Briefly put: as much as the doctrine of two kingdoms is different in *approach* from its modern version, the ethics of intention,[30] the impression nevertheless remains that a consistent line extends from one to the other.[31] The retreat to the intention which is also a retreat from praxis is, in my opinion, *also* a result of the distinction between a Christian as such and a Christian *in relatione* who is bound with other people and must protect their interests. In praxis, it cannot be maintained in any other way than by distinguishing between inside and outside, and that means then, between intention and praxis. It does not have to be demonstrated at length how far one has then removed oneself from Matthew, for whom everything depends on deeds.[32]

      c. The third question to the Reformers' interpretation of the Sermon on the Mount concerns the relationship of the individual to the community. For the Anabaptists, it was basic to build community according to the will of Christ. Luther, in connection with his interpretation of the Sermon on the Mount, turns again and again to the individual Christian. Christians are individual and rare birds.[33] The idea, so central for Matthew, that the *community* of brothers and sisters is the place where the Sermon on the Mount has to be practiced, is more distant from him. He could not yet actualize the community of those who "want to be Christians in earnest" because he did not consider the time ripe for it and in order that no "sect of reckless people" should arise.[34] Thus, the community can hardly become for Luther the place of visible realization of God's commandments to his "dear Christians."[35] Understood as a word to the individual Christian, the Sermon on the Mount remains without application for the shape of the church.

      All three questions try to find reasons why a real praxis of Christianity based on the Sermon on the Mount did not spread widely in the realm of the churches of the Reformation. It played a secondary role and was more of theological than practical interest. On the basis of Troeltsch's distinction between "church" and "sect," it must be asked whether the Reformers' interpretation has not been a typical "ecclesiastical" interpretation to a much higher degree than the Catholic two-level ethic, namely, a successful attempt at domesticating a text which provided difficulties in a territorial church. Is then the Reformers' interpretation of the Sermon on the Mount *actually* the attempt of a folk church to deal theologically with a text which in its deepest essence

---

[29]Luther*, *LW* 21, 111.

[30]Classical documents of the ethics of intention are W. Herrmann, *Ethik*, 5th ed. (Tübingen, 1921), § 24, e.g., 154: The commandments of Jesus "all basically demand one thing, complete dedication to God in ethical independence" (decisive is the overcoming of the heteronomy of conduct); Baumgarten* 118: "Make a pure heaven between your sinful, guilty way and the eternal, holy goodness, then the unrest of the world can no longer touch your souls" (on 6:33).

[31]Luther* writes, "You are not forbidden to go to court and lodge a complaint against injustice or violence, just as long as you do not have a false heart" (*LW* 21, 111).

[32]Cf. Luz* 58-60.

[33]Cf. Luther, "Temporal Authority: To What Extent It Should Be Obeyed," 1523, LW 45, 90ff.

[34]Luther, "The German Mass," LW 53, 64.

[35]Luther, "Temporal Authority," LW 45, 99f.

contradicted it? Deliberately I formulate this as a question, and I think that this is not all that can be said of the Reformers' interpretation of the Sermon on the Mount. But this much has to be said.

The fascination which has emanated and continues to emanate from the Sermon on the Mount precisely in the churches of the Reformation is all the more understandable. Among the interpreters of our century, D. Bonhoeffer and L. Ragaz probably play the largest role. In such a way that they cannot be ignored, they both demand the total practice of the Sermon on the Mount and warn of an internalized grace. Among the interpreters of the last century, the radicality of Leo Tolstoy is widely known, while the memory of the interpretations by W. Herrmann or A. v. Harnack,[36] great in their own way, has completely faded outside of the interested circles. But the text of the Sermon on the Mount itself is the most fascinating of all. All this points to the fact that the domestication of the Sermon on the Mount has failed thoroughly.

1. INTRODUCTION (5:1-16)

1.1. Jesus Goes up on the Mountain (5:1–2)

Literature*

See above pp. 209-211.

Text

1 But when he saw the crowds, he went up on the mountain; and as he sat down, his disciples came to him.

2 He opened his mouth, taught them, and said:

Analysis

The text is linked immediately with 4:25, and no new beginning is apparent. The material which is used by the evangelist comes from Mark 1:21; Matthew also uses the going up on the mountain from Mark 3:13.[1] But, despite these returns to the Markan source, he formulates here relatively freely.[2] In locating the Sermon on the Mount in this place, he makes his own intention felt. In his Markan source, Matthew is still standing at the introduction to the healing of the demoniac in Capernaum. He omits it and substitutes for it, in a manner of speaking, the Sermon on the Mount. There are hardly cogent reasons

---

[36]W. Hermann, loc.cit. (above, n. 31); A. Harnack, *What Is Christianity?* (New York: Putnam, 1901), 4th lecture (toward the end) - 7th lecture.

[1]Matthew 4:25 already had gone back to 3:7f. Here also Matthew uses once again more than one Markan text "synoptically."

[2]The following are Matthean expressions (cf. introduction 3,2): ἰδὼν δέ, with ὄχλος cf 8:18; 9:36; ὄχλοι plural; προσέρχομαι + dative; λέγων.

for the omission of Mark 1:23-28.[3]

Interpretation

From the formulation it does not become clear whether Jesus escaped from the crowds or whether he taught them. Only the ending of the Sermon on the Mount (7:28f.) makes clear that the latter is meant. Thus the Sermon on the Mount has two concentric circles of hearers, disciples and multitudes. This excludes certain interpretations of the Sermon on the Mount: It can not be an ethics for the disciples in the *more narrow* sense, not an ethics only of the perfect. A two-level ethic is excluded. The Sermon on the Mount is ethics for the disciples but this applies also to the listening people. At most one might understand the Sermon on the Mount as a promotional speech which would make the gospel of the kingdom accessible to the people, who are already proleptically following.[4] The mountain in Matthew is a place of prayer (14:23), of healings (15:29), of revelation (17:1; 28:16), and of teaching (24:3). It does not have a fixed meaning. But it is probable that the association with the ascent of Moses on Mount Sinai is connected with the phrase ἀναβαίνω εἰς τὸ ὄρος (Exod. 19:3,12; 24:15,18; 34:1f., 4). The conclusion of the Sermon on the Mount, 7:28f., again recalls these texts.[5] This does not mean that the evangelist wants to place Jesus antithetically to Moses or understands the law of the second Moses as the invalidation of the first law.[6] The recalling of the basic history of Israel is clear: Now God, through Jesus, will again speak in a fundamental way to Israel as at that time on Mt. Sinai. Only the Sermon on the Mount itself will show how Jesus' gospel of the kingdom is related to the law of Moses. Jesus sits down, as is customary for teachers in the synagogue service. Through the biblical expression ἀνοίγω τὸ στόμα αὐτοῦ[7] not only is the solemnity increased but also the recall of the biblical character of the scene is strengthened. The Son of God now for the first time, after his brief seminal utterances in 3:15 and 4:17, will proclaim his gospel to Israel.

1.2. The Beatitudes (5:3-12)

Literature

Best, E. "Matthew 5,3," *NTS* 6 (1960/61) 255-58.

---

[3]It is not correct that Matthew in chs. 8f. "invariably cites only one instance of each type" of healing narratives (Schweizer 73) so that one could say that Mark 1:23-28 is superfluous alongside of 8:28-34, cf. 9:32 and 8:6 next to 9:2! A healing in a synagogue would even have been quite suitable for Matthew's conception of salvation history.

[4]Cf. *Opus imperfectum* 9.1 = 679f.: "altitudo virtutum, altitudo bonorum operum, mons Ecclesiae" (the height of virtues, the height of good works, the mountain of the church).

[5]Cf. the interpretation of 7:28f. and J. Jeremias, "Μωϋσῆς," *TDNT* IV 871; Bacon, *Studies* 339; Ogawa, *Histoire* 126f.; Lohfink* 278. Leo the Great, *Sermo* 95.1 = *BKV* I/55 293 puts Jesus in parallel with God, the apostles with Moses on Mt. Sinai. Cf. also Bullinger 50B (surpassing by larger crowds); Wolzogen 200.

[6]Cf. also 23:2; 24:3.

[7]Cf. introduction 3.2 s.v. ἀνοίγω.

Betz, H. D., "Die Makarismen der Bergpredigt (Matthäus 5,3-12)," *ZTK* 75 (1978) 1-19.

Braumann, G., "Zum traditionsgeschichtlichen Problem der Seligpreisungen Mt V 3-12," *NovT* 4 (1960) 253-60.

Dirichlet, G., *De veterum macarismis,* RVV 14/4 (Giessen: Töpelmann 1914).

Dodd, C. H., "The Beatitudes: A Form-critical Study," in idem, *More New Testament Studies,* pp. 1-10 (Grand Rapids: Eerdmans, 1968).

Dupont, J., "Les πτωχοί τῷ πνεύματι de Matthieu 5,3 et les עֲנָוֵי רוּחַ de Qumrân," in *Neutestamentliche Aufsätze* (FS J. Schmid), ed. J. Blinzler et al., pp. 53-64 (Regensburg: Pustet, 1963).

————. *Béatitudes* I-III.

Frankemölle, H., "Die Makarismen (5,1-12; Lk 6,20-23). Motive und Umfang der redaktionellen Komposition," *BZ* NF 15 (1971) 52-75.

George, A., "La 'forme' des Béatitudes jusqu'à Jésus," in *Mélanges Bibliques* (FS A. Robert), pp. 398-403 (Paris: Bloud et Gay, 1957).

Giesen, *Handeln* 79-121.

Gregory of Nyssa, *De Beatitudinibus, PG* 44, 1194-1302, tr. and cited from *Acht Homilien über die acht Seligkeiten,* pp. 153–240. BKV I/56 (1927).

Harnack, A. "Sanftmut, Huld und Demut in der alten Kirche," in *Festgabe für J. Kaftan,* pp. 113-29 (Tübingen 1920).

Jacob, G., "Die Proklamation der messianischen Gemeinde," *ThV* 12 (1981) 47-85.

Kähler, C., "Studien zur Form- und Traditionsgeschichte der biblischen Makarismen," Diss., Jena (1974).

Kieffer, R., "Wisdom and Blessing in the Beatitudes of St. Matthew and St. Luke," *SE* 6, 1973 (TU 112), 291-95.

————. "Weisheit und Segen als Grundmotive der Seligpreisungen bei Matthäus und Lukas," in *Theologie aus dem Norden,* SNTU, A2 (1977), 29-43.

Koch, K. *The Growth of the Biblical Tradition: The Form-Critical Method* (New York: Scribners, 1969), 6-8, 16-18, 28, 38, 44.

Maahs, C. H., "The Makarisms in the New Testament," Diss., Tübingen (1965).

McEleney, N., "The Beatitudes of the Sermon on the Mount/Plain," *CBQ* 43 (1981) 1-13.

Michaelis, C., "Die π-Alliteration der Subjektsworte der ersten 4 Seligpreisungen . . .," *NovT* 10 (1968) 148-61.

Neuhäusler, E., *Anspruch und Antwort Gottes,* pp. 141–169 (Düsseldorf: Patmos, 1962).

Schnackenburg, R., "Die Seligpreisung der Friedensstifter (Mt 5,9) im matthäischen Kontext," *BZ* NF 26 (1982) 161-78.

Schweizer, E., "Formgeschichtliches zu den Seligpreisungen," in idem, *Matthäus und seine Gemeinde,* pp. 69–77 (Stuttgart: KBW, 1974).

Strecker, G., "Die Makarismen der Bergpredigt," *NTS* 17 (1970/71) 255-75.

Trilling, W., *Christusverkündigung in den synoptischen Evangelien,* pp. 64-85 (Munich: Kösel, 1969).

Walter, N., "Die Bearbeitung der Seligpreisungen durch Matthäus," *SE* 4, pp. 246-58 (TU 102) (Berlin: Akademie, 1968).

Windisch, H., "Friedensbringer–Gottessöhne," *ZNW* 24 (1925) 240-60.

Zimmerli, W., "Die Seligpreisungen der Bergpredigt und das Alte Testament," in *Donum Gentilicium* (FS D. Daube), ed. E. Bammel et al., pp. 8-26 (Oxford: Clarendon, 1978).

Text

3 Happy are the poor in spirit,
for theirs is the kingdom of heaven.

4 Happy are those who mourn,
   for they will be comforted.
5 Happy are the kind,
   for they will inherit the earth.[1]
6 Happy are those who hunger and thirst for righteousness,
   for they will be satisfied.
7 Happy are the merciful,
   for they will obtain mercy.
8 Happy are the pure in heart,
   for they will see God.
9 Happy are the peacemakers,
   for they will be called sons of God.
10 Happy are those who are persecuted for righteousness' sake,
   for theirs is the kingdom of heaven.
11 Happy are you if they slander and persecute you
   and, lying, say all kinds of evil things against you for my sake.
12 Rejoice and be glad, for your reward is great in the heavens.
   Just so they have also persecuted the prophets before you.

Analysis

1. *Context and Structure*. The Beatitudes are a unit in themselves and were composed as such. The first and the eighth beatitudes are framed by the same apodosis ("for theirs is the kingdom of heaven"). These two apodoses also are the longest. Length and frame composition show that the theme "kingdom of heaven" remains important in the Sermon on the Mount; Matthew takes up again the central catchword of the proclamation of Jesus which was given in 4:17,23 and desires to unfold now what "gospel of the kingdom of heaven" means in terms of content.[2] The first eight beatitudes present themselves, through the word δικαιοσύνη at the end of the fourth and eighth beatitudes, as two "stanzas"[3] of exactly equal length.[4] In the first four beatitudes, moreover, the terms for those who are pronounced happy begin with π-.[5] The last, ninth beatitude is longer than the others and contains a direct address in the second person plural. Its emphatic address to the community is continued in the following pericope, 5:13-16. It is connected with the preceding one by the catchword διώκω. This obviously is important to Matthew, for it is taken up again in v. 44 along with the promise of future sonship of God (vv. 9,45).

2. *Redaction*. Are the beatitudes which Matthew has in addition to Q (vv. 5,7-10) redactional? Scholarship is divided.[6] Linguistically only the addition of τὴν

---

[1]Verses 4 and 5 are reversed in Western text witnesses, presumably for the sake of the parallels in the apodosis which is created in this way (3/5: οὐρανοί - γῆ; 4/6 ending in -θήσονται). For McEleney* 3:12f., v. 5 is a later gloss of a post-Matthean redactor.

[2]Cf. the excursus on 4:23-25.

[3]There is no strict rhythm, or perhaps it has been destroyed by Matthew through his additions. But the strictness of the form shows itself in the identical beginnings of the lines (μακάριοι οἱ or ὅτι αὐτοί or αὐτῶν, also in v. 9) and the identical conclusion of the apodosis with a future form of the third person plural middle/passive.

[4]Twice 36 words with a few uncertainties in the text; v. 11f. contain 35 words.

[5]Michaelis*.

[6]E.g., Frankemölle*, especially 73-75; Walter* 248,256f. think of Matthean authorship; e.g., Hoffmann** II 118f., Dupont, *Béatitudes* I 260,296f. think of redactional insertion of special material; e.g. Strecker* 259, Guelich** 113-15 think of a Q section which was enlarged already before Matthew.

226

δικαιοσύνην (v. 6), all of v. 10,[7] and βασιλεία τῶν οὐρανῶν can be demonstrated as redactional. Such a demonstration is not possible for the addition of τῷ πνεύματι in v. 3, which often is considered redactional. Thus more speaks in favor of assigning the remaining additions and changes to a text recension prior to the redaction. It must be admitted that in the additional beatitudes there is language which is strongly influenced by the Old Testament,[8] which may point to Matthew or the community before him. The new formulation of the second beatitude, which is based on Isa. 61:2, is clearly pre-Matthean.[9] Such new formulations in the light of the Old Testament commenced already at an early time. Two hapax legomena[10] speak in favor of the formulation of vv. 7-9 prior to the redaction. As for the rest, additional beatitudes correspond thematically to general Christian community parenesis.[11] Therefore we assume that Matthew has found a list of seven beatitudes which had already been enlarged.

3. The *history of transmission* can be reconstructed most likely as follows:

a. The three first beatitudes, transmitted in Q (Luke 6:20b,21) might go back to Jesus in their Lukan form of text (perhaps without the Lukan νῦν in v. 21). The direct ascription of salvation to the déclassé and the lack both of an explicit Christology and of an ecclesiological limitation of the addressees speak in favor of this thought.

The question of whether Jesus' beatitudes were formulated *in the second or in the third person plural* is very difficult. The third person belongs to the genre of macarism. In the second person, they would be direct addresses of Jesus to the suffering ones. Later, presumably before Matthew, they would have been adapted again to the third person, which is usual for macarisms. Or did Luke assimilate the macarisms which were formulated in the third person to the woes and to the last, secondary macarism (vv. 22f.)? Although Luke prefers direct addresses,[12] the first thesis seems more probable to me. The Lukan beatitudes are a peculiar mixed form between third person (in the protasis) and second person (in the apodosis). An adaptation to vv. 22f. would

---

[7]Matthean vocabulary (cf. introduction 3.2): διώκω, δικαιοσύνη. The contacts with vv. 3,11 are decisive.

[8]Verse 5: Ps. 36:11; v.8: Ps. 23:4, cf. Ps. 73:1 (Hebrew text). Frequent Old Testament phrases are: Κληρονομέω . . . γῆν (LXX c. 37 times, without pronoun passages); "to see God" (especially in the cultic language and usage which is derived from it); ἐλεέω as God's address or with God as the subject.

[9]The woes Luke 6:24,25b presuppose v. 4 probably already in the Matthean form since it cannot be assumed that Matthew at the same time has connected the formulations of two different woes in a newly formed beatitude and created the association with Isa. 61:1f. (against Schürmann, *Lukasevangelium* 339f.). R. Guelich advocates the opinion that only the evangelist has created the association with Isa. 61:1f. and thus has understood the Beatitudes, which before were interpreted ethically, (again) as based on the idea of fulfillment, "The Matthean Beatitudes: 'Entrance Requirements' or Eschatological Blessings?" *JBL* 95 (1976) 426-34, cf. idem, 117f.

[10] Ἐλεήμων, εἰρηνοποιός.

[11]Cf., e.g., 1 Peter 3:4 (πραΰς); Did. 3:8 1 Clem. 60:1 (ἐλεήμων,); James 4:8; 1 Peter 1:22; 3:4; 2 Clem 11:1; Herm. Vis. 3.9.8 (pure heart).

[12]Examples in H. J. Cadbury, *The Style and Literary Method of Luke* (Cambridge: Harvard University, 1920), 124-26.

necessarily look different.[13] Neither does the Lukan text form agree with the beatitudes in the second person which occur in Aramaic and Hebrew.[14] Presumably an "anomalous" Aramaic text form was the reason for the "anomalous" Greek text form. But in Matthew, the content shift to parenesis and the choice of the third person fit together.

b. In Q, the original series of three beatitudes was enlarged by the fourth beatitude (Matt. vv. 11f.), which arose in the community. At the same time the promise of salvation—in all beatitudes—is referred to the Christian community.

c. Between the Sayings Source and the redaction of Matthew the broadening of the three original beatitudes by a fourth one (v. 5) to a π- series and the addition of vv. 7-9 took place.

Since the π- series probably owed its form to oral tradition and also influenced the wording of the pre-Lukan woes Luke 6:24f., we have to reckon not with a unilinear development of the text but with a juxtaposition of written and oral transmission in Greek. In this phase of transmission, the Beatitudes were formulated in the light of Isa. 61:1-3 and various psalms.

4. There are special investigations of the *genre beatitude*.[15] Beatitudes in Judaism were used primarily in wisdom parenesis as an expression of the connection between deed and fate.[16] Most of the time they were formulated in the third person, i.e., without concrete addressees.[17] The future apodosis with eschatological sense can be documented since apocalypticism, when the formulation of the connection between deed and fate was possible only by taking into account the eschaton.[18] Also beginning with apocalyptic literature, there is the brief nominal protasis which no longer describes the behavior of those praised in detail in wisdom style.[19] The emphasis then lies on the apodosis.

Jesus' beatitudes therefore are connected with this alteration of this original wisdom genre in apocalyptic, but are distinctive—by the use of the second person, by

---

[13]The Lukan text form is unique in Greek. According to Dupont, *Béatitudes* I 277, beatitudes in the second person plural do not exist in secular Greek. Beatitudes in the singular are relatively rare and do not follow a definite formal pattern. There are several examples for μακάριος + relative clause in the second person singular (Pindar, *Pyth.* 5.46-49; Euripides, fragment 446 [*TGF*]; μακάριος + name in vocative case [Homer I 3.182; Aristophanes, *Av.* 1725; *Vesp.* 1275.1512; *Nu.* 1206; *Pax.* 715]). Further examples in Dupont, *Béatitudes* I 277 n. 1 and Strecker* 257 n. 1.

[14]The rare Aramaic and Hebrew macarisms in the second person plural are always formulated with a suffix (e.g., Isa. 32:30). Literally translated, this would be μακάριοι ὑμεῖς, so, e.g., *Herm. Vis.* 2.2.7; see 9.29.3.

[15]Cf. Dirichlet*; Dodd*; George*; Kieffer, *Weisheit*; Kieffer, *Wisdom*; Koch* 6-8,16-18; Maahs*; Schweizer*; Zimmerli*; and especially Kähler*.

[16]Kähler* passim, especially 69 no. 1; 167ff. no. 1,3-5,7f.,13; 232ff. no. 1-5,7-9,11f.

[17]Exceptions 1 Enoch 58:2: "Blessed are you righteous and elect ones, for your fate will be glorious"; Isa. 32:20 (plural); Eccles. 10:17; Deut. 33:29; Ps. 127:2; As. Mos. 10:8 (?) (singular); in the NT: Matt. 13:16; John 13:17; 1 Peter 3:14; 4:14 (plural); Matt. 16:17; Luke 14:14 (singular); rabbinical and Samaritan examples in Str-B I 189 and in Kähler* 179 n. 243.

[18]1 Enoch 58:2 (cf. n. 17); Wis. 3:13; 1 Enoch 99: 10, cf. 2 Enoch 52:15; in the NT: Luke 14:14; James 1:12; Rev. 14:13, cf. 1,3.

[19]1 Enoch 58:2 (cf. n. 17), cf. Bar. 4:4; 2 Apoc. Bar. 11:6; As. Mos. 10:8.

stringing them together,[20] and by the paradoxically formulated protasis: precisely those of whom one would expect it are not called happy. For the Matthean beatitudes, because of the adaptation to the linguistic usage of wisdom, the parenesis is the *Sitz im Leben*.[21]

5. It is almost impossible to make secure assertions about the prehistory of the last beatitude, vv. 11f. It is probable that the saying was formed in the community (situation of persecution, explicit Christology); it is certain that it stood in Q.

In v. 11, Matthew probably replaced the title of Son of man by ἕνεκεν ἐμοῦ.[22] In Luke, the situation of the exclusion from the synagogue is addressed (ἀφορίζω, ἐκβάλλω τὸ ὄνομα); Matthew formulates in a more general manner. The generalizing πᾶν (πονηρόν) is probably Matthean.[23] The hapax legomenon ψευδόμενοι, which makes it more precise, is probably secondary but does not permit of further definition.[24] In v. 12 the generalization is shown with the present imperatives. It is particularly noticeable how pointedly Matthew speaks of persecution (διώκω twice, cf. vv. 10,44).

History of influence

The history of interpretation recognizes three basic types which also may supplement each other:

a. A first basic type puts the emphasis on the *impartation of grace* in the Beatitudes.

This interpretation is based mainly on the first four beatitudes. People are called happy who are in a certain *situation*: "That they are poor and sad and meek and empty and in need of righteousness is only the situation which has come to them."[25] Especially in Protestant interpretations grace is often spiritualized, "It is . . . the empty before God . . ., to whom the promise is made."[26] The Beatitudes "all designate . . . the same contrast . . . between those who are righteous of themselves and those for whom there is righteousness only out of grace."[27]

b. A second basic type understands the Beatitudes primarily as *ethical admonition*.

The mass of the interpretations of the early church and of the Middle Ages represents this type, as well as most of the Catholic interpretations of more recent times.

---

[20]There are only few series, without exception with wisdom parenetic tendency: Sir. 25:7-10 (an enumerating saying); Tob. 13:14-16; 2 Enoch 41:2-42:14; 52:6-13 (macarism and curse). In the OT there are only series of two macarisms (Zimmerli 10).

[21]Koch* 28f.: the sermon.

[22]Matthew replaced also in 10:32 υἱὸς τοῦ ἀνθρώπου by ἐγώ, cf. 23:34.

[23]Generalizing πᾶς without article and πονηρός are Matthean, cf. introduction 3.2.

[24]Matthew 15:19; 26:59 might argue in favor of redaction.

[25]Barth, *CD* IV/2, 190.

[26]G. Barth, "Matthew's Understanding of the Law," 124.

[27]Bornhäuser* 23.

   In the early church and in the Middle Ages the sequence of the Beatitudes was understood as a royal *way of ascending steps*. The way from the first to the last Beatitude is identical with the way from repentance to perfection. Gregory of Nyssa puts his interpretation clearly into the frame of a way or steps to the top of a mountain.[28] In more recent times, M. Dibelius interprets the Beatitudes as "table of virtues," Windisch as "entrance requirements" into the kingdom of God.[29] According to Neuhäusler, the listener is to be led by them to the question, "Am I like this?";[30] for Trilling they are to be put under the title of 5:48—"Be perfect."[31] According to Dupont all Beatitudes are in the last analysis concerned about *one* subject, righteousness.[32] Walter sees the Beatitudes as a counterpart of the decalog, divided like it into two tables.[33]

   c. A third basic type recognizes in the Beatitudes the *order for the life of the community*. They aim at the life (5th-8th beatitudes) which comes from grace (1st-4th beatitudes).

   Zinzendorf, in a sermon of 1725, impressively understands the eight beatitudes as the description of the way of those who "hunger and thirst for grace" and learn exactly from this "how they should act with other people."[34] In more recent times, similar attempts usually proceed from the Matthean division of the Beatitudes into two strophes. The first strophe perhaps concerns those who are waiting or in need, the second those who act.[35] Or the first stanza deals with attitude, the second with activities.[36] There also are attempts to understand the Beatitudes as an order for the life of the community, attempts which interpret all eight beatitudes in a unified manner. For Bonhoeffer it is completely irrelevant whether the Beatitudes speak of an action or a suffering of the disciples; important alone is that they speak of the life with Christ in discipleship: "The community which is the subject of the beatitudes is the community of the crucified. With Him it has lost all, and with Him it has found all."[37] Luther interprets the Beatitudes *ethically*, as the early church, but understands their commandments as the content of the *gospel:* "This gospel . . contains also commandment, namely, how one should be poor in spirit, meek, merciful, etc." The interpretation of the law by Jesus through the Beatitudes is "the greatest benefaction of all."[38] Others understand the Beatitudes indeed ethically but put the emphasis on the "remembrance of the promise" in the apodoses, for "not the demands . . ., but the rationales for them which make one

---

[28]Next to Gregory, Ambrosius, *In Luc* 5.49-82 (especially 52.60 = *BKV* I/21 230-47, especially 231f.,235f.) is to be mentioned, furthermore, Hilary 931-34.

[29]M. Dibelius, *Jesus*, 2nd ed. (Berlin 1949), 95; Windisch** 63 n. 1.

[30]Neuhäusler*, 145.

[31]Trilling I 90.

[32]Dupont, *Béatitudes* III 667.

[33]Walter* 256.

[34]Zinzendorff I 155-71, quotations from pp. 158,166.

[35]Windisch** 63.

[36]Zahn 185f.; Michaelis I 215, cf. Walter* 256.

[37]Bonhoeffer** 97.

[38]Luther II 56. Cf. on Luther's imperatival but unlegalistic interpretation of the beatitudes Heintze** 154-56.

blessed'' are emphasized.[39]

If the three types of interpretation are compared with the statements of the texts, one has to differentiate in regard to the history of the tradition. Certain interpretations have special support in certain nuances of the text.

Interpretation: Jesus

For *Jesus* the unconditional, categorical bestowal of grace on people who arc in a desperate situation is decisive. The three authentic beatitudes have a paradoxical character. They are not to be interpreted from the connection of deed and fate in the wisdom tradition, for they neither put human behavior in the foreground nor is the promise in any way the result of the behavior of those who are called blessed. On the contrary, the daily experience that they are not satisfied speaks against the palpability of the beatitude, e.g., of the hungering. Rather the background of these three beatitudes is the apocalyptic hope for a total reversal of the circumstances. Jesus' beatitudes are distinguished from apocalyptic expectation of the future through his proclamation of the kingdom of God: the promised glorious future begins in the now of his ministry. A portion of the salvation which is promised to the poor, the hungry, and the mourning becomes already a reality in Jesus' turning to the déclassé, in his meals with them and in the joy celebrating the love of God which is experienced now.

5:3

On the original meaning of the first beatitude we make the following observations. With its general statement of the addressees as "poor" and its general apodosis "to you belongs the kingdom of God" it presumably had the function of a title already in the original series of three pronounced by Jesus; the second and third beatitudes are concrete examples of the first.[40] "Poor," according to Semitic usage, means indeed not only those who are lacking in money but, more comprehensively, the oppressed, miserable, dependent, humiliated—but by no means *only* a certain type of piety and/or *only* a poverty which is separated from external circumstances and is internal. Philological data point rather clearly in this direction,[41] as also the parallel beatitudes of the weeping and hungering, descriptions which cannot be separated from external circumstances. Finally, the translation by the Greek word πτωχός, the strongest available Greek word for social poverty, speaks in favor of this interpretation. The basic rule is: The πένης has to work, the πτωχός has to beg.[42] Πτωχός is in the LXX the translation of עָנִי and דַּל, but practically never of עָנָו. This translation emphasizes the social aspect of the beatitude, corresponding to its meaning in Jesus' usage. When the Matthean text qualifies the word πτωχός by τῷ πνεύματι, then it emphasizes an aspect which cannot be expected on the basis of πτωχός and therefore sounds surprising. The addition indicates that one has to

---

[39]Burchard** 418,417. A similar thesis is advocated by Eichholz** 44 and Trilling* 81.

[40]Observation of Migaku Sato.

[41]Cf. E. Bammel, "πτωχός κτλ." *TDNT* VI 888f.; E. Jenni, art. "עָנָה," *THAT* II 334f.; Dupont, *Béatitudes* II 24-34,49: In the Jewish examples, the religious sense of עָנִי does not inhere in the term but in the context; and even then a social element almost always is included.

[42]F. Hauck, "πτωχός κτλ," *TDNT* VI 886ff.

interpret πτωχός alone differently![43] Thus a shift in meaning has taken place. If our interpretation of the original meaning of the first beatitude is correct, then one has to assume that Luke remained true to it and Matthew did not.[44] The beatitude of the hungering ones points in the same direction.

With this, the *main problem* of the interpretation of the Matthean beatitudes is described: through the pre-Matthean additions and through the Matthean interpretations, a *shift in the meaning of the beatitudes in the direction of parenesis* apparently has taken place. The exegesis has to determine this precisely and ask for proof of its legitimacy.

Interpretation: Matthew

5:3

Μακάριος, originally in Greek an expression reserved for the gods, is in the later period barely distinguished from εὐδαίμων and means "happy" in the full, unsurpassable sense.[45] The *"poor in spirit"* were interpreted in various ways:

Does πτωχός (1) take here the meaning of real, economic poverty? Or does it mean (2) metaphorically "lowly" or in general "not having," "lacking"? The dative can be interpreted (A) as a dative of means or (B) as a dative of reference. Finally, πνεῦμα may mean (a) the Holy Spirit or (b) the human spirit. Various possibilities of explanation result from this analysis.

If one takes the dative as instrumental (A), then πτωχός means real poverty (1A). If one then understands πνεῦμα as the human spirit (b), then one has the interpretation "poor through one's own spirit," i.e., "voluntarily poor" (1Ab). Frequently this interpretation was advocated; but the formulation would be difficult.[46] The other possibility would be: "poor by (effect of) the divine Spirit" (1Aa). Much speaks against this interpretation too.[47] Thus it is better to understand the dative as a dative of reference (B). It then determines πτωχός in the direction of a general or metaphorical understanding (2B). The interpretation as the divine Spirit becomes then difficult; it has been proposed: "poor in divine Spirit" (2Ba). But this is philologically impossible. Thus the interpretation in

---

[43]It is understandable only on the basis of the Semitic עֲנָוֵי רוּחַ.

[44]Guelich** 74f. sees in πτωχοὶ τῷ πνεύματι a linguistic modification of the original text by the evangelist in light of Isa. 61:1 in the sense of religious poverty, as already with Jesus, according to him (loc.cit. 71f.). But then either the translation by πτωχός was a misunderstanding or the modification by τῷ πνεύματι, which is not suggested by Isa. 61:1, is unnecessary. More consistently therefore, Schweizer* 76, n. 13, speaks of the "danger" of a misunderstanding which is inherent in the Greek translation.

[45]F. Hauck, "μακάριος κτλ," *TDNT* IV 362-370.

[46]Schlatter 133; Lohmeyer 83 (intentional affirmation of the fate of poverty). The thought of *voluntary poverty* would be expressed differently both in the Semitic and in the Greek language, namely, Hebrew/Aramaic with נדב or רצון, Greek with ἑκών.

[47]Verse 8 does not suggest to think of the *divine spirit* (καθαροὶ τῇ καρδίᾳ). The Matthean usage of πνεῦμα also speaks against it: Matthew characterizes the divine Spirit always by an attribute, except where the meaning is completely clear by the context. Poor "in" divine Spirit is impossible; one would expect the Greek genitive (Liddell-Scott, s.v. πτωχός II 1).

terms of the human spirit remains (2Bb). Depending on the understanding of "poor" and "spirit," there are different nuances: Either τῷ πνεύματι shifts the meaning of "poor." Then it means: poor not only economically but in regard to the heart, i.e., "lacking courage," "desperate."[48] Or one can interpret πνεῦμα of the inner life as such; the "poor in spirit" are then "those who stand before God as beggars in regard to their inner life . . . in the feeling of their inability to help themselves."[49] Often reference was made to the Galilean "people of the land" who religiously were considered as nothing. If one proceeds from the metaphorical nuance "lowly," which is linked rather with the Semitic עָנָו than with the Greek πτωχός, then one understands "lowly in regard to the spirit" not as a circumstance but as an attitude: Blessed are the lowly in spirit, i.e., the humble.[50] The decision is difficult because the nuances may overlap each other.

Are there related Semitic expressions or even a Semitic equivalent to πτωχοὶ τῷ πνεύματι? The Old Testament contains related expressions which, however, are formulated with different word stems.[51] The only direct parallels are found in the Qumran writings (1QH 14.3; 1 QM 14.7). They are formulated with עָנָו and not with עָנִי. In middle Hebrew, עָנִי is the economically poor one, עָנָו the lowly, humble one.[52] 1QH 14.3 can no longer be explained. 1QM 14.7 is uncertain: the preceding context interprets עַנְוֵי רוּחַ in the sense of "despondency," "despair," the immediate parallel תְּמִימֵי דֶרֶךְ in the sense of "humble."[53] Both nuances, "poverty in heart" = despair and "lowliness in heart" = humility, overlap. Thus an ethical element cannot be excluded. The same conclusion follows from the other Matthean beatitudes.[54]

Thus we observe not only a linguistic change but also a shift in content. Social poverty moves to the background; inner need moves to the foreground.[55] It reaches over into the ethical attitude of humility. Thus one has to speak of a tendency to internalize and ethicize the first beatitude. Where the evangelist

---

[48]Best* 256f.

[49]Zahn 183, cf. Str-B I 190; J. Weiss 259f.; Soiron** 146f.; Klostermann 34; BAGD s.v. πνεῦμα 3b ("because they do not have a Pharisaic pride in their own spiritual riches"!).

[50]E.g., Dupont, *Béatitudes* III 457-71; Strecker* 262, Kähler* 179 ("deliberately chosen attitude").

[51]Most closely related is שְׁפַל רוּחַ = humble in Prov. 16:19; 29:23; 'Abot 4:4,10; b. Sota 5a and often. The opposite is גְּבַה–רוּחַ (ὑψηλὸς τῷ πνεύματι Eccl. 7:8. Related are נְכֵה רוּחַ (of a contrite spirit, Isa. 66:2) and דַּכְּאֵי רוּחַ (ταπεινοὶ τῷ πνεύματι, Ps. 34:19) which combine an ethical element with the thought of a condition. שֵׁבֶר (fracture, anguish) in Isa. 65:14 stresses the condition alone. Cf. furthermore similar expressions in Isa. 61:3; Prov. 15:13; 17:22; Ps. 51:19; with καρδία, e.g., Ps. 10:2; 23:4; 31:11; 35:11. In all cases the word which is determined by רוּחַ is used metaphorically.

[52]An investigation of the linguistic usage of עָנִי and עָנָו in post-biblical Hebrew is an urgent desideratum! Cf. below n. 70.

[53]Dupont* interprets it this way.

[54]Perhaps with exception of the second beatitude.

[55]Schottroff, *Volk* 162-66, wants to maintain the idea of social poverty with Matthew. But the thought of the unified Old Testament anthropology must not, in my opinion, be used to empty רוּחַ of all concrete content and to make it an expression for the totality of the person. רוּחַ means, I think, a very concrete *aspect* of this totality, namely, the heart (R. Albertz and C. Westermann, "רוּחַ," *THAT* II 738).

belongs in this development cannot be determined unambiguously. The expression "poor in spirit" does not indicate whether the humble are poor or rich.

History of influence

The early church took up this interpretation. The great majority of the fathers understood the spiritual poverty as *humility*.[56] The distance from the original "social" interpretation is increased: spiritual poverty precisely does *not* mean *necessitate pauperes* (poor by necessity).[57] In any event "spiritually poor" refers to the inner attitude to riches: one should not set one's confidence in riches. But in principle the rich are just as blessed as the poor, for there is no distinction of persons before God.[58] The partiality of the original beatitude as Jesus spoke it is completely left behind. The internalizing of poverty achieves its greatest depth and at the same time a new quality in mysticism. Meister Eckhart, in an impressive sermon on Matt. 5:3, spoke of a triple poverty: "Poor in spirit" is the one who "does not want anything"—not even "to fulfill God's dear will"—who "does not know anything"—not even about the work of God in him—and who "does not have anything"—not even room in himself in which God is to work.[59]

Alongside this interpretation, in the early church the interpretation of *voluntary poverty* (rejected above, 1Aa, 1Ab) plays a considerable role. However, the first beatitude then no longer refers to all Christians but only to the *religiosi*, clerics and monks.[60] It found entrance also into monastic rules.[61] It was in most cases not the only

---

[56]Material in Dupont, *Béatitudes* III 399-411. That is quite astonishing, for this understanding is not suggested by the Greek word πτωχός. Obviously, there is an unbroken *knowledge* of the meaning of the text which does not depend simply on its wording. By the way, the Reformers also interpret in the sense of humility, e.g., Zwingli 219 (*spiritus humilis* [humble spirit]); Calvin I 171 (humility under the discipline of the cross).

[57]Thomas, *Lectura* no. 416: "Et dicit 'Spiritu': quia quidam pauperes necessitate sunt, sed non debetur illis beatitudo" (And it says "in the spirit," because some are poor by necessity, but the beatitude does not apply to those).

[58]Pseudo-Clementine *Homilies* 15,10,1; Clement of Alexandria *Quis Div. salv.* 17.5 (the poor who do not have a share in God are not blessed); Ambrose, *In Luc* 5,33 = *BKV* I/21 232 (not all the poor are blessed). For Leo the Great, *Sermo* 95,2 = *BKV* I/55 294 it is a matter of that poverty "which is not captured by love for temporal things." Luther II 58: "Poor means: not to cling to possessions with heart and mind whether you have them or not." Thus David and Solomon can become examples for the poor while beggars can be spiritually rich, for their "whole mind is directed toward money and possessions." Poor and rich can become blessed in an equal way!

[59]*Meister Eckeharts Schriften und Predigten*, ed. H. Büttner, I (Jena: Diedrich, 1925), 180-85.

[60]This interpretation is widespread since Pseudo-Clementine *Recognitions* 2.28.3, Gregory of Nyssa 1.5 = 163f., Chromatius 332, and Jerome on this passage ("qui propter spiritum sanctum voluntate sunt pauperes" [those who for the sake of the Holy Spirit are voluntarily poor]). Emperor Julian who threatened the Christians with the confiscation of their possessions "in order that they can enter the kingdom of heaven as the poor" seems to presuppose it (quoted by O. Pank, *Das Evangelium Matthäi in Predigten und Homilien* I, 3d ed. [Bremen: Ed. Müller, 1896], 83). It was maintained particularly in Catholicism until the modern period (cf. Maldonat 97; Lapide 207). Protestant interpretations of voluntary poverty are found among the Anabaptists (P. Walpot, *Das grosse Artikelbuch* 3,22 = *QGT* XII/2 181) and in Pietism, e.g., P. M. Hahn, *Die gute Botschaft vom Königreich Gottes*, (*Zeugnisse der Schwabenväter* VIII) (Metzingen, 1963) 38 (chosen poverty by acceptance of the call to teach!).

[61]Basilius, *Regula brevius* 205 = *PG* 31,1217; *Die endgültige Regel der Minderen Brüder des Heiligen Franziskus von* Assisi 6 (in *Die grossen Ordensregeln*, ed. H. U. v. Balthasar, 3d ed. [Einsiedeln: Johannes, 1974], 317).

interpretation but stood *alongside* the more general understanding of humility, because the beatitudes, spoken before the whole people, by no means apply only to the *religiosi*. This interpretation is now usually abandoned, even in Catholicism.

The humble are promised the "kingdom of heaven." Matthew with this promise sets a bracket around all the beatitudes (vv. 3,10); the other apodoses unfold what "kingdom of heaven" means. At the same time he reverts to using the title of the proclamation of Jesus which he had set in 4:17,23: the Sermon on the Mount is the unfolding of the "gospel of the kingdom."[62] As, e.g., in 21:43 and 25:34, the kingdom is clearly the content of salvation. Matthew 4:17 and the future tenses of vv. 4-9 make clear that it is still in the future. It also is clear that the designation "kingdom of heaven" does not mean that the promise is spiritualized or moved to the beyond: It is described in vv. 4-9 with partially concrete eschatological images and comprises *also* the earth if one may interpret the juxtaposition of v. 3 and v. 5 in this way.

5:4

With the second beatitude addressed to those who mourn we can also observe a tendency to spiritualization. If in Jesus' original form the literally weeping ones were meant, then in the post-Matthean church interpretation the beatitude is referred not at all to *saecularis tristitia* (worldly mourning)[63] but to mourning over one's own sin and that of others.[64] The question is what is Matthew's position in this line of development. Without question, the replacement of "weeping" by the more general "mourning" already before Matthew had made possible the later religious interpretation, but it was not the motivation for the change. Πενθέω (and παρακαλέω) rather come from Isa. 61:2f.; there the subject is mourning in this world quite generally, certainly the mourning for Jerusalem.[65] Neither are there, in my view, any examples from contemporary literature in which πενθέω without further additional definition carries the meaning of mourning over imperfection or sin.[66] Thus the meaning in Matthew is probably still the same as in Luke: With "mourning" is encompassed mourning of this eon which in the coming eon will be replaced by comfort. This finding is important since it demonstrates how cautiously Matthew changes his tradition: he himself has intensified the ethicizing tendency which was already given to him in his tradition (v. 6) but he has not taken it to the end. Thus it is unlikely that there is for Matthew a unified religious or ethical meaning in the first four beatitudes.

---

[62]Differently Burchard** 415,432: The Sermon on the Mount is only a "section" of the ethics, namely, community ethics under a missionary aspect. Where else is then the "gospel of the kingdom," if not in the Sermon on the Mount?

[63]Bede 23; Theophylact 188.

[64]Since Origen, *Comm. in Psalmos* 37.7 (= J. B. Pitra, *Analecta Sacra Spicilegio Solesmensi parata*, vol. III [Venice 1883], 21) with almost all interpreters.

[65]Cf. also the macarism for those who were saddened by the defeat of Jerusalem, Tob. 13:16; further passages in Str-B I 195-97.

[66]With additional definitions: T. Reuben 1:10 (ἐπὶ τῇ ἁμαρτίᾳ μου; James 4:8 (clear from the context).

5:5

The understanding of the beatitude of the πραεῖς is made extraordinarily difficult by the semantic open-endedness of this word. It is not by accident that in it the ideal of piety of each interpreter can be reflected: "surrender to God," so Gaechter; "passive resistance" (in contrast to the Zealots), Schalom ben Chorin. The Greek Gregory of Nyssa speaks of the mastering of wrath by reason. "Meekness . . . does not permit that . . . violence and injustice be done to someone" and has to be distinguished from softness, so says the politician Zwingli, and the socialist Ragaz followed him.[67]

In early Christian parenesis, πραΰς is parallel to ἡσύχιος (1 Peter 3:4; 1 Clem. 13:4; Barn. 19:4), μακρόθυμος, ἐλεήμων (Did. 3:7f.) and ἐπιεικής (Tit. 3:2; 1 Clem. 21:7; cf. 2 Cor. 10:1; 1 Clem. 30:8). Primarily it is contrasted with wrath (Ignatius, *Eph.* 10:2). This is in agreement with Greek usage,[68] but is probably less informative for Matthew than for the tradition of ecclesiastical interpretation.[69] The Jewish-Christian usage influences Matthew, for the beatitude is a quotation of Ps. 36:11. There πραΰς usually stands for Hebrew עָנָו,[70] particularly when it was understood in the sense of an ethical attitude. Πραΰς for people who lived in the proximity of Semitic languages came to mean "humble."[71] It also is not unknown to Matthew; 11:29 and 21:5 demonstrate this. In 21:5 the element of nonviolence, in 11:29 that of kindness is included. A look at Jewish parenesis shows that the nuances of humility and kindness can hardly be separated from each other.[72] Thus, πραΰτης is humility which is demonstrated in kindness.[73] The third beatitude stands in content approximately between the first and the seventh. The earth, not only the land of Israel, will belong to those who are kind, for the traditional promise of the land had long been transposed into the cosmic realm,[74] but not also to the beyond, for the promise of the earth makes clear that the kingdom of heaven also comprises a new "this world."

---

[67]Gaechter 148; Ben-Chorin, *Bruder* 71; Gregory of Nyssa* 2.3 = 169f.; Zwingli 220; Ragaz** 18.

[68]Aristotle, *Eth. Nic.* 4.11 = 1125b = -1126a defines πραΰτης as the mean between ὀργιλότης and ἀοργησία, i.e., as well-measured, regulated mastering of wrath.

[69]Cf. Gregory of Nyssa above at n. 67; Ambrose, *In Luc* 5.54 = *BKV* I/21 233 (deliberate suppression of passion). In general, there is in the interpretation by the early church a shift of the Aristotelian μεσότης in the direction of ἀοργησία, e.g., in Peter of Laodicea 37.

[70]In the LXX, πραΰς is used 9 times for עָנָו, 3 times for עָנִי; πτωχός 4 times for עָנָו, 39 times for עָנִי; πένης 3 times for עָנָו, 12 times for עָנִי.

[71]The Semitic influence is shown in making πραΰς and ταπεινός or πραΰτης and ταπεινοφροσύνη parallel: Matt. 11:29; 2 Cor. 10:1; Col. 3:12; Eph. 4:2; for the early church cf. Harnack 114f.,120-27, for the LXX ibid. 118f.

[72]Montefiore, *Literature* 17.

[73]Πραΰς in Matthew is not contrasted with an affect (wrath); therefore, the usual translation "meek" is not appropriate. Πραΰς also does not mean "nonviolence" in the sense of renunciation of the exercise of power, neither in the sense of a political strategy of pacifism (so the pacifist Erasmus, *Paraphrasis* 24B: "qui nulli vim faciunt" [who do violence to no one]) nor in the sense of political subordination (thus Luther II 59: "they are not to become masters and rule the world").

[74]Cf. already Isa. 60:21; Jub. 22:14; 32:19; Did. 3:7 (reminiscence of Matt. 5:5).

5:6

Matthew has inserted his key term δικαιοσύνη into the fourth beatitude as the object[75] of hunger and thirst. There are three possibilities of interpretation: Δικαιοσύνη may mean (1) human behavior,[76] (2) a divine gift or God's power,[77] (3) a combination of the two, God's covenant order as gift and task.[78]

In the *history of interpretation* the first two types can easily be located: The first is the classical interpretation of the early church and the "Catholic" interpretation. "Righteousness" then stands for a human behavior, most of the time not so much for the principle of *suum cuique* (to each his or her own), but either for a special virtue in contrast to avarice[79] or as the essence of virtue as such.[80] This type of interpretation understands "hunger and thirst" usually in an active sense: it is a question of works and not merely a desiring.[81] Especially because of the exegesis of the Reformation, the trend was reversed in Protestantism,[82] and the verse was read on the basis of Paul: The righteousness for which the human being longs is then not so much God's eschatological power of recompense but his grace here and now, the *iustitia imputata* (imputed righteousness).[83] "Hunger and thirst" receives a passive note; because it is a matter of the righteousness of God, namely, the imputed *iustitia passiva* (passive righteousness), hunger and thirst can mean only human longing.

It seems to me that the alternative is to be decided unambiguously in favor of the first, i.e., the interpretation of the early church. Δικαιοσύνη *can* be understood in all Matthean passages as human behavior, in some it *must* be so understood. Since the first and the second strophe of the Beatitudes end with this catchword, everything speaks in favor of interpreting δικαιοσύνη in vv. 6 and 10 in the same way; in v. 10 the interpretation of human behavior is much

---

[75]Examples for the (rare) construction of πεινάω and διψάω with accusative in Strecker* 265 n. 2.

[76]E.g., A. Descamps, "Les justes et la justice dans les Évangiles . . .," Univ. Cath. Lov. diss II/43 (Louvain 1950), 172; Strecker* 265f.; Kähler* 184f.; Sand, *Gesetz* 202; Dupont, *Béatitudes* III 355-84 ("l'idéal de la perfection," 384); Guelich** 87 ("right relationship with God and others" in Christ).

[77]E.g., Schniewind 44; Schlatter 137 (gift); Lohmeyer 88 ("like the air of God which all breathe"); Eichholz** 44 ("primarily . . . God's acting"); Gundry 70; Bonnard 57 ("le verdict souverain de Dieu"); Fiedler, *Gerechtigkeit* 66 (eschatological gift of salvation); Stuhlmacher, *Gerechtigkeit* 190f.; Giesen, *Handeln* 88-102 (102: "especially . . . the character of a gift").

[78]Schweizer 53. Already Bullinger 52A interpreted it this way ("iustitia bipertita" [twofold righteousness]).

[79]E.g., John Chrysostom 15.3 = 245f.

[80]E.g., Gregory of Nyssa 4.5 = 191f.

[81]Jerome on the passage: "Non nobis sufficit velle iustitiam . . . sed . . . esurire iustitiae opere" (it is not sufficient for us to will justice but to hunger for justice by the deed).

[82]With the Reformers themselves, the interpretation of the early church is influential. Luther II 60: "Who strive with all their actions . . . that they become pious"; Zwingli 220: "iustitiam asserit et vindicat" (he asserts and claims righteousness).

[83]Melanchthon 152 ("gratia caelestis" [heavenly grace]); Calov 179 ("iustitia imputata" [imputed righteousness]); Cocceius 9 ("absolutio conscientiae" [the absolution of the conscience], "obsignatio filiorum" [the sealing of the sons], "spes gloriae" [the hope of glory]); Bengel 38 ("non dicit beati iusti" [he does not say: blessed are the righteous]); Olshausen 208f.

more probable. The context also speaks in favor of this, especially beginning with the third beatitude, and so does 3:15. This leaves only the question whether this interpretation can be combined with the metaphor of "hunger and thirst" or whether, on the basis of these verbs, an interpretation in the direction of God's righteousness is suggested. The Jewish and Hellenistic parallels show that "hunger and thirst" may mean both "to long for"[84] and "to make an effort for."[85] Thus nothing impedes the ethical interpretation which the early church, with good sensitivity, advocated almost exclusively. With this, the Old Testament structure of "righteousness" is preserved: righteousness is the behavior commanded by God in his covenant. As to content, it is described more closely in 5:20-48. The attempt to connect the "active" and the "passive" interpretation on the basis of a more comprehensive meaning of the word δικαιοσύνη, one that would embrace God and humans, is an unnecessary complication which is more reflective than Matthew himself.

With the following three beatitudes we come close to central concerns of Jewish wisdom parenesis.

5:7

The fifth beatitude, which speaks of the merciful, formulates protasis and apodosis in exact correspondence. It thereby approaches both the Old Testament "law of the 'fate-determining dimension of deeds' "[86] and the parenetical motif of the correspondence of divine and human behavior. Since the demand of mercy represents the essence of Jewish works of love,[87] there are numerous Jewish parallels.[88] Matthew speaks of the priority of mercy over sacrifice (9:13; 12:7), for ἔλεος belongs to the βαρύτερα τοῦ νόμου (23:23). In the miracle narratives he will show that the mercy of the Son of David corresponds to the mercy which is demanded of people. The relationship of the meaning of salvation in the protasis to the promise in the apodosis remains unsettled, as in the other beatitudes. It is neither unambiguously so that God's mercy precedes and motivates human action (thus 18:23-35), nor unambiguously so that human mercy has the *purpose* to effect divine mercy, as it is stated a little later in church parenesis.[89]

5:8

"Pure in heart" or a "pure heart" is a Jewish expression which comes from Old

---

[84]Amos 8:11; Jer. 38:25; Bar. 2:18 (δόξα, δικαιοσύνη); *'Abot* 1:4 (words of the wise); *b. Sanh.* 100a (Torah); Aristotle, *Cael.* 2.12 = 291b (philosophy); Philo, *Virt.* 79 (σοφία), etc.

[85]Sirach 24:21f.; Philo, *Fug.* 139 (καλοκαγαθία); Philo, *Poster.* C 172 (ἀρετή); Plato, *Rep.* 562c (freedom); Horace, *Ep.* 1.18.23 (money); Cicero, *Ep. ad Quint.* 3.5 (honor); Claudius Aelianus, *Var. Hist.* 14.22 (destruction of the monarchy), etc. Often the alternative cannot be decided.

[86]Zimmerli* 20, following K. Koch, "Gibt es ein Vergeltungsdogma im Alten Testament?" *ZTK* 52 (1955) 1-42.

[87]Str-B IV/1 559-610.

[88]Prov. 17:5; *b. Sabb.* 151b = Str-B I 203; *pBQ* 8,6c,19 (ibid.); *Tos.B.Q.* 9,30,366 (ibid.). Montefiore, *Literature* 23: "Jesus says here what lots of Rabbis said in all ages."

[89]First Clement 13:2; Polycarp, Phil. 2:3.

Testament psalm piety.[90] This means undivided obedience toward God without sin. "Heart" designates in Jewish usage not an internal area of the human being but the center of human wanting, thinking, and feeling. Since the expression is tied to an established Jewish linguistic usage, one must not read an anti-cultic polemic into it. Judaism has always—along with the more narrow cultic usage—spoken of the purity of the human being in a comprehensive sense.[91] Matthew also is aware of purity wholistically understood, which indeed relativizes the cultic realm but by no means invalidates it (cf. 5:23f.; 23:25f.: πρῶτον). The reference to Ps. 23:4, i.e., that psalm which is sung at the entrance in the *temple*, also points to the inner unity of the concept of purity, not to polemic against the cult.[92] The promise is meant eschatologically, just as in the other beatitudes. Judaism and early Christianity hope that God, who was in this world invisible even to Moses, can be seen face to face in the eschaton.[93] Then all separation from God and all obscurity will disappear.

History of influence

This beatitude has a very intensive history of interpretation, because in its linguistic expression it was closer to the Greek sense of late antiquity than any other one. As K. Beyschlag says,[94] it becomes the "essence of all Christian mysticism and asceticism." Only few things can be mentioned here. In late antiquity the ascetic interpretation of purity of heart predominated. Valentinus sees the human heart as the place of the demons. But when the good Father looks at it, it becomes light; thus the one who is pure in heart can be called blessed.[95] For Clement, this word is the Alpha and Omega of his ideal of the perfect gnostic. Purity of heart is the suppression of wild desires. In the hard fight against the drives of one's own body, God's promise for the gnostic is fulfilled.[96] Gregory of Nyssa also is a witness for this interpretation. At question here is the purification of the heart from all passion and all sins of thought; thus the image of God in humans will shine again and God will become visible.[97] Matthew 5:8 is a key word in the *Life of Anthony* by Athanasius and describes his path to perfection.[98]

The Reformation offers—not exclusively but very clearly—examples for a

---

[90]Psalm 23:4; Ps. 50:12; Ps. 73:1, Hebrew text; cf. Str-B I 205f.; in early Christianity *Herm. Vis.* 3.9.8; 5.7; *Man.* 12.6.5.

[91]Survey in R. Meyer, "καθαρός κτλ.," *TDNT* III 423.

[92]The polemic against the cult was gladly read into the text by Christian interpretation which was concerned to establish an anti-Jewish profile of the Beatitudes, cf., e.g., Bengel 38 ("non sufficit puritas caeremonialis" [ceremonial purity is not sufficient]); Bornhäuser** 35 ("woe to those who are only externally pure").

[93]Cf., e.g., 4 Ezra 7:91,98; Jub. 1:28; Str-B I 207-15; 1 Cor. 13:12; 1 John 3:2; Rev. 22:4; further Jewish examples in W. Michaelis, ὁράω κτλ., *TDNT* V 339ff.

[94]*ZTK* 1977** 302.

[95]Fragment 2 = Clement of Alexandria, *Strom.* 2.20.

[96]K. Holl, "Die schriftstellerische Form des griechischen Heiligenlebens," in *Gesammelte Aufsätze zur Kirchengeschichte* II, *Der Osten*, reprint (Darmstadt: Wissenschaftliche Buchgesellschaft, 1964), 256f.

[97]6.3 = 213-15.

[98]Holl, ibid. (above n. 96) 250f.

differently accented, so to speak "secular" interpretation of purity of heart. One should strive not into the height but into the depth, Luther says, as God himself has done; and one should "seek God in the miserable, erring and laboring ones"; "that's where one sees God, there the heart becomes pure, and all arrogance lies down." Purity of heart means that each in his or her place in the world "thinks what God says and puts God's thought in the place of his or her own thoughts."[99] In post-Reformation interpretation purity of heart becomes the inner-worldly attitude; it means *simplicitas* (simplicity) and *integritas* (integrity).[100]

The promise to see God has occupied the interpretation even more intensively. "To say that eternal life will consist in the vision of God"[101] had almost at all times a special power. A root of this power lies in the philosophy of Plato and Aristotle for which the true sense of being is realized in seeing God.[102] This may be the reason for the fact that the distinction between the present and the eschaton, in which the viewing of God will be granted, often is broken through just a little; the viewing of God is now already realized, in the radiance of the image of God in the perfected Christians.[103] The purified soul sees "God within, as in a mirror."[104] To see God is granted to the eye of the spirit, the heart which is purified from evil thought and deeds—not alone by decision and will but by the help of God.[105] Along with the thought of the possible seeing of God already indirectly in the present, there is throughout the entire tradition of interpretation always the hope of the final seeing of God by those who "have become immortal through seeing and are immersed in God."[106]

This beatitude discloses an immense wealth of Christian self-understanding and Christian hope. It would be wrong to delete simply as illegitimate everything which appears exegetically not justified before the forum of the biblical text. Rather it belongs to the power inherent in the central biblical texts to disclose new dimensions in new people. Nevertheless, these new dimensions and new hopes have to engage in constant debate with the old views of the text. On the basis of the original meaning of the text one must constantly be on guard that purity of heart and the seeing of God will not lead to removal from the world or to private piety of the one who is religiously gifted,[107] but will manifest itself as obedience toward God in the world and as hope for a future seeing of God which is more than private individual experience. The sixth beatitude stands in a context which speaks of interhuman relationships and does

---

[99]II 55 (Sermon of 1519); the same**, 324-30, quot. 325.

[100]Bucer 43B. Cf. 1 Tim. 1:5; 2:22.

[101]F. Schleiermacher, *The Christian Faith* §163,2 (Edinburgh: T & T Clark, 1928), 213.

[102]Passages like Plato, *Rep.* 7.527D-E. 533D (eye of the soul); *Symp.* 211D-E; Aristotle, *Eth. Euc.* 7.15 = 1249b,16ff. are fundamental.

[103]Gregory of Nyssa (above n. 97).

[104]Athanasius, *Contra Gentes* 2 = BKV I/31 14.

[105]Origen, *Cels.* 7.33 = BKV I/53 250.

[106]Quotation from the influential section Irenaeus, *Haer.* 4.20, § 6 = BKV I/4 387.

[107]Cf. the beautiful story from *Vita patrum* 10. 194 = *PL* 74,223, related by Beyschlag, ZTK 1977** 301 n. 21: An ascetic who lived for more than 30 years in the wilderness meets a younger brother in an inn in the city and blames him because he exposes himself to temptation. The younger brother answers: "Deus non quaerit nisi cor mundum" (God only seeks a pure heart).

not attempt to distance the person and lead into religious self-sufficiency. Here, it seems to me, the interpretation of the Reformation has come particularly close to the Matthean sense of the text.

5:9

The seventh beatitude, which speaks of peacemakers, also breathes of Jewish coloring.

> The admonition to make peace has a central place in wisdom and in rabbinical parenesis.[108] In each case, concrete steps in interhuman relationships are meant. The connection of peacemaking with an eschatological promise can be demonstrated frequently.[109] But the admonition to make peace is never coupled with the eschatological promise of being children of God. However, there are statements which articulate Israel's sonship with God as future hope.[110]

Εἰρηνηποιός means something active, not just readiness for peace. Our beatitude, together with the following ones, points to the commandment of love of enemies 5:44-48. There also the promise is made that they shall be children of God (5:45); there also, the subject is, as in vv. 10-12, enemies and persecutors. Thus, Matthew is thinking not only of a peaceful living together of members of the community, but thinks beyond the limits of the community.[111] A direct Christological reference is lacking; only when reading the whole Gospel will the reader see clearly how faithfully the Son of God has already lived that which he demands. The promise to be children of God does not stand in direct relationship to making peace.[112] The reader of the Gospel of Matthew probably understands it not primarily from the background of Jewish analogies but on the basis of 3:13–4:11: How Jesus, the Son of God, proves himself in obedience toward the Father, so obedience toward his will leads the disciples to the point that they also—in the eschaton—can be called children of the Father.

5:10

The redactional beatitude of the persecuted in v. 10 does not go beyond v. 3 and vv. 11f. It reinforces once more the two main aspects of the whole series, δικαιοσύνη and kingdom of heaven. The perfect participle δεδιωγμένοι lifts

---

[108]*Abot* 1:12,18 (Str-B I 217f.); P. Lapide, "Zukunftserwartung und Frieden im Judentum," in *Eschatologie und Frieden* II, ed. G. Liedke et al., TM.FEST A7 (Heidelberg: Forschungsstätte der Evang. Studiengemeinschaft, 1978), 127-78. Cf. especially the rabbinical "tractate" on peace *S. Num.* 6.26, § 42 [131-37], transl. K. G. Kuhn).

[109]2 Enoch 52:11-13 as a macarism; *Pe'a* 1:1; *b. Ta'an* 22a (Str-B I 218); *Mek. Exod.* 20.255 (81a = Str-B I 215).

[110]Jubilees 1:24f.; T. Judah 24:3; Pss. Sol. 17:27 (future!); cf. Wis. 5:5. On eschatological sonship with God in the NT, cf. E. Schweizer, υἱός κτλ., *TDNT* VIII 390f.

[111]Schnackenburg* 173f. The problem of war lies outside of the horizon which our beatitude reflects directly, cf. N. H. Soe, *Christliche Ethik*, 2d ed. (Munich, 1957), 353.

[112]Windisch* 254-57 sees two possible bridges between beatitude and promise: (1) a messianic one concerning Solomon, son of God and man of peace, 1 Chr. 22:9f., and (2) one by way of the imperial cult where the imperial son of God has the title "peacemaker" (however, only since Commodus).

the actual event of persecution as described in vv. 11f. into a more universal sphere. Matthew, looking back to a persecution which happened earlier,[113] understands persecution almost as a general sign of being a Christian.[114] Δικαιοσύνη means human behavior. One can be persecuted only because of such behavior, not because of mere longing for (divine) righteousness. Christian practice and confession of Jesus belong to righteousness; persecution for the sake of righteousness in v. 10 and, also redactionally formulated, persecution "for my sake" in v. 11 interpret each other mutually: the confession of Christ manifests itself in deeds (7:21-23; 25:31-46).

5:11–12a

The last beatitude addresses the disciples directly. Matthew again has generalized. Instead of ἀφορίζω and ἐκβάλλω τὸ ὄνομα he has the much more general διώκω and λέγω πονηρόν.[115] The community fundamentally has to reckon with defamation and persecution. That is realistic, particularly in the time of Domitian;[116] the persecution pareneses, numerous in the New Testament, illustrate this clearly (Heb. 10:32-34; 1 Peter 2:12; 3:14,16f.; 4:12-17; cf. 2 Tim.). Ψευδόμενοι throws light on the ethical interest: a promise applies not to any persecution but to persecution which happens for the sake of Christ, i.e., for the sake of righteousness (cf. 1 Peter 3:14,17; 4:14f.). Verse 12 takes up μακάριοι and interprets it: there will be joy and jubilation in the community over suffering.[117] The reason for joy is the reversal of circumstances which the future will bring: Your reward in heaven will be great. "Reward" in Matthew is always bestowed in the beyond, in the last judgment.[118]

5:12b

Verse 12b is an appendix. It remains unclear how the persecution of the Old Testament prophets lays the foundation for the promise of heavenly reward. While Luke mentions only Old Testament prophets, Matthew—like Q—speaks of the persecution of the "prophets before you." Wandering prophets play a relatively large role in Matthew (cf. 10:41; 23:34,37). He has taken over the prophetically influenced traditions of the Q community more faithfully than Luke.

On the *history of influence* of vv. 11f.: Matthew looks back to the persecution of the community by the Jews. In the present his community probably is persecuted by

---

[113]Cf. introduction p. 67.

[114]Cf. on 10:17,22,24f. Rabanus 790: vv. 3-10 are valid for all times, vv. 11f. are directed only to the disciples at that time.

[115]Cf. Dupont, *Béatitudes* III 331: the Matthean formulation can be applied to very different situations.

[116]L. Goppelt, *Der erste Petrusbrief*, KEK 12/1 (1978), 60-64: Since the Neronian persecution such actions are possible practically in the whole empire.

[117]As in 2 Apoc. Bar. 52:5-7 and 1 Peter 4:13f. (perhaps an echo of our beatitude, cf. introduction, §5.6).

[118]Strecker, *Weg* 162.

Gentiles.[119] Therefore the logia on persecution retain their actuality. We can observe what is just the beginning of a fateful development: the persecutors, following the tradition in v. 12b, still are "Jews," even if after 70 they are in reality probably no longer Jews. This means that through the Matthean generalization of the persecution tradition the Jews became the representatives "of the persecutors," as in the Gospel of John they become representatives of the hostile world. Here it becomes understandable how the Jews became the scapegoat representing the world that is hostile to the Christians.

Summary

The Matthean interpretation of the Beatitudes belongs to a long history of interpretation but is not yet the end point. First it must be characterized by the key word *ethicizing*; the beatitudes become a catalog of virtues. The second key word *internalizing*; religious virtues, humility, renunciation of the world and of sin, faithfulness move increasingly to the foreground. This tendency unfolded fully only after Matthew. The interpretation in the Reformation to a certain extent reversed the ethicizing tendency and to that extent came closer to the original sense (but not the Matthean sense!); however, it has not reversed the internalizing of the Beatitudes. This internalizing has progressed further in modern times because the concreteness of the promise of salvation also has been more and more spiritualized.[120]

The Matthean Beatitudes thus involve a series of uncompromising demands. They confront us with the question of whether we are still in a position to accomplish their specific promise of salvation. They confront particularly the Protestant interpreters with the question of whether they take seriously the connection of the promise of salvation with an actively lived Christian life.[121] Finally, it is a demand in which, not religious inwardness is praised as blessed, but Christians who practice their faith *in the world* in their relationships with other people.

Conversely, there also are questions which must be asked of the Matthean Beatitudes, specifically on the basis of the Protestant tradition of interpretation. They coincide with the questions which resulted from the development of the tradition from Jesus to Matthew: Was Jesus' gift of grace betrayed by the Matthean reinterpretation? Was the message of grace redefined

---

[119]Matthew 24:9-14 applies to the time of the author of Matthew.

[120]J. G. Herder, *Christliche Reden* 22, Werke 36 (Karlsruhe: Bureau der deutschen Klassiker, 1826), 11, is an example of this internalization: "Blessed are those who can do without . . ., for heaven is in their soul." For F. C. Baur, the fulfillment of the promise lies in the pure ideal of Christian consciousness which expresses itself in the Beatitudes, the "feeling of the need for salvation which as such already carries the full reality of salvation in itself" (*Das Christentum und die christliche Kirche der ersten drei Jahrhunderte*, Werke III, reprint [Bad Canstatt 1966], 27). The "poor in spirit" according to Bultmann (*This World and the Beyond*, [London: Lutterworth, 1960], 204) are they who wait completely for God's unworldly future "and by such an attitude of waiting on God have inwardly freed themselves from their attachment to the here and now."

[121]The problem of the Protestant type of interpretation becomes clear as an example in Zinzendorf I 182 who argues exactly against the Matthean meaning of the first beatitude: "It is a very agreeable matter with the beatitude of the poor. One must not think at all of something virtuous or truly humble, of that which is called virtue or humility which has come upon the children of God. . . ."

as an aspect of Christian ethics? Does the evangelist Matthew really take grace seriously?

History of influence

We look once more at the *history of influence* in order to clarify this basic question. It is striking how often in the interpretations grace was added. It seems to be missing in the Matthean text, and precisely for that reason it was added in the interpretation of the early and medieval church.[122] The paralleling since Augustine of the seven beatitudes with the sevenfold effects of the Holy Spirit according to Isa. 11:2f. probably is the most impressive and important.[123] This connection has determined the entire medieval exegesis.[124] It is anything but frivolous. Behind it stands as a basic concern the connection of grace and virtue or, if one adds the often adduced seven petitions of the Lord's Prayer, of petition, grace, and virtue. For medieval theology this order is irreversible: "He gave the order of life not according to commands, but truly also (according to) gifts and prayer."[125] Thus the combination of gifts of the Spirit and demands of the Beatitudes makes clear that their concern is "dona *virtutum*" (the gifts of virtues).

The same concern stands behind the many attempts of interpreting the Beatitudes *Christologically*. Origen comes closest to the frame of the Matthean pattern of thought when he emphasizes that Jesus in his ministry has given an example of the fulfillment of the Beatitudes, in his kindness, in his weeping over Jerusalem, in his reconciling love.[126] Gregory of Nyssa at first sees the help of Jesus on the way to the mountain in the fact that he promises blessedness and shows the way,[127] but at the finish he has to surmount this interpretation Christologically because it is obviously insufficient: "He is the giver of the inheritance, he is the beautiful inheritance, he is the good portion, he who makes us rich, he is wealth, he who shows you the treasure and wants to be your treasure who in you awakens the desire of the precious pearl and at the same time the hope that you will be able to acquire it."[128] And in a different passage he opines "that the Lord, in speaking of virtue and righteousness, offers himself to his disciples as the object of the desire."[129] Matthew says none of this.

---

[122]Since the early church interprets a text always on the basis of the entire faith, such "additions" do not show a weakness but a factual strength.

[123]The passage is mentioned by U. Duchrow, "Der Aufbau von Augustins Schriften Confessiones und De trinitate," *ZTK* 62 (1965) 344f. Augustine conceives of a schema of gifts of grace, beginning with the fear of God and ending with wisdom, which probably has put its stamp on the conception of both the *Confessions* and *De trinitate* (loc.cit. 348-67).

[124]Stoll** 169f.: "One of the most successful" schemes of interpretation of the Sermon on the Mount in the Middle Ages.

[125]"Non modo mandatorum tradidit disciplinam, verum etiam donorum et precum" (Paschasius Radbertus 344 = 300), cf. idem 341 = 298: "Habemus . . . in principibus eadem (i.e., the Beatitudes) ut impetremus dona, in donis vero, ut operemus Spiritus sancti mandata" (we have . . . in the principles [i.e., the Beatitudes] the same as we receive as gifts, and in gifts, indeed, as we perform the commands of the Holy Spirit).

[126]*Hom. in Luc* 38 = *PG* 13,152. Additional texts from Origen to Augustine are brought together by P. Rollero, *La "expositio Evangelii secundum Lucam" di Ambrogio come fonte della esegesi Agostiniana*, Univ. Torino, Publ. Facolt. Lett. X/4 (Torino 1958), 39f.

[127]Gregory of Nyssa* 6.6 = 218.

[128]Ibid.,* 8.6 = 240.

[129]Ibid.,* 4.7 = 194.

Such attempts demonstrate how ancient and medieval interpreters spoke very intensively of grace even if they did not negate the ethical dimension of the Matthean Beatitudes as did later Protestant interpreters. The question arises whether they picked up in their own way a concern of Matthew or whether they corrected a deficiency. I would like to try to demonstrate with a few deliberations that the ethical reworking of the Beatitudes in the Gospel of Matthew by no means entailed an elimination of grace.[130]

1. We have to consider the situation of the Matthean community. It looks back perhaps 50 years to the continuous history of Christian preaching of grace. A message of grace which is repeated without ceasing can become "cheap grace."[131] In ethicizing the beatitude, Matthew or the community before him has taken its changed situation into account. The text thus shows how Christian proclamation must always be determined also by the situation in which it takes place. Whether, e.g., a preacher of today decides in favor of Jesus' original form of the Beatitudes or of the Matthean form has to be evaluated, it seems to me, less on the basis of the "correctness" of the theological approach than on the basis of the situation of the community. Obviously it was a basic problem for the Matthean community how to remain loyal to the faith given to it. And in this situation Matthew wanted to help the community precisely through his ethical interpretation.

2. The initial proclamation of grace is prior not only in the history of the Matthean community, but also in the Gospel of Matthew. The "ethical" Sermon on the Mount belongs to the history of God's actions with Jesus. The narrative frame of the whole Gospel is for Matthew an expression of the priority of grace which makes his ethical beatitudes "dona virtutum" (gifts of virtues). The demands of Jesus are the demands of the "Immanuel" who accompanies and helps his community.

3. An element of the promise of grace also is found in the apodoses of the Beatitudes. All are to be understood eschatologically and not anticipated by the grace of the presence of God which is experienced now. Matthew has understood "images" like "kingdom of God," "heirs of the land," "see God," etc., very concretely. The church interpretation had the tendency to see an aspect of the promises of the Beatitudes realized already in the present.[132] The price which had to be paid for it was that the promises threatened to lose their concreteness and their world-embracing character and to shrink into the personal possession of salvation of the individual.[133] This was not the opinion of

---

[130]The "addition" of grace by the exegesis of the early church thus is correct as far as the matter itself is concerned, not exegetically!

[131]Cf. Bonhoeffer** 13-27.

[132]Cf. above nn. 103-106. In scholasticism, this is systematized: Thomas, *ST* I/II qu. 69 art. 2 speaks of the "beatitudo inchoata" (the blessedness which has begun) and the "beatitudo perfecta" (perfect blessedness). For Matthew, on the other hand, the promises lie in the future and the joy about them in the present. The experience of the helping presence of the Lord, whose expression consists, e.g., in the miracle narratives, also lies in the present.

[133]Examples above, nn. 103f. Schleiermacher, above n. 101, also is impressive: He can picture the seeing of God only as "the perfect fullness of the liveliest consciousness of God" and can hardly distinguish that which is still to come from that which is present.

Matthew. In the Protestant tradition of interpretation, there is another difficulty for the comprehension of the grace character of the Matthean promises: God's promises in the Beatitudes apply to the Christian, "who strives and makes an effort." Nevertheless they are for Matthew a full and pure bestowal of grace. Here probably there are comparable Protestant difficulties of understanding, similar to those faced in responding to the Catholic doctrine of grace. The Christian who makes an effort, who is supported by God, to whom Matthew promises "reward" *horribile dictu*, is precisely not the one who wishes to be righteous by his or her own works.

    4. Finally God's demanding will itself is for Matthew an element of grace. For him it is "gospel" that the Son of God proclaims God's will. "Matthew does not distinguish between indicative and imperative, . . . but he conveys to the human being his demand as gift."[134] His understanding of the gospel agrees with the Old Testament-Jewish understanding of the Torah as an aid in *remaining* in the covenant which God has made for his people.[135] In this sense, Jesus' commandments also are a part of the gospel. "As (the gospel) elsewhere spreads his benefaction, namely, how he has made the blind to see, has awakened the dead, has made the lame well, so it (!) presents us here also the benefaction that he interprets the law for us." The command is not alien to the gospel, rather "the gospel also contains commandments, namely, how one should strive to be poor in spirit, meek, merciful, etc." Matthew has understood the "ethical" Beatitudes approximately in this way, and none other than Martin Luther has stated it likewise.[136]

1.3. "You are the salt of the earth . . ." (5:13-16)

Literature

Cullmann, O., "Das Gleichnis vom Salz," in idem, *Vorträge und Aufsätze, 1952-1962*, pp. 192-201 (Tübingen: Mohr, 1966).

Hahn, F., "Die Worte vom Licht Lk 11,33-36," in *Orientierung an Jesus* (FS J. Schmid), ed. P. Hoffmann, pp. 107-38 (Freiburg: Herder, 1973).

Heiligenthal, R., *Werke als Zeichen*, WUNT II/9, pp. 115-23 (Tübingen: Mohr, 1983).

Jeremias, J., "Die Lampe unter dem Scheffel," in idem, *Abba* 99-102.

Krämer, M., "Ihr seid das Salz der Erde . . . Ihr seid das Licht der Welt," *MTZ* 28 (1977) 133-57.

Nauck, W., "Salt as a Metaphor in Instructions for Discipleship," *StTh* 6 (1953) 165-78.

Schnackenburg, R., "Ihr seid das Salz der Erde, das Licht der Welt," in idem, *Schriften zum Neuen Testament*, pp. 177-200 (Munich: Kösel, 1971).

Schneider, G., "Das Bildwort von der Lampe. Zur Traditionsgeschichte eines Jesus-Wortes," *ZNW* 61 (1970) 183-209.

Soucek, J., "Salz der Erde und Licht der Welt," *TZ* 19 (1963) 169-79.

Further literature** on the Sermon on the Mount, above pp. 209-211.

---

[134]Strecker* 274.

[135]Formulation following M. Buber's understanding of the Jewish faith (*Zwei Glaubensweisen*, especially section 17).

[136]II 56 (Wittenberg Sermon of 1522).

Text

13 You are the salt of the earth.
But when the salt becomes dumb,[1] with what will it[2] be salted?
It it good for nothing except[3] to be thrown out and to be trampled under
foot by people.
14 You are the light of the world.
It is impossible that a city which lies on top of a mountain remain hidden.
15 One also does not light a lamp
and put it under a bushel
but puts it on a lampstand,
then it will give light to all in the house.
16 Thus your light should shine before people so that they see your good
works and praise your Father in the heavens.

Analysis

1. *Structure.* In comparison with the structure of the Sermon on the Plain, there follows
here a longer interruption (5:13-37). Our section is linked by an emphatic ὑμεῖς with vv.
11f. Thus it deals again principally with the disciples. The concluding verse 16 is often
and rightfully considered a type of heading for vv. 17-48:[4] there it is explained what
"good works" are. Moreover, Matthew in 6:1 points back to 5:16 (ἔμπροσθεν τῶν
ἀνθρώπων, πατὴρ ὑμῶν ὁ ἐν τοῖς οὐρανοῖς), in order to prevent a misunderstanding of
v. 16.
The section is structured clearly: A shorter negative statement, ending with a
threat of judgment, and a longer positive statement, which considers the missionary
dimension of the community, are both introduced by ὑμεῖς ἐστε τὸ . . . + genitive in
final position (13,14-16). Within both parts there is a chiastic correspondence which is
characterized by the key words λάμπω (15d, 16a), φῶς (14a, 16a) and ἄνθρωποι (13c,
16a). The conclusion 16bc, with the "look up" to the Father in heaven, presents itself
structurally as "excess," which therefore has special meaning.
2. *Redaction and Sources.* The following thesis is frequent: vv. 13a, 14a and
16[5] are redaction. The logia of salt (14bc) and of the lamp (15) come from Q. Matthew,
who omits the Mark variants of these logia (9:50; 4:21), preserves the Q text more
faithfully than Luke. The latter has the lamp saying twice (8:16; 11:33) but he intervenes
more strongly in redacting and assimilates the texts to each other. The saying about the
city (14b) comes from the special material.
This thesis requires only a few precisions. The image of the city (v. 14b) has
hardly been inserted by Matthew, for it fits neither the introduction (v. 14a, light!) nor
the application in v. 16 where he speaks of behavior, not of a condition. Probably Q was

---

[1]Semitism: Hebr./Aram. תפל = 1. to be saltless, 2. to speak stupidly.

[2]It is syntactically the simplest, referring to Mark 9:50 (αὐτό!) and to the trend of the image which is
concerned about the salt alone, to supplement ἅλας as the subject of ἁλισθήσεται.

[3]Εἰ μή means "except." Meaning: the only possibility which is left to the salt which has become dumb
is to be thrown out. Cf. Herodotus 1.200: οὐδὲν . . . εἰ μὴ ἰχθῦς = nothing . . . except fish.

[4]Zahn 206: "Basic thought of the whole remaining discourse"; Burchard** 420.

[5]The following are Matthean in v. 16: οὕτως, λάμπω, ἔργον, ἔμπροσθεν, ἄνθρωποι?, ὅπως, πατὴρ
ὑμῶν ἐν τοῖς οὐρανοῖς. Cf. introduction 3.2.

supplemented before Matthew (QMt?).[6] It is difficult to determine how far there were other changes of the Q sayings before Matthew. The close parallel between 1 Peter 2:12 and v. 16 is, I think, not due to common Jewish basic thoughts[7] but to the fact that 1 Peter presupposes the Gospel of Matthew.[8]

    3. *Origin.* To be sure, definite statements concerning the origin of the logia of salt and light are hardly possible. In my opinion, nothing impedes the view that both go back to Jesus. The decision depends in the last analysis on their interpretation; we can only make conjectures.

Interpretation

One can no longer determine for certain the *original meaning* of these wisdom logia. The *salt saying* has to be understood in the probably older Q version as a minatory saying, on the basis of its ending, while Mark 9:50b interprets it secondarily in a parenetic way. Luke 14:34f. also refers it to the disciples. Perhaps it was a threatening word of Jesus originally directed to Israel. Nothing can be stated about the origin and original meaning of the *saying about the city.*[9] The word about *light* is similarly difficult. No unambiguously oldest form can be determined between Matthew and Mark 4:21.[10] The meaning also is uncertain: Jeremias interprets καίω as "kindle" and the putting it under a bushel as "extinguish," so that the metaphor says, "One does not light a lamp only in order to extinguish it immediately."[11] But one can certainly not assert that a bushel is a suitable and customary instrument for extinguishing an oil lamp.[12] But it is just as senseless to hide a light under a bushel. For what reason would it not be extinguished when it is no longer needed? Briefly, the image evokes a senseless behavior that can no longer be anchored in an everyday event. It is therefore difficult to know what it referred to originally. There are some proposals: Jesus[13] speaks of his own activity which must

---

[6]Or does the Matthean favorite word οὐδέ (15a) speak in favor of the idea that the linking of the two metaphors of the city and the lampstand is due to the evangelist?

[7]T. Naph. 8:4 (God will be glorified through you among the nations); *Mek. Exod.* 44b on 15:2 ("if the Israelites do the will of God, his name will be made great in the world"); Midr. Ps. 67:6 (the nations praise God because of the righteousness of the Israelites). In addition, certain statements on the Qiddush ha-shem are important (cf. Str-B I 414-17).

[8]Literal agreements: Καλὰ ἔργα, δοξάζω. E. Best, "1 Peter and the Gospel Tradition," *NTS* 16 (1969/70), who otherwise comes to a different result and attributes the remaining peculiarities of 1 Peter 2:12 to the linguistic usage of 1 Peter (109f.). 1 Peter 3:14 is just as close a parallel to Matt. 5:10. Cf. introduction 5.6.

[9]Jeremias, *Parables* 215, understands the word as a word of comfort for the disciples, the "citizens . . . of the eschatological city of God . . ., whose light shines in the night without needing human effort."

[10]Schneider* 191; Hahn* 111f. The (altogether uncertain) Semitisms do not lead to a result: the Markan question form corresponds to wisdom style (Bultmann, *Tradition* 82). But it excludes the Aramaizing impersonal plural καίουσιν (cf. Black, *An Aramaic Approach,* 126f.) and the paratactic final clause καὶ λάμπει.

[11]Jeremias* 102. Luke thinks of kindling (ἅπτω). Καίω occasionally *may* mean "kindle" (Liddell-Scott, s.v. καίω I.II), but only occasionally.

[12]The examples mentioned by Jeremias* 101, *Sabb.* 16:7 (Str-B I 238f) and *b. Besa* 22a speak only of the fact that in emergencies one may smother a light on the Sabbath with a vessel when extinguishing is not permitted. There is not a single example for supposing that the extinguishing of a lamp by means of a bushel was "something done every day" (102); for practical reasons (sooty bushel basket) it is improbable.

[13]Hahn* 112f. traces it back to Jesus, but only because the opposite cannot be proved.

not remain hidden.[14] He is thinking of the kingdom of God which arrives in him.[15] He opposes the Jewish leaders who withhold the kingdom of God from the people (cf. Matt. 23:13).[16]

These deliberations show where the difficulty of the explanation lies: the images are general. Salt, city, and light can be used almost for anything, and the history of interpretation shows that this has actually happened.

5:13

In his redactional introduction, Matthew puts ὑμεῖς emphatically in the first place.[17] The total community is addressed, as in vv. 11f., not only the apostles or the proclaimers.[18] The emphatic "you" resumes vv. 11f.: precisely you who are persecuted and slandered are the salt of the earth.[19] Verses 13-16 point the persecuted community to its missionary commission. "Salt of the earth" is a metaphor which sounds strange. It is not immediately obvious what is meant; precisely for this reason, one is curious.[20] The reader who ponders the meanings probably refers γῆ to the world and not to the soil, if not already on the basis of 5:5, then at least because of the parallel κόσμος in v. 14. The two logia are to be understood in the sense of Matthean universalism. It is unclear how the evangelist has understood (a) the metaphor "salt" and (b) the parable of the "becoming dumb" of the salt.

a. In imitation especially of the Jewish metaphorical use of salt, various allegories were proposed in early as well as in more recent times: On the basis of the function, it was thought that salt seasons, purifies, and preserves.[21] As far as the content is concerned, salt refers to the wisdom of the disciples,[22] their proclamation,[23] their

---

[14]Jeremias* 102; Schneider* 192f.

[15]Soucek* 172 (on the basis of Mark 4:21—ἔρχεται).

[16]Dodd, *Parables* 108.

[17]Putting ὑμεῖς first: 10:30; 13:11,16,18; 15:5,16; 16:15; 23:8f., cf. 5:20; 20:26, usually with clear emphasis. Cf. introduction 3.2.

[18]Cf. below in notes 51-56 and Schnackenburg* 194.

[19]Since Augustine** 1.6 (16) this reference is seen clearly. Often therefore also vv. 11-16 are taken together as one pericope.

[20]Gundry 75 has called attention to the fact that one uses salt in small amounts as fertilizer. But the power of the metaphor, it seems to me, lies exactly in the fact that with salt and earth two things are brought together which have nothing in common, just as a single light cannot lighten the whole world. Besides, salt is not the normal, necessary fertilizer but at most an additive.

[21]See Soiron** 217. I. Blümner, "Salz," in *RECA* IA 2088-95 presents information about the use of salt in antiquity. Naturally, salt as seasoning stood foremost. The pickling of meat, fish, and vegetables with salt as preservative also was widespread. Only in third place would the thought of purifying arise (cf. 2 Kings 2:21f.; Ezek. 16:4).

[22]Examples in Nauck* 166-68 and in Fiebig* 20 no. 58. The Latin *sal*, less frequently the Greek ἅλς (Plutarch, *Aristophanes and Menander* II 854C), and the adjective *salsus* may mean "witty," "clever," cf. Col. 4:6. In the exegesis of the church, the interpretation of wisdom is widespread: Origen, *Hom.* 6 on Ezek. 16:4 = *PG* 13,114; Cyril of Alexandria, fragment 41 = Reuss 165 (= φρόνησις) and many later authors; the Valentinians, according to Irenaeus, *Haer.* 1.6.1, interpret it of

willingness to sacrifice,[24] and their manner of living. Jülicher wanted to end the allegorical interpretations radically: The *tertium comparationis* is only the opposition between usefulness and uselessness of salt.[25] But Jülicher's assertion that the metaphor "salt" could be replaced by any other is an absurdity; it can not be said as he proposes, "You are the coal of the earth" nor, as Ragaz rejects rightfully, can sugar be substituted for salt.[26] Result: The choice of the metaphor is not arbitrary but has to be interpreted. But how? The everyday use of salt as seasoning is the most suggestive one. This meaning is assured by ἀρτύω for Mark 9:49 and Luke 14:34. It cannot be demonstrated for Matthew, but because seasoning is the most common use of salt, it is probable. With salt as seasoning, its necessity and irreplaceability are given.[27]

     b. Two possibilities exist for the interpretation of the parable of the salt "becoming dumb."[28] Perhaps the evangelist understood it simply as a picturesque expression for an impossible possibility, since salt chemically cannot lose its quality. The much-discussed Jewish parallel in *b. Bek.* 8b might speak in its favor,[29] also verses 14b and 15, both of which refer to something impossible. But the following speaks against it: if salt can never become saltless, neither is it thrown out and trampled under foot. The agreement of the listener to the illustration, which is necessary for the understanding, would not be assured if in reality there were no case where salt had to be thrown out. Thus, Matthew must think of a real possibility, perhaps of physical disintegration of salt by moisture which can take place if salt (e.g., at the storekeeper) is kept in the open air. Since only one-third of the Dead Sea salt contains table salt and could not be sold in trade without additives,[30] the easily dissociated components of the salt mixture can affect the

---

the πνευματικόν. In the history of liturgy, we must remember the "salt of wisdom" at infant baptism.

[23]Cf. below n. 53. The interpretation of salt as meaning the Torah can be documented in Jewish literature (*Sop.* 15:8 = Str-B I 235).

[24]Salt was used for sacrifices in Judaism as in Hellenistic antiquity, cf. Str-B II 21-23 and I. Blümner, "Salz," *RECA* IA 2093f. Krämer* 134f. interprets salt as meaning the disciples, whose presence makes the world a pleasing sacrificial gift, similarly Soucek* 174. Cullmann* 199 and Schnackenburg* 195f. interpret it of the sacrificial spirit of the disciples. The interpretation of S. Kierkegaard, "Der Augenblick," *Ges. Werke* 34 (Düsseldorf 1959), is impressive: To be a Christian means "to be salt and to be sacrificed." The opposites of salt are mediocrity and "prattle."

[25]*Gleichnisreden* II 70.

[26]*Gleichnisreden* II 71; Ragaz** 32.

[27]Sirach 39:26 (salt belongs to the things necessary for life); Pliny, *Hist. Nat.* 31.45 ("nihil . . . utilius sale et sole" [nothing is more useful than salt and sun]). Plutarch, *Quaest. Conv.* 4.4 = II 668F (salt, the only indispensable seasoning, as indispensable for taste as light is for colors).

[28]A third interpretation, presented among others by L. Köhler, *Kleine Lichter* (Zürich 1945), 73-76, is to be rejected. According to it, the reference is to salt plates with which the baking ovens were lined and which became unusable after approximately 15 years and had to be thrown out. According to Mark/ Luke, salt is for seasoning (ἀρτύω).

[29]Joshua ben Hananiah (c. 90) as an example of something impossible: " 'When salt loses its savor, with what should it be salted?' . . . 'With the afterbirth of a mule.' 'Does a mule have an afterbirth?' 'Can salt lose its savor?' " Str-B I 236 interpret the passage as a "cynical mockery of Mary and Jesus, with reference to Matt. 5:13. That is quite improbable, since the reference to the virgin birth is unclear and Matt. 5:13 is not dealing with it. I also consider it improbable that *b. Bek.* refers back to Matt. 5:13; in this manner, e.g., *b. B. Mes.* also would have to refer to Mark 10:25! It is more likely that this is a proverbial idiom for something impossible, cf. Abrahams, *Studies* II 183f.

[30]One liter of water of the Dead Sea contains 170 g $MgCl_2$, 103 g NaCl (table salt), 47 g $CaCl_2$, 14.5 g KCl, 6 g $MgBr_2$ and further salts in small amounts (according to J. H. Meyer, "Leben aus dem Toten

table salt through the effect of moisture and impair its taste.[31]

The importance of the logion lies in its threat. "To be thrown out"[32] and "to be trampled under foot"[33] suggest associations with the terminology of judgment. What is demanded is only indirectly indicated by the metaphor "salt of the earth." Salt is not salt for itself but seasoning for food. So the disciples are not existing for themselves but for the earth. What Matthew means exactly he will say in v. 16, which summarizes our verse too.

5:14

Verse 14 begins again with a metaphor, the hyperbolic character of which is still clearer than in v. 13. You, the small group of disciples, are the light of the world. The metaphor is not made clear until vv. 15f.; the evangelist first adduces the image of the city on a mountain, which does not completely fit the thought of works. The lack of articles in v. 14bc shows that the idea is hardly that of *the* city of God—Jerusalem on Mt. Zion[34]— but simply of any city located on a mountain. All metaphorical or allegorical interpretations of the city are to be rejected; it is only the thought that the city is visible from afar.

5:15

With that it corresponds to the oil lamp placed on a lampstand, which nobody would put under a bushel[35] because it is there in order to give light. The meaning of the metaphor "light of the world" is here made clear as a first stage; it is the brightness which light radiates in the world of which Matthew is thinking.

"Light" is an "open" metaphor whose sense only the context makes clear. In Judaism we encounter it in varied application. Israel,[36] individual righteous persons and teachers,[37] the Torah,[38] the Servant of the Lord,[39] or Jerusalem[40] can be designated as

---

[31]Suggestion by R. Gorski.

Meer," in Merian, *Israel* 12 [1978] 142). The salt is, as Krauss, *Archäologie* I, 119, reports, strongly caustic and therefore was not sold as pure table salt.

[31]Suggestion by R. Gorski.

[32]Βάλλω in connection with the annihilating judgment is especially frequent in Matthew: 3:10; 5:29; 7:19; 13:42,48 (ἔξω!); 18:8f; ἐκβάλλω 8:12; 22:13;25:30.

[33]Cf. the Old Testament judgment image of the wine-press (Isa. 10:6; 25:10; 63:3,6 with καταπατέω).

[34]G. v. Rad, "Die Stadt auf dem Berge," in *Gesammelte Studien zum Alten Testament* (I) (Munich: Kaiser, 1958), 224; K. M. Campbell, "The New Jerusalem in Matt 5:14," *SJT* 31 (1978) 335- 63. The interpretation of the early church of the city as the church follows the Jerusalem typology. It can be found beginning with Ps.-Clem. *Hom.* 3.67.1.

[35]Vessel for measuring, 8.75 litres.

[36]*Midr. Qoh.* 1:3 (85a); 1:15 (94a) in Str-B I 237.

[37]Rabbinic material in Str-B I 237f.; also *T. Levi* 14:3 (sons of Levi); 11QPs 27.2 (David); Rom. 2:19; 2 Apoc. Bar. 77:13 (shepherds of Israel); *b. Ber.* 28b (Yohanan ben Zakkai).

[38]*b. B. Bat.* 4a (Str-B I 237); 2 Apoc. Bar. 77:16.

[39]Isa. 42:6; 49:6.

light (of the world). The variegated use does not permit us to interpret the statement "You are the light of the world" as a polemic opposing a certain Jewish self-understanding of Israel as the light of the world.

The reader of the Gospel of Matthew will remember 4:16 where Isaiah spoke of the light seen by the people sitting in darkness. The commission to the disciples thus corresponds to the mission of Christ himself. For the rest, the sense of the parable still remains hidden. Only the imperative of v. 16 will make clear what meaning it has: the community which is the light of the world should let this light shine, otherwise it is something as absurd as the oil lamp under the bushel. Only on the basis of v. 16 does it become clear why Matthew—in distinction from Q—introduces a universal feature even in the image: the light on the lampstand shines for *all* in the house.

5:16

Verse 16 is the summarizing key of the pericope. The perspective shifts from the persons addressed to their works. The linguistic sign for this is the transition from λάμπει to λαμψάτω (vv. 15-16). But for Matthew this does not mean the introduction of a new category, for the person is for him constituted by, and lives by, his or her deeds. The disciples, i.e., the Christians, are the light of the world *by* letting their works shine,[41] just as the salt is salt only when it salts. The indicative "You are the light of the world" is thus at the same time a demand which must be realized by deeds.

"*Good works*" is an established expression which can be understood in two ways. If one understands it as a translation of the Jewish מַעֲשִׂים טוֹבִים, then it is concerned with the demands of God which are not prescribed by the Torah, namely, especially works of love and almsgiving.[42] On the other hand, in later writings of the early church (Pastoral Epistles, Hebrews, 1-2 Peter, 2 Clement) the expression refers to Christian ethics in general. It seems to me that Matthew here connects with a Jewish topic of proving oneself before people by good works which is not specifically rabbinic and makes one think rather in a general sense of good deeds.[43] First Peter also is centrally characterized by this idea; it is interesting that Matthew and 1 Peter (influenced by Matthew?) are in agreement that precisely in the situation of persecution (Matt. 5:11f.) mission activity and the demonstration of works in consistent conduct of life are decisive.

The "good works" receive their content from the preceding Beatitudes and from the following Antitheses. If the first eight Beatitudes were a general

---

[40]*GenR* 59 (37b) in Str-B I 237.

[41]This is expressed quite similarly in the Pseudo-Clementine letters *Ad Virgines*, which are centrally influenced by Matthew (1.2.3-5): The "ways of the righteous shine" . . . . "through good works so that they are in truth the light of the world" . . . "through the light of the good works of the fear of God so that they see our good works and praise our father in heaven. For a man of God must . . . be perfect" (cf. Matt. 5:48).

[42]מַעֲשִׂים טוֹבִים is a broad term which can stand among the rabbis alongside of מִצְוֹת (fulfilling of commands), תּוֹרָה (study of the Torah!), תְּשׁוּבָה (repentance), cf. the examples in Str-B IV/1 536f.

[43]Cf. *T. Naph.* 8:4 ("If you do that which is good, humans and angels will bless you"); *T. Benj.* 5:3 ("the light of good works"). Early Christianity applies this idea to mission, cf. also 1 Peter 2:12; 2 *Clem.* 13:1; further (remote) material in Heiligenthal* 119.

reflection of Christian virtues, then one could understand the section vv. 11-16 so to speak as a specific admonition to the persecuted community to take them seriously in its situation. Verse 16b states the goal of Christian conduct: the works of the Christians have a missionary function. Here the Matthean priority of the deed over the word becomes clear. Just as discipleship means fulfillment of the commands of Jesus, so in the proclamation the *life* of the Christians receives a—not to say *the*—decisive place. In such a conception of "Christianity of deed" a special office of proclamation cannot push itself imperiously into the foreground; witness by living remains the task of the whole community.

Matthew thinks of indicative and imperative together differently from Paul. The condition of salvation, granted by God ("salt," "light"), is at the same time an exhortation to action. Matthew speaks without embarrassment of good works, without meaning self-justification by works. There are only few texts in the New Testament where the honor of God [44] is so clearly the goal of Christian conduct as such. At the same time, God is here for the first time in the Gospel of Matthew designated as "your Father in heaven." Presumably, this expression was not surprising for the readers; it became customary in the synagogue at that time[45] and was the designation for God which was familiar to the community from its own worship services.[46] Nevertheless, it deserves our attention, for the designation of God as "Father" plays an extraordinarily important role in the Sermon on the Mount. It determines the center, i.e., that part where Matthew unfolds the relationship to the Father as the "inside" of the Christian way to perfection (6:8f.,14f.; cf. 6:1,4,6,18). Thus our passage points to this center, particularly the dimension of prayer. A "signal" which points to the relationship to God, so central to the practice of the Sermon on the Mount, flashes like a beacon in v. 16.

History of influence

Two misunderstandings in the history of interpretation of our text call attention to aspects which are important to our situation:

1. *Luther* was unable to do justice to the text because of his opposition to works-righteousness. The text is spoken "in accordance with St. Matthew's way of speaking; he usually talks this way about works" and cannot speak of faith in Christ, like Paul and John. In order to vindicate the text Luther suggested that it does not speak so much of the works of love, as Matt. 25:31-46, but "rather principally about the distinctly Christian work of teaching correctly, of stressing faith, and of showing how to strengthen and preserve it."[47] It is not possible to misunderstand the text more thoroughly! I am not aware of any interpretation in *the early and medieval church* which constitutes a threat of something like "works-righteousness." On the contrary! As an example, Theodore of

---

[44]Here we have a common feature between this verse and 6:1-18 although there is a noticeable tension because there the concern is precisely conduct that is *not* to be seen.

[45]Cf. on Matt. 6:9-13 n. 60.

[46]Cf. introduction, § 4.2.1.

[47]II 79f. = WA 32,352f = *LW* 21, 64ff.

Heraclea speaks of the thought that the text leads away from one's own glory seeking.[48] The *Glossa ordinaria* states as the goal of v. 16: "ut non finem boni operis in laudibus hominum constituatis" (that you do not determine the goal of the good work in the praise of people).[49] A modern Catholic interpreter writes: "The works are simply the light which has invaded life and has been realized. They are truth which has taken shape, lived faith. They do not stand alongside faith. . . . The good works altogether are the active Christian life. . . which streams incessantly as from a volcano."[50]

2. Another reinterpretation also was influential in the whole history of interpretation. The text was *applied to the narrower circle of disciples*, and then by extension *to the officebearers*.[51] Salt sometimes,[52] and light most of the time, were understood as proclamation.[53] This tradition of interpretation has found a very clear embodiment on Protestant soil. According to Luther, the text deals with the office of apostle or of preaching whereby salt has to be understood as the biting preaching of judgment, light as "the other part of the office," the enlightenment to eternal life.[54] According to Zwingli, it refers "in primis" (first of all) to apostles and pastors whose concern is public preaching.[55] It is understandable that the anticlergy criticism of the church could also make use of the text in this manner. Wycliff's *Opus Evangelicum* is especially impressive on our text and culminates in the demand of poverty of the proclaimers of the word who cover their light under the bushel of worldly money interests.[56]

Summary

Matthew's projection is that the life of the Christians should function as a testimony of faith to the glory of God. In looking at Protestant theology, it is striking that there is for him no hiddenness of the Christian life *sub contrario* (under the opposite), no narrowing of Christian single-mindedness to the word of proclamation alone, no indication of an ecclesiological variant of the two-

---

[48]Fragment 25 = Reuss 64. E.g., Albertus Magnus 172 is emphatic: "non propriae gloriae intuitu, nec lucri praetextu, vel ambitionis intentione, sed ut glorificaretur Pater coelestis" (not in view of one's own glory, not with the pretext of gain, nor with the intention of ambition but in order that the heavenly Father be glorified).

[49]Strabo 92.

[50]Trilling I 106.

[51]So usually; by Tostatus preferably to the prelates (116-18 et passim), by Bullinger to the pastors and doctors (53f.), by Pseudo-Cyprian, *De aleatoribus* 2 = PL 4,828 to the bishops. Outstanding exceptions are, e.g.: Origen, *Cels.* 7.51; 8.70; Theodore of Mopsuestia, fragment 24 = Reuss 104f.; Wolzogen 208; Calov 182; Grotius I 90.

[52]The nuance salt = wisdom is widespread (e.g., Bede 25; Paschasius 231; Tostatus 116; Maldonat 67). The interpretation of salt as works and light as proclamation also is not infrequent.

[53]Already among the Naassenes, the lamp is the kerygma (Hippolytus, *Ref.* 5.7.28); similarly, e.g., Jerome on the passage; Gregory of Nazianzus, *Or.* 40 = PG 36,412; *Opus imperfectum* 10 = 685; Christian von Stavelot 1306; Luther II 77; Zwingli 223 ("verbo veritatis" [by the word of truth]); Brenz 251; Calov 183; Chemnitz 431. On this interpretation the influence of Mark 4:21 has to be considered.

[54]II 77.

[55]222.

[56]Wyclif** 109-15, cf. G. A Benrath, *Wyclifs Bibelkommentar*, AGK 36 (1966), 121-23.

kingdoms doctrine.[57] Rather the light of the world takes shape in the *works* of the Christians. By this he means, in the first place, love as he interprets it by means of the Beatitudes and through the Antitheses. It is the works of the Christians through which the demand "to keep all that I have commanded you" (28:20) is to be carried into all the world, encountering people as light. In this way, Matthew has made clear throughout his whole theology the open and variously usable images of salt and light. At the same time it is noteworthy, in contrast to Catholic and Protestant interpretation, how for Matthew the community is obviously the entirety of its members and how unthinkable it is for him to reserve the address and the claim of Jesus for a certain circle of special members of the community. "Salt of the earth" and "light of the world" are, so to speak, the "Christian infantry," which is united on the way of righteousness which Jesus has made possible.

2. THE MAIN PART (5:17—7:12)

Verses 17-20 introduce the main part of the Sermon on the Mount. Matthew 5:17 and 7:12 form an inclusion with the catchwords νόμος and προφῆται. The main part consists of sections 5:21–48 and 6:19–7:11, which are of exactly equal length, and the shorter central part 6:1-18.

2.1. The Preamble (5:17-20)

Literature

Banks, R., *Jesus and the Law in the Synoptic Tradition*, SNTSMS 28, pp. 204-26 (Cambridge: At the University Press, 1975).

Barth, *Gesetzesverständnis*, 60-68.

Betz, H. D., "Die hermeneutischen Prinzipien in der Bergpredigt (Mt 5,17-20)," in *Verifikationen* (FS G. Ebeling), ed. E. Jüngel et al., pp. 27-41 (Tübingen: Mohr, 1982).

Bornkamm, G., "Wandlungen im alt- und neutestamentlichen Gesetzesverständnis," in idem, *Geschichte und Glaube* II (= Aufs. IV), BEvT 53, pp. 73-80 (Munich: Kaiser, 1968).

Broer, I., *Freiheit vom Gesetz und Radikalisierung des Gesetzes*, SBS 98, pp. 11-74 (Stuttgart: Katholisches Bibelwerk, 1980).

Davies, W. D., "Matthew 5,17-20," in *Mélanges Bibliques* (FS A. Robert), pp. 428-56 (Paris: Bloud et Gay, 1957).

Giesen, *Handeln* 122-46.

Hahn, F., "Mt 5,17—Anmerkungen zum Erfüllungsgedanken bei Matthäus," in *Die Mitte des Neuen Testaments* (FS E. Schweizer), ed. U. Luz and H. Weder, pp. 42-54 (Göttingen: Vandenhoeck & Ruprecht, 1983).

Hamerton-Kelly, R. G., "Attitudes to the Law in Matthew's Gospel: A Discussion of Matthew 5,18," *BR* 17 (1972) 19-32.

Harnack, A. "Geschichte eines programmatischen Worts Jesu (Mt 5,17) in der ältesten Kirche," *SPAW* (1912), 184-207.

Heubült, C., "Mt 5,17-20. Ein Beitrag zur Theologie des Evangelisten Matthäus," *ZNW* 71 (1980) 143-49.

---

[57]Bonhoeffer* 93: The *theologia crucis* of the Reformers has the tendency to prefer a "modest" invisibility, in the form of a total absorption in conformity to the world, to "Pharisaic" ostentation.

Holtzmann, *Theologie* I 502-08.

Hoppe, R., *Der theologische Hintergrund des Jakobusbriefes*, FzB, pp. 123-30 (1977).

Hübner, *Gesetz* 15-39.

Légasse, S., "Mt 5,17 et la prétendue tradition paracanonique," in *Begegnung mit dem Wort* (FS H. Zimmermann), ed. J. Zmijewski, BBB 53, pp. 11-21 (Bonn: Haustein, 1980).

Ljungman, H., "Das Gesetz erfüllen," *Lunds Universitets Aarsskrift* N. F. Adv. 1,50/6, Lund 1954, 7-76.

Luz, U., "Die Erfüllung des Gesetzes bei Matthäus (5,17-20)," *ZTK* 75 (1978) 398-435.

Marguerat, *Jugement* 110-141.

McConnel, *Law* 6-41.

Meier, *Law* 41-124.

Pregeant, *Christology* 63-83.

Schürmann, H., " 'Wer daher eines dieser geringsten Gebote auflöst . . .'. Wo fand Matthäus das Logion Mt 5,19?" in idem, *Untersuchungen* 126-36.

Schweizer, E., "Matthäus 5,17-20. Anmerkungen zum Gesetzesverständnis des Matthäus," in idem, *Neotestamentica*, pp. 399-406 (Zurich: Zwingli, 1963).

———, "Noch einmal Mt 5,17-20," in *Matthäus und seine Gemeinde* 78-85.

Strecker, *Weg* 143-52.

Trilling, *Israel* 167-86.

Further Literature** on the Sermon on the Mount see above pp. 209-211.

Text

17 Do not think that I have come to dissolve the law or the prophets; I have not come to dissolve but to fulfill.

18 Amen, for I say to you: Until heaven and earth pass away, not a single iota or not a single little pen stroke of the law will pass away until everything happens.

19 Whoever therefore looses one of the least of these commandments and teaches people such
   will be called least in the kingdom of heaven.
   But whoever does and teaches them,
   that one[1] will be called great in the kingdom of heaven.

20 For I say to you: Unless your righteousness surpasses by far that of the scribes and Pharisees, you will not enter into the kingdom of heaven.

Analysis

1. *Structure*. The section is not unified in theme and form. It consists of four individual logia. The last one, v. 20, is clearly the title of the Antitheses, after the rabbinic pattern of the prefixed summary,[2] and is connected with vv. 22,28,32,34,39,44 by means of λέγω ὑμῖν and with v. 47 through περισσεύσῃ/περισσόν (an inclusion). In addition, v. 20 points back to vv. 4,10 and forward to 6:1,33 (δικαιοσύνη) and 7:13,21 (εἰσέρχεσθαι εἰς τὴν βασιλείαν τῶν οὐρανῶν. Thus v. 20 has a key position. Verses 17-19, conversely, are not directly connected with the Antitheses. Their theme also is different. They deal with the validity of the law, not with the righteousness of the disciples. Thus one might ask whether it would be correct to interpret vv. 17-19

---

[1] It is tempting to conjecture οὕτως instead of οὗτος, cf. Beyer, *Syntax* 172.

[2] A *kelal*, cf. introduction p. 21.

independently and to understand v. 20 as a new beginning.³ This would have considerable consequences for the interpretation of v. 17: it is not the Antitheses that clarify what is meant by the fulfilling of law and prophets, but vv. 18f. On the other hand, v. 20 does not start afresh but is linked immediately with v. 19 by γάρ. Already v. 19 speaks of the conduct of the disciples and only indirectly of the law. Through the emphatic λέγω ὑμῖν, v. 20 is closely connected with v. 18, through βασιλεία τῶν οὐρανῶν with v. 19. Λέγω ὑμῖν in v. 18 is at the same time a small bridge between the opening section on the law vv. 17-19 and the Antitheses. Again it is shown that Matthew composes not through delimitations but through transitions.⁴ Thus vv. 17-19 cannot be clearly separated from v. 20 and the Antitheses, even though v. 20 signifies a new thematic beginning. That makes the interpretation of vv. 17-19 difficult.

The individual logia are different in form. Verse 19 contains an antithetical parallelism; but the second part is abbreviated. Verse 17 also contains an antithesis which, however, is still further removed from a clear parallelism. Verse 18, with the two conflicting ἕως ἄν phrases, is "deformed." Verse 20 is a saying concerning "entering into the kingdom of God," formulated negatively, as is 18:3.

2. *Sources and origin.* The prehistory of the individual sayings varies. Matthew has edited heavily in this section.

a. *Verse 17:* Much is redactional: πληρόω, νόμος/προφῆται, their connection with ἤ.⁵ How to judge the formal relationship with 10:34⁶ and whether the evangelist has edited a traditional saying are disputed matters. But how it had read we can scarcely now say. That has two consequences:

1. It is rash to trace this saying back to Jesus and to make it the anchor of the interpretation of Jesus' understanding of the law.⁷

2. It is hazardous to (re)construct from this saying an Aramaic original and to make such a (re)construction the foundation of an interpretation of the difficult word πληρόω.⁸ That would mean explaining difficult material by totally hypothetical suggestions!

b. *Verse 18:* The situation of the tradition is hopelessly unclear. Does the verse

---

³The proposal by Pregeant, *Christology* 63, to see in v. 17 the key verse to vv. 21-48 and in v. 20 the key verse to 6:1-18, is untenable. However, Broer* 73 is worth considering: vv. 18-20 develop the negative side of v. 17 (no καταλῦσαι of the law), vv. 21-48 the positive side (πληρῶσαι).

⁴Thus v. 20 is a transitional verse (Luz* 423).

⁵Cf. the detailed redaction historical analyses in Meier, *Law* 41-115, and Broer* 16-24, 35-42, 49-51, 57f. and the introduction 3.2. Guelich** 137f. considers only the addition of ἤ τοὺς προφήτας as Matthean.

⁶It is clear neither in 10:34 nor in 5:17 whether μὴ νομίσητε ὅτι is redactional. Besides, the one passage would not prove anything for the other, for the evangelist can repeat even a traditional introduction to a logion in a different place.

⁷E.g., Lapide** 24f. on the basis of *b. Sabb.* 116b = Str-B I 241f. But this text is certainly not a witness to an original text of Matt. 5:17, for it comes from אָוֶן גִּלָּיוֹן, i.e., a disparaging pun on εὐαγγέλιον, and thus betrays the fact that it presupposes the Greek language tradition (i.e., Matt. 5:17), not a Hebrew or Aramaic original text.

⁸Since Dalman, *Jesus*, there is the thesis that behind πληρόω may stand the Aramaic קַם (piel = to confirm, establish). This is not "doubtless" (53), for LXX most of the time translates מְלָא with πληρόω; the Syriac translations also translate Matt. 5:17 with this stem. The most probable (not certain) conclusion from this and from the observation of Lapide** 24 that מְלָא in reference to the law is not Semitic is that there was no Semitic original of Matt. 5:17.

come from Q (cf. Luke 16:17)?[9] There is in Luke 16:17 no Lukan redaction, in Matt. 5:18 only an uncertain Matthean redaction; there is no common syntactical basic pattern, no common wording and no meaningful place in the Sayings Source for this isolated word.[10] It is more likely that v. 18 goes back to a Jewish-Christian special tradition. But then it remains open which of the two conflicting ἕως ἄν phrases is redactional. Vocabulary statistics offer no proof.[11] The customary thesis that v. 18d is redactional[12] depends on the Q hypothesis. K. Berger has discovered a New Testament form-schema of sentences which are built according to the pattern ἀμὴν λέγω ὑμῖν — οὐ μή + prophetic future + temporal clause with ἕως or μέχρις.[13] If Matthew used such a sentence, then the first ἕως ἄν clause would have to be a Matthean addition.[14] But an isolated logion with the temporal clause ἕως ἄν πάντα γένηται would be puzzling and would need a context.[15] A traditional logion which contained the first ἕως ἄν clause (18b), on the contrary, would be understandable in itself.[16] Besides, v. 18b as Matthean redaction would be very difficult to interpret. *Result*: I consider the problem unsolvable, and there is nothing else to do except to interpret the verse as it stands.

    c. *Verse 19*: Quite a great deal is linguistically Matthean.[17] The judgment of many interpreters that the verse is completely traditional often comes from the fact that they dislike the thought of attributing such a legalistic logion to the evangelist. On the other hand, it is improbable that the logion is completely redactional.[18] There are some indications that the second part of the parallelism, i.e., the positive formulation in 19cd, is due to the evangelist.[19] According to the consensus of opinion, v. 18 and v. 19 come

---

[9]So most interpreters. The strongest argument is the fact that the following verse, Luke 16:18, is taken up by Matt. 5:32. But that was—after the second antithesis—natural anyway.

[10]Schürmann* 130-32 thinks that Matthew has read Luke 16:14-18 in Q and finds reminiscences (unconvincing to me) of the (redactional?) verse Luke 16:15 in Matt. 5:20 and of Luke 16:16 in Matt. 5:17.

[11]The following are redactional: ἕως ἄν, the contrast of οὐρανός and γῆ in the singular, but not πάντα without accompanying ταῦτα, cf. introduction 3.2. Ἀμήν . . . λέγω ὑμῖν . . . οὐ μὴ παρέλθῃ . . . ἕως ἄν πάντα . . . γένηται is covered by Matt. 24:34, ὁ οὐρανὸς καὶ ἡ γῆ (παρέλθῃ) by Matt. 24:35. In that place, except for ἕως ἄν everything is traditional. On the basis of 24:34f., an imitation by Matthew is possible for both ἕως ἄν phrases.

[12]E.g., Meier, *Law* 55-61, and Broer* 35-42 (both count on Q variants).

[13]*Amenworte* 73f.

[14]Schweizer, "Noch einmal"* 82f.; Luz* 406f.

[15]Schweizer, ibid. 80f., thinks that the logion originally stood in the context of an eschatological discourse. Hypothetical!

[16]Therefore Marguerat, *Jugement* 114f., thinks that the traditional v. 18b originally stood in final position and was shifted by Matthew (combination of solution above n. 12 with solution above n. 13f.). This combination of all possibilities is the most complex. It seems to me now (in distinction from above n. 14), that the linguistic arguments speak indeed rather for the addition of 18b (cf. above n. 11), but that 18d on the basis of the interpretation can more easily be understood as redaction. Result: non liquet.

[17]Ὃς ἄν — ὃς δ' ἄν, διδάσκω, ἄνθρωπος, οὕτως, βασιλεία τῶν οὐρανῶν, anaphoric οὗτος, cf. introduction 3.2. Uncertain is εἰς . . . τούτων (redactional only in 18:10,14, otherwise often special material) and the positive μέγας instead of the superlative. The avoidance of superlative and comparative is a characteristic of the popular language of the time (BDF § 60 n. 1) and also strengthened by the influence of the Semitic language where there is no comparison, but particularly noteworthy in Matthew (Schlatter 158).

[18]So Heubült* 144; Gundry 81f.

[19]Luz* 408; Marguerat, *Jugement* 115.

from strict Jewish-Christian law-observing circles, perhaps from debates and intra-Christian polemic about the validity of the Mosaic law. It is difficult to assign the amen saying (v. 18) to Jesus; he transgressed the law for the sake of love in many individual cases.[20] It is disputed whether v. 19 is an originally independent logion or whether it first originated as a commentary on v. 18.[21] It is conceivable that both sayings were handed down together before Matthew.

d. *Verse 20* is redactional according to almost universal judgment,[22] a saying that speaks of entering the kingdom of heaven, especially beloved by the evangelist.

Interpretation

Our verses belong to the most difficult ones of the Gospel. Matthew makes clear by their position at the beginning of the main part of the Sermon on the Mount before the Antitheses that they are for him foundationally important. His relationship to the Mosaic law—and with that to Judaism—is in debate here. The same question is at stake in the Antitheses, to which vv. 17-20 want to lead. How they are related to the law in the understanding of Matthew is highly controversial. The Matthean principle that Jesus has come to "fulfill" the law is formulated so generally that it hardly permits us to exclude specific interpretations cogently. All the more important is the question of how vv. 18f., which are strongly redacted by the evangelist, assist in the understanding of v. 17.

Most of the time they lead to a dilemma. In the liberal theology of the 19th century it was customary to interpret v. 17 and the Antitheses in such a way that Jesus makes the law complete "by deepening it in going back to the intention—ultimately to love and inner truthfulness."[23] Verses 18f. fitted poorly into such an interpretation. While vv. 18f. represent "rabbinical orthodoxy," the Antitheses sound almost Marcionite.[24] Verses 18f. had a "destructive effect for the developed meaning of the whole."[25] But yet: from which meaning of v. 17 are we to proceed?

Various possible solutions are offered. F. C. Baur had understood the Gospel of Matthew as a representative of an ancient Jewish Christianity which was not yet particularistic. The two-source theory suggested that it originated after 70. Now the

---

[20]Examples of the difficulties with the "Jesus saying" 18: Manson, *Sayings* 25, understands the verse as an ironic mockery of the scribes; Banks* 218f. as a "rhetorical statement emphasising how difficult it was for the law to perish."

[21]An argument in favor: "these commandments" need a reference. But it could be an Aramaism (Dalman, Jesus 58f.). Negatively it is significant that v. 19 speaks of ἐντολή instead of νόμος.

[22]The following are Matthean: connecting γάρ, περισσεύω, δικαιοσύνη cf. introduction 3.2; redactional sayings concerning entrance into the kingdom of heaven: 7:21 and 18:3, both formulated negatively.

[23]Harnack* 185. De Wette 31 interprets v. 20 of the "righteousness of intention," F. C. Baur, *Vorlesungen über die neutestamentliche Theologie* (Leipzig 1864), 48, speaks of "inner intention," which "rests on the unconditionedness of the moral consciousness" and which he distinguishes from the Judaistic redaction of the Gospel (ibid. 55). Admirably A. Ritschl, *Die Entstehung der altkatholischen Kirche* (Bonn: Markus, 1857), 35-46: Jesus liberates the commandments of the love of God and of humans from the individualization in which they stood in the law of Moses and makes them the principle of the law. Those laws which cannot be coordinated with love he eliminates.

[24]Windisch** 52f.

[25]Holtzmann, *Theologie* I, 504.

unclarity of vv. 17-20,21-48 was understood as an expression of the difficulty of the evangelist to extract himself from his Jewish-legalistic background,[26] or, conversely, of his difficulty to do justice to the different groups in his community, which was strongly characterized as Jewish-Christian.[27] Matthew 5:17-20 as the expression of the not-quite-successful synthesis of Baur's great opposition between Jewish and Gentile Christianity? It would be easier to eliminate vv. 18f. as an interpolation.[28] Our century furnished additional possibilities of dealing with the problem: vv. 18f. now widely became a piece of Jewish-Christian tradition, carried along, which the evangelist indeed handed down but which was in actuality meaningless to him.[29]

Compared with this, our analysis has determined that Matthew has also reworked vv. 18 and 19 to a considerable extent. Already for this reason they cannot have been completely unimportant to him. The analysis of the structure demonstrated that all four sayings are linked closely with each other. Verses 18 and 20 are highlighted especially through λέγω ὑμῖν. In addition, the supposition that the evangelist simply handed down—and that in such a conspicuous place—material which he himself could basically no longer support is awkward from the start. Thus we are looking for an interpretation which can take vv. 18f. seriously. Here the historical situation of the evangelist has to be taken into consideration. He belongs to a Jewish-Christian community which is characterized by traditions with fundamental observance of the law.[30] But in his community the Gospel of Mark, which stood rather free toward the law of Moses, was also known. In this tension between different traditions—all *Jesus* traditions—and various possibilities of praxis, Matthew had to point the way.

5:17

The introductory μὴ νομίσητε addresses the community directly. A direct polemic, perhaps against antinomians, cannot be proved; Matthew argues principles.[31] The difficulties of interpretation are culminating in the two verbs καταλύω and πληρόω. If one refers καταλύω and πληρόω

1. to the *teachings of Jesus*, then one may further ask whether the teachings of Jesus change anything of the law or not. If Jesus does not change anything of the law, then πληρόω might mean

a. *"to bring out in its true meaning," "to bring to full expression."*[32] But if Jesus' fulfilling changes the law itself, then one could understand πληρόω either more quantitatively in the sense of

---

[26]Cf. J. Weiss, *Earliest Christianity* (New York: Harper & Row, 1959), vol. 2, 753f.

[27]Cf. Holtzmann, *Theologie* I 505.

[28]E.g., E. Wendling, "Zu Mt 5,18.19," *ZNW* 5 (1904) 253-56.

[29]Pointed thesis in Walker, *Heilsgeschichte* 135: Matthew is a " 'radical antinomian' who does not at all take 5:18f. literally." How convenient it would be if he had not adduced the two verses at all!

[30]Cf. introduction 5.1.

[31]Cf. Strecker, *Weg* 137 n. 4; Trilling, *Israel* 171. It seems to me that it cannot be proved in 7:15-23 either that the opponents were theoretical theological antonomians. Direct polemic against Jewish accusations that Jesus was an opponent of the law is improbable because the Matthean community stood no longer in direct discussion with the synagogue. Thus the sentence is best explained as a principal thesis.

[32]E.g., W. G. Kümmel, "Jesus und der jüdische Traditionsgedanke," in idem, *Heilsgeschehen* I 34; Dupont, *Béatitudes* I 142f.; Klostermann 41; Zumstein, *Condition* 120. The interpretation on the basis of the Aramaic קים is related, cf. above n. 8.

b. *"to add,"* *"to supply"* (something missing)[33] or more qualitatively in the sense of

c. "complete," "make perfect."[34]

If one refers καταλύω and πληρόω

2. to the *ministry of Jesus*, then πληρόω may mean either that the story of Jesus

a. *"fulfills"* in the *sense of salvation history* the promises of the law and the prophets[35] or that Jesus

b. in his life *"fulfills"* the demands of law and prophets *through his obedience*, i.e., that he *keeps the law*.[36] Finally, one may also

c. think of the death and resurrection of Jesus: Jesus has *"fulfilled" the law through his death and his resurrection* and so also brought it to its goal and end.[37]

History of Influence

The alternatives gain their shape on the basis of the *history of interpretation*.[38] There were two epochs in church history when the focus centered on the interpretation of Matt. 5:17. The debate with Marcion—who wanted to eliminate the verse—was decisive.[39] The ecclesiastical interpretation of Matt. 5:17 by Irenaeus and the Christian gnostic interpretation by the Valentinians opposed Marcion. Both were closely related. For Ptolemy, the teacher of Flora, Matt 5:17 meant the *perfection* of the law which originally was imperfect (ἀτελής) and in need of being perfected (ἐνδεής πληρωθῆναι) and corresponds to the perfect God only conditionally. Ptolemy developed this thought by his differentiation of the commands of God, of Moses, and of the elders.[40] Irenaeus, in *Haer.* 4.13.1, understood the fulfillment of the law by Jesus as an extension (*extensio*); the "more" which Jesus brings is faith and the extension of the law's validity from the deed to the desire. He distinguishes the ceremonial law from the moral law; the fulfillment of the former took place in a different manner: Abolished as a literally

---

[33]In comprehensive sense J. Weiss 266f.; Jeremias, *Theology* I 84f.

[34]E.g., Dibelius 125; Merklein, *Gottesherrschaft* 77 ("something is to happen with the law"); A. Feuillet, "Morale ancienne et morale chrétienne d'après Mt 5,17-20," *NTS* 17 (1970/71) 124 ("conserver en perfectionnant et en dépassant").

[35]Schweizer, "Anmerkungen"* 400; C. F. D. Moule, "Fulfilment-Words in the New Testament: Use and Abuse," *NTS* 14 (1967/68) 317-19; pointedly Guelich 141f., 162-64 (on the basis of the thesis that Matthew has inserted only ἢ τοὺς προφήτας into a traditional logion).

[36]Schlatter 154; A. Descamps, "Les justes et la justice dans les Évangiles et le Christianisme primitif," Université Catholique de Louvain Diss II/43 (Louvain 1950), 131 ("observer entièrement"); Luz* 414f. (as basic meaning).

[37]Cf. below n. 81.

[38]For the most ancient time cf. Harnack*. I owe much material on the history of interpretation to A. Ennulat.

[39]Tertullian, *Marcion* 5.14.14 = *PL* 2,508 ("frustra de ista sententia neganda Pontus laboravit" [Pontus has labored in vain on negating that sentence]). Later Marcionites turned the sentence around: Christ came in order to tear down the law (cf. Isidore of Pelusium, *Epist.* 1.371 = *PG* 78, 393; Adamantius, *Dial* 2.15 = GCS 4, 88). The Manicheans took over the Marcionite critique of the law (Harnack 191f.).

[40]Ptolemy, *Ad Flor.* = Epiphanius, *Haer.* 33.3.4.

understood command, it remains as a sign of Christ (4:16). Predominant since Irenaeus is the interpretation of Matt. 5:17 that puts the perfection of the imperfect law by Jesus in the center.[41] Origen compared the development from the old law to the new with the development of a child into an adult, during which the child is changed but not destroyed.[42] Grace is added to the law.[43] Since the high Middle Ages it usually was said: that the *consilia Evangelica* (the evangelical counsels) were added.[44]

It is noteworthy that hardly any traces of a Jewish-Christian legalistic way of interpretation have been preserved. Such an interpretation would have to emphasize that Jesus kept the law in his life and confirmed it through his teaching. Leaving aside for now *b. Šabb.* 116b, where the text is very uncertain,[45] there are only general witnesses for completely law-observant Jewish Christians, but hardly interpretations of Matt. 5:17. In the Pseudo-Clementines, Matt. 5:17 with v. 18 indeed is quoted frequently, but their community does not keep the entire law because some pericopes are falsified.[46] The Syriac *Didascalia* polemicizes in ch. 26 against those who still keep the ceremonial law: "But in the gospel he (Jesus) has renewed, fulfilled and confirmed the law, and he has dissolved and abolished the repetition of the law."[47] Indirectly one can conclude from this that the Jewish Christians, against whom the author here polemicizes, have appealed to Matt. 5:17. Our text plays a central role in the Jewish-Christian writing which is preserved by Abd al Jabbar. One must not take anything away from the law. "The one who lessens any part of it shall be called 'least.' "[48] This interpretation of Matt. 5:17 is no longer reflected in the church fathers. This agrees with the fact that law-observant Jewish Christians were a marginal group of which there is little known.

---

[41]Tertullian, *Or.* 1 = BKV I/7 248 formulates a "fourfold cycle" of abolition (e.g., of circumcision), supplement (of the moral law), fulfillment (of the promise) and perfection (by faith). For him as a rigorist, the enlargement of the law (interpretation 1b) is especially important, e.g., *Pud.* 6 = BKV I/24 738; *Monog.* 7 = ibid. 835.

[42]Fragment 97 = 55f.; fragment 98 (ibid.): Jesus dissolved the γράμμα of the law but not the πνεῦμα.

[43]John Chrysostom 16.2 = 275: The law lacks the power. Christ introduced justification by faith and thus fulfilled the purpose of the law; Gregory the Great, *De Expositione* 3.1.11 = *PL* 79,1028: "legis iustitiae gratiam addidit" (he has added grace to the justice of the law).

[44]Thomas, *Lectura* no. 467; Albertus Magnus 82 ("moralia addendo" [by adding morals]).

[45]It is unclear whether one has to read אלא (but) or ולא (and not), i.e., whether Jesus "does not subtract from the Torah but adds" (so Str-B I 1242) or whether he "does not subtract and not add anything" from or to the Torah (so Lapide** 24). The former interpretation corresponds to the interpretation of the early church, e.g., n. 41. But M. Güdemann, "Die Logia des Matthäus als Gegenstand einer talmudischen Satyre," in idem, *Religionsgeschichtliche Studien* (Leipzig 1876), 65-97, correctly calls attention to the fact that only ולא fits as far as the content is concerned (differently Légasse* 18, n. 60). But then *b. Šabb.* 116a-b could be a witness for a Jewish-Christian interpretation of Matt. 5:17 which understands "fulfill" in the sense of strict faithfulness to the law: "Neither to subtract nor to add anything." The Jewish-Christian source of the anecdote contains also apocryphal material and therefore (and because of n. 7) cannot be the Aramaic primitive Matthew (against Güdemann 94-97). Possibly Deut. 4:2 has influenced this Jewish-Christian reading of Matt. 5:17.

[46]*Ep. Petr. ad Jac.* 2:3-7; *Hom.* 3.51.1-3 ("what he dissolved did not belong to the law," 51.2). Cf. Strecker, *Judenchristentum* 162-87.

[47]Cited by Achelis-Flemming 132. The thought obviously is that the original law was identical with the decalogue while the "repetition" became necessary because of the golden calf and comprised the ceremonial law of Exod. 35-41. The Jewish Christians who are here opposed have kept exactly this.

[48]S. Pines, *The Jewish Christians of the Early Centuries of Christianity according to a New Source* (1966), 5.

In the *time of the Reformation*, Matt. 5:17 again became a central text in the struggle with the Anabaptists. In the interpretation of the Reformers and post-Reformation readers, the accents shift. No longer the *perfection* of the law of the medieval exegesis but its correct *interpretation* by Jesus is now in the center. This is already foreshadowed in Luther. The *perfectio*, the central term in the exegesis of Matt. 5:17, is by him applied to Jesus' *interpretation* of the law: "Christ does not only recite the law of Moses but interprets it . . . perfectly" *(perfecte explicat)*.[49] The *Wochenpredigten* formulate emphatically, "I do not intend to bring another or a new law, but to take the very Scriptures which you have and to emphasize them, dealing with them in such a way as to teach you how to behave."[50] Calvin emphasized the unity of the covenant or the "holy linking of law and gospel."[51] It is in agreement with this interpretation that, according to the Reformers, Jesus interprets in the Antitheses the decalogue in its true sense against the distortions of it by the Jews; Jesus speaks his "but I say to you" no longer against the Old Testament itself.[52] In Calvin it is especially clear in what situation this interpretation became relevant: It was not Christ's will to abolish the old religion. For then only "the frivolous and confused spirits . . . would have taken advantage of the opportunity and . . . attempted to cause all order of religion to waver."[53] The application to the time of Calvin is obvious. In contrast, the Anabaptists defended the thesis of the fundamental difference between the Old and the New Testaments. The Sermon on the Mount is for them more than an interpretation of the Old Testament; rather, between "the office of the law and the office of Christ . . . [there is] a wide difference."[54] In the numerous disputations with the Anabaptists, Matt. 5:17—as an argument against the Anabaptists—played a large role.[55] The latter asserted nothing but a pointed version of the theses of the early church of the *perfectio legis* (perfection of the law). But the Reformers had basically returned to the old Jewish-Christian thesis of the *interpretation* of the law of Moses by Christ, but now on the basis of the conviction of the church that the ceremonial law never was meant in any other sense than figuratively.[56]

The other possible explanations have supplemented the history of interpretation, as it were, as occasional or permanent accompanying music. It seems to me that one cannot detect any special centers of gravity. It is in any case characteristic that *at no time did various possibilities of interpretation exclude each other*; rather they were always perceived as aspects.[57] This is also the reason why the new Reformation accent on our text did not become a confessional point of contention. To give some examples: John

---

[49]*Antinomerdisputation* III 32 = WA 39/I,351.

[50]WA 32**,356 = *LW* 21,69. "With their glosses the Jews have distorted and corrupted the Law, and I have come to set it straight" (ibid. 355 = *LW* 21,68).

[51]I 182.

[52]Cf. below p. 248 on 5:21-48.

[53]I 180. On Calvin's anti-Anabaptist application of Matt. 5:17 cf. Stadtland-Neumann** 15-21.

[54]P. Walpot, *Das grosse Artikelbuch, Vom Schwert* 4, 75 (QGT 12/II 275).

[55]Cf., e.g., the discussion between P. Marbeck and M. Bucer, QGT 7,448f. (Christ does not benefit the person who still wants to be under the literal law) or the debate with H. Marquardt, QGT Switzerland 2,657.

[56]The post-Reformation interpretation advocates this new accentuation only partially, e.g., Aretius 51 (Jesus restores the law "suo genuino sensu" [in its genuine sense]); Cocceius 10 (Christ did not fulfill the law so "ut ex minus perfecta faceret consummatiorem" [that he would make that which was less perfect more complete]).

[57]Almost always one hears of the *manifold* fulfillment of the law. Cf., e.g., Tertullian (above, n. 41).

Chrysostom speaks of the threefold fulfillment of the law—through the fact that Christ never trespassed it (according to 3:15), through Christ's expiatory death (according to Rom. 8:3f.) and through his deepening of it in the Antitheses.[58] John of Damascus said that Christ fulfilled the law in being circumcised, in keeping the Sabbath, and in effecting salvation to which all Scriptures give testimony.[59] Thomas even speaks of a sevenfold fulfilling of the law by Jesus.[60]

The history of interpretation shows how difficult it is to find a *precise* meaning for Matt. 5:17 and how much the context of the Antitheses, the total witness of the Bible, and one's own situation played a role from the beginning in the interpretations. Decisive for the interpretation are (a) the meaning of the words πληρόω and καταλύω and (b) the Matthean context.

a. On the *meaning of the words*. Καταλύω in connection with νόμος and similar words is frequent in Greek and Hellenistic Jewish texts, almost idiomatic. The meaning wavers between "abolish" in the sense of "invalidate" and "abolish" in the sense of "not to keep," "break."[61] It is difficult to combine this with interpretation 2a—that Jesus fulfills the promises of law and prophets.[62] Πληρόω in connection with "law" and similar words also is documented. All this suggests to the Greek-speaking reader especially deeds, and not the teaching, of Jesus.[63]

b. On the *context*: The reader of the Gospel of Matthew naturally associates the fulfillment formulas 1:22; 2:15,17,23; 4:14 with πληρόω. But important also is the reminiscence of 3:15 where Jesus fulfills "all righteousness." Here it concerned his actions. The immediate context of our passage also makes one think of Jesus' actions (5:16,20).[64] But the Antitheses suggest that 5:17 has a relationship with the teaching of Jesus.

Thus on the basis of the meaning of both verbs it is easiest to think of the fulfillment of the law through Jesus' acting (interpretation 2). Καταλύω suggests thinking of a fulfillment through Jesus' obedient practice of the law (interpretation 2b), not of a fulfillment of the promises of law and prophets (interpretation 2a). Both interpretations could be connected with the phrase "law or[65] prophets" since both predict[66] and command. But if Matthew is thinking here primarily of the *demands* of the prophets, then he may be thinking, e.g., of the prophetic command of mercy, Hos. 6:6 (= Matt. 9:13;

---

[58]16,2f = 274f.

[59]*Exp. fidei* 4,25 = BKV I/44 257f.; 4,17 = 230.

[60]*Lectura* no. 467.

[61]Examples in Luz* 415 n. 82f.

[62]Rightly noted by Guelich** 142f.

[63]Combination of πληρόω with νόμος: Herodotus 1.199; 4.117 (both times ἐκπλῆσαι); Sib. 3.246; *T. Naph.* 8:7; Rom. 13:8; 8:4; Gal. 5:14; 6:2; further examples with ἐντολή and related words in Luz* 415 n. 84.

[64]On 5:18d cf. below pp. 266f.

[65]"Η between nouns connects members of equal kind and is hardly different from καί (5:10; 10:11,14,37; 12:25; 18:8, *pace* Guelich** 137f.).

[66]Deuteronomy 18 (Moses as prophet).

12:7). He uses the phrase "law and prophets" similarly in 7:12[67] and 22:40. If he then thinks *primarily* of the obedience and the life of Jesus, this does not mean that he wants to reject the idea of prediction. The thought of teaching also belongs to the broader "field of association" of 5:17. Thus v. 19 already emphasized the unity of teaching and practice, and vv. 20-48 speak of the teaching which is the basis of the praxis of Jesus and of the higher righteousness of the disciples. Our interpretation therefore does not want to exclude such subsidiary thoughts. But praxis is prior to teaching (cf. 7:15-23!).

Particularly if one thinks primarily of the praxis of Jesus, then it is striking that Matthew uses πληρόω and not perhaps τηρέω or ποιέω. Πληρόω is for him—different from the secular examples and from Paul[68]—an exclusively Christological verb. Only Jesus (and John the Baptist) "fulfills" the law. A unique element of totality and fullness is implied. It is in agreement with this that v. 17 is an ἦλθον-word: it is the very special mission of Jesus to fulfill law and prophets completely and comprehensively. Verse 17 thus contains a Christological element,[69] even if Matthew is not thinking of the death and resurrection of Jesus. It is then carried on in vv. 18 and 20 by the emphatic "I say to you" and especially through the ἐγώ of the Antitheses.

5:18

The interpretation of v. 17 is made more precise through vv. 18 and 19. "Iota" is the smallest letter of the Hebrew square script but also in Greek a small letter. Κεραία might mean the decorative stroke in Hebrew letters.[70] In Greek, "little pen strokes" can be accents or breathing marks or anything proverbially small.[71] "Until heaven and earth pass away" can either be a popular circumlocution for "never"[72] or limit the validity of the law until the end of the world.[73]

The decision is very difficult. Matthew 24:35 speaks explicitly of the fact that Jesus' words will outlast heaven and earth. Does the evangelist mean that—in contrast to the words of Jesus—the law is to be valid *only* until the passing of heaven and earth? Matthew then would follow a sparsely documented Jewish idea that the law would be

---

[67]Matthew 7:12, as the second part of the bracket around the Sermon on the Mount, is particularly important. Matthew 11:13 is accented differently; Matthew therefore has deliberately changed it in comparison with Q, put the prophets first and added the verb προφητεύω.

[68]Rom. 8:4; 13:8; Gal. 5:14.

[69]Lohmeyer 107 (Christ is not "servant," but "Lord and 'fulfiller' " of law and prophets); Bornkamm* 78 (Jesus legitimizes the law, not vice versa). Also Ljungman's* involved exegesis leads to this: Jesus fills the Scripture, conceived as a whole, through his life.

[70]Str-B I 248f.

[71]BAGD, s.v.; Philo, *Flacc.* 131. It is an unnecessary assumption that the authority of the Scripture is tied to the Hebrew text of the Torah (so Betz* 33).

[72]Banks* 215; Strecker* 144. Wettstein I 294 speaks of a "locutio proverbialis" (proverbial expression). Cf. on the (sparse) examples below, n. 76.

[73]That is the interpretation which is predominant since the early church until today, cf. those mentioned by Broer* 43 n. 87.

abolished in the future eon.[74] But what reader would notice that Matthew is already now thinking of a situation which comes much later? But especially: the temporal limitation of the Torah scarcely suited the context, where the idea is that of an *unrestricted* validity. Unless one wants to resort to the probably false assumption that for Matthew the end of heaven and earth is still in the distant future,[75] then the only way is to understand the phrase in the sense of "never." This is possible on the basis of the Old Testament and Jewish background.[76]

The last purpose clause "until all takes place" is just as difficult. Since one does not want to impute to the evangelist a mere material repetition of the first purpose clause, which would be linguistically very awkward, the ethical explanation is today widely accepted: "until all takes place" means "until all that which is commanded in the law is done."[77] Γίνομαι may in Matthew mean "to be done" (cf. 6:10; 26:42), even if this is not the most probable sense. Matthew then would point in this final little sentence to the necessity of practical fulfillment of the law.[78] However, the temporal ἕως ἄν remains difficult. As far as the content is concerned, v. 18d does not name a clear terminal point for the validity of the law. Does Matthew, like many Jews, mean that the new eon will come when Israel keeps one single Sabbath?[79] But this would be singular in Matthew and would also not fit well into the context. Thus the verse remains difficult.

All other interpretations are still more difficult. A salvation-historical interpretation, meaning the fulfillment of the Old Testament promises, would be possible only if v. 17 also is to be understood similarly.[80] There remains the attempt to interpret 18d Christologically: in Christ's death and resurrection "all" that was predicted in the Old Testament "has taken place." However, this would require complicated eisegeses into the text [81]—to say nothing of the difficulty that the law then according to 18b would

---

[74]Cf. Luz* 407 n. 48 and the literature mentioned there.

[75]Against Luz* 418.

[76]A. Vögtle, *Das Neue Testament und die Zukunft des Kosmos*, KBANT (1970), 102-04 rightly points to the material parallels Jer. 31:35f.; 33:20f.,25; Ps. 148:2-6. In the Jewish realm, one must compare ExR. 6.1 = Str-B I 249; GenR. 10.1 on 2:1 (heaven and earth have a measure, only the Torah has no measure). Linguistic parallels are sparser; cf. Job 14:12; Ps. 72:5,7,17. Naturally Matthew does not postulate philosophically the eternity of heaven and earth. He only wants to take into consideration the longest possible period of time and not to set a temporal limit for the validity of the Torah. Cf. Broer* 43-45.

[77]Rare in the early church, e.g., Augustine** 1.8 (20); among the more recent interpreters, e.g., Barth, *Gesetzesverständnis* 65; Marguerat, *Jugement* 131, there further n. 79.

[78]It would be still more appealing if ἕως ἄν had the meaning of purpose ("in order that all take place"). Schweizer interprets it in this sense, "Noch einmal,"* 83. But his examples are for ἕως, with ἄν only *T. Job* 21:2; 22:3 (not in all MSS).

[79]Cf. the examples Str-B I 600.

[80]In the ancient church, e.g., in the *Opus imperfectum* 10 = 688, among the more recent interpreters, e.g., Schweizer, *Anmerkungen** 399f., on the basis of passages like 1:22; 21:4; 26:54,56.

[81]In the ancient church most impressively Afrahat, *Hom.* (transl. G. Bert, Leipzig 1888) 2,6f.: Christ has abolished the temple sacrifices through his sacrifice so that law and prophets hang only on two commandments now (the double commandment of love, Matt. 24:40); Matt. 5:18 refers to them! More

be valid until the end of the world, according to 18d, on the other hand, only until Christ.

5:19

Λύω in v. 19 takes up καταλύω of v. 17 and may mean both the transgressing and the invalidating of a commandment. What is meant by the "least commandments"? The rabbis distinguished between "light" and "weighty" commandments, a distinction that involves, on the one hand, the effort demanded of the believer, on the other hand, the reward promised for keeping it.[82] Our logion agrees with them in the fact that it urges the keeping even of the least commandments, for in the last analysis one cannot—thus the rabbis—know how much reward each commandment brings.[83] Thus the keeping of all commandments, independent of their content and their relationship to the center of the Torah, is demanded explicitly. The least commandments correspond to the iota and the little pen stroke of the law which will not pass away (v. 18). The promise to be "great" or "the least" in the kingdom of heaven is striking.

We ask first for the *original meaning*. (a) Does it mean that there are different places in heaven? Such thoughts existed in Judaism; they correspond to the need for individual retribution in eternity.[84] Thus understood, our logion has a peculiar "half radical" attitude: whoever transgresses the little commandments of the Torah and teaches in this manner, will receive the least place in the kingdom of heaven but still can enter it. Käsemann assumed that here Jewish-Christian prophets wanted to deny their opponents—who in regard to the law thought more liberally, as, e.g., Pauline Christians[85]—earthly church fellowship but not the kingdom of heaven as such.[86] (b) The other possibility is that the apodosis "will be called the least" has been formulated only for reasons of rhetorical harmony and the correspondence of deed and fate[87] in parallel with the protasis. Then it would mean actually an exclusion from the kingdom of

---

recent attempts: Hamerton-Kelly* 30 (on the basis of 28:11: ἅπαντα τὰ γενόμενα); Davies* 440-456 (for Jesus, on the basis of a Christology of the servant of the Lord, ibid. 450); Meier, *Law*, especially 61-65 (on the basis of the problematic thesis that 28:16-20 is to be interpreted as a proleptic parousia). The difficulties are great; thus, e.g., Davies must interpret the passing of heaven and earth figuratively of the death and resurrection of Jesus (453-56)—at least he sees the problem!

[82]Cf. Str-B I 901-05. The shedding of blood, idolatry, Sabbath, the honoring of the parents belonged to the weighty commandments; tabernacles, the bird mother (Deut. 22:7), or the eating of blood belonged to the light commandments (= מִצְוָֹת קַלּוֹת, thus not literally the same as Matt. 5:19).

[83]Cf. *'Abot* 2:1; Str-B I 249 and 903 on this passage.

[84]Cf. *2 Enoch* 3-22; *3 Apoc. Bar.* passim; rabbinical material in Str-B III 531-33.

[85]Matthew 5:19 was variously interpreted, especially in the 19th century as an antithesis to Paul; in our century, e.g., by J. Weiss 267; Montefiore II 494; Manson, *Sayings* 24f.; Betz* 38f.; Heubült* 145, especially on the basis of ἐλάχιστος, cf. 1 Cor. 15:9. Yet Paul belongs into a much broader stream of law-free Christianity.

[86]"The Beginnings of Christian Theology," in idem, *New Testament Questions of Today* (Philadelphia: Fortress, 1969), 87.

[87]This correspondence is constitutive for the "sentences of holy law."

heaven.[88]

The possibilities of proof are meager. In the latter case we would have the self-testimony of a radical law-observant Jewish Christianity, e.g., of such Christians who made many difficulties for Paul around the year 50 because they were of the opinion that there was salvation for the Gentile Christian Galatians only in the obedience to the Torah. Yes, the Jewish Christians of Matt. 5:18f. seem to be still stricter than the Galatian Jewish Christians—whom Paul has to remind in any case that whoever demands circumcision then also must fulfill the *entire* law in *all* its prescriptions (Gal. 5:3). But if the Jewish Christians of Matt. 5:19 assign their more freely thinking opponents only the last places in heaven, then we encounter according to Jewish categories a special "half-liberal" type. The rabbis strictly maintained in their teaching that all commandments of God, even the least, are valid. In practice, however, they were— especially the Hillelites—realists who entrusted something to God's grace and by no means demanded the keeping of *all* commandments as a condition for entry into the kingdom of God. To keep a majority of the commandments or true repentance was entirely sufficient.[89] People who insisted on the keeping of all commandments or said, "cursed is the one who does not remain *in all things* that are written in the book of the law in order to do it,"[90] were fanatics and exceptions in Judaism. Our Jewish Christians perhaps were such fanatics; perhaps they were "half-liberal." A decision seems impossible.

On the Matthean level the verse is difficult also. Since Matthew is familiar with the conception of different ranks in heaven (11:11; 18:1,4; 20:21), one may prefer to believe he belongs in the first interpretation and to count him among the "half-liberal" Jewish Christians faithful to the law.

5:17-19

This changes little for the basic problem of 5:17-19. Matthew has received a Jewish-Christian tradition which demands the keeping of *all* individual commandments of the Torah and excludes content critique of Torah commandments. He has not only received it but also intensively emended it redactionally and placed it in a prominent place in his Sermon on the Mount. This fits well with the basic intention of the Matthean verse 17 which first of all spoke of the fulfillment of the law through Jesus' obedience and life. The conclusion seems unavoidable that the "fulfilling of the law" in v. 17 first has to be interpreted on the basis of vv. 18f. Then the content means the faithfulness to each individual commandment of the Torah. This interpretation is not in opposition to the Christological accent of vv. 17 and 18 ("Amen I say to you"). The mission of Jesus consists exactly in his establishing of the Torah through his

---

[88]This interpretation is widespread in the early church, e.g., Chromatius 6.2 = 344; John Chrysostom 16.4 = 278 ("hell and damnation"); Luther, WA 32**, 358 = *LW* 21,72ff.(expelled from the kingdom of heaven), recently, e.g., Schweizer 62.

[89]Cf. Broer* 56f. For the rabbis, principally the entire Torah, including each subtlety, is from heaven, cf. *b. Sanh.* 99a. God will decide in the judgment according to the majority of the deeds of a person (Str-B IV 1041f.). In *b. Sanh.* 81a, Gamaliel advocates a maximalist, Akiba a minimalist position (the one who keeps *one* commandment will live), cf. *b. Mak.* 24a; *p. Qidd.* 1,10,61d; *Midr. Pss.* 15, §7 (60a). On the power of repentance cf. Nissen, *Gott* 131-34.

[90]Galatians 3:10 = Deut. 27:26 (πᾶσιν = LXX). It is characteristic of the Qumran sect that a person has to do *everything* demanded in the law.

obedience, up to the last and least commandment. Jesus is not servant but Lord of the Torah but he exercises his lordship in such a way that he lets the Torah remain valid without restrictions.

This cannot be harmonized with an interpretation which in vv. 18f. sees only insignificant Jewish-Christian traditional material.[91] But also the thesis—which has become a classic through Christian doctrine and practice of centuries—that Matthew affirms the moral law and leaves the ceremonial law out of consideration,[92] is not in agreement with this view. Exegetical attempts to see in the "least" commandments the decalogue[93] or, what is more, the Antitheses[94] at least betray the fact that here the wording of the texts is taken seriously.

There are sufficient passages in Matthew to show that for him the ritual commandments of the Torah also are valid, e.g., 23:23,26 or 24:20. These passages make clear what the difference between the Matthean community and Judaism does consist in: Matthew takes it as clear in principle that, on the basis of Jesus' teaching, "justice, mercy, and faith"—thus indeed the love commandment—are the chief commandment and that commandments like that of tithing (23:23) or that of the purification of the outside of the cup (23:26) are iotas and little pen strokes. The love commandment stands in the center; the ceremonial laws are of secondary rank. But they also are parts of the law which Jesus fulfills as a whole. Verses 17-19 are a "Jewish-Christian program"[95] of great uniformity.

5:20

The interpretation of the Antitheses and of v. 20 has not become easier thereby. The progressive connection with γάρ makes clear that the law belongs into the "higher righteousness" of which he is now speaking, that it even is its central part. Δικαιοσύνη is righteousness which the human performs, as in 3:15.[96] The comparative περισσεύειν . . . πλεῖον is curious;[97] μᾶλλον would be more commonly used. Πλεῖον suggests a quantitative interpretation: Unless your righteousness is present to a measurably higher degree than that of the scribes

---

[91]Cf. above n. 29.

[92]Strecker, *Weg* 30-33; Schulz, *Stunde* 174-190; Hoppe* 123. I cannot harmonize Matthew and the epistle of James in their position on the ceremonial law (against Hoppe* 123-29).

[93]Calvin I 182; Lapide 133. F. Dibelius, "Zwei Worte Jesu," *ZNW* 11 (1910) 188-92, is thinking of the short commandments of the second table of the decalogue; but it does not say: ἐντολαὶ βραχύταται! Since again the least commandments of v. 19 were combined with the iota and little pen stroke of v. 18, one has interpreted these of the decalogue (already *Didascalia* 26 = Achelis-Flemming 129,132).

[94]Οὗτος then is referred to what follows, cf. already John Chrysostom 16.4 = 278, among recent interpreters, e.g., O. Carlston, "The Things that Defile," *NTS* 15 (1968/69) 79.

[95]Luz 421*.

[96]Cf. on 3:15 and 5:6.

[97]A pleonastically formulated comparative is completely possible in Greek, cf. Kühner-Blass-Gerth II/1 26; BDF § 246 n. 2. However, the intensification through μᾶλλον is the customary one. Πλεῖον corresponds to the Latin *plus*, not *magis*.

and Pharisees,[98] you will not enter the kingdom of heaven. A quantitative comparison between the righteousness of the disciples and the Pharisees and scribes lies in the text in any case. It corresponds to insisting on the fulfillment also of the individual commandments of the law in vv. 17-19. Thus the higher righteousness of the disciples means, on the basis of vv. 17-19, first of all a quantitative more of fulfilling the Torah. The reader who is influenced by Jewish thinking now expects the "fence surrounding the Torah," which the "teacher" Jesus will erect.[99] The Antitheses follow. They are a "fence" of a very special kind. They are not only concerned—in the Jewish way—with a radical intensification of individual Old Testament commands. Instead, the decisive element for Matthew is that the love commandment becomes the center of these intensified individual commandments. With the first and last Antitheses, it furnishes, in a way, the frame of all Antitheses. Based on the Antitheses, the higher righteousness of the disciples is not only a quantitative increase of the fulfilling of the law—measured on the Torah—but primarily a qualitative intensification of the life before God—measured on love. Verse 20 stands, so to speak, in the middle between these two conceptions, different in sense, dependent on whether it is read "from the front" or "from the back." Not only in a literary sense but also in regard to content, the verse has a transitional, a hinge function.[100]

Summary

How can these basic conceptions—seemingly so divergent—be brought together?

1. Matthew obviously does not sense the tension between the qualitative *fulfillment* of the will of God in the Antitheses, which is infinitely intensified through the love commandment, and the obedience toward all individual prescriptions of the Torah, which is demanded by vv. 17-19. The transition takes place smoothly and inconspicuously. In practice, the Matthean community has subordinated the many individual commandments of the Torah to the love commandment as the center. In theory, they probably were not able to see a tension. The iotas and little pen strokes of the ritual law did not for them imply the impression of opaqueness and unclarity, and the prescriptions of the law did not suggest the idea of heteronomy and lack of freedom. Matthew did not have the liberals' need to break through from the slavery of individual commandments to spirit and morality.[101] The instructions given by Jesus in the Antitheses were for him obligatory ἐντολαί (cf. 28:20), thus principally nothing

---

[98]On the typifying paired listing of the Jewish opponent, cf. the comment on 3:7.

[99]Cf. Przybylski, *Righteousness* 81-87.

[100]Luz* 423 n. 108.

[101]Cf. the material above n. 23. The explicit statement that Jesus in Matt. 5:18f. did not want to dissolve the ceremonial law occurred for the first time in H. S. Reimarus: "I also wanted to show that Jesus neither attempted nor commanded that ceremonial laws should be abandoned, nor did he himself introduce any new ceremonies" (*The Goal of Jesus and His Disciples* [Leiden: Brill, 1970], 59). But the disciples did not live according to the teaching of the master and dissolved not only little pen strokes, but whole laws (ibid. 71). Matt. 5:18f. was considered as negative by Enlightenment criticism; the abolition of the negative took place through fraud.

other than the Old Testament commandments. And vice versa, the iotas and little pen strokes, as parts of that law which Jesus had come to fulfill, were salutary and good. Matthew would never have arrived at the thinking that the law was the opposite of grace. For him law belongs to grace, even the Old Testament law in all its prescriptions, specifically after Jesus had revealed its center and its depth. Therefore, it would be impossible for him to connect the idea of works-righteousness with the gift of the law fulfilled by Jesus. Individual prescriptions and intensification of the law on the basis of love are not mutually opposed but belong to each other and make the *offer* of God's will concrete. Matthew is rooted in this understanding of God's will as grace in Judaism.

2. Preamble (17-19) and Antitheses (21-48) belong together under a Christological prefix. The sovereign "But I say to you" of Jesus connects vv. 17-19 with the Antitheses. Thus it becomes clear that the Old Testament law is not simply the Jewish law as it always was in force. Rather, the Old Testament law has its authority not from itself but through Jesus. The Antitheses make this completely clear. They underline, so to speak, the ἦλθον of v. 17 in its full significance. Jesus is not the servant but the Lord of the law. The Matthean understanding of the law belongs to the more weighty and basic theme of Christology. In the same way, the Matthean Sermon on the Mount, including 5:17-19, belongs to the story of Jesus, the Son of God, which is superior to it.

3. Conversely, the preamble 17-19 also offers an important indication for the interpretation of the Antitheses. Why did Matthew provide this introduction for them? In order to insure that they must in no case be interpreted as antinomian, as a break with the heritage of Israel. The Matthean community had experienced the painful break with the synagogue and was situated outside of Judaism. In this situation, Matthew programmatically had to make a claim to the Old Testament for the sake of the identity of God, the Father of Jesus. The formula quotations raise the programmatic claim to the *predictions*; our passage raises the programmatic claim to the *law*.

The concept that law and prophets are fulfilled completely and perfectly by Jesus means at the same time that for Matthew there is no longer any other way of access to the Bible of Israel than by way of Jesus. Therefore, the preamble to the Antitheses has at the same time the effect of a reprimand of Israel. Matthew, for whom the authority of the Bible is fixed through Jesus, can do no other than measure the scribes and Pharisees by the standard of the higher righteousness which is set by Jesus. Measured by this standard, which is not theirs, their righteousness is found as not enough. Matthean theology unavoidably has an anti-Jewish effect which can be seen only to a small extent in the history of the influence of *this* text but very well in that of other texts which agree with this principle.

Thus our text is a statement of principle which endeavors to interpret and safeguard the Antitheses. The history of interpretation shows that its basic significance was rarely recognized except when the Old Testament seemed to be endangered as a basic text of the church.[102] It further demonstrated that it was

---

[102]Marcion; the Anabaptists in the view of the Reformers. Our text played a role also in the debate with the "German Christians" of the Nazi period. Examples: "Richtlinien der Kirchenbewegung Deutsche Christen . . . in Thüringen vom 11. Dez. 1933," in *Die Bekenntnisse . . . des Jahres 1933*, ed. K. D. Schmidt (Göttingen: Vandenhoeck & Ruprecht, 1934), 102: "The way to the fulfilling of the German

difficult for the church, which had become non-Jewish, in all times to recognize the real meaning of our text. Access to Matt. 5:17-20 was made almost impossible, not only by the Pauline prefix under which the text had often been read, but especially by the fact that for the Gentile-Christian Great Church the law actually was reduced to the "royal" law "of liberty" (James 2:8-13, cf. 11:25), namely, the moral law, particularly the decalogue.

For the Matthean community, difficulties also arose here. After the failure of the mission in Israel it had to be open to the Gentile mission. With that, not only the question of the further validity of the iotas and tittles of the ritual law but also, e.g., that of the validity of such a fundamental commandment as that of circumcision arose. There is no indication that Matthean Christians practiced circumcision in the Gentile mission. This means that the incipient Gentile mission unavoidably had to lead to a revision of Matt. 5:17-19. It evidently was carried out by those parts of Jewish Christianity which after the end of the mission to Israel decided for integration into the Great Church.[103] The Matthean community belonged to them. This historical development then further means that a Gentile-Christian community which is no longer bound to the law can also no longer directly accept the Matthean principle.

Meaning for Today

But the basic Matthean statement, it seems to me, remains fundamental. The relationship of the Gentile-Christian church to the Old Testament always was like a walk on a mountain ridge. It was threatened by the danger of works-righteousness and by the danger—perhaps still more widespread—of a lowest-common-denominator ethic, respected on all sides, on the basis, e.g., of the decalogue. It was threatened also by the danger of a flight from the reality of the world into inwardness or into the conventicle. Despite the very large differences, there is here a common thread among Marcion, the Manicheans, the spiritualists of the Reformation period, and the Anabaptists. The history of interpretation demonstrates that Matt. 5:17 moved into central focus always where the church, along with a devaluation of the Old Testament, was threatened with, or was offered, withdrawal from the world. The function of the text today consists perhaps in reminding the church that Christian faith is praxis *in the world*. There is a valid will of the Father for this world. Its concrete pillars are the divine commandments which cannot be evaded by any principle of morality, as "complete" as it may be, or by a departure from the world, however it may be shaped.

I conclude with two summary references to the history of interpretation. Among all the Reformers *Calvin* gave the law most clearly a central, positive place in his

---

law is the faithful German community." Opposed to this, there is, e.g., the word of the presidium of the Evangelical-Reformed Church of Hannover of March 31, 1935, in *Die Bekenntnisse . . . des Jahres 1935*, 85: "We reject . . . any attempt to devaluate the Bible as a book of the Jews. Attempts to interpret the destinies of peoples . . . without the light of the word of God (Matt. 5:17-19) lead into error."

[103]Cf. introduction pp. 68f. The history of such Christians might be reflected in Ps. Clem. *Rec.* 1.64: "The temple will be destroyed and the abomination of desolation will stand in the holy place *and then* the gospel will be preached to the Gentiles, as a testimony to you that out of their faith your unbelief will be condemned."

thinking. He spoke most clearly of the similarity, even the unity, of the old and the new covenants. With all the differences, there is here an analogous basic structure between the theology of Matthew and that of Calvin. It led both of them to a practical piety which took seriously the existence of the community in the world.[104] The other reference is to *Hans Denck*, a Bavarian theologian of the Reformation, who died early (1527) and who, despite great affinity to Anabaptists and spiritualists, is not to be equated with them. Matthew 5:17 stands in the center of his brief, but most important theological writing, "On the Law of God."[105] Denck was deeply concerned over the thesis that "Christ has fulfilled the law so that we do not need to," which leads to the devaluation of Christian praxis. It is the Christians "through whose good works the Gentiles should be motivated to praise God the Father in heaven"! He knows that "No law was ever understood and written so highly but that it is and must be fulfilled *in the body of Christ.*" He was concerned about the *life of the community,* and in that he is a theological brother of Matthew.

2.2. The Higher Righteousness I: The Antitheses (5:21-48)

Literature

Banks, R., *Jesus and the Law in the Synoptic Tradition,* pp. 182-203, SNTSMS 28 (Cambridge: At the University Press, 1975).

Berger, K., "Die Gesetzesauslegung Jesu in der synoptischen Tradition und ihr Hintergrund im Alten Testament und Spätjudentum," pp. 149-82, diss. Munich (1966).

Broer, I., "Die Antithesen und der Evangelist Matthäus," *BZ* NF 19 (1975) 50-63.

_____, *Freiheit vom Gesetz und Radikalisierung des Gesetzes,* pp. 75-113, SBS 98 (Stuttgart: KBW, 1980).

Daube, *New Testament* 55-62.

Descamps, A., "Essai d'interprétation de Mt 5,17-48. 'Formgeschichte' ou 'Redaktions-geschichte'?" *SE* I, pp. 156-73 1959 (TU 73).

Dietzfelbinger, C., *Die Antithesen der Bergpredigt,* TEH 186 (Munich: Kaiser, 1975).

_____, "Die Antithesen der Bergpredigt im Verständnis des Matthäus," *ZNW* 70 (1979) 1-15.

Guelich, R. A., "Not to Annul the Law, Rather to Fulfil the Law and the Prophets," diss. Hamburg (1967), pp. 117-215.

_____, "The Antitheses of Matthew 5,21-48: Traditional or Redactional?" *NTS* 22 (1975/76) 444-57.

Hasler, V., "Das Herzstück der Bergpredigt," *TZ* 15 (1959) 90-106.

Hübner, H., *Das Gesetz in der synoptischen Tradition,* pp. 40-112 (Witten: Luther-Verlag, 1973).

Légasse, S., *Les pauvres en esprit,* pp. 57-98, LD 78 (Paris: Éditions de Cerf, 1974).

Lohse, E., "Ich aber sage euch,' " in *Der Ruf Jesu und die Antwort der Gemeinde* (FS J. Jeremias), ed. E. Lohse et al., pp. 189-203 (Göttingen: Vandenhoeck & Ruprecht, 1970). 189-203 (= idem, *Die Einheit des Neuen Testaments,* pp. 73-87 [Göttingen: Vandenhoeck & Ruprecht, 1973]).

---

[104]In a certain way, the tension between Matt. 5:17-19 and 21-48 becomes a conflict in the debate between Calvin and the Anabaptists, cf. Stadtland-Neumann** 23: "The Reformer surrenders . . . large passages of the Sermon on the Mount to the Anabaptists and withdraws to the Old Testament."

[105]In *Schriften, 2. Teil: Religiöse Schriften* ed. W. Fellmann, p. 52, QFRG 24 (Gütersloh: Bertelsmann, 1956).

Meier, *Law* 125-61.
Merklein, *Gottesherrschaft* 253-93.
Percy, *Botschaft* 123-65.
Sand, *Gesetz* 46-56.
Schmahl, G., "Die Antithesen der Bergpredigt," *TTZ* 83 (1974) 284-97.
Strecker, G., "Die Antithesen der Bergpredigt (Mt 5,21-48 par)," *ZNW* 69 (1978) 36-72.
Suggs, M. J., "The Antitheses as Redactional Products," in *Jesus Christus in Historie und Theologie* (FS H. Conzelmann), ed. G. Strecker, pp. 433-44 (Tübingen: Mohr, 1975).
Further literature** on the Sermon on the Mount at Matthew 5-7 see above pp. 209-211.

1. *The formal structure.* Only the first and the fourth antitheses contain the full introductory formula ἠκούσατε ὅτι ἐρρέθη τοῖς ἀρχαίοις (vv. 21,33). Moreover, the new beginning in v. 33 is stressed by πάλιν. Thus they are divided into two blocks of three antitheses of equal length (vv. 21-32,33-48).[1] In the first two cases the antithesis is introduced with πᾶς (vv. 22,28), in the fourth and fifth it has the form of a prohibition (μή with infinitive, vv. 34,39). Matthew divides the Antitheses into two blocks and in this way obliterates the varied literary origin of the material. Finally the special length of the first and of the last antitheses is not accidental; the evangelist evidently wanted to stress them particularly. The third antithesis is the shortest, also in its introduction; thematically it is closely connected with the second one.

2. *Questions of literary criticism.* The first, second, and fourth (perhaps fifth, vv. 38f.) antitheses are unique material. Matthew has supplemented them through materials from Q (vv. 25f.,29f.?, cf. 31f.). This corresponds to the situation in general: the antitheses from the special material come first (vv. 21-37; the third antithesis was inserted here only because it belongs thematically to the second one), only then those from Q. Q therefore was not the primary source, but, as also in chs. 13; 18; 24 in comparison with Mark, a collection of material for supplementation. This speaks in favor of the hypothesis that Matthew had found in written form a collection of antitheses which contained the first two and the fourth and was perhaps already connected with 6:2-18, and that he supplemented it by Q materials. From this collection Matthew also took over the antithetical form.

3. *History of tradition.* The origin and originality of the Antitheses are controverted. The following theses vie with each other:

a. The so-called "*normal hypothesis*": The first, second, and fourth antitheses, which come from the special material, are "primary," the third, fifth, and sixth are "secondary" antitheses.[2]

Only with the primary antitheses does the possibility exist that the antithetical form goes back to Jesus; the secondary ones have most probably been formed by

---

[1]The two parts have 258/244 words and 1131/1130 letters, respectively.

[2]Bultmann, *Tradition* 143f.; Albertz, *Streitgespräche* 146-51; Eichholz** 69f.; Guelich, *Not** 117-215; Strecker* 47.

Matthew as such.[3] A thesis regarding the content often is combined with it: the primary antitheses make the Old Testament commandment more radical, the secondary ones invalidate it.

b. The *"tradition hypothesis"*: All six antitheses were already available to the evangelist as antitheses.[4]

The most important starting point for this hypothesis is the theological relation of the Antitheses to 5:17. If it was the concern of Matthew that Jesus has fulfilled the whole law, then he himself cannot have formed antitheses, which would indicate that he puts himself above the law! This is intensified by the (probably wrong but widespread) assumption of the "normal hypothesis" that especially the secondary, Matthean, antitheses abrogate the Torah. The "tradition hypothesis" has literary-critical consequences and its weakness in this point: it either has to assume that the Sayings Source did not exist (Jeremias, Wrege), or has to accept a far-reaching emendation of Q prior to Matthew to which then all antitheses would be due.[5] The question is to be taken seriously whether vv. 38f. is not already a pre-Matthean antithesis.

c. The *"redaction hypothesis"* is today more frequently maintained: All six antitheses come from the evangelist Matthew.[6]

Only Broer* has attempted a real proof. Of his arguments the reference to other "antithetical" formulations in Matthew,[7] or to 19:9[8] or to ἐγώ, which is often emphasized in the Matthean redaction,[9] should probably not be taken seriously; but the reference to the parallelism between 5:21-32 and the catalog of vices in 15:19 (φόνοι, μοιχεῖαι, πορνεῖαι) definitely should be considered. But 15:19 shows only that Matthew repeated the sequence of the first three antitheses, which came from him anyway. Otherwise, this hypothesis faces a double difficulty: It has to prove for *all* antitheses that the combination of thesis and antithesis is secondary, and it has to interpret 5:17-20 in such a way that *all* antitheses fit with it.[10] *Result:* This hypothesis, despite the increasing number of its advocates, is the most improbable one.

---

[3]In English-language scholarship it is often advocated that only the third antithesis is formed redactionally, e.g., Bacon, *Studies* 181; Branscomb, *Jesus* 235f.; Streeter, *Gospels* 252f. (mostly on the basis of a special source M), cf. similarly Kilpatrick, *Origins* 18-20,24; Davies, *Setting* 387f.

[4]Jeremias, *Theology* 251f.; Wrege** 56f.; Sand, *Gesetz* 48; Lührmann, *Redaktion* 118.

[5]Sand, *Gesetz* 48. It speaks against this view that the incorporation of the Q materials into the pre-Matthean antitheses betrays Matthean theological concerns (vv. 25f.: love of enemies; vv. 29f.: threat of judgment).

[6]Stauffer, *Botschaft* 39; Hasler, *Amen* 79f.; Suggs, *Wisdom* 109-14; Suggs*; Broer, *BZ* 19*, 56-63, etc. Berger* 175-82 is inventive: the origin of the Matthean antitheses lies in the contrasting of Moses and Jesus in Mark 10:2-10, i.e., at the third antithesis.

[7]However, antitheses of a quite different kind. Broer, *BZ* 19, 57, points to 10:34; 15:11,17f.,20; 19:8f. and even to 5:17.

[8]Loc. cit. 61. But Jesus argues there on an Old Testament foundation.

[9]Matthew 10:16; 23:34; 28:20. But Matthew elsewhere never combines λέγω ὑμῖν—which he uses frequently—with ἐγώ.

[10]Suggs, *Wisdom* 114, does not see here a problem because Jesus is "Wisdom-Torah." But why then does he turn antithetically against the Mosaic Torah, which is also identified with wisdom?

My own position can here only be indicated. Like the "normal hypothesis," I consider the third, fifth, and sixth antitheses as redactional. But it seems probable to me, in distinction from the "normal hypothesis," that the fourth antithesis also is secondary, even if there the antithetical formulation is due to the source which was taken over by the evangelist.

4. *Redaction.* Aside from some redactional formulations and the new formation of the antitheses in vv. 31f., 38f., 43f., the most important achievement of the evangelist lies in the composition. Through the formulation of the sixth antithesis and the new grouping of the Q material from Luke 6:27-36 he achieves the framing of the antitheses by the love commandment, more precisely: by the command of the love of enemies (vv. 25! 44). The last antithesis, culminating in the key word τέλειος thus shows itself as the climax. Otherwise Matthew has indulged in his "conservatism"[11] not only in the formulation but also in the composition: The Q block Luke 6:27-36 as well as the special material block vv. 21-37 remain together despite some transpositions. In the formulation of new antitheses Matthew has carried on the antithesis form as it was given to him from the tradition of the special material.

5. *Origin of the antithesis formula.* There are Jewish parallels to the antithesis formula:

a. Rabbis may contrast two possibilities of the interpretation of a biblical text, often a literal one and a free one, through the formula שׁוֹמֵעַ אֲנִי . . . אָמַרְתָ (I could understand . . . but you shall say).[12]

b. Rabbis may oppose their own interpretation to that of other rabbis by an emphatic וַאֲנִי אוֹמֵר (But *I* say . . .).[13] The rejected interpretation is here not introduced by a fixed phrase. These parallels are very close to Matthew through their use of the first person.

c. "But I say to you" without an antithetical contrast has parallels in Jewish wisdom[14] and apocalyptic[15] writings.

Result: The introductory phrase in the Antitheses is definitely an independent new formulation, in comparison with Jewish parallels, even if a certain closeness to Jewish exegetical terminology can be found.

6. The *meaning of the antithesis formula.* The main question is whether the antithesis refers to the Jewish-Pharisaic interpretation of the Old Testament—i.e., to the halakah[16]—or to the Old Testament.[17] It is not only

---

[11]Strecker* 46.

[12]*Mek.* Exod. 20:22 = Jithro 9. The passage is unique; normally the introduction of the correct interpretation goes: תַּלְמוּד לוֹמַר (Bacher, *Terminologie* I 189). Daube, *New Testament* 55-62, is inclined to this analogy.

[13]Sipre Num. = 11.21f. par. 95; *Sipre Deut.* 6:4f. = par. 312; further examples in Smith, *Parallels* 29f.; Lohse* 193- 96; Dalman, *Jesus* 68.

[14]*T. Reub.* 1:7, cf. 4:5; 6:5; *T. Levi* 16:4; *T. Benj.* 9:1, cf. Berger, *Amen-Worte* 91-93.

[15]*I Enoch* 94:1,3,10; 99:13; 102:9; cf. Sato, *Q* 273-79.

[16]E.g., Zahn 221; Barth, *Gesetzesverständnis* 88 (with limitations); Burchard** 423; Dietzfelbinger, *ZNW* 1979* 3 (only for the evangelist).

[17]E.g., Schlatter 165f.; W. G. Kümmel, "Jesus und der jüdische Traditionsgedanke," in idem, *Heilsgeschehen* I 32 ("to cut off the root of the Jewish faith in the law"); Lohse* 198; Merklein,

today that here the interpretation is split. At least since the Reformation there has been an alternative. The interpretation to a large extent went along confessional lines.

After the rejection of the Old Testament law by the Marcionites and its differentiated rejection by the Gnostics,[18] an exegesis prevailed in the early and medieval church which understands the Antitheses as the *contrast of old and new law*. Then the positive relation between the two laws is brought out in nuances; the decisive concepts are those of perfection[19] and extension.[20] It is said rather with restraint that individual commandments have been abolished through Jesus.[21] This understanding of the Antitheses usually asserts itself in post-Reformation Catholic exegesis.[22] It is intensified by interpreters of the free churches: The law of the Old Testament which, e.g., permits use of force and oaths is no longer valid for the Christians, but the law of the New Testament is unqualifiedly valid.[23]

There are new tones[24] in the exegesis of the Reformers. Here throughout, by Luther, Calvin and in the post-Reformation interpretation, the agreement of Jesus with the Old Testament and his *opposition to contemporary, Jewish-Pharisaic interpretation*

Gottesherrschaft 256. According to Hummel, *Auseinandersetzung* 74, the word of Jesus, "spoken on another mountain," stands over against the Sinai Torah and is the foundation of a proper Christian halakah.

[18] According to Ptolemy, *Ad Flor.* = Epiphanius, *Haer.* 33.6.1, the prohibition of murder, of adultery, and of false oaths is part of the "pure" law of God, but the principle of retaliation a part of that law of God which is connected with injustice and was therefore abolished by Jesus.

[19] Thomas, *STh* 1/II qu 107 art 2: "Nova lex comparatur ad veterem sicut perfectum ad imperfectum" (The new law is being compared to the old as the perfect to the imperfect).

[20] Cf. above n. 41 on 5:17-20. "Lex nova adimplet veterem legem, inquantum supplet illud quod veteri legi deerat" (The new law fulfills the old law, inasmuch as it supplies that which was missing in the old law) (Thomas, see above n. 19).

[21] Irenaeus, *Haer.* 4.13.2, distinguishes between the "bodily" regulations for servants and the "commandments of freedom" of the Sermon on the Mount. John Chrysostom 16.7 = 187: God has "adapted the difference of the two laws to the difference of the times."

[22] E.g., Maldonat 110-13, with sharp polemic even against several unnamed Catholics who fall prey to the teaching of the heretics; Lapide 135 (partly against the δευτέρωσις of the Pharisees, partly against the imperfect Mosaic law).

[23] E.g., Wolzogen 213-15; Socinus** 13. On the understanding of the Old Testament by the Anabaptists, cf. C. Bauman, *Gewaltlosigkeit im Täufertum*, SHCT 3 (1968), 155-70.

[24] There are pre-Reformation anticipations of the interpretation of the Reformers. Maldonat 61 mentions the Pelagians. Nicolaus of Lyra, *Postilla*, on the passage: "Salvator nova praecepta moralia non dedit; praecepta decalogi replicavit" (The Savior did not give new moral precepts; he unfolded the precepts of the decalogue). Similarly Tostatus 19,132f: "Replicavit ipsa praecepta Decalogi . . . induxit . . . homines ad . . . verum intellectum ipsorum . . . errores Iudaeorum . . . excludendo" (he unfolded the precepts of the decalogue themselves . . . he led . . . the people to . . . the true insight of them . . . by excluding the errors of the Jews). It is a fact that the Humanists interpret like this. Erasmus, *Paraphrasis* 29-35 (e.g., on 5:39: "At ego Legem hanc [sc. the retaliation] non abrogo, sed confirmo" [But I do not abrogate this law but confirm it]); Faber Stapulensis 24 (The ancient [fathers] kept the decalog "ad sensum literae" [to the meaning of the letter], Christ "perficit ad spiritum" [has perfected it to the spirit]). Perhaps Wyclif also belongs in this line, cf. G. Benrath, *Wyclifs Bibelkommentar*, AKG 36 (1966) 114.

is emphasized.[25] The Old Testament commandment is then interpreted on the basis of the New Testament, thus, e.g., the 5th commandment on the basis of Matt. 5:21f.[26] As the motive of this interpretation, the interest to see the superiority of the new covenant not in a new law but in the gospel becomes apparent, e.g., in Calov.[27] Calvin does not want to make Christ a new lawgiver and to release the Old Testament from the guilt of the sin of humans over against God.[28] According to him, the Jews, who have in a fundamental way misunderstood the sense of the law and are scolded accordingly, cannot be exonerated.[29] They have to bear the burden of this theology.

"To hear," in rabbinical terminology, can be understood in the sense of "to receive as tradition."[30] But to interpret it as meaning the tradition in distinction from the Old Testament is improbable because the content of the second and fifth, probably also that of the first, third, and fourth theses is literally or according to sense an Old Testament sentence and not a rabbinical interpretation. With that, the idea of the tradition naturally is not simply excluded; only ἀκούω is not a technical term but "open" (= you have heard, e.g., in the synagogue or at home). It agrees with this that the λέγω of the antithesis is contrasted not with the ἠκούσατε but with the ἐρρέθη of the thesis. But ἐρρέθη both on the basis of the rabbinical exegetical usage[31] and on the basis of Matthean usage is to be interpreted as a divine passive for God's speaking in the Scripture. This is as good as certain for Matthew and probable for earlier layers of the tradition both on the basis of rabbinical usage and because of the content of the theses. Then "those of old" probably are to be understood, in the sense of the rabbinical רִאשׁוֹנִים, as the Sinai generation.[32] Thus, the antithesis formula put the word of Jesus against the Old Testament itself. In this important question, the interpretation of the early church and the Catholic and Free Church interpretations basically remain correct, in contrast to the classical Protestant interpretation.

---

[25]Luther II 93 ("Christ does not abolish the law but imposes more than Moses"); Calvin, *Inst.* 2.8.7 (Christ is "the best interpreter" of the law and not a lawgiver who would have filled out a lack of the Mosaic law); Formula of Concord, Epitome 5,7 (*Book of Concord,* ed. T. Tappert [Philadelphia: Fortress, 1959] 479) (Christ "takes . . . the law into his own hands and explains it spiritually" for the knowledge of sin and of the wrath of God); Bullinger I 56 ("restituit . . . sensum genuinum" [he restored . . . the genuine sense]); Hunnius 99; Calov 19; Chemnitz 440 ("vera legis interpretatio" [the true interpretation of the law]); Bengel 42 ("Mosis legem non excedit sermo Christi" [the word of Christ did not deviate from the law of Moses); Olshausen 219 (only the inward interpretation of the law meets its full sense).

[26]Cf. Luther, *Large Catechism (Book of Concord,* p. 389); Calvin, *Inst.* 2.8.39.

[27]Calov 197.

[28]"As if here a weak point on the law would be mended by Christ!" (I 185).

[29]Calvin I 184: "Immeasurable accumulation of their errors . . . with a godless pleasure and corresponding arrogance throw their lies instead of the Scripture among the people."

[30]Str-B I 253; Bacher, *Terminologie* I 192; II 219,222. שְׁמוּעָה is a technical term for halakic tradition. The aorist ἠκούσατε speaks against the understanding of ἀκούω as "explain, interpret" (cf. Bacher ibid. I 189).

[31]Bacher, *Terminologie* I 6: נֶאֱמַר "is the most frequent form of citation of biblical passages."

[32]Str-B I 253f.; Schlatter 165; examples from Qumran in Lohse* 197.

7. *Origin of the antithesis formula.* The possibility that Jesus himself formulated antitheses is relatively strong. In favor of this belief is, on the one hand, the proximity to Jewish traditional terminology and, on the other hand, the difference from Jewish statements: in the Antitheses the Old Testament is not interpreted but surpassed. Something comparable is perhaps found in Judaism in the understanding of law in the Temple Scroll but this is not in antithetical form.[33] Therefore we assume that the antithetical formulation of the first and second antitheses is due to Jesus. The antitheses formula is then not simply a new variant of rabbinical formulae of interpretation but something new. In my opinion, it is of great significance for the determination of Jesus' self-understanding. Jesus appears here, it seems, with a claim which ''was for Jewish sensitivity an intervention into the divine prerogative.''[34] It is the more surprising that at least some antitheses contain nothing that could not be found also in Jewish tradition. This poses a decisive problem of interpretation.

8. *The Antitheses in the frame of Matthean theology.*[35] Why has Matthew even increased the number of antitheses although he had to protect them in vv. 17-19 against a misunderstanding? They bring out the Christological dimension of the commandments of Jesus[36] and make precise the ''I came'' of v. 17 and the ''I say to you'' of vv. 18,20. They demonstrate how the Son of God fulfills in complete sovereignty God's word of law and prophets in putting his word over against Moses. Matthew had indicated this already through the localizing of Jesus' first proclamation of the gospel ''on the mountain.'' Now 5:17-48 make clear that this does not mean that a second Moses abolished the Torah of the first Moses. Instead, Jesus' proclamation of the will of God is the ''door'' to the Old Testament.

The framing of the series of Antitheses through the first and sixth antitheses makes clear that Matthew sees the center of the Old Testament in love. Love is the fulfillment, not the abolition of law and prophets (5:17). The love commandment does not abolish the ''least commandments'' (5:18f.) but relativizes them from case to case. In this sense, law and prophets ''hang'' on the love commandment (22:40).

2.2.1. First Antithesis: On Killing (5:21-26)

Literature

Dalman, *Jesus* 69-79.
Fridrichsen, A., ''Exegetisches zum Neuen Testament,'' *SO* 13 (1934) 38-46.

---

[33]The Temple Scroll presents itself as a direct revelation of God at Sinai (according to Exodus 34, cf. 11QTemple 2), to that extent comparable to Deuteronomy (and the Book of Jubilees), with formula of authorization (11QTemple 54,6f., cf. Deut. 4:2). The claim of revelation is documented through the use of the first person for the speech of God, increased in comparison with Deuteronomy. However, in the Temple Scroll the I of the revealer remains anonymous, and there is no language form comparable with the Antitheses.

[34]Dalman, *Worte Jesu* I 258, cf. Merklein, *Gottesherrschaft* 256.

[35]Cf. p. 271 on 5:17-19.

[36]This has been pointed out especially by Guelich**, cf., e.g., 260-63.

Guelich, R. A., "Mt 5,22: Its Meaning and Integrity," *ZNW* 64 (1973) 39-52.
Jeremias, J., "ῥακά," *TDNT* VI 973-76.
Köhler, K., "Zu Mt 5,22," *ZNW* 19 (1920) 91-95.
Marguerat, *Jugement* 151-67.
Moule, C. F. D., "The Angry Word: Mt 5,21f," *ET* 81 (1969) 10-13.
Trilling, W., *Christusverkündigung in den synoptischen Evangelien,* pp. 86-107 (Munich: Kösel, 1969).
Weise, M., "Mt 5,21f—ein Zeugnis sakraler Rechtsprechung in der Urgemeinde," *ZNW* 49 (1958) 116-23.
Zeller, *Mahnsprüche* 62-67.
Further literature** at 5:21-48, above pp. 273-274.
Further literature on the Sermon on the Mount at Matthew 5-7, above p. 209-211.

Text

21 You have heard that it was said to those of old:
   "You shall not kill."
   But one who kills is subject to judgment.
22 But I say to you:
   Everyone who is angry with his brother is subject to judgment.
   But whoever says to his brother, "Raka," is subject to the Sanhedrin.
   But whoever says "Fool," is subject to the hell of fire.
23 When you bring your sacrifice to the altar,
   and remember there that your brother has something against you,
24 then leave your sacrifice there before the altar,
   first go, reconcile yourself with your brother,
   and then come and offer your sacrifice.
25 Be well-disposed to your opponent, immediately, while you are on the way with him, lest the opponent turn you over to the judge and the judge to the guard and you be thrown into prison.
26 Amen, I say to you: You will not get out of there until you have paid back the last penny.[1]

Analysis

1. *Structure.* The section is divided into three parts: vv. 21f., 23f. and 25f. Through λέγω (vv. 22, 26) a loose bracket around the whole is created; the key word ἀδελφός (4 times) is central for the two first parts. The change from the second person plural to the second person singular, occasioned especially by literary-critical considerations, is striking.[2] It intensifies the address (9 times σου etc. in vv. 23-26!). Verse 21f. is structured very stringently: The antithesis in v. 22 is varied threefold and intensified through the line from κρίσις by way of συνέδριον to γέεννα τοῦ πυρός. It is connected with the thesis v. 21 in a double manner: through the equivalent punishment, ἔνοχος ἔσται τῇ κρίσει vv. 21/22a and through the introduction ὃς δ' ἄν vv. 21/22b,c.

Literary criticism. Verses 23f. are an independent piece of tradition; differently from vv. 21f. the brother is the angry one. Verses 25f. (with parallel in Luke 12:57-59 = Q) also are an independent unit. It is not certain when these traditional pieces have been merged; probably Matthew is responsible at least for the addition of vv. 25f. since he has

---

[1]Κοδράντης (*quadrans*), as a Latin loan-word also in rabbinic usage = 1/4 of an as = 1/64 of a denarius; smallest Roman coin.

[2]A similar change also in vv. 27-30, 38-42.

created a bracket to the last antithesis under the theme of "love of enemy."

3. *Verses 21f.* pose difficult problems in regard to the history of tradition: (a) Did the thesis and the antithesis originally belong together? Verse 22a is closely connected with v. 21b through ἔνοχος ἔσται τῇ κρίσει.[3] Wrath and (as a result) murder were linked already in Jewish tradition.[4] Thus there is no reason to separate v. 22 from its connection with the thesis.[5] (b) Is v. 22 unified? It is singular that the antithesis v. 22 is divided into three parallel sentences. The first is connectd with v. 20b by the formulation of the punishment, the second and the third by ὃς δ' ἄν. This finding gave rise to numerous attempts at dissections in the history of tradition. Most of the time v. 22b,c are considered as secondary additions.[6] In my opinion, v. 22 is an original unit which cannot be further dissected.[7] The variation of πᾶς δ' to ὃς δ' ἄν was required stylistically.[8] Verse 22b,c furthermore contain a rhetorically extremely effective intensification of the punishment. It seems to me that this unified piece of tradition has its origin with Jesus.

4. *Verses 23-24.* The two verses come from pre-Matthean time since they presuppose the existence of the cult. The relatively dense Mattheisms[9] could point to an oral tradition which the evangelist formulated in a relatively free manner. Our text is not a mere variant of Mark 11:25.[10] The interpretation will give the reason for thinking that it comes from Jesus.

5. Verses 25f. come from Q. Matthew has preserved the wording more faithfully than Luke, who adapts the saying to a Hellenistic financial lawsuit. Probably only τάχυ and ἀμήν, intensifying the parenesis, are due to Matthew. The text is not a crisis parable—the redactional introduction Luke 12:57 probably is responsible for this widespread wrong characterization—but a wisdom admonition.[11] The peculiarly doubled reference to "judgment" is striking. Just for this reason it fits into the proclamation of Jesus.

---

[3]An identical word in thesis and antithesis is necessary in the positive formulation of the antithesis in order to express the intensification, cf. the repeated μοιχεύω vv. 27/28, pace Berger** 153.

[4] Sirach 22:24; *T. Dan* 1:7f.; *T. Sim.* 2:11; *T. Zeb.* 4:11; *Did.* 3:2 (ὁδηγεῖ . . . ἡ ὀργὴ πρὸς τὸν φόνον).

[5]That v. 22 *can* have stood by itself is not yet a reason to assume that it actually was by itself.

[6]E.g., Bultmann, *Tradition* 134; Strecker** 47f.; Merklein, *Gottesherrschaft* 260f.; Beare 146f.; Marguerat, *Jugement* 153. Köhler* considers v. 22b a later gloss (with references to quotations of the church fathers, which, however, often are abbreviated and therefore not fully convincing), similarly Moule*. According to Fridrichsen*, v. 22c is a post-Matthean gloss of a copyist who misread the reference to eternal punishment. According to Schweizer 68f., v. 21b also could be an addition. Neile 62 and Lohmeyer 119 figure that two logia were combined with each other.

[7]Likewise Guelich* 47-49. A law according to which all antitheses must have contained only one member does not exist. But there is a law according to which tradition-historical dissections should be undertaken only if they are really unavoidable!

[8]Verse 22a contains the general case which can be formulated as a participle, v. 22b,c concrete individual cases as examples which are better formulated with the aorist subjunctive. Moreover, λέγω δὲ ὑμῖν ὅτι ὃς ἄν would be very awkward.

[9]Cf. introduction 3.2. The following are Matthean: v. 23: οὖν, προσφέρω, ἐκεῖ, μιμνήσκομαι?; v. 24: ἄφες (aorist imperative), ἐκεῖ, ἔμπροσθεν, ὑπάγω (imperative?) τότε, ἐλθών + verb, προσφέρω. Πρῶτον corresponds to 23:26.

[10]Pace Wellhausen 20.

[11]Correctly Zeller, *Mahnsprüche* 64f. The wisdom parallels and the phrase λέγω σοι, which belongs to the admonition to the individual, speak against an original parable.

Interpretation

5:21

The bipartite thesis v. 21 consists only in its first half of an Old Testament quotation (5th [6th] commandment). Its second half is a free rendering of the order of law as it is stated in Exod. 21:12; Lev. 24:17, cf. Num. 35:16-18. Thus Jesus does not allude to a contemporary halakic regulation which is distinguished from an Old Testament regulation. Κρίσις most likely means, based on the Old Testament, the punishing judgment of the murderer.[12] Ἔνοχος in Greek is a legal term and means "to be subject."

5:22

The tripartite antithesis v. 22 poses some lexical problems: ῥακά is most probably a transcription of the Aramaic word רֵיקָא,[13] a frequently used, relatively harmless[14] word of abuse which had perhaps the meaning of "hollow head." Μωρός is a customary Greek word of abuse, with a disrespectful nuance, but without great intensity.[15] The Aramaic equivalent is perhaps שָׁטְיָא ("insane," "crazy"),[16] also a very frequently used word of abuse. There is no significant difference in meaning, let alone an intensification between the two.

With the punishments, συνέδριον in the New Testament means almost always the Jerusalem Sanhedrin of the 71; our passage too, especially with the article, probably should be understood as this.[17] Γέεννα (the addition of τοῦ πυρός comes probably from Matthew, who intensifies the idea of judgment)[18] rests on the Aramaic גֵּיהִנָּם and is a familiar designation for hell as the eschatological[19] place of punishment.

What is the interrelationship of the three sentences v. 22a,b,c?

---

[12]M. McNamara, *The New Testament and the Palestinian Targum to the Pentateuch*, AnBib 27, 130 points out that in the *Tg. Isa* and in the *Tg. Onq.* on Gen. 9:6 judgment is mentioned.

[13]The vocalisation ῥακα (instead of ρεκα) causes difficulties. Jeremias 974,5-10 explains it plausibly as due to the influence of the Syriac *raqa'* (home of Matthew in Syria!).

[14]John Chrysostom 16,7 = 289 who knows Syria explains ῥακά as a deprecatory expression, used toward servants, such as "you there." Basilius, *Reg. brev.* 51 = *PG* 31,1117: a word of relatively friendly condescension, used toward members of the household.

[15]Examples in BAGD, s.v. μωρός no. 3.

[16]Jeremias* 975,3ff.

[17]Weise* 116-21; Wrege*** 59f. and Dietzfelbinger, *Antithesen*** 17f. interpret συνέδριον, following Ignatius, *Magn.* 6:1; *Phld.* 8:1; *Trall.* 3:1, on the basis of Matt. 18:15-18 and in analogy to the legal setting of the Qumran community, as the "council of the community." The entire usage of the NT speaks against this view. This interpretation is not found until the *Didascalia* 9 (= 18 Achelis/Flemming) and the Syriac translations (which translate *knusta'*).

[18]Cf. introduction 3.2 s.v. The thought that fire belongs to the Gehinnom is widespread among Jews (*1 Enoch* 90:26f.; 4 Ezra 7:36); The formulation γέεννα τοῦ πυρός is impossible in Aramaic (Dalman, *Jesus* 73).

[19]Cf. Str-B IV 1029-43, as purgatory between the eons only since the 2nd century, cf. Str-B IV 1043f.

Since the time of the early church a type of interpretation has been dominant which attempts to find in the series of three offenses and punishments an intensification by stages: "To be angry" refers to inward wrath, hidden in the heart; the two words of abuse designate increasing degrees of insults.[20] In regard to the punishments, the punishment of hell would surpass the preceding words κρίσις and συνέδριον. Again and again, κρίσις was interpreted as a local court[21] and συνέδριον as the highest human court to which is added the divine judgment as the last court. But this interpretation is difficult. Κρίσις designates only very rarely a court[22] and has to be interpreted in v. 22 in the same manner as in v. 21. Between συνέδριον and γέεννα τοῦ πυρός there is not an increase but a qualitative shift from human-earthly to divine-eschatological judgment.

Thus the thesis of a continuing increase in v. 22a,b,c must be discarded. Another determination of the relationship is more likely: v. 22a is a general statement, v. 22b,c are sharpening concretions.[23] They make clear how seriously v. 22a is meant and let "wrath" begin already with the most banal words of abuse. The examples of v. 22b,c are chosen to be as radical and coarse as possible. The only increase is found in the expression γέεννα in v. 22c. But it does not mean that only one specific word of abuse would be punished by hell. Rather the punishments in 22a,b are first related to the earthly area because the Old Testament order of law in v. 21b also gave its judgment on this level. The concluding v. 22c then makes clear that for Jesus wrath is punishable not only on the earthly level. Thus the increase here has not just a rhetorical character.

If this is correct, then any thought of casuistry has to be excluded from the succession of the three sentences. Verse 22b,c is not the expression of a legal practice of the Matthean community, not practiced halakah,[24] but exemplary sharpening of God's demand which was meant unconditionally. Matthew is not located on the trajectory that made this antithesis into a law, a trajectory which, through the introduction of a gradual intensification of offenses and punishments, ended with the classification of most utterances of

---

[20]Examples: Augustine*** 1,9 (24): Feeling enclosed in the heart; uncertain, vehement word; personal insult; Thomas, *Lectura* no. 485: "Ira . . . intus latens" (anger, lying hidden inside) (22a) and "exterius apparens" (appearing outwardly) (22b,c); the latter is divided into a spontaneous "vox indignationis" (word of indignation) and the "affectio irascibilis cum certa malitia" (irate feeling with certain malice). The gradation of the punishments is corresponding: Augustine*** ibid. distinguishes thus: human judgment with possibility of defense, definite sentencing, fire of hell.

[21]Most frequently, the court of 23, provided for capital crimes according to *Sanh.* 1:4, was mentioned (e.g., Klostermann 43; Schlatter 170; Schweizer 72, Strecker** 49).

[22]Among the examples given by BAGD, s.v. κρίσις, only Diodorus *Siculus* 17.80.2 is cogent; ἔνοχος with the dative, according to widespread usage, is to be referred to the punishment (Guelich* 45); just as little can the Aramaic formulations, which probably lie behind it, be referred to courts (Jeremias* 975,11- 30).

[23]The relationship of the three partial sentences of v. 22 to each other is then similar to the relationship of the three original beatitudes to each other: a general statement, two concretions. Cf. Marguerat, *Jugement* 154-60.

[24]This thesis is widespread. Cf. those mentioned above n. 17 and Strecker** 49 (v. 22b,c give "a legal structure . . . to the antithesis"); Hoffmann III*** 182 ("legal scheme of thought") Trilling* 97 ("casuistic sentences of law").

wrath as venial sins.[25] The punishment of hell stands as a perspective behind the earthly punishments and above *all* deeds of wrath.

Only a comparison of this sharpened demand of Jesus with *Jewish ethics* makes clearer in what the "antithesis" to the Torah could consist.

In the Old Testament and in the early Jewish writings, particularly wisdom writings, there is a great deal of discussion about *wrath*. The community rule of Qumran contains exactly defined punishments for outbreaks of wrath against members of the sect which break the foundation of communion (1QS 6,25-27; 7,2-5.8f, cf. 5,25f). Jesus' contemporary Hillel, in contrast to the "wrathful" Shammai, embodied for many the ideal of the "gentle," patient, even-tempered Jew.[26] In rabbinical texts, there are statements which understand wrath in extreme cases as such a grave offense that there is no human but only a divine punishment for it.[27] Public shaming of the neighbor is an offense which cannot be compensated for by good works.[28] In wrath, wisdom leaves the wise so that even Moses forgot the halakah when he was wrathful.[29] In *b. Qidd.* 28a[30] there is handed down a *baraita* in the style of a sentence of law which threatens one who calls his neighbor "slave," "bastard," or "ungodly" with banishment, 40 lashes, and revenge.

Wisdom parallels which contain as "broad" an interpretation of the 5th commandment as that of Jesus are still more important. The sentence of Eliezer ben Hyrcanus is handed down: "The one who hates his neighbor, behold, belongs to those who shed blood."[31] Already Sir. 34:21f. LXX designated the one who withholds the necessities of life from the poor as a murderer. A series comparable to Matt. 5:22 is found also in *2 Enoch* 44:2f.: "He who expresses anger to any person without provocation will reap anger in the great judgment. He who spits on any person's face, insultingly, will reap the same at the LORD's great judgment."[32]

The parallels show that Jesus' demand is nothing new within contemporary Jewish parenesis. They remind us of the fact that in Pharisaic Judaism Torah was not only the basis of a system of law, or "civil order" or "outward duty,"[33] that it comprised not only the realm of the measurable commandments (מְצְוֹת) but was direction of God for the whole person. Precisely in Pharisaic Judaism it was not new that the Torah must be read "within the line of law," i.e., on the basis of the demand of mercy and the love

---

[25]Cf. the examples below n. 49.

[26]Cf. the examples in Str-B I 198f.

[27]*TBQam.* 9,31 (366) = Str-B I 278 (for shaming actions in anger); *b. Yoma* 9b = ibid. (unfounded hatred weighs just as heavily as the three basic sins of idolatry, immorality, and shedding of blood).

[28]*'Abot* 3:11: Whoever publicly shames the neighbor has no share in the future world, even with knowledge of the Torah and good works; cf. also *b. B. Mess.* 58b = Str-B I 282; *b. Hal.* 18a = ibid.

[29]*b. Pesah.* 66b = Str-B I, 277.

[30]Str-B I 280. In comparison with Matt. 5:22, the words of abuse are coarser and the punishments are adapted to the offense.

[31]*Derek Erez* 10 = Str-B I 282.

[32] Longer recension; *The Old Testament Pseudepigrapha*, ed. J. H. Charlesworth (Garden City: Doubleday, 1983), I 170.

[33]Calvin I 185.

commandment,[34] and that it was "entrusted to the heart."[35] Torah as demand of law and Torah as the will of God which claims the whole person do not exclude but include each other in Judaism. Christians must not give in to the temptation to construct a picture of Judaism which makes light of the whole realm of parenesis that is influenced by wisdom as "legally not obligatory" and to push it to the margin only in order to safeguard the originality of Jesus.[36] Thus, as far as the content is concerned, the first antithesis is by no means original. Jesus only formulates more pointedly and arrestingly than Jewish parenesis. Most of all he wraps his admonition in the form of a sentence of law.[37] Thus he emphasizes its absolutely obligatory character. But this does not yet make it a real antithesis to Judaism and to the Old Testament. Is the newness in Jesus' admonition only in its antithetical dress? But what does this say if Jesus, in opposition to the Torah, by virtue of his special authority as messenger of the kingdom of God proclaims something which was generally known? In that case there is a break between the pathos of the antithesis formula and the self-evident nature of the antithesis content.

It seems to me one has to begin with the *intimate connection* in Judaism of demand of law and parenesis. Jesus, by *opposing antithetically* the parenesis—in the obligatory form of "sentences of law"—to the prevailing order of law, creates newness. While in Judaism the nation's order of law given by God and the more demanding parenesis to the individual supplement each other harmoniously, Jesus sets them in opposition to each other. The Old Testament order of law is not radical enough and does not yet fully correspond to the will of God; but the radically formulated wisdom admonition is God's proper will. This devaluation of law fits into the proclamation of Jesus. Jesus was hardly interested in valid and practicable orders of law for his society, probably because he was concerned with the gathering of the *eschatological* people of Israel in light of the inbreaking of the kingdom of God and the proclamation of the divine will corresponding to the kingdom of God. Although it is not said in the text, I think that one can understand the *antithetical* relationship of (traditional) law of God and (traditional) parenesis which appears

---

[34]Montefiore, *Gospels* II 499, correctly points to the rabbinical principle לְפָנִים מִשּׁוּרַת הַדִּין. The expression probably comes from Eleazar from Modaim (Mek. Exod. 18.20), c. 100, and refers as a rule to works of love which "cannot be sued for." That "remaining within the line of law" does not simply mean an arbitrary possibility is shown by the important saying of R. Yohanan *b. B. Mess.* 30b = Str-B I 345: Jerusalem has been destroyed because they judged according to the law of the Torah and did not remain within its line of law.

[35]Sifra Lev. 19.14 (Qedoshim 2); *b. B. Mes.* 58b: Of various actions which cannot be sued for, it is said, "Of the things which are entrusted to the heart, it says: you shall be afraid of your God." On the whole cf. Urbach, *Sages* I 330-32.

[36]An example: For Judaism it is valid: "A statute of law which fences in life from all sides, and yet it applies: as many fence boards, as many fence gaps." Then Jesus comes and "liberates the will of God from its petrification in tables of stone, and reaches for the heart of man" (Bornkamm, *Jesus of Nazareth* 105).

[37]Against K. Berger, "Zu den sogenannten Sätzen heiligen Rechts," *NTS* 17 (1970/71) 25-27, the origin of these sentences does not lie in wisdom literature (B. refers to *T. Levi* 13:9 as an example) but in the Old Testament language of law as is suggested already by the protasis 21b and as is shown by many examples (e.g. Exod. 31:14f.; 35:2; Lev. 6:11,20; 7:25; 11:31; 15:21; 21;21). The protasis deals with a *specific* action, the apodosis with a penalty.

in the Antitheses only in light of the kingdom of God breaking into the world.[38]

History of influence

The history of influence of the first antithesis is largely a history of mitigating its harshness.

     a. Notably the Western text tradition since Irenaeus *limits the applicability of the antithesis to unjustified wrath*. Since the variant εἰκῇ[39] became the *textus receptus*,[40] the exegesis deals with the question of defining justified wrath. Such tendencies were strengthened by Aristotelian philosophy which, in contrast with the Stoa,[41] did not condemn wrath as such as long as it occurred for the right thing and in right measure.[42] Thus there also is such a thing as justifiable wrath, even useful and necessary wrath.[43]
     b. This included *religiously motivated wrath*, "holy hatred."[44] Thus the attempt was made to understand why Jesus despite his antithesis scolds his Jewish opponents as "fools and blind" (Matt. 23:17) and Paul excoriates the Galatians as "foolish" (Gal. 3:1). One must distinguish between wrath against sin and that against sinners.[45] It is correct that this side of the problem is not considered by the first antithesis. Nevertheless, the widespread sentiment that the word of abuse "fool," "where it proceeds from a good caring heart . . . [is] no sin,"[46] *may* prove itself to be an avoidance of its demand.
     c. Most of all, the *"wrath" of the officebearer of the state* remained excluded. The problem was seen long before the Reformation, e.g., if the *Opus imperfectum* maintains in convincing simplicity that without wrath there is "neither teaching . . . nor court sentencing" nor a restriction of crimes. Result: "Iracundia quae cum causa est, non iracundia est, sed iudicium" (Wrath which is with cause is not wrath but judgment).[47] Naturally, the Reformers emphasize this in their distinction of the two kingdoms: "If

---

[38]Cf. Goppelt*** 40: "The antithesis, precisely because God's new world comes in secret . . . has salvation historical, eschatological significance."

[39]D W it sy co 𝔐.

[40]Jerome on the passage rejects the gloss εἰκῇ which since that time is not uncontroversial in the Western tradition. The Reformers strike it; on the other hand Grotius I 116: "merito hoc additum" (this is added deservedly).

[41]Representative example: Seneca, *De ira* (wrath is completely rejected because it is opposed to *ratio* [reason]).

[42]Representative example: Aristotle, *Eth. Nic.* 4.11. The philosophical theses have a strong effect, particularly through the little writing by Lactantius on the wrath of God. Lactantius' own thesis: "Wrath is . . . a demand of reason; for it makes an end to violations of duty . . ." (17 = BKV I/36 110).

[43]John Chrysostom 16.7 = 288 refers to the example of Paul in Corinth and Galatia. Basilius, *Or.* 8.6f. = BKV I/47 285-58, refers to Old Testament zealous persons from Moses to Elijah in order to call to wrath against Satan, not against the brother or sister; Thomas, *STh* 2/II qu 158 art 1, formulates: "Si autem aliquis irascatur secundum rationem rectam, tunc irasci est laudabile" (But if someone becomes angry according to a right reason, then it is praiseworthy to become angry).

[44]Ragaz*** 55.

[45]Luther, WA 32***, 362: "It is the dear wrath which does not allow evil to anyone, which is friendly to the person but hostile to sin."

[46]Luther, WA 32, 364.

[47]11 = 690.

father, mother, judge and preacher would keep silent and their hand relaxed and would not fend off or steer away evil, then government and Christianity and everything good would fall to pieces because of the evil of the world. Therefore it says here: Enemy of the thing and friend of the person.''[48]

d. The interpretation of the three little sentences of v. 22 as stages of offenses and punishment was cause for another kind of mitigation: wrath which remains hidden in the heart or shows itself only in spontaneous words of abuse *without malicious intention* is not so great an offense and is not punished so harshly. The *distinction between venial sins and mortal sins* could commence from this series of steps and reduce the mortal sin to the more serious cases of wrath as described in v. 22c.[49] Or, with the interpretation of Zwingli: Because Jesus knew that complete freedom from wrath is impossible, he has added v. 22b,c, which attempts to assure that one at least does not release the wrath even if one cannot banish it from the heart.[50] Not too far removed from this, as far as the content is concerned, is the apostrophized expression of Luther: "to forgive, but not forget.''[51]

It is easy to take an exegetical position on the interpretations. One has to reject any interpretation which does not take v. 22 literally as a serious demand which is valid for all. Its exemplary character in v. 22b,c also is missed if it is understood in the sense of a moderation. The distinction between justifiable and unjustifiable wrath does not recommend itself at all, as Matthew lets us see through the examples in vv. 23f. and 25f., in which it is totally missing. At best one might ask whether the restricting of freedom from wrath to the personal and interpersonal realm can be defended on the basis of the wisdom background of the parenesis. But since in Jesus precisely this is new, that this parenesis, which is influenced by wisdom, is directed antithetically against the existing law of God of the old eon, one has to be skeptical also about this view. Even assertions such as that our antithesis basically implies a rejection of capital punishment and of war[52] cannot simply be discarded if they are formulated on the basis of the kingdom of God.

A *systematic* position is much more difficult. What follows from the fact that the kingdom of God, in whose light Jesus formulated his antithesis and in whose anticipation he required of his listeners absolute humaneness, has not appeared? Its anticipation has paled in the meantime.

In this world, are not the attempts at mitigation, as seen in the history of interpretation, something very human? "You shall not only not kill, you shall not *want* to kill. You shall not permit in you the impulse which, if you were to follow it, would

---

[48]Luther, WA 32***, 364f.; Large Catechism, *Book of Concord*, p. 389; *Hauspostille* 1544 = WA 52,411 and often, but also Zwingli 224 ("non . . . de iudice, . . . sed de privato" [not . . . of the judge, . . . but of the private individual]).

[49]Instructive is, e.g., Thomas, *STh* 2/II qu 158 art 3 (utrum omnis ira sit peccatum mortale [whether all anger is a mortal sin]), where Thomas must argue against Matt. 5:22 and comes to the conclusion that Jesus has spoken only of a wrath which "appetit proximi occisionem" (strives for the killing of the neighbor).

[50]225.

[51]WA 32***, 361.

[52]Ragaz*** 55.

kill.''[53] This demand of the first antithesis, taken by itself, amounts to an absolute self-control of the person, involving the innermost impulses, through his or her superego. Is it possible and helpful, or is it expecting immensely too much? Does grace consist perhaps in not demanding so much as was attempted in the history of interpretation? Zwingli has interrupted his interpretation of the Antitheses, which he understood as an expression of divine justice, again and again by the lapidary sentence ''as we do not keep it (for we are briefly not without temptation)''[54] and then introduced the minimal commandment of the ''custodian''[55] which, with its ''death for death, life for life, eye for eye, . . . wound for wound,'' indeed does not agree with divine righteousness but at least prevents the worst that could happen. Is then the righteousness of the Old Testament, which is so much more *humane*, an inkling of grace?

The question is concentrated on the issue of what for Matthew—and also for us—is taking the place of the anticipation of the kingdom of God which would support the human being. The Matthean answer is double: It is the story of Jesus the Son of God whom his Father has accompanied on the way through obedience until the resurrection. And it is the community which takes this journey after him and experiences that the story of the Son of God is a story of God with the community. Only in the midst of the experience of the presence of the living Lord is a radical demand helpful. Thus it is the presupposition of the Matthean Antitheses that their demands are made by the one who is with his community until the end of the world.

On this basis, another type of moderation of the demands, not yet discussed, moves closer to Matthew than all others, namely, their *limitation to the community*. The prohibition of wrath refers to the Christian brother or sister, ''in whom Christ lives.''[56] Yes, wrath against fellow-Christians can even be declared as the sin against the Holy Spirit.[57]

However, for Matthew the reference to the community does not mean a limitation of its validity. But the key word ἀδελφός shows that he is thinking of the community. The community is for him the place which makes radical obedience toward the will of the Father possible. The obedience itself aims beyond its borders. Matthew has indicated this already in 5:16 where he spoke of the missionary dimension of Christian obedience. He will then burst open the boundaries of the community especially in the last antithesis, which takes up again the theme of the first one.

---

[53]C. F. v. Weizsäcker, ''Bergpredigt, Altes Testament und modernes Bewusstsein,'' in *Der Garten des Menschlichen* (Munich: Hansen, 1978; pocket book edition Frankfurt 1980), 335 (Engl. trans. *The Ambivalence of Progress*, New York: Paragon, 1988).

[54]Zwingli, ''Von göttlicher und menschlicher Gerechtigkeit,'' in *Hauptschriften* ed. R. Pfister, (Zurich 1942), 57.

[55]Ibid. He is thinking of the ''pedagogue'' of Gal. 3:24.

[56]*Didascalia* 9 = 48 Achelis-Flemming; similarly Apollinaris of Laodicea, fragment 20 = Reuss 7; Theodore of Heraclea, fragment 27 = ibid. 64.

[57]Hilarius 937.

5:23–24

The two following verses interpret our antithesis. They formulate positively what the antithesis itself formulated negatively: Now it is no longer just the issue of avoiding words that kill but positively of reconciliation, i.e., of love for the brother or sister. There has been a preference for understanding these verses as an example of the way Matthew made the demands of the first antithesis concrete in a realistic way. The opposite is true. A comparison with Jewish parallels shows that our example is by no means realistic.

One should not refer to the rabbinical regulations about the interruption of the guilt sacrifice in cases where the return of stolen goods has not yet taken place (*b. B. Qam.* 9.12; Tos. *Pes.* 3.1)[58] as the *closest Jewish background*, for there the issue is the correct carrying out of the sacrifice. Neither do the statements of Philo about self-examination prior to the sacrifice (*Spec. Leg.*) offer material parallels. Important are rather the statements concerning the unity of ethics and cult, made particularly in wisdom tradition: Sacrifices by godless people are an abomination to God; the one who shows mercy offers sacrifices (Prov. 15:8; 21:3,27; Sir. 31[34]:21-24; 35:1-3; etc.).[59] In these texts also, the cult takes second place to ethics, without being abrogated. In rabbinic Judaism, such thinking found a place, e.g., in the familiar principle that the Day of Atonement alone does not expiate offenses against fellow humans (*Yoma* 8:9).[60] Indeed, for Matthew prophetic traditions, which he himself formulates with Hos. 6:6, are important.

With such a background our verses are at the same time understandable and strange. Their sharp point is unusual: Whether the brother or sister is angry justly or unjustly does not play a role. It may have sounded especially harsh to Galileans, for whom the command to be reconciled with the brother or sister prior to sacrifice would, as a rule, have meant a return journey of several days to Galilee. As often with Jesus, so we have here a categorical, hyperbolically sharpened exemplary demand which aims at a new basic attitude to the fellow human and, as such, enjoins *more* than its literal fulfillment. It is valid for Jesus and for Matthew that the cultic law is not abrogated by the command of reconciliation; but the πρῶτον, which appears again in 23:26, applies to reconciliation.

The *interpretation by the church* furnishes *possibilities of application.* The turning to the neighbor is a criterion and presupposition for the prayer of thanksgiving[61] and for the eucharist.[62] Luther extends it to politics: Sacrifice without reconciliation is ''just as if someone has started war and murder and shed much blood and then gives a

---

[58]J. Jeremias informs us about this, '' 'Lass allda deine Gabe' (Mt 5,23f),'' in idem, *Abba* 104-06.

[59]Cf. G. v. Rad, *Wisdom in Israel* (Nashville: Abingdon, 1972), 186-89.

[60]This and other passages in Str-B I 287f.

[61]E.g., *Didascalia* 11 - 69 Achelis-Flemming; Strabo on v. 23.

[62]E.g., John Chrysostom 16.9 = 294. Both ideas go back to *Did.* 14:1f.: Nobody shall participate in the confession of sins and the eucharist of the community who has not been reconciled with the neighbor. An early effect of our text, which perhaps already mirrors the practice of the Matthean community.

thousand guilder for it for soul masses.''[63] Augustine formulates comprehensively: "All our thinking and intending must agree with what we confess with the mouth.''[64]

5:25–26

The last piece of tradition, concerning reconciliation with the trial opponent before the court session, lets an exhortation that begins in everyday life take a sudden and surprising turn which lets the last judgment shine through behind the trial situation. In the foreground, this text is really pragmatic and finds its parallels in similar "counsels of expediency" in the wisdom tradition.[65] Guards (court officers, as administrators of torture?)[66] and trials were just as familiar to the community of Matthew living in Syria as the Greek common word εὐνόω. But the depth dimension is decisive. It becomes tangible in the threatening description of the trial. In Jewish law imprisonment for debt was unknown;[67] so it is the situation of the terror of a Gentile trial where the poor debtor is kept in prison until the last penny is paid. This threatening situation points to the metaphorical depth level: Matthew indicates it through his favorite word ἀμήν, which points almost always to an eschatological statement concerning the final judgment,[68] and through the word λέγω, which is used similarly in many passages.[69] Behind the trial there becomes visible the final judgment, in which there is no grace. Thus the "everyday advice" receives an eschatological dimension, namely, that which, according to the Gospel of Matthew, hovers over all of daily life, the final judgment. Here one of the two concerns which Matthew had with this text becomes visible: the perspective—almost always threatening—of the final judgment under which he puts the actions commanded by Jesus.[70] The other concern lies in the catchword ἀντίδικος, which opens a view ahead to the last antithesis and secures the interpretation of the whole first antithesis in the sense of the comprehensive love which includes even enemies.

2.2.2. Second Antithesis: On Adultery (5:27-30)

Literature

Haacker, K., "Der Rechtssatz Jesu zum Thema Ehebruch (Mt 55,28)," *BZ* NF 21 (1977) 113-16.

---

[63]WA 32***, 366.

[64]Augustine***1,10 (27).

[65]Cf. Prov. 6:1-5; 25:7f.; Sir. 18:19f. (with transparence of everyday advice for the relationship to God similar to Matt. 5:25f.).

[66]Josephus, *Ant.* 4.214; 16.232 (for tortures); Greek Diodorus Siculus, 15.6,1f.; 17.30.4; Appian, *Bell. Civ.* 1.31 §138.

[67]On the problem of such imprisonment cf. Deissmann, *Light from the Ancient East* 229-31; Jeremias, *Parables* 180.

[68]Exceptions in Matthew only 8:10; 13:17; 17:20; 18:13,18f.; 21:21; 26:13,21,34.

[69]Λέγω in connection with a statement about the final judgment or reward: 5:20; 6:2,5,16; 8:11; 10:15,42; 11:22,24; 12:36; 19:23,28; 21:43; etc.

[70]The closest parallel is 18:35; but cf. also 7:26f.

Hommel, H., "Herrenworte im Lichte sokratischer Überlieferung," *ZNW* 57 (1966) 1-23.

Niederwimmer, K., *Askese und Mysterium*, FRLANT 113, pp. 24-33 (Göttingen: Vandenhoeck & Ruprecht, 1975).

Schattenmann, J., "Jesus und Pythagoras," *Kairos* 21 (1979) 215-220.

Stauffer, *Botschaft* 82-85.

Further literature** cf. at Matt. 5:21-48 above pp. 273-274. Literature *** on the Sermon on the Mount at Matt. 5-7 above pp. 209-211.

Text

27 You have heard that it was said:
"You shall not commit adultery."
28 But I say to you:
Everyone who looks at a woman with lustful intention
has already committed adultery with her in his heart.
29 If your right eye seduces you,
tear it out and throw it from you;
for it is better for you that one of your members perish
and your whole body not be thrown into hell.
30 And if your right hand seduces you,
cut it off and throw it from you;
for it is better for you that one of your members perish
and your whole body not go to hell.[1]

Analysis

1. *Structure.* The second antithesis is structured similarly to the first one. After the true antithesis (vv. 27f.) an addition follows (vv. 29f.) with frequent address in the second person singular (12 times σου, etc., in vv. 29f.). The introductory phrase and the thesis itself are shorter in comparison with v. 21. Again thesis and antithesis are related linguistically to each other. This time the connection is done with the aid of the punishable fact of committed adultery (μοιχεύω vv. 27/28). Through this word-stem the third antithesis also is connected with the second one.

2. *Redaction and prehistory of vv. 27f.* There are few Matthean additions discernible.[2] As in vv. 21f. the antithesis probably cannot be further dissected. In addition to the close connection between thesis and antithesis, given through μοιχεύω, there is the fact that already in Judaism the 6th commandment and the prohibition to desire the wife of the neighbor (10th commandment) had come together;[3] in regard to the history of tradition the antithesis is built on a given tradition of interpretation and turns it antithetically. Content deliberations speak in favor of attributing it to Jesus.

3. *Redaction and prehistory of vv. 29f.* The verses have a parallel in Mark 9:43,45,47 (parallel to Matt. 18:8f.). They are found twice in Matthew. This and certain peculiarities of the two Matthean text-forms show that the evangelist took over our

---

[1] Verse 30 is missing in D et al. Did they not see a connection between "hand" and adultery?

[2] Does perhaps ἐν τῇ καρδίᾳ αὐτοῦ come from Matthew (Strecker** 51)? But 13:19 (redaction) is hardly comparable.

[3] Cf. Berger, *Gesetzesauslegung* I 327, 346.

version of the sayings probably not from Mark but from elsewhere, perhaps from Q.[4] Here also, Matthew has chosen his special source as the foundational text and supplemented it through Q material. The "bridge" between the antithesis and the addition was here the "eye" in v. 28, which is understood as the instrument of seduction. The reconstruction of the wording of Q is very difficult: Luke has omitted the logion completely; perhaps it was unpleasantly radical for him. Probably the imperatives βάλε ἀπὸ σοῦ and ἔξελε, the introduction with εἰ, and the construction with συμφέρει . . . σοι ἵνα . . . καὶ μή belong to the particularities of the Q version in comparison with Mark.[5] Redactional additions can at most be conjectured.[6] The Semitic language background, the double tradition, and the fact that Jesus often has formed sayings in a similarly hyperbolic way speak for the origin of the logion with Jesus.

History of influence

The history of interpretation shows a peculiar ambivalence between (a) a tendency to broaden the text in dualistic distaste for sexuality and (b) another tendency to ameliorate this antithesis also in order to be able to live with it.

a. The *intensification and broadening* may start in different places:

1. γυνή was understood not as wife but as *woman* in general. The Vulgate translates with *mulier* (woman) and not with *uxor* (wife). As a consequence, the prohibition of the lustful look was referred not only to the wives of others but also to other women, virgins,[7] even to one's own wife.[8] Μοιχεία gains a broader meaning and means sexual immorality as such,[9] in actuality simply intercourse.

2. The interpretation concentrates on the verb ἐπιθυμέω, which is understood in the sense of *concupiscence* as the root of all sin. Thus the antithesis can indicate further connections: It ultimately prohibits any "inordinate" desire.[10] The medieval interpretation sometimes comes close to dualism: Thus the *Opus imperfectum* distinguishes between the *concupiscentiae carnis* (desires of the flesh) and the *concupiscentiae animae* (desires of the soul); the former are principally reprehensible.[11]

---

[4]It is difficult to find a place for this saying in Q since Luke does not have a parallel. Was it behind Luke 17:2, i.e., in a context similar to Mark 9:42-50, since Matthew in 18:6f. is also influenced by Luke 17:1f?

[5]The construction with the dative and ἵνα is Semitic in comparison with the Markan construction (accusative with infinitive) (Beyer, *Syntax* 80f.).

[6]Possibly redactional are the following: ἀπόλλυσθαι, εἰς . . . τούτων, δεξιός, cf. introduction 3.2. Yet the finding is nowhere very clear.

[7]E.g., Euthymius Zigabenus 216 (married, divorced woman, or virgin); Lapide 140; Beza 22; Calov 206. Jerome, *Ep.* 22.5 = *PL* 22,397 applies the passage to the virgin Eustochium. The humanists, Erasmus, *Paraphrasis* 31BC, and Grotius I 135 decidedly limit the antithesis to the wife.

[8]The most famous example is L. Tolstoy, *The Kreutzer Sonata* (New York: Ogilvie, 1890), toward the end of the 11th chapter; but also already Tertullian, *Cast.* 9 = BKV I/7 340f. states with revulsion that the same act makes a woman a wife and an adulteress.

[9]Paschasius Radbertus 248; Jansen 44; Barth, *CD* III/4,233 ("all thinking and speaking, action and conduct" of man and woman "which is inconsistent with and destructive of marriage").

[10]Augustine*** 1.12 (36). Luther's Large Catechism also interprets the 6th commandment as referring to all unchastity (T. Tappert, ed., *Book of Concord* [Philadelphia: Fortress, 1969], 342-95), with the reasoning that with the obligatory and early marriage in Judaism adultery was practically the only form of unchastity.

[11]*Opus imperfectum* 12 = 694.

A broad and ancient interpretative tradition introduces instead of ἐπιθυμία the word ἡδονή: pleasure is the truly reprehensible element which Jesus wants to oppose.[12] Thus the antithesis comes into the undertow of tendencies hostile to pleasure and marriage.[13] Actually it can lead to the avoidance of dealing with women as far as possible.[14]

3. It is a broadening of a different kind if, especially in the interpretive tradition coming from Chrysostom, not only men but evidently also *women* are considered as addressed.[15] To speak here of an intensification is perhaps incorrect, because the greater freedom of the woman in the cities of late antiquity in comparison with the rural Jewish Palestine created a new situation.

b. The counter-tendencies are circumscribed insufficiently with the key word "weakening." Two elements are important for it, namely, primarily in the tradition of the early, medieval, and Catholic church the conviction that sin has not destroyed completely the human nature created by God, and in the interpretation of the Reformation the high evaluation of marriage together with the disinclination against monkish and priestly asceticism.

1. The definition of πρὸς τὸ ἐπιθυμῆσαι αὐτήν has played an essential role in the interpretation. Πρός was understood as a rule as purposive and not as consecutive.[16] Thus the *reprehensible intention* has to be combined with the looking at a woman in order for it to be sin. Jerome and the medieval tradition distinguish between προπάθεια and πάθος, the former being an "animi subitus affectus . . . amoris" (the soul's sudden feeling . . . of love), the latter "deliberatio ex consensu" (deliberation by consensus).[17] Thus in the interpretation, concepts like "finis" (end, purpose), "deliberatio" (deliberation), "consensus" (consensus), etc., play a great role.[18] After the Council of Trent, concupiscence against which the baptized struggles with God's help is not a mortal sin, and Luther also lets it "stand: 'If an evil thought is involuntary, it is not a mortal sin.' "[19]

The Reformers are concerned for the *protection of marriage*. Married love is the best way of obedience vis-à-vis the demand of Jesus: "It would be a real art and strong safeguard against all this . . . if everyone learned to look at his (or her) spouse correctly,

---

[12]Origen, *Hom. in Lev* 6:3 = *PG* 12,470; Gregory of Nyssa, *Virg.* 21 (against all pleasure and sense perception); Basilius, in Cramer I 38. Bonhoeffer*** 108 still can say that Jesus liberates "the marriage from . . . pleasure" which he understands as "selfish" and "evil" and contrasts with the "service of love" in discipleship.

[13]Already Tertullian, *Cast.* 9 (cf. above n. 8) states that the text is directed not only against the second marriage but really against marriage as such.

[14]Francis of Assisi, *Frühere Regel* no. 12 (H. U. v. Balthasar, *Die grossen Ordensregeln* [Einsiedeln: Johannes, 1980], 299f.): One should not counsel with women, nor eat with them out of one dish, nor accept obedience from them. That is mindful of the practice of several rabbis, cf. below, p. 295.

[15]John Chrysostom 17.2 = 307; cf. Clement of Alexandria, *Paed.* 3.70.1f. = BKV II/8 1966. But μοιχεύειν in the active is used almost exclusively of the man.

[16]Consecutive understanding of πρός in Calvin (?) I 190; Calov 207; Paulus I 524.

[17]Jerome 30f.; Strabo 94 (quotation); Thomas, *Lectura* no. 506.

[18]Augustine*** 1.12 (33); *Opus imperfectum* 12 = 694.

[19]*Sessio* 5,5 (= Denzinger no. 792); Luther, WA 32*** 373 = *LW* 21, 85. "I cannot keep a bird from flying over my head. But I can certainly keep it from nesting in my hair or from biting my nose off" (ibid.).

according to God's word, which is the dearest treasure and the loveliest ornament you can find in a man or a woman.''[20] Luther is placed in confrontation on two fronts: On the one hand he emphasizes that we must not run from each other but live together part of which also is marrying;[21] he fights against monkish perfection. On the other hand he fights against the corruption of morals, especially "in Italy."[22] The emphasis on marriage has been preserved in post-Reformation exegesis and becomes visible today also in significant Catholic statements.[23]

The history of interpretation makes clear how and how strongly we are here influenced by our tradition—and sometimes also by the attempt of an emancipation from it. How does the text confront the tradition?

Interpretation

5:27–28

Γυνή means the wife and not any woman. This follows from the area of validity of the 6th (7th) commandment and the literal meaning of μοιχεύω, which means "to commit adultery" and not simply "to act immorally." Πρός with infinitive designates according to Matthean usage (6:1; 23:5; 26:12 redactional, 13:30 traditional) the intention and not the result. On this basis, caution is indicated toward all intensifying and broadening interpretations. It deals with intentional looking with the aim of breaking the marriage of another man.[24]

Πρός τὸ ἐπιθυμῆσαι αὐτήν is difficult, because desiring really can only be the result of an (evaluating) look but not its intention. Therefore Haacker proposes a different translation: "in order that she (i.e., the woman = αὐτήν) desires," i.e., "in order to stimulate lust in her."[25] The Matthean usage of πρός with infinitive (never accusative with infinitive) and the already Jewish combination of the 6th with the 10th commandment speak against this view.[26] Matthew probably wanted to avoid an unintentional "seeing" and speak of an intentional "looking," i.e., of a human *act*. Therefore he adds to βλέπων the explicit purposive additional phrase.[27]

What is the meaning of the antithetical contrast? The Jewish *judiciary order* had made more difficult the possibilities of sentencing somebody as

---

[20]Luther, WA 32***, 372 = *LW* 21, 87.

[21]WA 32***, 371.

[22]WA 32***, 370 = *LW* 21, 85.

[23]E.g., Pius XI, Denzinger no. 2231.

[24]The Jewish husband cannot break his own marriage but only that of another Jew, cf. on vv. 31f.

[25]A further argument of Haacker* is the transitive from of ἐπιθυμέω. Indeed the genitive is more common, but the accusative also is used, e.g., Exod. 20:17; Deut. 5:21.

[26]Cf. above n. 3.

[27]Βλέπω may mean "to see" and "to look"; the meaning becomes clear only in those (sparse) manuscripts which put ἐμβλέπω, instead of βλέπω.

adulterer to death by shifting the burden of proof in favor of the accused.[28] Since Jesus is not concerned with the establishing of a different judiciary order, one must compare in the first place the parenetic interpretations of the 6th commandment in Jewish tradition. Here one detects that Jesus has expressed something with his antithesis which would have found support not only in the entire ancient world,[29] but especially in Judaism of the time.[30]

Particularly in Hellenistic Judaism, under the influence of the four Stoic πάθη lust often became the reason for all sin.[31] The connection of the eyes with lust and immorality is taken for granted in antiquity[32] and in Judaism, particularly under the influence of wisdom literature.[33] It can be documented in rabbinical Judaism that sin in thought is still worse than committed sin.[34] Statements as *T. Benj.* 8:2 come perhaps close to our antithesis: "For the person with a mind that is pure with love does not look on a woman for the purpose of having sexual relations;" *b.Hal.* 1: "Whoever looks at a woman with (lustful) intention is counted as one who sleeps with her;"[35] Lev.R. 23 (122b): "Even the one who commits adultery with his eyes is called an adulterer."[36] Such passages are not unique; in any case they are more frequent than parallels to the first antithesis.

Christian interpretation should not attempt to assert at any price the originality of the demand of Jesus.[37] Taken by itself it is not original. It also does not protect the rights of the woman but at most those of the other husband whose marriage is already broken by the lustful look.[38] It fits into the intensified

---

[28]Cf. Str-B I 297f.

[29]Hellenistic parallels in Hommel* 5. Probably Epictetus, *Diss.* 2.18.15 (text in Klostermann on the passage) and Epictetus, *Diss.* 4.9.3 come closest.

[30]Material in Str-B I 298-301; Fiebig*** 51-55; Moore, *Judaism* II 167-72. Montefiore, *Gospels* II 506 summarizes: "No simple Rabbinic Jew . . . would find in it (i.e. in vv. 27f.) anything startling except the implication that there was any opposition between the old Law and the new."

[31]Philo, *Op. Mund.* 152 (πόθος); *Omn. Prob. Lib.* 159; *Spec. Leg.* 4.84; *Decal.* 142; *Vit. Ad.* 19; Rom. 7:7; James 1:15; Berger, *Gesetzesauslegung* I 346f. In the Rabbinate, the evil impulse corresponds to lust.

[32]E.g., *Prop.* 2.15.12.

[33]Sirach 16:9,11; *Pss. Sol.* 4:4f.; *T. Iss.* 7:2 (whoring by lifting the eyes); *Jub.* 20:4 (whoring with eyes and hearts); 1QS 1.6 (eyes of immorality). Further passages in Niederwimmer 27 n. 75. Cf. 1 John 2:16f.; 2 Peter 2:14.

[34]*b. Yoma* 29a = Str-B III 373 (thinking of sin is worse than sin itself); against this *b. Qidd.* 40a (God does not count evil thoughts).

[35]Str-B I 299, similarly Pesiq.R. 24 = 124b.

[36]Str-B ibid.

[37]Loymeyer 128: In Judaism such statements are "scattered, . . . a boast of specially pious people"; Gaechter 178: No Jewish teacher "thought" in such terms "of the 6th commandment" (which is wrong!); Strecker** 52: Overcoming of Pharisaic hypocrisy between outside and inside. One also should not, out of consternation that Jesus perhaps once was not creative, deny that he spoke this antithesis (Stauffer, *Botschaft* 82-85; Percy, *Botschaft* 143f.).

[38]Merklein, *Gottesherrschaft* 264.

interpretation of the 6th commandment which we can observe in connection with the concept of purity in Judaism of the time.

Is there something special in this demand of Jesus? The context of Jesus' own behavior could be special: Jesus obviously had a very relaxed relationship to women who were at a disadvantage according to the Israelite law of God. His freedom even to turn to prostitutes, the—probable—discipleship of women, and the—undisputed—support of the circle of Jesus by them testify to it.

The behavior which is reported of many rabbis is different: One should beware of unnecessary contact with women; this results from the intensified interpretation of the 6th commandment. One should not speak with a woman unnecessarily, not even with one's own (*'Abot* 1:5). On the street one should not walk behind a woman, not greet her and not be served by a woman,[39] not be alone with another woman,[40] for already the voice and the hair of a woman are immoral.[41] Of course, one should not look at a woman, not even at an unmarried one,[42] for one is in danger by doing so. These Jewish statements belong to a tendency which was intensifying at the time, to keep women, out of public life, even the religious life.[43] Without question, Jesus is *not* to be counted in this tendency, despite ascetic inclinations.[44]

Because Jesus did not avoid contacts with women, as many rabbis did for religious reasons, his demand means something different from that of the rabbis. However, what this difference was must unfortunately remain uncertain. Was Jesus concerned for the protection of the disadvantaged woman? Was he concerned to liberate her and to "integrate" her through an open, common life which was characterized neither by sexual desire nor by fear of it?[45] Opposed is the thesis that Jesus was primarily concerned about the sanctity of marriage. It seems to me that the prohibition of divorce which Matthew adds immediately and the formulation of the text as an antithesis to the 6th commandment of the decalogue point in this direction. These two need not exclude each other.

The antithetical form is to be interpreted as in vv. 21f.: On the basis of the kingdom of God, the integrity of the woman and/or the sanctity of God-ordained marriage is so important for Jesus that already the lustful look of a man at a married woman amounts to the act of adultery. That means on the one hand that the act of adultery, in the sense of the Old Testament-Jewish law, is displaced to the background. In the light of the kingdom of God Jesus is not interested in it. Such adulteries are not worth considering in any case if the

---

[39]*b. Ber.* 61a; *b. 'Erub.* 18b; *b. Qidd.* 70a (these and other passages in Str-B I 299f.).

[40]*T.Reub.* 3:10.

[41]*b. Ber.* 24a = Str-B I 299.

[42]Sirach 9:5,7-9; *b. 'Abod. Zar.* 20a = Str-B I 300.

[43]At that time, e.g., the balcony for women in the synagogue was introduced.

[44]Niederwimmer* 28 speaks correctly of an intensified "fear of concupiscence" in the Pharisaic Judaism of the time. Berger, *Gesetzesauslegung* I 326, emphasizes the ascendancy of the Levitical concept of purity since the Chronicler and its transfer to the relation to women.

[45]E.g., Braun, *Radikalismus* II 86 ("a command for the protection of the neighbor"); Jeremias, *Theology* 227 ("Jesus accepts women into the group of disciples"); Schweizer 74 (the subject is "the right and the life of the woman") tend in this direction.

sanctity of a marriage is already destroyed through a lustful look. On the other hand, this demand of Jesus, which is expressed as a sentence of absolutely binding law, again avoids making an unfulfillable demand on humans only if it is heard together with the presupposition corresponding to it: With Jesus this presupposition is the arrival of the kingdom of God, in the anticipation of which a partial integration of the disadvantaged woman takes place; with Matthew it is the community standing under the support of the exalted Lord in which precisely the "little ones" have a special weight.

5:29–30

The addition of vv. 29–30 confirms that Matthew understands v. 28 as a radical demand of obedience. It is not just a mirror of the soul which reveals one's own sin. There is here no tendency toward a moderation of the demands to a practicable level.

Are these logia meant to be taken realistically or symbolically? A "realistic" interpretation is possible insofar as the cutting off of the hands is demanded occasionally in rabbinical texts precisely in the case of sexual offenses.[46] However, we hear little of its being carried out. In the history of interpretation the literal explanation[47] was rejected just about unanimously. An interpretation of "tear out" and "cut off" as hyperbole is more discussable: one should no longer use eye and hand for sinful purposes. But, as already the interpretation of the early church stated,[48] the addition of δεξιός to the eye speaks against both interpretations. Why should the right eye play a special role at the seduction to sin? "Right" stands symbolically for "good," "precious," "important."[49] The double saying is a warning against sin, perhaps related to standing phrases:[50] In order to avoid it, one is to give everything, even the most important and precious thing, away. The perspective is that of judgment which makes even physical integrity a matter of second rank. A limitation to sexual offenses probably was alien to the original saying; such sayings are usable in many fields of application.

Matthew has referred the saying to the seduction to commit adultery and understood eye and hand as instruments for it. For him, the reference to the condemnation in judgment at the end was probably especially important. It is

---

[46]*Nid.* 2:1 and *b. Nid.* 13b (expressly as judicial punishment and not as a curse); *b. Šabb.* 108b (both texts in Str-B I 302f.); *b. Sanh.* 58b (for violence; Hona is supposed really to have caused the cutting off of the hand); *b. Pesah.* 57b (because of lese majesty, an anecdote); Philo, *Spec. Leg.* 3.175 in accordance with Deut. 25:11f.

[47]Democritus (in Plutarch II 521D; Tertullian, *Apol.* 46 = BKV I/24 161) is supposed to have blinded himself in order not to be distracted by women from philosophy. In modern interpretation, G. Stählin, "κοπετός κτλ.," *TDNT* III 859ff., cf. 852f., is the most important advocate of a literal interpretation. Already Tholuck 208 notes against it with horror it would let the "Christian church become a house of invalids."

[48]John Chrysostom 17.3 = 308.

[49]W. Grundmann, "δεξιός," *TDNT* II 37ff.

[50]In Hellenism there are examples of a similar usage, cf., e.g., Heliodorus, *Aeth.* 2.16.1ff.; Plato *Symp.* 205e (ἐπεὶ αὑτῶν γε καὶ πόδας καὶ χεῖρας ἐθέλουσιν ἀποτέμνεσθαι οἱ ἄνθρωποι, ἐὰν αὑτοῖς δοκῇ' τὰ ἑαυτῶν πονηρὰ εἶναι); Aristotle, *Eth. Eud.* 1235a; Saying of Sextus in Origen on Matt. 19:12 = GCS 40,354: πᾶν μέρος τοῦ σώματος τὸ ἀναπεῖθόν σε εἰς τὸ μὴ σωφρονεῖν ῥῖψον; Seneca, *Ep.* 51.13; Ovid, *Ex Pont.* 4.14.17f.

not by accident that the word γέεννα occurs in both the first and the second antithesis and both end with a look at the possibility of condemnation in the final judgment.

History of influence

The church tradition has interpreted the sayings allegorically and asked especially for the meaning of "eye" and "hand." The interpretations are interesting. The exegetically wrong allegorical interpretations of the "open" saying give indications to possible fields of application. The interpretation of the lustful spirit, evil thought, wrong aims of the will from which one must separate is widespread.[51] Following Chrysostom, the interpretation of false friends, perhaps even relatives and kin from whom one should separate for the sake of the gospel,[52] even if one loves them like the apple of the eye,[53] is frequent. Finally, the interpretation of the body of Christ, the church, has to be mentioned which, for the sake of the life of the whole body, must under certain circumstances abandon some of its members.[54]

2.2.3. Third Antithesis: On Divorce (5:31-32)

Literature

Baltensweiler, H., *Die Ehe im Neuen Testament* (Zurich: Zwingli, 1967).
Berger, *Gesetzesauslegung* I 508-75
Bonsirven, J., *Le divorce dans le Nouveau Testament* (Paris: Société de S. Jean l'Évangéliste, 1948).
Bauer, J. B., "Bemerkungen zu den matthäischen Unzuchtklauseln (Mt 5,32; 19,9)," in *Begegnung mit dem Wort* (FS H. Zimmermann), ed. J. Zmijewski et al., BBB 53, pp. 23-33 (Bonn: Hanstein, 1980).
Crouzel, H., *L'Église primitive face au divorce*, ThH 13 (Paris: Beauchesne, 1971).
Delling, G., "Ehescheidung," *RAC* IV 707-19.
Denner, M., *Die Ehescheidung im Neuen Testamente* (Paderborn/Würzburg: Schöningh, 1910).
Dieterich, H., *Das protestantische Eherecht in Deutschland bis zur Mitte des 17. Jahrhunderts*, Jus Ecc 10 (Munich: Claudius, 1970).
Dombois, H., *Unscheidbarkeit und Ehescheidung in den Traditionen der Kirche*, TEH 190 (Munich: Kaiser, 1976).
Dungan, D. *The Sayings of Jesus in the Churches of Paul*, pp. 102-31 (Philadelphia: Fortress, 1971).
Dupont, J. *Mariage et divorce dans L'Évangile* (Bruges: Desclee de Brouwer, 1959).
Eheverständnis und Ehescheidung. Empfehlungen des Interkonfessionellen Arbeitskreises für Ehe- und Familienfragen (Mainz-Munich, 1971).
Fitzmyer, J., "The Matthean Divorce-Texts and Some New Palestinian Evidence," in idem, *To Advance the Gospel*, pp. 79-111 (New York: Crossroad, 1981).

---

[51]John Chrysostom 17.3 = 308 (will, understanding); Ps.-Clem. *Rec.* 7.37.3-7 (*sensus* [senses] and *cogitatio* [thought]); Ephraim 6.7 = 126f. (evil thoughts); Isaac of Antioch, *Hom.* 36 (51) = BKV I/6 166-168. Bengel 45 broadens it and speaks of "sui abnegatio (self-denial)."

[52]John Chrysostom ibid. (the two interpretations are often side by side!); Isidore of Pelusium, *Ep.* I 83 = *PG* 778,240 (relatives).

[53]Augustine*** 1,13 (37): "illud . . . quod ita diligis ut pro dextro oculo habeas" (that . . . which you love so much that you have it before your right eye).

[54]Hilarius 4.21 = 939; Origen on Matt. 18:8f. = 244.

298

Greeven, H., "Ehe nach dem Neuen Testament," *NTS* 15 (1968/69) 365-88.

Hoffmann, P., "Jesu Wort von der Ehescheidung und seine Auslegung in der neutestamentlichen Überlieferung," *Conc* 6 (1970) 326-32.

Hoffmann-Eid, *Jesus* 109-46.

Isaksson, A., *Marriage and Ministry in the New Temple*, ASNU (Lund: Gleerup, 1965).

Lövestam, E. "Divorce and Remarriage in the New Testament," *The Jewish Law Annual* 11 (1981) 47-665.

Lohfink, G., "Jesus und die Ehescheidung. Zur Gattung und Sprachintention von Mt 5,32," in *Biblische Randbemerkungen* (Schüler-FS R. Schnackenburg), ed. H. Merklein, et al., 2d ed., pp. 207-17 (Würzburg: Echter, 1974).

Moingt, J., "Le divorce 'pour motif d'impudicité' (Mt 5,32; 19,9)," *RSR* 56 (1968) 337-84.

Nautin, P. "Divorce et remariage dans la tradition de L'Église latine," *RSR* 62 (1974) 7-554.

Niederwimmer, K., *Askese und Mysterium*, FRLANT 113, pp. 12-41 (Göttingen: Vandenhoeck & Ruprecht, 1975).

Olsen, V. N., *The New Testament Logia on Divorce: A Study of Their Interpretation from Erasmus to Milton*, BGBE 10 (Tübingen: Mohr, 1971).

Ott, A., *Die Auslegung der neutestamentlichen Texte über die Ehescheidung*, NTAbh 3, 1-3 (Münster: Aschendorff, 1911).

Pesch, R., *Freie Treue. Die Christen und die Ehescheidung* (Freiburg: Herder, 1971).

Riedel-Spangenberger, I., *Die Trennung von Tisch, Bett und Wohnung (cc 1128-1132 CIC) und das Herrenwort Mk 10,9*, EHS.T 102 (Frankfurt: Lang, 1978).

Sand, A., "Die Unzuchtklausel in Mt 5,31.32 und 19,3-9," *MTZ* 20 (1969) 118-29.

Schaller, B., "Die Sprüche über Ehescheidung und Wiederheirat in der synoptischen Überlieferung," in *Der Ruf Jesu und die Antwort der Gemeinde* (FS J. Jeremias), ed. E. Lohse et al., pp. 226-46 (Göttingen: Vandenhoeck & Ruprecht, 1970).

Sigal, P. "The Halakhah of Jesus of Nazareth according to the Gospel of Matthew," Ph.D. diss. (Pittsburgh 1979).

Vogt, F., *Das Ehegesetz Jesu* (Leipzig: Bibliographisches Institut, 1910).

Further literature in B. Reicke, "Ehe, Eherecht, Ehescheidung," *TRE* 9,324f.

Further literature** at Matt. 5:21-48 above pp. 273-274. Literature*** on the Sermon on the Mount at Matt. 5-7 above pp. 209-211.

Text

31 But it was said:
"Whoever dismisses his wife must give her a bill of divorce."
32 But I say to you:
Everyone who dismisses his wife, except for fornication, drives her to adultery;
and whoever marries a dismissed woman commits adultery.

Analysis

1. *Structure.* The introductory phrase is formulated very briefly, partly because this antithesis is closely connected with the preceding one,[1] and partly because the symmetry of the Antitheses[2] forced a brief formulation. Verse 32a and b is formulated as a mashal with synthetical parallelism. This parallelism becomes still clearer if one omits

---

[1]Connecting catchwords: πᾶς ὁ + participle, μοιχεύω, γυνή. Through μοιχεύω the third antithesis is related to the same commandment of the decalogue as the second one.

[2]Cf. above at 5:21-48 n. 1.

παρεκτὸς λόγου πορνείας, which is special material beyond Luke 16:18 and Mark 10:11, and assumes that a short Aramaic *afel* form was the basis for the formulation ποιεῖ αὐτὴν μοιχευθῆναι.[3]

2. *Sources and redaction.* Verse 32 was given to Matthew in two forms, in that of Mark 10:11 (= Matt. 19:9) and in one similar to Luke 16:18. But it is very uncertain to assume a Q text: Neither can the wording be reconstructed exactly nor can the logion be situated in Q in a meaningful context. Probably the clause of fornication was already available to Matthew: It is formulated in language different from 19:9, where the evangelist presumably has inserted it into the Markan text.[4] Moreover, 19:3-9 demonstrates that the theological weight of Matthean reflection on the prohibition of divorce is located elsewhere and that the clause of fornication is not without tension included in the Matthean scope. Presumably the possibility of divorce in the case of fornication agreed with the practice of the Jewish-Christian Matthean community. Ὅς ἐάν in v. 32 is due to Matthew.[5] We also owe him the formulation of the thesis in v. 31: he took the abbreviated formula of introduction from the traditional primary antitheses, the free paraphrase of Deut. 24:1 from Mark 10:2-9. We have here again a prime example of redaction which is determined completely by the tradition!

3. *History of tradition and origin.* The original form of the logion v. 32; Luke 16:18; Mark 10:11 is strongly disputed. It seems to me that the suggestion that Mark 10:11 comes closest to the original form is most improbable.[6] Luke 16:18 and Matt. 5:32 have in common that they address only the man and forbid the marriage of a divorced woman. Leaving aside the certainly secondary clause of fornication, there are the following differences:

(1) The passive formulation ποιεῖ αὐτὴν μοιχευθῆναι in Matt. 5:32a presupposes the basic Jewish conviction that the husband cannot break his own marriage. Is that a later moderation and adaptation of a Jewish-Christian community to its environment? Then the hidden provocation of the original word of Jesus in Luke 16:18 would consist in the fact that it presupposes tacitly that the husband can break his own marriage.[7] Or is the active μοιχεύω Luke 16:18 a secondary adaptation to non-Jewish conditions? If the Lukan version were more original, then the word would be "more revolutionary." The question can hardly be decided; but the desire to gain a saying of Jesus which is as un-Jewish as possible must not lead to a preference for the Lukan version.

(2) Was καὶ γαμῶν ἑτέραν in Luke 16:18a original and in Matt. 5:32a omitted, when the clause of fornication was inserted, perhaps because of the length of the saying? Or is it an addition, perhaps on the basis of Mark 10:11, mitigating the saying and at the same time formulating legally in a more practicable way: Only through the remarriage of the man does the divorce become final and thus constitute adultery? The symmetry of the two members, Matt. 5:32a,b; Luke 16:18a,b, speaks in favor of the thesis that the saying originally did not refer to the remarriage of the man.

---

[3]Cf. Greeven 383 no. 1. Such a form is conceivable from the stem גוז which in *Tg. Onq.* Exod. 20:13 has taken the place of נוף, little used in Aramaic, which does not have *hiphil* forms. Sy[cu] formulates similarly with the stem *gwr*.

[4]Cf., e.g., Schaller* 230; Wrege*** 68f.

[5]Cf. introduction 3.2.

[6]Schaller* 238-43 considers μοιχάομαι ἐπί (Mark 10:11) as an Aramaism (גור with ב or ל). But Mark 10:11 does not want to say that the man commits adultery *with* the new wife but "in relation" to the first wife, with whom his marriage still continues to exist before God. That can be expressed in Greek in no other way than with ἐπί.

[7]Hoffmann-Eid, *Jesus,* suggestively argues for this solution.

This amounts to a prior decision on the *main problem*: Does the prohibition of the marriage of a divorced woman Matt. 5:32b belong to the original logion, which then from the beginning would have contained a parallelism? Matthew and Luke hand down this prohibition. In or before Mark it was secondarily replaced by v. 12. There is, in my opinion, no reason to consider Matt. 5:32b; Luke 16:18b as secondary.[8] If Jesus indeed forbade the marriage of a divorced woman, then it is difficult to understand his prohibition of divorce as taking the side of the disadvantaged woman. The prohibition to marry a divorced woman is absolutely not in the interest of the disadvantaged woman.[9] The Jewish command to the husband to pay the marriage bond at a divorce, on the other hand, meant at the same time practicable and effective protection for the woman.[10]

Explanation

Fully two-thirds of the scholarly essays or books published on our text in the last twenty years (about 60!) come from Catholic pens and have the main or subsidiary purpose to declare it in harmony with Catholic marriage law. Thus with this text we enter an area of sensitive and controversial theology. It becomes less manifest from the literature that it could also put Protestant divorce practice in question.

5:31

The third antithesis is distinguished from the two preceding ones. It does not happen here that a command of the decalogue is radicalized by an ethical demand. Instead, the thesis, v. 31, contains a very special Old Testament regulation; it paraphrases in a free way the Old Testament regulation of divorce, Deut. 24:1. Strictly speaking, it is not a command there; the regular divorce with a bill of divorce is mentioned only in connection with the prohibition for the man to marry his divorced ex-wife a second time (Deut. 24:4). Matthew presents a contrasting regulation, namely, Jesus' qualification of divorce as adultery, except in the case of πορνεία. How can one still speak of "fulfillment of the law" in the sense of 5:17-19 with this antithesis formed by Matthew himself? Our text gives an answer only implicitly: with the possibility of a divorce for πορνεία, a case is left in which one writes a bill of divorce in the

---

[8]On the contrary: while there are parallels to the prohibition of divorce in Qumran, the prohibition of marrying a divorced woman is singular in its environment. In Judaism there is such a prohibition only for the priest (Lev. 21:7); cf. a unique warning of R. Akiba for practical reasons (*b. Pesah.* 112a = Str-B I 321). Josephus, *Ant.* 4.244 demands that marriage be to virgins. In Greece also there were no reservations against a second marriage, differently from Rome where the old ideal of the *univira* (with only one man) was alive, cf. B. Kötting, "*Digamus*," *RAC* III 1017-20. Cf. the demand that bishop, deacon, and widow are to have only one wife or husband (1 Tim. 3:2,12; 5:9; Tit. 1:6).

[9]We know little about the fate of the divorced woman at the time of Jesus. Lev. 22:13 reckons that she would return into the house of her parents. For the later time, cf. the examples in Krauss, *Archäologie* II 53 and n. 396. Financially she was taken care of for at least a year through the *Ketubah* . In the house of her father she is *persona sui iuris* (a person in her own right), i.e., no longer under the *patria potestas* (authority of the father). D. W. Amram, *The Jewish Law of Divorce according to Bible and Talmud*, 2d ed. (New York: Hermon, 1968), 104f., points out that a divorced woman was always in bad circumstances because it was assumed that she was not divorced without reason.

[10]How frequent were divorces in Judaism? We know no instances which would be comparable to the complaints from Rome about the increase of divorces.

sense of Deut. 24:1. Not until 19:3-9 does the evangelist clarify how he thinks of the relationship of Jesus' will to the Old Testament regulation about the bill of divorce: Jesus' demand corresponds to the original will of God, the commandment of Moses about the bill of divorce is a mere permission, the validity of which continues in restricted measure. Moses' permission (19:8 = ἐρρέθη 5:31) is coordinated with and subordinated to Jesus' proclamation of the original will of God (ἐγὼ δὲ λέγω ὑμῖν 5:32 = 19:9).

5:32

With v. 32, Matthew inserts a traditional word of Jesus as an antithesis.

For Jesus

The interpretation of the prohibition of divorce within the framework of the proclamation of Jesus is not simple. Among exegetes the inclination is most widespread to associate it with Jesus' kindliness to women, who were at that time "in every respect"[11] scorned: by understanding marriage as a "unity which cannot be abolished through the law," Jesus liberates the woman from her dependence as an object of law and as possession of the husband and uncovers "the reality of the interhuman relationship" of marriage.[12] The prohibition of divorce would then be an expression of the love of Jesus and of God for the disadvantaged woman.[13] But there are some things which puzzle us. There also was a general rejection of divorce in Qumran[14] but not out of love for the disadvantaged woman. The Jesus logion indeed combines the prohibition of divorce with the prohibition of marrying a divorced woman. That is indeed consistent, since in Judaism ordinary divorce was intended to make a remarriage possible. This prohibition could be devastating for the divorced woman. It is—to put it mildly—"naive"[15] and understandable only if one assumes that Jesus consistently proclaimed God's will on the basis of the kingdom of God without considering that there were in Israel despite this will of God numerous unmarried divorced women. Thus it is probable that Jesus thinks on the basis of the pure, unconditional will of God, i.e., on the basis of marriage, not of love for the disadvantaged woman. To this extent the controversy dialog in Mark

---

[11]Josephus, *Ap.* 2.201: γυνὴ χείρων . . . ἀνδρὸς εἰς ἅπαντα.

[12]Hoffmann* 326.

[13]Schweizer 75 ("protection of the woman"); Hoffmann-Eid, *Jesus* 119 ("Jesus uncovers here the right of the woman against the one-sided right of the man"); Pesch* 15 ("marriage . . . as mutual binding"); Braun, *Jesus* 98 ("is partial . . . in favor of the disadvantaged woman").

[14]11QTemple 57.17-19 (right of the king; monogamy; permanent marriage for the entire life; remarriage after the death of the woman); CD 4.21-5.2 (law for the ordinary person and for the king; no two women during their life times; proof from Scripture, Gen. 1:27). The Temple Scroll supports the interpretation of CD 4.21ff. which includes a prohibition of divorce, cf. Fitzmyer* 91-97.

[15]Pesch* 21 (Jesus presupposes that people are "truly 'healthy' "; divorce belongs in the context of the kingdom of God, cf. ibid. 20). Dietzfelbinger, *Antithesen* 28-30, evaluates much more harshly: The prohibition of divorce takes away from the woman the minimal protection of law which she still has; it ruthlessly abolishes regulations which are indispensable for human society and leads to unbearable, untruthful circumstances.

10:2-12 has understood him correctly. But all of this does not make the integration of the prohibition of divorce into the totality of the proclamation of Jesus easier. There seems to be here a Qumran-like feature.

Another thesis also must be examined critically. Frequently it is said that Jesus' prohibition of divorce is not a sentence of law but a principle,[16] a provocation,[17] a bit of parenesis[18] in form of a sentence of law, in analogy to 5:22,28—"alienated" language of law[19]—which wanted to mediate a fundamental, incontrovertible ethical demand.[20] The relevance of this thesis for the present debate concerning the laws of divorce of the various churches is considerable. Formally, v. 32 is an apodictic sentence of law which ends with a statement of guilt and not with a statement of punishment.[21] Matthew 5:22,28 shows that such sentences of law can be used parenetically; then the sentence of law intensifies the parenesis. But 5:32 has a different character from 5:22,28: in distinction from a word of abuse or a seductive look, the prohibition of divorce can be enforced and checked by law; that is shown in the community order of Qumran. Therefore all early Christian communities have drawn legal consequences from Jesus' prohibition of divorce; Mark 10:11, through the addition of "and marries another," specifies the time when the divorce is final and liable to judgment. Paul through his "privilege," 1 Cor. 7:12-17, does not invalidate the prohibition of the Lord, but he came out with an opinion at the point where the community, standing under the command of the Lord, and the world intersect. In any case, Matthew clearly shows through his "clause" that he understands Jesus' prohibition of divorce as an order valid in his community[22] and precisely for this reason can formulate an exception. In view of this unanimous finding in early Christianity it seems problematic to charge him with making a law of an ethical demand of Jesus.[23] Of course, Jesus has not

---

[16]G. Delling, "Das Logion Markus 10,11 und seine Abwandlungen im Neuen Testament," in idem, *Studien zum Neuen Testament und zum hellenistischen Judentum* (Göttingen: Vandenhoeck & Ruprecht, 1970), 226.

[17]Lohfink* 210f.; Pesch* 19 (Jesus is a "prophetic provocateur, . . . not a legislator"). In view of Qumran, can this be said?

[18]Schaller* 245; Niederwimmer* 21 speaks of "*hokmah* parenesis," which appeals to the insight of the listener.

[19]Cf. Hoffmann* 326.

[20]K. Barth interprets not only the first two but also the third antithesis as an ethical radicalizing of an Old Testament command (*CD* III/4, 233): " 'Adultery' in the mind of Jesus . . . is . . . everything which is inconsistent with . . . marriage . . . thinking and speaking, action and conduct—and beyond this all perversion, depletion, falsification and corruption, all unreason, laziness and wickedness in the life and relation of the sexes."

[21]Cf. in the Old Testament Lev. 17:3f.; 20:9,11,16,27; Num. 35:16f. The Old Testament parallels contain always a statement of guilt and of punishment.

[22]Hummel, *Auseinandersetzung* 49-51, speaks of halakah, Niederwimmer* 52 of "lex" (law), Greeven 385 of "holy sentence of law."

[23]Cf. Niederwimmer* 52. Pesch* 74-76 evaluates this development to church law already in the NT in a very differentiated way. I would like to refer to this expressly, precisely because—to my regret—I cannot see in Jesus' prohibition of divorce only an "appeal to our heart, our conscience, our love," to "free loyalty" (77).

founded a community with a legal form. But his demand is, so to speak, a "potential" law for eschatological Israel at the dawn of the kingdom of God. The contrast between law and parenesis does not fit the matter.

For Matthew

In the community of Matthew, the principle of Jesus was practiced in such a way that divorce was permitted only in the case of πορνεία. The literature on this clause of exception is immense. What is the result of the discussion?

1. Παρεκτός cannot be understood in any other sense than that of an exception: in the case of πορνεία the prohibition of divorce is not valid.

Other interpretations, like the "inclusive one" ("the man who dismisses his wife commits adultery, even in the case of unchastity")[24] and the "preteritive one" ("the man who dismisses his wife—let the case of unchastity be disregarded for now— commits adultery"),[25] have today just about disappeared from the discussion, because the philological finding is unambiguous. J. Dupont states correctly that the true difficulty does not consist in the interpretation of the biblical text but in the fact that so many good authors did not understand it.[26]

2. Πορνεία can mean only sexual misbehavior, and as a rule that means—with a married woman—adultery.

Πορνεία is a general word for "every kind of illegitimate sexual intercourse."[27] If a certain kind of unchastity is meant, it becomes clear each time by the context. Besides, πορνεία in the figurative sense in the Old Testament tradition can mean idolatry.

a. These statements, it seems to me, include a definite negation of an interpretation which is already quite old,[28] was renewed by Bonsirven and Baltensweiler,[29] and is today very popular, especially in Catholic exegesis.[30] This interpretation attempts to understand πορνεία on the basis of the prohibitions of incest in Leviticus 18. Since for the rabbis a proselyte was like a newborn, marriages of relatives of former Gentiles in Judaism were not in all cases considered as incestuous, because

---

[24]Ott* 289-99; Vogt* 149-53; Ljungman (cf. literature on Matt. 5:17-20) 81 ("the λόγος πορνείας does not change anything" about adultery). But Matt. 19:9 would have to have μηδέ and not μή. Παρεκτός cannot have inclusive meaning; that would be possible only in an enumeration (Dupont* 104).

[25]Zahn 238, 583; Lohmeyer 130. This interpretation is impossible in 19:9 and therefore must be dropped for 5:32 also.

[26]Dupont* 103.

[27]BAGD, s.v.

[28]Survey of the early history of this interpretation advocated since 1844 in Ott*, 261-66.

[29]Bonsirven* 43-60; Baltensweiler* 87-102.

[30]Represented, e.g., by J. B. Bauer, "Die matthäische Ehescheidungsklausel (Mt 5,32 und 19,9)," in *Evangelienforschung* (Graz: Styria, 1968), 147-58 (with reservation); Bonnard 283; Guelich ***210 (only for the Matthew redaction); Fitzmyer* 97 (on the basis of the prohibition of marriages with nieces in Qumran in the context of the prohibitions of divorce); Meier, *Law* 147-50 (there many further representatives of this interpretation n. 54); R. Schnackenburg, "Die Ehe nach dem Neuen Testament," in idem, *Schriften zum Neuen Testament* (Munich: Kösel, 1971), 419f.

Gentile relatives of the "newborn" proselyte just were no longer considered as such.[31] Matthew then would have declared— perhaps similarly to Acts 15:20,29—marriages of relatives entered according to Gentile custom as illegitimate. But, in my opinion, this interpretation is quite improbable, for: (1) The context does not indicate at all that Matthew wants to take πορνεία in such a narrow sense and to refer his exception only to former Gentiles. (2) Correspondingly, no single church father and no single interpreter up until the modern time would have understood what he was truly concerned about. (3) In Leviticus 18, the word πορνεία is missing. (4) Παρεκτὸς λόγου πορνείας is a clear reference to Deut. 24:1;[32] but then it must deal with the reasons for the divorce of legitimate and not with the invalidity of illegitimate marriages. *Result*: This exegesis is an "artifice"[33] which can recommend itself alone through the fact that it does not raise a conflict (in my opinion, an imaginary one) of our passage with the Catholic church law.

b. The general sense of πορνεία makes it impossible to define "unchastity" more closely. Πορνεία cannot be delimited as unchastity during the engagement,[34] as premarital intercourse,[35] as continuing unrepented adultery or prostitution of the wife,[36] as concubinage,[37] as "wild licentiousness,"[38] or as flirting with another man.[39] Almost always the sexual morality of the exegete is the godfather of such thoughts.

c. Πορνεία means in our passage sexual activity of the woman outside of marriage, i.e., actually adultery.[40] That results from the context: it speaks of married women. Besides, this best fits the controversy over the interpretation of the "disgraceful matter" in Judaism, which is presupposed in Matt. 19:3-9.[41] At most one has to explain

---

[31]Str-B III 353-58.

[32]The reference to Deut. 24:1 is unambiguous since the rendering of the *nomen rectum* דָּבָר as *nomen regens* can be documented rabbinically in connection with Deut. 24:1, cf. Schaller* 235 n. 33.

[33]Pesch* 39.

[34]Isaksson* 135-40.

[35]A. Fridrichsen, "Excepta fornicationis causa," *SEA* 9 (1944) 54-58; similarly already Paulus I 530-35.

[36]Sand* 127f. (following the OT prophets); A. Kretzer, "Die Frage: Ehe auf Dauer und ihre mögliche Trennung nach Mt 19,3-12," in *Biblische Randbemerkungen* (Schüler-FS R. Schnackenburg), ed. H. Merklein et al., 2d ed. (Würzburg: Echter, 1974), 220 (continuing unfaithfulness).

[37]A. Vaccari, "O divorcio nos Evangelhos,"*RCB* 7 (1963) 60-79 (the woman must be dismissed if she is not the wife).

[38]Bornhäuser 82.

[39]Zahn 239f.: "all amorous behavior with another man."

[40]The most important problem in the history of interpretation was always whether πορνεία alone means a sexual act outside of marriage, so, e.g., John Chrysostom 17.4 = 312; Luther II 642 (however, Luther, for reasons of pastoral care, permitted other grounds for divorce also, e.g., malicious desertion, refusal of sexual intercourse in marriage, giving cause for serious sin, cf. Dieterich* 69-74); Calvin I 189-90; Maldonat 118-20, or whether πορνεία could be understood in a figurative sense or stand as an example for other sins. *Herm. Man.* 4.1.9 extends it to the sins of the Gentiles. Augustine*** discusses the question in detail (1.16 [43-50]) and mentions beside adultery unbelief (44), idolatry (45), avarice, and dissolute passion (46) as well as the cause of it (47). In the Reformation period, e.g., Zwingli 228 ("non ut caeteras causas divortii excludat" [not that he would exclude other causes for divorce]), H. Bullinger, *Der christliche Ehestand* (Zürich 1540, ch. 25,5) advocates a broad interpretation, Calvin a narrow one (Schellong*** 60f.). Exegetically, extensions to nonsexual sins are not covered by the text of Matt. 5:32; 19:9.

[41]To this and to the position of the school of Shammai, which is particularly close to the Matthean community, cf. on Matt. 19:1-12.

why πορνεία and not μοιχεία is used. There are three reasons: (1) In the biblical language tradition the stem μοιχ- is used more of men, the stem πορν- more of women.[42] (2) The two stems do not have different meanings, but μοιχεία is a specific form of πορνεία so that both words can be used also as synonyms.[43] (3) Double μοιχεία/μοιχεύω would be awkward.

Thus, in the Matthean community Jesus' prohibition of divorce was promulgated, unless there was a case of adultery. With this, it took up a basic Jewish conviction: unchastity is an abomination which desecrates the land of Israel.[44] The question of whether adultery could not also be forgiven in the light of God's love did not arise for the community at all.[45] Rather, the community seems to think in cultic-ritual terms, as in Judaism: adultery and unchastity are a contamination which destroy marriage. Through adultery, the marriage *is* already destroyed. Therefore for Judaism, divorce in the case of adultery is mandatory.[46] The Matthean unchastity clause leaves it linguistically open whether in the case of unchastity a marriage *must* be or only *may* be divorced. Both the Jewish background and the earliest Christian history of interpretation make the former more easily understandable.[47] For it was scarcely considered by the community as a liberalizing of an otherwise too strict commandment but rather as the command of God which protects marriage against impurity. The practice of the Matthean community thus is close to that of the Shammaites, while Jesus himself is perhaps closer to the Essenes.

---

[42]Examples in BAGD 27.

[43]Examples for synonymous use of πορνεία and μοιχεία in F. Hauck and S. Schulz, "πόρνη κτλ." *TDNT* VI 584ff.; 587ff.

[44]Cf. Lev. 18:25,28; 19:29; Deut. 24:4; Hos. 4:2f.; Jer. 3:1-3,9.

[45]In the discussion concerning the prohibition of remarriage, the thought that through a remarriage the reconciliation of the separated spouses would be excluded has played a role already at an early time, but only after Matthew, for the first time in *Herm. Man.* 4.7f.,10f., classically Thomas, *ST* (Suppl.!) 3, qu. 62 art. 6. Therefore, an adulteress should not be dismissed if she repents; if she does not repent, she *must* be dismissed in order that sin be not treated as unimportant ("ne peccato eius consentire videatur" [in order that he does not seem to consent to her sin]). In the texts of the Reformers on marriage the aim of reconciliation plays a large role, cf. Luther II 643f.; WA 32f., 379 (= *LW* 21, 96) (in distinction from the secular law of divorce, the Christians are to be admonished to forgiveness and reconciliation to the extent that malicious sin "that takes mercy and forgiveness for granted" does not arise from it); Bullinger (above n. 40), ch. 25,2.4. But it is clear that this thought is missing in Matthew. It is, in my opinion, an important but secondary attempt to motivate the prohibition of remarriage as centrally Christian. In Judaism, the reconciliation of divorced people is despised, cf. Philo, *Spec. Leg.* 3.31.

[46]*Sota* 5:1 (the adulteress is forbidden to her husband for reasons of purity), cf. *b. Git.* 90b ("commandment of Torah"); Prov. (LXX) 18:22 (ὁ . . . κατέχων μοιχαλίδα . . . ἀσεβής).

[47]*Herm. Man.* 4.1.5 (if the husband knows of the adultery of the wife and does not effect a separation, he shares in the sin); cf. further Theodoret of Cyrus, *Graec. aff. cur.* 9 = *PG* 83, 1053f. (κελεύει); Euthymius Zigabenus on 19:9 = 517; in the West, Justin, *Apol.* 2.2 (Flora [?] considers it sin to continue living with her immoral husband); Tertullian, *Marc.* 4.34.7 (*macula* [stain]) Hilarius 940 (*perscribens* [prescribing]); *Opus imperfectum* 32,9 = 802. This, by the way, also corresponds to Attic feeling for what is right and to the *lex Iulia* which makes the expulsion of adulterous women obligatory (F. Hauck, μοιχεύω κτλ., *TDNT* IV 700f.; 733ff.).

5:32b

The prohibition of marriage to a divorced woman extends the Old Testament prohibition of the husband marrying his own divorced wife a second time (Deut. 24:4) to all divorced women. This prohibition also has a cultic-ritual air. Its catastrophic consequences for the divorced women are alleviated in the Matthean community, at least for wives of Christians: since divorce is possible only in the case of unchastity, it amounts to a prohibition to marry an adulteress.

The antithesis thus reflects the practice of marital law in the Matthean community. The voice of the evangelist is reflected only to the extent that he explicitly contrasts this practice with the Old Testament. Matthew 19:3-9 will make clear how. It remains remarkable that the evangelist does not subordinate the practice of his community here, as, e.g., at the order of excommunication in 18:15-17, under the principle of the forgiveness of God. To this degree, our text is not specifically Matthean. But it is Matthean that the evangelist supports the practice of his community.

History of influence

The history of influence[48] mirrors the varying legal regulations of divorce in the different denominations. The basic position of the major confessional traditions is familiar; every pastor experiences its consequences. I would like to indicate only some main lines and limit myself to the position of the major churches.

a. The *Catholic position*, which provides for the possibility of a separation of table, bed, and living quarters with a remaining *vinculum* (bond) of the marriage,[49] especially approaches the Matthean position, it seems to me. This is perhaps surprising, in view of the flood of Catholic literature which is probably an expression of its great uncertainty. Certainly there are differences. Matthew speaks of the ἀπόλυσις[50] and does not distinguish between the possible separation and the impossible divorce—when the marriage bond still exists. On the other hand, the πορνεία aspect no longer plays a central role for the *separatio tori, mensae et habitationis* (separation of bed, board, and

---

[48]Ott* is classical and indispensable. Denner* is conditionally helpful (only for the patristic period), also Vogt* (for the post-Tridentine Catholic exegesis). The relevant canonical law texts are treated well by Riedel-Spangenberger* 23-30,34-36,79-130. Dieterich* gives information about the theory and practice of earlier Protestantism. Good material for the history of interpretation especially in the ancient church is offered also by Dupont* (passim), Moingt*, Nautin*, and especially Crouzel*. Olsen* goes beyond Dieterich* in dealing with the Catholic exegesis of the Reformation period and the English Reformation with special reference to the history of interpretation, church law. Dombois* is very much worth reading, thanks to his general view. Basic in church law are CIC Can 1128-1132 (old edition; the "reformed" CIC was not accessible to me). I owe here much to the help of Andreas Ennulat.

[49]It is formulated clearly by Augustine and Jerome. Cf., e.g., Augustine, *Nupt. concup.* 1.10, trans. A. Fingerle (Würzburg 1977), 86; *Adult coni.* 2.4, trans. J. Schmid (Würzburg 1949), 46; on Augustine as a whole, M. F. Berrouard, "Saint Augustin et l'indissolubilité du mariage," in *St. Patr.* 11 (TU 108), 291-306. For Jerome, the two letters 77 to Oceanus and 55 to Amandus are particularly important, where he points to the prohibition of the marriage of a divorced woman (Matt. 5:32)—and divorced for whatever reason (*Ep* 55,4 = BKV II/18 348). The following council texts are especially important: Elvira Can. 8-10 (cf. Denzinger no. 52a), Arles Can. 10 (complete texts in Dombois* 24f.); the "hard" line of the Latin church is enforced since the *Decretum Gratiani* (12th century); cf. Riedel-Spangenberger* 97ff.

[50]On ἀπολύω as a technical term for "divorce" cf. Fitzmyer* 90f.

residence). But the decisive point, in which Matthew and the Catholic practice converge, lies in the prohibition to marry a divorced woman. With it agrees the no to a second marriage which the church fathers in general maintained with great decisiveness;[51] not until the 4th century does a change take place in the East.[52] Since then the tendency to put man and woman on an equal level, as far as church law is concerned, is important.[53] Matthew 5:32 was formulated only as an address of the husband. In relation to the wife, it results from Matt. 5:32b that no woman may marry a divorced man. This means that Matt. 5:32, with the thoroughgoing equalization of man and woman, leads to the demand to marry neither divorced men nor divorced women, i.e., to a form of "divorce" (only in the case of unchastity!) which is distinguished from the Jewish form principally by the fact that it does not include the possibility of a second marriage. In regard to content, if not terminology, this corresponds precisely to the separation of bed, table, and residence.[54] Therefore, no legal ecclesiastical solution is as close to the Matthean one as the Catholic one. That becomes clear as soon as one takes v. 32b also into consideration.[55] The numerous "evasions"[56] on Matt. 5:32, in the last analysis motivated apologetically, especially on the Catholic side, are, in my opinion, an unnecessary labor of love.

b. In the *Orthodox churches*, divorce makes it possible to enter with repentance into a second marriage. The second marriage is cautiously affirmed already by some Greek fathers.[57] In the Eastern tradition, the conviction was always important that through adultery a marriage is actually destroyed.[58] Thus, the possibility of a second marriage for divorced persons is granted, not according to divine law (τάξις) but

---

[51]Examples: *Herm. Man.* 4.6; Justin, *Apol.* 1,15; Athenagoras, *Suppl.* 33 = BKV I/12 322 (the second marriage is only disguised adultery; that is valid even beyond the death of the first wife); Clement of Alexandria, *Strom.* II.23 (145,3 = BKV II/17 255); Tertullian, *Monog.* 9 = BKV I/24 496 (separation only through the tribute of death, etc.).

[52]The practice of the remarriage of divorced persons has existed in the East and the West repeatedly (cf., e.g., Origen on Matt. 14:23 = 340 or Augustine's debate with Pollentius in *De adulterinis coniugiis* [cf. above n. 49]). But even in the East, the remarriage of divorced persons is permitted only reluctantly by the church fathers, cf. Basil, *Ep.* 188 ad Amphiloch = BKV I/46 193 (penance limited in time at repeated marriage of divorced persons); in addition, canon 9; *Ep.* 199 canon 21,35,41,48; *Ep.* 217 canon 68f.; Epiphanius, *Haer.* 59.4.9 = *PG* 41,1024f. (because of weakness); Ambrosiaster on 1 Cor. 7:11 = *PL* 17,218.225 (only for the man is a remarriage after divorce possible). Crouzel* 361 speaks of the "extreme rarity" of explicit favorable statements.

[53]"Nec viro licet quod mulieri non licet" (What is not permitted to the woman is also not permitted to the man) (Ambrose, *Abraham* 1.4.25 = CSEL 32 I/2,519); Jerome, *Ep.* 77.3 ("quidquid viris iubetur, hoc consequenter redundat ad feminas" [whatever is commanded to the men, that consequently flows over to the women]). Similar tones are found in very many, especially Latin, authors.

[54]The formulation appears for the first time in Justin, *Apol.* 2.2 (separation of table and bed).

[55]Dupont* is almost the only Catholic author who has seen this, cf. especially 136-57. Crouzel* 379f. asks correctly what it means that the church fathers did not have the problems which more recent (Catholic!) exegetes have with the clause of unchastity.

[56]Dupont* 114.

[57]Cf. above n. 51.

[58]Classical formulation in Theodor of Heraclea, fragment 34 = Reuss 66: "οὐ τὸ . . . ῥεπούδιον λύει τὸν γάμον . . . , ἀλλὰ ἡ ἄτοπος πρᾶξις"; similarly Cyril of Alexandria, fragment 61 = Reuss 172; Erasmus, Paraphrasis on 19:9 ("quae alteri viro sui fecit copiam [possibility], jam uxor esse desiit" [the woman who gives another man the possibility of herself has already ceased to be a wife]). Cf. Crouzel* 363-66.

according to the pastoral principle of fairness (ἐπιείκεια, οἰκονομία).[59] The grounds for divorce are here taken as restrictive but not limited to adultery. From Matt. 5:32, πορνεία as a ground for divorce is taken seriously but the prohibition to marry divorced persons is neglected with respect to the weakness of the human being (cf. Matt. 19:8).[60]

c. The Orthodox position became alive anew in the *churches of the Reformation*, perhaps through mediation of Erasmus.[61] The Reformers also emphasize that a marriage is destroyed through adultery; therefore a divorce is possible.[62] A factor which is essential for the further development and new in contrast to the Eastern churches is the understanding of marriage by the Reformers as a "secular thing."[63] This understanding had different consequences: it led first of all to a great uncertainty over the question how the problem of divorce was to be solved as a problem of *church law*. The mixed ecclesiastical-secular courts of the Reformation period were a brief result.[64] Already after a certain time, the legal competency for divorce became a secular matter alongside of which binding regulations of church law existed only in an initial stage. Theologically, the basic conviction that Jesus' prohibition of divorce was not a law but an ethical demand, which must be well distinguished from civil law,[65] corresponds to this development. This made it possible to minister openly in pastoral care, guided by love, and to take seriously the concrete situation of a marriage, but it led at the same time to the actual adaptation of the church to secular marriage law or to the secular (sinful!) reality of marriage and to its proclamation of God's grace in all situations without distinction.[66]

The need in all confessional traditions is great. The immovable ecclesiastical *law* concerning divorce in Catholicism appears to many people as the opposite of the love and forgiveness of God. The lack of a practiced

---

[59] Cf. Dombois* 17f.,37f. The introduction of the concept of οἰκονομία seems to me important as an expression of the attempt to understand all formulated law in its relation to the human being.

[60] Is Matt. 19:9 closer to the Orthodox position?

[61] Cf. Olsen* 20-27. Similarly, e.g., Cajetan or Ambrosius Catharinus advocated the "Eastern" position (cf. Ott* 164-72) which was not condemned formally at the Council of Trent (Denzinger no. 977, sess 24, can 7).

[62] Luther, WA 32f., 379 (= *LW* 21, 96) and more often.

[63] Cf. Luther, *De Capt. Babyl.*, WA 6,550 (= *LW* 36, 92); "Vom ehelichen Leben," WA 10/II,283; *Traubüchlein für die einfältigen Pfarrherren*, BSLK[4] 528, cf. Dieterich* 21f.

[64] Dieterich* 83-92; on the Reformed area M. E. Schild, "Ehe, Eherecht, Ehescheidung" VII, *TRE* 9,342.

[65] Examples: "EKD-Denkschrift of 1969," in *Die Denkschriften der EKD*, vol. 3. *Ehe, Familie, Sexualität, Jugend* (Gütersloh: Mohn, 1981) (GTB 416) 28: ". . . not an instruction for the practice of law but a new ethos"; H. Soe, *Christliche Ethik* (Munich: Kaiser, 1957), 305f.: ". . . a misunderstanding if one would want to understand the words of Jesus as law"; A. Stein, "Ehe, Eherecht, Ehescheidung" IX, *TRE* 9,360 recommends to orient oneself for divorce on John 8:1-11 and not on our text.

[66] Particularly in Luther, to whom divorce is such an abomination that he would prefer bigamy to it if necessary (*De Capt. Babyl.*, WA 6,559 [= *LW* 36, 104-06]), it is striking how much he is oriented not so much by Bible and tradition but by his experiences in the care of souls. Therefore, e.g., malicious desertion as ground for divorce or the pedagogic idea of the prevention of still greater sin plays a large role in his thinking. Calvin, on the other hand, recognizes on the basis of the Bible only adultery as grounds for divorce for Christians (Schellong*** 58-61).

ecclesiastical law of divorce in Protestantism[67] on the other hand leads to the fact that the individual pastor is left alone and must choose most of the time the way of least resistance, i.e., the blessing of all that has happened. He experiences the reverse of Luther's grandiose principal thesis that love by no means needs laws,[68] and may ask himself or herself whether laws also could provide help to love so that it does not accept everything and remain silent in face of everything. For a Protestant who experiences the ambiguity of his or her own church, it is moving to see how Catholic brothers or sisters who suffer under the situation in their church reach for the thesis that Jesus' prohibition of divorce is not a sentence of law,[69] i.e., for that problematical basic Protestant thesis in which the Protestant recognizes a reason for the predicament of his or her own church.

   The history of influence of Matt. 5:32 in Catholic church law makes clear that the reference to the biblical text alone does not solve the problems. On the contrary: if the Catholic looks in a merely biblicistic way to the order of Matt. 5:32, then he or she can be quite satisfied with the continuation of the status quo in his or her own church. But does not a tension exist between the realization of Matt. 5:32 in the Catholic church and the center of the proclamation of Jesus, the unconditional love of God for the human being? Then one also must ask critically about Matt. 5:32 as a possible source of this tension. Already in Jesus' own absolute rejection of divorce and marriage of divorced persons there was an element of potential lovelessness. On the other hand, the Protestant who suffers under the indifference of his or her church, feels the clear ecclesiastical order of Matthew and the absoluteness of Jesus' demand of life-long monogamy as a positive challenge for thought. The immovable pillars of divine order which in the Catholic church become a burden and compulsion for many people keep alive in the Protestant churches the urgently necessary question whether there are not orienting pointers set by God which the Christian can in no way neglect.

   Thus the question is how the love of God for humans and the absolute demand of the indissolubility of marriage are related to each other. With Jesus both are present but not combined in systematic reflection. One might take up R. Pesch's key word of "free loyalty"[70] and formulate as follows: The question is for both confessions how the faithfulness in marriage demanded by God remains free without becoming relative.

2.2.4. Fourth Antithesis: On Swearing (5:33-37)

Literature

Bauernfeind, O., "Der Eid in der Sicht des Neuen Testaments," in *Eid, Gewissen, Treuepflicht,* ed. H. Bethke, pp. 79-112 (Frankfurt: Stimme, 1965).
Dautzenberg, G., "Ist das Schwurverbot Mt 5,33-37; Jak 5,12 ein Beispiel für die

---

[67]Cf. on the situation in the Protestant realm: *Eheverständnis** 32-46.

[68]*De Capt. Babyl.,* WA 6,554 (= *LW* 36, 97-98).

[69]Cf. above n. 17.

[70]Pesch*.

Torakritik Jesu?'' *BZ* NF 25 (1981) 47-66.

Hirzel, R. *Der Eid. Ein Beitrag zu seiner Geschichte* (Leipzig: Hirzel, 1902).

Honecker, M., ''Der Eid heute angesichts seiner reformatorischen Beurteilung und der abendländischen Eidestradition,'' in *Ich schwöre,* ed. G. Niemeier, pp. 27-92 (Munich: Kaiser, 1968).

Kutsch, E., '' 'Eure Rede aber sei ja ja, nein nein,' '' *EvT* 20 (1960) 206-18.

Stählin, G., ''Zum Gebrauch von Beteuerungsformeln im Neuen Testament,'' *NovT* 5 (1962) 115-43.

Zeller, *Mahnsprüche* 124-26.

Further literature** cf. at 5:21-48 above pp. 273-274; literature on the Sermon on the Mount at Matthew 5-7 above, pp. 209-211.

Text

33 Again you have heard that it was said to those of old,
"You shall not swear a false oath,
but you shall fulfill your oaths to the Lord."

34 But I say to you,
Do not swear at all,
not even[1] by heaven,
for it "is the throne of God,"

35 nor by the earth,
for it "is the footstool of his feet,"
nor toward Jerusalem,[2]
For it "is the city of the great king";

36 neither shall you swear by your head,
for you cannot make a single hair white or black.

37 Your word shall be, "Yes, yes," "No, no";
what is more than that comes from evil.

Analysis

1. *Structure.* The thesis recalls v. 21 (as there, it has a full introductory formula, a two-part formulation). It introduces the second half of the Matthean series of Antitheses. For the first time the antithesis is formulated as a prohibition (as v. 39). The general prohibition (ὅλως!) is unfolded in four little sentences introduced by μήτε. Three are symmetrical: heaven, earth, and Jerusalem fit together; each of the explanatory ὅτι sentences contains an Old Testament allusion and ends with a reference to God, which in the last one is very sonorous. The fourth sentence (v. 36) introduced with μήτε is out of step in content and form.[3] Verse 37 is a new main clause with an address in the second person plural, as v. 34.

---

[1] Μήτε here means (additively) ''also not'' (= μηδέ) and not (partitively) ''neither'' (—''nor''). Cf. Rev. 7:1,3; 9:21 (οὔτε); Arrian, *Anabasis,* ed. G. Roos (Leipzig 1907) 7,14,3 (οὔτε = not even); Mayser II/3 172 b. Μήτε and μηδέ are often confused in the Mss of the NT (BDF §445, n. 1).

[2] Εἰς in the midst of the series with ἐν is striking. Is the idea that of a solemn oath with ''prayer orientation'' toward Jerusalem? A formula of swearing with the name of Jerusalem is not documented in Jewish writings, cf. Str-B I 333.

[3] Form: second person sing., repetition of ὀμνύω; content: ''human'' instead of ''superhuman'' substitute in the oath, different foundation, lack of an allusion to the OT.

2. *History of tradition.* The antithesis is not homogeneous. Verse 36 is striking. It is unique that Jesus argues with the scripture (vv. 34f.). Verses 34f., 37 have a variant in James 5:12, which is not formulated as an antithesis.

2.1. *The fragment of original tradition* has to be reconstructed with the aid of James 5:12.[4] This verse contains a basic element of the "specification" of vv. 34f., but without the allusions to Scripture and without v. 36. Its second part corresponds to the positive admonition, Matt. 5:37. But it does not speak of a double yes or no, but formulates with a predicate, "Let your yes be a yes and your no a no." The conclusion is quite different from Matt. 5:37b.

In my opinion, James 5:12 permits the following conclusions: (1) Matt. 5:36 is a secondary addition. (2) The antithetical formulation is presumably[5] not original. It is in favor of this view that the thesis does not contain a clear Old Testament reference in v. 33 and that there are no linguistic correspondences between thesis and antithesis. Thus 5:33f. is different from 5:21f. and 5:27f. (3) A basic piece of vv. 34f. may have belonged to the original text. Especially the Old Testament motivations are secondary. If this is correct, then the prohibition part and the command part of the admonition, as in James 5:12, would be approximately of equal length.[6] (4) The predicative formulation of the double yes and no which occurs in James 5:12 is original. It speaks for this view that it is found overwhelmingly in the tradition of the early church, even in places where Matt. 5:37 is clearly effective.[7] (5) The concluding part is quite uncertain: Matt. 5:37b could be formulated in the redaction;[8] but the final phrase of James 5:12 ("in order that you do not come into judgment") is probably not old either.[9]

Result: At the beginning of this tradition there was a hortatory saying in the second person plural of two parts, preserved in its basic structure in James 5:12.

2.2. *Secondary text parts.*

---

[4]A further close parallel is found in *2 Enoch* 49:1 (long recension): "I (Enoch) am swearing to you, . . . neither by heaven nor by earth . . . For [the Lord] said, 'There is no oath in me, nor any unrighteousness, but only truth.' So, if there is no truth in human beings, then let them make an oath by means of the words 'Yes, Yes!' or, if it should be the other way around, 'No, No!' " (trans. F. I. Andersen, in *The Old Testament Pseudepigrapha: Apocalyptic Literature & Testaments*, ed. J. H. Charlesworth). The passage, which can easily be detached from its context, is a Christian addition, according to A. Vaillant, *Le Livre des secrets d'Hénoch* (Paris: Institut d'études slaves, 1952), 109 n. 7, and U. Fischer, *Eschatologie und Jenseitserwartung im hellenistischen Diasporajudentum* (Berlin: de Gruyter, 1978), 37-39.

[5]E.g., Strecker** 58,61 (v. 37 is a secondary, "ethicizing accretion to the original antithesis 33-34a") or Guelich*** 211-16,249 (original antithesis 33a,34a,37a; 33b speaks in contrast to 33a of promissory oaths and is together with 34b-36 secondary) are in favor of the genuineness of the antithesis form. According to Ogawa, *Histoire* 131, and Stendahl 679h, the antithesis is redactional, according to Wrege*** 74 pre-Matthean, but very late ("Gentile-Christian circles . . . for whom the problem of the Torah is solved christologically").

[6]The following features are in favor of assuming that the Old Testament allusions are a secondary accretion. In wisdom admonitions there are normally no Old Testament quotations. Ἱεροσόλυμα is the Greek form of the name. The parallel Matt. 23:22 also is relatively late.

[7]Justin, *Apol.* 1.16.5; Clement of Alexandria, *Strom.* 5.99.1; 7.67.5; Pseudo Clement, *Hom.* 3.55.1; 19.2.4; *Apostolic Constitutions* 5.12.6; Jeû 2,43 = GCS 45,305; Epiphanius *Haer.* 19.6.2 = *PG* 41,269. Justin and Jeû do not know James, Ps. Clem. probably not, Clement of Alexandria probably knows James but does not quote it (cf. F. Mussner, *Der Jakobusbrief* [Freiburg: Herder, 1964] 39. It is the more striking that here the original text is influential on the basis of oral tradition because in most places mentioned Matt. 5:37 is quoted, cf. Guelich, "Not to Annul,"** 159-63; G. Strecker, "Eine Evangelienharmonie bei Justin und Pseudoklemens?" *NTS* 24 (1977/78) 308.

[8]Cf. introduction 3.2. Πονηρός and the stem περισσ- are Matthean.

[9]Matthew hardly would have suppressed this reference to the last judgment, cf. 5:26,30.

2.2.1. *Verse 33.* Οὐκ ἐπιορκήσεις is not in the Old Testament and has linguistic relations neither to the decalogue commandment concerning the name of God (Exod. 20:7) nor to Lev. 19:12. But this prohibition occurs in Hellenistic Jewish parenesis (Pseudo-Phocylides 16; *Sib. Or.* 2.68; cf. Philo, *Spec. Leg.* 2.224; *Did.* 2:3). The second part distantly recalls the wording of Ps. 49:14 (Eng., 50:14), but there vows (εὐχαί) are the subject. The two parts of the thesis are related unequally to the antithesis: the prohibition (v. 33a) is rather intensified, the command (v. 33b) is abolished. Ἀποδίδωμι ὅρκον is unusual in Jewish-Christian writings but is a Greek phrase.[10] Probably v. 33 comes from a Greek-speaking Jewish-Christian community which, following the first and second antithesis[11] and recalling the second commandment of the decalogue (Exod. 20:7)[12] and similar series of ethical prohibitions,[13] formulated the prohibition of swearing antithetically. It is an unnecessary assumption to suppose that v. 33b is secondary in comparison with v. 33a.[14]

2.2.2. The expansions from the Old Testament of the three substitute swearing formulas in vv. 34f. are secondary. Since they are beautifully symmetrical, they have been formulated in one process. It can no longer be stated whether the Hebrew or the Greek text is presupposed.

2.2.3. Verse 36, which formally follows vv. 34f. is very late. It has numerous Hellenistic and Jewish parallels.[15]

Origin. Since the categorical prohibition of swearing is unique in Judaism, it probably comes from Jesus.[16]

Interpretation

Jesus in v. 34 articulates a fundamental and unrestricted (ὅλως)[17] prohibition of

---

[10]E.g., Demosthenes, *Or.* 19.318; Aeschinus, *Or.* 3.74; W. Dittenberger, *Sylloge Inscriptionum Graecarum*[4] 150,166; P.Oxy. 1026.6 (to fulfill an oath).

[11]Was the two-part structure of v. 21 imitated in v. 33?

[12]Jewish interpretation of the second commandment in regard to swearing in Philo, *Decal.* 82-95 and Str-B I 326.

[13]Cf. Jer. 7:9; *3 Apoc. Bar.* 4:17 (φόνοι, μοιχεῖαι, πορνεῖαι, ἐπιορκεῖαι = Antitheses 1-4!), cf. also 13:4.

[14]E.g., in Manson, *Sayings* 158; Guelich*** 213f.; Merklein, *Gottesherrschaft* 266. Usually exegetes understand ὅρκοι then, in indirect link with Ps. 50:14 as promissory oaths. Verse 33a would speak of assertive, v. 33b of promissory oaths. It is difficult for me to understand this argumentation. One cannot argue with Ps. 50:14, for it speaks of vows; in the Greek text, only the word ἀποδίδωμι is in common (with different verb forms). There is no deliberate reminiscence of Ps. 50:14; v. 33b is formulated on the basis of the Old Testament just as little as v. 33a.

[15]Wettstein I 305f.; Jewish: *Sanh.* 3:2 = Str-B I 334; *b. Ber.* 3a (Fiebig*** no. 185).

[16]Dautzenberg*, especially 65, considers it seriously possible that the prohibition of swearing could have had its origin in a Jewish-Christian community, because ''as an instruction of Jesus it was widely unknown in early Christianity.'' Is a prohibition of swearing—not by Jesus but also not (cf. below) Jewish—really conceivable as the contribution of a Jewish-Christian community to the Jewish discussion of oaths? In my opinion this is a classical instance of the criterion of dissimilarity.

[17]There were again and again attempts to evade ὅλως. Examples: Calvin I 193; Beza 23 (it is only the issue of oaths ''per rem creatam, ut apparet ex proxime sequentibus . . formulis'' [by a created thing, as is apparent from the next following . . . formulas]). It is nice but impossible to replace ὅλως with the aid of sy[sin] (cf. Merx, *Evangelien* II/1, 101f.) by ὑμᾶς.

oaths. Probably he was the first person[18] to draw from the critical attitude toward oaths which was widespread in antiquity the consequence of a fundamental prohibition.

In Hellenism, the critique of oaths is widespread. The oath contradicts basic ethical principles. The person should himself or herself be reliable and not be bound by heteronomous authority. Oaths are undignified for a free human being.[19] Critique of oaths may take on an enlightenment, antireligious note: appeal to the gods is superfluous because the reliability of the human being alone is decisive.[20] The support of truth by religion has decayed.[21] The critique of oaths, however, may also—especially in late antiquity—have a religious character: the true sage does not need oaths because he carries God in himself.[22] To swear an oath means to pull God down into human affairs.[23]

Many of these Hellenistic motifs are found again in *Philo*. Because he is a Jew, he thinks about the oath question theologically, based on the holiness of God. No one can swear by God since no one has a direct knowledge of God's nature (*Leg. All.* 3.207). To swear means a defilement and desecration of the divine name (*Spec. Leg.* 4.40; *Decal.* 93). The law means that the mere word of an upright person is an oath (*Spec. Leg.* 2.2). Even to swear truthfully is only the second best possibility (*Decal.* 84). Not to swear would really be according to reason (*Decal.* 84), for "frequent swearing is for the rational person a proof . . . of untrustworthiness" (*Spec. Leg.* 2.8).

The *Essenes*, according to the report of Josephus (*War* 2.135) reject oaths and were excused by Herod from the fealty oath of subjects (*Ant.* 15.371). But in reality, they not only know the oath at entering the sect (1QS 5.8-11), but also the oath before court; their peculiar custom seems to have been to prohibit a private oath but to permit the oath before a judicial court (*CDC* 9.8-12; 15.3f.) and to avoid the name of God (*CDC* 15.1).

In *rabbinical Judaism*, prophetic (e.g., Hos. 4:2) and wisdom (Sir. 23:9-11) critique of frequent swearing had an effect. They made a "fence around the Torah" by attempting, through regulations and penalties, to prevent the misuse of the divine name by false or superfluous oaths,[24] but also by impressively warning in parenesis against

---

[18]The evaluation of the Pythagoreans is difficult. According to Diodorus Siculus 10.9.1 Pythagoras recommends to swear only rarely. The neo-Pythagorean "Golden Verses" know of an oath of the Pythagorean community which may have to do with the secret discipline (cf. B. L. van der Waerden, *Die Pythagoräer* [Munich: Artemis, 1979], 149, 151) and may come from very ancient times (cf. the oath formula, ibid. 104). Only according to reports of late antiquity did the Pythagoreans refuse the oath (Diogenes Laertius 8.22; Iamblichus *Vit. Pyth.* 9.47). The prohibition of oaths of the *Praecepta Delphica* in Ditt. Syll.[4] III 396 (= no. 1268, I 8) is difficult to classify historically.

[19]Examples: Sophocles, *Oed. Col.* 650; Choerilus Epicus in Johannes Stobaeus, Ecl. 3.27.1; Menander, *Sententiae* 592, ed. S. Jaekel (Leipzig: Teubner, 1964), 67; Plut II 275C (βάσανος . . . ἐλευθέρων); Epictetus, *Ench.* 33.5 (avoidance of oaths as far as possible); Quintilianus, *Inst. Orat.* 9.2.98 ("gravi viro parum convenit" [it suits a serious person little]). Already father Zeus—in distinction from Yahweh who swears by himself— has nodded his head as a sign of his trustworthy statement (Homer, *Iliad* 1.524-28). Cf. Hirzel* 109-24.

[20]Aeschylus, fragment 394 (TGF 114); οὐκ ἀνδρὸς ὅρκοι πίστις, ἀλλ᾽ ὅρκων ἀνήρ; Cicero, *Or.* 36.5 (12): "Graeci . . . noluerint religione videri potius, quam veritate" (The Greeks did not want to seem stronger in religion than in truthfulness).

[21]Examples in Hirzel* 113-23.

[22]Marcus Aurelius 3.5.

[23]Simplicius, in Epictetus 33.5 (= Dübner 114).

[24] *Šeb.* 3:7 (punishment by scourging for violation of an oath); *b. Šeb.* 38a (Str-B I 323f.).

careless swearing.[25] The second commandment is understood as prohibiting false and unnecessary oaths.[26] Statements which draw the "fence" around the Torah so wide that they reject swearing as such are very rare.[27]

5:34, 37

Jesus, like the rabbis and Philo, speaks against misuse of oaths as a flowery formula of confirmation in everyday life.[28] The form of the saying and the prohibition of substitute expressions (vv. 34f.) point in this direction. We know that at that time oaths were used at the most trifling occasions, much more frequently than today.[29] Jesus thus stands completely in the tendency of Jewish parenesis but goes beyond it by categorically prohibiting oaths. Oaths to be sworn before court[30] and official loyalty oaths[31] are probably affected only indirectly by his comprehensive formulation. The concrete examples "not by heaven, not by earth, not by Jerusalem" intensify the prohibition. It is valid under all circumstances, even with substitute formulas. "By heaven" or "by earth" were favorite formulas in Judaism in order to avoid the name of God while swearing. Even "harmless" oaths are included in the prohibition.[32] Jesus does not go the way of Philo, who recommends for the protection of God's name the substitutionary formulas as a lesser evil.[33]

Positively, Jesus demands unrestricted truthfulness of the human word. "He eliminated the distinction between words which have to be true and those which do not have to be true."[34] There are not to be two kinds of truth among

---

[25]Str-B I 328-30; impressively also *b. Ber.* 33a = Str-B I 326: Even the one who speaks an unnecessary blessing transgresses the second commandment; *p. Šeb.* 6,37a,54 = Str-B I 329: a proverb: Whether pure or guilty, do not get involved with an oath. Further examples in Montefiore, *Literature* 48-50.

[26]Str-B I 326f.

[27]Tanch. 126: "Do not think that it is permitted to swear by my name. Not even for the affirmation of truth is it permitted; even there it is not fitting for humans to swear that they may not learn to play with vows and and to deceive their neighbor by oaths" (Bischoff*** 54); Tanch B § 1 79a (Str-B I 330) makes the permission to swear dependent on complete piety; *b. Šebu.* 36a = Str-B I 336: "No" is an oath and "Yes" is an oath. Orthodox Jews do not swear before court (Lapide*** 76).

[28]Cf. Zeller, *Mahnsprüche* 126.

[29]Philo, *Decal.* 92 ("bad habit," "at any occasion"). The oaths which are enumerated in the foundational chapter *Šeb.* 3:1-9 are instructive, e.g., "I swear that I will eat"; "I swear that I will give this to such a man" or "that I will not give it," or "that I will sleep" or "that I will not sleep" or "that I will throw a stone into the sea"; somebody swears to neglect a commandment, not to take a *lulab* or not to put on the *tephilim*, etc.

[30]Cf. Str-B I 322-25.

[31]Cf. J. Schneider, "ὅρκος κτλ.," *TDNT* V 459ff.; E. Seidl, *Der Eid im römisch-ägyptischen Provinzialrecht* I (Munich: Beck, 1933), 44ff. passim; for Palestine cf. Josephus *Ant.* 15.368-72.

[32]Meier, *Law* 156.

[33]Cf. *Spec. Leg.* 2.3-5.

[34]Schlatter 181.

people. In this, Jesus is in agreement with old and new philosophy[35] and humanism.[36] The human being in the whole of everyday life is bound to God without any limitation.

Nevertheless, the entirety of Jesus' demand is not yet seen. Jesus' prohibition of oaths is more than a categorical rejection of lies. The specific examples in vv. 34f. show that he, just as Judaism on the whole, is concerned about the sanctification of God's name and about God's majesty.[37] In other words, Jesus is not only concerned about truthfulness so that the case of the oath would exemplify what truthfulness is. But he is concerned about the oath because here the name of God is invoked. The anthropological aspect, the command of truthfulness, has its theological correlative in the demand of sanctification of God's name. In this, Jesus is in accord with Jewish thinking concerning the oath. By prohibiting oaths in principle,[38] he is more radical than his Jewish contemporaries.[39]

As with other categorical demands of Jesus, this one also is somewhat unrealistic. Jesus does not consider what an absolute prohibition of oaths would involve, namely, consequences of a very problematic kind.[40] Jesus considers this as little as he does with his demand to renounce force or with his prohibition of divorce. The will of God has priority over everything else. In this radicality one may see a sign of the eschatological kingdom of God to which Jesus knew himself bound, although the text does not speak explicitly of it.[41]

---

[35]An impressive example of a philosophical interpretation of the fourth antithesis is given by I. Kant, *Religion within the Limits of Reason Alone* (New York: Harper & Brothers, 1934), 147: The oath relies on superstition because it presupposes that a person whom one does not trust to tell the truth ''is yet expected to be persuaded to speak truly, by the use of a formula.'' The bad effect of oaths which Jesus had in mind is ''that the greater importance attached to them almost sanctions the common lie.''

[36]Example: Shakespeare, Julius Caesar, Act II/1 (Brutus): ''What need we . . . / . . . other oath / than honesty to honesty engag'd / . . .? / Swear priests and cowards and men cautelous, / old feeble carrions . . . ?''

[37]Meier, *Law* 155, points correctly to ''the well-known axiom beloved of the Germans: . . . God is not at our disposal.''

[38]Zeller, *Mahnsprüche,* opines that Jesus' prohibition is limited to interhuman relationships *only* and therefore does not come into conflict with the Old Testament command of the oath before court. The principal formulation (ὅλως) speaks against this view. The community also, which formulated the antithesis, has understood Jesus differently, it seems to me.

[39]How little Jesus' prohibition of oaths was felt as un-Jewish can be seen by the fact that the Jew Josephus, who sees complete renunciation of oaths among the Essenes, nevertheless considers them a very excellent Jewish school of philosophers.

[40]E.g., the oaths of purification for debtors, the oaths of deposits (sworn declaration of innocence of an accused when witnesses are lacking), also the oaths of fulfillment for wronged laborers, robbed persons, or wounded persons (against perjured opponents in law suits) or the possibility of oaths for women in suits of divorce would be negated.

[41]This proposal of interpretation presupposes the incorrectness of two other interpretations: Berger** 163f. sees the decisive motive in an ''increased fear of defilement'' of the divine name which he wants to find in numerous early Jewish texts. Schweizer 128 sees in the antithesis the liberation ''from the painstaking discrimination between innocuous formulas and those that use God's name or tacitly include it.'' When did Judaism consider this as laborious?

5:33

The *community* has interpreted Jesus' prohibition of oaths in various ways.
Verse 33 determines its relationship to the Old Testament. Through the form of
antitheses the community has indicated that the Old Testament law of God has
been surpassed by Jesus' proclamation. This surpassing involves not only an
element of deepening, namely, a more comprehensive sanctification of the name
of God but also an element of abrogation, namely, the rejection of the oath.
Thus, a prohibition of oaths can obviously not only be considered as a consistent
sanctification of the name of God by Jewish eyes, as by Philo, Josephus, and
others, but also more critically because the oath in the Old Testament is an
established component of the law of God and an obligatory command (cf., e.g.,
Num. 5:19-22). In the antithetical formulation, there is some ambivalence:
Jesus' prohibition of swearing is indeed the most consistent avoidance of a false
oath (v. 33a); but the one who obeys it does no longer render to the Lord oaths
and vows (v. 33b).

5:34-35

The additions of the community to vv. 34f. intensify the original meaning but
do not yet change it: In remembrance of Isa. 66:1 and Ps. 48:3, the community
intensifies the idea of the majesty of God who stands behind the substitute
formulas (cf. 23:22).

5:36

Beginning in v. 36, the accents are shifted. First, the verse shows that the
prohibition of oaths is really to be understood as specific and not only in a
Platonic general way by taking up still another common formula.[42] But the
argumentation has shifted: the concern is no longer primarily the power of God
but the powerlessness of human beings, who cannot even change the color of
their hair.[43] The tone of the verse is one of wisdomlike resignation, similarly to
Matt. 6:27, 34.

5:37

Verse 37 is newly formulated in the Matthew tradition. What is meant by the
double yes or no? There are two Jewish examples which understand a double
yes as a substitute for an oath.[44] On this basis it was thought that v. 37 could be
understood as an expression of the initial softening of the prohibition of oaths:
Matthew still is maintaining the prohibition of oaths, but gives his community a
special formula of confirmation.[45] Probably this is wrong; duplication of the

---

[42]*Sanh.* 3:2 = Str-B I 334; numerous Hellenistic examples in Wettstein I 305f.

[43]In the early church, a prohibition of dying one's hair was seen in the verse (Tertullian, *Cult. fem.* 2.6;
Cyprian, *Hab. Virg.* 16). But from the chosen formulation one can conclude at most (sociologically)
that this problem was no longer alive in the Matthean communities.

[44]*2 Enoch* 49:1 (= above n. 4); *b. Šeb.* 36a = Str-B I 336 (4th century).

[45] Hoffmann III*** 184; Strecker, *Weg* 133f.; Wrege*** 73, etc.

word as a rule provides intensification in Greek[46] as well as in Semitic languages.[47] "Yes, yes" means nothing but a true yes, a yes which is valid and has solidity.[48] Thus, one cannot speak of an evasion of the prohibition of oaths in the Matthean version either.

We can hardly say for sure how Matthew himself has interpreted the text. Through his concluding "what is more is of evil" he points out that he wants to understand the prohibition and the command of Jesus literally. He makes Jesus keep his own command: when the high priest "adjures" Jesus to confess himself as Son of God, which is to be understood most likely as an exhortation to an oath, Jesus does not answer with an oath but with σὺ εἶπας, which leaves the responsibility for the statement with the high priest without contesting its truth (26:63).

History of Influence

Once again, the history of influence[49] is characterized by attempts to remove the sting of the text and to make its demand easier or to evade it. However, in the early church it was interpreted almost always literally,[50] in the Greek-speaking church for a very long time, since John Chrysostom had emphasized it strongly with his whole authority.[51] In the Latin church the attempts at mitigation began already early.[52] Striking is its temporal connection with the Constantinian reversal, when on the imperial level oaths of officers or oaths to the flag under Christian emperors were introduced.[53] The church now sees in the rejection of Gentile oath formulas and in the insistence on a "Christian" oath an urgent concern. The attempts to adapt Matt. 5:33-37 to the new reality are manifold.

a. In various ways, as far as the subject matter is concerned, the rabbinic thesis of the "*fence around the law*" is reactivated. That which Jesus' prohibition wants to

---

[46]Intensifying ναί ναί in Preis, *Zaub* I pap 1 line 90 (p. 6); Aristophanes, *Nub.* 1468; Theocritus, *Idyll* 4.54; Archilochus, fragment 990; Petronius, *Sat.* (ed. M. Heseltine, Cambridge: Harvard University, 1961) 25,1 (*ita ita*), probably also 2 Cor. 1:17. On the intensifying character of duplication as such cf. Stählin 119f. n. 2; BDF § 493.

[47]Intensifying שׁ֗י, ךְי֗ה and similar words: 2 Kings 10:15; *Mekh. Exod.* 20:3 = Fiebig*** no. 203; further examples Str-B I 337. To reach back to Assyrian texts of the 7th century (Kutsch*) is unnecessary.

[48]In favor of this view is also the fact that the interpretation of the early church has never understood ναί ναί as a Christian formula of affirmation, as far as I know.

[49]On the history of oaths in Christianity (not only as posthistory of Matt. 5:33-37) cf. Honecker*; useful collection of texts in H. Bethke, *Eid, Gewissen, Treuepflicht*, Antworten 8 (Frankfurt: Stimme, 1965), 155-300.

[50]Justin, *Apol.* 1.16.5; Ireneus, *Haer.* 2.32.1; Ptolemy ad Flor = Epiphanius, *Haer.* 33.6.1; Clement of Alexandria, *Strom* 7.50.1 = BKV II/20 56; Basil, *Ep.* 59 (199, Amphilochius) *can* 29 = BKV I/46 210, etc.

[51]John Chrysostom 17.5-7 = 313-22; idem, *Stat.* 15.5 = *PG* 49,160f.; following him, e.g., *opus imperfectum* 12 = 697; Dionysius bar Salibi 167; Theophylact 200.

[52]Cyprian, *De Mort.* 4 = BKV I/34 237; idem, *Test.* 3.12 = *PL* 4,741, is one of the few Latin fathers who consistently rejects the oath.

[53]P. Hofmeister, *Die christlichen Eidesformen* (Munich 1957), 10f.

prevent is the *false oath*. In order to prevent it, he prohibits oaths as such.[54] Or: Jesus is concerned only with preventing the *thoughtless oath*;[55] he forbids the oath, for a frivolous oath leads to habit, and habit leads to false oaths. "Therefore, the Savior, out of respect for oaths, has forbidden swearing."[56] Paul is an example of thoughtful application of the oath—only in his letters, i.e., in writing and after deliberation, but never in his sermons did he swear.[57] With this interpretation, Jesus' prohibition of oaths has been brought again to the level of rabbinic parenesis and of the Old Testament. Only few advocates of this interpretation have recognized this, most clearly Calvin, who deliberately affirmed the orientation by the Mosaic law as the final measure: Jesus forbids "only such oaths . . . which also were forbidden by the law."[58]

b. The thesis is frequent that Jesus has not *forbidden* oaths by the name of God but *only the substitute formulas* enumerated in vv. 34b-36.[59] The Christian aversion against "substitute formulas" was based first of all probably on the aversion against "Gentile" oath formulas,[60] later in Protestantism on the aversion against the veneration of saints.[61]

c. The model of a *two-level ethics* was transferred to the fourth antithesis. Several monastic rules, e.g., the rule of Benedict (ch. 4), prohibit the oath of monks. Priests also in the Middle Ages often were freed from the duty to swear oaths. It is interesting that kings and the nobility up to the modern period tried to claim the same privilege for themselves.[62]

d. The *distinction of the two kingdoms* is decisive in the interpretation of the Reformers. The prohibition of oaths does not apply to the realm of the state. Luther can bring the distinction to the simple but fatal formula, as far as the history of its influence is concerned, that oaths that one is ordered to take are not touched by Jesus' prohibition.[63] The necessity of oaths in the area of the state moves more and more to the center of the statements of the Reformers, especially in opposition to the Anabaptists. If one prohibits oaths, then this is "a destruction of secular government and justice. For government and justice are constituted on the oath."[64] Thus the normal practice of

---

[54]Augustine, *Mend.* 28 = *PL* 40,507; Gregory of Nazianzus, *Or.* 4 *contra Jul.* 1.123 = *PG* 35,661-63; Thomas, *STh* 1/II qu 107 art 2; Strabo on 5:37, etc.

[55]Thomas, *STh* 2/I qu 89 art 3 ("sine necessitate et cautela" [without necessity and caution]; Zwingli 229f.; *Catechismus Genevensis* 160 (BSKORK 19); Maldonat 123; Wolzogen 225 (against voluntary oath).

[56]Zinzendorf I 271.

[57]Augustine, *Mend.* 15 = *PL* 40,507.

[58]Calvin, *Inst.* 2.8.27.

[59]Cyril of Alexandria 380f.; Jerome on 5:34; Beza 24.

[60]*Opus imperfectum* 12 - 698 ("quia deificat per quem iurat" [because it deifies him by whom he swears]).

[61]*Heidelberg Catechism*, question 102.

[62]Gregory of Nazianzus, *Or.* 53.8 = *PG* 10,1008: Gregory himself does not swear but he does not make this a duty. On the prohibition of oaths for monks, priests, and the nobility, cf. Hofmeister (above n. 53) 83-89.

[63]"Nobody shall swear of himself . . . Where it is a matter of God's word, there everything is accept-able, swearing, being angry . . . But that means to have God's word regarding it, when he commands me officially and for his sake or demands it through those who bear office" (WA 32***, 384).

[64]Melanchthon, *Verlegung etlicher unchristlicher Artikel . . .*, *Werke* I, ed. R. Stupperich (Gütersloh: Mohn, 1951), 311.

Protestantism is formed which considers oaths as permissible when one of the following conditions is met: It has to (a) deal with an important matter, (b) involve the honor of God, (c) be for the best of the fellow human being, or (d) be an oath commanded by the authority.[65]

    e. Closely related with this interpretation is another type which understands the difference of the two kingdoms as the *difference between this eon and the kingdom of God*. Because of sin our antithesis is now hardly usable.[66] One accepts oaths as an "emergency measure"[67] and states with regret, "infirmitas . . . cogit (weakness makes it necessary)."[68] The oath is necessary, as medicine is for the sick person.[69]

    f. Finally, a type of recent origin must be mentioned, one that attempts to limit prohibited oaths to *promissory oaths* and wants to except affirmative ones.[70]

    g. *Reference to other New Testament passages* with which our antithesis was to be harmonized plays a considerable role in the whole interpretation. Aside from the reference to Jesus' own oath before the high priest (Matt. 26:63),[71] exegetically probably a wrong reference, and the reference to Heb. 6:16, it is especially Paul who, in different ways, plays a role, especially in his efforts for the gospel, in calling on God as witness (Rom. 1:9; 2 Cor. 1:23; Gal. 1:20; Phil. 1:8; 1 Thess. 2:4).

The entire tradition of the Great Church since the early Middle Ages almost unanimously set Matt. 5:33-37 aside and accepted oaths, even though often with a bad conscience. Some few nonconformist groups and individuals stand in contrast with this history.

    In the Middle Ages it was notably the *Cathari*[72] and the *Waldensians* who refused oaths. Since the Reformation, the *Humanists* also rendered the text its right.[73] The seriousness which our text and with it the prohibition of oaths received among the *Anabaptists* lies on a completely different level.[74] The *Schleitheim Confession* says in a simple manner, well worth consideration, "He says: Let your speech or your word be Yes and No, which cannot be understood in such a way as if he had permitted oaths. Christ is simply Yes and No, and all those who seek him sincerely will understand his

---

[65]According to P. J. Spener, *Kurtze Catechismuspredigten* (1689), Schriften II/2 (reprint Hildesheim and New York: Olms 1982), 52.

[66]Olshausen 226f.: Oaths are necessary in the world of lies. Zwingli, "Von göttlicher und menschlicher Gerechtigkeit," *Hauptschriften* 7, ed. R. Pfister (Zürich: Zwingli, 1942), 58: "But if we do not do this (i.e., true speaking and acting), but deceive each other, then he (i.e., God) commands to force us by an oath."

[67]H. Thielicke, *Theological Ethics*, vol. 2: *Politics* (Philadelphia: Fortress,1969), 384.

[68]Strabo 96.

[69]Thomas, *STh* 2/II qu 89 art. 5.

[70]H. Grotius, *De iure belli et pacis* (Amsterdam: Janssonium, 1651), 250f. (= 2,13 par. 21); Wolzogen 225; F. Tillmann, *Handbuch der kath. Sittenlehre* IV/1, 4th ed. (Düsseldorf: Patmos, 1950), 256.

[71]Cf. above p. 318.

[72]H. Borst, *Die Katharer*, SMGH 12 (Stuttgart: Hiersemann, 1953), 185f.

[73]Erasmus, *Paraphrasis* 33C; Grotius I 161.

[74]H. J. Hillerbrand, *Die politische Ethik des oberdeutschen Täufertums* (Leiden: Brill, 1962), 60-69; E. Bernhofer-Pippert, *Täuferische Denkweisen und Lebensformen im Spiegel oberdeutscher Täuferverhöre*, RStT 96 (Münster: Aschendorf, 1967), 135-37; H. A. Hertzler, "Die Verweigerung des Eides," in *Die Mennoniten*, ed. H. J. Goertz, KW 8 (Stuttgart: Evangelisches Verlagswerk, 1971), 100-08; C. Neff, "Eid," *Menn Lex* I 535-46.

word."[75] After clear knowledge of the commandment, only obedience can follow. With Menno Simons[76] the emphasis is shifted to the problem of the subjective truthfulness of the person. If here perhaps the ancient-humanist tradition plays a role, then this is all the more the case with the *Quaker* William Penn, whose effective book on oaths works with the entire ancient tradition. According to him, swearing is forbidden by Christ, is detrimental for human nature because it creates two kinds of truths, and is unnecessary.[77] It is not surprising that *Tolstoy* joins the chorus of the nonconformists and rejects oaths, even as a basis of war (pledge of allegiance to the flag!).[78]

Summary

The survey of the history of interpretation and its errors is disturbing. It does not take much power of persuasion to demonstrate that the interpretation of the nonconformists comes closest to the text. Nevertheless, even considering the fact that in the major churches, obviously under the influences of external circumstances, the text was missed, it should not be overlooked that the simple obedience of nonconformism does not solve all the hermeneutical problems of the text.

    a. There remain questions posed by the total data of the New Testament. Jesus' prohibition of oaths was already in early Christianity obeyed only in a limited sense. Paul and Matt. 23:16-22 testify to this. In contrast to fasting (Mark 2:20) and the renunciation of force (Luke 22:35f.), the distinction from Jesus is never reflected upon. Was the prohibition of oaths by Jesus known only sparsely?[79] The fasting commandment, the rule of provisions, or the prohibition of divorce show that in early Christianity Jesus' commandments were nuanced and—in a positive or negative sense—adapted.[80] What would this mean for the prohibition of oaths?

    b. Jesus' rejection of oaths may come into conflict with the center of the gospel of love. Therefore in Catholic tradition, according to Jer. 4:2, truth, judgment, and justice became the criteria of oaths.[81] The interpretation of the Reformation is still clearer; it makes love the measure for the rendering of oaths: "Thus, one may swear out of duty of love, namely, if one neighbor swears to the other to be faithful to him if the other desires it, not . . . only in spiritual matters."[82] Calvin formulates in the sense of the double commandment: our

---

[75]*Schleitheim Confession*, art. 7 (text in *Der linke Flügel der Reformation*, ed. H. Fast, Klassiker des Protestantismus 4 [Bremen: Schünemann, 1962], 69f.).

[76]Hertzler (above n. 74) 103.

[77]Cf. W. Comfort, *Just among Friends* (New York: Macmillan, 1941), 62ff.; *Principles of Quakerism: A Collection of Essays* (Philadelphia, 1909), 163-79 (official self-description with much material on the history of influence).

[78]Tolstoy*** 245-63 (= ch. 12).

[79]Cf. on this Stählin* and Bauernfeind*.

[80]An example of the nuanced application is given in the Martyrdom of Apollonius 6 = BKV I/14 320: Although oaths are principally eliminated in favor of the simple "Yes," Apollonius is willing to demonstrate his homage to the emperor by an oath but not to sacrifice to him.

[81]*Veritas, iudicium, iustitia*: Thomas, *STh* 2/II qu 89 art 3; *CIC* Can 1316.

[82]Luther, *Predigten über das 2. Buch Mose 1524-1527*, WA 16,475.

oath is to "... be made to serve a just necessity; in other words, to vindicate the glory of God, or promote the edification of a brother [or sister]."[83] With this, the Reformers came to that point where Matthew himself through his arrangement of the Antitheses put the center of the individual commands of Christ (but not a reason for their elimination!). Unfortunately, he reflects about the relationship of the individual commandments to the commandment of love just as little as about the relationship of the Old Testament iotas and little pen strokes to it. Probably they are subordinated to the commandment of love from case to case while in the major churches the tendency prevailed actually to eliminate them.

Questions also result from the eschatological character of the demands of Jesus. They were "law of the kingdom of God," not of the world. The question of how far, despite the delay of the kingdom of God, they should be practiced as a sign pointing to it, must be answered in the light of faith in the risen Lord. Matthew has given his answer with the offer of the way to "perfection," on which the risen one helps his community. It is not in harmony with this answer that today not even in the ecclesiastical realm have oaths completely disappeared.[84]

2.2.5. Fifth Antithesis: On Nonviolence (5:38-42)

Literature

On 5:38-48

Blank, J., "Gewaltlosigkeit—Krieg—Militärdienst," *Orient* 46 (1982) 157-63, 213-16, 220-23.

Dihle, A., *Die goldene Regel,* SAW 7 (Göttingen: Vandenhoeck & Ruprecht, 1962).

Fiebig, P., "Jesu Worte über die Feindesliebe," *TSK* 91 (1918) 30-64.

Lienemann, W., *Gewalt und Gewaltlosigkeit. Studien zur abendländischen Vorge-schichte der gegenwärtigen Wahrnehmung von Gewalt,* FBESG 36 (Munich: Kaiser, 1982).

Lührmann, D., "Liebet eure Feinde (Lk 6,27-36; Mt 5,39-48)," *ZTK* 69 (1972) 412-38.

Piper, J., *Love Your Enemies,* SNTSMS 38 (Cambridge: At the University Press, 1979).

Schottroff, L., "Gewaltverzicht und Feindesliebe in der urchristlichen Jesustradition (Mt 5,38-48; Lk 6,27-36)," in *Jesus Christus in Historie und Theologie* (FS H. Conzelmann), ed. G. Strecker, pp. 197-221 (Tübingen: Mohr, 1975).

Strecker, G., "Compliance—Love of One's Enemy—The Golden Rule," *ABR* 29 (1981) 38-46.

Theissen, G., "Gewaltverzicht und Feindesliebe (Mt 5,38-48; Lk 6,27-38) und deren sozialgeschichtlicher Hintergrund," in idem, *Studien* 160-97.

On 5:38-42:

Clavier, H., "Matthieu 5,39 et la non-résistance," *RHPR* 37 (1957) 44-57.

---

[83]Calvin, *Inst.* 2.8.27.

[84]In the *CIC*, the oath is solidly anchored (cf. index). On the situation in the Protestant Churches of Germany, G. Niemeier, "Eid und Gelöbnis im Recht der Kirche," in idem, ed., *Ich schwöre* (Munich: Kaiser, 1968), 103-119, is informative.

Currie, S., "Matthew 5,39f—Resistance or Protest?" *HTR* 57 (1964) 140-45.

Daube, *New Testament* 254-65.

Fiebig, P. "ἀγγαρεύω," *ZNW* 18 (1917/18) 64-72.

Lohfink, G., "Der ekklesiale Sitz im Leben der Aufforderung Jesu zum Gewaltverzicht (Mt 5,39b-42; Lk 6,29f)," *TQ* 1662 (1982) 1236-53.

Sahlin, H., "Traditionskritische Bemerkungen zu zwei Evangelienperikopen," *ST* 33 (1979) 69-84.

Schulz, *Q* 120-27.

Tannehill, R., "The 'Focal Instance' as a Form of New Testament Speech: A Study of Matthew 5,39b-42," *JR* 50 (1970) 372-85.

Wolbert, W., "Bergpredigt und Gewaltlosigkeit," *TP* 57 (1982) 498-525.

Zeller, *Mahnsprüche* 55-60.

Further literature** cf. on 5:21-48 above pp. 273-274. Literature*** on the Sermon on the Mount at Matt. 5-7 above pp. 209-211.

Text

38 You have heard that it was said,
   "An eye for an eye and a tooth for a tooth!"
39 But I say to you,
   Do not resist evil.
   But whoever slaps you on your right cheek,
   offer him or her the other also.
40 And the one who wants to sue you and take away your tunic,
   let him or her have the cloak also.
41 And whoever forces you to a mile of compulsory service
   go two with him.
42 Give to the one who asks you.
   And do not turn away from the one who wants to borrow from you.

Analysis

1. *Structure.* The introductory phrase is again abbreviated, verbally identical to 5:43. The prohibition of Jesus is formulated with μή + infinitive, as in 5:34. Thus the fifth antithesis is connected backward and forward. After the true antithesis vv. 38-39a there is a transition to the second person singular with four admonitory sayings as concretions, alternately introduced with ὅστις and the participle. Thus, the whole text is formally very unified; only v. 42 is exempt from the symmetry of the concretions: it contains a double imperative in final position. This gives v. 42 a special accent.

2. *Redaction and sources.* Aside from vv. 38-39a, Q lies at the basis. Matthew has isolated the logia Luke 6:29f. from the whole of the Q composition on love of enemy (Luke 6:27-36) and shaped from it the explanation of the fifth antithesis. The reconstruction of the wording of Q is difficult. The numerous variants in the Apostolic Fathers and in the Apologists hardly help in this reconstruction.[1]

2.1. The *antithesis (vv. 38-39a)* probably is due to the evangelist.[2] Reasons: The quotation (from Exod. 21:24; Lev. 24:20; Deut. 19:21) corresponds to the LXX text.

---

[1] *Didache* 1:3-5; Ignatius, *Pol.* 2:1; *2 Clem.* 13:4; Polycarp, *Phil.* 12:3; Justin, *Apol.* 1.15.9-13; 16,1f.; *Dial.* 96.3. In all cases one has to count, it seems to me, at least *also* with direct or indirect influence of the Matthean text.

[2] Jeremias, *Theology* 251, and Wrege*** 80-82, who reject the Q hypothesis, count on a pre-Matthean "primary" antithesis; according to Percy, *Botschaft* 150; Hübner 95; and Dietzfelbinger, *Antithesen* 39, it goes back to Jesus.

In v. 39 μή + infinitive formally resumes v. 34. The verb ἀνθίστημι indeed is unique in Matthew, but it was necessary because in almost all antitheses (and all redactional ones!) there is a verbal connection between thesis and antithesis (ἀντί - ἀνθιστῆναι). Πονηρός is Matthean.[3]

2.2. In *vv. 39b, 41*, Matthew changes the participial construction; he has a fondness for ὅστις and also knows the Semitizing resumption of the relative pronouns through an αὐτός in the oblique case which is not congruent.[4] In *v. 39b* the addition of δεξιός may go back to Matthew[5] and the remaining linguistic differences to Luke. In *v. 40*,[6] it has to remain moot whether the Matthean version (situation of a lawsuit, order tunic-cloak) or the Lukan version (situation of a mugging?, the sequence cloak-tunic) is more original.[7] Neither of the two versions is redactional.

2.3. *Verse 41* is usually seen as a preredactional addition in QMt.[8] It is possible that Luke has omitted this verse, having lived in either a senatorial province or Rome where forced service did not occur because no troops were stationed there.[9]

2.4. *Verse 42*: The Matthean version of 42b is less radical than the Lukan version which again presupposes the situation of a robbery. By most commentators, the Matthean version is considered as older, and in Luke 6:34 a reminiscence of the original Q version (Matt. 5:42) is assumed.[10] The reverse seems to me more probable: Matthew had to shorten Luke 6:32-34 for reasons of symmetry;[11] he reformulated v. 42b in his language,[12] took over the otherwise missing theme of loaning from the omitted verse Luke 6:34, and shaped it into a command which was practicable in his community. Similarly in vv. 43, 46f. he took over the key words "hate" and "reward" from Luke 6:27,24.

3. *History of tradition and origin*. The four sayings 39b-42 are to be counted as parenetical hortatory sayings, formulated in the second person singular imperative. It is noteworthy—even if by no means unique in the framework of wisdom sayings—that the admonition is lacking an argumentation which makes it convincing. The verses 39b and 40 are formulated so pointedly that their origin with Jesus, on the basis of the "criterion of dissimilarity" is very probable; this judgment could apply also to v. 41, despite its

---

[3]Cf. introduction 3.2

[4]On ὅστις cf. introduction 3.2; Semitizing αὐτός as an anaphoron in an oblique case also 10:32f.; 13:12, cf. 12:50.

[5]Cf. 5:29f.

[6]The following could be Matthean (cf. introduction 3.2): θέλω, λαμβάνω, but not ἄφες which is used here differently from the customary usage.

[7]The Lukan situation is taken up again in 6:30b; but Matt. 5:40 and 42b also fit together since v. 40 is presumably concerned with a debtor's trial and with tunic and cloak as a pledge (cf. Exod. 22:26f.; Deut. 24:12f., with rules about lending Exod. 22:25; Deut. 24:10f.).

[8]Μίλιον does not speak in favor of this addition being made in a Greek-speaking area (so Strecker 64), for this Latin word is also a rabbinic loanword. If it is a matter of demands for assistance by officials or soldiers, it is a stylistic refinement.

[9]Thus Schweizer 67. However, the parallel Epictetus, *Diss.* 4.1.79, shows how little this argument is convincing.

[10]E.g., Schürmann, "Sprachliche Reminiszenzen an abgeänderte oder ausgelassene Bestandteile der Redequelle . . .," in idem, *Untersuchungen* 115; Merklein, *Gottesherrschaft* 225.

[11]Cf. above at 5:21-48 n. 1.

[12]The following might be Matthean: θέλω, ἀποστρέφω, cf. introduction 3.2. 'Από (usual with δανείζω) σοῦ points back to 5:29f., like δεξιός v. 39.

narrower base of tradition. Verse 42 is an originally independent exhortation whose origin—especially because of the uncertain relationships of the tradition—cannot be stated with assurance.

Explanation

The most important questions are: (1) To what degree are these commandments meant literally and to what extent do they "only" aim at a direction of acting or an attitude? (2) What is their area of applicability?

5:39b

The three sayings 39b-41 are to be interpreted by themselves at first. A slap in the face (v. 39b) was considered as an expression of hate and insult; the insult and not the pain stands in the foreground.[13] The addition of *right*, which perhaps comes from the evangelist to make it more precise, could mean an especially vehement insult. The slap on the *right* cheek is not the ordinary thing; for that one either has to be left-handed or slap with the back of the hand.[14] But it is more probable that it was made more precise arbitrarily for rhetorical reasons.[15] No special situation is in view. It is neither the issue that a master beats his slave or the oppressor the oppressed nor the waiver of legal retribution for insults[16] nor slaps on the cheek which the disciples receive during the mission ("as heretics"),[17] but rather any kind of violent altercation possible in everyday life. Slaps are so widespread that it is unnecessary to awaken special reminiscences of the servant of God of Isa. 50:6, who was beaten.[18]

5:40

Verse 40 is mindful of the situation of a debtor's suit. The tunic of a poor person is to be used as a pledge. That he should give his cloak also indicates an immense heightening, for the cloak is much more valuable than the tunic. In addition an indirect opposition to the Old Testament law of pledging is opened

---

[13]Cf. Isa. 50:6; Lam. 3:30. Wettstein I 309 gives examples for the proverbial phrase "os praebere contumeliis" (to offer the face for insults).

[14]*B. Qam.* 8:6 = Str-B I 342: For a slap with the back of the hand, a double penance is required. 1 Esdr. 4:30 (LXX) mentions a slap with the left hand as special insult.

[15]Otherwise, it would lead to an awkward anticlimax: After you have suffered the greater injustice (the slap on the right cheek), you shall accept also the smaller one. Cf. Maldonat 125: "Non caedendi, sed loquendi consuetudinem secutus est" (he has followed the custom not of hitting but of speaking).

[16]Guelich*** 221f., following Daube, *New Testament* 260-63, on the basis of *B. Qam.* 8:6 (above n. 14). The antithesis vv. 38-40 would then refer specifically to the realm of jurisdiction. That is improbable (a) because vv. 41f. would not longer fit, (b) because the "active" character of the actions commanded by Jesus would remain unexplained if it were a mere waiver of a lawsuit, and (c) because v. 39a also is not to be interpreted like this, cf. below at n. 37.

[17]Jeremias, *The Sermon on the Mount* (London: Athlone, 1961), 27.

[18]‘Ράπισμα/ῥαπίζω and σιαγών remind the reader of Isa. 50:6 and Hos. 11:4 but also of Lam. 3:30 and 1 Esdr. 4:30 (LXX). Dietzfelbinger, *ZNW* 1979** 12 bases his understanding of the fulfillment of Torah on these passages: Matthew leads his readers from retaliation on to these passages. If he only had said this more clearly!

here: to the poor man, who must give his cloak as a pledge, one must return this cloak every evening so that he can sleep in it (Exod. 22:26f.; Deut. 24:12f.). Thus the logion means that one should not get involved in such lawsuits at all, and even as a debtor one should voluntarily give up even the minimum of the right of the poor.

5:41

Verse 41 speaks of services demanded by force. Ἀγγαρεύω—perhaps a Persian loanword,[19] which occurs also in Latin and among the rabbis[20]—means services which are demanded as obligatory by the army or by officials, services like transportation and accompanying the group,[21] but also provisions and finally any kind of forced labor demanded even by others.[22] Thus the verse perhaps but not definitely implies a point against the Roman power of occupation. It is most likely that we should think of accompaniment—perhaps in insecure areas or for the transport of cargo.

5:39b-41

With this, our verses are "understood" only quite externally. What does Jesus intend with his surprising demands? Whom do they address? Out of which situation are they to be understood?

The general admonition to suffer injustice is widespread in all antiquity.[23] In Judaism, the exhortation to endure, to forgo revenge and to suffer vis-à-vis the individual enemy is especially evident when no infraction of the law of God is connected with it.[24] Often the idea of one's own renunciation of revenge is combined with that of the judgment of God.[25]

If one attempts to determine the peculiarity of our three sayings, then it is obvious that a motivation for the renunciation of force is lacking. A resigned element is missing: "Give in, for there is no other course of action."[26] An

---

[19]R. Schmitt, " 'Méconnaissance' altiranischen Sprachgutes im Griechischen," *Glotta* 49 (1971) 97-101.

[20]Examples in Fiebig*, *ZNW* 18.

[21]Mitteis-Wilcken I/1 372-80; M. Rostowzew, "Angariae," *Klio* 6 (1906) 250f.,253-57.

[22]*b. Yoma* 35b; *b. Ned.* 32a (= Str-B I 344) show that ἀγγάρεια was demanded also by private citizens.

[23]The examples are found in Platonic (cf. Plato, *Gorg.* 469c ἑλοίμην ἄν μᾶλλον ἀδικεῖσθαι ἤ ἀδικεῖν) and Stoic tradition (e.g., Seneca, *De ira* 2.33.2; Marcus Aurelius, 9.27; Epictus, *Diss.* 3.22.54); the references to nonviolent testimony to truth among philosophers (Socrates) are numerous, cf. Schottroff* 11-13.

[24]Nissen, *Gott* 266f., cf. his examples on giving up revenge, ibid. 304-16.

[25]E.g., *2 Enoch* 50:4 (no revenge because the Lord will avenge you on the day of judgment); *'Abot* 4:19 (cf. Str-B I 369); 1QS 10.17f. ("for judgment belongs to God"); Sir. 28:1 ("he that takes vengeance will suffer vengeance from the Lord"); *Midr.Ps.* 41 (131a, par. 8) = Str-B I 370 ("I will pay them back good for evil, then God will punish them").

[26]Examples in Schottroff* 207f.

optimistic calculating is missing: "By giving in, you make friends of your enemies."[27] Any hint which could explain these demands as prudent and reasonable is missing.[28] That is the more conspicuous since they are formulated very pointedly and concretely.[29] In a direct sense, it seems to me, they are not convincing. Whether through offering the other cheek in an altercation one can overcome the enemy inwardly so that he truly feels the "fiery coals" on his head (Rom. 12:20) is quite uncertain; shortly after the writing of Matthew, Ignatius had contrary experiences in this regard.[30] Particularly the passion narrative shows that this calculation does not necessarily come out right. Why should the poor person in a suit of lien give also the cloak? Neither does eager collaboration with the power of occupation mean to remain unharmed—it is better to remain unobtrusive and to do only the minimum— nor does it aid in the conversion of a political foe nor is it a means of passive resistance! No, as prudent counsels to practice a "love for reconciling the enemy,"[31] Jesus' demands do not convince; it is better to remain, e.g., with the Pharisees. At the least, Jesus' demands do not consider their consequences, which might be very ambivalent: it also could happen that the one who strikes winds up for another hit, that the poor person without a cloak has to freeze and that the hostile occupation power is strengthened!

There is a piece of conscious provocation in our logia. It is a matter of alienation, of shocking,[32] a symbolic protest against the regular rule of force.

---

[27]Examples in Schottroff* 208-11 (waiver of revenge by the ruler as a "powerful means for the protection of rulership" [Seneca, *De ira* 3.23.2]), cf. *Did.* 1:3: At the conclusion of the admonition to love the enemies it says: καὶ οὐχ ἕξετε ἐχθρόν (and you will not have an enemy). The speech of Agrippa to the Jews illustrates this in the political area (Josephus, *War* 2.350f.): "Now here you ought to be submissive to those in authority, and not give them any provocation . . . Now nothing so much damps the force of strokes as bearing them with patience, and the quietness of those who are injured diverts the injurious persons from afflicting." Precisely such motivations are not indicated in the text. The victim not only is to endure silently but to offer the other cheek, a highly impressive form of activity! The reference to the readiness of the Jews to die when Caligula desired images erected in the temple contributes little (Josephus, *Ant.* 18.261-88): The Roman governor Petronius was not a violent person but a very reasonable man. Pilate also (cf. Josephus, *War* 2.169-74) calculated very exactly the political cost at this point.

[28]John Chrysostom attempts to make the command of v. 40 plausible to his readers in an especially "beautiful" manner (18.2 = 327): any number of people would give afterwards a garment to a person who acts as nobly as Matt. 5:40 demands!

[29]There are only few parallels for pointed, hyperbolic formulations. Cf. *Counsels of Wisdom* (= Ziller 57): "smile," "feed him"; Aramaic *Words of Ahiqar* (Pritchard, *Ancient Near East* 249: "If the wicked man seize the corner of thy garment, leave it in his hand."); Papyrus Insinger 21 (= W. v. Bisping, *Altägyptische Lebensweisheit* [Zürich 1955], 113f.): "If one strips a prudent man, he gives his clothes and says a blessing in addition." Jewish: *Tos.BQ* 9,29f. = Str-B I 342 (the injured asks on behalf of the injurer); *b. Yebam.* 121a (when scoundrels attack a person, he or she should nod the head).

[30]Ignatius, *Rom.* 5:1: The soldiers became progressively worse through good deeds shown to them.

[31]"*Entfeindungsliebe*" Lapide*** 99-137. He speaks of a "theopolitics of little steps of love which aims at making the enemy cease to be your enemy" (101), in reference to 5:39 of "generous realism" and that "even a brutal collector of debts can be moved to shame by the generosity of a defeated person which might bring him to his senses, perhaps by the aid of the judge" (115), and in reference to 5:38b of a counsel to "passive resistance" (128). This may be helpful as an attempt to actualize the Sermon on the Mount within history but not as an interpretation of Jesus.

[32]The catchword "irony" (Clavier* 54) makes it seem harmless.

Their evidence lies not in the fact that the behavior demanded by them would be plausible but rather in the fact that they are "a sigh of the oppressed,"[33] insofar as one understands this formulation in a rather broad and not only in an economic-political sense. They are the expression of a protest against any kind of the spiraling of force which dehumanizes the human being and of hope for a different behavior of the person from that which is the everyday experience. But they do not stop there, for they demand an active behavior. In them is to be found a gentle protest and an element of provocative contrast to the force which rules the world.

It also is obvious that Jesus' demands aim at more than they require. The three examples make clear, "as a form of focus,"[34] what Jesus intends for a much broader realm of life. They are, so to speak, intensified images of a behavior which must be discovered and realized in all realms of life. To this extent it is true that these commands intend to be obeyed, not simply literally but in such a way that what they demand is to be "discovered" anew in new situations, in freedom but in a similar radicality.

In our logia any direct pointer to the kingdom of God is missing. Yet it seems to me that the contrast between kingdom of God and world breaks open in them. Only in this way can their contrast character—deliberately protesting and reversing normal behavior—be understood. Thus they are indirectly determined by the arrival of the kingdom of God.[35] That fits well into the eschatology of Jesus, who again and again speaks not of the kingdom of God itself but of the everyday life which is influenced by the kingdom of God (parables). If this is correct, then one may dare still a further statement: For Jesus, the arrival of the kingdom of God is manifested as limitless love of God for the people which on its part makes possible the love of humans among themselves and even for their enemies. Does a relationship exist between our demands for the renunciation of force and this love? The Sayings Source was the first to point it out clearly by framing our logia by the commandment of love of enemies (Luke 6:27f.,35). For Jesus, we can only postulate it. It meant that provocative renunciation of force has to be understood as an expression of love,[36] but also that love of the neighbor must not be understood in a narrow

---

[33]Formulation of K. Tagawa.

[34]Tannehill* 378-80 speaks correctly of an "extreme instance" or "focal instance," which Jesus has chosen in order to put his listeners on the basis of the "deliberate tension with ordinary human behaviour" in an "imaginative shock" (382). Characteristic for these logia is their openness which invites the listener "to extend . . . this pattern to new situations."

[35]The "indirect" eschatological reference of the admonition to love the enemy and to renounce the use of force is brought out with special clarity in the Marxist interpretations of Jesus by Machoveč and Bloch. Machoveč, *Jesus* 131: "see . . . the guilty . . . already through the 'prism of the kingdom' . . . through the prism of that radical . . . change"; E. Bloch, *Atheism in Christianity* (New York: Herder & Herder, 1972) speaks of Jesus' demand of love which at first is interpreted as an interim demand; but "still more: in its deepest parts it participates already in the eschatological content of the kingdom."

[36]Cf. Hoffmann*** IV 267, similarly Marklein, *Gottesherrschaft* 273-75. Wolbert* 522 formulates very beautifully but in a sense that can, in my opinion, unfortunately only be postulated for Jesus: "Nonviolence is not legitimate in itself; it has to be justified by a legitimate goal." "The admonitions of the 5th antithesis show paradigmatically how far love must be willing to go."

sense, purely between people, but includes a protest against the force which rules the world and a breaking through the mechanisms of behavior which are determined by it.

5:42

The admonition to give and lend (v. 42) is much more general and lacks in its Matthean formulation the pointedness which is characteristic of vv. 39b-41. It fits into the tradition of Jewish exhortations to benevolence.[37] It stands in loose connection with the trial of attachment in v. 40, but addresses only the one who has possessions. In distinction from vv. 39b-41 and also from the more original Lukan version, the problem of force is no longer in view in our verse. Is v. 42 an attempt of the evangelist to discover anew Jesus' demand for renunciation of one's own rights in the situation of the community in which one does not rob but one asks and lends? The radicality of the first three examples, however, has been lost here.

5:38-39a

Matthew formulates the introductory antithesis vv. 38-39a and thus summarizes the exemplary demands in his "do not resist evil." The summary indicates a generalization. What can be determined about the total Matthean perspective?

a. Matthew intends no narrowing of the area of validity of the demands.

Such a narrowing would be in view if πονηρός referred to the opponent in the trial, and the demand not to resist him could only mean the forgoing of the suit.[38] But such a limitation is not possible. Ἀνθίστημι means in general "to give resistance"; juridical usage is relatively seldom. Πονερῷ is probably to be understood—as in v. 37 and most of the time in Matthew—as a neuter, in the sense of "evil" and not as a masculine as might possibly be suggested by ὅστις.

Μὴ ἀντιστῆναι τῷ πονηρῷ thus makes clear that the following commandments are meant as examples of a behavior which is valid beyond them. They are taken from completely different areas of life. The principle of retaliation, "an eye for an eye," also stands not only for the limited area of the judicial treatment of injuries, where Judaism referred to it especially frequently, but as a comprehensive, foundational principle of law and behavior which, indeed, is an Old Testament law but is valid not only in Judaism.[39]

b. A certain shift in the accent toward a Christian passivity is clearly to be found in Matthew. It signifies a new tone that he summarizes the *positive* exhortation of vv. 39b-42 in the *negative* formulation, "do not resist." It has kept the upper hand in the history of interpretation and influence. The motto in the church tradition will be not "contrast," "provocation" but (at most!) "distancing" (*no* military service, *no* acceptance of the office of judge, etc.).

---

[37]Cf. Str-B I 346-53; Moore, *Judaism* II 162-79; Nissen *Gott*, especially 267-77.

[38]Many interpreters understand it in this way, cf. particularly Currie* and Guelich*** 219f.

[39]Aeschylus, *Choeph.* 309-13 quotes as an ancient saying: ἀντὶ μὲν ἐχθρᾶς γλώσσης ἐχθρὰ γλῶσσα τελείσθω . . . ἀντὶ δὲ πληγῆς φονίας πληγὴν τινέτω. Dihle* 30-40 gives examples from popular ethics for the basic principle, "As you do to me, so will I do to you."

c. The definition of the relationship to the Old Testament in this antithesis is most difficult. In distinction from the first two antitheses, which intensify but do not abolish its basic commandments, Matthew introduces here redactionally an Old Testament principle which can be understood only as a contrast to the words of Jesus. Can it still be said with this antithesis that Christ has "fulfilled" the law?

The most viable attempt to ease this tension is still the contention—passed on since the time of Tertullian[40]—that Old Testament retaliation was already a limitation of revenge and thus a positive approach in the direction of Jesus' overcoming of force. Was Matthew conscious of this? The Jewish-Christian Matthew would know this just as well as the church fathers; it was also known to him that the rabbis in the name of retaliation limited the use of force; e.g., they made the payment of money legitimate as restitution.[41] This explanatory attempt of the early church convinces quite a few modern interpreters.[42] There still remains discomfort on the basis of the Matthean formulation: Ὀφθαλμὸν ἀντὶ ὀφθαλμοῦ, etc., is taken up by v. 39a exactly with a negative association: μὴ ἀντιστῆναι. The formulation by the evangelist leads (misleads?) in any case to the conclusion that the thinking is less that of fulfillment than of an antithesis to the Old Testament. It is granted that in Judaism individual Old Testament commandments may be invalidated and yet the whole Torah be fulfilled, e.g., when a commandment no longer corresponds to the new situation or when the life which God creates through the Torah would be destroyed by an individual commandment.[43] Perhaps Matthew thinks of it in this way. But there remains a strong state of tension with 5:18f.

d. In the meaning of Matthew, this antithesis also applies to the community. The individual whom the words in v. 39-42 address resides in a community.[44] In it, the demand to renounce force applies. Jesus commands the disciple who hurries to him with the sword to put it away (26:51-54). The history of the community is a history of suffering, persecutions, scourgings, and dying (23:34). Experience of violence is a reality for it; renunciation of resistance is an absolute commission. It is possible because Jesus himself has taken this path. Matthew tells his story as that of the πραΰς . . . βασιλεὺς who exemplified in his passion nonviolence and was led through it by God to the resurrection. *Here*—and only here—is for him the opportunity and possibility of nonviolence.

Matthew did not think primarily and specifically in political terms of the renunciation of force. However, one also must not exclude the political realm. It is

---

[40]Tertullian, *Marcion* 4.16 = *PL* 2,395-98. In this connection one encounters again and again the Christian concession that the morality of the Pharisees is relatively high (cf. Augustine*** 1.18 [56f.]).

[41]Str-B I 339f.

[42]Cf., e.g., Dietzfelbinger** above n. 18. Daube, *New Testament* 259-65, solves the problem by assigning the retaliation exclusively to the law of damage, the slap to the insult. Thus he can say that the antithesis does not contradict the thesis (the OT and Jewish law) because it deals with a different matter. A counter-example would be, e.g., *Sifra on Lev.* 24,19af = Fiebig*** no. 242 (slap with result of restitution). Lapide*** 132 points out that the OT speaks of the *giving* of restitution by the one who did the damage and not of *taking* by the one who was damaged. Unfortunately, Matthew omits the δώσει in his quotation!

[43]Cf. Nissen, *Gott* 381-89.

[44]That is the basic thesis of Lohfink*.

touched on in v. 41, just as the area of jurisdiction in v. 40.[45] But it must be especially emphasized that for the community the renunciation of violence is not an internal sectarian principle but a demand of and an offer for all people. Nonviolence and giving up one's rights thus determine the behavior of the community toward the world, as an example of lived discipleship which may lead to the people beginning to praise the Father (Matt. 5:16).

e. By arranging nonviolence and forgoing of rights within the whole of the six Antitheses, Matthew coordinates them also with love. Verse 42 makes this most clear, but also vv. 39-41 are illuminated once more anew from the love of *enemy* which is proclaimed in v. 44. Just as in the first antithesis with vv. 22,23f., so also Matthew contrasts at the end of his Antitheses deeds of love with each other under a negative and a positive aspect. Negatively, love means renunciation of counterforce and resistance (vv. 39-41). What it means positively will be made clear in vv. 44-47. To this extent, the "negative"formulation of the antithesis of v. 39a does not mean only a moderating interpretation but requires its supplement by the sixth antithesis.

History of influence

Our text, especially the principle of v. 39a, has had a wide-reaching history of influence and has remained hotly controversial in its consequences until today. Very simplified, (a) a "rigorist" and (b) a "mitigating" line of interpretation confront each other.

a. *Rigorist line of interpretation.* The church in the pre-Constantine period had always rejected the entrance of a Christian into the army, even in the third century, when many soldiers had converted to Christianity.[46] The problem of killing was probably more important than that of idolatry.[47] The fact that always the literal interpretation of our words of Jesus was predominant is consistent with this. Examples: Tertullian extends v. 40 to all possessions and even is willing to give away his clothes if only his faith is not threatened.[48] The author of the *Opus imperfectum*, who is interested in practice and is in many ways very close to Matthew, formulates: "For if you hit back, you have . . . denied that you are a disciple of Christ, not with words but with deeds."[49]

---

[45]Cf. on the area of jurisdiction 1 Cor. 6:7f.; on the political application, one may remember that the Christians in the rebellion of 66-70 belonged to the party of peace, cf. Schottroff* 219.

[46]Surveys in A. Harnack, *Militia Christi*, reprint (Darmstadt: Wissenschaftliche Buchgesellschaft, 1963 [= 1905]), 46-92; J. Cadoux, *The Early Christian Attitude to War* (London: Headly, 1919), 49-243; H. v. Campenhausen, "Der Kriegsdienst der Christen in der Kirche des Altertums," in idem, *Tradition und Leben* (Tübingen: Mohr, 1960), 203-15 (= *Tradition and Life in the Church* [Philadelphia: Fortress, 1968]); R. A. Bainton, "Die frühe Kirche und der Krieg," in *Das frühe Christentum im römischen Staat*, ed. R. Klein (Darmstadt: Wissenschaftliche Buchgesellschaft, 1971), 187- 216; Blank* 220-23; Lienemann* 87-98.

[47]*Canones Hippolyti* 13f.: "Persons who have the authority to kill or soldiers should not kill at all, even if they are ordered to. . . . No Christian shall go and become a soldier . . . A superior who has a sword shall not become guilty of shedding blood" (*Die Kirchenrechtsquellen des Patriarchats von Alexandrien*, ed. W. Riedel, [Leipzig 1900], 206f.).

[48]*Fuga* 13 = *PL* 2,117-19.

[49]12 = 699.

In the post-Constantinian period a significant turn of events commenced:[50] The advocates of a literal interpretation of our text are now to be found in the circles of the heretics, minority churches or groups: Waldensians, Francis of Assisi, Wycliffites, Erasmus, Schwenkfeld, the Anabaptists, the Quakers, Tolstoy, Gandhi (who is influenced by Tolstoy),[51] Albert Schweitzer, Christian pacifists and many representatives of the so-called ''Black theology,'' Jehovah's Witnesses—in short, those who from the perspective of the Reformation are easily qualified as ''Enthusiasts'' but who in this matter are in agreement with the overwhelming testimony of the early church. The *Anabaptists* in their early period—not without considerable influence from Matthew[52]—reject the participation of believing Christians, whose citizenship is in heaven and whose weapons are spiritual,[53] in court procedures and in the army.[54] They do this for the most part, not because they dispute the God-willed character of the state and the validity of secular standards for its realm, but because as Christians they do not see their task in this realm.[55] They give testimony not so much to the basic *conflict* between secular law and the law of Christ as to a more relaxed *distance* between the two which may last for centuries. For Tolstoy, Matt. 5:39 is ''the very essence of Christianity.''[56] But he argues against a cult of suffering for its own sake and understands ''that Christ does not at all demand that one offer the cheek and give up the cloak only for the sake of suffering.'' Even Tolstoy is not simply ''legalistic''; he can explicate the formula ''never use force'' as ''never do anything contrary to the law of love,''[57] i.e., in a way similar to the interpretation which comes from Augustine. Only love cannot coexist so simply with evil for him. It is true that a certain biblicism is present with most representatives of this type of interpretation,[58] but most of the time it is not an absolute biblicism and often belongs together with alarm about what Christian collaboration with force was able to tolerate or even to do in the name of love. The Waldensians are to be seen vis-à-vis the papacy of the Middle Ages, the Anabaptists

---

[50]The decisive turning points are the Synod of Arles (314), which excommunicates Christians who in times of peace desert military service (Blank* 157), and the *Codex Theodosianus* of 416 which excludes Gentiles from the army (*Cod. Theod.* 16.10.21, quoted by Ritter, *Alte Kirche*, KThQ I, 189).

[51]The most important text of Gandhi on his relation to Christianity is probably the 20th chapter of his autobiography (M. Gandhi, *An Autobiography* [Ahmedabad 1937], 50-52); further texts are conveniently collected in M. Gandhi, *What Jesus Means to Me*, ed. R. Prabhu (Ahmedabad 1959).

[52]Konrad Grebel was occupied with the Greek Gospel of Matthew in the earliest Bible circles from which the Anabaptist movement originated in the Reformation period; cf. L. v. Muralt - W. Schmid, *QGT* Schweiz I (Zürich 1952), 12.

[53]*Schleitheim Confession*, art. 6 (in Fast [above n. 75 on 5:33-37] 67).

[54]Examples of polemics on Matt. 5:38-42: Bern Disputation of 1532: The controversial point is how far the OT is still valid. For the Anabaptists the cancellation of Lev. 24:19f. through Matt. 5:38-42 was meant not only for the individual (*QGT* Schweiz IV 192f.). P. Walpot, *Artikelbuch* 4,28: Among the Christians there are no longer to be courts, but ''alone the power of the keys and not the power of the hangman''; God alone will resist the enemy (*QGT* XII 249f.).

[55]Lienemann* 183-85 summarizes: For the Anabaptists, it is more important that the means of proclamation are in harmony with the gospel than that they consider the consequences, and the evangelical testimony is more important for the world than the loving care for its preservation.

[56]Tolstoy*** 13 (Sec. 2, beg.).

[57]Tolstoy*** 9, 13.

[58]Tolstoy*** 10: ''I do not intend to comment on the law of Jesus; I desire only that all comment shall be forever done away with.''

vis-à-vis the Reformation, George Fox vis-à-vis Cromwell, Tolstoy vis-à-vis the Russian Orthodox church, and Martin Luther King vis-à-vis the Christian West.

b. The father of the *"mitigating" interpretation* of Catholic and Protestant shape is *Augustine*. In his sketch of the relationship of *civitas Dei* and *civitas terrena* (*CivD* 19) he does not discuss our text. Rather he was impelled to make his most important statement on Matt. 5:38f. in warding off the objection of Marcellinus that the teaching of Jesus "in no way agrees with the customs of the state."[59] In his answer, Augustine attempts to defuse the conflict between the demands of Jesus and the requirements of the state: Those regulations refer "more to the preparation of the heart which is internal . . ., than to the word which happens in public."[60] The person living in the state ruled by Christians is in the same situation as a father who must punish his son: sometimes it is necessary to carry out actions "benigna quadam asperitate" (with a certain benign roughness) where one "has to act more by usefulness than according to the will" of God. Among these things are the "merciful" war—"if it can be" conducted as such[61]—which, in the *City of God* [62] is designated "just war," and punishment which is to be carried out in the right spirit, i.e., without hatred—even if it were capital punishment.[63] The harshness of the commandments of Jesus has been evaded in different ways in the early church. E.g., the offering of the cheek can allegorically be interpreted as the offering of the right doctrine over against heretical objections.[64] In the later two-level ethic, the prohibition of arms is valid for clerics, that of suing only for monks.[65] Public injustice has to be opposed in any case.

The *interpretation of the Reformers*, despite its harsh polemic against the two-level ethic, comes to a similar practice. Our text plays a central role in Luther's writing "Temporal Authority: To What Extent It Should Be Obeyed."[66] Indeed, Jesus' commands apply to all people and are not only counsels of perfection. However, the law applies to the world, the commandments of the Sermon on the Mount only to the Christians (92). Although "Christians among themselves and by and for themselves need no law or sword"(94),[67] Luther speaks of the "Christian-in-relation: not about his being a Christian, but about this life and his obligation in it to some other person . . . like a lord or a lady, a wife or children or neighbors." In all these relationships—not only in the state but also in community and family—one must not be a fool like that crazy saint "who let the lice nibble at him and refused to kill any of them on account of this text."[68]

---

[59]Letter of Marcellinus to Augustine (Augustine, *Ep.* 136.2 = *PL* 33,515).

[60]Augustine, *Ep.* 138 (ad Marcellinum), 2.13 = *PL* 33,530.

[61]Loc. cit. 2.14 = 531.

[62]*CivD* 19.7.

[63]Augustine*** 1.20 (64). The decisive point of view, however, is the improvement of the one to be punished, i.e., mercy which regulates the dealing with the commandments of Matt.5:39-42 (loc.cit. 1,19 [58]; 1,20 [63]).

[64]Jerome on 5:40.

[65]Thomas, *Lectura* no. 542,544.

[66]WA 11,245-80 = *LW* 45, 81-129 (page references to this edition).

[67]A remarkable quotation which would offer an opening to an order in the Christian community which would not stand under the protection of the sword. This approach is, however, already in the next sentence overlaid by the alternative that the Christian on earth does not live "for himself (or herself) alone but for his (or her) neighbor." In this way, not the Christian community but the Christian alone becomes the subject of the command of Matt. 5:39-42.

[68]WA 32***, 390 = *LW* 21, 109-10.

For the interpretation of the Reformation it is decisive that participation of Christians in the preservation of law and peace takes place out of responsibility toward the neighbor.[69] Thus, for the sake of the neighbor, the Christian must be able to forgo practicing Jesus' command of the renunciation of force. This applies first of all to the officials: "Do you want to know what your duty is as a prince or a judge or a lord or a lady . . .? You do not have to ask Christ. . . ."[70] For the sake of the neighbor, Luther can even accept the status of the warrior and his occupation like any other office.[71] But the consequences are far-reaching: Since a Christian is always "in relationship," there is really no Christian who would not be at the same time the bearer of an office. Indeed, since no human action happens independently of relationship to other humans[72]—the commandments of the Sermon on the Mount are not meant for hermits—one *can* on the basis of this belief legitimize their waiver in any situation. It is to be granted that Luther did not want this as a consequence. Calvin, on the basis of his high admiration of the Old Testament law goes still further than Luther. He opines on our text, e.g., that the Christians should "with entire friendship for their enemies, use the aid of the magistrate for the preservation of their goods."[73] This type of interpretation then became widely habitual in the churches of the Reformation.[74]

Finally, *v. 42*, which is close to being practical, has given rise to manifold and influential attenuations. To give away spiritual gifts hurts less, as Jerome testifies involuntarily in all honesty: "Money . . ., which is not lacking when given away, namely . . . wisdom"![75] The greatest gift is pity.[76] You must be aware of possible harm to yourself (!) or to another through your gift,[77] or, somewhat more in general: dignity and justice[78] have to be determinative in the praxis of this command. Also an *ordo caritatis* (order of love), which begins with the next involved persons, is a frequently occurring guideline.[79] In short, a mocking remark of Julian the Apostate, who wondered

---

[69]*Von weltlicher Obrigkeit* (above n. 66) 94. Cf. Lienemann* 154.

[70]WA 32***, 391 = *LW* 21, 110.

[71]"Whether Soldiers, Too, Can Be Saved," WA 19, 623-62 = *LW* 46, 93-137.

[72]Even at the renunciation of one's possessions, relatives, e.g., in any case the order of law, are involved.

[73]*Inst.* 4,20,20.

[74]Cf., e.g., the typical pragmatic argumentation in F. Schleiermacher, *Die christliche Sitte* (Berlin: Reimer, 1843), 259-63: General willingness to suffer injustice means the end of civil society as long as there are evildoers in it. It can by no means agree with the will of Christ that they would assert themselves. The "ancestor" of this argumentation is—Celsus! (below n. 82).

[75]Quoted according to Thomas, *Lectura* no. 549.

[76]"Plus est compati ex corde quam dare" (It is more to have compassion from the heart than to give) (Gregory the Great, quoted according to Thomas, *Lectura* no. 548). Cf. Strabo 97: "si deest facultas, da affectum" (when the means are lacking, give love).

[77]Augustine*** 1,20 (67).

[78]Cyril of Alexandria, fragment 66 = Reuss 173 (the suppliant must be ἄξιος, the request δικαία; Strabo 97 ("quae honeste et iuste possunt dari" [what can be given honestly and justly]). Already Tertullian, *Fuga* 13 = *PL* 2,118 urges reason when giving: One does not give wine to somebody suffering a fever or a sword to a candidate for suicide.

[79]E.g., in Maldonat 126. Relatives and friends come before strangers and unknown people.

what would happen if the Christians would take this commandment seriously,[80] has remained effective throughout many centuries and has sheltered Christianity from an all-too-literal interpretation of and obedience to this commandment!

Summary

It is easy to distance oneself from this virtual ecumenical weakening of this text, at least theoretically. But this was not the purpose of these comments. Rather the history of influence should make us aware of some basic problems which are important for the application of the text in the situation today.

1. Nowhere, not even in Matthew, has Jesus' impact been maintained in its full authority. Jesus' commands aimed at nothing less than at a consistent living and suffering of the truth of the kingdom of God in the situation of its coming in contrast to and provocation of the world and over against the world. The kingdom of God has not come in the manner in which Jesus thought. The community has remained steadfast to Jesus in a different way, namely, under the sign of faith in the risen Lord. This basic change makes necessary a new evaluation of the demands of Jesus. It is made easier by the fact that they were meant not as law but as examples and with the intent of leaving from the beginning room for creative fancy. *A simple back-to-Jesus thus is impossible for basic theological reasons*; it is necessary on the basis of the exemplary nature of the text to take one's own situation into account. The history of influence testifies to this necessity of change and the freedom which is given by the text itself.

2. The history of influence demonstrated that a fundamental change took place at the Constantinian reversal, a change which *had to* have its effects on the interpretation of our text if it really is to be discovered *anew* in each situation. Until then, the Christians were confronted only with the question of how they should carry out and live their testimony in the world of law and politics, a world for which the Christians were not at all responsible. "Wars were a characteristic mark of that world,"[81] from which the Christians knew themselves to be separated and which they did not have to justify. But since the Constantinian reversal there was the possibility of direct Christian participation in the shaping of politics, the pursuit of which could principally be the duty of love. Only now a tension existed between (1) the Christian commission to carry the testimony of the gospel to the world and to live in the community itself and (2) the Christian commission to help in shaping the realm of the world, including politics, for the best of humankind.

One cannot avoid this conflict. The Anabaptists, partly because of outside forces, gave priority to the proclamation and realization of the gospel in the community before they participated in shaping the world. Already Celsus blamed such an attitude for leaving "the government on earth to the most lawless and wildest barbarians" who

---

[80]In Gregory Nazianzus, *Or.* 4.97 = BKV I/59 136. Julian interprets the demands of Jesus literally and concludes, not quite incorrectly, that they call for "living in another world." Origen, 4.99 = BKV I/59 137f. contends against this with the argument "that some regulations of our law have obligatory validity . . . while others . . . leave a free choice." A preliminary form of the "two-level" ethic!

[81]Lienemann* 87.

neither respect the worship of God nor true wisdom among people.[82] The accusation that Christian pacifism thrives on the fact that others take care of the dirty business of politics has a tradition! But who would dare to doubt in the final analysis that the prime decision of the nonconformists to bring the gospel to the world is not *also* a decision full of love and responsibility for the world?

Conversely, the decisions in the major churches show how great the danger was that through the responsible participation in secular power the proclamation of the kingdom of God was obscured and these demands of Jesus which belong to it were practically invalidated.[83] No interpretation of the Sermon on the Mount was ever completely protected from justifying what actually happened in the church in its time. E.g., the interpretation of the Sermon on the Mount by the Reformation, not in its intention but definitely in its effect, distances itself from the intent of the Preacher on the Mount. But who would care to assert that adaptation and opportunism and the decision of the Reformers to participate in worldly authority was not primarily an attempt of *evangelical* love for the neighbor?

The opportunity to participate responsibly in secular authority is (most of the time) still granted to the Christians. Therefore, we also confront by necessity the described dilemma, in distinction from Jesus and Matthew, who did not confront it.

3. The history of influence finally indicated the situation in which we ourselves deal with our text. For very many, it is the situation of a Great Church which is determined by traditions of the interpretation of the Sermon on the Mount that have become normative, whose task it is to assist in laying the foundation for the church's own participation in secular power. These churches are not able to make real the gospel of the renunciation of law and force in the shape of the church itself, as long as they are pure *Volkskirchen* (national churches).[84] In the present, most national churches have actually become minority churches which must preach the gospel to a world perhaps still nominally Christian. Thus the missionary opposition to the world, which makes even the practice of the church become an element of proclamation (cf. Matt. 5:16), is the same now as it was in the pre-Constantine period. But the possibilities for Christians and churches to participate in the political shaping of the world are often still those of the post-Constantinian time. In this situation it is no longer sufficient, in my opinion, to orient oneself by the normative tradition of the interpretation of the Sermon on the Mount in the main churches, but it is necessary, in conversation with other traditions of interpretation and particularly with the biblical texts, to draw up a new interpretation which corresponds to our own situation of today.

---

[82]Origen, *Cels.* 8.68 = BKV I/53 816.

[83]I deliberately accept the risk of the accusation that I am inadequately presenting the *intention* of the two-kingdoms doctrine of the Reformation, because I am here concerned not primarily for its intention but for its *effect*. We meet its effects today in two standard arguments: (1) The "distinctive sayings of the Sermon on the Mount do not (have) the character of sentences of law" and are therefore addressed only to the individual; (2) they "presuppose a different human being . . . than the one with whom we have to deal today" (sin!). But "perfection (Matt. 5:48) cannot be achieved on earth" (J. Fulda, "Pacifismus und Bergpredigt," *Allgemeine Schweizerische Militärzeitschrift*, 1982/6).

[84]The Catholic church differs to a certain extent from the Protestant churches since it has retained the ability to integrate its own nonconformists (monasticism!) within itself. The two-level ethic is the expression of this integration.

The following thrusts of the text seem to me especially important:

1. To forgo the use of force is a "contrasting sign" of the kingdom of God or a part of a new way of righteousness which has been opened up by Jesus. On this basis any realization of our text will have to make clear that "use of force . . . " belongs "to the signature of the unredeemed world" which "urgently is in need of salvation and therefore . . . of the signs of renunciation of force."[85] It is not so important for the church that its pacifists are dependent for their survival on responsible politics, but it is important that its politicians are dependent for the sake of the gospel on Christian pacifists. The practice of our text today must express this credibly.

2. Renunciation of force is understood by Jesus and by Matthew as an expression of love. Love has the freedom to think ahead to the consequences. On this basis there cannot be, in the last analysis, an alternative between an ethics of intention and an ethics of responsibility,[86] neither in the actions of the Christian nor in the coexistence of Christians in the church or in the ecumenical movement.

3. The juxtaposition of renunciation of force and commandment of love in Jesus and Matthew is a reminder to Christian love of its origin from the kingdom of God and the radicality which is derived from it.[87] It is able to preserve love from being *only* a secular aid to survival.

2.2.6. Sixth Antithesis: On the Love of Enemies (5:43-48)

Literature

(Cf. also the bibliography on 5:38-48.)

Bauer, W., " Das Gebot der Feindesliebe und die alten Christen," in idem, *Aufsätze und kleine Schriften*, pp. 235-52 (Tübingen: Mohr, 1967).
Dupont, J., " 'Soyez parfaits' (Mt 5,48), 'soyez miséricordieux' (Lc 6,36)," *Sacra Pagina* 2, pp. 150-62, BETL 12/13 (Gembloux: Duculot, 1959).
Fiedler, *Jesus* 185-94.
Fuchs, E., "Die vollkommene Gewissheit," in idem, *Zur Frage nach dem historischen Jesus*, pp. 126-35 (Tübingen: Mohr, 1960).
Haas, H., *Idee und Ideal der Feindesliebe in der ausserchristlichen Welt, Rede zur Feier des Reformationsfestes und des Übergangs des Rektorats* (Leipzig: 1927).
Hasenfratz, H. P., *Die Rede von der Auferstehung Jesu Christi*, Forum theologiae linguisticae 10, pp. 238-42 (Bonn: Linguistica Biblica, 1975).
Hoffmann-Eid, *Jesus* 147-85.
Huber, W., "Feindschaft und Feindesliebe," *ZEE* 26 (1982) 128-58.
Linton, O. "St. Matthew 5,43," *ST* 18 (1964) 66-79.

---

[85]Blank* 161.

[86]Cf. M. Weber, "Politik als Beruf," *Gesammelte politische Schriften*, 2d ed. (Berlin: Duncker and Humblot, 1958), 539: "The Christian does what is right and leaves the success up to God" (ethics of intention); on the other hand, the ethicist of responsibility (politician) knows "that one has to give account for the (foreseeable) consequences of one's actions."

[87]Cf. Wolbert, above n. 36.

Luz, U., "Jesu Gebot der Feindesliebe und die kirchliche Verantwortung für den Frieden," *Ref.* 31 (1982) 253-66.

Merklein, *Gottesherrschaft* 222-37.

Nissen, *Gott* 278-329.

Randlinger, S., *Die Feindesliebe nach dem natürlichen und positiven Sittengesetz* (Paderborn: 1906).

Reuter, R., "Liebet eure Feinde," *ZEE* 26 (1982) 159-87.

Schnackenburg, R., "Die Vollkommenheit des Christen nach den Evangelien," *GuL* 32 (1959) 420-33.

Schulz, *Q* 127-39.

Seitz, O., "Love Your Enemies," *NTS* 16 (1969/70) 39-54.

Unnik, W. C. van, "Die Motivierung der Feindesliebe in Lukas 6,32-35," *NovT* 8 (1966) 284-300.

Waldmann, M., *Die Feindesliebe*, Theologische Studien der Leo-Gesellschaft 1 (Vienna: Mayer, 1902).

Weizsäcker, C. F. v., "Intelligente Feindesliebe," *Ref.* 29 (1980) 413-18.

Zeller, *Mahnsprüche* 101-13.

Cf. also the literature** on 5:21-48 above, pp. 273-274; Literature*** on the Sermon on the Mount above pp. 209-211.

Text

43 You have heard that it was said:
"You shall love your neighbor"
and hate your enemy.
44 But I say to you:
Love your enemies
and pray for your persecutors,[1]
45 so that you become sons of your Father in the heavens
because he lets his sun rise over evil and good.
46 For if you love those who love you,
what reward will you then have?
Do not the tax collectors do the same?
47 And if you salute only your brothers,
What are you doing special?
Do not the Gentiles do the same?
48 So be perfect, as your heavenly Father is perfect.

Analysis

1. *Structure.* After thesis and antithesis (vv. 43-45), a double saying follows as an additional reasoning (vv. 46f.) and the concluding verse 48. Important key words from the preceding section are taken up: διώκω (vv. 10, 11, 44), υἱοὶ θεοῦ (v. 9), πατὴρ ὁ ἐν τοῖς οὐρανοῖς (v. 16), μισθός (v. 12) and περισσο– (v. 20). This points to the fact that our antithesis bundles up preceding material. Verse 48 has a special position: it no longer contains the leading key word ἀγαπάω and introduces a new one with τέλειος. In this manner it seems unconnected and abstract in comparison with that which precedes. The previously characteristic division into three parts is broken off. That shows that this verse has a special position. It is a *kelal*,[2] a summarizing transitional verse. With

---

[1] Most manuscripts (and the *textus receptus*) follow the four-part long form of Luke 6:27f.

[2] Cf. introduction, p.39.

ὁ πατὴρ ὑμῶν ὁ οὐράνιος, which is taken from v. 16 and v. 45, it is the transition to the following section on prayer (6:1-18), where this designation for God becomes the center.

2. *Redaction and source.* Matthew uses the Q logia Luke 6:27f.,35, 32-34. In order to create the symmetry between the two blocks of antitheses, vv. 21-32 and 34-48,[3] he is forced to abbreviate and tighten. Verse 48, in Q (= Luke 6:36) presumably the introduction to Luke 6:37-42, is, on the whole, formulated anew by him,[4] in order that he may at the same time conclude the whole series of Antitheses and make a back reference to v. 20. Several details remain uncertain:

2.1. Again the antithetical formulation, i.e., in this case the thesis *v. 43,* may be due to the evangelist. The command to love one's enemies is elsewhere in early Christian literature never handed down in the context of an antithesis. Linguistically, the proof of redaction cannot be demonstrated: Μισέω is a reminder of the shortened verse 27 of Luke. Ἐχθρός creates an additional verbal connection to the traditional v. 44 (ἐχθρούς) which is rhetorically effective.

2.2. *Verse 44:* The tradition outside the New Testament frequently points back to all four members of Luke 6:27f.[5] This speaks in favor of the theory that it was only Matthew who has abbreviated the logion to these two parts. The actualizing intensification to the situation of persecution also is due to him.[6] The combination of the commandment of love of enemies with its theological foundation in v. 45, which Luke does not bring until 6:35, is probably old; v. 45 presupposes something!

2.3. In *v. 45* Matthew, who speaks in concrete pictures, deserves priority to Luke, who formulated theologically.[7]

2.4. *Verses 46f.* are completely uncertain. The shortening to two parts is probably again due to Matthew. The secondary generalizations (ἁμαρτωλός instead of τελώνης/ἐθνικός; ἀγαθοποιέω instead of ἀσπάζομαι) are Lukan or pre-Lukan. It is difficult to decide whether the Matthean reference to reward or the Lukan formulation with χάρις is more original.[8] Usually χάρις is considered as Lukan redaction.[9] On the other hand, the reward is important for Matthew.[10] It seems to me more likely that Matthew has altered the Q text. But he proceeded again "conservatively": the reference to reward was available to him from Q (Luke 6:35b). Matthew, who for formal reasons was forced to abridge, has taken up in a new way an important topic from Q, as he did in v. 42 with regard to the "borrowing."

---

[3]Cf. above on 5:21-48, n. 1.

[4]Τέλειος elsewhere only Matt. 19:21; on οὖν, πατὴρ οὐράνιος cf. introduction 3.2.

[5]Cf. the survey in Wrege*** 84f.

[6]Cf. 5:10f. and introduction 3.2 s. v. διώκω.

[7]The following could be Matthean, cf. introduction 3.2: Ὅπως, γίνομαι(?), πατὴρ ὁ ἐν τοῖς οὐρανοῖς, ἀγαθός//πονηρός, δίκαιος.

[8]Cf. introduction 3.2. Μόνον, περισσόν are Matthean.

[9]But the usage does not agree completely with the Lukan usage. Χάρις in Luke most of the time means "grace" (but then usually in connection with θεός , therefore probably not in Luke 6:33f.), more infrequently "favor, thanks," as for instance in 17:9; Acts 2:47; cf. Sir. 12:1; 20:16. Only that fits here. Could it be that Luke struck out a theological term μισθός which fits well into the context (Luke 6:23,35!)? The secular examples which v. Unnik* 290,292-96 furnishes on the rule of mutuality do not fit, since they document the meaning "gift," "counter-gift."

[10]Μισθός is always understood in Matthew in the sense of the heavenly reward and is an important theme, especially in the Sermon on the Mount (5:12,46; 66:1 [redaction],2,5,16).

3. *Origin.* The two *meshalim* Luke 6:27f.,35 and Luke 6:32-34 belong together only thematically but not literarily. The first saying is almost certainly spoken by Jesus, the second one probably.[11] Verse 36 agrees with a Jewish principle; no statements concerning its origin are possible.

Interpretation

5:44-45
Jesus

The commandment of love of enemies is one of the most central of Christian texts. It is not only quoted frequently in early Christian parenesis[12] and in most Christian areas,[13] but is considered *the* Christian distinction and innovation,[14] in which the Gentiles marvel.[15] It was a decisive factor for the Christian missionary preaching,[16] for the Apologists and the early Latin fathers to present Christianity as a religion of action; love of enemies was not only taught but also practiced.[17] The central position of love of enemies in the early church agrees with the intention of the Sayings Source and particularly of Matthew who gave it a priority position in his last, concluding antithesis. With that, he presents the love commandment as the center of the "higher" righteousness of the Christians which he summarizes in v. 48 with "perfection."

The opinion of the church fathers that Jesus' commandment to love one's enemies is something new is only conditionally correct. There are similar statements in many places, in Judaism, among the Greeks, especially the Stoics, in India, in Buddhism, in Taoism.[18] Possible differences are very relative but help to make the *original sense of the logion Luke 6:27f.,35; Matt. 5:44f.* clearer. In the *Jewish examples* the catchword of "love" of enemies is missing. This difference is considered significant by the Jews themselves: Jewish texts are cautious in the use of exaggerated formulations

---

[11]The negative evaluation of the tax collectors and sinners is not a counter-argument, since the logion, precisely for the sake of an effect of alienating, connects with common judgments.

[12]In the NT possibly Rom. 12:14; 1 Peter 3:9 are reminiscences of the command of Jesus, cf. Piper* 100-133. On early Christian occurrences cf. Bauer* 240-52.

[13]Beyschlag, *ZTK* 1977*** 314 notes a lack of it in Gnosticism but not in Marcion.

[14]Justin *Apol.* 1.15.9 (τί καινόν); Tertullian, *Pat.* 6 = BKV I/7 44 ("principiale praeceptum" [the principal commandment]); *Scap.* 1 = *PL* 1,698 ("diligere . . . inimicos solorum Christianorum" [to love . . . the enemies of Christians alone]), cf. also John 13:34 (ἐντολὴ καινή).

[15]*2 Clement* 13:4. The early church understood the "enemies" mainly (like Matthew) in a religious sense and also referred to the Gentiles, cf. Beyschlag*** 314,316.

[16]Love of enemies played an essential role in mission, cf., e.g., Justin, *Apol.* 1.14.3; Clement of Alexandria, *Strom.* 7.86.1.

[17]Cf., e.g., Aristides, *Apol.* 15.5; *Ep. Diognet.* 6.6; Cyprian, *Bon. pat.* 3 = *PL* 4,623 (Christians as "philosophi non verbis sed factis" (philosophers not with words but deeds); the Scripture refers under the catchword *patientia* (patience) essentially to Matt. 5:34-48); Athenagoras, *Suppl.* 11 (with us you will find private individuals, workmen, mothers who fulfill by their deeds what they hardly understand).

[18]Detailed compilations of the material in Waldmann* 19-88; Heinrici*** 148-59; Schottroff* 207-11; Dihle* 61-71 (especially for antiquity); Randlinger* 22-65; Haas* passim (entire history of religion); Fiebig, *TSK* 55-64; Str-B I 353-71; Nissen, *Gott.* especially 304-29 (for Judaism); Piper* 19-49.

and require what is realistically possible.[19] They speak mostly of individual concrete ways of behavior toward the enemy.[20]

In contrast, the original four-part logion of Jesus formulates exaggeratedly: Loving and enemies, doing good and haters, blessing and cursers, praying and wrongdoers are opposites which, like a placard, point out the contrast element in the behavior demanded by Jesus. The first part of the saying is probably once again[21] the basic title for the three following parts; it then is exemplified with individual cases. "Love" is thus something comprehensive. It is correct that one must think not primarily of friendly feelings but of concrete deeds;[22] but it is still more important that "love" is a behavior of the *entire* person which does not exclude feelings. If one gathers together the many individual Jewish statements which point in a similar direction—there are also others[23]—then one can most likely say that Jesus makes what is also in Judaism (alongside of others) a possible statement into an extreme absolute.

In *Greek philosophy*, particularly in the Platonic and Stoic tradition, there are basic statements similar to those of Jesus. The motto of unrestricted love of other humans,[24] which includes sympathy with the one who is unpleasant, evil, or hostile, has fundamental validity. Here it is basic that every one has a share in the same divine origin so that universal love of human beings is in agreement with nature. The wise person rests in himself or herself and can not suffer damage through external enmity.[25] Hellenistic parallels can also speak of the imitation of God in this connection.[26] Finally, the undifferentiating love of God is for the Stoic an expression of astonishment over the harmony of the cosmos, which is not made by humans but is perceived as grace and to which the human being responds through the general love of all.

---

[19]Cf. the Jewish voices in Nissen, *Gott* 317, and in Haas* 21-24. P. Lapide's sketch of Jesus' "Entfeindungsliebe" (love which removes enmity) (***99-108) which has Jesus require not "sympathy . . . " or "self-sacrifice" but "only and alone 'the performance' " of small steps of love (ibid. 100) thus interprets completely correctly—the Jewish tradition!

[20]Examples in interpretation of Exod. 23:4f. and Prov. 25:21f. in Str-B I 369f.

[21]Cf. Luke 6:20f.; Matt. 5:22.

[22]The word ἀγαπάω was not chosen in order to exclude with it ἐράω or φιλέω. It does not mean *only* a practical or *only* a caritative love in distinction from friendship or sexual love. Rather the word was chosen because in Jewish Greek, e.g., in the LXX (through the phonetic similarity to the Hebrew אהב ?) ἀγαπάω is the most frequent vocable for love. It is conceivable that here from the beginning, perhaps by Jesus himself, a reference to Lev. 19:18 was implied, which Matthew then brought out explicitly.

[23]Cf. below nn. 42,45.

[24]On φιλανθρωπία as a widespread ethical concept of Hellenism, which also contains the idea of the *imitatio Dei* within itself, cf. U. Luck, art. "φιλανθρωπία κτλ." *TDNT* IX 107-12; on the acceptance by Philo, Nissen, *Gott* 466-70, 485-97.

[25]An impressive example is Marcus Aurelius 2.1 which expresses all these elements, cf. Epictetus, *Diss.* 3.22.54 (the Cynic loves [φιλέω] like a father or brother the human beings who mistreat him or her).

[26]Seneca, *Ben.* 4.26.1 (give benefits also to the ungrateful in imitation of God); Marcus Aurelius 9.11 (the gods are kind even against the unjust and give them health, riches, etc.); Sallustius (in Hasenfratz* 239: the sun also does not turn away from the blind).

In contrast with this it is striking that Jesus speaks explicitly of the love of *enemies*. The four hyperbolic imperatives cannot be seen as extreme cases of a general commandment of love of human beings. Jesus speaks emphatically of the *enemy* in all his or her maliciousness. The secret reservation that the enemy could be made a friend through love is missing. It is inappropriate to limit the enemy to the sense of personal enemy; the Greek ἐχθρός is a comprehensive word for enemy on the basis of the LXX.[27] The intensification which lies in the three examples of Luke 6:27[28] speaks in favor of including even quite extreme types of enmity. Jesus' demand is a demand of contrast.[29]

A further distinction from the Hellenistic parallels lies in the concept of God, despite identically sounding formulations. Jesus speaks of a personal God who acts in history uniquely. His commandment does not agree with world harmony but with God's will. The extreme demand of love of enemies corresponds especially to the extreme love of God in the coming of his kingdom over against sinners and the underclass.

The motivation (v. 45) is hardly to be interpreted as distinctive to Jesus.[30] It takes up a wisdom form of argumentation.[31] God's goodness toward both the good and the evil is not really a motivating factor for demanding love, particularly of enemies.[32] There is here a certain incongruity. It remains unclear how the reference to God's actions in his creation is related to the promise of sonship with God (v. 45a). The motivation of the love of enemies is theological, not eschatological. At most one may remember that with Jesus eschatology and theology are not in opposition to each other: The eschatology of *Jesus* discloses a new experience of the present world and precisely with this comes the possibility of speaking of God's creative action in an unbroken, theological manner. The parables of Jesus, which in principle belong to the realm of theology, not eschatology, are a form of speech which is made possible through Jesus' special eschatology.[33]

Matthew

Matthew shortens the commandment of four parts and thus achieves a more precise form. The contrast to πλησίον and to the narrow Jewish interpretation

---

[27]Cf. particularly Huber* 135f. He debates with C. Schmitt (*Der Begriff des Politischen* [Munich: Duncker & Humblot, 1932]) who, under reference to the Greek distinction between πολέμιος (= *hostis*) and ἐχθρός (= *inimicus*) restricted the commandment of Jesus to personal enemies. Not the secular Greek usage but the Jewish-Christian usage, especially of the LXX, is normative.

[28]"Hate"; "curse" (verbal); "abuse" (physical).

[29]Cf. Reuter* 167.

[30]It is uncertain whether v. 45 was already in Jesus' saying connected with the love of enemies.

[31]Cf. Zeller, *Mahnreden* 104-11.

[32]The rabbis also speak in connection with Ps. 145:9 ("Yahweh is good to *all*") not of the duty of loving enemies but at most of the duty of showing mercy to all, but especially to the righteous, cf. Str-B I 374,376f.

[33]Cf. Merklein, *Gottesherrschaft* 235-37.

of Lev. 19:18 suggests that with "enemy" he is thinking also of the Gentiles.[34] The key word διώκω, taken over from vv. 10f., makes clear that he is thinking of the enemies of the community and in this sense summarizes the statements of Q ("hate," "curse," "mistreat"). National enemies in a war are hardly in the foreground of his thinking, although the basic understanding of enemy in the word of Jesus and probably also the experiences of the community in the Jewish War by no means exclude such an interpretation.[35] It is conceivable that in the worship of the community there was intercession for enemies and persecutors.[36] In v. 45 it is unclear whether the sonship with God of the believers refers to the eschaton[37] or is to be understood as present, in the sense of rabbinic parallels.[38] Since the eschatological passage 5:9 is still remembered by the reader, since the Sayings Source also understood sonship with God eschatologically,[39] and since in early Christianity there was a general reluctance to equate the Christians with the Son of God Jesus,[40] the eschatological interpretation is to be preferred. Thus those who do love their enemies will be revealed in the last judgment as children of God. The traditional reasoning for the love of enemies—God's goodness toward both the good and the evil—Matthew perhaps understood in the sense of his idea of the *corpus permixtum* (mixed body): The world and also the community are fields in which both weeds and wheat grow (13:36-43; cf. 22:9). Thus God is now gracious toward all; only the judgment will reveal the children of God. Matthew therefore perhaps sees his admonition to love enemies and his reference to God's goodness directed against the evil under his eschatological reservation: They are valid for the present; the judgment will make an end of them. That would be different from Jesus, who understood the unrestricted love of God and its human correspondence, the love of enemies, as a sign of the coming of the kingdom itself.

5:43/44a

Matthew interprets the command of love of enemies more clearly through the antithetical frame (vv. 43-44aα). It provides a double difficulty for interpretation: (a) The second part of the thesis, "and you shall hate your enemy," is not found in the Old Testament; (b) it remains uncertain whom the evangelist means to address with this thesis.

On (a) the reference back to Lev. 19:18 suggests itself because this passage was familiar to Matthew and because it could formally very well be contrasted with the

---

[34]Cf. v. 47 and *b. Ber.* 17a = Str-B I 382 (Yohanan ben Zakkai also greets a Goy first). Mek.Exod. 23:4 = 104b in Str-B I 368 shows that even among Jews this text could be referred to the cattle of the Gentile.

[35]Cf. the attractive conjecture by Theissen* 179. The profiled interpretation by Tolstoy*** 256-68, which puts the national enemy into the foreground, overdraws the text.

[36]Polycarp, *Phil.* 12:3 with reference to our passage.

[37]In the sense of *Jub.* 1:24f; *T. Judah* 24:3; *Pss. Sol.* 17:27.

[38]In E. Lohse, "υἱός κτλ.," *TDNT* VIII 359ff. Theissen* 162 interprets it as not eschatological.

[39]Cf. the parallel ἔσται ὁ μισθός ὑμῶν πολύς, Luke 6:35.

[40]E. Schweizer, "υἱός κτλ.," *TDNT* VIII 389ff.

demand of the love of enemies (common key word ἀγαπάω). But since the command of love of neighbor for him is precisely the "highest commandment" which Jesus affirms (22:34-40), he could not simply contrast it with the Old Testament saying without explication. Therefore he had to make the biblical word more precise through an exegetical addition[41] without opening himself to the accusation that he has considered this addition (formulated by himself!) as an Old Testament saying. Therefore it means: To those of old, the commandment of the love of neighbor has been said in terms of a specific interpretation, namely, one which expressly excludes enemies. Jesus will make clear in 22:34-40 that there are also different interpretations.

No one antithesis expresses as clearly as this one the anti-Jewish front which is so important to Matthew. None "fulfills" the law as clearly without invalidating it. But therefore it comes into tension with the antithesis formula. With none of the other antitheses does the "Protestant" thesis that the Antitheses are not directed against the Old Testament but against its Jewish interpretation have as much support.

On (b) against whom is the Matthean thesis directed? Occasionally in Old Testament or Jewish texts, not the personal enemy but the enemy of God and of the people is the object of hatred.[42] But such statements are rare. In many cases, as in the community of Qumran, which often has been suspected as the secret addressee of Matt. 5:34,[43] the hatred against the enemies of God does not lead to corresponding behavior, for one does not want to anticipate the wrath of God through one's own revenge.[44] More numerous are the statements which although they do not speak of hatred against the enemies, nevertheless limit the love command to Israel and exempt the enemies of God, e.g., the Gentiles, from it.[45] Beyond this, v. 43 touches the Hellenistic principle of popular ethics to pay back equally, i.e., to return love for love and hatred for hatred.[46]

---

[41]P. Fiebig, *Altjüdische Gleichnisse und die Gleichnisse Jesu* (Tübingen: Mohr, 1904), 35, offers a Jewish example of a similar procedure.

[42]Psalms 119:113-115; 139:21f.; Deut. 23:6; 25:19; etc. Jewish texts in Str-B I 365f. The warnings against hatred predominate by far in Judaism, cf. only *T. Gad.*

[43]E.g., Stauffer, *Botschaft* 128-32; Davies, *Setting* 245-48; Seitz* 49-51.

[44]Cf., e.g. 1 QS 1.10 (hatred against the sons of darkness, each according to his or her guilt) with 10.17f. (pursue everyone with good—for the judgment belongs to God). The practical synthesis is shown in 9.21f.: unremitting hatred towards all men of perdition (= ill repute?) in a spirit of secrecy.

[45]Str-B and Nissen, *Gott* 322-27, quote numerous passages which are unfriendly toward Gentiles. Nissen distinguishes religiously motivated enmity from personal enmity. But there are numerous counter-voices, e.g., Mek.Exod. 23:4 (104b) = Str-B I 368; *b. Sanh.* 105b = Str-B I 370; *b. Ber.* 10a = ibid., or those rabbinic voices which—probably occurring since Hillel, *Ab.* 1:12— interpret Lev. 19:18 universally. The situation in Judaism is illustrated very beautifully, it seems to me, through the story used by Fiedler, *Jesus* 194, from *b. Ber.* 10a = Str-B I 370, of Beruriah, the wife of R. Meir: Meir has to be admonished by his wife Beruriah to intercede for his enemies, for God's enemy is sin, not the sinner. The story shows: (1) such intercession is intended in Judaism, but (2) not taken for granted (where is it?), and (3) Judaism can also transmit rather negative information about its great teachers. *Result*: There are great differences within Judaism.

[46]Plato, *Menander* 71E (τοὺς μὲν φίλους εὖ ποιεῖν, τοὺς δ᾽ ἐχθροὺς κακῶς); *Resp.* 336a (ὠφελέω/ βλάπτω); Archilochos, P. Oxy. 22,2310 fr 1 (a) col. 1,14f. (ed. M. Treu [Munich: Heimeran, 1959], 10) (τὸν φιλέοντα . . . φιλέειν, τὸν ἐχθρὸν ἐχθαίρειν). Numerous further examples, also on the popular ethical praxis of the principle of retaliation, in Dihle* 30-40; H. Bolkestein, *Wohltätigkeit und Armenpflege im vorchristlichen Altertum* [Utrecht: Osthoek, 1939], 158-60; v. Unnik 294-300.

So v. 43b presumably does not have in mind a certain position or group which advocates enmity but quite generally the restricted interpretation of the love command in the sense of Jewish particularism or in the sense of popular ethical common sense. "Hate your enemy" is a rhetorical counter-formulation,[47] called forth by Lev. 19:18, which wants to address the hearer. In point of fact, it does mean the hatred of the enemy if one understands the love command in a particularistic or popular ethical way.

5:46-47

The two following logia make clear that the love of enemies does not exclude the love of friends (μόνον, v. 47; naturally one should greet friends!) but it means: Your love must extend so far that it comprehends also the enemies.[48] The love of enemies is the περισσόν which belongs to the higher righteousness (cf. 5:20).[49] The reward consists in the promise that those whose righteousness surpasses that of the Pharisees and scribes may enter the kingdom of heaven. The negative contrast is provided by the tax collectors and Gentiles: Matthew takes them over from the tradition; the fact that he keeps this reference (Luke supplants them by the more general expression "sinners") shows that his community still lives in the horizon of Jewish thinking. Through its love of enemies it demarcates itself from "the others" and thus points already ahead to the interpretation of the early church where Christian love became the topic of apologetics.[50] The idea of the missionary effect of the practice (5:16) and the danger of confirming oneself through one's own περισσόν are located close together—especially in a situation of persecution.

5:48

The *Q saying Luke 6:36* serves as the basis. This verse is one of the earliest formulations of the Jewish principle of the *imitatio Dei*[51] on Palestinian soil.[52] This

---

[47]Even if in Semitic languages "very often" in contrasting pairs the negative part is only the negation of the positive part, the Greek (!) text of Matt. 5:43b cannot be translated by "you don't have to love your enemy," pace Jeremias, *Theology* 212 n. 6.

[48]Against Linton*. Verse 45b also points in the same direction: Evil *and* good.

[49]Nicely, Bonhoeffer*** 131f.: "the 'extraordinary,' the 'unusual,' that which is not 'a matter of course' . . . the 'beyond-all-that.' "

[50]Cf. above n. 14-17.

[51]Literature: H. Kosmala, "Nachfolge und Nachahmung Gottes. I. Im griechischen Denken," *ASTI* 2 (1963) 38-85; II. "Im jüdischen Denken," *ASTI* 3 (1964) 65-110; H. D. Betz, *Nachfolge und Nachahmung Jesu Christi im Neuen Testament*, BHTh 37 (Tübingen: Mohr, 1967), 107-136, 84-101; on Judaism: A. Marmorstein, "The Imitation of God (imitatio Dei) in the Haggadah," in *Studies in Jewish Theology, A. Marmorstein Memorial Volume* (London: Oxford, 1950), 106-121; M. Buber, "Nachahmung Gottes," in *Werke* II (Munich: Kösel, 1964), 1053-65; H. J. Schoeps, "Von der Imitatio Dei zur Nachfolge Christi," in idem, *Aus frühchristlicher Zeit* (Tübingen: Mohr, 1950), 286-301; on general history of religions: I. Abrahams, "The Imitation of God," in idem, *Studies in Pharisaism and the Gospels* (New York: Ktav, 1967), II 138-82.

[52]The next following Palestinian passage is dated c. 150 (Abba Schaul, *Sifra* Lev. 19:2 [342a] = Str-B I 372 [ethical interpretation of Lev. 19:2]). *Tg. Yer.* I Lev. 22:8 = Str-B II 159 is a literal parallel to Luke 6:36; further similar passages in Str-B I 372. Examples from Hellenistic Judaism which reflect

principle arose perhaps not without Hellenistic influence. Matthew has formulated it completely anew. Statements about the perfection of God are found particularly among the Greeks.[53] But Matthew also may be mindful of Old Testament statements.[54]

The key for understanding is the word τέλειος which, outside of our passage, occurs in 19:21.[55] It is rightly emphasized that the term must not be interpreted on the basis of the Greek doctrine of virtues but on the basis of its Jewish background. In Jewish texts, individual believers can be designated as perfect because of their piety and their obedience, e.g., Noah or Abraham.[56] The Hebrew equivalent תָּמִים occurs frequently in the Qumran texts; it is the self-designation of this group which walks on the "perfect way," i.e., keeps the rigorously intensified Torah.[57] Two elements belong to perfection: as a subjective element the idea that the heart must not be divided and that obedience must be entire; as an objective element the complete fulfilling of all demands of the law. The quantitative element in the Matthean conception of righteousness, already sounded in v. 20 and once more in v. 47 with the word περισσόν, is found also in 19:20f., where it is the issue of keeping the one command which is still lacking for perfection. This makes it probable that the quantitative element must not be neglected in our passage either. "Perfect" is the one who keeps God's commandments without any reduction.[58] The Didache, which follows in the Matthean tradition, understands it in the same way: Perfection means "to bear the whole yoke of the Lord" (6:2). Most likely Matthew is thinking concretely of the love of enemies in particular; when he is speaking of the perfection of God, he probably refers to God's goodness on the basis of v. 45. Lifted out is ὑμεῖς: the community is to be distinguished from the Gentiles by its perfection (v. 47).

Why did Matthew change the Q tradition if he also was concerned about mercy? Through τέλειος he stresses the foundational significance of the love of enemies. It is not a demand next to others but the center and point of all commands, which leads to perfection. Perfection thus is not a special status of a few, "special" Christians. Our passage, precisely at this point, seems to stand in superficial tension with 19:20f., where the renunciation of possessions is

---

presumably the influence of Platonic thinking on ὁμοίωσις θεοῦ are older: *Ep. Ar.* 188.208-210 (imitation of God's mildness and mercy by the king); Philo, *Spec. Leg.* 4.73; *Leg.All.* 1.48 (benevolence). Hellenistic parallels above n. 26.

[53] G. Delling, τέλειος κτλ., *TDNT* VIII 68ff.; 69ff.; 70ff.

[54] L. Sabourin, "Why Is God Called 'Perfect' in Mt 5,48?" *BZ* NF 24 (1980) 266 refers to Judg. 9:5; 2 Kings 15:32 (name); Job 37:16 (insight); Ps. 18:30 (way) and to Ugaritic designations of El as perfect.

[55] On the history of interpretation and the history of influence of τέλειος, see at 19:21.

[56] *b. Ned.* 32a; TanchB § 23 (40a) = Str-B I 386 (perfection of Abraham through circumcision as a plus beyond the fulfilling of the commandments); further, Gen. 6:9; Sir. 44:17 (Noah; parallel δίκαιος).

[57] Characteristic is, e.g., 1QS 1.8.13f. (not to trespass a single one of all the words of God); 8.17f.,20 (perfect holiness without trespassing a commandment); further references in Delling (above n. 53) 73ff.

[58] Similarly Dupont*; Barth, *Gesetzesverständnis* 91; Strecker, *Weg* 142; Schnackenburg* 424f. stresses the subjective element more strongly. Luck*** passim, especially 36, wants to understand the Antitheses on the basis of a sapiential understanding of the law, which sees the law as the "beginning of the way to perfection."

emphasized and the closeness to a two-level ethic is greater. This tension can be bridged if one recognizes that perfection is for Matthew a *task* which all Christians face and which motivates all. The righteousness, which is greater (περισσεύση . . . πλεῖον, 5:20) than that of the Pharisees and scribes, includes in its quantifying element the possibility that different Christians can variously advance far on this way. But the goal is the same for all; Matthew has set it up through the Antitheses. In this sense, Matthew is definitely a perfectionist. The word "Do what you can" of the Didache is already valid for him, although its acquiescent overtone is not yet heard.[59]

With v. 48 Matthew finally directs the parenesis of the Antitheses back to God himself. *He* is perfect, the one who gives gifts to "righteous and unrighteous" (v. 45). Therefore Matthew calls him "your heavenly Father." This designation of God is here much more than a common phrase. It stands at the beginning of the central part of the Sermon on the Mount, where the evangelist speaks of the prayer to the Father and thereby states the internal aspect and the point of reference of the Christian struggle for the better righteousness. With this, the evangelist points to the basic fact which makes the whole Sermon on the Mount possible and which he expresses in another way by putting the ethical demand of our chapter into the history of the path on which God has set out with his Son.

History of influence[60]

First, it is noteworthy how it was taken for granted in the early church that this "basic law"[61] of faith can be and is practiced.[62] *Second Clement* 13–14 is a good example, where it is said clearly that the one who does not love the person who hates him is not a Christian but stands under the judgment of God. But there are early indications that the practice did not always live up to the demand. The inclination to mitigate the commandment can be traced through the whole history of interpretation.

a. *Second Clement* 13–14 is instructive: The community has to be admonished, not only because it does not love those who hate it, but because it does not love even those who love it (13:4). Harmony within the community was not the best! The author reminds the community that whoever does not do the will of the Father does not belong to the church (14:1). The first mitigation comes from Origen: Since vis-à-vis the love of enemies it is not said "love them as yourself," it is sufficient, in contrast with the love of neighbor, not to hate enemies.[63] This interpretation, which is indeed energetically

---

[59]*Didache* 6:2: "For if you can bear the whole yoke of the Lord, you will be perfect; but if you cannot, do what you can" (E. J. Goodspeed, *The Apostolic Fathers* [New York: Harper & Brothers, 1950], 14). Similarly with mitigating tendency Augustine (below n. 67) and Maldonat 128: "Non vult nos eo usque (i.e., to the perfect unity with the Father) progredi, sed non stare" (He does not want us to progress so far, but he does not want us to stand still).

[60]Literature: Bauer* for the early period; Waldmann* 150-178; Randlinger* 122-63.

[61]Tertullian, *Pat.* 6 = BKV I/7 44.

[62]Theodore of Heraclea, fragment 50 = Reuss 68: "Christ does not give any laws which cannot be carried out."

[63]Origen, *Hom. in Cant.* 2.8 = PG 13,53f.

rejected by most, nevertheless left its traces. Naturally, love of enemies does not mean that I must love enemies as much as blood relatives and friends in such a way that any distinction between them would be removed.[64]

b. Attempts to overcome the problem by means of the *two-level ethic* are manifold. Ambrose arranges in his teaching of duties the love of enemies among the "perfect duties" which he distinguishes from the "medium" ones.[65] In the *Liber Graduum*, the love of enemies belongs to the *via perfecta* (perfect way).[66] According to Augustine it is "only a gift of the perfect children of God, although indeed every believer should strive for this perfection."[67] In Scholasticism it was never made a mere "counsel" without distinctions. But with the aid of Stoic traditions, distinctions were made: enemies indeed must not be excluded from the general love of humans and from general intercession. Everybody is required to have spiritual preparation to be ready for the love of enemies "si necessitas occurreret" (if the necessity should arise). But to love an enemy "absque articulo necessitatis" (without the element of necessity) "pertinet ad perfectionem caritatis" (pertains to the perfection of love) which is not necessary for salvation.[68] Thus love of enemies is no longer the center but a borderline case of Christian practice.

c. The restriction of the command of love of enemies to the *personal area* enjoys ecumenical preference. The opponent in a war is explicitly exempted,[69] love of enemies is articulated for individual morality. It is a question of overcoming personal feelings of hatred against "the unfriendly neighbor, the competitor in one's job," "whom the simple farmer or tradesman hates with all the ardor of his heart," not, as Tolstoy, e.g., thought, the overcoming of national hatred.[70] "Hatred against the national enemy is" in any case "less intensive and develops with greater difficulty."[71] "His (Jesus') words hit like lightning the oppressive air of thoughts of revenge and bring to expression the idea that the attitude which he demands should be completely free from all thought of retribution and revenge. Jesus wants to strike out at the *intention*."[72] The weight is shifted from acts of love to enemies to the feelings of the individual. The problem of war thus can be dropped from the area of the love of enemies; one does not feel evil against the national enemy as a human being.[73] The ethics of intention has its continuation in the area of the existentialist interpretation. Love of enemies means "the surrender of one's own claim."[74] In contrast, love of enemies means for Matthew a tangible *deed*.

---

[64]Jerome, *Pelag.* 1.30 = BKV I/15 385.

[65]Ambrose, *Off.* 1.11 (37) = BKV I/32 28.

[66]*Liber Graduum* (ed. M. Kmosko, 1926 [PS 1/3]) 19.32 = 508f.

[67]Augustine, *Ench.* 19 (73) = BKV I/49 460. Since the great masses of Christians do not achieve the high good of the love of enemies, they pray the Lord's Prayer, Matt. 6:12!

[68]Thomas, *STh* 2/II qu 25 art 8f.; citation from art. 8 corpus.

[69]J. Mausbach and G. Ermecke, *Katholische Moraltheologie* II/I (Münster: Aschendorf, 1954), 145; C. Schmitt, cf. above n. 27.

[70]Cf. above n. 35.

[71]Dibelius*** 115.

[72]Fiebig, *TSK** 53.

[73]"Yet the fight is decontaminated for the person who in the midst of the struggle stands before God" (Schniewind 72).

[74]Rudolf Bultmann, *Jesus and the Word* (New York: Scribners, 1934), 112. Fuchs* 132-35 misses the text when he portrays the perfection of Matt. 5:48 with the guideline of self-consciousness.

Summary

All this leads to the question of whether love of enemies does not demand too much of a person. The New Testament presents us not only with the love of enemies but also with Paul, who is not at all squeamish toward his opponents—not to mention the author of 2 Peter and his manner of dealing with enemies (2 Peter 2:12-22!). Many interpreters have here had to confess their difficulty.[75] But the Gospel of Matthew itself is especially illustrative of the problems. The same author who puts the love of enemies on the top of his series of Antitheses not only has received from his tradition the great discourse of woes against the Pharisees (Matthew 23) as words of Jesus but has refashioned them in a powerful way. Certainly one may list various explanations of how this discourse came about; but it certainly is not a testimony for the love of enemies toward Pharisees and scribes, not even of fairness against opponents whom the Jewish-Christian Matthew really could have known better. Is then the evangelist Matthew himself a prime witness for the problematic of this commandment?

Let me put the question with the words of a—well-intentioned—Jew, since the Jews have suffered most from the Christian deficit of love of enemies: "The defect in the ethical teaching of Jesus is that it is strung so high that it has failed to produce solid and practical results just where its admirers vaunt that it differs from, and is superior to, the ethical codes of the Pentateuch, the Prophets and the Rabbis."[76] According to this critic, a less absolute and more realistic ethics, perhaps in the manner of the rabbis, would have been more useful.

Is then the love of enemies a utopian demand which is ambivalent because it contradicts basic anthropological and psychological presuppositions of the human being? Is it a "saying which violates nature"?[77]

H. Heine says: "If the dear God wants to make me quite happy, he lets me experience the joy of seeing that on these trees about six or seven of my enemies are hanged. With a sentimental heart I will forgive them all injustice before their death. . . . Yes, one must forgive one's enemies, but not before they are hanged."[78] For *F. Nietzsche*, love of enemies is weakness and dishonesty: "Not to be able to take revenge means not to want to take revenge. . . . They also speak of the 'love of one's enemies' and sweat at it."[79] For *S. Freud*, the command of love of enemies is an attempt of the culture superego to change the need of aggression into guilt feelings and so to fight

---

[75]J. de Valdes 91f. thinks that Paul and Christ did not have thoughts of revenge in their heart, but it would be better for him (de Valdes) and the preacher not to strive after them: "It is safer to say evil of no one, for human nature is very much inclined toward passion." The interpretation of the Reformers here distinguishes between personal love of enemies and the need to "rebuke . . . vigorously and attack" which is demanded of the office of the word (Luther, WA 32***, 398 = *LW*, 21, 119).

[76]Montefiore, *Gospels* II 523.

[77]L. Kolakowski in Lapide*** 101.

[78]H. Heine, "Gedanken und Einfälle," in *Sämtliche Schriften* VI/1, ed. K. Briegleb (Munich: Hanser, 1975), 653.

[79]F. Nietzsche, "Genealogie der Moral," 1st treatise, sec. 14, in *Werke* vol. 7 (Leipzig, 1923), 326 (Engl.: "Genealogy of Morals").

against it, an attempt which was indeed successful but is hostile to happiness.[80] Measured by human nature, the command of love of enemies belongs to the "Credo quia absurdum" (I believe because it is absurd). Its problematic becomes visible in Christian history: The love of the neighbor, of which the extreme case is the love of enemies, was to be realized always only in palpable communities. Its price is an intensified aggression toward the outside. "When once the Apostle Paul had posited universal love between men as the foundation of his Christian community, extreme intolerance on the part of Christendom toward those who remained outside it became the inevitable consequence."[81]

An observation on the history of interpretation: again and again it becomes clear in the early church that the enemy of Matt. 5:44 who is to be loved is the Gentile, while Matt. 7:1-5 deals with the relationships among the members of the community.[82] Thus the enemy to be loved is the potential brother or sister under the missionary aspect.[83] In this way, the "enemy" is no longer loved for his or her own sake but in order that he or she might be won for Christ. But what if the one who is loved *in this manner* is not won over for Christ? If he or she persists in enmity? Church history furnishes many examples how in this case "love of enemies" turns into aggression; the attitudes of Matthew and of Luther to the Jews are only two of these examples.

According to Matthew, the true and the false prophets are to be distinguished by their fruits (7:15-23). One can evaluate fruits in different ways. "Nowhere have I seen the true loving . . . of the enemy who is in full bloom and continues to harm us," says a not-so-well-meaning critic, Gottfried Keller.[84] The account which church history renders is in any case ambiguous. There are not *only* crusades, wars of faith, forced missionary endeavors, and Christian anti-Judaism, but they definitely do exist *also*. What do they have to do with Jesus' command to love one's enemies? The questions of history and of psychology are indispensable for the reflection on the fruits demanded by Matthew.

They lead to two observations. One of them is self-critical: Jesus spoke of the enemy in all his harshness and brutality.[85] He did not combine love with a goal. Love of enemy was not a chance or a test for the enemy to become something better. The Gospel of Matthew also does not intend it differently. It is an expression of Christian failure with respect to this command that it has been combined so widely with the goal of mission. Love-with-the-goal-of is not love and not that which Jesus has intended.

---

[80]S. Freud, "Civilization and Its Discontents," in *Standard Edition of the Complete Psychological Works of Sigmund Freud* (London: Hogarth, 1961), vol. 21, 57-145, especially 108-16 (sec. 5), 134-45 (sec. 8).

[81]Freud, ibid. 114.

[82]Beyschlag, *ZTK* 1977** 314f.

[83]Cf. already Ignatius, *Eph.* 10:1 (for them there is hope of repentance). A classic statement: Clement of Alexandria, *Strom.* 7.86.1 (we don't know yet whether the one who is now hostile against us will later find faith).

[84]*Der grüne Heinrich* I 387, according to J. Weiss, *Die Predigt Jesu vom Reiche Gottes* (Göttingen: Vandenhoeck & Ruprecht, 1971), 149.

[85]Bonhoeffer*** 127: "By our enemies Jesus means those who are quite intractable and utterly unresponsive to our love."

The second observation leads deeper: Jesus, Matthew, and the critics of the command of the love of enemies are in agreement on the fact that this command is not a "natural" demand. How could it be? Jesus had formulated it in a mottolike contrast to "natural" behavior. It is not the tactic of a fighter, not the generosity of a victor, not the resignation of a defeated one, and also not the solitariness of a sage. Rather Jesus has made his demand under the completely "unnatural" presupposition that the kingdom of God is breaking in and that the human being should be in harmony with it. Therefore it must not be understood, as has often been done in the history of interpretation, as the acme of the "natural" human love. Matthew has not advocated it because it is reasonable or natural or promises success but because the one who makes it is as the risen Lord with his community all the days to the close of the age. Thus the question is not directly whether it is tactically or psychically realistic but whether the experience of grace which is presupposed in it is so strong that the human being can become free for such a love.

Here also is the central difference from the Marxist evaluation of the love of enemies. Mao Tse-tung has stated in a poignant reflection that it is not yet possible under the conditions of the class struggle. "Genuine love of mankind will be born only when class distinctions have been eliminated throughout the world. The classes have caused the division of society into many opposites, and as soon as they are eliminated there will be love of all mankind, but not now. We cannot love our enemies, we cannot love social evils, and our aim is to exterminate them."[86] The distinction between a yes to the sinner and a no to sin,[87] which is so fundamental in the Christian realm, has no analogy here. Instead, humans are so identified with their social class and the viewpoint of this class that love of enemy would only threaten to weaken the struggle against evil. But the Christian faith attempts to erect signs of God's unconditional yes to the human being, on the basis of the kingdom of God and in a world which is characterized by struggle. That is what is meant by love of enemies.

This last reflection makes it clear that such unconditional signs of God's yes to the human being can not and are not meant to answer the questions of the strategy to be applied in the struggle for social justice or concerning the survival of humankind. Their legitimacy and strength lie on a different level. "Intelligent love of enemies"[88] as political strategy or political alternatives to the class *struggle* is necessary for the sake of the love of human beings; however, they are not "love of enemies" in the sense of Jesus but only a perspective resulting from it. It was not the intention of Jesus to improve the situation of the world. Acts of love toward enemies are, in Jesus' view, an expression of the unconditional yes of God for the human beings for their own sake. They are necessary in a fundamental sense and stand alongside of and *before* all realistic strategies of "intelligent" love.

---

[86]Mao Tse-tung, "Talks at the Yenan Forum on Art and Literature," in *Mao Tse-tung: An Anthology of His Writings*, ed. A. Fremantle (New York: New American Library, 1962), 260.

[87]A classic statement: e.g., Clement of Alexandria, *Strom.* 4.93.3 ("sinning consists . . . in doing, not in being").

[88]Weizsäcker's attempt to sketch political lines under this cue from the Sermon on the Mount shows in an impressive manner that there cannot be a direct application of the Sermon on the Mount in politics, but only an attempt to transmute it. His point of contact is less the eschatological radical love of enemies of Matt. 5:44 than the much more communicable Golden Rule of Matt. 7:12. Cf. below on Matt. 7:12.

2.3. The Higher Righteousness II: The Attitude toward God (6:1-18)

The central section of the Sermon on the Mount (6:1-18) is shorter than 5:21-48 and 6:19—7:11. It consists of a three-strophe admonition to right piety. A title is put in front (6:1). After the second strophe, there follows an insertion. The evangelist has inserted the Lord's Prayer (6:9-13) and framed it with two sayings (6:7f.,14f.). All admonitions have the same structure: after a negative part (vv. 2,5,7f.,16) a positive antithesis follows (vv. 3f.,6,9-13,17f.). Thus the Lord's Prayer is in form the positive antithesis to the warning of babbling prayer (vv. 7f.); as far as the content is concerned, however, it breaks its frame. It is emphasized once more through the appendix (vv. 14f.). Thus the Lord's Prayer is the center of the section and so of the entire Sermon on the Mount. Its title word "Father (in the heavens)" is the guiding word of the whole section; it is repeated throughout and thus imposes itself on the reader (vv. 1, 4, 6, 8, 9, 14, 15, 18). Through this word our section is bracketed with the preceding and the following sections of the Sermon on the Mount (5:16,45,48; 6:26,32; 7:11,21). The frequency of the word πατήρ shows quite externally where the center is. Despite its composite character, the section makes a unified impression: The key word προσεύχεσθαι creates a close connection between vv. 5f. and vv. 7-13. The appendix (vv. 14f.) takes up linguistically and in terms of content the longest petition of the Lord's Prayer, the petition for forgiveness of v. 12.

For the commentary it is advisable to depart from the order of pericopes, in this one case, and to anticipate the three-strophe admonition, 6:2-6,16-18.

2.3.1. On Almsgiving, Prayer, and Fasting (6:1-6, 16-18)

Literature

Betz, H. D., "Eine judenchristliche Kult-Didache in Matthäus 6,1-18," in *Jesus Christus in Historie und Theologie* (FS H. Conzelmann), ed. G. Strecker, pp. 445-57 (Tübingen: Mohr, 1975).

Dupont, *Béatitudes* III 260-72.

George, A., "La justice à faire dans le secret (Matthieu 6,1-6 et 16-18)," *Bib* 40 (1959) 590-98.

Gerhardsson, B., "Geistiger Opferdienst nach Matth 6,1-6.16-21," in *Neues Testament und Geschichte* (FS O. Cullmann,), ed. H. Baltensweiler et al., pp. 69-77 (Tübingen: Mohr, 1972).

Klostermann, E., "Zum Verständnis von Mt 6,2," *ZNW* 47 (1956) 280f.

Nagel, W., "Gerechtigkeit—oder Almosen? (Mt 6,1)," *VC* 15 (1961) 141-45.

Schweizer, E., " 'Der Jude im Verborgenen . . ., dessen Lob nicht von Menschen, sondern von Gott kommt'. Zu Röm 2,28f und Mt 6,1-18," in idem, *Matthäus und seine Gemeinde* 86-97.

Tannehill, R., *The Sword of his Mouth*, 1975 (Semeia S 1), 78-88.

Tilborg, *Jewish Leaders* 8-13.

Zeller, *Mahnsprüche* 71-74.

Further literature** on the Sermon on the Mount at Matt. 5-7 above, pp. 209-211.

Text

1 But beware of practicing your righteousness[1] before the people in order
  to be noticed by them. Otherwise you have no reward with your Father in
  the heavens.

2 So when you practice benevolence,
  do not sound the trumpet before yourself
  as the hypocrites do in the synagogues and on the little streets
  in order to be praised by the people.
  Amen, I say to you: They already have[2] their reward.

3 But you, when you practice benevolence,
  let not your left hand know what your right hand is doing,

4 in order that your benevolence be done in secret.
  And your Father who sees into the secret things,[3] will reward you.[4]

5 And when you pray,
  do not be like the hypocrites:
  for they like to stand in the synagogues and at the street corners and
  pray
  in order to seem[5] pious to the people.
  Amen, I say to you: They already have their reward.

6 But you, when you pray,
  "go into your room and close the door,"
  in order to pray to your Father who is in secret.
  And your Father who sees into the secret things will reward you.

16 But when you fast,
  do not be like the dismal looking hypocrites,
  for they make their faces unseemly,
  in order to seem[5] pious to the people as fasting.
  Amen, I say to you: They already have their reward.

17 But you, when fasting,
  anoint your head and wash your face,

18 In order that you not seem pious to the people because of your fasting,
  but to your Father who is in secret.
  And your Father who sees into the secret things will reward you.

Analysis

1. *Structure*. The pericope is connected with 5:16 and 20 by δικαιοσύνη (6:1),
ἔμπροσθεν τῶν ἀνθρώπων, πατήρ . . . ἐν τοῖς οὐρανοῖς (6:1), and δοξάζω, with
6:19-24 by the rare word ἀφανίζω (6:16,19,20). In addition, v. 7 (ἐθνικοί!) contains a

---

[1]The variant reading ἐλεημοσύνη·of the textus receptus (defended by Nagel*) probably came in from
vv. 2-4.

[2]Ἀπέχω is a term of business language: "to have received," "to have a receipt."

[3]Literally: *in* the secret things, as v. 4a. The literal translation is meaningless since the Father is not in
the dark. Explanations: (a) equalizing formulation in v. 4a and 4b because ἐν and εἰς were used inter-
changeably; (b) Aramaism; but Aram. חמא ב in the meaning of "to see something" is not usual (pace
Jeremias, *Theology* 216).

[4]The textus receptus adds: ἐν τῷ φανερῷ and thus testifies to the eschatological interpretation of the
future tense.

[5]Really: "shine." The German translation, "sie machen ihre Gesichter unansehnlich, um vor den
Menschen als Fastende angesehen zu sein," was chosen in order to resemble the pun ἀφανίζω – φαίνω.

reference back to 5:47. Again it can be seen that the evangelist, despite a clear new beginning, connects sections with each other. The theme of "righteousness," given in 5:20, is treated further but under a different aspect, already foreshadowed in 5:16. Besides, the key word "hypocrites" and especially πρὸς τὸ θεαθῆναι αὐτοῖς (v. 1) is a "signal," pointing ahead to chapter 23 (cf. 23:5). There will be the final accounting with the hypocrites.

The verses 2-4,5f. and 16-18 are a unified composition, consisting of three strophes. Each strophe consists of a negative and a positive part. Both the negative and the positive part contain each (1) a statement of the situation (almsgiving, prayer, fasting), (2) a prohibition or a command, (3) a statement of intention, and (4) the divine promise or the Amen saying which negates the promise. Each warning contains a comparison with the "hypocrites"; therefore it is in each case a little longer than the positive corresponding part. The language is strictly constructed prose, not poetry; we have neither rhythms nor parallelisms in the strict sense of the word but only corresponding parts. The last, concluding admonition to right fasting is a bit longer than is suitable for a conclusion. All three strophes are characterized by the same opposites: publicly —hidden; people—Father; present (ἀπέχουσιν τὸν μισθὸν αὐτῶν) and future (ὁ πατὴρ . . . ἀποδώσει) reward. It is especially impressive that only in the second half of each strophe, at almsgiving, praying, and fasting in secret, the heavenly Father is introduced while the behavior of the hypocrites, which hankers after recognition by the people, ends on a dead track, seen religiously. The linguistic terseness is impressive. The oversharp metaphor of trumpeting (v. 2), the pun φαίνω — ἀφανίζω in v. 16,[6] or the cutting formulation ἀπέχουσιν τὸν μισθὸν betray a master. Several proverbial phrases have entered our language from our text;[7] this also testifies to its power of language.[8]

2. *Redaction.* That v. 1 comes from the evangelist is probable through the numerous cross-references and is supported by the linguistic analysis.[9] For vv. 2-6,16-18 a written source is probable, one that Matthew has changed relatively little. But the text contains a number of linguistic peculiarities which Matthew himself also uses frequently,[10] e.g., the designation of God as Father.[11] The evangelist is rooted linguistically and theologically in his community. It is conceivable that the source here

---

[6]Can it be translated as a pun into Aramaic? Or is it an indication that the text arose in Greek-speaking Jewish Christianity?

[7]"To sound the trumpet" (Matt. 6:2); "do not let your left hand know what the right hand is doing" (Matt. 6:3); "in the quiet chamber" (Matt. 6:6).

[8]Schweizer* 88f. and Hoffmann V** 91 attempt to trace back some of the sharpest formulations to Jesus, while the text as a whole comes from Jewish Christianity. A problematic attempt! The text is so concise and unified that one would prefer *one* author. Why must Jesus have been the only early Christian teacher who was able to formulate sayings "like goads and like nails firmly fixed" (Eccl. 12:11)?

[9]The following are Matthean: προσέχω, δικαιοσύνη, μή with infinitive, ἔμπροσθεν . . . ἀνθρώπων, πρός with infinitive, θεάομαι (?), εἰ δὲ μή γε (?), μισθός (?), πατὴρ . . . ἐν τοῖς οὐρανοῖς; cf. introduction 3.2. Detailed analysis in Tilborg, *Leaders* 10f., and Dupont, *Béatitudes* III 260-62.

[10]The following are Matthean: οὖν, ἔμπροσθεν, ὅπως, ὥσπερ, ὑποκριτής, βλέπω, μισθός, ἀμήν, πατήρ, ἀποδίδωμι, ἑστώς (?), φαίνω. But in addition the text contains many hapax legomena. Gundry 102 believes that Matthew has put it into writing.

[11]Πατήρ as the designation for God without the addition of "heavenly" or something similar is not Matthean; but the essential closeness to Matthew is great. Moreover, the idea of reward and the motif of hypocrisy are constitutive for our text and for the evangelist.

was connected with the one for the primary Antitheses.[12]

3. *Development of tradition and form.* It seems to me that the text cannot be dissected. Between the individual strophes there are small asymmetries; but is it necessary that the original form was strictly symmetrical? Perhaps one can assume that it was formulated throughout in the second person singular, since Matthew prefers the plural, as is shown in vv. 1,7-15.[13] The solitary allusion to Scripture in the middle strophe[14] does not suggest that the text was reworked. The section is of one cast.

It does not fit any previously available genre completely. The sapiential hortatory saying is akin to it. The second person singular, the definiteness which leans toward hyperbole, and the confrontation of prohibition and command are typical of it.[15] The eschatological conception of the heavenly reward (vv. 4,6,18 at the end), the conclusion of the prohibition by an Amen word (vv. 2,5,16 at the end), and the solid styling of the opposing type, the hypocrite, are atypical. The admonition does not have a general meaning, like wisdom sayings elsewhere, but a real addressee and a tangible opposition. The connection of three different themes in three strophes also is atypical for sapiential hortatory sayings. All this points to a situation in which comprehensive polemical instruction concerning the basic dimensions of piety became necessary. The symmetrical styling in strophes makes it easier to learn by heart.

4. *Origin.* Does our text come from Jesus? On the basis of the criterion of dissimilarity, the answer was easy: the text has been felt to be Jewish[16] or reform-Jewish[17] and therefore not authentic to Jesus. But the post-Easter origin is by no means certain.[18] The most important argument against authenticity is the difference from Mark 2:19a where the disciples do not fast. There are possible explanations: Matt. 6:16-18 could be a general instruction to the people, Mark 2:19a could refer to the special situation of the disciples. Or Mark 2:19a could have in mind the praxis of the disciples as a group while Matt. 6:16-18 speaks of the private fasting of the individual. Ἀμὴν λέγω ὑμῖν and "Father" as a designation for God are (Jesus or) "Christ language." Thus the author *could* have been a Jewish Christian who was influenced by the language of Jesus. But the text does not contain a trace of Christology as could have been expected, precisely for fasting (cf. Mark 2:20). Does it come from Jesus after all? The hyperbolic formulations[19] and the address only to the individual would speak in favor of it. It is not merely the case that the temple or synagogue worship, the Pharisaic days of fasting, or the beginnings of Jewish care for the community are of no interest to the text, but—what weighs even more heavily in this case—not even the Christian worship services with their communal prayers, the presumably quite ancient Christian practice of days of

---

[12]Thus within a different overall conception, e.g., Dupont, *Béatitudes* I 161f.,181; Kilpatrick, *Origins* 26; Soiron** 129f. Cf. section 2 on 5:21-48.

[13]Schweizer 86.

[14]The singular τὴν θύραν corresponds to the LXX Isa. 26:20, against the Hebrew text. Again a (weak) indication for the original Greek composition of our text?

[15]Cf. Zeller, *Mahnsprüche* passim.

[16]Haenchen, *Weg* 117, with view to the "Pharisaic" idea of reward.

[17]Betz* 456, cf. G. Schille, *Das vorsynoptische Judenchristentum*, AzTh I 43 (Stuttgart: Calwer, 1970), 44f.

[18]Betz* makes the dilemma clear: According to him, those who handed down this text, not authentic to Jesus, must have "stood close . . . in time and theology" to Jesus; "in no place" can Christian influence be found (456.450).

[19]Cf. on this below, pp. 357, 359.

fasting,[20] and the Christian care for the community. Can all this be explained by the style of wisdom exhortation alone? Thus many questions concerning the origin of our text remain moot, questions which earlier scholarship, determined only by the "criterion of dissimilarity," was easily able to solve. Naturally it would be simplest if one could assume, on the basis of the very scarce linguistic observations,[21] that the original text was Greek. Then it would come from a very gifted Jewish-Christian teacher who—in the spirit and language of Jesus—composed it at a time when the followers of Jesus within the synagogue community had to come to terms with Jewish practices of piety. But this also is uncertain, and origin with Jesus remains possible.

Interpretation

6:2

We are dealing here with three forms of Jewish expression of piety,[22] which also were of central importance in the Christian communities.[23] The first strophe deals with private benevolence. Ἐλεημοσύνη—the German word "Almosen" and the English "almsgiving" are derived from this Greek word[24]—besides the general meaning "mercy," in Jewish-Greek language had also the more special meaning of "welfare," "almsgiving."[25] In the period of early Christianity, there was not yet the care of the poor in the synagogue which was organized on the community level and was unique in antiquity, but the distribution of the tithe for the poor was left to the judgment of the individual. Benevolence was recommended all the more strongly.[26] Jewish sources demonstrate that almsgiving was also abused and offered opportunity for advantageous public self-display.

It did *not* occur that a trumpet was blown at spectacular benevolence.[27] Here the

---

[20]Betz* considers this "cult didache" as anti-Pharisaic and critically inclined toward the temple cult (456f.).—a difficult thesis, because it would have to be applied under changed circumstances also to Christian communal services. This question rightly was always of interest to the history of interpretation, cf. below nn. 55-58. The numerous Pharisaic-rabbinical parallels to our text speak against the idea of an anti-Pharisaic frontline, cf. below p. 358. It is correct that Matt. 6:2-6,16-18 is an admonition to the individual and therefore excludes the public cult of any kind.

[21]Cf. above nn. 3,6,14.

[22]Tobit 12:8 names prayer, fasting, deeds of mercy with righteousness. Among the rabbis, there is the triad of prayer, almsgiving, repentance (Str-B I 454; IV 553f.). The combination of prayer and fasting is frequent among Jews and early Christians. A similar combination is found also in *2 Clem.* 16:4.

[23]Gerhardsson's* association (73f.) with Deut. 6:5 is artificial: Prayer = loving God from the heart; fasting = chastising of the soul (!); almsgiving = worship with "might" (notice the order in Deut. 6:5!).

[24]*BE* I, 17th ed. (1966), 362.

[25]Przybylski, *Righteousness* 100f., points out that the Matthean differentiation between δικαιοσύνη and ἐλεημοσύνη corresponds to the contemporary distinction between צֶדֶק and צְדָקָה among the early Tannaites.

[26]Str = B IV 537-45; Moore, *Judaism* II 162-74.

[27]Cf., below n. 59.

text speaks in irony and caricature, by taking up a widespread metaphor.[28] But it is well known that gifts could be pledged publicly in the synagogue or at worship services of fasting.[29] The person who pledged a large amount was especially honored and was permitted, e.g., to sit next to the rabbi.[30]

The text apostrophizes such possibilities as hyprocrisy. Ὑποκριτής is a neutral word in Greek usage and means "actor." Transferred to the realm of ethics, it receives in Greek as in Jewish usage[31] a negative sense and designates a person who does or is something else than what he or she says. In distinction from Matthew 23, not the deed of the Jewish opponents is attacked but their motivation: almsgivers are reproached for giving the promised alms not out of love to the neighbor or for God's sake but for their own sake. They have already received—with the honor accorded to them—their reward. In the background stands the rabbinical conception of God's balancing justice: some, chiefly Gentiles and evildoers, are paid the reward for good deeds on earth, and then in heaven the punishment will take place, while the just often suffer on earth and will gain their reward in heaven for it.[32] The hypocrites are not identified with a certain group but remain a general negative type. However, the evangelist Matthew most likely is thinking of the Pharisees and scribes.[33]

6:3-4

The text also formulates the counter-position pointedly and hyperbolically:[34] The left hand is not to know what the right hand is doing. This saying, which has become a proverb,[35] must not be pressed. It does not mean that "even the person who practices mercy may not know that he or she practices mercy."[36] The ideal conception of doing "entirely spontaneous and unpremeditated"[37] good is alien to the text. The image only means: Nobody, not even the closest confidant, needs to know about your almsgiving. Benevolence happens before

---

[28]Demosthenes, *Or.* 25.90 (797); Achilles Tatius, 8.10.10; Dio Chrysostom, *Or.* 8.2; Cicero, *Epistulae ad Diversos* 16.21.2; Juvenal, 14.152; cf. German "ausposaunen," French "trompetter," English "trumpet forth," "sound one's own trumpet."

[29]Str-B IV 548-50, at η, ζ, θ, ι, λ.

[30]*p. Hor.* 3.48a,57 (Str–B IV 550). Cf. Sir. 31:11: "the assembly will relate his acts of charity."

[31]There is no fundamental difference between Greek (often neutral) and Jewish (often negative) usage. Where the concept appears in Greek metaphorically in ethical contexts, it is also negative (examples in U. Wilckens, ὑποκρίνομαι κτλ., *TDNT* VIII 562). In Judaism, where there was less interest in theater, this metaphorical usage predominates. In most cases, ὑποκριτής is not simply "evildoer," but refers to a person who pretends something; cf., e.g., 2 Macc. 6:21-28; Sir. 1:28f.; Job 36:13. The translation "hypocrisy" therefore is very frequently accurate (against Wilckens loc.cit. 564,29f.).

[32]Str-B I 390f.; II 231f.

[33]This follows from the relationships between 6:1 and 5:20 or 23:5.

[34]In the exegesis of the early church John Chrysostom 19.2 = 344 and exegetes dependent on him are practically the only ones who have retained the hyperbolic interpretation.

[35]*GinzaR* I 104 = Lidz *Ginza* 17,27f. is dependent on Matthew.

[36]Clement of Alexandria, *Strom.* 4.138.2.

[37]Bonhoeffer** 138.

God alone who—again a Jewish thought[38]—will make public, reward, and punish secret deeds in the last judgment. It is the perspective of the eschatological judgment according to works, as in Paul in Rom. 2:16,28f. Thus the text counts on the fact that the benefactors will receive a reward from God.[39] But it does not encourage the people to calculate simply in a more skillful way and to live with a more subtle—namely, a religious—form of self-affirmation, but it uses the reference to the reward, given by God—in actuality—in order to unmask human self-presentation as the secret goal of good deeds.

Numerous Jewish and Hellenistic texts make similar demands. Sapiential texts warn against religious hypocrisy (Sir. 1:28f.) and recommend "a secret gift" (Prov. 21:14). Rabbi Zadok (first century) warns against making the Torah into a crown with which one can boast (*m.'Abot* 4:5). The principle to give the poor alms secretly in order not to shame them is advocated repeatedly.[40] Therefore one also is supposed to put money in the "chamber of secrets" standing in the temple (*m.Šeqal.* 5:6). The practice to pledge alms publicly is criticized by the Shammaites.[41] Benevolence for one's own glory was felt to be a definitely Gentile practice.[42] In Hellenistic, especially Stoic texts, similar tones are also found. "That which I did well I did not in order to be seen but for my own sake . . . to please myself and God" (Epictetus, *Diss.* 4.8.17). However, God is here not the court which judges from the outside, but is identical with the human being himself or herself in the conscience. "No audience for virtue (is) higher than the conscience" (Cicero, *Tusc.* 2.26[64]). The special feature of the Jewish texts, in comparison with the Stoic materials, namely, giving up the claim to self-perfection of the wise person, is due to the concept of God. It is expressed in our text precisely in the thought of reward!

Our text can be distinguished from its Jewish parallels only with difficulty. The pointedness of the demand, which is generally characteristic of Jesus, is striking. It is also in the style of Jesus that the hyperbolic-figurative demand, "Let not the left hand know what the right hand is doing," excludes a legal-juridical setting; it is left to the creative fantasy of the hearer how this demand is to be fulfilled.[43] Finally, in the designation of God as "your Father," there is the reminiscence for the community of Jesus' relationship to God, i.e., the knowledge of the loving God who is near at hand.

6:5

In the second strophe, the subject is the proper way of praying. In Judaism the place of prayer is preferably the synagogue.[44] But since it is not understood as

---

[38]Examples in Schweizer* 90f.; the eschatological element is evident especially in 2 Macc. 12:41; Rom. 2:16; rabbinical material in Str-B I 391,396.

[39]Against Calvin I 216: "figurative manner of speaking."

[40]Examples in Str-B I 391f.; further *b. Ketub.* 67b (toward the end, Simeon ben Yoḥai).

[41]*t. Schab.* 16.22 (136) = Str-B IV 548.

[42]*p. B. Bat.* 10b = Str-B I 204.

[43]Cf. Tannehill* 85-88.

[44]Προσευχή may mean directly the synagogue.

a sacred space, one may on principle pray at any place.[45] The text probably is thinking of the regular prayers, i.e., the morning, noon, and evening prayer. Since the times for prayer are not fixed exactly, as, e.g., in Islam, but prayers only need to be performed within a certain interval of time,[46] people who would pray visibly[47] at the street corners[48] would cause attention. In the synagogue the idea is perhaps that of the loud, free prayer of individuals in the worship services.[49] In Jewish texts, this is not seen as a problem, although praying on the streets seems to have occurred frequently.[50] Praying presumably was something too obvious for most Jews and not suitable as a means for *special* self-presentation. It is difficult to say from where this special sensitivity of the text precisely toward prayer as a potential act of self-presentation is derived.[51]

6:6

Again the positive application is given in a drastic figurative way: "Go into your room." Ταμεῖον normally is the storage room which was always present in the Palestinian farmhouse,[52] but, in the wider sense, any private chamber not visible from the street. But the command does not simply want to prescribe certain places for prayer. To that extent the interpretation of the early church is correct: "Not the place (τόπος) does damage, but the manner (τρόπος) and the aim (σκόπος)."[53] Instead, it wants to urge through pictures and hyperboles the right attitude for prayer: even prayer itself *can* become a means for pious self-presentation. The intention of our text is to call attention to this danger and to teach to pray correctly. Prayer has to be oriented alone on God, who again is designated as Father and so as the God of Jesus. The statement that he will reward right prayers,[54] which is due to the symmetry of the strophes, is very troublesome.

---

[45]Str-B I 399f. sub *e*.

[46]*M.Ber.* 4:1—"The morning *Tefillah* [may be said any time] until midday. . . . The afternoon *Tefillah* [may be said any time] until sunset. . . . The evening *Tefillah* has no set time; and the Additional *Tefillah* [may be said] any time during the day" (trans. Danby).

[47]Standing while praying is the customary Jewish attitude of prayer.

[48]Πλατεῖα = main street, distinguished from the unspecified ὁδός.

[49]Cf. J. Heinemann, *Prayer in the Talmud*, SJ 9 (Berlin: de Gruyter, 1977), especially 191f.

[50]Str-B I 399f.

[51]Luke 18:13 makes the tax collector stand quite far in back in the temple, in distinction from the Pharisee. The tradition reports frequently of Jesus that he had prayed in a lonely place (Mark 1:35; Luke 5:16) by himself (Matt. 14:23; Luke 9:18, cf. Mark 14:32-42). Naturally these passages are not direct historical testimonies, but they could still reflect historical reality. Then the sensitivity toward praying in public could be a heritage from Jesus—if indeed our text itself is not derived from Jesus.

[52]Krauss, *Archäologie* I 44.

[53]Theophylact 204, similarly, e.g., *Opus imperfectum* 13 = 709. The church interpretation emphasizes since Origen, fragment 116 = 62 that one may pray in any place. This conviction was decisive for the allegorical interpretation: The text *can* not be meant literally!

[54]It is not a question of the promise of answering prayers in the quiet little room but of the reward for such praying in the last judgment.

History of influence

The question of Christian community prayer is addressed in our text just as little as the question of Jewish community prayer in the synagogue or in the temple. The interpretation of the church sought, on the one hand, to exempt Christian community prayer explicitly from the critical questions of the text while it was taken for granted, on the other hand, that Jewish prayer practice as a whole was condemned by Jesus.

a. The generally advocated opinion is that the common prayer of Christians in the worship service does not offer an opportunity for presenting one's own piety.[55] Even in the communal services the praying believer should only have God before his or her eyes.[56] The metaphors of v. 6 were interpreted allegorically. The chambers of the heart and the doors of the senses are meant.[57] It was not until the period of Pietism that our text was understood literally, namely as a call to worship in houses and "collegia" in the quiet chamber.[58]

b. Alongside this interpretation, there is the tendency to condemn Jewish prayers altogether. All three strophes of our text are interpreted completely as anti-Jewish. Already in *Did.* 8:1 the "hypocrites" are identified with the Jews as such, who fast on Monday and Thursday. With the first strophe, the interpretation of "trumpeting" offers a grotesque example: for a millennium, despite many protests, the legend was entertained that in the synagogue trumpets were sounded at the giving of alms in order to attract the poor;[59] and even a scholar of our century had high hopes that we would sometime find the missing documentation for such a hullabaloo.[60] In Origen, Jewish prayer becomes inferior even where it is not distinguished from Christian prayer: Since there is a difference in principle between the community which is without spot and the synagogue, the one who prays in the synagogue is "not far removed from the 'street corners.' But the Christian is not of such a kind," for he or she prays in the Christian community.[61] "Synagogue" becomes here an abstract word of abuse.

On the other hand, if our text would be a product of the community it is striking that it does not put Christian against Jewish praying. Since in our text not the prayer but the praying person is the subject, it is not directed against any—Christian or Jewish—community prayer. Rather it is the question of *how* one should pray for oneself and under changed circumstances also in the assembly of the community. In the perspective of our specific, illustrative text, it can be said: Prayer should never have another purpose than to speak with God. For the communal service, this may mean: "Prayer as a demonstration of faith, as disguised sermon," prayer as didactic preparation of the listener for the sermon or as a summarizing resumé of the content of the sermon, "prayer . . .as

---

[55]Maldonat I 133.

[56]Calvin I 204.

[57]Cf. Hilarius 5 = 943f.

[58]Lapide 157 turns against this "ridicula haeresis" (ridiculous heresy).

[59]E.g., Anselm (in Thomas, *Lectura* no. 563); Anselm of Laon 1304; Peter of Laodicea 57; Strabo 98f.; Euthymius Zigabenus 229 ("τινές"); Nicolaus of Lyra, 3rd column on chapter 6; Tostatus, vol. 20,16f.; Calvin I 202; Chemnitz 466; Cocceius 13; Lapide 155; Bengel 48; Paulus I 560; etc.

[60]Bornhäuser** 122f.

[61]Origen (cf. bib. at 6:9-13) 20.1.

an instrument of edification, is obviously *not* prayer at all. Prayer is *not* prayer if it is addressed to anyone else but God."[62]

6:16

The third strophe of fasting also sketches the opposite type, the hypocrite, in an exaggerated way. The idea seems to be that of donning sackcloth, of omitting ointments, and of sprinkling ashes on the head, customs which were practiced at public fasting only in extreme situations, e.g., during a drought.[63] But our text is thinking of individual fasting as an expression of mourning, of repentance, as an act of humility or for intensifying prayer,[64] which was quite popular.[65] By practicing private fasting in such an extreme way, one could acquire the reputation of a saint.[66]

6:17-18

The instruction of the text, by contrast, is to wash and anoint the face when fasting. Whether this command is meant, as the preceding strophes, in an exaggerated way—then one might think of festive garb[67]—is questionable. The washing of the face, the frequent visit to baths, recommended by the rabbis, and the anointing with oil rather were a part of daily hygiene.[68] Thus, the command might also be meant realistically: When you fast, act precisely in such a way that one does not notice any symptom of your fasting. Washing is not only an expression of everyday life but also a figurative illustration of hiddenness, exactly like the "quiet room" and the saying of the left and the right hand. The listener himself or herself has to determine what "washing and anointing" means tangibly. Again, such stirring "focal-point formulations"[69] appeal to creative fantasy and to the liberty of the listener. As such, they fit not only formally but also in terms of content with Jesus.

The text thinks not only of the problematic of fasting in itself; it also does not give a special Christian motivation, perhaps in the sense of Mark 2:20, but simply presupposes it as an expression of piety in order to inculcate the right

---

[62]Barth, *CD* III/4, 88.

[63]*Ta'an.* 1:2-7; cf. *Ta'an.* 2:1 = Str-B IV 83-85 and the examples in Str-B IV 103f. (no. *b*). 105 (no. *e*).

[64]Cf. *Ta'an.* 1:3-7 = Str-B IV 83f. (in the case of failing rain) *b. B. Mes.* 85a = Str-B IV 96 (fasting in especially difficult cases); *b. Ta'an.* 12b = ibid. (fasting for getting rid of dreams); see also the examples in Str-B IV 108.

[65]Str-B IV 94-100 (on private fasting in general); on the extension of fasting Str-B II 241-44. Beginning in the second century, the rabbis warned against excessive fasting, cf. Abrahams, *Studies* I 121f.; Str-B IV 99f.

[66]Cf. the hermit Bannus (Josephus, *Vita* 11f.).

[67]So, e.g., Schweizer 91. Eccl. 9:7f. or Ps. 45:8 shows that ointments could be an expression of special festive joy; but this cannot be documented about washing.

[68]On the daily hygiene of the Jews cf. Krauss, *Archäologie* I 209-33, on anointing particularly 229f. Str-B IV 385 documents the positive attitude of the rabbis to Roman baths; *b. Sanh.* even demands that a rabbi may not live in a city where there is no bath house.

[69]Cf. Tannehill* and at 5:38-42 no. 34.

orientation of the fasting person to God alone. The subject is the human being and not the religious custom.[70]

History of influence

The text is concerned neither with a justification of nor a critique of fasting, as was sometimes thought, especially in the Reformed tradition.[71] The allegorical interpretation also demands too much of the text in a different way. Thus, it was said, e.g., that "washing and anointing" refers to the removal of sin; oil is the oil of spiritual joy, of love, of pity, or even Christ himself.[72] Nevertheless, precisely these allegorical interpretations are important because they attempt in their own way to integrate fasting into a comphrehensive understanding of what it is to be a Christian.[73] With this, the allegorical interpretation is an important attempt to integrate an individual text into the entirety of the Christian faith. In a deeper sense it does justice to the paradigmatic character of the three examples.

6:1

The Matthean introductory verse is a summarizing title. Its function is twofold: First, it is intended to generalize. Almsgiving, prayer, and fasting are exemplary possibilities of clarifying the right relationship to God. Δικαιοσύνη means again[74] the human acting as God the Father wills. One can translate the word here actually by "religiosity" or "piety."[75] Second, it is intended to anchor our section in its context. It points ahead to 23:5 and thus secures from the beginning the parenetic dimension of the great discourse of woes against Pharisees and scribes. But, most of all, it refers back to 5:20; from there it takes up again "your righteousness."

Summary

Here the evangelist gives what is indeed the deepest insight into his understanding of righteousness. Not only in the quantity of the fulfillment of the law (5:20) or in the radicality of obedience (5:21-48) is Christian righteousness to be better than that of the scribes and Pharisees (5:20), but also internally, in its intention and basic attitude. The church fathers pointed out correctly that here, after 5:21-48, the right intention of actions is addressed.[76] After

---

[70]Again, a feature typical of Jesus in the depth of the text!

[71]Calvin I 216; similarly Aretius 62: Fasting is (obviously in distinction from almsgiving and praying, which are commanded by the Lord) a "res media" (a neutral matter).

[72]Strabo 103.

[73]Cf. *Opus imperfectum* 15 = 718: A hypocrite is one who fasts "a cibis" (from food) but not "ab operibus malis" (from evil deeds).

[74]Cf. above on 3:15; 5:4; 5:20.

[75]Cf. Davies, *Setting* 307.

[76]Examples: Augustine, *Sermo* 3 = *PL* 38,374 (the sermon deals with the relationship of 5:16 to 6:1); Thomas, *Lectura* no. 474. J. Wesley, *Wesley's Standard Sermons* (London: Epworth, 1921), vol. I, no. XXI, II, 57, formulates succinctly that Matthew proceeds "to show how all our actions, likewise, even those that are indifferent in their nature, may be made holy, good, and acceptable to God, by a

developing in ch. 5 *what* the divine will is, the concern in ch. 6 is to preserve the person who does the divine will from a danger which threatens precisely *him or her*. In the words of Bonhoeffer: Matthew 6 "takes up the theme of the περισσόν (i.e., 5:20,47) and lays bare its ambiguity . . . The call to the 'extraordinary' is the *risk* (!) men must take when they follow Christ."[77] Matthew is aware of the danger of good deeds: "In each human action the devil can perform a fraud; alone in the conscience, cunning is impossible."[78] To this extent he does not progress in ch. 6 to another theme, viz., perhaps that of piety or religious practices, but he is concerned about the inwardness of the same righteousness of which he spoke in the Antitheses. Without reflection concerning this inwardness it would remain a deeply ambiguous matter. In this respect, 6:1-18, with the Lord's Prayer in the center, and not yet 5:21-48, is the high point of the Sermon on the Mount.

This center of the Sermon on the Mount brings Matthew into clear proximity to Paul.[79] In Matthew also, we find knowledge of the fact that a human deed is not qualified simply by its agreement with God's demand but only by the basic intention of the heart. The analogy to the Pauline idea that precisely *righteousness* as one's own righteousness before God may be sin (Rom. 9:30–10:3) suggests itself. It is of the greatest significance for the understanding of the Gospel of Matthew that the evangelist, driven by the quest for wholehearted, and not only external, obedience toward God's will, reflects on the question of the right direction of the heart as a decisive problem of the higher righteousness.

It is still more important that in *this* connection he stresses prayer as the decisive center of obedience and of righteousness. If in the traditional hortatory discourse almsgiving, prayer, and fasting stood equally side by side, then Matthew himself lifts out prayer as the center of the Christian life. He does this by referring, in the added logion on the answer to prayer (vv. 7f.) and the Lord's Prayer, to that which alone is able, in the last analysis, to direct the human being into the right, not self-related attitude toward God, namely, prayer. Perhaps he has reflected in this direction as the *Opus imperfectum* understands him: There "is no remedy against vainglory but prayer alone. . . . Thus mercy is the preparation for prayer and fasting an aid to prayer."[80]

---

pure and holy intention." But also the pious intention to achieve something from God in secret, with renunciation of one's self-presentation before human beings, is thwarted by the evangelist, since he put the prayer to that Father "who already knows before your prayer what you have need of," into the center of the whole section (6:7-13).

[77] Bonhoeffer ** 134,136.

[78] *Opus imperfectum* 13 = 707.

[79] This text has found too little attention for the determination of the relationship between Matthew and Paul.

[80] 15 = 715.

2.3.2. Against Babbling Prayer (6:7-8)

Literature

Delling, G., art. "βατταλογέω," *TDNT* I 597f.
Zeller, *Mahnsprüche* 133-35.
Further literature** on the Sermon on the Mount at Matt. 5-7 above, pp. 209-211.

Text

7 When you pray, do not babble like the Gentiles; for they think they will be heard because of their torrent of words.
8 Do not make yourselves their equal, for your Father knows what you need before you ask him.

Analysis

This is an independent logion which is linguistically so distinctive[1] that the evangelist can hardly be considered its author.[2] It also argues against Matthean authorship that the saying has its unique scope in v. 8b, which Matthew does not take up directly in v. 9. As for the content, it could come from Jesus.[3]

Interpretation

6:7

The meaning and the etymology of the very rare word βατταλογέω are disputed. A connection with the noun βάτταλος or βάττος (stutterer) or the verb βατταρίζω (stutter) is most probable. It likely refers to a repetition of syllables which are in themselves senseless.[4] The content of the word is taken up in πολυλογία. The prohibition probably has Gentile prayers in view, which through the accumulation of epithets of God or also of magical words give the impression of babbling.[5] In comparison with this, Matthew lifts out the Lord's Prayer positively as a short prayer.

---

[1]The following are Matthean: ὥσπερ, οὖν, ὁμοιόω (?), cf. introduction 3.2. There is also much that is non-Matthean: the hapax legomena βατταλογέω, εἰσακούω, πολυλογία, as well as πρό with infinitive and πατήρ for God without "heavenly," "in the heavens," or "my." The comparison of v. 8 (end) with 6:32, in view of the different statement and of the partly different linguistic expression, speaks more for than against tradition. However, as far as the content is concerned, it is important for Matthew; cf. on 6:31f.

[2]Against Bultmann, *Tradition* 133; Klostermann 54.

[3]Βατταλογέω does not speak against an Aramaic original text since the (also onomatopoetic) Aramaic *palpel* בטבט could have occasioned the translation by its sound similarity.

[4]Hesychius B 340,346f. puts in parallel: ἀργολογία, ἀκαιρολογία, ποππύζειν, τραυλίζειν, φλυαρισμός; *Etymologieum Gudianum* M (ed. F. Sylburg [Leipzig 1816], 173): μόλις λαλεῖν; Suidas I 462 (Adler): πολυλογία. On the subject: Delling*.

[5]Cf. E. Norden, *Agnostos Theos*, reprint (Darmstadt: Wissenschaftliche Buchgesellschaft, 1956), 146-49. An example of the heaping up of epithets is furnished by the hymn to Isis, Apuleius, *Met.* 11.2; also Acts 19:34 (two hours); Vergil, *Aen.* 4.510 (300 gods). Mockingly Terentius, 5.1.6f. ("idem dictum est centies" [the same thing is said a hundred times]); Lucianus, *Tim.* 11; Martialus, 7.60.3.

This meaning, which seems to suggest itself, has been obscured in the Greek tradition of interpretation. There βατταλογέω was interpreted in the sense of φλυαρία (senseless babbling) and the warning was referred not to the length but to the content of the prayer.[6] It was said that the text prohibits asking for unseemly things, namely, unspiritual, lowly, earthly things,[7] things below,[8] for which one should not pray. The Latin tradition of interpretation rightly has never followed this exegesis,[9] although it came into difficulties through its correct interpretation, in view of the wordiness of ecclesiastical prayers.

If in our logion there were *only* an admonition to brief prayer, then it would agree with many a Jewish text[10] and also many a Hellenistic statement.[11] But it means more. Already the last part, 7b, shows that wordy prayers are not rejected in themselves but as a means to win God's hearing.

6:8

The parallel reasoning in v. 8b takes up this facet. The central theme of our logion is not the length of prayer but the answer to prayer. Long prayers are not necessary, because God knows what humans need before they ask. It is not simply a rejection of manipulation, also not simply that God knows everything anyway and that therefore prayer is no longer truly necessary, but the issue is that God is with the human being with his love *before* he or she prays so that he or she does not have to pray in a wordy manner. Our text belongs together with others which speak of the unconditional certainty of answer to prayer and of the nearness of God to humans (cf. Matt. 7:7-11; Luke 11:5-8; 18:2-7; and the address of the Lord's Prayer). Jesus is unique with this absolute certainty of answer to prayer.[12] Probably he makes contact with the Jewish expectation that

---

[6]Origen, fragment 118 = 62.

[7]Gregory of Nyssa, *Or.* (cf. bib. on 6:9-13) 1.5 = 101f. (temporary, lowly, paltry earthly happiness, perishable, foolish, useless); John Chrysostom 19.3 = 349 (power, glory, victory over the enemies, riches).

[8]Τὰ κάτω (Origen, *Or.* [cf. bib. on 6:9-13] 21.1).

[9]Vulgate: *multum loqui* (to say much).

[10]Str-B I 403-05 states correctly that rabbinical tradition has different opinions concerning the length of prayers and can also recommend long prayers. The recommendation of brief prayers is rooted in the wisdom tradition: Eccl. 5:1; Sir. 7:14.

[11]The aversion against the "fatigare Deos" (to wear out the gods) is widespread: Seneca, *Ep. ad Lucilium* 31.5; Horatius Flaccus, *Carm.* 1.2.26. For short prayers: Plautus, *Poenulus* 1.2.203 ("paucis verbis rem divinam facito" [you should make the divine matter in few words]); Marcus Aurelius, 5.7 (either not pray at all or do so simply).

[12]There are parallels which argue on the basis of the omniscience of God: "God knows the answers of the tongue before questions . . . are posed" (Papyrus Insinger 124, in W. v. Bisping, *Altägyptische Lebensweisheit* [Zürich 1955], 117); Xenophon, *Mem.* 1.3.2 reports that Socrates had asked the gods simply for that which is good. In Exod. Rab. 21:3 (on 14:15), Eleazar ben Pedath interprets Isa. 65:24 (cf. below n. 13) of God's omniscience: God knows the heart.

in the new world God answers humans before they call on him.[13] To validate this expectation for the present is part of the coming of the kingdom of God. Of course, Jesus does not want to make prayer superfluous but wants to encourage the believers to pray. The interpretation of the church, which again and again had to deal with the question whether praying would be necessary at all, has understood this very well, in contrast with modern enlightenment.[14] Cocceius formulates very pregnantly: "Our prayer is not the reason for the gifts of God which we receive but rather a sign that God has prepared his gifts for us," i.e., the prayer commanded by God *is based* on the promise of answer.[15]

History of influence

    a. The criticism of long prayers led to *confessional polemics*: Luther directed his criticism against the "merely enforced work of the mouth or the tongue"[16] of the monastic prayers. It is understandable that criticism was directed especially against the rosary and litanies.[17] The judgment of H. E. G. Paulus is fair: "Whether . . . Hail Marys are prayed by number or so many recitations of our desires and 'Have mercy, dear Lord God' have become liturgical in and outside of our (i.e., Protestant) churches, it is clear that one, like the other, is against the simply noble word of Jesus: 'God knows what you need before you ask.' "[18] The apologetic of Christian practice appealed to the Pauline "Pray without ceasing" (1 Thess. 5:17, cf. Rom. 12:12). But the usual thesis that long prayers "cum cordis devotione" (with the devotion of the heart)[19] are permitted does not do justice to Matt. 6:7a.

    b. Our text also came into the undertow of the *polemic against Judaism*. Since it is formulated against Gentile babbling prayer, the misinterpretation is especially ironic. Sometimes vv. 5f. still are effective. So Origen can say: "Whoever babbles in praying is . . . in the lower stage, that of the 'synagogue.' "[20] "Synagogue" has become the type of the negative path which has been overcome by the Christian church, but a type with which the real Jews of any time had to identify themselves. With this interpretation, it is then not incomprehensible if again and again—from Chromatius to Adolf Schlatter—the Pharisees or "Jewry" become those whose wordy prayer Jesus is censuring.[21]

---

[13]Isaiah 65:24 is related ("Before they call I will answer"—in the eschaton). This expectation is demonstrated also in the old Habinenu prayer: "Before we call you will answer" (*p. Ber.* 4,81a,45; *b. Ber.* 29a, in Str-B IV 222). Tanch. 97b.117a; Tanch.B § 9 (43b); § 23 (49b) (= Str-B IV 926) expects this for the time of the Messiah.

[14]Braun, *Jesus* 83: The passage "taken strictly" eliminates "the necessity of the act of a petitioning prayer."

[15]Cocceius 13.

[16]WA 32***, 417.

[17]G. Voetius, De pseudo-precationibus, rosariis, litaniis, horis canonicis, et officiis ecclesiae Romanae (Pseudo-prayers, rosaries, litanies, canonical hours, and offices of the Roman church); in *Selectarum disputationum Theologicarum* III (Ultrajecti: Waesberge, 1659), 1013-76.

[18]I 565.

[19]Thomas, *Lectura* no. 579, following Anselm.

[20]Origen (cf. bib. at 6:9-13) 21.1.

[21]Chromatius 358; Schlatter 206f.

2.3.3. The Lord's Prayer (6:9–13)

Literature

Abrahams, I., "The Lord's Prayer," in idem, *Studies* II, 94-108.

Brown, R., "The Pater Noster as an Eschatological Prayer," in idem, *New Testament Essays*, pp. 275-320 (Garden City: Doubleday 1968).

Carmignac, J., *Recherches sur le "Notre Père"* (Paris: Letouzey & Ané, 1969).

Dalman, *WJ* I 283-365.

Debrunner, A., "'Επιούσιος," *Glotta* 4 (1913) 249-53.

Dewailly, L. M., " 'Donne-nous notre pain': quel pain? Notes sur la quatrième demande du Pater," *RSPT* 64 (1980) 561-88.

Fiebig, P., *Das Vaterunser. Ursprung, Sinn und Bedeutung des christlichen Hauptgebetes*, BFCT 30/3 (Gütersloh: Bertelsmann, 1927).

Foerster, W., "ἐπιούσιος, *TDNT* II 590-99.

Freudenberger, R., "Zum Text der zweiten Vaterunserbitte," *NTS* 15 (1968/69) 419-32.

Fridrichsen, A., "'Άρτος ἐπιούσιος," *SO* 2 (1924) 31-41.

———, "'Άρτος ἐπιούσιος. Eine Nachlese," *SO* 9 (1930) 62-68.

Grässer, *Parusieverzögerung* 95-113.

Greeven, H., *Gebet und Eschatologie im Neuen Testament* (Neutestamentliche Forschung III/1, pp. 72-101 (Gütersloh: Bertelsmann, 1931).

Grelot, P., "La quatrième demande du 'Pater' et son arrière-plan sémitique," *NTS* 25 (1978/79) 299-314.

Harnack, A., "Über einige Worte Jesu, die nicht in den kanonischen Evangelien stehen, nebst einem Anhang über die ursprüngliche Gestalt des Vater-Unsers," *SPAW* (1904) 170-208.

———, "Zwei Worte Jesu (Mt 6,13 = Lk 11,4; Mt 11,12f = Lk 16,16)," *SPAW* 1907, 942-57.

Heinemann, J., *Prayer in the Talmud*, SJ 9 (Berlin: de Gruyter, 1977).

Jeremias, J., "The Lord's Prayer in the Light of Recent Research," in idem, *The Prayers of Jesus*, pp. 82-107 (Naperville: Allenson, 1967).

———, *Theology* 188-96.

———, Kuhn, K. G., *Achtzehngebet und Vaterunser und der Reim*, WUNT 1 (Tübingen: Mohr, 1950).

Leaney, R., "The Lucan Text of the Lord's Prayer," *NovT* 1 (1956) 103-11.

Lohmeyer, E., *Das Vater-Unser*, 5th ed. (Göttingen: Vandenhoeck & Ruprecht, 1962).

Manson, T. W., "The Lord's Prayer," *BJRL* 38 (1955/56) 99-113.

Ott, W., *Gebet und Heil*, SANT 12, pp. 91-99 (Munich: Kösel, 1965).

Schelbert, G., "Sprachgeschichtliches zu 'abba'," in *Mélanges Dominique Barthélemy*, ed. P. Casetti et al., OBO 38, pp. 395-447 (Göttingen: Vandenhoeck & Ruprecht, 1981).

Schlosser, J., *Le règne de Dieu dans les dits de Jésus* I, EBib, pp. 247-322 (Paris: Gabalda, 1980).

Schürmann, H., *Praying with Christ: The "Our Father" for Today* (New York: Herder & Herder, 1964).

Schulz, *Q* 84-93.

Schwarz, G., "Matthäus VI 9-13; Lukas XI 2-4," *NTS* 15 (1968/69) 233-47.

Starcky, J., "La quatrième demande du Pater," *HTR* 64 (1971) 401-09.

Strecker, G., "Vaterunser und Glaube," in *Glaube im Neuen Testament* (FS H. Binder), ed. F. Hahn and H. Klein, BTS 7, pp. 11-28 (Neukirchen-Vluyn: Neukirchener, 1982).

Tilborg, S. van, "A Form-Criticism of the Lord's Prayer," *NovT* 14 (1972) 94-105.

Vögtle, A., "Der 'eschatologische' Bezug der Wir-Bitten des Vaterunser," in *Jesus und Paulus* (FS W. G. Kümmel), ed. E. Ellis and E. Grässer, pp. 344-62 (Göttingen: Vandenhoeck & Ruprecht, 1975).

Zeller, D., "God as Father in the Proclamation and in the Prayer of Jesus," in *Standing before God* (FS J. M. Oesterreicher), ed. A. Finkel and L. Frizzell, pp. 117-29 (New York: Ktav, 1981).

Further literature** on the Sermon on the Mount at Matt. 5-7 above, pp. 209-211.

Bibliography on the history of interpretation and the history of influence:

Aner, K. *Das Vaterunser in der Geschichte der evangelischen Frömmigkeit*, SGV 109 (1924).

Angénieux, J., "Les différents types de structure du 'Pater' dans l'histoire de son exégèse," *ETL* 36 (1970) 40-77, 325-59.

Bock, J., *Die Brotbitte des Vaterunsers. Ein Beitrag zum Verständnis dieses Universalgebetes und einschlägiger patristisch-liturgischer Fragen* (Paderborn, 1911).

Chase, F., *The Lord's Prayer in the Early Church*, Texts and Studies I/3 (Cambridge: Cambridge University, 1891).

Dibelius, O., *Das Vaterunser. Umrisse zu einer Geschichte des Gebets in der Alten und Mittleren Kirche* (Giessen: Ricker, 1903).

Fendt, L., *Einführung in die Liturgiewissenschaft*, STö.T 5 (Berlin: Töpelmann, 1958).

Furberg, I., *Pater Noster in der Messe*, Bibliotheca theologiae practicae 21 (Lund: Gleerup, 1968).

Hamman, A., "Le Notre Père dans la catéchèse des pères de l'Eglise," *MD* no. 85 (1965) 41-63.

Kuss, O., "Das Vaterunser," in idem, *Auslegung und Verkündigung* II, pp. 277-333 (Regensburg: Pustet, 1967).

Rietschel, G., *Lehrbuch der Liturgik*, ed. P. Graff, I, 2d ed. (Göttingen: Vandenhoeck & Ruprecht, 1951), and II, 2d ed. (Göttingen: Vandenhoeck & Ruprecht, 1952) (index).

Rordorf, W., "The Lord's Prayer in the Light of Its Liturgical Use in the Early Church," *StLi* 14 (1980/81) 1-19.

Vokes, F., "The Lord's Prayer in the First Three Centuries," *StPatr* 10, pp. 253-60 (1970) (TU 1107).

Walther, G., *Untersuchungen zur Geschichte der griechischen Vaterunser-Exegese*, TU 40/3 (Leipzig: Hinrichs, 1914).

Important interpretations of the Lord's Prayer by the fathers in monographs:

Cyprian, *De Dominica Oratione*, PL 4, 535-62, trans. BKV I/34 161-97 = "The Lord's Prayer," in *St. Cyprian–Treatises.*, The Fathers of the Church, 36, pp. 125-62 (New York: Fathers of the Church, Inc.).

Eckart, *Tractatus super Oratione Dominica*, in *Die lateinischen Werke*, ed. E. Seeberg, vol. 5, pp. 101-29 (Stuttgart 1936).

Gregory of Nyssa, *De Oratione Dominica*, PG 44, 1120-93; trans. BKV I/56 89-150 = "The Lord's Prayer," *St. Gregory of Nyssa*, Ancient Christian Writers, vol. 18, pp. 21-84 (Westminster: Newman 1954).

Luther, M., *Auslegung deutsch des Vater unser fuer dye einfeltigen leyen*, WA 2, 80-130 = "An Exposition of the Lord's Prayer for the Simple Laymen," *LW* 42, 15-81.

Origen, *De Oratione*, PG 11, 416-561; trans. BKV I/48 7-148 = "Prayer," *Origen*, Ancient Christian Writers, vol. 19, pp. 15-64 (Westminster: Newman, 1954).

Tertullian, *De Oratione*, PL 1, 1153-65; trans. BKV I/7 248-73 = "Prayer," *Tertullian–Disciplinary, Moral and Ascetical Works*, The Fathers of the Church, vol.

40, pp. 153-90 (New York: Fathers of the Church, Inc., 1959).

Text

9 This is how you should pray:
   Our Father[1] in the heavens,
   hallowed be your name,
10 your kingdom come,
   your will be done,
   as in heaven, (so) also on earth.
11 Our bread for tomorrow
   give us today;
12 and forgive us our debts,
   as we also have forgiven our debtors;
13 and lead us not into temptation,
   but preserve us from evil.

Analysis

1. *Structure*. The Lord's Prayer is handed down to us in three variations, namely, the Lukan short version, consisting of only five petitions (Luke 11:2-4) and two closely related long versions (Matt. 6:9-13; *Did*. 8:2). The long version shows greater symmetry, liturgically a fuller language and a clearer rhythm. It is easiest to divide the Matthean Lord's Prayer into two main parts, the three you-petitions (second person singular, vv. 9c-10) and the somewhat longer three we-petitions (first person plural, vv. 11-13).[2] The three you-petitions begin with an imperative aorist in the third person and in Greek still show traces of final rhyme (3 x σου). The we-petitions are determined by the first person plural pronoun (7 x). All of them[3] have two parts, in distinction from the you-petitions where only the last one has two parts. Beginning with v. 11, the sentence structure changes; after the resonant conclusion (v. 10c) the bread petition is sensed as a clear new entrance. The address, which in the Matthean version is just as long as the two first you-petitions, stands over the whole prayer and so has great weight.

2. *Redaction*. The question arises whether the evangelist has emended redactionally a text which is so anchored in the liturgy of the community as the Lord's Prayer.[4] This does not seem to be excluded on principle and is, in my opinion, even probable in the case of Luke whose version of the Lord's Prayer is not documented as the

---

[1]The translation "Vater unser"—used among Lutherans and Catholics—which follows the word order of the Vulgate is linguistically incorrect in German. The "reformed" translation "Unser Vater" was, by the way, also preferred by Luther in the Bible translation.

[2]Most Greek fathers count six petitions, which presumably agrees with the intention of Matthew; cf. Strecker* 15 (on the number *three* in Matthew!). The Catholic and the Lutheran counting with seven petitions follows Augustine (*Enchiridion* 31.115 = BKV I/49 496).

[3]This applies also to the petition for bread, because the position of the verb (δός at the beginning of the second line) shows that it also has two parts.

[4]Rejected by Jeremias* 89: "No author would have dared to make such alteration in the Prayer on his own." The compilation of two words of institution in Luke 22:15-20, however, which probably took place not in the community worship service but at the desk, speaks against him. Jewish communal prayers at the time were not fixed in their wording but could be changed and supplemented, cf. below n. 14; in the formulation of private prayers, there was freedom anyway. Besides, Jeremias gets into conflict with his own presuppositions since he nevertheless proceeds from *one* original version of the Lord's Prayer and thus attributes the freedom, which he denies the evangelists, to some anonymous member of the community.

part of a communal liturgy. Probably the placing of the prayer following vv. 7-8 should be ascribed to Matthew.[5] Whether the two additional petitions vv. 10b and 13b and the enlarged address are due to him is not yet obvious from the text of the Didache; *Did.* 8:1f. belongs to those passages which make it probable that the author of the Didache presupposes Matthew, for the connection of the Lord's Prayer with Matt. 6:5f.,16f. is familiar to him. The Didache, however, does not copy Matthew but receives the Matthean texts in the form in which they remained in the memory of the community.[6] The peculiarities of the Didache text, which are small in comparison with Matthew, cannot be traced with certainty to a text version which is older than the Matthean.[7] But the Matthean text itself gives indications: The language of the additional petitions on the whole is indeed Matthean,[8] but some details speak against Matthean authorship.[9] Moreover, the Matthean text version is documented very early, even through writings which otherwise show no contact with the Gospel of Matthew.[10] Thus it is most probable that the two additional petitions were already found by the evangelist.[11] If this is correct, then precisely the special petitions illustrate how much the evangelist in his own diction takes up the language of his community.[12]

     3. *History of tradition.* In seeking the original wording of the Lord's Prayer the often-advocated thesis might prove correct that on the whole Luke is more original in the number of the petitions and in the address, but Matthew in the wording. Indeed one must consider seriously the old thesis, proposed for the first time by Origen, of two different original recensions of the Lord's Prayer.[13] But the reference to spontaneous variations of Jewish prayers is more helpful.[14] They make understandable both the additional petitions

---

[5]Οὕτως οὖν προσεύχεσθε ὑμεῖς v. 9a is probably formulated by him: the οὕτως οὖν in first position and ὑμεῖς at the end are redactional, cf. introduction 3.2.

[6]Cf. introduction p. 75. The main thrust of the Didache text, namely, the judicial regulation of fasting twice a week and of praying of the Lord's Prayer three times a day is new in comparison with Matthew. Only the key words fasting, praying, hypocrites come from Matthew.

[7]Cf. Köster, *Überlieferung* 206f.

[8]Πάτερ . . . ὁ ἐν τοῖς οὐρανοῖς, γίνομαι (especially γενηθήτω), θέλημα τοῦ πατρός, οὐρανός (singular)//γῆ, πονηρός. Cf. introduction 3.2.

[9]The article with γῆ is missing (otherwise in the meaning "world" or "land" always determined; the same with ἐπί; possible exception is only the passage 28:18 which is text-critically uncertain). Ὡς . . . καί, (v. 10!) is not found in Matthew elsewhere.

[10]2 Tim. 4:18 is a reminiscence of the Matthean concluding petition, even though Matthew is not known to the author. The address to the "Father in heaven" is documented in Mark 11:25 (cf. Matt. 6:14) in a logion which comes close to the petition for forgiveness. Since it is unique in Mark, it is probably a reminiscence of the Lord's Prayer. Less certain are reminiscences of the Lord's Prayer in Mark 14:36,38; John 12:28; 17:15. Among the Apostolic Fathers, Polycarp 6:2; 7:2 must be mentioned; but Polycarp is familiar with Matthew. Altogether there is hardly a New Testament text which is so widely known within the NT as the Lord's Prayer. Cf. Vokes* on the history of the Lord's Prayer in the time immediately after the New Testament.

[11]The plural οὐρανοί in the address and the ὡς καί in the petition for forgiveness might be Matthean (cf. 18:33; 20:14); but that remains very uncertain. Kilpatrick, *Origins* 21; Frankemölle, *Jahwebund* 275f., count on a far-reaching Matthean shaping of the Lord's Prayer.

[12]Cf. introduction 4.2.1.

[13]Origen* 18.2f. Among contemporary scholars, Lohmeyer 15-17,208f., who associates Matthew 6 with the Galilean, Luke 11 with the Jerusalem community.

[14]Heinemann* 43, cf. 46,63. I. Abrahams, "Some Rabbinic Ideas of Prayer," in idem, *Studies* II 84 n. 2, points to rabbinical texts which actually forbid the literal fixation of the prayers: *m. 'Abot* 2:13; *m.*

in Matthew and the possible alterations of the wording. The supplements in the pre-Matthean Lord's Prayer are all easily understandable as secondary variations: The address was enlarged, according to the example of the Jewish prayer address "Father in the heavens," which was becoming prominent at that time.[15] The asymmetrical brief beginning part of the two you-petitions was enlarged by a third petition which appropriately concluded the first part of the prayer. A positively formulated parallel sentence was added to the last we-petition whereby the closeness to the other we-petitions and the symmetry of the whole became greater. The beautiful rounding of the pre-Matthean Lord's Prayer and the continuing rhythmic character point to its liturgical use.[16] By contrast, the changes of Luke in the wording of the two we-petitions are secondary; they mirror the delay of the parousia (δίδου, imperative present; τὸ καθ' ἡμέραν,) and the parenetical use (παντὶ ὀφείλοντι). Further attempts at dissection,[17] as far as the history of tradition is concerned, are not really plausible. Therefore we proceed from the assumption that the count of five petitions agrees with the oldest achievable version. Like the later Matthean version, so it also is formally compact. After the brief address πάτερ follow the two brief you-petitions, introduced by an imperative aorist and ending with a possessive suffix. The three we-petitions are not formulated as evenly but are shown as belonging together by the connective καί.

4. Aramaic has to be assumed as the *original language* of the Lord's Prayer. Occasionally Hebrew is advocated as the original language,[18] yet there is no indication for it except for the uncontroverted fact that most extant prayers in the Judaism of that time were formulated in Hebrew. Besides אַבָּא [19] which most likely was the source for the Lukan πάτερ, there is a second indication for original Aramaic language: 'Οφείλημα in Greek means only "debt of money"; the metaphorical use in v. 12 is understandable only on the basis of Aramaic חוֹבָא which may mean at the same time "debt" and "sin." Besides, the Jewish Qaddish prayer, from which the Lord's Prayer borrows in the first part, also was formulated in Aramaic. When the prayer is retranslated into Aramaic, scholars are in broad consensus on approximately half of the text. There is a high probability that the Aramaic Lord's Prayer was formulated rhythmically: The first, second, and fifth petitions consists of a line with two stresses, the petition for bread and the petition for forgiveness of two lines with two stresses.[20] As in later Jewish prayers, there are traces of a final rhyme which as a rule is constituted by the final suffixes of the

---

Ber 4:4; *b. Ber.* 29b. *p. Ber.* 4,8a = German trans. Horowitz 127: "Only (one may) not (recite the prayer) in such a way as if one were reading a letter . . . One should on every day add new words to (the prescribed prayer)."

[15]Cf. below n. 60.

[16]In the present, the priority of the Matthean version is seldom advocated even by Catholics, since a plausible reason for the omission of petitions cannot be found. Cf. Carmignac* 24-26.

[17]Harnack, *SPAW* 1904* 1955-208, considers the petition for the Spirit, which is handed down by the minuscules 162 and 700 and by Gregory of Nyssa and probably Marcion, as the original Lukan text. He concludes from the great differences between Matthew and Luke which arise in this way that only the we-petitions but not the you-petitions, which are "closely related to the official Jewish prayers" (203), belonged to the original Lord's Prayer.

[18]Ben Chorin, *Bruder;* Carmignac* 30-33; Starcky*.

[19]Middle Aramaic examples on ostraca from approximately the time of Herod the Great; later also Middle Hebrew documents (Schelbert * 406-09,416-28).

[20]Cf. the retranslation by Jeremias, *Theology* 196, which is, in my opinion, plausible.

second person singular or the first person plural.[21] But a complete rhymed form of the Lord's Prayer cannot be produced because we are completely in the dark at the retranslation of the petition for bread: the Aramaic equivalent of the Greek ἐπιούσιος is as unclear as the latter itself. Precisely this obscure ἐπιούσιος provides important information: Since this word unquestionably occurs in all Greek versions of the Lord's Prayer, it is not to be assumed that there were different translations from the Aramaic. The assumption of *one* Greek original translation from which the variants can be explained is more probable. It is improbable that the uniquely Matthean petitions existed at any time in Aramaic. Ὡς . . . καί (v. 12) is a common phrase in Koine,[22] but cannot be translated literally into Aramaic.[23]

    5. *Origin.* The Lord's Prayer comes from Jesus. This assumption, shared by most interpreters, results from the following interpretation.

Interpretation

Tertullian sees in the Lord's Prayer a summary of the entire teaching of faith and morals, a "brevarium totius Evangelii" (a breviary of the whole gospel).[24] For him, a new form of prayer is appropriate for the new covenant; it is the new wineskin in which the new wine is kept. Thus it is understandable that the Lord's Prayer not only becomes the central Christian prayer but also one of the most central dogmatic texts. As already Cyprian formulated it,[25] "coelestis doctrinae compendium" (a compendium of the heavenly doctrine). In the early church it was solemnly "handed over" to the candidates for baptism before baptism and spoken by them as the first prayer after baptism.[26] From the third century on, it even was part of the secret discipline for a time.[27]

History of influence[28]

This basic understanding and the constant use of the Lord's Prayer have led to the fact that there is hardly a Christian text which has had greater effect in piety, worship, instruction, and dogmatics.

    a. *Worship.* It can no longer be determined for certain at what time the Lord's Prayer received its firm place in the liturgy. In Cyril of Jerusalem it stands after the intercessory prayer and before communion.[29] It has its place in the liturgy of the African

---

[21]Kuhn*, especially 30-40. The final rhyme is otherwise not widespread in ancient poetry and probably entered from Jewish prayers in Christian texts.

[22]Examples in Lohmeyer* 77.

[23]Aramaic, the phrase is not ὡς . . . καί but כְּמָא . . . כֵּן. Moreover, the anarthrous οὐρανός and γῆ cannot be rendered in Aramaic (Dalman* 315f.).

[24]Tertullian * 1.

[25]Cyprian* 9.

[26]*Apostolic Constitutions* 7.45; Chrysostom, *Hom. in Col.* 6.4 = *PG* 62,342; Rordorf* 2-5.

[27]"Beware of disclosing the secret of the confession or of the Lord's Prayer out of carelessness." (Ambrose, *Cain et Abel* I.9.37 = *PL* 14,355). Further examples in Vokes* 255.

[28]This section is based on a draft by W. D. Köhler.

[29]Cyril, *Cat. Myst.* 5.11-18 = BKV I/41 387-90.

church ca. 400 after the "fractio" directly before the kiss of peace.[30] Through the reform of the mass by Gregory the Great it is connected immediately with the canon and receives an introduction.[31] Presumably Gregory has inserted the Lord's Prayer in its place used today in order that it be spoken "over the body and blood of the Savior." Gregory considers the Lord's Prayer as an integral part of the epiclesis of the canon of the Mass and together with it as the table grace in the Eucharist.[32] In the Protestant churches, it obtains a fourfold meaning after the reforms of the Mass in the 16th century: It may be the conclusion of the intercessory prayer,[33] the conclusion of the substitute for the canon of the Mass,[34] the confession of sins,[35] or simply the conclusion of the worship service.

b. *Instruction.* The Lord's Prayer has had an important place in catechesis since the earliest times. It was understood, on the one hand, as an excerpt and compendium of the Christian doctrine, but, on the other hand, as an instruction for prayer, according to the words of Peter Chrysologus as the "shortest instruction" for the "understanding of supplication."[36] It is the common opinion since the early church that the Lord's Prayer is the norm for prayer and that Christian praying has to follow it. Thus it is not surprising that the Lord's Prayer is an indispensable part of the catechisms of all confessions. For Luther, in whose catechisms it occupies a large portion, there is no better prayer than the Lord's Prayer, this "oratio pro pueris et simplicibus" (prayer for children and the simple people).[37] In the Catholic catechisms of this time too, the Lord's Prayer belongs to the main tenets of Christian teaching.[38] The Bern Synod of 1532 formulates impressively: "The Lord's Prayer is the true Christian prayer, and the water pitcher or bucket with which blessed grace is drawn out of the fountain of grace of Jesus Christ and poured into the heart."[39]

c. *Piety.* Already at the time of the Didache, i.e., shortly after the writing of the Gospel of Matthew, praying the Lord's Prayer three times a day is proposed (*Did.* 8:3). To these three times of the tradition, Cyprian adds two further times, at sunrise and sunset. Augustine thinks that no day should pass by on which the Christians do not say this prayer.[40] In the Middle Ages the Lord's Prayer played an important role in the monastic prayer of the hours,[41] while the laity's familiarity with it receded.[42] Exactly for

---

[30]Rietschel-Graff* I 255. Therefore many Western text witnesses read in v. 12 ἀφίομεν instead of ἀφήκαμεν, according to Rordorf* 13.

[31]"Praeceptis salutaribus moniti et divina institutione formati audemus dicere . . ." (After having been admonished with the salutary precepts and formed by the divine institution we dare to say . . .).

[32]J. Pascher, *Eucharistia, Gestalt und Vollzug,* 2d ed. (Münster: Aschendorf, 1953), 228-30.

[33]Primarily in the Zwinglian preaching service. In the Calvinistic preaching service, a paraphrase of the Lord's Prayer follows the general prayer of the church (Rietschel-Graff* I 357).

[34]In the Anglican Church (Fendt* 220-22).

[35]Cf. Luther's *Formula Missae* of 1523 = WA 12,205-220, there 213 = *LW* 53, 15-40, there 28-29. In the Large Catechism, Luther says, "Indeed, the whole Lord's Prayer is nothing else than such a confession" (*Book of Concord,* 459).

[36]Peter Chrysologus 70 = 94f.

[37]Catechism sermon of 1528, WA 30/1, 50.

[38]C. Moufang, *Katholische Katechismen des 16. Jahrhunderts in deutscher Sprache* (Hildesheim: Olms, 1964), passim.

[39]BSRK 53.

[40]Cyprian* 35; Augustine, *Civitas Dei* 21.27.

[41]*Regula Benedicti* 13 = BKV I/20 42f.

this reason it was used as a formula for magic and conjuration.[43] Since the late Middle Ages, the Reformation and Counter-Reformation, its significance for the piety of lay people has increased. Catechetical instruction and the practice of the rosary (since the Crusades) have contributed to this popularity. For Luther, the Lord's Prayer is not only a central text for instruction but a constant source of his piety.[44] A new evaluation of the Lord's Prayer is connected with Pietism: It remains decisive in instruction; but freely formulated prayer is a more mature expression of piety.[45]

Interpretation

The brief resumé of the history of influence poses questions for interpretation:

1. The Lord's Prayer is handed over to the baptized as the essence of the new truth in which they stand. Zinzendorf has stated pregnantly: The Lord's Prayer is the prayer of the born again, of those who are born "from the Holy Spirit" . . . "anew."[46] We ask: To what extent is the Christian faith the presupposition and content of the Lord's Prayer? In view of the fact that today it has become widely a Christian remainder in a post-Christian world,[47] this question leads immediately to the problematic of our own dealing with it.

2. As the prayer of the new covenant, the Lord's Prayer is considered as un-Jewish. Not until the Enlightenment, when a new recognition of Judaism became possible, did a contrary trend set in. Now the Lord's Prayer was discovered to be as a Jewish, even an original Jewish prayer.[48] We ask: How is the Lord's Prayer related to Jewish prayers? Is it "new" and if so, in what is it new? Since it is a text from Jesus, this question leads immediately into the attempts of today to determine anew the relationship between Judaism and Christianity, in controversy and in the common participation in the Jew Jesus.

3. The Lord's Prayer was a multifunctional text, suitable as a model prayer, as a dogmatic compendium, as a catechetical synthesis, as a private and

---

[42]In the empire of Charlemagne, not even all the clergy knew it, cf. J. N. D. Kelly, *Early Christian Creeds*, 3d ed. (New York: McKay, 1972), 422-23.

[43]R. Knopf, "Eine Tonscherbe mit dem Texte des Vaterunsers," *ZNW* 2 (1901) 228-33; A. M. Schneider, "Vaterunser," *HWDA* 8, col. 1513-15.

[44]"To this day I suckle at the Lord's Prayer like a child, and as an old man eat and drink from it and never get my fill" ("Eine einfältige Weise zu beten für einen guten Freund," WA 38, 364 = *LW* 43, 200).

[45]Aner* 24-27.

[46]"Dear friends, who can pray like this? Can a person before he or she is born anew from the Holy Spirit, before the divine light of faith has been kindled in his or her soul?" (I 297).

[47]According to a poll of the *Spiegel* (no. 52, 1967, 41), 86% of all Germans pray at least occasionally, i.e., more than believe in the existence of God (68%). Unfortunately there are no figures for the scope of use of the Lord's Prayer.

[48]Grotius I 223: In the Lord's Prayer there is written in a concentrated way "quicquid in Hebraeorum precibus erat laudabile. . . . Tam longe abfuit ipse Dominus . . . ab omni affectatione non necessariae novitatis" (whatever was laudable in the prayers of the Hebrews . . . . The Lord himself for so very long kept away . . . from every striving for unnecessary novelty). Wettstein I 323: The Lord's Prayer is "tota . . ex formulis Hebraeorum concinnata" (completely . . . composed out of formulas of the Hebrews).

public church prayer, etc. We ask: What does it mean for the understanding of the Lord's Prayer that it is a prayer text? Is this prayer text transferable into other forms of usage?

Essentially *three basic types of interpretations* in various mixed forms can be discerned. Two are already suggested by Tertullian. Since Tertullian, the Lord's Prayer has been understood as a sum of the "sermo Domini" (sermon of the Lord), i.e., as a summary of the Christian proclamation, and as a "commemoratio disciplinae" (remembrance of the discipline), i.e., as a basic text of ethics. In the history of interpretation, this is reflected in (a) the dogmatic and (b) the ethical interpretation. The ethical interpretation, whose most significant representative in the early church probably was Gregory of Nyssa, understood the Lord's Prayer not only as an instruction for praying but as a "guide to a blessed life" as a whole.[49] These two possibilities of interpretation, which do not exclude each other, were supplemented since the rise of the history of religions school by (c) the eschatological interpretation,[50] which relates the individual petitions more or less consistently to the eschaton and interprets the Lord's Prayer, without regard to its relevance, from the situation of the eschatological proclamation of Jesus. In what follows, the justification for these three basic patterns of interpretation is to be investigated.

6:9b

The *address*: The original Lukan πάτερ probably rendered the Aramaic form of address אַבָּא. It comes from familial language and is used as the address of small and adult children to their fathers and also as a respectful address to aged men.[51] In the time after Jesus it completely displaced the usual forms of address אָבִי (my father) and אַבָּא (*status emphaticus*).[52] From Jewish prayers manifold forms of the address of God as Father are extant, but not אַבָּא.[53] Thus the selection of this address of God is unique.[54]

---

[49]Gregory of Nyssa* 5.3.

[50]For the first three petitions, the eschatological interpretation is advocated by Zahn 268-74, for the whole Lord's Prayer by A. Schweitzer, *The Mysticism of Paul the Apostle* (New York: Macmillan, 1955), 239-41, Loisy I 603f., and R. Eisler, "Das letzte Abendmahl," *ZNW* 24 (1925) 190-92, in beautiful harmony. The eschatological interpretation has become the (still?) predominant one today especially through Greeven*, Jeremias*, Lohmeyer*, Schürmann*, Brown*, and Schulz*.

[51]The assertion, which is often found following an (earlier!) thesis of J. Jeremias, that אַבָּא corresponds to the German "Papi" (English perhaps "Daddy") of the small child, is wrong in this one-sidedness.

[52]Schelbert* 405-07 demonstrates on the basis of archeological material that in the time of Jesus אָבִי (and 'aba' which is indistinguishable from 'abba'?) were still common as an address.

[53]Πάτερ in the prayer of an individual: Sir. 23:1,4; Wis. 14:3; 3 Macc. 6:3,8, cf. Wis. 2:16; πάτερ in the prayer of the community: 3 Macc. 5:7; Tob. 13:4, cf. 1 Chr. 29:10 LXX. Hebrew: אָבִי Sir. 51:10; further examples Str-B I 410 sub a, cf. G. Schrenk, πατήρ etc. *TDNT* V 980 n. 220-223. Rather frequent are the examples for אָבִינוּ in the prayer of the community; cf. the material in Dalman* 296-302; Schrenk loc.cit. 979-81; Montefiore, *Literature* 125-29; J. Jeremias, "Abba," in *The Prayers of Jesus* (Philadelphia: Fortress, 1967), 11-65.

[54]The research of Schelbert* is now fundamental. According to him, the choice of the address 'abba' for God (linguistically possible alongside of other forms of address) is unique in the context of contemporary Palestinian Middle Aramaic (405-07). In the frame of later targum Aramaic, this choice is not

J. Jeremias saw in it a central characteristic of the *ipsissima vox Jesu* (Jesus' actual words) and an expression of the unique relationship to God of the Son Jesus.[55] Even if his thesis, in its exclusive concentration on the historical Jesus, cannot be maintained,[56] it still must be asked whether Jesus' אַבָּא is not an expression of a special relationship of Jesus to God, characterized by the idea of closeness to and love of God—a relationship, however, that applies to every person. Since written Aramaic prayers from the Judaism of that time are rare, the lack of Jewish parallels does not weigh so heavily. Thus it is likely that the thesis of Jeremias is correct in this general form: The Aramaic address of God, which is preserved in Greek New Testament texts as ἀββά (Rom. 8:15; Gal. 4:6 in obviously liturgically shaped texts; Mark 14:36), shows that the Christian communities saw something special in this address of God by Jesus. The continuing use of '*abba*' as an address of God in the Diatessaron and in the Old Syriac translations points in this direction. In the Lord's Prayer itself, the break in rhythm—אַבָּא standing by itself is not integrated into the double rhythm and really demands a pause afterwards—shows what importance rests on this address. It fits into Jesus' proclamation of God, who is close with his love to the poor, sinners, and the underclass; it also fits the parables of the father, so important for Jesus (Luke 11:11-13; 15:11-32) and his certainty that God hears prayer, a certainty that comes strikingly to the forefront (Matt. 6:7f. [Father!]; Luke 11:5-13 [Father!]; 18:1-8).

Thus, when the Lord's Prayer begins with the address πάτερ, it is a promise of salvation; it is a prayer of the children of God.[57] God wants to "encourage us to believe that he is truly our Father and we are his children. We therefore are to pray to him with complete confidence, just as children speak to their loving father."[58]

As little as the prayer address '*abba*' betrays an exclusive Christological consciousness of being the Son, so little does Jesus want to distinguish himself by it from Judaism. The opposite is true: Jesus moves within a Jewish *possibility* of speaking. With '*abba*' he addresses God, who for Judaism was always Father. The fact that Jesus addresses the God of Israel in everyday language and with great simplicity and directness as "Father" demonstrates how close and familiar he is with him; but it is certainly not an un-Jewish understanding of God. One may—one even must—speak of a *special* understanding of God by

---

unique but only unexpected: Here '*abba*' becomes the only habitual form of address to people, and there are a few examples where '*abba*' is used of God, however never as an address (*b. Ta'an.* 23b [Jewish-Babylonian Aramaic]; *Tg. Ps.* 89:27; *Tg. Mal.* 2:10; *Tg. Job* 34:36 [late!]). In Middle Hebrew, '*abba*' is a possible form of address and is never used of God (431f.).

[55]Cf. Jeremias, "Abba" (above n. 53) 60f.

[56]The basic passage for Jeremias is Matt. 11:27 (in my opinion, not genuine). According to him a series of "my Father" words can be traced to Jesus and are an expression of his specific relationship to God. Jeremias believes that Jesus never included himself with the disciples in a common "our Father" (ibid. 52 and n. 103). The last thesis, very frequently advocated, is untenable for Jesus (because of the lack of material) and for Matthew (the frequent πατὴρ ὑμῶν does not seek to exclude Jesus; πάτερ μου 26:42 has an exemplary character).

[57]Cyprian* 9. When Cyprian adds that the little word "our" implies a rejection of the Jews, it is in no way compatible with the intention of Jesus.

[58]Luther, *The Small Catechism* (Minneapolis: Augsburg, 1960), 15; cf. *Book of Concord*, 346.

Jesus, but should not confuse this with an un-Jewish understanding of God.[59]

This is also the thinking of the Matthean community, which calls the Father of Jesus "our Father in the heavens" and so follows Jewish linguistic expression which became important in the synagogue,[60] and thus does not distance itself from it. In the debate with Israel, this designation of God means for Matthew that the "Father" of Jesus is none other than the God of Israel invoked in the synagogue. Matthew distances himself from the synagogue, not from its God. "In the heavens" designates the difference from the earthly father; no reflection on the transcendence of God is connected with this expression. "Our" coordinates the praying believer with the community; this also is customary in Jewish prayers.[61]

The two you-petitions of the original Lord's Prayer form the nucleus of the eschatological interpretation of the Lord's Prayer.

6:10a

This eschatological interpretation is without doubt secured with the petition *"your kingdom come."* The coming reign of God is frequently prayed for in Jewish prayers;[62] it is even remarkable how often the future reign of God is the subject of petitions of the rabbis, with whom elsewhere the present aspect of God's rule is more in the foreground. In comparison with Jewish parallels, Jesus' way of speaking of the coming of the kingdom of God is striking: Jesus understands it as something dynamic, powerful.[63] The lapidary brevity of the petition also is noteworthy: in the Jewish prayer of the Eighteen Benedictions, the 11th and 12th berakoth speak of the return of the judges and the destruction of Rome; the Qaddish prayer asks for the hastening of God's reign. Such tones

---

[59]Thus the address does not indicate, e.g., a conscious universalizing of the idea of God (correctly Zeller* 119f.). Jesus' conception of God did not lie "crosswise to Judaism" and did not want to "collide with the rooting of Judaism in Israel's history of salvation" (thus J. Becker, "Das Gottesbild Jesu und die älteste Auslegung von Ostern," in *Jesus Christus in Historie und Theologie* [FS H. Conzelmann], ed. G. Strecker [Tübingen: Mohr, 1975], 110). To emphasize this does not yet mean to overlook that which is special in the Lord's Prayer of the Jew Jesus, as this is done by F. Mussner, *Tractate on the Jews* (Philadelphia: Fortress, 1984), 123-30.

[60]The oldest examples: *Mek. Exod.* 81a on 20:25 = Str-B I 283 (Yohanan ben Zakkai, ca. 70); *Seder Elij. R.* 28.149 = Str-B I 394 (Eliezer ben Hyrcanus, ca. 90); cf. Schelbert * 418f.,421-28.

[61]The examples from Jewish prayers with אָבִינוּ are much more frequent than those with אָבִי, "because the human being (while praying) always unites his or her soul with the community" (*b. Ber.* 29b = Str-B I 410 [Abbaye, 4th century]), not perhaps because "the personal address of God, 'my Father,' " was unthinkable "in the literature of ancient Palestinian Judaism" (pace Jeremias, "Abba" [above n. 53] 29). The difference between the vocative and the predicative אָבִי (thus Sir. 51:10) and the distinction between "my Father" and "my Father in the heavens," which is found frequently, is not a principal one; moreover, Sir. 23:1,4 (κύριε πάτερ) remain as possible examples for the address "my Father."

[62]Shemoneh-Esreh, 11th Berakah; Qaddish; Musaph prayer for Rosh Hashana; Alenu prayer (all texts in Str-B I 418f.); Al-hakkol prayer (cf. below n. 71); *Targ. Obad.* 14; Seder Rab Amram 1 (9a) (cf. below n. 71) (all texts in Dalman* 311-13).

[63]Dalman* 88; Schlosser* I 261-84. Luke 11:20 is to be compared. Schlosser reminds us of the Jewish statements of the coming of God which, e.g., in the targums, are rather limited (Dalman* 83). The reign of God obviously is for Jesus not something static which only "will become visible" (*Sib. Or.* 3:47; *As. Mos.* 10:1; rabbinical examples in Dalman* 83).

are lacking in the Lord's Prayer. That fits well for Jesus: He does not elsewhere describe in detail the coming of the reign of God, does not fix it in time, and lets its political and national dimensions recede.[64] Perhaps the open formulation also is typical of Jesus: It does not prescribe a definite understanding of the reign of God for the praying believer. The eschatological element of this petition cannot be doubted, although the tradition of the interpretation of the church has most of the time gone separate ways.[65]

6:9c

The explanation of the first petition, "Hallowed be your name," is more difficult. If one interprets it eschatologically, then the passive would be a divine passive; it would pray that God do something for his name in an eschatological self-manifestation. The meaning of the two first petitions would be identical. But one must not push the imperative aorist ἁγιασθήτω in the sense that a *unique* intervention of God for his name would be requested. The imperative aorist corresponds to the Greek style of prayer;[66] no conclusions can be drawn from the Aramaic imperfect. Thus it is equally possible that God is asked for the hallowing of his name here and now in history, not only in the eschaton. Finally, it must be asked whether the passive is really a divine passive or whether human beings also could be the subject of the hallowing of the name. Then God would be asked that humans would hallow his name through the right use of the name of God and obedience to his will. The petition would come close to an admonition of oneself: Let us hallow God's name. This proposed interpretation corresponds to the parenetic tradition of interpretation which was predominant until the rise of the eschatological explanation of the Lord's Prayer: "God possesses . . . in himself the fullness of all glory . . .; nevertheless, he commands . . . that we ask that he also be glorified by our life." [67] A decision has to be made with the aid of the Jewish parallels.

---

[64]Caution is advised at the evaluation. If the petition is read in the context of the proclamation of Jesus, then the receding of the national and political element is pronounced. If it is read in the context of Jewish prayers, then it is simply a brief formulation in the frame of a "short" prayer (cf. below n. 112).

[65]Particularly in the Greek tradition of interpretation, the reference to the *regnum gratiae* (reign of grace), which manifested itself in the proclamation of the word, the sacraments, prayer, mission, and Christian life, was predominant. In the Latin tradition of interpretation the knowledge of the eschatological sense of the kingdom petition is better preserved—the Vulgate translates *adveniat* (may arrive). The Reformers interpret it usually of the double advent of the kingdom, in combining the two possibilities of interpretation—which overloads the three words of the petition. The *Catechismus Romanus* 4.11.13 offers a classical Catholic interpretation: "Petimus . . . ut regnum Christi, quod est ecclesia, propagetur . . . schismatici ac haeretici redeant ad sanitatem" (We pray . . . that the reign of Christ which is the church . . . may be propagated . . . that the schismatics and heretics may be brought to sanity).

[66]BDF §337 n. 4; Schwyzer II 341.

[67]John Chrysostom 19,4 - 351. Luther: "God's name certainly is holy in itself, but we ask . . . that we may keep it holy" (*Small Catechism*, p. 16; cf. *Book of Concord*, 346). Survey of the history of interpretation in Tholuck** 346.

a. On the basis of the Old Testament passages, one may think of both the sanctification of the name by God himself (cf. Lev. 10:13; Ezek. 36:22f.; 38:23; 39:7) and of the sanctification of God's name by humans (Exod. 20:7; Lev. 22:32; Isa. 29:23). In several passages, both aspects occur.

b. In Jewish texts, the prayers in which humans are the subject of the hallowing of the name are the majority. But many passages cannot be interpreted unambiguously: Hallowing of the name by God and by humans belong together.[68]

c. Probably the most important parallel to the Lord's Prayer is the *Aramaic Qaddish prayer*, which was spoken at the end of the preaching section of the synagogue service. Its time of origin is unclear, but because of its closeness to the temple liturgy and the lack of any reference to the destruction of the temple it is dated by many scholars[69] in the period before 70 C.E. Its beginning is parallel to the two first petitions of the Lord's Prayer:

> His great name may be magnified and hallowed in the world which he has created according to his will.
> May he let his royal reign rule in your life and in your days and in the life of the whole house of Israel, in haste and in the near future.

According to Fiebig and Jeremias,[70] the first part of the Lord's Prayer can be understood directly as a summary of the Qaddish. Jesus then would have added the unique, new elements in the three we-petitions. The Lord's Prayer is seen as distinctive adaptation of the Qaddish by Jesus. But since the juxtaposition of a petition about the name and about the royal reign is frequent in other prayers also[71] and since Jewish private prayers often are positively modeled on synagogue prayers,[72] a *polemical* adaption of the Qaddish by Jesus is improbable. But most likely the contemporaries of Jesus felt reminded by the Lord's Prayer of the Qaddish and had to understand it in the same way, particularly since the first two petitions in their brevity do not contain any further hints at interpretation.

At the first Qaddish petition, the idea is probably rather that of the hallowing of the name by humans: (1) The juxtaposition of *Hithpa'el* (יִתְקַדַּשׁ) and *Pe'al* (בְּרָא) does not suggest a divine passive. (2) The origin of the Qaddish from the doxology (Dan. 2:20) makes one think rather of a hallowing by humans. But probably the first Qaddish petition is so open that it does not exclude the idea of the hallowing of the name by God.

d. The "hallowing of the name" is a widespread expression which means obedience toward God's commands, especially the speaking of prayers and the keeping

---

[68]God hallows his name when humans hallow it (Sifra Lev. 18:6 [339a] = Str-B I 413). God hallows his name by bringing humans to obedience. God is asked to hallow his name because of the people who hallow his name (*Tanna debe Eliyahu* 21 = Str-B I 409).

[69]Cf. D. de Sola Pool, *The Old Jewish-Aramaic Prayer: The Kaddish* (Leipzig: Rudolph Haupt, 1909), 21-24; I. Elbogen, *Der jüdische Gottesdienst in seiner geschichtlichen Entwicklung*, reprint (Hildesheim: Olms, 1967), 93f.

[70]Fiebig* 34-36; Jeremias* 164 points particularly to the lack of the little word "and" between the first two petitions of the Qaddish and the Lord's Prayer.

[71]Prayer Seder Rab Amram 1 (91): "Make your name unique in your world; make your royal reign unique in your world"; Al-hakkol prayer: "Hallowed be your name among us before the eyes of all that lives; his kingly reign over us be revealed and visible in haste in the near future"; Musaph prayer for the new year: "We know . . . that the reign (שָׁלְטָן) is with you . . . and your terrible name above everything which you have created" (texts in W. Staerk, *Altjüdische liturgische Gebete* [Bonn: Marcus und Weber, 1910], KIT 58, 22); Alenu prayer of Rab (text in Str-B I 419). Cf. also the juxtaposition of the prescription of Rab that every Berakah must contain a reference to the divine name and of that of Yohanan who demands the same concerning the kingly rule of Yahweh (*b. Ber.* 40b = Str-B I 419).

[72]Cf. Heinemann* 51,172,175.

of the second commandment of the decalog. It had its apex for the Jews in martyrdom.[73]

Result: All this speaks in favor of an "open" interpretation. The petition is so general and formulated so briefly that it allows us to think both of human and divine action. However, the majority of parallels point in the former direction, so that the ethical element must by no means be excluded. But there are no arguments for an exclusively eschatological interpretation of the petition. Thus we place ourselves alongside the tradition of interpretation which was dominant from the early church until the 19th century and against the eschatological interpretation of the petition dominant today.

6:10b,c

With the third petition, *your will be done,* the problems are similar. Does the petition mean an action of the human being (your will be done *through* people)? Or does it mean an action of God (*you* do your will *among* the people)? A special case of the latter possibility is the eschatological interpretation that God may assert his will in the eschaton. Again this does not correspond to the meaning of the Jewish parallels,[74] nor does it follow from the wording. The attached sentence, "as in heaven, so on earth," puts the weight on the second part. As the will of God is done in heaven, so may it be done on earth.[75] Matthew 6:33 gives a hint at the Matthean understanding, where the evangelist adds δικαιοσύνη to the kingdom of God (as 10a + b,c). Seek the kingdom by practicing the righteousness which is suitable for it. The Gethsemane scene in 26:42 is still more important: Jesus, in praying, "Your will be done," not only asks that God do what he wants but at the same time he asks for the strength to subordinate himself actively to this will of God. Thus our petition aims at the active behavior of the person. But it is not a hidden imperative; instead, it lays the human action before God's feet in the shape of a petition. In the realm of Old Testament–Jewish thinking the will of the active God is always understood as the claim on an active partner. It is not surrender to an impermeable fate which is to be accepted simply in faith.[76] It seems to me that an alternative between divine action and human action would be a false alternative.[77]

6:11

The *petition for bread* cannot be interpreted with certainty because the meaning of the word ἐπιούσιος cannot be determined. It occurs elsewhere (perhaps) in

---

[73]Cf. Str-B I 411-18.

[74]The Jewish parallels from prayer texts are sparse; the short prayer of Eliezer, *b. Ber.* 29b, comes closest (c. 65?, text in Str-B I 419f.). Other parallel texts in Dalman* 314f.

[75]Dalman* 317f.

[76]Cf. Lohmeyer* 79f. and the Stoic parallels mentioned there.

[77]The ethical dimension of the will of God is shown most clearly in 7:21; 12:50, the salvation-historical dimension in 18:14.

all of non-Christian antiquity only once, in a late Hawara papyrus.[78] A retranslation into Aramaic also fails as an aid for a decision, since a word whose meaning cannot be determined can be translated in many different ways. Helps for interpretation are (a) the etymological derivation of the word, (b) possible inferences from the sentence, i.e., the whole petition for bread, and (c) the oldest interpretations. Five interpretations vie with each other:

1. Derived from ἐπί and οὐσία (substance), ἄρτος ἐπιούσιος is the bread which unites with our substance[79] or goes beyond all substances.[80] On this basis, the church fathers and the medieval exegetes have almost always—supported by the liturgical use of the Lord's Prayer before communion—interpreted the bread as referring to the Eucharist or viewed it Christologically in the sense of John 6. This intensified a fatal tendency to the spiritualizing of the Lord's Prayer which is seen clearly, e.g., in Jerome.[81] The sacramental interpretation was so much taken for granted that even specific deductions were drawn from it: the demand for daily communion or the withholding of the cup from the laity.[82] Reversion toward a literal interpretation was introduced by the Reformers;[83] but this took root only hesitantly in the Catholic Church.[84] On this point, exegesis was split for a long time along confessional lines. This interpretation is not plausible, since it presupposes the Christology, the understanding of the Eucharist, and the concept of substance of a later period.

2. If one understands οὐσία as *"existence,"* "sustenance,"[85] then ἐπιούσιος, could be interpreted as "necessary for existence." Since the time of the Old Syriac translations, many interpreters follow this interpretation because it is in keeping with the entire petition.[86] Etymology speaks against it. The detailed philological discussion seems to come to the conclusion that all combinations of ἐπί with derivatives of the stem εἶναι have to lead to the elision of the ι; thus ἐπούσιος would be correct. The ι is retained

---

[78]Preisigke, *Sammelbuch* I no. 5224. The word is fragmented, the papyrus is now lost. It speaks perhaps for interpretation no. 2.

[79]Origen* 27,2.

[80]Jerome on the passage. Vulgate: *supersubstantialis* (above substance).

[81]"Absit ut nos . . . de pane isto, qui post paululum concoquendus et abiiciendus est in secessum, in prece dominica rogare iubeamur" (May it be far from us that we . . . would be commanded in the Lord's Prayer to ask in regard to that bread which after a little while is to be digested and eliminated) (in *Tit.* 3.12 = *PL* 25,588).

[82]Since the time of Cyprian* 18, daily communion was demanded on the basis of Matt. 6:11. Arguments against the Utraquists (who demanded the Lord's Supper in both forms) were based on Matt. 6:11 at the Councils of Basel and Trent (Bock* 290,294: "de Sanguine . . . nulla ibi fit mentio!" (no mention is made there of the blood).

[83]Cf. Carmignac * 166-75. Luther changed between 1523 and 1528 from the spiritual to the material interpretation while Zwingli stayed with the spiritual interpretation. A presupposition was the turning away from the Vulgate by the Reformation. In patristic literature, the interpretation of the Reformers has its predecessors in the School of Antioch (Carmignac* 153-56).

[84]Carmignac* 182-85.

[85]Οὐσία = existence, e.g., in Aristotle, *Part. An.*, who speaks of the οὐσία (existence) of living beings, in contrast to γένεσις (1.1 = 640a; 5.1 = 778b) or to ἔργα = activities (2.2 = 648a, cf. 647b). An example for nonphilosophical use: Aristotle *Eth. M.* 1.20 = 1191a: κίνδυνος . . . ἀναιρετικὸς τῆς οὐσίας (dangerous to life). In my opinion, objections to this interpretation are not possible on the basis of the meaning of οὐσία.

[86]Foerster* 594,17ff. points out that beside σήμερον a further statement of time is superfluous.

when the main stem begins with a vowel only if before the opening vowel an aspiration or an original digamma is to be assumed. One also would have to ask why a more common Greek word such as ἐπιτήδειος or ἀναγκαῖος was not chosen.

3. A further interpretation proceeds from ἐπὶ τὴν οὖσαν (ἡμέραν) and understands ἐπιούσιος as "for today."[87] This interpretation is doubly problematical. The fact that ἡ οὖσα without ἡμέρα is never documented as an expression for "the present day" speaks against this interpretation; and here also it would have to be written ἐπούσιος. The Greek ἐφήμερος would be common. The manna tradition of Exodus 16 would fit very beautifully into this interpretation: the people of Israel are forbidden, other than on Friday, to collect bread for the morrow.[88] But there is no reason to interpret the petition on the basis of Exodus 16.

4. Linguistically the only possibility is a derivation from ἐπιέναι (come to) or from ἡ ἐπιοῦσα (the coming day). Ἡ ἐπιοῦσα occurs very frequently in the New Testament world.[89] Derived from it, the adjective ἐπιούσιος is a completely normal formation, understandable even better since there is no other Greek *adjective* with the meaning "of tomorrow."[90] Besides, the understanding, "Give us today our bread for the morrow," is documented by the Gospel of the Nazareans for the first half of the second century.[91] Even if the Gospel of the Nazareans is a translation from Greek, the word מָחָר occurring there probably agrees with the text of the community liturgy and thus is older than the second century. A little later, the same interpretation is found in the Coptic translation and in Origen* (*Orat.* 27.13).

5. The last interpretation also is based on the derivation from ἐπιέναι and proceeds either from τὸ ἐπιόν (the *future*) or from the fact that the Semitic מָחָר can also have the meaning of the adjective "future."[92] The bread asked for is then the future heavenly bread, the bread of the eschatological meal in the kingdom of God. This conception is widespread in the Jesus tradition (Mark 14:25; Matthew 8:11f.; Luke 22:30). Also the connection of the heavenly meal of glory with the everyday nourishment of bread, which is not obvious in the Jewish background, is documented (Luke 14:15). But it speaks against this interpretation that לחמן דלמחר in the first place would have been understood differently by any unprejudiced listener, certainly with the possessive suffix, *our* bread. But also the little word "today," which presupposes the expectation of the extremely imminent end, speaks against it.

Result: Etymologically the fourth interpretation is most probable. It is supported by the old testimony of the Gospel of the Nazareans and is also the best one to be connected with σήμερον. Thus probably we should translate: Give us today our bread for tomorrow.

The fourth petition of the Lord's Prayer belongs to a situation of social urgency in which the nourishment for the following day could not simply be

---

[87]Debrunner* under reference to Sophocles, *Oed. Tyr.* 781 (τὴν μὲν οὖσαν ἡμέραν).

[88]Mek.Exod. 55b on 16:4 = Str-B I 420f.: "The person who has food to eat today and says, What will I eat tomorrow? is of little faith!" (El'azar of Modiim before 135). But the passage refers to the Exodus situation. Starcky* and Grelot* understand Luke 11:3 (ἐπιούσιον/τὸ καθ᾽ ἡμέραν) and Matt. 6:11 (ἐπιούσιον/σήμερον) as translation variants of Hebrew יוֹם בְּיוֹמוֹ (= Exod. 16:4). But LXX formulates: ἡμέρα εἰς ἡμέραν. How would one explain the translation by two different Greek expressions in Matthew and Luke?

[89]Twice in LXX, 3 times in Revelation, 46 times in Josephus.

[90]There only is αὔριον, as an adverb, or, as a noun, ἡ αὔριον.

[91]Hennecke I 139-52.

[92]Cf. Jeremias* 165-67; Brown* 301-08.

taken for granted. "Bread" as the most important food in Semitic idiom can stand as *pars pro toto* for "nourishment" as such, but should not be extended beyond this to any sort of necessities for life.[93] One may perhaps think of the situation of a day laborer who does not yet know whether he will find work again on the next day so that he can live with his family. "Bread for tomorrow" implies at the same time a limitation: It is a question, not of riches, but only of being able to survive. In this respect this interpretation is in content very close to the second interpretation, regarding the minimum necessary for existence, which was rejected above. "Today" is by no means superfluous but makes us feel the urgency of the petition. There is a characteristic difference between this petition and the ninth Berakah of the Shemoneh Esreh in which, from the perspective of the farmer, prayer is made for the produce of the year.

This includes the assumption that the bread petition does not reflect the special situation of the Jesus disciples who became poor for the sake of the proclamation of the kingdom of God, i.e., of the itinerant radicals. That this is not the case results probably also from Luke 10:4,7f.: The itinerant messengers of Jesus are not permitted to carry something "today" with them, not even the nourishment for the following day, but live alone from hospitality. Naturally they may pray for the food for the following day; but the petition is not formulated for their situation. This is important for the question of whether the Lord's Prayer is a prayer for the disciples. For otherwise there are only *argumenta e silentio*, namely, there is no indication for supposing that the situation of the successors is specifically mirrored in the petitions. It is much more the case that all petitions of the Lord's Prayer are formulated very openly so that many people can find themselves in them. The bread petition seems to confirm this. It is not a special need of the circle of Jesus' disciples.

6:12

If the Jewish parallels to the bread petition—at least in comparable concreteness—are sparse, with the *petition for forgiveness* we come again to a central theme of Jewish praying.[94] The outstanding part of it is the concluding sentence.[95] Indeed, the idea that divine forgiveness is tied to human forgiveness is widespread in Judaism,[96] but there is, to my knowledge, no case where

---

[93]Luther expands: "food and clothing, home and property, work and income, a devoted family, an orderly community, good government, favorable weather, peace and health, a good name, and true friends and neighbors" (*Small Catechism*, p. 19; *Book of Concord*, 347). This does not agree with the intention of the text. The strong rooting of this petition in the situation of the poor makes us ask naturally how a socially secure inhabitant of an industrial nation can pray it. My answer: by making it into an "alien" petition and identifying in it with the truly poor and their need rather than by expanding it to other needs in disagreement with the text.

[94]Shemoneh-Esreh, 6th Berakah; Abinu Malkenu; Habinenu (texts in Str-B (421); further parallels in Dalman* 337. The prayers for the Day of Atonement also offer rich material, e.g., in Str-B I 113f.

[95]It excludes the eschatological interpretation of the petition for forgiveness. If one looks back to the human forgiveness which has already happened (aorist), then the petition for God's forgiveness cannot refer only to the eschaton.

[96]The most important Jewish passages are Sir. 28:2-5; *m. Yoma* 8:9 (God does not expiate the sins of a person against his or her fellow human beings on the Day of Atonement until that person has obtained the forgiveness of the other people). The principle that heaven has mercy on those who have mercy on people is found often, cf. Str-B I 425.

human acting is taken into a central prayer text in this manner.[97] What has already so far been implied in our interpretation becomes clear here as an example: prayer and human acting do not exclude each other. On the contrary, prayer is the speaking of the *active* human being with God.

It is difficult to determine exactly the relationship of the subordinate clause to the main clause. While, in view of the Aramaic tenses, the aorist ἀφήκαμεν cannot be pushed, for Matthew it probably indicates a condition in the sense of 5:23f.; 6:14f.; 7:1. This relationship obviously applies in parenesis when one speaks from the perspective of the human being, in distinction from the parable of the unmerciful servant (18:23-35), where the effectiveness of God's action also is tied to the human action but precedes it. The paradoxical unity of prevenient grace and a condition to be fulfilled by human beings is destroyed only if people by their forgiving raise a claim so that they could hope that God will imitate their example.[98] It is also important that the community which prays the Lord's Prayer presupposes that its members even as Christians still sin and need forgiveness.

6:13

An eschatological interpretation has been proposed also for the concluding petition of the original Lord's Prayer, the *temptation petition*: Πειρασμός would mean the tribulation of the end time. Almost all evidence speaks against this view: Neither in Jewish apocalyptic nor in the New Testament[99] is πειρασμός an apocalyptical technical term. The expected definite article is missing. The Jewish parallels[100] also speak in favor of thinking of the temptations which occur in everyday life. Life in its entirety is here not seen negatively, as this is done later, often in ascetically influenced interpretations of the early church.[101] Πειρασμός can also mean "affliction" or "suffering" in general,[102] but it is better to think here of the usual meaning "temptation."[103] Much deep thought has been applied to the question of how one can avoid the statement that it is God who leads into temptation.[104] Even if it is perhaps

---

[97]Cf. Abrahams* 96.

[98]So Gregory of Nyssa* 5.1f.

[99]Only Rev. 3:10.

[100]*B.Ber.* 60b = Str-B I 422: "Do not bring me into the power of sin . . . of guilt . . . of temptation . . . of contempt"; 11 QPs 24,11f.: "Do not bring me into situations which are too hard for me; remove the sins of my youth from me and let my transgressions not be remembered against me."

[101]"The whole human life on earth (is) a temptation" (Origen* 29.2).

[102]Harnack, *SPAW* 1907*, 944-47.

[103]In English one can differentiate between "testing" and "temptation," but not in German. It does not mean, in the sense of wisdom literature, the "testing" (that would be in Greek πεῖρα), but the temptation behind which stands the power of evil from which one wishes to be protected. The parallel petition, v. 13b, makes this clear and corresponds to the customary application of the LXX word πειρασμός = נִסָּה. Cf. also 4:1; 26:41 and Spicq, *Notes* III 552-59.

[104]Some Old Latin MSS read "ne patiaris nos induci in temptationem" (do not permit us to be led into temptation), also Tertullian* 8, Cyprian* 25, and perhaps already Marcion (Harnack, *Marcion* 207*), further passages in Chase* 60ff., obviously under the influence of 1 Cor. 10:13 and James 1:13. According to Ps. 119:8 numerous interpreters understand as follows: "a temptation which we are not able

possible to keep the idea of God's sole responsibility away from an Aramaic causative ("make it so that we do not come into temptation," instead of "lead us not into temptation"),[105] the fact remains that the Greek translator obviously did not have these problems. Instead, it is understandable that in prayer God's absolute power is simply presupposed. The petition does not make a philosophical judgment on the question of who effects the evil. Instead, there applies here also that which was already found in the initiatory petitions: human beings ask for something which they determine by their behavior.

The petition "but preserve us from evil," which brings the temptation petition to the length of the other we-petitions, is found only in Matthew. It stands in parallel position to the preceding petition and carries it further by emphasizing the reality of the power of evil which stands behind the temptation and by asking for liberation from it. Since ancient times, it has been disputed whether πονηροῦ in this final petition is to be understood as a masculine or as a neuter.[106] The neuter interpretation is supported by the majority of the Matthean[107] and New Testament examples, the parallelism to the temptation petition, the oldest probable interpretations of the petition in 1 Tim. 4:18 and *Did.* 10:5 as well as the Jewish parallels—in Judaism "the evil one" as a designation for Satan is not found. On the basis of the Jewish texts it is suggestive to think of everyday experiences: illness, affliction, evil people, the evil impulse.[108] The Matthean concluding petition thus contains an intensification and generalization of the temptation petition and rounds off the Lord's Prayer through a positive formulation.

The three-member *doxology,* which is usual in our services, is missing in the best manuscripts. But 2 Tim. 4:18 and the doxology in *Did.* 8:2 which, according to the custom of the Didache (10:5) has two members, show that the Lord's Prayer was prayed in the Greek church from the beginning with a doxology. Jewish prayers also without a concluding doxology are unthinkable; there is a certain amount of freedom in the wording of private prayers,[109] which makes it understandable why the doxology did not need to be written down. In those older text witnesses which contain the doxology, the breadth of variation in the text is great.

---

to bear" (examples in Lohmeyer* 135). Origen* 29,1.4.9 interprets: Do not let us succumb in temptation. The difficulties of the interpreters (not of the text!) have left their traces down into modern translations (e.g. Jeremias* 155: "let us not . . . fall victim").

[105]So Jeremias* 169 ("permissive nuance" of the causative); Carmignac* 292-94. The expert Dalman* 347, however, thinks that the "Aramaic *Aphel a'ēl* everywhere . . . means not a mere letting [something] come but an active bringing."

[106]Neuter: The Latin fathers, particularly since Augustine (Vulgate: *a malo* [from evil]), most Catholics, and many Lutherans. Luther accepts the masculine interpretation also (Large Catechism, *Book of Concord,* 435). The Reformed, with most Greek fathers, interpret it as a masculine.

[107]Differently, in my opinion, only 13:19 (tradition) and, following it, 13:38.

[108]Shemoneh-Esreh, 7th Berakah: poverty; *b. Ber.* 60b (cf. above n. 98): evil encounters, suffering, bad dreams, evil thoughts; *b. Ber.* 16b: the impudent, evil people, evil encounters, evil impulse, evil companions, bad neighbors, Satan, harsh judgment (texts in Str-B I 422f.; Dalman* 352-54.

[109]Heinemann* 172-77 shows that frequently free formulated private prayers were concluded with "normative" doxologies. On the other hand, there is freedom: "R. Abbahu spoke a new benediction every day" (*p. Ber.* 4.8a, trans. Horowitz 127).

Summary

We asked: How new is the Lord's Prayer in comparison with Jewish prayers? The question seems to bypass the essential character of the Lord's Prayer.

Several peculiarities of the Lord's Prayer fit into Judaism:

a. The Lord's Prayer was *Aramaic*, while most extant Jewish prayers are Hebrew. But since it never was intended to be an official synagogue prayer, the Aramaic language is not unusual. Numerous Jewish private prayers were formulated in Aramaic,[110] leaving aside the untransmitted private prayers of the ordinary people. One can say only that Jesus used the language of the people and not that of the synagogue prayer liturgy. He did not share the rejection of the use of Aramaic which was prevalent among some scholars of his time. On the other hand, the scholars expressly did permit the Aramaic language for private prayers.[111]

b. The Lord's Prayer is a very *brief and simple prayer*. That is interesting but scarcely uncommon in the Judaism of the time. The Lord's Prayer, with its avoidance of unnecessary words, epithets for God, and Berakoth belongs together with other Jewish "brief prayers."[112] Such prayers were frequent, as summaries of longer prayers or as free formulations.

c. The Lord's Prayer is an *individual prayer*. But individual prayers from many rabbis are handed down.[113] It is in accord with this observation that many topics of Jewish community prayers are missing: the appeal to the patriarchs, the mention of Israel, any national coloring of the petitions, the concrete description of the future hope. Certainly this is typical of Jesus, but precisely these motifs recede in Jewish private prayers.[114]

Although such peculiarities are Jewish, they belong integrally to the Lord's Prayer. Another thought can help us further: *The Lord's Prayer bears the impress of Jesus*. It is stamped by Jesus, the man and the messenger of God, both where it is Jewish as well as where it is distinctive in relation to Judaism. Both together determine the special character of the Lord's Prayer.

The Aramaic language and the simple formulations are typical of Jesus. They agree with the fundamental—not un-Jewish—basic feature of the proclamation and ministry of Jesus, who was close to the people, spoke their language, and told stories of the kingdom of God out of his everyday world. In the context of the activity of Jesus his simple language becomes an expression of the nearness of God whom Jesus proclaimed and whom he addressed by *'abba'*. The way Jesus placed the petition of the poor for bread for the morrow

---

[110]Heinemann* 159,190,265f.

[111]Cf. the discussion on the language of prayer in *m. Sota* 7:1 and *b. Sota* 33a: The daily prayer of the individual and other private prayers in Aramaic language are explicitly permitted. The thesis according to which the ministering angels did not understand Aramaic has been contradicted.

[112]Jewish examples of brief prayers: The short prayer of Eliezer, *b. Ber.* 29b = Str-B I 419f.; the short prayer of Joshua, *m. Ber.* 4:4 = Str-B IV 222 and the *habinenu* prayer as an abbreviation of the Shemoneh-Esreh = Str-B ibid. Heinemann* 190f. puts the Lord's Prayer into the series of Jewish private prayers of which he says in general: "This genre of prayer is characterized by its stylistic simplicity and its lack of formal requirements" (190).

[113]I. Abrahams, "Some Rabbinic Ideas on Prayer," in idem, *Studies* II 85: "Nothing is more remarkable than the extraordinary number of original individual prayers in the Talmud."

[114]Abrahams* 104. The rabbinical prayer conclusions in *b. Ber.* 16b-17a are a good illustration.

into the center of his prayer is a distinctive expression of the nearness of God and is in agreement with the first beatitude. The particular piety of Jesus is shown in his address of God as Father, which points to the nearness and love of God. The demand to forgive, which is incorporated in the prayer and which sets an entirely distinctive accent in the realm of Jewish piety, is also characteristic of Jesus. The receding of national, salvation-historical, and political dimensions of the prayer agrees with a fundamental feature of Jesus' proclamation, the center of which is the kingdom of God and not the history of Israel's salvation. Finally, the eschatology of the Lord's Prayer is characteristic of Jesus. It corresponds to the eschatology of the parables of the kingdom of God which also do not speak of the kingdom of God but attempt to determine everyday life from the perspective of the kingdom. In brief, one must put the *entirety* of the Lord's Prayer into the proclamation and activity of Jesus. Then it becomes obvious how the Jewish element and the special accents *together* result in that which is typical of Jesus. In view of the Christian endeavor to present it hastily as the compendium of one's own *doctrina* (doctrine, teaching),[115] this means first of all an invitation to stop and reflect.

The Lord's Prayer has proved itself also relatively unyielding toward attempts to understand it as the prayer of the regenerated or as "formula, a token of recognition" of the community of salvation.[116] It does not reflect the particular situation of the circle of disciples. It is formulated openly. In its formulations, many people can find themselves; for it does not prescribe to those who pray it what desires, hopes, or views they need to have. In this respect it not only presupposes grace through its address but it is itself an expression of grace and of the nearness of God. By including many people in its words, it *makes* prayer *possible*. In exaggeration, one might say that it is not the sign by which the circle of disciples is to be recognized but the expression of the grace which precedes the circle of disciples.

Thus the Lord's Prayer is an *aid in praying* and is intended to help the person who recites it to discover the loving closeness of the Father. It wants to make prayer possible. If today the Lord's Prayer remains a significant text even beyond a consciously practicing churchly Christianity, then this is in agreement with its own power. This means for the church today that it should not use *its* Lord's Prayer as a concise expression of its own status of salvation but as a basic text which, beyond the borders of the church, can help people in praying and discovering the love of God.

History of influence

A rather considerable part of the history of Christian interpretation and the history of influence comes here into question. Very often, Christian interpretation made the Lord's Prayer a stranger to itself by treating and interpreting it as a compendium of Christian doctrine. The interpretation then became the attempt subtly to elicit from the Lord's Prayer divine mysteries. Understood as a dogmatic basic text, it reflected, e.g., the doctrine of the Trinity. The first and fourth petitions concerned God the Father, the

---

[115]Cf. Cyprian, above n. 25.

[116]Pace Jeremias, *Theology* 196f.

second and fifth the Savior, the third and sixth the Holy Spirit.[117] Maximus Confessor understood the Lord's Prayer as a compendium of dogmatics, of mysticism, and of philosophy.[118] In view of this interpretation of the Lord's Prayer as a basic text of ecclesiastical doctrine, one must not be surprised that the Enlightenment reversed the thrust; here the Lord's Prayer became the basic text of Christian doctrine precisely because it did *not* contain the traditional subjects of Christian dogmatics, as, e.g., the doctrine of the Trinity![119] The misunderstanding basically is the same in both instances.[120]

The Lord's Prayer is not intended to make theology possible, but prayer. Matthew was very much aware of this. Deliberately he led the disciples in his Sermon on the Mount, after confronting them with the demand of higher righteousness and perfection, into the inner space of prayer. Here is the center of the Sermon on the Mount. Thus Matthew leads the human being through action to grace. The person who is on the way to perfection (5:20-48) learns in the heart of the sermon to understand the will of God which makes demands on him or her, as the will of *the Father*. And that means: not as a destroying will which demands too much but as the will of God that brings salvation. The way from the practice of perfection into prayer to the Father and then back again to the fruits of good works, which Matthew traverses in the course of the Sermon on the Mount, has immense depth. Matthew knows of the depth of the connection of practice and grace in prayer. With that he picks up ideas which are inherent in Jesus' prayer.

Meaning today

The Matthean combination of prayer and action is of fundamental significance in view of the critical questions which are raised today about prayer. Two examples from the more recent history of influence may make this clear: For Kant, praying is a "superstitious illusion" and has at most "the value of a means whereby that disposition within us may be . . . quickened," namely, to execute all actions "*as though* they were being executed in the service of God." And about the Lord's Prayer he says: It is a formula "which has at once rendered dispensable not only all this, but also prayer itself . . . . One finds in it nothing but the resolution to good life-conduct."[121] Prayer makes itself superfluous when it enables action and thus transcends superstition. B. Brecht stands more or less at the other end. In a grandiose scene toward the conclusion of *Mother Courage* he confronts the mute Cattrin and a farmer's family. At a nocturnal attack of the enemies against the defenseless city of Halle, the farmers fall on their knees and pray their Lord's Prayers while Cattrin climbs on the roof in order to warn the sleeping people with her

---

[117]Tholuck** 340f.

[118]Maximus Confessor "Expositio orationis Dominicae," *PG* 90,872-909; cf. Walther* 83. On the systematic theological interpretation of the Lord's Prayer cf. especially Angénieux*.

[119]Aner* 28f.

[120]A recent monograph on the Lord's Prayer demonstrates that such attempts have not died out even today. K. F. Althoff, *Das Vaterunser* (Stuttgart: Vrachhaus, 1978), is an attempt to gain hidden depths from this "prayer of humanity" by means of number speculations and star symbolism. This kind of thing is exegetically absurd. It would not deserve mention if such obscurantism did not enjoy increasing popularity in many "neognostic" circles.

[121]I. Kant, *Religion within the Limits of Reason Alone* (New York: Harper & Brothers, 1934), 183 (Book Four, General Observation under no. 1 and note).

drum.[122] Prayer is here understood and rejected as a false alternative to action, as a flight from action.

For Matthew, prayer is not a flight from practice but its innermost side. Prayer makes it possible for the disciples of Jesus to experience the demands of Jesus as the will of the Father and to draw strength from this. Prayer does not become superfluous by acting, but the acting remains constantly dependent on prayer. Matthew shows here a depth and a richness of content in comparison with today's critical questioners, which it is well to consider.

2.3.4. Of Forgiveness of Sins (6:14-15)

Text

14 For if you forgive people their transgressions,
   then your heavenly Father will forgive you also.
15 But if you do not forgive others,
   then your Father will not forgive you your transgressions either.

Analysis

The logion has the form of a *mashal* of two members with beautiful parallelism. It has an independent variant in Mark 11:25, which Matthew omits later. In content, it corresponds to the petition for forgiveness in the Lord's Prayer and may well go back to Jesus—like the petition itself.[1]

Interpretation

Matthew resumes with this logion the petition for forgiveness of the Lord's Prayer and formulates it parenetically. Both the conditional formulation and the "negative" v. 15, which is missing in Mark 11:25, make clear that human forgiving is a condition for divine forgiving. Thus the evangelist lifts out exactly that passage of the Lord's Prayer in which human action was most directly envisaged. In distinction from the logion vv. 7f., stressing the nearness of God, which points to the Lord's Prayer, the issue in this logion, which concludes the Lord's Prayer, is to safeguard the connection of prayer with action. Matthew makes clear that prayer is also a part of Christian practice, an emphasis that will be the subject again in 6:19–7:27. The command to forgive corresponds in content to the center of his ethics, the love commandment.

2.4.

Literature

Giavini, G., "Abbiamo forse in Mt 6,19-7,11 il primo commento al 'Pater Noster'?"
   RivB 13 (1965) 171-77.
Further literature** on the Sermon on the Mount at Matt. 5-7 above, pp. 209-211.

---

[122]B. Brecht, *Mother Courage* (New York: Grove, 1955), scene 11.

[1]Cf. Pesch, *Markusevangelium* II 207.

1. *Survey.* The major section that now follows precisely corresponds in its length to the Antitheses. Matthew obviously intended this and has seen it as a unity. It is not simple to provide a clear title for its content. In distinction from the Antitheses, questions about the life of the community are more strongly taken into view. Two main parts are clearly visible: 6:19-34 deals with questions of possessions, 7:1-11 with various questions. It is difficult to say how the section is connected with the entirety of the Sermon on the Mount. Matthew 6:19–7:11 has always given the impression of being a "disorganized heap of 'supplements.' "[1] Formally, the section is unified by the fourfold μή + prohibition in the second person plural as an introduction to a new section (vv. 19,25; 7:1,6). The key word ἀφανίζω forms a bridge between 6:16 and 19, ὀφθαλμός a bridge between 6:22f. and 7:3-5. As to content, intepreters have pointed out in various ways the relationship to the central Lord's Prayer: 6:31-33 and 7:7-11 go back to 6:7-15. But it seems to me that it is not successful to interpret the whole section as a continuing exposition of the petitions of the Lord's Prayer.[2]

2. *Matthew 6:19-34* consists of one longer section and three short sections which Matthew himself has put together. Two of the four text pieces belonged together already in Q but in reverse order (6:25-33,19-21 = Luke 12:22-31,33f.).[3] The third piece (vv. 22-23) comes from a Q context which Matthew had used already and which therefore was familiar to him (= Luke 11:34-36, cf. Matt. 5:15 = Luke 11:33). Verse 24 has a correspondence in Luke 16:13 (Q?). The detailed analysis will show that Matthew followed the source not only in the order of the material but also in the formulation; he is a conservative redactor. The theme which is emphasized by the Matthean composition is the relation of the disciples to possessions. Since Matthew, after the central section 6:1-18, puts a *new* section, which is not as a whole arranged according to the Lord's Prayer and which deals with the relationship of the disciples to possessions, in the midst of his programmatic Sermon on the Mount, he demonstrates that for him as well as for Luke, this question is fundamental.

3. *Matthew 7:1-11* does not have a clearly redactional connection. Again, I believe that an interpretation on the basis of the last two petitions of the Lord's Prayer fails:[4] Between the petition for forgiveness and vv. 1-5 there is only a general closeness, and the attempt to see the common denominator between 6:13 and 7:6 in the warning of defection restricts both texts too much. Only 7:7-11 speaks again of prayer and thus reminds us of the Lord's Prayer, particularly of 6:8.

Matthew, after the section which he himself composed, 6:19-34, takes up again the thread of Luke's Sermon on the Plain. He follows it until v. 5. The two sections on judging and on the log, 7:1-2 and 3-5, are thematically closely related. Verse 6 stands in this context without connection. The only bridge to vv. 3-5 is the common word stem

---

[1]Bornkamm** 425.

[2]The thesis was already advocated before Bornkamm** by Giavini*, in the following arrangement: Matt. 6:9-11 - Matt. 6:19-34; Matt. 6:12 - Matt. 7:1-5; Matt. 6:13 - Matt. 7:6. Bornkamm**, who was not familiar with Giavini, advocated the same thesis. In my opinion, 6:19-24 cannot be made plausible in detail as an interpretation of the first three petitions.

[3]In Q there was a connection by key words: μεριμνάω (Luke 12:11,22-31); κλέπτης, διορύσσω (Luke 12:33 [cf. Matt. 6:20],39).

[4]Advocated by Bornkamm** 427-30 and Guelich** 356,377.

βαλ(λ)–.[5] Since also in our section the Q recension available to Matthew is different from the one of Luke, one can debate whether v.6 was already attached in QMt to vv. 3-5 with the word βάλλω. Verses 7-11 come from a different place in Q and have been put here deliberately by Matthew. Matthew showed through the central position of the Lord's Prayer how important prayer is for him. Now he rounds off the parenesis of the Sermon on the Mount once more by a reference to prayer.

2.4.1. Do Not Collect Earthly Treasures (6:19-24)

Literature

Amstutz, J., ΑΠΛΟΤΗΣ. Eine begriffsgeschichtliche Studie zum jüdisch-christlichen Griechisch, Theoph. 19, pp. 96-103 (Bonn: Hanstein, 1968).

Betz, H. D., "Matthew vi.22f and Ancient Greek Theories of Vision," in *Text and Interpretation* (FS M. Black), ed. R. Mc. L. Wilson, pp. 43-56 (Cambridge: Cambridge University, 1979).

Degenhardt, H. J., *Lukas, Evangelist der Armen,* pp. 88-93, 127-31 (Stuttgart: Katholisches Bibelwerk, 1965).

Edlund, C. J., *Das Auge der Einfalt (Mt 6,22f; Lk 11,34f)*, ASNU19 (Copenhagen: Munksgaard, 1952).

Hahn, F., "Die Worte vom Licht Lk 11,33-36," in *Orientierung an Jesus* (FS J. Schmid), ed. P. Hoffmann, pp. 107-38 (Freiburg: Herder, 1973).

Jülicher, *Gleichnisreden* II 98-115.

Mees, M., "Das Sprichwort Mt 6,21; Lk 12,24 und seine ausserkanonischen Parallelen," *Aug.* 14 (1974) 67-89.

Pesch, W., "Zur Exegese von Mt 6,19-21 und Lk 12,33-34," *Bib* 40 (1960 356-78.

Rüger, H. P., "Μαμωνᾶς," *ZNW* 64 (1973) 127-31.

Sjöberg, E., "Das Licht in dir. Zur Deutung von Mt 6,22f Par.," *ST* 5 (1952) 89-105.

Zeller, *Mahnsprüche* 77-82.

Further literature** on the Sermon on the Mount at Matt. 5-7 above p. 000.

Text

19 Do not collect for yourselves treasures on earth,
    where moth and rust destroy them
    and where thieves break in and steal;
20 But collect treasures in heaven,
    where neither moth nor rust destroy them
    and where no thieves break in and steal.
21 For where your treasure is, there your heart will be also.
22 The lamp of the body is the eye.
    If your eye is sincere,
    your whole body will be full of light.
23 But if your eye is evil,
    then your whole body will be full of darkness.

---

[5]Attempts at a relationship in regard to content between 1-5 and 6: According to J. Weiss 296, v. 6 is to avoid misinterpretations of 1-5; the evangelist would not want to endanger church discipline (18:15-18) by the forgoing of judging. Bengel on the passage already expresses this classically: The apostle seeks a middle way between two extremes, "nimia severitas" (too much severity) and "nimia laxitas" (too much laxity). But the evangelist was, as is shown by 13:36-43 and 18:21f, not interested in church discipline. Verse 6 is thus at most a *pre-Matthean* "Gemara," which restricts vv. 1-5 (Davies, *Setting* 326,396).

> So if the light in you is dark,
> how great will the darkness be!
> 24 Nobody can serve two masters.
> Either he will hate the one and love the other,
> or he will cling to the one and despise the other.
> You cannot serve God and mammon.

Analysis

1. *Structure.* Three originally independent logia are discernible (19-21,22-23,24). They all are permeated by parallelisms and repeat entire clauses. The first logion contains in v. 21 a concluding clause which dissolves the symmetry but is the most weighty one. The second and the third logion are structured similarly: an antithetical (22b.c/23a.b) or synonymous (24b/c) parallelism is framed by two nonparallel (22a,23c) or not quite (24a,d) parallel framing pieces. Matthew often displays a high measure of Semitic feeling for form where he works redactionally with logia.

2. *Redaction.* (a) In *vv. 19-21* the Q text is taken over literally; Luke has formulated redactionally the whole introduction with his admonition to sell one's possessions and give alms (v. 33). The only place where Matthew changed the Q wording may be in v. 20: Q formulated in the plural ἐν τοῖς οὐρανοῖς. [1] (b) In *vv. 22-23* the reconstruction of the Q text is difficult. Outside of ἐὰν οὖν and (ἐὰν) δέ there are no Mattheisms. Yet the assumption is justified that behind Matt. 6:23c and Luke 11:36 a further part of an old antithetical parallelism becomes apparent. [2] The final clause (v. 23c,d) also is the result of a secondary shortening. But the question is to whom it is due. While the parenetic formulation σκόπει οὖν (Luke 11:35) might very well be due to Matthew, we are groping in the dark at the threatening question τὸ σκότος πόσον (Matt. 6:23d): The language is not Matthean; it might be QMt. (c) *Matt. 6:24* agrees almost literally with Luke 16:13. Matthew only omitted οἰκέτης and thus understood, as already in 5:25f. and 6:22f., an illustrative text as direct parenesis.

3. *History of tradition.* (a) *Vv. 19-21:* Often it is proposed to see in v. 21 a secondary addition to an originally stylistically pure wisdom admonition. [3] But one should not make the postulate of the originally pure genre the starting point for attempts at analyzing the composition. Verse 21 is not so much a "supplementary comment" [4] as a "controlling motif" [5]: The transition into the singular in v. 21 is intended; it intensifies the address and sharpens the warning to its inner dimension. Verse 21 has not been added as a proverb to vv. 19-20 but has *become* a proverb only in the history of influence of 6:19-21 because it was applicable in so many ways. [6] (b) *Vv. 22-23:* The change from λύχνος (v. 22a) to τὸ φῶς τὸ ἐν σοί (v. 23c) is striking. With this is connected the difficulty that the eye as a *source* of light (= λύχνος!) of the body cannot be documented anywhere in Judaism, but only in Greek writings. [7] Λύχνος instead of

---

[1] When contrasted with γῆ, Matthew uses οὐρανός in the singular. The plural οὐρανοί in Q (Luke 12:33) is supported by the asymmetry with γῆ and perhaps also through a possible reminiscence in Luke 18:22 (according to Schürmann, *Untersuchungen* 115).

[2] Evidence in Hahn* 114-17.

[3] Bultmann, *Tradition* 83f.; Zeller, *Mahnsprüche* 77f.; Schweizer 102.

[4] Beare 180.

[5] Guelich** 328.

[6] Survey of the patristic examples in Mees*.

[7] Examples in Betz* 48.53 and Spicq, *Notes* I/126 n. 3 (Empedocles, Archimedes, Plato).

"light" came into the text only, it seems to me, when the word (in Q?) was added as a "word of commentary"[8] on the logion of the "lampstand" under the bushel (Luke 11:33). Verse 22a was therefore not an independent original nucleus but probably, as introduction, a part of the entire saying from the beginning. (c) *V. 24*: The problem is similar to vv. 19-21: Has an original popular proverb[9] received a new function as an address by a secondary parenetical conclusion?[10] Again the postulate of the pure genre (in this case the *mashal* without address) must not be taken as a starting point for a reconstruction of the history of tradition; the address v. 24d belongs—already for reasons of the symmetry of the clauses—to the original logion.

4. *Origin*. None of these logia contains an explicit reference to the kingdom of God which might be characteristic of Jesus. On the other hand, the occupation with the history of tradition has taken the ground out from that widespread argumentation which reduced these logia first to a purely sapiential kernel without address and then consistently *had to* deny that they were spoken by Jesus because they are completely general.[11] In their sharp opposition to riches, vv. 19-21 and v. 24 are different from a more positive attitude toward riches, widespread in rabbinical Judaism, without being therefore un-Jewish. They fit into Jesus' social critique; they *can* be from him. In contrast, a statement on vv. 22-23 is difficult; the decision would have to consider the Lukan v. 36 which is not discussed here.

History of influence

With 6:19-34 Matthew formulates in a central place in the Sermon on the Mount his *critique of possessions*. The central question for interpretation is whether and in what way he makes the demand on his community to renounce possessions. The history of interpretation furnishes examples of how this center of the text could be evaded.

a. One tendency of interpretation which has already some support in the text itself, namely, in vv. 22-23, which speak of the interior of the person, is *internalization*. The attempts regularly begin with vv. 22-23: the "light in you," following the comparison of reason with the eye, which was widespread in antiquity,[12] was interpreted as meaning the νοῦς.[13] For Matthew's meaning, the frequent explanation of the inner light as referring to the human heart is more correct.[14] But this interpretation is connected with the dualism and hostility to the body of late antiquity. The darkness becomes identical with the *sensus carnales* (carnal senses),[15] and the decisive question is then whether the human heart is obligated to the earth which is impure in itself or to heaven

---

[8]Wanke, "Bezugs- und Kommentarworte" 61-66.

[9]Often repeated in the entire history of interpretation and never proved.

[10]Bultmann, *Tradition* 87f.

[11]Cf., e.g., the thought of Zeller, *Mahnsprüche* 81.

[12]Aristotle, *Topica* 1.17 (108a); Philo, *Op. Mund.* 53; further examples in Wettstein I 330.

[13]Since Justin, *Apol.* 1.15,16 widespread. Examples: Theodore of Heraclea, fragment 45; Cyril of Alexandria, fragment 77 = Reuss 69,176; Dionysius bar Salibi 176; Thomas, *Lectura* no. 616; Erasmus, *Paraphrasis* 39.

[14]Examples in Knabenbauer I 332. Καρδία is suggested by v. 21.

[15]*Opus imperfectum* 15 = 721.

which is pure in itself.[16] The human being is asked whether his or her own heart has the "lumen fidei" (light of faith)[17] or, formulated in regard to the will, whether he or she would do something "bono animo" (in a good spirit) or "pura intentione" (with a pure intention). Later also the concept of conscience appears in this place.[18] The result then is that "the good conscience justifies every action." Or in regard to possessions: "The direction of our heart toward God" can be demonstrated not only in renunciation but just as well in the acquisition of possessions.[19] If one in such a way takes the starting point with vv. 22-23 and internalizes the Matthean demand, then the interpretation of v. 24, which is widespread throughout the entire history of the church, becomes conceivable: "Aliud est . . . *habere* divitias, aliud autem *servire* divitiis" (It is one thing to *have* wealth, but another thing to *be enslaved* to wealth).[20] The rich person whose heart does not cling to wealth is willing to give away his or her possessions, but naturally in moderation so that still enough is left for his or her family.[21] Thomas and Zwingli are agreed on the practical consequences: It is the question of the right measure.[22] But for us the question is: Do the central verses 22-23 give us a handle for such an internalizing of the demands of Jesus?

b. A tendency toward *expansion* of the text is parallel to this internalizing. As to method, it becomes possible through allegorical interpretation: it opens for the text new fields of application in regard to morality. At the same time it separates it at least so far from its literal sense that the latter is only one possibility of interpretation among others. Rust, moth, thieves can be interpreted allegorically, e.g., of pride, envy, and the heretics.[23] The allegorization makes it possible to evade the precise sense of the text: "One has to understand it not only in regard to money but to all passions." The treasure on earth may be not only money but also the belly, feasting, theater, sex. "Each individual is a slave where he or she is overcome."[24] Mammon is then not only gold but "any very attractive figure on earth."[25] In comparison with such widespread tendencies,

---

[16]Augustine** 2.13 (44).

[17]Ibid. 2.13 (46); Strabo on 6:22 = 104.

[18]"With that he has . . . reminded all of us of our conscience" (Luther II 174). Cf. also, e.g., Brenz 337: "Si opera alioqui bona fiunt mala, ex malo corde" (If works in general good become evil, they are done out of an evil heart).

[19]Quotations from Bossuet I 52 (29th day): "La bonne intention sanctifie toutes les actions de l'âme" (the good intention sanctifies all the actions of the soul); A. Schlatter, *Die christliche Ethik*, 4th ed. (Stuttgart: Calwer, 1961), 427.

[20]*Opus imperfectum* 16 = 722, similarly already John Chrysostom 21.1 = 383; Jerome on 6:24. In this way not even David is a servant of mammon (Luther, *Predigt* no. 71 of 1528, WA 27,343).

[21]Beautifully carried out by Wesley, *Wesley's Standard Sermons* I 481: Providing for children and one's own house is a "duty"; but there is a limit: "the plain necessities of life; . . . not superfluities."

[22]Thomas, *Lectura* no. 611, distinguishes on 6:19-21 between *necessarium* (that which is necessary) and *superflua* (that which is superfluous). That which is necessary depends on the situation and may mean one thing, e.g., for a king but something else for a "normal" person. Zwingli 237 thinks that Christ has commanded "modum . . . quendam in . . . temporariis rebus" (a certain moderation in temporary things) and makes himself an advocate of a "media via" (middle way). His definition of the Christian rich person is classical and useful: "Dives est, qui satis habet. Et hic habet satis, qui modum servat" (A rich person is the one who has enough. And enough has the person who observes moderation).

[23]E.g., in Rabanus Maurus 834.

[24]Jerome on 6:21.

[25]Cramer I 48 (Theodoros Monachos).

it is truly striking that, e.g., Jacob of Sarug (c. 500) designates very pointedly the service to mammon as *the* form of idolatry with which the devil operates after the old idols lost their attraction for the Christianized population.[26]

We are faced with the question: To what extent does our text have an exemplary character? As such, with "possessions" as an example, it would warn against any conformity to the world. Conversely: How far is it concerned exactly and exclusively about possessions?

Interpretation

6:19-20

Verses 19-20 appeal to good common sense: It does not pay to collect treasures. The moth—an almost symbolic animal for earthly destruction[27] —will eat accumulated clothes. Clothes are in the Near East an obvious expression of wealth for women; consider the rich dowry in textiles. The meaning of βρῶσις (eating as a process; food) unfortunately is not clear: Presumably it is here a misleading translation of a Semitic word which meant the "eater," i.e., a certain eating insect, e.g., the death-watch beetle.[28] Then it would refer, e.g., to the destruction of wooden boxes in which all kinds of things were preserved.[29] The διορύσσειν, which literally means "digging," is not necessarily a reference to the digging up of money by thieves which in Palestine was often hidden in the ground,[30] or to the criminal digging of underground passages[31] or to breaking into houses with adobe walls;[32] the word διορύσσω has become a term for "breaking and entering."[33] Positively, the text recommends the collecting of heavenly treasures. With this, the idea of reward is taken up without modification; it refers to almsgiving, works of love, or other good deeds.[34] The purely sapiential critique of perishable riches of Prov. 23:4f.

---

[26]Poem on the fall of the idol images 390-580 = BKV I/16 175-83.

[27]Cf. Isa. 51:8; Sir. 42:13; Jas. 5:2 (to my way of thinking neither directly nor indirectly influenced by Matthew).

[28] אָכַל Mal. 3:11, LXX βρῶσις, meaning the locust. מַאֲכֹלֶת among the rabbis may mean "death-watch beetle" (Jastrow s.v.). The widespread translation "rust" relies on the Vulgate translation "aerugo" (copper rust, verdigris) instead of the older Latin "comestura" (eater).

[29]K. Koch, "Der Schatz im Himmel," in *Leben angesichts des Todes* (FS H. Thielicke) (Tübingen: Mohr, 1968), 47-60, there 49-52. אוֹצָר means "storage, storage place"; thus it is not a heavenly "fortune," but rather the good works themselves which "are envisioned as materially present in heaven" (52).

[30]Str-B I 971f.

[31]Διῶρυξ = ditch, canal, underground passage.

[32]Guelich** 327 thinks of Palestinian mud-brick houses. But the generalized expression permits neither conclusions about the origin nor social historical conclusions.

[33]Examples in BAGD, s.v. τοιχωρύχος = housebreaker, burglar. Biblically: Job 24:16.

[34]Tob. 4:9f. (mercy); *Pss. Sol.* 9:5 (the one who does justice θησαυρίζει ζωήν); 4 Ezra 6:5 (treasures of faith); 7:77; *2 Bar.* 14:12 (treasure of works); *2 Enoch* 50:5 (inexhaustible treasure in judgment by

(and perhaps Sir. 29:9-13) is here heightened eschatologically; but one cannot say that the judgment is emphasized as, e.g., in *1 Enoch* 94:7-10.

6:21

The sharpening of the admonition occurs through v. 21. Although there are no direct Jewish parallels to this sentence, the thought is Jewish: καρδία is the center of the human being; the "treasure" makes clear where the person's "center" is located and what is most important to him or her. Verse 21 is intended to sharpen the admonition of vv. 19-20 radically. With the question of money, human existence as such is at stake. Thus v. 21 is not a general maxim which could be applied to manifold forms of earthly ties of human beings, but an intensified warning against earthly treasures.[35]

6:22-23

The two following verses concerning the eye are difficult. Verse 22a may be an illustration or a metaphor, depending whether one understands "eye" literally or figuratively. Verses 22b,c and 23a,b also can be interpreted in two ways:
   1. They may be a parable: with the person it is as with the body. When the eye is well, the whole body is doing well. Verse 23c,d then indicates the meaning intended:[36] the inner light of the person. The illustration most likely does not involve the Greek idea that the eye has a fiery character, but probably means rather the simple experience that without the eye the human being (= σῶμα) cannot see anything, is in darkness.[37] On the basis of the illustration one would think of the contrast between a healthy and a sick eye. A smaller difficulty of this interpretation consists in the fact that πονηρός in Greek may well mean "sick," but ἁπλοῦς does not mean "healthy." For the interpretation one would have to go back to the Hebrew תָּם or the Aramaic שְׁלַם, which frequently correspond to Greek ἁπλοῦς, and may mean "healthy." But the greater difficulty is the interpretation of the real meaning. What is the "light in yourself"? The soul? Reference to the inner light cannot be documented as a Jewish expression for the soul.[38] Other interpreters refer to the share of the

---

giving up gold and silver for the sake of the brother, cf. Luke 12:33f.). Rabbinical examples in Str-B I 430f. Polemics against the heaping up of earthly treasures: *1 Enoch* 94:7-10; 97:8-10.

[35]Rightly: Guelich** 328: "The focus turns to the person rather than to the treasure." Because in v. 21 repeatedly the original and specifically Christian element of 19-21 was seen (Pesch* 366; Degenhardt* 92), we have to warn of over-interpreting the text: It does not (yet, see v. 24) deal with God and his kingdom (pace Schweizer 103). The future tense ἔσται does not anchor the human heart in heaven (against Zeller, *Mahnsprüche* 80f.), but is in form a maxim, in content parenetic.

[36]Clear representatives from the early church: John Chrysostom 20.3 = 373f. (bodily illustration for spiritual things. What the eye is for the body, the spirit is for the soul); from the present: Sjöberg* 90-103; Guelich** 329.

[37]Greek parallels above n. 12. Correctly Luther II 173: The one who does not have an eye and is supposed to walk will break the neck or drown in water because he or she does not see.

[38]The examples listed by Str-B I 432 are (a) all late and (b) all dependent on Prov. 20:27. Sjöberg* 97 makes plausible the thought that our passage is not at all influenced by Prov. 20:27.

human person in the world of light[39] or the share in the kingdom of God.[40] Such interpretations presuppose a context which in any case is not present in the Matthean form of the text.[41] But the greater difficulty consists in the fact that the reader who (a) speaks Greek and not Aramaic, (b) has in mind the Septuagint and later Jewish metaphorical meaning of the "eye," and (c) reads this after Matt. 6:19-21 will understand our text certainly in a different way. Therefore, this interpretation is to be rejected for the extant text of Matthew, even if not absolutely for the original form of our saying.

2. Our verses are metaphorical. The text "does not speak of the bodily eye."[42] "Eye" is in Judaism always metaphorical; in the eyes, the character and the moral quality of a person are reflected.[43] A fixed contrast is that of the "evil" and the "good" eye; the texts usually think of avarice and calculation versus generosity and honesty.[44] The Jewish-Christian readers of the Gospel of Matthew probably thought of this contrast, after reading 6:19-21, although a certain element of surprise consists in the use of the "sincere" eye instead of the "good" eye. Ἁπλοῦς in Greek is often freighted rather negatively ("simple," "uneducated," "uncomplicated," "simpleton," "barbaric," "indistinguished," but also "direct," "open"), but in Jewish-Christian thought usually understood positively ("integral," "without envy," "open," "pure," "obedient," "perfect");[45] the Hebrew תָּם or the Aramaic שְׁלַם stands behind it. Thus the "sincere" eye means a form of human behavior, primarily generosity, but, beyond it, honesty and uprightness in obedience toward God as such.[46] Thus our text is not concerned with the *nature* of human beings[47] but with their

---

[39]Sjöberg* 103 on the basis of Qumran.

[40]Guelich** 332.367 on the basis of Q.

[41]For Luke or Q, on the other hand, a Christological interpretation is probable, since 11:33-36 follow the saying of the sign of Jonah (11:29-32).

[42]*Opus imperfectum* 15 = 720. The insight that the text speaks of the eye "per metaphoram" (metaphorically) (Bucer 72) has been preserved throughout the history of interpretation. The most splendid representative of the metaphorical interpretation today is still Jülicher, *Gleichnisreden* II 98-108.

[43]W. Michaelis, "ὁράω κτλ.," *TDNT* V 375f. Important is, e.g., Sir. 13:25f. (the heart of a person changes the face); 14:8-10 (the eye expresses disfavor); *T. Gad* 5:7 (μετάνοια . . . φωτίζει τοὺς ὀφθαλμούς); Philo speaks frequently of the eyes of the διάνοια or the ψυχή.

[44]Prov. 22:9 (generosity); 23:6 (evil eye, calculating); 28:22 (evil eye—riches); Sir. 35:9 (generosity); *'Abot* 2:9,11, cf. already Deut. 15:9. Further rabbinical examples in Str-B I 833-35. Matthew is familiar with this usage: 20:15!

[45]Cf. especially the research of Edlund* 661-78 and Amstutz* 16-966. In the *T. 12 Patr.* ἁπλότης becomes a cardinal virtue, cf. *T. Iss.* 3:2–5:1, especially 4:6 (ἁπλότης ψυχῆς parallel to εὐθύτης καρδίας, opposite to ὀφθαλμοὶ πονηροί and πλάνη τοῦ κόσμου); *T. Benj.* 6:4-7.

[46]Edlund* 104-13 (wholeness!); Baumbach, *Verständnis* 78f. Amstutz* 96-102, there 99, understands it, on the basis of 20:15, as "without envy."

[47]Betz* 55f. emphasizes that v. 23 is directed against Greek anthropology and its concept of the divine soul. Hardly! Behind v. 23, there is, quite unpolemically and incidentally, the Jewish and Matthean basic conviction that the activity of the persons determines what they are. Therefore, our text cannot be used for the question of polemical theology whether, after the fall of Adam, reason was preserved for the human being as "lumen internum" (internal light); cf. the polemic of Calvin against the position of

actions which make them full of light or darkness. The "light in yourself" (v. 23c) probably means nothing else than "the lamp of the body" of v. 22a, but now formulated very specifically: "that which should be light in you."[48] The meaning of v. 23c,d. is: If everything is not right with your acting, your obedience, especially your generosity, then the darkness is total.

Thus vv. 22-23 are not intended to lead the reader away from human acting to an internal level. They also are not intended to detract from the questions of possessions. In the contrast between the "evil" and the "sincere" eye, the relationship to possessions remains central. But they want to sharpen the thought, similarly to v. 21: In human dealings with money, the total existence of the person is at stake; it is here a question of light and darkness, of wholeness and perfection. Verse 24 then does not indicate a return to a superficial level but follows exactly.

6:24

The verse again connects with an experience: No one can serve two masters without conflicts. Matthew no longer speaks of the slave; this text also is not a parable for him but a direct parenesis, supported by wisdom from experience.

The Aramaic מָמוֹנָא[49] means "possessions," "money."[50] The Aramaic word is a rhetorically very effective vestige in the Greek saying, which is formulated very compactly and scarcely changed. Μισέω and ἀγαπάω could mean in a weakened way "decide against" and "prefer."[51] But this assumption is not necessary for Matthew. Almost automatically, the reader associates with ἀγαπάω the basic command of love for God. But this is said explicitly only at the end: Verse 24d for the first and only time in our section brings God into the picture. With this, the high point is reached; after v. 21 and v. 23c,d called attention to the fact that human existence is at stake in one's attitude to possessions, now once more the thought is sharpened: It is a question of correct worship of God.

Summary

In what, specifically, does this worship of God which is not to be worship of mammon consist? It causes us to think that in Judaism, with its often poor rabbis, we do not find such coarse tones, but certainly do in the very rich

---

"papists" who asserted on the basis of our passage that the human being, thanks to reason, has the possibility to choose between good and evil (I 219).

[48]Amstutz* 102. Jülicher, *Gleichnisreden* II,99: an "oxymoron."

[49]*Status emphaticus.* The form makes clear that this logion was formulated originally in Aramaic and not in Hebrew.

[50]Rüger* 130f; מָמוֹן is a Canaanite loanword, having relatively late entered into Hebrew and Aramaic, whose root מוֹן means something like "provisions, stored goods." The derivations from אָמַן are popular but wrong.

[51]Str-B I 434.

Philo.[52] But probably neither the burdened conscience of a well-to-do city community[53] nor the piety of the poor, of the "little people," speaks in the Gospel of Matthew, but rather the knowledge of Jesus' renunciation of possessions for the sake of the kingdom of God. What did Matthew specifically demand from his community? Two sayings which emphasize human action precede v. 24. The following section (vv. 25-34) concerning freedom from worry speaks of itinerant radicals; it is possible that this was not clear to the Matthean community. The admonition not to collect earthly treasures and to practice benevolence instead (vv. 19f.) stands emphatically at the beginning of a newly composed section on possessions, immediately after the center of the Sermon on the Mount. And finally Matthew resumes the theme of renunciation of possessions once more in his Gospel, namely, in the narrative of the rich young man 19:16-30, where he links the selling of goods not only as Mark with discipleship but in 19:19 also with the command of the love of neighbor. All this shows that the proved distinction between the *having* of possessions, which would be permitted, and the absolutely forbidden worship of mammon is not in agreement with the thinking of Matthew. For him, worship of God as well as worship of mammon become visible in *deeds* involving money. It is not stated definitely here in what they should consist. Matthew obviously proceeds similarly to Luke who in his writings shapes the total renunciation of possessions in the circle of the disciples as an appeal to his readers to do as much as possible. Thus it also agrees with his own understanding of Jesus in the Sermon on the Mount, who makes exemplary demands and also gives a freedom to determine for yourself the way and manner of fulfillment. But this fulfillment has to aim at a maximum: also on the question of possessions, there stands in the intention of Matthew the principle that perfection is the goal and that on the way to it the righteousness of the disciples must be greater than that of the Pharisees and scribes.[54] In Matthew's perspective, one may not turn aside by generalizing to other areas than the question of possessions. Matthew has too clearly pointed out through the section 6:19-34 in the heart of the Sermon on the Mount that precisely the question of the relationship of Christians to possessions is a central question of the higher righteousness.

2.4.2. Seek the Kingdom of God (6:25-34)

Literature

Bultmann, R., "μεριμνάω κτλ.," *TDNT* IV 589-93.
Degenhardt, H. J., *Lukas, Evangelist der Armen,* pp. 80-85 (Stuttgart: Katholisches Bibelwerk, 1965).
Dupont, *Béatitudes,* III, 272-304.

---

[52]Fragment II,649 in Klostermann 62: It is inconceivable that love of the world can exist with love of God. Greeks also warn against becoming a δοῦλος χρημάτων (a slave of possessions) (Euripides, *Hec.* 865, cf. Plato, *Resp.* 555c; Seneca, *De Vita Beata* 16), however, not for the sake of worship of God but of the internal freedom of the wise person.

[53]Against Kilpatrick, *Origins* 124, cf. introduction n. 198.

[54]This means that 6:19-24 in Matthew's view is an example of discipleship ethics, as Bornhäuser** 145 correctly emphasizes.

Merklein, *Gottesherrschaft* 174-83.

Olsthoorn, F. M., *The Jewish Background and the Synoptic Setting of Mt 6,25-33 and Lk 12,22-31*, SBFA 10 (Jerusalem: Franciscan Printing Press, 1975).

Schottroff, L. and Stegemann, W., *Jesus and the Hope of the Poor*, UB 639, pp. 39-45 (Maryknoll: Orbis, 1986).

Tannehill, R., *The Sword of His Mouth*, Semeia S, pp. 60-67 (Philadelphia: Fortress, 1975).

Zeller, *Mahnsprüche* 82-94.

Further literature** on the Sermon on the Mount at Matthew 5-7 above, pp. 209-211.

Text

25 Therefore *I say to you:*[1]
Do not be concerned for your *life, what* you *eat* or *what* you *drink,*[2]
also not for your *body, what* you *put on.*
Is not the *life* more than *food* and the *body* more than *clothing?*

26 **Look** to the birds **of the sky:**
They do *not* sow and do *not* harvest and do not gather into barns,
and *your heavenly Father* **feeds** them.
Are you not *more* than they?

27 Who among you can add a single cubit to his height by being *concerned?*

28 And *what are* you *concerned* about *clothing?*
Observe the lilies *of the* field, how they grow:
They do *not* toil and do *not* spin.[3]

29 But *I say to you:* Solomon in all his glory was not *clothed* like one of these.

30 But if God so clothes the plants on the field which are today and will be thrown into the fire *tomorrow,*
will he not much *more* (clothe) you, people of little faith?

31 *Do not be concerned* by saying, *What* shall we *eat?*
What shall we *drink? What* shall we *put on?*

32 For the Gentiles **seek** *all these* things.
For *your heavenly Father* knows that you need all this.

33 **Seek** first the kingdom and his[4] righteousness,
and *all of this* will be granted to you.

34 Therefore do not be *concerned* about *tomorrow,* for *tomorrow* will be *concerned* about itself. It is sufficient that each day have its own trouble.

---

[1]Italics in the translation designates relationships of key words internal to the text; bold face indicates relationships in the word stem.

[2]Since the long version with ἢ τί πίητε does not agree with the Lukan parallel, is in form asymmetrical and is not taken up again by τροφῆς, it might be original despite the correspondence to v. 31 (ἢ· τί πίωμεν).

[3]I do not consider the much discussed original text version of the Sinaiticus and perhaps of the supplemented Oxyrhynchus papyrus 655 to be original. They read: οὐ ξένουσιν (orthographic error for ξαίνω = to card wool) οὐδὲ νήθουσιν οὐδὲ κοπιῶσιν (cf. K. Brunner, "Textkritisches zu Mt 6,28," *ZKT* 100 [1978] 251-56). This is either a variant which intruded from POxy 655 into ℵ or a unique copying error which arose spontaneously and was corrected immediately.

[4]The Greek means unambiguously, despite Calvin I 225, the righteousness of God (and not of the kingdom). The surprising text has to be explained by literary critical means: Matthew wanted to treat the Q model as conservatively as possible when he inserted καὶ τὴν δικαιοσύνην. This is how βασιλεία arose, seemingly without attribute (unusual for Matthew), which was promptly corrected by numerous manuscripts.

Analysis

1. *Structure*. The numerous internal connections by key words or word stems give the text a considerable unity. The imperative or prohibitions (μεριμνᾶτε, ἐμβλέψατε, καταμάθετε, ζητεῖτε) are determinative; the text has an imperatival and not an instructive character.[5] A rough arrangement follows: introductory prohibition (25); first argument from experience (26); second, parallel argument from experience (28b-30) with brief introduction (28a); admonition, resuming the prohibition and summarizing (31-33). It is not possible to create strict formal symmetry among the individual clauses; one should not speak of a "didactic poem"[6] with several strophes. In this unified text, vv. 27 and 34, which break the formal scheme, are particularly impressive.

2. *Redaction*. The text comes from Q. It probably existed there in various recensions, because the reconstruction of a completely identical Q text does not seem possible. Verse 34 and Luke v. 32 are both preredactional, and thus come probably from QMt and QLk. Τὰ πετεινὰ τοῦ οὐρανοῦ, ὁ πατὴρ ὁ οὐράνιος and αὐτῶν in v. 26, οὖν and λέγοντες in v. 31, ὁ οὐράνιος v. 32, καὶ τὴν δικαιοσύνην v. 33 are Matthean redaction; perhaps also ἢ τί πίητε in v. 25, τοῦ ἀγροῦ v. 28, πρῶτον and πάντα in v. 33.[7] The most important interventions of the Lukan redaction are: the introduction v. 22aα, the formulation οἷς οὐκ ἔστιν . . . v. 24, the generalizing τὰ λοιπά v. 26, the stylistically caused transposition in v. 28, the avoidance of the rhetorical questions, and perhaps the whole of verse 26a.

The following features are noteworthy in the Matthean redaction: (a) It stays conservatively with the preexisting formal characteristics by strengthening the connecting key words within the text.[8] (b) It is conservative, receiving given formulations and not formulating them anew (in distinction from Luke!): Τὰ πετεινά available to Matthew from Q (Luke v. 24),[9] also the word πατήρ (Luke v. 30) which is stressed by οὐράνιος. It also is important that Matthew found his favorite word "of little faith" here in the tradition; his redactional use of this word will begin only from here on. (c) It takes up Old Testament phrases: πετεινὰ τοῦ οὐρανοῦ, χόρτος τοῦ ἀγροῦ.[10] (d) For the rest, the few redactional changes are stylistic smoothings. A truly content alteration is created only by the insertion of δικαιοσύνη in v. 33. Precisely because this is the only "innovation" in the text, it is noteworthy.

3. *History of tradition*. The interpretation of the original text sense and also the question of whether the text comes from Jesus depend on the reconstruction of the history of tradition. The most important question is whether v. 33, with the key word "kingdom of God," belongs to the oldest text. I only will indicate here the status of the debate and my own view.

1. There is broad *consensus* on the following items: In v. 25, διὰ τοῦτο ties it to what precedes. Διὰ τοῦτο in Q referred to the preceding logion of being concerned, Luke 12:11f. Verse 17 is distinguished in purport and linguistic shape from the remaining verses and is a secondary interpretation, influenced by the wisdom traditions. Is Matthew

---

[5]Merklein, *Gottesherrschaft* 175f.

[6]Degenhardt* 80; Grundmann 215. The text is prose.

[7]On the individual key words, cf. introduction 3.2.

[8]The correspondences and key word connections in vv. 26/28 (τοῦ), vv. 26a,c/32b (πατήρ, οὐράνιος or οὐρανός) and perhaps in vv. 25b/31 (πίνω) are due to Matthew.

[9]It probably was characteristic of the Q text that in both images the specific term (κόραξ, κρίνον) was taken up by a general term (πετεινόν, χόρτος) (observation in a seminar paper by S. Rothen- Pfunder). On the conservative character of the Matthean redaction, cf. also above n. 4.

[10]Πετεινὰ τοῦ οὐρανοῦ LXX c. 34 times; χόρτος τοῦ ἀγροῦ 2 Kings 19:26; Jer. 12:4.

v. 28a a secondary transition which turns back to the second argument from experience (28b-30)? Verse 34 is an addition in QMt. The additions pick up key words of the "main text," so that they are not originally independent logia but interpretations of the text.

2. The analysis of 25b-26,28(b)-33 is *disputed*. There is agreement only on the fact that all arguments are weak. The original kernel of the text is seen either (a) in v. 25[11] or (b) in vv. 26,28-30[12] or (c) in vv. 26,28-32b without 32a.[13] (d) A fourth group of exegetes forgoes a further dissection and considers 25f.,28-33 the oldest text.[14] The tight composition with the many key words and determinative imperatives speaks in favor of this view. Again, in my opinion, one should not eliminate in a purist fashion the eschatological element (v. 33!) and reconstruct a purely sapiential text which does not contain anything specifically typical of Jesus. It is well known that sapiential admonition could be combined in various ways with prophetic and apocalyptic eschatological preaching.[15] In this, at least, Jesus is not at all new. Besides, in our text the consistent address in the second person plural is unusual—"normal" for sapiential admonitions is the second person singular[16]—combined with the designation of the addressees as "of little faith." That points to the possibility that definite addressees may be (not: must be) meant in a concrete situation. Precisely this is presupposed in v. 33, which can be directed only to listeners who have already heard of Jesus' proclamation of the kingdom of God. For these reasons, I would follow the fourth thesis. Secondary interpretations might be present at most in v. 25d,e and in v. 32a.

4. *Origin.* The analysis of the history of tradition shows that there are no decisive reasons not to consider the basic text vv. 25f.,28-33 (perhaps without vv. 25d,e and 32a) as spoken by Jesus. In favor of this view is also the fact that this basic text was already interpreted before Q by additions in the style of wisdom.

Interpretation

There are few Gospel texts which have called forth such a harsh critique. Each "starved sparrow" refutes Jesus,[17] let alone every famine and every war. The text seems externally simple: it pretends that there are no economic but only ethical problems[18] and it is a good symbol for the economic naïveté[19] which characterized Christianity in the course of its history. It is applicable only in the special situation of an unmarried Jesus, living with friends in sunny Galilee. [20] It is problematic also in the ethical aspect: It speaks of work "in the most

---

[11]Bultmann, *Tradition* 88, as a possibility; similarly Klostermann 92.

[12]E. Fuchs, "Jesus' Understanding of Time," in *Studies of the Historical Jesus* (Naperville: Allenson, 1964), 105.

[13]Zeller, *Mahnsprüche* 86f.

[14]Schulz, *Q* 154 (early Christian prophetic product); Merklein, *Gottesherrschaft* 179 (word of Jesus).

[15]Cf. Sato, *Q*, especially 254-64.

[16]Zeller, *Mahnsprüche* 142. On our text ibid. 85, "One is more accustomed to such directness in the prophetic word of reproach."

[17]J. Weiss 293.

[18]Montefiore, *Literature* 141.

[19]Cf. E. Bloch, *Atheism in Christianity* (New York: Herder & Herder, 1972), 138.

[20]Cf. J. Weiss 294f.

disdainful manner''[21] and supports laziness.[22] The admonition not to be
concerned for tomorrow seems naive, and not only in the age of global nuclear
threat; rather, in the opinion of many interpreters, already the provision of
Joseph for the seven lean years in Egypt shows that there are more reflective
statements in the Bible on the subject "be concerned, care" than Matthew
6:25-34. Therefore, the history of interpretation can be read widely as the
attempt to defend the text against attacks.

But what is to be defended? The one main question of interpretation is
what is really meant by the warning against "concern, care." Is it a warning
against anxiety, against inward lack of freedom, against being a prisoner of
worry? Is it a warning against avarice and greed? Or is it a matter not only of an
internal attitude but also of concrete behavior, e.g., of the admonition to
renounce possessions or to forgo work? The other main question is that of the
persons addressed. Is it addressed to the disciples who have to proclaim the
kingdom of God? Or do the sapiential elements show that it is addressed to
pious people in general, not merely to the apostles?[23] Or is the comfort of this
text addressed only to the "poorest of the poor," an indirect expression of the
material "concerns of the little people"?[24] Earlier centuries were almost united
on the Christian duty to work and therefore read our text under the
presupposition of the divine (Gen. 3:17-19) and apostolic command of work (2
Thess. 3:10-12).[25] Therefore frequently it was asserted as the scope of the text
that one should be concerned for the soul and not for food.[26] Today, there is
widespread uncertainty.

6:25a,b,c

The introductory clause "therefore I say to you" is neither prophetic[27] nor
simply an intensification of the authority of a wisdom speaker,[28] but deliberate
"Jesus language." Behind the following words stands the authority of the Lord
Jesus. Ψυχή is not "soul," since it eats and drinks, but (Semitically) "life."
But what is the content of μεριμνάω?

---

[21]K. Kautsky, *Foundations of Christianity* (New York: Russell, 1953), 293.

[22]Schleiermacher, *Predigten* I 153.

[23]Klostermann 63.

[24]Beare 185; Schottroff-Stegemann* 55,59.

[25]Cf. below n. 71 and the remarks on the history of influence by W. Trilling, *Der zweite Brief an die Thessalonicher*, EKK 14 (Zürich: Benziger, and Neukirchen-Vluyn: Neukirchener, 1980), 148f.

[26]Bengel 54 formulates it classically on v. 34: "God makes his children see the temporary as something alien which is not true and not their own, in contrast to the solid eternal goods. So it is no longer heavenly but earthly goods which appear to them as a dream. . . . They work also . . ., but with a detached soul." Similarly Johannes Tauler, *Predigt* no. 62: One should definitely make prudent and reasonable provision and seek the kingdom internally (Mokrosch-Walz, *Mittelalter* [KTQ II] 182f.).

[27]Schulz, *Q* 57-61.

[28]In a differentiated form in K. Berger, "Zur Geschichte der Einleitungsformel 'Amen, ich sage euch,' " *ZNW* 663 (1972), especially 61; Zeller, *Mahnsprüche*, especially 156.

Bultmann, in his brief but effective article, interprets the word as an expression of the basic structure of human existence to "secure" life in this world. Conquering one's concern in faith means "eschatological existence."[29] In reference to him, especially Bornhäuser and Jeremias have pointed out that the behavior, the effort of human beings stands in the forefront, based on the Old Testament and the context.[30] The history of the term does not furnish an unambiguous answer.[31] In the Semitic parallels also, the element of anxiety and of worry stands in the forefront.[32] Basically, the Semitic examples[33] do not provide a different finding from that of the Greek examples.[34] Not the history of the term but the context is decisive for the interpretation of our passage. The two illustrations (vv. 26 and 28) speak in favor of active human behavior: the birds do not sow and harvest, the lilies do not toil and spin. The "active" counter-term ζητέω (v. 33) also speaks in favor of this interpretation.[35] But more indications speak in favor of the idea that the conquering of *anxiety* is an essential element of our text: The Lukan μετεωρίζομαι (Luke v. 29 = be anxious), the motif of little faith (v. 30), the formulation of the question, "What shall we eat? What shall we drink? What shall we put on?" (v. 31).

One must not separate the two elements of "caring"—anxiety over existence and active effort-making. "Worry" is an acting from anxiety, practiced anxiety for existence. Whoever "worries," "cares" for a thing. He or she acts—but with worry, anxiety, and pain.

6:25d,e

Verse 25d,e states a first reason why one should not be concerned. The half-verse is disturbing in the context, for one is concerned about eating and drinking precisely *because* one cares for the ψυχή, about clothes exactly *because* one cares for the σῶμα. What should we then make of the statement that life or body is more than food or clothes? One can interpret it theologically: It is *God* who takes care of the "higher," of life and body; therefore he will take care also for the smaller, food and clothing.[36] But this thought, familiar from 10:28-31, would here not be sufficiently clear, especially since the two illustrations vv. 26 and 28-30, which are similar but more clear, follow only later. Therefore, it is better to interpret in terms of wisdom, i.e., as a warning against excessive concern: What does a person have in life if he or she constantly drudges

---

[29]R. Bultmann* especially 592.

[30]Bornhäuser** 150; Jeremias, *Parables* 214.

[31]Semitic equivalents of μεριμνάω are דאג, כעס, רגז, עשׂה, שׂעה. On the Semitic prehistory, which is treated very briefly by Bultmann, cf. Zeller, *Mahnsprüche* 87f.

[32]Examples in Zeller, loc.cit. nn. 251,252.

[33]Exod. 5:9; Prov. 14:23; Bar. 3:18; Sir. 38:29 (the potter working with his hands in distinction from the scribe); Luke 10:41 (Martha).

[34]Cf. the "acting" concern, care in the Greek examples in Bultmann* 589 and n. 2.

[35]On the active sense of ζητέω cf. Guelich** 342f. In addition, the insertion of the narrative of the rich fool 12:16-21 into the Q context in Luke points to the fact that the element of acting belongs to caring.

[36]E.g., in Augustine** 2.15 (49); Maldonat 147 ("quis vobis animam et corpus dedit, nisi Deus?" [Who gave you the soul and the body if not God?]) and others.

or worries?[37] This thought has a certain parallel in Luke 12:16-21. Be that as it may, both the first interpretation—which implicitly anticipates the thought of God's care which is afterward explicitly enunciated—and the second—which, with its motto of a moderate *carpe-diem* (use the day well), does not seem to fit well into the context—are disturbing in this context. This part of the verse is a secondary addition!

6:26

The exhortation is motivated by a double illustration. Matthew speaks in biblical language of the birds of the sky,[38] for whom the heavenly Father of the community cares. The text makes a strange statement concerning the birds, which really comes from the human world: they do not sow and do not harvest. This mentions two characteristic kinds of work of the male. Does this mean: "In distinction from you, the birds do not sow and harvest; how much more will then God care for you who do work?"[39] But God is not more concerned about humans than about birds and lilies because humans on their part contribute to their livelihood, but because he is their Father. Besides, human labor is not mentioned at all. On the other hand, the nonworking birds are "no . . . example, but . . . testimony to God's concern."[40] Thus, the issue is not that those addressed *should* not work. But why then is it said at all that the birds do not sow and gather? Probably because here is a point of contact to those addressed, i.e., they also do not sow and gather into barns.

6:28-30

The second illustration is a little more detailed and so intensifies the effect of the first one. What kind of flowers is meant by "lilies" we do not know; κρίνον may also be used in general for "flower."[41] It is important that field flowers are kept in view, i.e., "weeds," not garden flowers. With "toil" and especially with "spin" the labor of the woman is mentioned.[42] Solomon as a glorious king is proverbial. Verse 30 heightens the effect: the field flowers belong to the

---

[37]Wisdom examples in Zeller, *Mahnsprüche* 88. Luther II 186 formulates a parenetic variant of the same thought: "the food is to serve the body, but with you, the body serves the food."

[38]Cf. above n. 10. It does not seem probable to me that Matthew wanted to avoid the ritually unclean raven, just as I do not believe it can be demonstrated that in the original version the raven was chosen deliberately because it is an unclean animal. The raven is already a biblical illustration of God's concern (Job 38:41).

[39]Cf. Bultmann* 592: The illustration of birds and flowers which do not labor presupposes (!) that humans work.

[40]Heinrici** 76.

[41]Dalman, *Orte* 139 would prefer to have purple anemones instead of the white lilies, rare in Palestine, because high thistles and therefore much material for making fire could be gathered from the former (cf. v. 30). Well thought out!

[42]*Ketub.* 5:5 = Str-B I 955 enumerates the obligatory labors of the woman, cf. *b. Yebam.* 63a; *b. Yoma* 66b: Work with wool such as spinning is the duty of the woman under all circumstances. The general κοπιάω cannot be interpreted of the labor of the man, pace *Opus imperfectum* 16 = 723. If our interpretation of the text as a whole is correct, then it is an argument for supposing that women also followed Jesus.

perishable plants, i.e., not to woody plants of the field which furnish fire material for the poor people.[43] We are here dealing with the milieu of the poor country population of Galilee who have to use straw as material for fire. But it is not merely a matter of poor people being addressed and their cares verbalized. If the illustration is to fit truly, women are addressed who also do not "toil and spin." The direct address ὀλιγόπιστοι (of little faith) indicates that specific people are addressed. People with deficient faith (מְחוּסְרֵי אֱמָנָה), according to old rabbinical traditions are, e.g., those Israelites who wanted to gather manna and quail on the sabbath in the wilderness.[44] For Matthew, this traditional expression became important; it characterizes the situation of the community as standing between unbelief and faith which can be helped again in its doubt by the power of Jesus (8:26; 14:31).

6:27

The two illustrations are interrupted by a digression which sounds sapiential and pessimistic. Its meaning has been disputed since the beginning. Ἡλικία may mean "age" or "height." It was understood to mean either that nobody can add even a little to his lifetime or that nobody can add a cubit to his height. The common interpretation today is the former since the prolonging of life is a goal worthy of effort and an object of concern, but lengthening of one's body is not. But it seems to me that the better interpretation is the second,[45] since πῆχυς is not used figuratively in the temporal sense[46] and ἡλικία does not mean the length of life in general but a certain age.[47] There is the conviction in Judaism that Adam because of the fall had lost his original height.[48]

---

[43]Krauss, Archäologie I 84f. The baking oven (κλίβανος = תַּנּוּר) is found in every household and consists as a rule of a simple fired ceramic pot (ibid. 87f.).

[44]Mek.Exod. on 16:4 (55b) in Str-B I 420f.; on 16:19f. (58a) in Str-B I 439; on 16:27 (58b) ibid. Cf.*Tg. Ps. Jon.* on Num. 11:32 ibid. Later the expression קטן אמנה is predominant.

[45]It is the generally adopted interpretation in the early church and finds expression also in the translations. Itala: *statura* (stature); Vulgate: the same; Peshitta: *qwmth'*. Only the African version (= k) reads: *aetas* (age). The temporal interpretation is found in Erasmus, *Annotationes* 38f.; Theodore of Beza rejects it explicitly (30). According to Tholuck** 411 it was advocated almost exclusively in his time.

[46]BAGD, s.v. πῆχυς, only cites the adjective πήχυιος (χρόνος) from Mimnermus; there seem to be no other examples. It is a difficulty that the lengthening of the body by a cubit (52cm = 21in.!) is anything but a small detail (ἐλάχιστον Luke 12:25!); why does it not say "finger" (2cm = 1in.)? But the cubit is simply the normal measurement for the body. The person of antiquity does not seem to have conceived of cubit as a large measure (German "ellenlang") but as something small, cf. the πήχεις (little children) in Liddell and Scott s.v. πῆχυς VI.

[47]Ἡλικία in the temporal meaning is *age* of life (e.g.: young age) and not *length* of life. Although the transitions may be fluid, this alone speaks decisively against the translation "add a yard to the length of his life" (e.g., Schweizer 160). Understood in a temporal sense, the sentence would have to say: "to add a cubit to the *age* of his life," i.e., to make his age older by a small amount of time. And who would want that?

[48]Olsthoorn* 44 refers to this. In the messianic age, people are to be 100 or 200 cubits in height (*b. B. Bat.* 75a; *b. Sanh.* 100a). But the sapiential principle of evidence speaks against an interpretation of a future hope which is not at all indicated by the text. But it is entirely possible that one wants to be a little taller already in this eon, cf., e.g., Zacchaeus in Luke 19:3!

To become taller is quite a conceivable desire.[49] This digression, in distinction from the two illustrations, breathes a submissive mood. No human being can alter the measure which God has set for him or her!

6:31-32
Verses 31-32 summarize the admonition. Important for Matthew is the reference back to his framing of the Lord's Prayer, 6:7f.[50] The following verses are to be understood in the light of the faith of the praying community, whose heavenly Father knows what they need even before they ask. This is to be considered most of all for the interpretation of βασιλεία and δικαιοσύνη in v. 33.

6:33
Βασιλεία is, as elsewhere in Matthew, the coming reign of God, which the community hopes to enter through judgment.[51] Δικαιοσύνη means the activity of righteousness which humans are to perform, i.e., that action which agrees with God and his kingdom.[52] Through the insertion of "righteousness" Matthew wanted to clarify that the seeking of the kingdom is not a passive waiting, not an only internal religious attitude, but a tangible practice of righteousness as the Sermon on the Mount unfolds it. The relationship of righteousness and kingdom of God is, in the sense of 5:20, the relation of human practice and promised reward: "His righteousness is that we are taught to act rightly; his kingdom that we know what is the reward which is established for work and patience."[53] Nevertheless, it does not mean works-righteousness, for what is demanded of the community is an acting toward the heavenly Father who knows their needs and listens to them before they ask. The juxtaposition of βασιλεία and δικαιοσύνη thus corresponds to the juxtaposition of the second and third petition of the Lord's Prayer, except that here the task of the person, there the asked-for action of God for and through the person stands in the foreground. Human acting includes the action of God: God will create his kingdom and, already now, simultaneously as an additional gift,[54] grant his disciples food and clothing (cf. Mark 10:30; 1 Tim. 4:8).

Summary
Verse 31-33 make clear finally that *Jesus* here is not concerned with humanity in general but that definite people are addressed. They are men and women who

---

[49]Wellhausen 29 ironically comments, "There are giants among the exegetes who find (this) wish . . . inconceivable."

[50]Olsthoorn* 71.

[51]Cf. above on 5:3 and 5:20.

[52]Cf. above on 3:15 and 5:6; detailed exegesis in Dupont, *Béatitudes* III, especially 288-304.

[53]So expressly *Ps-Clem. Rec.* 2.20 and Strecker, *Weg* 154.

[54]Aretius 66: "Corollarium" (corollary). The earthly gifts of God are secondary in regard to the kingdom.

know of the kingdom of God and are seized by it.[55] The whole text stands under the sign of the coming kingdom of God. God's concern for his creature becomes, in Jesus, encouragement for the disciples at the coming of the kingdom. Sapiential sayings material is here put in the service of a specific statement about the kingdom of God.[56] Probably Jesus formulated this saying as comfort and claim to his disciples who, with him and for the sake of the kingdom of God, no longer practiced their trade. It is bound to Jesus and his message of the kingdom of God and is far removed from being an expression of general theological wisdom. The double λέγω ὑμῖν (vv. 25,29), which maintains the connection to Jesus, is appropriate.

In the *Sayings Source*, the text probably was related primarily to itinerant radicals.[57] That is shown by the connection with Luke 12:2-12, notably with Luke 12:11f. Yet already here an opening is indicated: The sapiential additions vv. 25d,e,27 (and 34) show that one could understand Jesus' comfort *also* as an expression of a generally valid truth. It is in agreement with this observation that in early Christianity there was, in my opinion, no separation in principle between wandering radicals, who gave up the practice of a trade and family life, and resident followers of Jesus. Instead all adherents of Jesus were potential itinerant radicals and called into following him, just as these knew themselves responsible for the communities.

Matthew understood the text as addressed to the whole community, as is implied, e.g., by the key words "of little faith" and "righteousness." He also has seen in it more than comfort and a demand only to those who, like Jesus, in the fashion of the birds and lilies, lived without a trade and only in the care of God and for his kingdom. But he still knew that this text truly was rooted in early Christian itinerant radicalism. This is shown by the observation that he combined it with 6:19-24 and thus with the demand to give up one's possessions. Thus the imperatival character is stressed in the face of the settled community. While for Jesus and in the Sayings Source the renunciation of the practice of a trade and, in connection with it, probably the renunciation of (use of) possessions was the presupposition for our text, within the composition of Matt. 6:19-34 it becomes at least indirectly again a demand which is combined with the comfort of God's help. The history of interpretation demonstrates how the Matthean question concerning the renunciation of possessions for the followers of Jesus remained connected with this text and was discussed again

---

[55]Cf. especially Merklein, *Gottesherrschaft* 180,182.

[56]Therefore, there are no parallels to our text which meet *precisely* its assertion. The Hellenistic parallels, e.g., from Epictetus (in Heinrici** 76-79) are oriented to the inner freedom of the sage. It probably does not have to be explained at length that the often-quoted saying of the exemplary industry of the ant who gathers her food herself (Prov. 6:6-11) in every respect is *no* parallel to our text. Naturally, a general belief in providence, as, e.g., in *Pss. Sol.* 5:9-12, is widespread. For R. Nehorai (*p. Ber.* 13c toward the end) the reason for the fact that God preserves human life much more than that of worms is that they are useful in a completely different way. *Qidd.* 4:14 = Str-B I 436f., when speaking of God's concern for the animals, calls attention to the fact that they do not have a trade and yet are nourished by God without concern. But precisely this is not an analogy for R. Simeon b. Elazar, since he himself, in distinction from the animals, stands under the curse of sin, i.e., has to work like Adam (*p. Qidd.* 4,66b,38 = Str-B ibid.).

[57]So, correctly, G. Theissen, "Wanderradikalismus," in idem, *Studien* 85: It is not a question of joy over birds, flowers, and meadows. It is not the mood of a Sunday afternoon walk.

and again anew, also because the sayings about mammon (v. 24 and 6:25-34) were put together in one preaching pericope.[58]

6:34

Verse 34 belongs to the secondary interpretations of our text in sapiential style. It is linguistically difficult. Αὔριον in the Semitic environment may mean not only the morrow but as *pars pro toto* the future as such.[59] While the preceding neuter predicative ἀρκετόν is possible in Greek,[60] the genitive formulation μεριμνήσει ἑαυτῆς is very unusual.[61] Κακία does not have the ordinary meaning of moral turpitude but the more general one of trouble or misery. The content is just as difficult. A rather optimistic and a rather pessimistic interpretation of the verse are alternatives: (a) Optimistically understood, our verse may open up the possibility to live for today.[62] (b) But the pessimistic interpretation is more likely, because the verse ends on a pessimistic note with 34c: All planning is in vain; it is enough to bear the burden of the day.[63] This verse is extraordinary, because immediately prior to it the seeking of the kingdom of God was mentioned. The juxtaposition of the two verses shows how in early Christianity the hope of the kingdom of God by no means determined life throughout, but eschatological hope and pessimistic realism could stand immediately side by side. Human reality is here also more complex than a theological theory.

History of influence

Roughly, one can distinguish between (a) interpretations which, like the Sayings Source or Jesus himself, understand our text as comfort for disciples of Jesus who know themselves committed to the gospel in a special way and (b) interpretations which, by picking up the Matthean additions but also changing them, relate our text to all Christians. Everywhere the question of the renunciation of possessions stands in the center of attention but is solved differently. Very frequently the question of work is raised.

    a. It belongs to the principal differences between early Christian itinerant radicalism and monasticism that in the latter from a very early time work was evaluated

---

[58]Matt. 6:24-34 is the pericope for the 15th Sunday after Trinity or (*LBW*) 8th Epiphany A.

[59]Cf., e.g., Gen. 30:33; Exod. 13:14; Josh. 4:6.

[60]BDF §131.

[61]BDF §176 n. 2. In Syriac it is constructed with *jzp* + *d* which is a literal translation. Is there an Aramaic construction behind v. 34? Cf. M'Neile 89.

[62]Wesley, *Wesley's Standard Sermons* I 512, offers an explicit interpretation in this direction: "Live thou to-day. . . . The past is nothing, as though it had never been. The future is nothing to you: it is not yours; perhaps it never will be." Schleiermacher, *Predigten* I 163-66, just as impressively castigates the tendency to understand the present moment always only as preparation for duties which are to be done later, e.g., in education. D. Bonhoeffer, *Letters and Papers from Prison* (New York: Macmillan, 1953), 31f., seeks on the basis of 6:34 the "narrow way, a way often hardly to be found, of living every day as if it were our last, yet in faith . . . living as though a splendid future still lay before us." Not appropriate for the text, but it is in accordance with the gospel!

[63]The pessimistic parallel *b. Sanh.* 100b, mentioned in Str-B I 441, is different because it takes into account, as does James 4:13f., the possibility that the person could die tomorrow.

positively and even became the basic element of monastic life.[64] Genesis 3:17-19; 2 Thess. 3:10-12 and the apostolic example of Paul are here effective. We find renunciation of work espoused by the earliest Egyptian hermits, who relied for their food exclusively on God, and a little later by the Euchites or Messalians, who demanded unceasing prayer. In the Syriac *Liber Graduum*, the way of the perfect and the "side-road," leading away from perfection, are contrasted. It is part of perfection not to be concerned in the sense of Matt. 6:25-34. But a "side-road" is the apostolic axiom of 2 Thess. 3:10-12: Work and eat your own bread![65] The eschatological perspective is here translated into a strictly ascetic principal conception. The *perfecti* (perfect) have, so to speak, already left the earth; when they care neither for their own nor for the life of their brothers and sisters, they are similar to angels.[66] Augustine's polemical writing against the Messalians, the tract *De opere monachorum*,[67] testifies to the fact that Matt. 6:25-34 must have been a central text for the Messalian monks who, as "birds of the sky" (22[25]), did no manual labor. Augustine's writing is essentially an interpretation of Matt. 6:25-34, not a simple matter, since, with all the polemicism against the work-shy monks, he wants to defend at the same time the right of the priests not to engage in work.[68] Similar tones emerge here and there in the Middle Ages. The Waldensians rejected any kind of work for their preachers under appeal to Matt. 6:24-34.[69] Next to Gen. 3:17-19, in the Middle Ages Matt. 6:25-34 contributed much to the negative evaluation of work.[70]

But the positive evaluation of work is characteristic of monasticism as a whole. Antony hears our text in the church, gives away all his possessions, and becomes an ascetic. But in the same chapter of his influential biography, the manual labor of the young ascetic appears in reference to 2 Thess. 3:10.[71] Pachomius and his brother distribute the superfluity of their manual labor to the poor in accordance with Matt. 6:34.[72] The emphasis on work becomes an integral part of all monastic rules from Basilius to Francis of Assisi. The interpretation of our text is for the first time connected with a reference to Matt. 19:16-22 and placed under the sign of a "consilium . . . perfectionis" (counsel of perfection) by Rupert of Deutz. Pathetically he exclaims: "These sparrows," which have renounced everything and desire only to follow their Lord, "shall build nests among you"; "construite coenobia, fundate ecclesias" (construct monasteries, found churches).[73] The ecclesiastical domestication of these radical birds under the sign of the *consilium Evangelicum* (counsel of the gospel) becomes clear at this point.

---

[64]Cf. to the whole subject: H. Dörries, "Mönchtum und Arbeit," in idem, *Wort und Stunde* I (Göttingen: Vandenhoeck & Ruprecht, 1966), 277-301. Examples on ἀμεριμνία and on feeding by God in the beginnings of monasticism ibid. 279-81.

[65]*Liber Graduum* (ed. M. Kmosko, 1926 [PS 1]) 19,13 = 494f.

[66]Ibid. 25,8 = 754.

[67]Translation in *Frühes Mönchtum im Abendland*, ed. K. S. Frank, vol. 1 (Zürich: Artemis, 1975), 48-106.

[68]Matt. 6:25-34 as Messalian central text: 1 (2); 23 (27-30); freedom from work for the priests: 21 (24).

[69]V. Vinay, "Waldenser," *RGG* VI 1531; K. V. Selge, *Die ersten Waldenser*, AKG 37/1 (Berlin: de Gruyter, 1967), 50f.

[70]J. le Goff, "Arbeit V. Mittelalter," *TRE* 3,627.

[71]Athanasius, *Vita Ant.* 3 = BKV I/31 691-93.

[72]*Vita Pachom.* 6 = BKV I/31 812f.

[73]Rupert of Deutz 1443f., cf. Stoll** 113.

b. The *interpretation* of our text *in reference to all Christians* makes us feel the unrest which it has brought into the churches. Again and again it is emphasized what the text does *not* say, and its teeth become increasingly blunt. Of course, work is permitted—even commanded—on the basis of our text. Jerome puts it in a brief, often repeated formula: "Labor exercendus est, sollicitudo tollenda" (work is to be carried out, worry to be removed).[74] Possessions also are permitted; the issue is only their use. Therefore our text is applied parenetically; it stands in the service of the admonition to benevolence and almsgiving.[75] But, most of all, anxiety cannot be something absolutely forbidden. It is important to distinguish between concern that is permitted, even commanded, and concern that is contrary to the gospel. Of immeasurable help is v. 34, a verse which becomes so important that it frequently occupies the greatest space in the interpretation of our text. Examples: concern over the present, and only it, is permitted.[76] There is a "tomorrow" only in time; temporal, earthly concerns are forbidden; we are to think of eternity.[77] Concern out of love is commanded.[78] God prohibits exaggerated concern.[79] One has to distinguish between active zeal (σπουδή) and anxious worry.[80] In the framework of the two-kingdoms doctrine, a distinction is made between the necessary concern of the official person and the prohibited concern for oneself: a king, the father of a family, a subject has to be concerned in the context of his or her office, and not only for today but also for tomorrow.[81]

Both types of interpretation, here only briefly sketched, are adaptations, even domestications of our text. The first type, with its stable, positive juxtaposition and mutuality of Christian radicals, of monks and priests, and of the Christian people, is specifically Catholic; the second basic type, which is much more widespread, is found both in Catholicism and in Protestantism. The domestication becomes the more apparent the more the contrast between the kingdom of God, which occasioned the anxiety-free existence of the followers, and the world gave room to an amicable, peaceful coexistence. Especially the second type of interpretation can empty the text almost completely: it can link the text with a Protestant work ethic, affirmation of possessions, and reasonable planning and provision, all of which serves the general interest. What remains is the warning of "discouraged worry" and a "despondent heart," no longer in harmony with Christian trust in God.[82]

---

[74]Jerome on 6:25. Very poignant and therefore worth quoting among many other interpretations of this kind is S. Kierkegaard's interpretation in *Consider the Lilies* (London: Daniel, 1940), 37 (citation from p. 209): The anxious soul receives "in his distraction with the bird, something altogether other to think about than his anxiety; he came to think rightly *how splendid it is to work, how splendid it is to be a man.* Should he again forget it as he labours, ah, then . . . the bird . . . will recall what he has forgotten."

[75]Already in Cyprian, *Elem.* 9 = BKV I/34 268f.; still more beautifully in John Chrysostom 22.4 = 389f., explicitly as a preliminary stage.

[76]"De praesentibus . . . concessit debere esse sollicitos" (He has conceded that one must be concerned . . . about present matters) (Jerome on the passage).

[77]Augustine** 2.17 (56).

[78]Luther, II 187.

[79]Calvin, in Stadtland-Neumann** 39-41.

[80]Lapide 173f.

[81]Luther, WA 32**, 459 = *LW* 21, 193-94.

[82]W. Herrmann, *Ethik,* 5th ed. (Tübingen: Mohr, 1921), 155.

Meaning today

The text, which was continually subject to depletion in the history of interpretation, appears to be gaining new fascination today. It seems to open up the chance of "untroubled liveliness" and "free spontaneity"[83] for the person who is swamped by planning and is boxed in on all sides institutionally by being "taken care of." The contemporary person who is tired of constant Christian justification of possessions and wary of the emphasis on the surpassing value of work feels a fresh breeze. The exegete, however, in the name of the text, must warn against hasty fascination. The alternative life, which is indeed the subject of this text, is service for the kingdom of God, not simply an alternative life-style. According to Matthew, this *service* involves trust in God in the renunciation of worldly security. Without establishing laws, it confronts the whole community with this demand. Thus, the church today also must be asked what significance poverty, the forgoing of vocation, or renunciation of work could have in the service of the kingdom of God. The text does not prescribe a solution, but it does give obligatory directions and opens up alternative possibilities which we ourselves have to actualize.

Hardly anyone has understood this better than S. Kierkegaard, among whose favorite texts was Matt. 6:25-34.[84] He tells in "The Instant, No. 7" a story which senses the demand of the text just as clearly as the distance of his own situation from it. It is the story of the candidate of theology Ludvig From who "first" (cf. Matt. 6:33!) seeks a royal position as a pastor, who therefore "first" has to pass examinations, then passes "first" the candidate's exam and the seminary, then gets "first" engaged and finally, after he "had to" bargain "first" for his salary, stands in the pulpit and preaches his first sermon on the text, "Seek 'first' the kingdom of God." The bishop is impressed by the "sound, unadulterated doctrine," proclaimed here, particularly by the "whole part how he elaborated on this 'first'!—But does it not seem to your Lordship that in this instance a correspondence between speech and life would be desirable?"[85]

2.4.3. Do Not Judge (7:1-5)

Literature

Zeller, *Mahnsprüche* 113-17.
Further literature** on the Sermon on the Mount at Matt. 5-7 above, pp. 209-211.

Text

1 Do not judge, then you will not be judged.
2 For with the judgment with which you judge, you will be judged, and with the measure with which you measure, it will be measured to you.
3 Why do you look at the splinter in the eye of your brother,
  but do not notice the log in your eye?

---

[83]Reuter** 96.

[84]Cf. above n. 74, also, e.g., *Christian Discourses* (London: Oxford, 1940), 7-93; *The Gospel of Suffering and The Lilies of the Field* (Minneapolis: Augsburg, 1948), 165-239.

[85]"The Instant, No. 7," in *Kierkegaard's Attack upon "Christendom" 1854–1855,* ed. W. Lowrie (Princeton: Princeton University Press, 1944), 208-11.

4 Or how will you say to your brother, "Let it be. I will pull the splinter from
   your eye,"
   and behold, the log is in your own eye!
5 Hypocrite, pull first the log from your own eye,
   and then you will see clearly so that you can pull the splinter from the eye
   of your brother.

Analysis

1. *Structure*. The piece consists of two different parts: vv. 1-2. and vv. 3-5. In
the present arrangement, the prohibition—in the plural and, as 6:19,25; 7:6, formulated
with μή—is a superscribed title. The sapiential admonition, vv. 3-5, formulated in the
singular, is an intensification, pointed to the individual (cf. the similar change in
5:21-26, 27-30, 38-42). Verses 3-5 consist of two double questions and a concluding
admonition, i.e., three parts of two phrases each. No strictly maintained parallelism can
be determined. Through the manifold repetition of κάρφος, δόκος, ὀφθαλμός,
–βάλλω, and ἀδελφός, the text makes a unified impression. The threefold ἀδελφός
indicates that the community is meant.

2. Matthean *redaction* can hardly be noticed. Verse 2a (missing in Luke) may
be secondary to v. 1 in the history of tradition, but was at hand for Matthew, just as for
the third evangelist (vv. 37b-38b, QMt or QLk). The Lukan logia vv. 39 and 40 appear
elsewhere in Matthew; there is in my opinion no definite clue that Matthew had read
them in his Q copy.[1] Verses 3-5 agree almost word for word with the Lukan parallel;
except for ἰδού (v. 4) nothing is redactional with any degree of probability.

3. *Origin*. Verse 1 is almost universally attributed to Jesus because of its
radicality, while v. 2a + b is considered a secondary argumentation.[2] Verses 3-5, it seems
to me, are a unified piece of tradition[3] which does not offer any clear indications for
analyzing its history of tradition.[4] The text is a prime example of how uncertain
judgments of genuineness can be. It fits well into the proclamation of Jesus which speaks
of love and forgiveness. Its hyperbolically pointed formulation and its direct address also
fit linguistically with Jesus.[5] It does not seem to be influenced by the problems of the
later community, e.g., the question of community discipline. On the other hand, it does
not show any direct traces of Jesus' proclamation of the kingdom of God and is in no way
original in comparison with several Jewish statements. We have here one of many
instances where the criterion of dissimilarity fails completely. Verses 3-5 are a Jewish
text which fits Jesus and therefore *can* be from Jesus!

---

[1]Schürmann, *Lukasevangelium* I 362, assumes on the basis of reminiscences that vv. 37bf. were already in Q; on pp. 369f. he argues the same thing for vv. 39f. Matthew knew and abbreviated these verses, he thinks. But that is only a vague possibility, it seems to me.

[2]Verse 2b is a generally known principle which has been handed down also in Mark 4:24 in a completely different context. Then v. 2a might have been added as a supplementary parallel verse to this earlier secondary argumentation (= Q), using the vocables of v. 1 and the structure of v. 2b.

[3]Zeller, *Mahnsprüche* 114, considers vv. 3-5 as a formulation of the community which explains vv. 1f. But why then the unmediated transition into the second person singular?

[4]For Schweizer 107 it is the original kernel, v. 4 (Hellenistic formulation because of ἄφες?) a first expansion, and v. 5 (interest of the community in "brotherly" criticism) a second expansion. There are no criteria for this thesis, it seems to me, in regard to the history of tradition and to form.

[5]Cf. 23:26 and Mark 10:25.

History of influence

The most important question is that of the extent of Jesus' prohibition to judge. Is it only an instruction for dealings between individuals? The metaphorical admonition of the splinter and the log (vv. 3-5) might speak in favor of this assumption. Or does it concern more, namely, a basic questioning of all judging, even judicial activity in the state and in society? The foundational formulation of v. 1 might speak in favor of this latter view.

a. The great majority of interpreters are in agreement that the judicial system of the state must not be disputed by our verses.[6] But even the judicial power of the church must not be limited. The interpreters point untiringly to Ananias and Sapphira (Acts 5:1-11) or the immoral person in Corinth (1 Cor. 5:1-8). Only in polemics, in regard to other churches, critical questions about the ecclesiastical legal system are raised.[7] Judging is not forbidden for those who have a church office.[8] The giving up of ecclesiastical jurisdiction or leniency would not lead to repentance but to moral indifference and general laxity.[9] Thus the field of application of our text is primarily the everyday life, the precipitate judgment of people on people, the "assessment, talking behind the back, and condemning."[10] Love and sisterly forgiveness are opposed to it. This understanding is old; already the combination of the prohibition of judging and the commandment of forgiveness in *1 Clem.* 13:2 and Pol. *Phil.* 2:3 points in this direction. But here also the prohibition is not absolutely valid. The measure for judging is love: in case of doubt, one should judge the neighbor "in meliorem partem" (to give the neighbor the benefit of doubt) and not draw hidden sin into the light.[11] The warning against hasty judging is found repeatedly.[12] Verse 5 is understood as a positive direction: the one who has reproved himself or herself and *then* reprimands others is not a "iudex perversus" (perverse judge) but does that which is commanded by the gospel.[13] All these examples demonstrate how this command of the Sermon on the Mount has been made practicable and has become a part of Christian personal ethics.

---

[6]I will forgo the listing of exemplary references and only point out that our text hardly plays a role in books on Christian ethics in our time when the problem of courts and punishment is discussed. H. Thielicke, *Theologische Ethic* III, (Tübingen, 1964), 377 (ET: *Theological Ethics,* vol. 3: *Sex* [Grand Rapids: Eerdmans, 1979]) is a noteworthy exception: Matt. 7:1f. is a reference to the fact that "the human being himself or herself transcends the order of law," so that all order of law is only a "way" for the human being, not a goal.

[7]Cocceius 15 argues against confession and papal jurisdiction.

[8]Already Irenaeus, *Haer.* 4.30.3 defends the internal ecclesiastical reprimand in light of Matt. 7:1f. Even earlier, according to *Didascalia* 9 (Achelis-Flemming 52), Matt. 7:1 applies only to the layperson, not to the bishop.

[9]Tertullian argues for a harsh penitential practice toward an episcopal opponent (Callistus?) who appeals for his lenient penitential practice to Matt. 7:1 (*Pud.* 2 = BKV I/24 728-31).

[10]Bullinger on the passage.

[11]Augustine** 2.18 (59); cf. Bengel on the passage: "Nolite iudicare sine scientia, amore, necessitate" (Do not judge without knowledge, love, necessity); Calvin I 227 encourages brotherly judging "ad regulam caritatis" (according to the rule of love) and opposes only the abusive judging of fellow believers.

[12]In some commentaries, the title of the exegesis even is: "Temerarium iudicium" (ill-advised judgment), i.e., in Lapide 175. Cf. already Augustine** 2.18 (61).

[13]Bengel on 7:5.

b. In monasticism, among the Anabaptists and other nonconformists, the prohibition of judgment was understood more radically. It is true that it was almost always applied only to the individual Christian (and to a certain extent to the community). But here something of the contrast between Christianity and secular structures becomes apparent. Syrian and Egyptian monasticism should be mentioned first. For the Anchorites this saying is absolutely the central theme, the focus of Christian existence as such. It is "as if there were for these people in the wilderness only this one word."[14] The stories which narrate how the fathers consistently have forgone any kind of judging are numerous.[15] F. von Lilienfeld says that "they are aware of the fact that Jesus' proclamation of the reign of God includes a reversal of the standards of the world and that they live out this reversal conscientiously. If they live in the 'practice' even of only one of the words of Jesus, then they have taken the step 'out of the world' toward the βασιλεία τοῦ θεοῦ."[16] However, this eschatological existence of the monks on the margin of the world in the wilderness does not put the world into question but leaves it alone. The *perfecti* (perfect) to whom the absolute prohibition of judging applies and the "children," the "little ones,"[17] live next to and for each other. Institutionalized monasticism, in whose rules the prohibition to judge is found,[18] thus also is one way in which the kingdom of God is successfully made at home as a marginal phenomenon of the world. The history of the Anabaptists shows similar results.[19]

Other cases where conflict arose are found in church history. The attempt of the radical nonconformists under Harrison to abolish courts of justice failed, because of the resistance of Cromwell and the moderates.[20] Tolstoy for philological reasons was forced to refer Matt. 7:1 to secular courts and began to doubt the honesty of all interpreters since the early church who had asserted the opposite.[21]

Interpretation

7:1

Verse 1, as the oldest part of the composition, has to be interpreted first by itself. Κρίνω has a wide field of meanings; the text does not give any indication for a restricted meaning. Therefore it is best to translate it in the general meaning as "judging," "being active as a judge," "to render judgments"; Luke then specifies the general κρίνω by means of καταδικάζω (condemn).

---

[14]Beyschlag, *ZTK* 1977**, 318.

[15]Examples in Beyschlag, *ZTK* 1977**, 319 and in the translation by B. Miller, *Weisung der Väter* (Freiburg: Lambertus, 1965) (Sophia 6), Index "Urteilen"; H. Dörries, *Wort und Stunde* I (Göttingen: Vandenhoeck & Ruprecht, 1966), 167, 268f.

[16]"Jesuslogion und Väterspruch. Die synoptischen Jesusreden in der Auslegung der Agroikoi der Wüste," *SB* 1 (1966), 174.

[17]*Liber Graduum*, ed. M. Kmosko (1926 [PS 1]) 11,3 = 278; cf. 5,10 = 118.

[18]Basilius, *Regulae brevius* 164 = *PG* 31,1189-91.

[19]Peter Walpot, *Das grosse Artikelbuch, Vom Schwert* no. 31 = QGT 12,251. Under Menno Simons the Anabaptists still were not permitted to accept the office of judge.

[20]Troeltsch** 818.

[21]Tolstoy** 21-37 (section III).

"In order that you be not judged" points to the eschatological equivalent:[22] in order that God does not judge you the same way in his judgment. Similar sapiential admonitions are directed at first to the individual;[23] but the sapiential dimension is ruptured by the eschatological apodosis. In the Sayings Source, this saying stood immediately after the section on the love of enemies—which was meant universally and as a principle and went beyond personal hostilities. With Jesus, we encounter not only a completely judgment-free fellowship with outcasts like sinners and toll collectors but also a noteworthy indifference toward the law of God prevalent in Israel, shown, e.g., in the story of the adulterous woman (John 7:53-8:11) or indirectly in the fact that Jesus was not greatly concerned for the halakah. All this speaks in favor of not limiting the application of our sentence to the personal realm. As the command to love one's enemies, so this demand probably should be understood in the context of Jesus' eschatology: The kingdom of God is coming; there must in principle be an end to the judging of human beings by others.[24]

7:2

Verse 2 in explanation makes reference to a principle which was generally held in business life,[25] in everyday life, in law, and also in regard to the last judgment: measure for measure. Verse 2a explains what that means for God's judgment: since we all will have to face God's judgment, those measures which we apply to others will be applied to us. These (perhaps secondary) clarifications do not absolutely signify a restriction in the sense of the warning: When you judge, think of the judgment of God. The idea also may be: If God in the judgment uses the principle "measure for measure," then all people are such "debtors" that they should forgo judging at all. A Matthean story which illustrates this and thus recommends limitless forgiving is Jesus' story of the unmerciful servant (18:23-35).[26]

---

[22]One cannot speak of a sentence of law (E. Käsemann, "The Beginnings of Christian Theology," in *NT Questions of Today*, 98-99), since it is neither a matter of a legal demand nor of a fixed form of a sentence of law. Rather it is the eschatological elaboration of a general Old Testament conception of correspondence. Cf. Sato, *Q* 310-26, who gives further examples for pre-Christian formulations of correspondence. Cf. above, n. 37 on 5:21-26.

[23]Zeller, *Mahnsprüche* 117, therefore thinks that the law is not at all in view in 7:1.

[24]There are no real Jewish parallels to v. 1. Parenetical admonitions like *'Abot* 1:6 = Str-B I 441 (judge everyone "in meliorem partem" [with the benefit of the doubt]); *'Abot* 2,4 = ibid. (judge only if you are yourself in the situation of the neighbor); *b. Šabb.* 127b (no precipitate inculpations); *2 Enoch* 44:4f. ("Happy is he who directs [his heart] toward every person, such as bringing help to him who has been condemned, . . . because on [the day of] the great judgment every measure and every weight . . . will be exposed as in the market").

[25]Examples from papyri in B. Couroyer, "De la mesure dont vous mesurez il vous sera mesuré," *RB* (1970) 366-70.

[26]Schlatter 240 correctly says: The forgiveness which the disciple in following Jesus has received as "his share in God and his kingdom" essentially is a presupposition for the prohibition to judge.

7:3-5

The admonition to think first of the log in one's own eye is—like the admonitions to forgo the use of force (Matt. 5:39-41)—an exemplary illustration of the principle of 7:1. Thus the verses by no means want to limit the principle of not judging *only* to the admonition to see first the log in one's own eye when one deals with the neighbor.[27] Rather it is a specific example in the area of interpersonal relations. The sharpness of the verses lies not in the fact that the ego of the judging individual is put in a new light. The judging one becomes one who is judged. The tangible power of the metaphors is impressive.[28] The hyperboles of the splinter and the log are "a blow struck at the heart of the man who knows good and evil."[29] The listener is questioned, is startled. The direct address with "you" (singular) intensifies this effect. On the basis of vv. 11f. you know the judgment which threatens your "log." The repeated expression ἀδελφός (brother or sister) intensifies in the Christian community the "thrust": the fellow human being whose little fault one likes to expose is a Christian brother or sister. The metaphors strengthen the grotesqueness: while it can happen that one has a little splinter in one's eye, the log in one's own eye bursts open all conceivable dimensions. The listeners are asked whether they would not have to see their own sin in this way. It is also a deliberate intensification that the log is in the eye. Whoever has a log in the eye is completely blind and therefore cannot at all judge concerning the splinter in the eye of the neighbor!

Verse 5 shows that this is thought through. Τότε διαβλέψεις means: Then you will see clearly. The appended infinitive must have purposive or consecutive meaning:[30] Only then will you be able to remove the splinter in the eye of the brother or sister. Verse 5 is not meant ironically: if you then still have the desire, you may find fault with your brother or sister![31] Instead, it clarifies that the meaning of our admonition is not the protection of the private sphere against unjustified interference by others. It does not simply mean that everybody should sweep before his or her own door or nobody should poke his or her nose into the affairs of the other. Rather the concern is a behavior in relation to the community in which even the splinter of the brother or sister remains a splinter.

---

[27]The church interpretation makes the exemplary application into a restrictive exclusivity by constantly arguing that the text does not refer to the judicial power of the state or the church, etc.

[28]Whether the hyperbole was newly created (by Jesus?) or follows a Jewish phrase is disputed. Since the closest Jewish parallel in Rabbi Tarphon (c. 110, *b. 'Arak.* 16b = Str-B I 446) stands in a polemic context, it is conceivable that Tarphon here polemicizes against the abuse of a saying coming from Jesus.

[29]D. Bonhoeffer, *Ethics* (New York: Macmillan, 1955), 154.

[30]BDF §§391-392.

[31]If you explain v. 5, because of the radicality of its statement ironically (e.g., Guelich** 352f.; Bonnard 97; Schürmann, *Lukasevangelium* I 371), you have difficulty with the future of the verb διαβλέπω: The verb is a compound with intensified meaning that signifies: "to look with wide open eyes," "to see clearly" (Liddell and Scott s.v.). With the ironic interpretation, the future tense is understood as a sort of mocking potential ("then you may try to see" = Schürmann, ibid. 367). But is there such a future tense in Greek? It is simplest to understand the future tense διαβλέψεις as a true future, cf. the translation.

The sin of the brothers and sisters is not simply a private matter. It seems to me questionable in Matthew's sense whether then the assistance of the brother or sister, whose log was removed, at the removal of the splinter can still have the character of "judging." Since he himself does not accentuate the section in his redaction, one may only ask on the basis of his entire Gospel what may have been important to him. Then it is remarkable that he interprets the admonition and the order for excommunication of his community (18:15-20) on the basis of forgiveness and perhaps also has criticized it indirectly (18:12-14,21-35). In his view, it probably also is appropriate when older and more recent interpreters think of the petition for forgiveness of the Lord's Prayer (6:12, cf. 14f.).[32]

Summary

Above all, this text also stands for Matthew under the demand of perfection (5:48). Then perhaps the radical attempt of the monks to actualize it would have had his approval. However, *programmatic* limitation of this command of Jesus to the personal relationship of the members of the community among themselves (which in the history of interpretation has taken the place of the *exemplary* application of vv. 1-2 by vv. 3-5) indicates a limitation of its thrust. Both for Jesus and for Matthew the text is to be understood in view of the kingdom of God.

2.4.4. Do Not Give What Is Holy to the Dogs (7:6)

Text

6 Do not give what is holy to the dogs,
   and do not throw your pearls before the swine,
   in order that they do not trample them under foot
   and turn around and tear you to pieces.

The logion is a riddle. Neither (a) its origin nor (b) its original meaning nor (c) its meaning in the Matthean context can be completely made clear.

a. It is a classical playground for Aramaists. Already J. A. Bolten in 1792 thought that behind τὸ ἅγιον stands a mistranslation of the Aramaic קְדָשָׁא or קָדְשָׁא (the ring) with "what is holy."[1] His proposal has been enhanced since then by various proposals by which the original text was reconstructed with additional mistranslations and with the aid of considerations of rhythm.[2] The various attempts threaten to cancel each other. Nevertheless, Bolten's proposal is still noteworthy. The logion might originally have warned, in a certain kinship to Prov. 11:22, against giving gold rings to dogs and pearls to swine. But for what purpose?

b. But the Greek text is decisive for the interpretation. In antiquity, dogs were not among the valued domestic animals but were often half-wild, roaming around, and

---

[32]John Chrysostom in Thomas, *Kette* I 282; *Opus imperfectum* 17,1 = 725.

[1]*Der Bericht des Matthäus von Jesu dem Messia* (Altona, 1792), 119. A. Meyer, *Jesu Muttersprache* (Freiburg: Mohr, 1896), 105-18, reports in detail about Bolten's work.

[2]I will only mention F. Perles, "Zur Erklärung von Mt 7,6" *ZNW* 25 (1926) 163f.; J. Jeremias, "Matthäus 7,6a," in idem, *Abba* 83-89; G. Schwarz, "Matthäus 7,6a," *NovT* 14 (1972) 18-25.

were usually despised.[3] The unclean pig, which is in rabbinical texts proscribed as unmentionable, was the quintessence of that which is abominable; in many a text, "swine" appears as a metaphor for "Gentiles" or "Rome."[4] In Jewish and non-Jewish texts, dog and swine are mentioned together.[5] Conversely, pearls are the most precious things one can think of.[6] That which is holy can be explained in general but also specifically as the sacrificial meat which should not be thrown to the dogs.[7]

All expressions are metaphorical. The verse could express a warning almost like a proverb: Words of the wise are not for blockheads. There are close parallels.[8] But one may also start out from the idea that swine and—to a lesser degree—dogs were common metaphors for Gentiles.[9] Then the verse would warn against giving the proclamation —perhaps even more exactly: the whole of the law and its "pearls," i.e., its interpretations[10]—to Gentiles. The word would come from a Jewish-Christian community. Less probable is the interpretation that it refers to Christian apostates,[11] on the basis of thought associations aroused by "dog" and "swine."

c. The meaning in the Matthean context is just as uncertain. The widespread allegorical interpretation as a warning against the Gentile mission is not fitting for Matthew.[12] The warning against Christian apostates fits just as little. A general wisdom saying, warning against blockheads, also is rather meaningless; what blockheads would be meant in the context? The thesis that v. 6 is a mitigating gloss which is intended to restrict vv. 3-5 is popular: There are limits to brotherliness. But in vv. 3-5 the subject was the reprimand of the sinful brother or sister, in v. 6 the subject is not sin but that which is holy.

I propose not to interpret the logion at all in its Matthean context. Matthew was a conservative author; he took it over from his tradition because it stood in his copy of Q.

d. Since our logion never was truly anchored in the Matthean context, it had to a high degree the same fate in its *history of interpretation* which we can observe elsewhere: The logia were separated again from their context and had an effect as individual sayings. Thus our saying could be used in a manifold way, for the protection of the gospel, of the perfect law, of the ecclesiastical *communio* (communion), of heavenly wisdom, of baptism, of the eucharist, against the Gentiles, heretics, mockers,

---

[3]O. Michel, "κύων κτλ., *TDNT* III 1101f.

[4]Str-B I 448-50.

[5]Horatius, *Ep.* 1.2.26; 2.2.75; Isa. 66:3; *b. Šabb.* 155b = Str-B I 448.

[6]Cf. Matt. 13:46.

[7]Cf. the rabbinic discussion whether the meat of sacrificial animals, if they have a blemish, can be thrown to the dogs: *m.Tem.* 6:5; *b. Bek.* 15a = Str-B I 447; further examples ibid. The answer normally was negative, but *b.Pesah* shows that the question was controversial. In *Jos.As.* 10:13, Asenath after her conversion throws her Gentile sacrifices to the dogs for food.

[8]Prov. 26:11; Ginza R 7,217 = Lidz. 218,30.

[9]Swine: Str-B I 449f.; dogs: Str-B I 724f.

[10]Pearls among the rabbis are beautiful sayings or interpretations by rabbis, Str-B I 447f.

[11] In 2 Peter 2:22, sayings on the dog and the swine are interpreted as referring to the heretics. In Phil. 3:2; Ign. *Eph.* 7:1, heretics are called dogs. In *Barn.* 10:3f. the Old Testament swine are allegorically interpreted as sinners. The widespread interpretation in the early church of the dogs as referring to apostates follows the verse Prov. 26:11, cited in 2 Peter 2:22, of the dog who returns to its vomit.

[12]Already Zwingli 240 and Calvin I 229 point to the New Testament command to mission in 28:16-20.

immoral children of the world, or ordinary believers. The use of the text in support of the secret discipline at the Lord's Supper, which is shown already in *Did.* 9:5, was very influential, in harmony with the later liturgical principle: That which is holy for the holy ones![13]

2.4.5. Courage to Pray (7:7-11)

Literature

Brox, N., "Suchen und Finden. Zur Nachgeschichte von Mt 7,7b; Lk 11,9b," in *Orientierung an Jesus* (FS J. Schmid), ed. P. Hoffmann, pp. 17-36 (Freiburg: Herder, 1973).

Koschorke, K., " 'Suchen und Finden' in der Auseinandersetzung zwischen gnostischem und kirchlichem Christentum," *WuD* 15 (1977) 51-65.

Piper, R., "Matthew 7,7-11 par. Luke 11,9-13: Evidence of Design and Argument in the Collection of Jesus' Sayings," in *Logia,* ed. J. Coppens and J. Delobel, BETL 59, pp. 411-18 (Leuven: University Press, 1982).

Theunissen, M., "'Ο αἰτῶν λαμβάνει. Der Gebetsglaube Jesu und die Zeitlichkeit des Christseins," in *Jesus, Ort der Erfahrung Gottes,* ed. B. Casper, 2d ed., pp.13-68 (Freiburg: Herder, 1976).

Zeller, *Mahnsprüche* 127-31.

Further literature** on the Sermon on the Mount at Matt. 5-7 above pp. 209-211.

Text

  7 Ask, and it will be given to you.
     Seek, and you will find.
     Knock, and it will be opened to you.
  8 For every one who asks receives,
     and the one who seeks finds,
     and to the one who knocks it will be opened.
  9 Or who among you is a person
     whom his son will ask for bread:
     Will he give him a stone[1]?
 10 Or he will ask him for a fish:
     Will he give him a serpent?
 11 If you then who are evil know to give good gifts to your children,
     how much more will your Father in the heavens give good things to those
     who ask him?

Analysis

    1. *Structure.* The pericope makes a unified impression. The triple exhortation (v. 7) is followed by a triple foundation (v. 8). A double parable follows, the symmetry of which is disturbed only by the fact that v. 10 is lightly shortened. The conclusion again is of two members and contains a conclusion *a minore* (from the smaller [to the greater]). The individual parts are closely connected by the key words αἰτέω (5 times)

---

[13]Cyril of Jerusalem, *Cat. Myst.* 5:19.

[1]The awkward translation of vv. 9f. attempts to render the un-Greek construction. There are clear Semitisms with an opening question instead of a conditional protasis, cf. Beyer, *Syntax* 287-93. The numerous textual-critical variants indicate the effort to make the text more precise.

and formations from the stem (δι)δο– (6 times). There is no strict rhythm.

2. *Redactional* are the formulation (πατήρ) ὑμῶν ὁ ἐν τοῖς οὐρανοῖς (v. 11) and perhaps ἄνθρωπος (v. 9).[2] The Matthean redaction of this Q text is again very modest; the most important Matthean alteration is his placing of this passage before the end of the main part of the Sermon on the Mount (cf. on 6:19–7:11). Only the second of the two parables in vv. 9f. has a parallel in Luke. The Lukan comparison with the egg and the scorpion is, according to most exegetes, secondary in comparison with Matthew.[3]

3. *Origin.* The section is a unit; a history of traditions analysis does not seem possible. It probably comes from Jesus.

Interpretation

7:7

The text begins with an admonition to ask. The tripartite variation heightens the urgency. All three verbs, αἰτέω, ζητέω,[4] and κρούω, have a religious dimension in Jewish-Christian usage: one asks or seeks God,[5] one knocks on the "gates of mercy."[6]

7:8

The reasoning for the exhortation is based on the certainty that God hears the one who prays. In comparison with v. 7, the accent has shifted; it now lies each time on the second verb. The Greek translator chose the present tense for two of the verbs in order to make clear that the promise of answer to prayer is valid not exclusively for the eschaton.[7] The text is formulated as openly as possible: *everyone* who asks, receives. Any limitation, e.g., to certain groups of praying people, contradicts its flow.

7:9-10

The promise of answer is explained through the two illustrations. They are taken

---

[2]Cf. introduction 3.2.

[3]But cf. below n. 10: does the comparison fish/serpent fit Syria, i.e., the home of the Matthean community?

[4]Cf. C. Westermann, "Die Begriffe für Fragen und Suchen im Alten Testament," *KD* 6 (1960), esp. 13f.

[5]To seek *God:* Jer. 29:13f. (parallel: find); Isa. 65:1 (not to seek / find); Isa. 55:6 (parallel: find); Sir. 32 (35):14 Hebrew; 1 QS 1:1f., cf. 5:11; of *wisdom:* Prov. 8:17; 4 Ezra 5:9f. (seek / not find). Greek examples: Plato, *Tim.* 28c (the heavenly is not easy to find; repeated by Justin *Apol.* 2.10.6 and by Tertullian, *Apol.* 46.9 in contrast to any Christian tradesman who has found God!); Clement of Alexandria, *Strom.* 4.5.1 = BKV II/19 13 (Pronouncement of Pythia); Epictetus, *Diss.* 1.28.20; 4.1.51 (ζήτει καὶ εὑρήσεις as admonition to philosophical searching). Especially the oft-cited passage of Plato makes understandable why Matt. 7:7b could have a history of influence which was widely independent from the context, cf. below nn. 26-30.

[6]Figurative usage only in rabbinical Judaism; examples in Str-B I 458; Fiebig** 141.

[7]No differentiation is possible in Aramaic; one has to assume either the imperfect or the participle, both of which probably were at that time neutral in regard to time.

from everyday life. Bread and fish belong to the basic food of the Jews.[8] The association of bread and stone is traditional;[9] they also have a similar appearance. The same applies in a certain way to serpent and fish.[10] The two illustrations are used because of the contrast "useless / useful," not, as in Luke, because of the contrast "dangerous / useful." Jesus' absolute formulation of the certainty of answer is not unheard-of for the believing Jew of his time. In contrast to the formulation in 6:7f. which is still more pointed, there are numerous Jewish parallels to our text.[11] Thus the function of the two parables is not that they explain something unknown or alienate people's expectations. By pointing up and sharpening a well-known Jewish statement of faith, their function is rhetorical.[12] They are intended—by means of the introduction to the parable, "who among you"—to attract the listener, so to speak, to have an effect on him or her.[13] The stylistic tool of duplication intensifies the effect.

7:11

The parables work with the principle of evidence. It is not simply lifted to the theological level, however, but is heightened through the πόσῳ μᾶλλον: the love of God is much more certain than the love of the earthly father. Only faith can formulate in this way; the "rational access" to "believing certainty"[14] is surpassed by faith. Already the choice of illustration—the father—was made under the presupposition of the faith of Jesus in his heavenly Father. The conception of God is not projected simply in such a way that a human experience of love with earthly fathers is transferred to God. Instead, the one who is founded on faith in the heavenly Father can, in the—admittedly ambiguous—experience of the love of earthly fathers, recognize helpful pointers to the heavenly Father. Faith in God stands at the beginning of this parable and is not its result. The reference to the evil of humans is a rhetorical means which

[8]On the eating of fish, cf. Krauss, *Archäologie* I 110f.

[9]Cf. Matt. 4:3; Prov. 20:17; Horatius Flaccus, *Sat.* 1.5.91; Seneca, *Ben.* 2.7.1 (*panis lapidosus* [stony bread] as a figure of speech); further examples in Wettstein I 270. Aristophanes, *Pax* 119, also is comparable (the children ask for bread and say πάππας).

[10]H. B. Tristram, *The Survey of Western Palestine: The Fauna and Flora of Palestine* (London: Committee of the Palestine Exploration Fund, 1889), gives a survey of the kinds of fish prevalent in the Jordan area: Eel-like fish, which are prima facie suggested, can apparently not be found; but they are "most abundant" in the lake of Antioch, ibid. 177! In Lake Gennesaret, on the other hand, there is the catfishlike "raven fish" (Josephus, *War* 3.520). Raven fish and eel are forbidden to the Jews according to Lev. 11:10. Result: the similarity between fish and serpent should not be overworked.

[11]Old Testament: Jer. 29:12f.; Isa. 49:15; Ps. 50:15; Job 22:27; Jewish, e.g., *Midr.Ps.* 4 § 3 (21b); *p. Ber.* 9,13b,7 (both Str-B I 453; contrast of God with a friend or patron who acts negatively); Lev.R. 34 (132a) = Str-B I 459 (comparison with a harsh man of flesh and blood; conclusion *a minore*). Only πᾶς, v. 8a, goes beyond the parallels.

[12]Jülicher's theory on parables does not fit all parables, but it fits formally this parable.

[13]The phrase τίς ἐξ ὑμῶν is a rhetorical appeal and not prophetic (thus H. Greeven, "Wer unter euch . . . ?" *WuD* 3 [1952] 100); it is found expressly in appeals to the evidence (cf. Luke 11:5; Matt. 6:27; 12:11; and Zeller, *Mahnsprüche* 84).

[14]In correcting Zeller, *Mahnsprüche* 130.

tends to intensify the certainty of faith.[15] "Good gifts"[16] is formulated in such a general way that any limitation of the promise (e.g.: *only* good gifts!) would contradict the scope of the text. As in 6:7f., so here also the point is to give courage to "childlike" prayer;[17] the certainty of answer does not make the prayer superfluous but possible.

Summary and history of influence

Again the unconditional trust of Jesus in the loving Father becomes apparent. Such faith awakens admiration but also criticism.[18] Is Jesus, in "the full magnificency and simplicity of his faith,"[19] not also naive and blind to reality?

One may understand the history of interpretation of our text as a struggle over this question and also as an attempt to relate our text to the reality of life. Usually the promise of our text is limited. The limitation occurs in three aspects:

a. Not every petition is answered! God gives only good gifts. The text refers to spiritual gifts.[20] Nor does God grant immediately that which is asked for.

b. The center of the text reverts back to the imperative in v. 7. The important consideration is *how* one prays! Thus the text is an exhortation to diligent, enduring, persistent prayer.[21] If prayer is not answered, the conclusion is simple: You simply have not prayed aright. "The one who does not find has not sought."[22] A widespread interpretation of v. 8 also is related to this making the text into a parenesis: the juxtaposition of asking, seeking, and knocking is no longer a juxtaposition of more intensive synonyms but a presentation of a *way* of praying, which, e.g., may lead from asking at the beginning to the final knocking at the heavenly "door," Christ.[23] In such limitations, real experiences are reflected. They must be considered seriously even where they do not maintain the absolute promise of God which lies in the text.

---

[15]Similar to Lev.R. 34 (132a) above n. 11. The history of interpretation spoke here (primarily only in Protestantism) occasionally of original sin (Bengel 55; "illustre testimonium de peccato originali"

[clear testimony to original sin]; cf. Jülicher, *Gleichnisreden* II 40: "an unforgiveable lack of good taste in the 19th century") but noted in most cases that the "evil" humans are mentioned only in rhetorical contrast to the one good God (19:17!).

[16]A rabbinic expression: *Mek. Exod.* 20.23 (79b) in Str.-B I 459.

[17]One also could have judged critically: Simeon b. Shetah in m. Ta'an. 3:8 criticizes the "childlike" importunity of Honi's prayer to his Father.

[18]Cf. the ambivalent utterance by Loisy I 631: "La foi ne connaît pas les scrupules de la théologie" (Faith does not know the scruples of theology).

[19]Montefiore, *Gospels* II 549.

[20]John Chrysostom 23.4 = 318 (the necessary, spiritual gifts); Thomas, *Lecture* no. 644 ("quod expedit" [that which is helpful]). Allegorical interpretation of bread: Christ, holy doctrine, love; of fish: "intelligentia in dogmatibus, fides" (insight in dogmatics, faith) (all in Thomas, ibid. no. 645). Very impressive the *Opus imperfectum* whose author—an exception in the early church—states emphatically that the fulfillment of the Sermon on the Mount is not completely possible: Christ now turns the people over to the one for whom nothing is impossible. He admonishes them to ask "ut quod ex vobis hominibus consummari non potest, per gratiam Dei adimpleatur" (that that which cannot be fulfilled by you humans, be fulfilled through the grace of God) (18 = 730).

[21]Especially emphasized are endurance and persistence (= seek), importunity and fervent desire (= knock), John Chrysostom 23.4 = 317.

[22]Origen, fragment 138 I = 69.

[23]Lapide 177 gives a fine survey.

c. A third kind of limitation of the promise of the text is less frequent: God only listens to Christians, not, e.g., to Jews and Turks[24]—a clear contradiction to v. 8a ($\pi\tilde{\alpha}\varsigma$!) and the expression of a theology which no longer thinks that the promise of God's love precedes in reality the formation of a community.

The exegesis can answer our question only partially on the basis of the history of interpretation. *Jesus'* certainty of answer belongs most likely with his hope for the coming of the kingdom of God, a hope unbroken until his death.[25] In a superficial sense it failed. Was it blind to reality? In any case, Jesus submitted to his death out of the power of this hope. For *Matthew*, answer to prayer means the presence of the Lord Jesus Christ with his community until the close of the age (Matt. 28:20). He makes this clear by his entire story of Jesus: God has led the Lord, who is present with his community, through suffering and dying to resurrection. Christian faith in prayer in no way means for Matthew that the heavenly Father will spare his community from all suffering and will fulfill all requests in a superficial sense. But this is not anywhere reflected explicitly. Rather, the evangelist shows at a different point how well thought out his theology of prayer is. Faith in prayer is for him not a substitute for proper human action but has its place alongside of it. Quite deliberately he speaks at the end of the main part of the Sermon on the Mount once more of prayer to the Father, as in its center, 6:6-15. Just as deliberately he will later on speak of the presence of the Lord Jesus with the one who takes the risk of faith and keeps the commandments (cf. 14:28-31; 28:19f.). Faith in prayer means the inextricable connection of an active Christian life with prayer to the loving Father. That shows how little the Matthean understanding of righteousness has in common with works-righteousness in the Pauline sense.

7:7a

Verse 7a has a special history of influence[26] which, independently of the text as a whole, builds on the traditional association of the verbs "seek" and "find." In Gnosticism, the seeking (and thus our logion) became the central description of Christian existence. The true gnostic is the one who seeks the invisible Father.[27] In contrast to this, the church's interpretation stresses that the Christians are those whose seeking has come to an end because they have found, namely, the *regula fidei* (rule of faith), the basis of faith.[28] The Christian gnostics Clement and Origen, who had to defend themselves against the implicit hostility of the anti-Gnostic church people to theology, attempted to tie the seeking to the faith of the church, not least by understanding it as seeking in the

---

[24]Brenz 357. Ps.-Clem. *Hom.* 3.56.2 ties the answer—Matthean only in formulation—to the doing of the divine will.

[25]Cf. the eschatological prospect at the eucharist, Mark 14:25.

[26]Cf. on this Brox*; Koschorke*.

[27]Examples especially in Brox* 21-25. The Greek Gospel of Thomas 5 formulates exaggeratedly: "It is enough for you to seek and not to find" (C. v. Tischendorf, *Evangelia Apocrypha* [Leipzig: Mendelssohn, 1876, reprint Hildesheim 1966], 144).

[28]Of prime importance is Tertullian's somewhat brusque explanation of this gnostic key passage (*Praescr.Haer.* 8-14 = BKV 1/24 660-68). The admonition to seek has to refer to the Jews, for the Christians have found already!

Scriptures, as exegesis.[29] The observer looking back notices: If the gnostics understood themselves as seekers, i.e., as such who even in their thought systems were still on the road and had not yet arrived at the Father beyond, then their relative tolerance toward church believers becomes understandable. At the same time, the diversity of their systems, as an expression of their seeking and probably also of their tentativeness, must be reevaluated differently from the evaluation by the church fathers.[30]

2.5. The Golden Rule (7:12)

Literature

Dihle, A., *Die goldene Regel*, Studienhefte zur Altertumswissenschaft 7 (Göttingen: Vandenhoeck & Ruprecht, 1962).

———, "Goldene Regel," *RAC* 11,930-40.

Erikson, E. H., "Die Goldene Regel im Lichte neuer Einsicht," in *Die Rolle des Ethischen in der Psychoanalyse* (Stuttgart, 1966), cited: *TB* (Hamburg, 1971) 192-215.

Hoche, H. U., "Die goldene Regel," *ZphF* 32 (1978) 355-75 (bibliography).

Mathys, H. P.; Heiligenthal, R.; Schrey, H. H., "Goldene Regel," *TRE* 13 (1984), 570-83.

Merklein, *Gottesherrschaft* 243-47.

Nissen, *Gott* 390-99.

Van Oyen, H., "Die goldene Regel und die Situationsethik," in J. Gründel and H. van Oyen, *Ethik ohne Normen?* ÖF, Kleine ökumenische Schriften 4 (1970), 91-135.

Philippidis, L, "Die 'Goldene Regel' religionsgeschichtlich untersucht," dissertation, Leipzig, 1929.

Reiner, H., "Die Goldene Regel. Die Bedeutung einer sittlichen Grundformel der Menschheit," in *Die Grundlagen der Sittlichkeit* (Meisenheim: Hain, 2d ed., 1974), 348-79.

Further literature** on the Sermon on the Mount at Matt. 5-7 above, pp. 209-211.

Text

12 Everything then that you wish that people do to you, do likewise to them; for this is the law and the prophets.

Analysis

1. *Redaction.* In Q, the Golden Rule most likely belonged in the section on love of enemies;[1] Matthew moved it to the end of the main part of the Sermon on the Mount. The apodosis, "for this[2] is the law and the prophets," comes from him; thus he refers back to the fulfillment of the law and the prophets by Jesus in 5:17 and creates a new bracket around the main part of the Sermon on the Mount. In addition, the intensifying

---

[29]Clement of Alexandria, *Strom.* 5.11-12 = BKV II/a9 126f; 16,6f. = ibid. 131 (seeking in love); Origen, fragment 138 II = 70 (seeking in the scripture).

[30]Cf. Koschorke* 61-63.

[1]Differently Polag, *Fragmenta* 36.

[2]Οὖτος γάρ with reference to the Scripture also 3:3, redactional; cf. 26:28.

πάντα comes from him; perhaps also οὕτως καί.[3]

2. *Origin.*[4] The Golden Rule is found universally. There are examples in Confucianism and in India just as in Greece from the time of Herodotus, particularly in nonphilosophical works, with rhetoricians, in collections of sayings, but also in almost all other literary genres. The Golden Rule was not indigenous to Judaism.[5] The first examples appear in Hellenistic-Jewish writings, e.g., the Letter of Aristeas, Sirach (LXX), Tobit, the Testaments of the 12 Patriarchs, and Philo.[6] Most of the non-Christian examples formulate the Golden Rule negatively: "That which you do not wish that people do to you, do not do to them." But positive formulations also occur.[7] The combination of the Golden Rule with the commandment of love of neighbor (Lev. 19:18) occurs already in Jewish thinking.[8] This is significant because at first it is a purely formal principle of correspondence, the content of which has to be filled in—perhaps in very different ways. As early as Hillel we find an anecdote which gives the understanding of the Golden Rule as the sum of the Torah.[9]

Interpretation: Q

This classical principle of universal wisdom appears in the *Sayings Source* in connection with Jesus' command of the love of enemies. It makes there a somewhat surprising impression: Luke 6:32-34 clarifies the problematic of the mutuality principle: "If you love those who love you in return," what is so special about it? Sinners and Gentiles do that too (cf. Matt. 5:47)! But precisely this mutuality principle, which is here rejected, is the foundation of the Golden Rule. Nevertheless, one probably should interpret the Golden Rule of Luke 6:31

---

[3]On πᾶς (πάντα ὅσα) and οὕτως (καὶ ὑμεῖς) cf. introduction 3.2 Πάντα was so important for Matthew that he put up with the awkward correspondence πάντα ὅσα – οὕτως.

[4]Philippidis* assembled the material; more briefly Dihle, *Regel* 8-13, 82-84, 94-102; idem, *RAC* 933-37. Augustine, *De Ordine* 2.25 = *PL* 32,1006: "vulgare proverbium" (a popular proverb).

[5]Does its abstractness not fit into Jewish sapiential thinking?

[6]Tob. 4:15; *Ep. Ar.* 207; Sir. 31:15 LXX; *T. Naph.*, Hebrew 1:6; Ahiqar, Aramaic B 53; Philo, *Hypothetica* = Eusebius, *Praep. Ev.* 8.7.6; *Tg. Ps. Jon.* Lev. 19:18; Ps. Menander 39 (referring to adultery); *2 Enoch* 61:1; *b. Šabb.* 31a; *'Abot* RN 15 (beginning, referring to the honor of the neighbor); 16 (beginning, referring to house and wife of the neighbor); *Death of Moses* = Wünsche, *Lehrhallen* I 151 (spoken by Moses); most passages in Str-B I 460 and 357.

[7]Positive formulations, e.g., in Dio Cassius 51.34.39; Isocrates, *Ad Nicocleam* (Cypr) 49; *2 Enoch* 61:1; Ahiqar, Aramaic B 53, cf. also *Ep. Ar.* 207; Dihle, *Regel* 103: The positive version is "just as popular" as the negative one.

[8]A certain closeness between Lev. 19:18 and the Golden Rule results from "as yourself." Sir. 31:15 in the Hebrew version is close to Lev. 19:18 and is in the Greek version influenced by the Golden Rule, according to Dihle, *Regel* 83f. *Tg. Ps. Jon.* on Lev. 19:18 adds the Golden Rule to the command of love of neighbor. A connection with the command of the love of neighbor is evident also in the *Death of Moses* (above n. 6), cf. Berger, *Gesetzesauslegung* I 134.

[9]*b. Šabb.* 31a: A Gentile comes to Hillel and demands to be taught the whole Torah while he stands on one foot. The man had been sent away earlier by Shammai. Hillel makes him a proselyte, tells him the Golden Rule and ends by saying, "Go, learn." A similar story can be found about Akiba in *'Abot RN* B 26; cf. Nissen, *Gott* 397.

as an imperative.[10] As to the content, it has to be filled by the love of enemies. But it is uncorrespondingly less radical and rather a turning of Jesus' command of love of enemies into a "pedagogy" which is not without problems.[11] If Jesus himself should have accepted it, then he deviated from his usual radicality.

One should not see great significance in the fact that the Golden Rule is formulated positively in the synoptic tradition and negatively by Hillel.[12] The positive formulation demands that the person addressed take the initiative, while the negative version may end with mere passivity. But the parallels demonstrate that the context of the content is much more decisive than the positive or negative formulation. Depending on the context, the sense of the two versions may be very different.[13] The positive formulation is Christian in itself just as little as the negative one.[14] Particularly the history of its reception in the early church demonstrates that quite arbitrarily both formulations were taken over.[15] Thus the early church saw nothing outstanding in the positive formulation.

---

[10]Dihle, *Regel** 113f. interprets Luke 6:31 as a statement: Thus you behave (i.e., sinners!). That is hardly possible (a) because of the introductory καί which connects with the imperatives of 27-30 and (b) because of Luke 3:11; 10:37; 17:31; 22:36.

[11]Hillel also (above n. 9) uses "pedagogy" by summarizing the whole Torah in the Golden Rule. Here also one must ask whether such a summary does not compress the Torah inadmissibly, cf. the deliberations in Nissen, *Gott* 390-99. As far as the content is concerned, it is impossible to "replace" the Torah by the Golden Rule for a Gentile, just as Matt. 7:12 does not "summarize," e.g., the Antitheses. Interpreted *in optimam partem* (to the best effect), Nissen can say of Hillel: He creates an "emergency bridge" for the Gentile (300); building on it he can say, "Go, learn."

[12]According to Jeremias, *Theology* 211f., Jesus refers to Hillel, so that his positive formulation is a deliberate surpassing of Hillel. A daring hypothesis!

[13]This is a typical case where anti-Judaic prejudices, noticeably in the 19th and 20th centuries, obscured for many exegetes the view of reality. Examples: For Zahn 209, the negative version of Hillel shows "what the Israelite . . . can get away with without getting into contradiction to the law," while Jesus interprets God's will as seen in the OT. According to Bischoff** 93 the difference between Hillel and Jesus is as great as that between "neminem laede" (do not injure anyone) and "omnes iuva" (help all people). Hillel's "commandment is best fulfilled by the dead in the grave! Only the person who is permeated by lively moral-religious energy can fulfill the command of Jesus"! Mathys* 572 reports on the Jewish counter-polemic which was made necessary: "Tempi passati?" (Have times changed?)

[14]Dihle, *Regel** 107, collects the material. Already *Did.* 1:2 and Acts 15:20,28 (Codex Bezae) formulate it negatively again.

[15]G. Hunold, "Identitätstheorie. Die sittliche Struktur des Individuellen im Sozialen," in *Handbuch der christlichen Ethik* I (Freiburg: Herder, 1978), 194f., distinguishes three possiblities of understanding on the basis of different basic types of interaction: (a) the interpretation in reference to the self with the goal to make the fellow human being an instrument for one's own purpose; (b) the interpretation which grants the fellow human being an equal right with the goal to make arrangements with him or her; (c) the high demand of love which is determined by a foundational "Yes." He associates interpretation (a) with the negative and interpretation (b) with the positive version. Similarly Reuter, *Orientierung*** 100, distinguishes the negative formulation as polemic morality, the positive one as an expression of a more sublime competition ("with it one can sell oneself at a gain according to the calculating principle: 'if you [do it] to me, then I [will do it] to you' "). The variations show how differently the Golden Rule can be interpreted. However, the differences, it seems to me, do not depend on the positive or negative version.

Interpretation and history of influence: Matthew

Thus to interpret Matt. 7:12 does not mean to ask for the meaning of the text in itself. Rather, we have to ask what meaning the positively formulated Golden Rule receives in the context of the Matthean Sermon on the Mount, and, conversely, what direction of interpretation it indicates for the Matthean Sermon on the Mount. Thus various interpretations, which would be possible on the basis of the wording, fall by the wayside. They cannot be interpreted in their Matthean context in the sense of a "naive" or also less naive "egoism."[16] That which I would like to experience myself motivates my acting, as Schopenhauer said in his critique of Kant: "Then on the basis of this standpoint my egoism decides for justice and love of people; not because it desires to *practice* it but because it desires to *experience* it." [17] In its Matthean context it also is not an expression of a polemical morality[18] or of the idea of retaliation which also could turn against the fellow human being. A classical expression of this thinking is the epitaph of Apusulena Geria[19]: "Quod quisque vestrum optaverit mihi, illi semper eveniat vivo et mortuo" (What each of you will wish for me shall happen to that person, during lifetime and after death). A "positive" formulation of the Golden Rule! Finally, on the basis of the Matthean context, it is not the expression of natural law or the expression of a behavior which is ultimately rational. As much as the element of intelligibility, even of self-evidence, belongs to the Golden Rule, as little is its significance in the context of the Matthean Sermon on the Mount exhausted by it.

Here we encounter one main thread in the *Christian history of influence* of Matt. 7:12.[20] The Golden Rule is in harmony with natural law, which law and gospel together presuppose: "To do good and to experience good is the natural law; and if this is completed, then the law of Moses also is fulfilled, for it consisted in this."[21] As a part of natural law it becomes a foundation for ecclesiastical law.[22] This idea is maintained also in the interpretation of the Reformation,[23] and then becomes very important in English, French, and German Enlightenment philosophy.[24] This basic thread is still effective today when *humanitas* and *Christianitas* are reconciled in the name of the Golden Rule: Jesus wanted "to say nothing new but something extremely old, nothing original but something generally valid, nothing surprising but something intelligible,

---

[16]Bultmann, *Tradition* 103.

[17]A. Schopenhauer, "Preisschrift über die Grundlage der Moral," in *Sämtliche Werke*, vol. 6 (Leipzig: Reclam edition, 1938), 279 (§ 7 beginning).

[18]Reuter, *Orientierung*** 100.

[19]In Wettstein I 341.

[20]The most important sources are Heiligenthal* and Schrey*. Van Oyen* 96-106 offers a brief survey.

[21]Origen, fragment 142 = 72; Photius, fragment 29 = Reuss 283f. is particularly impressive among Greek interpreters.

[22]*Decretum Gratiani* before I/1 = *PL* 187,30.

[23]Luther, *Lectures on Galatians, 1519*, on Gal. 5:14 = II 219 = *LW* 27, 354-55; Melanchthon 164f. impressively summarizes the eight central commands of his order of natural law.

[24]Schrey* 577f. refers to Th. Hobbes, *Leviathan*, ch. 15, Berkeley, Shaftesbury, J. St. Mill, Thomasius, Voltaire, and Leibniz.

incontestable, and inescapable. Jesus is only the messenger of an eternal truth which in principle is acknowledged always and everywhere and by all, semper et ubique et ab omnibus."[25]

But the *more recent ethical discussion* has made clear that the Golden Rule cannot be directly a normative ethical basic principle. It is capable of expression "that our humanity proceeds always communicatively, i.e., always as a mutual relationship, as an exchange with others,"[26] but it has no normative character. E.g., it is significant for H. van Oyen exactly because it is contingent to the situation and leaves the decisions "to the person who realizes himself or herself in the encounter with the neighbor."[27] Expressed differently: *The Golden Rule must already presuppose a standard of behavior.*[28] For it "does not contain the principle of duties to oneself, nor of the duties of benevolence to others (for many a one would gladly consent that others should not benefit him, provided only that he might be excused from showing benevolence to them), nor finally that of duties of strict obligation to one another, for on this principle the criminal might argue against the judge who punishes him, and so on."[29] For this reason, Kant extended the Golden Rule beyond the fellow human being addressed in it to *all* people and made the universally formulated categorical imperative the principle for acting.

In Christian interpretation also, this problem was felt. Augustine reports that many translators had inserted the word "bona" (good things) into the Golden Rule so that the text read: "All the good things which you desire that the people do for you," in order that not perhaps something pleasurable but dishonorable, as, e.g., voluptuous banquets, would become the content of mutual actions.[30] Therefore, in the history of interpretation of Matt. 7:12, the command of love of neighbor was put as a preceding clause before the Golden Rule from the very beginning. The Didache puts it in this sense at the start of the instruction, and Zwingli formulates with splendid power of illustration: "Christ has sugared the command of nature with love."[31]

What meaning does the Matthean Sermon on the Mount give to the Golden Rule? Through the addition of the evangelist, "for this is the law and the prophets," it is lifted out and made a foundational sentence. Matthew points back to 5:17, where Jesus spoke of fulfilling law and prophets through his life and teaching. In picking this up again, he makes clear that this fulfillment is

---

[25]Stauffer, *Botschaft* 59, quotation 57. The incursion of the negative version into the post-New Testament tradition is for him a kind of re-Judaizing of the message of Jesus. The thesis is among those mentioned in n. 13.

[26]Reuter, *Orientierung*** 99. It is modern to interpret it as bursting of the "self-encircling" and the "self-relationship" of the human being and as leading the disciple of Jesus to the Thou (Soiron** 422). The relationship to the fellow human being is common to all formulations, also the non-Christian ones.

[27]Van Oyen* 136, following situation ethicists like P. Lehmann and J. Fletcher.

[28]Schrey* 578 says that the Golden Rule "does not give a standard of behavior but presupposes it," following Leibniz (*Nouveaux essais sur l'entendement humain*).

[29]I. Kant, *Fundamental Principles of the Metaphysic of Ethics* (New York: Longmans, Green & Co., 10th ed., 1946), 57, n. 1 (second section).

[30]*Civitas Dei* 14.8 = BKV I/16 755f. Hoche* 362f. illustrates this with the example of the inebriated guest whom the host must prevent from driving a car although he himself also in this situation would like to use the car.

[31]Didache 1:2f.; Justin, *Dial.* 93.2f.; Clement of Alexandria, *Paed.* 3.12 (88,1) = BKV II/8 211; *Ep. Apostolorum* 18 (29) = Hennecke I 201f. Zwingli's quotation comes from "Von göttlicher und menschlicher Gerechtigkeit," 10 (= Hauptschriften 78, 1942, 62).

bundled up in the practice of the Golden Rule. At the same time, this concluding statement makes the first reference to that which could be meant by the Golden Rule: it is in harmony not only with general early Christian thinking (Gal. 5:14; Rom. 13:8-10; Jas. 2:8), but certainly Matthean thinking (22:40), to remember first of all love in connection with the fulfilling of the law. "Law and prophets" are here used in the same sense as in 5:17; he thinks primarily of the will of God,[32] which is proclaimed in both and is fulfilled by obedience.

The Golden Rule itself has been clarified by the evangelist only sparsely by further interpretation. Οὖν presumably is nothing more than a loose connector,[33] which perhaps lifts out the Golden Rule as a summarizing accumulation of the entire main part, 5:17–7:11.[34] Then again, the idea of the love commandment, which has such great significance in the main part of the Sermon on the Mount through the first and last antitheses, through the petition for forgiveness of the Lord's Prayer, and through the further explication in 7:1-5, moves into the foreground. It is the most central "preamble" of the Golden Rule in the Gospel of Matthew. That corresponds already with its interpretation in the Sayings Source, but also with Jewish thinking—from which Matthew originates.[35]

That means that the Golden Rule is radicalized by the Sermon on the Mount. Everything, without exception, which is demanded by love and the commandments of Jesus you should do for other people. Πάντα receives its meaning in the context of Matthean perfectionism. The higher righteousness and the command of perfection of the one who teaches his disciples to keep "all which I have commanded you" (28:20) is the subject. On the basis of the Matthean "preamble" the positive formulation of the Golden Rule[36] becomes important, maintaining that Christian practice is to be intitiative, not reactive behavior. The Christian is to be the first one to begin loving, in agreement with Jesus' commands, e.g., in 5:38-48. On the basis of the Sermon on the Mount, the Golden Rule is much more than common sense. Reuter says it well: "It is only the gospel which really (gilds) the Golden Rule."[37]

---

[32]Cf. on 5:17-20.

[33]Loosely connecting οὖν also in 10:32; 12:12; 18:29.

[34]Already Bucer 76D notes the reference backwards of 7:12 to 5:17.

[35]Cf. above n. 8. For Hillel also such a combination of Golden Rule and love would not fit badly. On the one hand, he teaches a Gentile the Golden Rule, on the other hand he left the principle "Be among the disciples of Aaron, loving peace and striving for peace, loving others and leading them to the Torah" ('Abot 1:12).

[36]Hoffmann-Eid, *Jesus* 150, says correctly that the Matthean Golden Rule "aims at a change of behavior" and therefore must be formulated positively. Therefore one must say: (1) The positive formulation of the Rule is not originally Christian; (2) it is nonetheless significant that the Jesus tradition brings the positive formulation; (3) the early Christian tradition, which frequently took up the negative formulation, often no longer recognized this significance.

[37]Reuter, *Orientierung* ** 103. But Reuter, it seems to me, in his very readable essay overlooks the fact that the "formulation of the Rule, picked up from the mutual relationship" (ibid.) is not yet the "ethics of the coming reign of God." It owes its power not to the coming of the kingdom of God but to its rational evidence. But it is correct that this rationally intelligible interpretation of the Sermon on the Mount is not self-evident but intends an initiative approach to the fellow human being and his or her desires.

But this also means that the Golden Rule on its part interprets the Sermon on the Mount. With its comprehensive formulation, it maintains that in the Sermon on the Mount a summa of Christian righteousness is proclaimed, a summa which is intended comprehensively to determine the entire life of Christians. It once more recalls that the individual directions of the Sermon on the Mount are living examples of perfection which are to be integrated and extended in the whole of life. It excludes the thought that *only* the commandments mentioned there are meant and it maintains the element of freedom, even of "autonomy"[38] of the human beings to invent for themselves in the light of love what is meant in the Sermon on the Mount. What you wish for yourself may be helpful in discovering the behavior that love demands in an actual situation. The Sermon on the Mount is not a bundle of prescriptions which legally obligate the Christian. Finally, it points to the fact that the horizon of Christian activity is universal: *human beings* are the partners. The Sermon on the Mount is by no means concerned with an ethics which is to be practiced only in the protected inner space of the Christian community.

Summary

With all due caution, one must ask whether the Golden Rule does not also include a further development and alteration of the commands of Jesus. Its evidence is not the same as that of the command of love of enemies or of the renunciation of force. There, the internal agreement of the listener to the truth of the commands was based on the contrast which they indicated to his or her own experience. For the human being who is caught up in lies, power, and hatred, the contrasting commands of Jesus meant a ray of hope for a new, better human being in the coming of the kingdom of God.[39] But the Golden Rule is plausible also without eschatology, because it assigns a place to one's own ego in the "exchange relationship"[40] of giving and receiving of love.

I would like to leave it open whether Matthew was aware of the fact that the Golden Rule is not only a summary but also at the same time an attempt at a translation of Jesus' radical commands into a situation of a slackened eschatology which is no longer immediately influenced by the coming of the kingdom of God in the immediate future. Jesus' exemplary radical demands, determined by the contrast between the kingdom of God and the world, become here the generally valid demand of initiatory, active love for each person. It is plausible to all people who do not consider others—in a Manichaean, not a Christian way!—as unalterably evil from the beginning.

Here the Golden Rule seems to give an indication to a possible practice for us today on the basis of the Sermon on the Mount. It takes the interpretation of Jesus' *radical* demands a step forward in the direction of "*intelligent* love of

---

[38]Nissen, *Gott* 392: The only premise of the Golden Rule is a formal one, namely, that of the autonomy of the human being.

[39]Cf. above, pp. 328-29, 341f.

[40]Cf. Reuter** above n. 37.

enemy.''[41] Therefore it is important for the translation of Jesus' demands in the direction of rationally communicable activity, e.g., also for the political realm.[42] At the same time, it becomes clear that this attempt at translation does not contain the entirety of Jesus' dialectical demands. The Golden Rule is plausible within the world; it is an attempt to design perspectives on the basis of Jesus' radical commandment of love. Jesus' commandment of the love of enemies was in agreement with God's radical love of the world and means the exhortation to erect contrast signs of hope in the world. The rationally communicable, active praxis of reasonable balance of the Golden Rule can be encouraged by such contrast signs but is not identical with them.

3. CONCLUDING ADMONITIONS (7:13-29)

The conclusion of the Sermon on the Mount is best divided into three sections:[1] The two ways (7:13-14), the warning against the false prophets (7:15-23), and the parable of building a house (7:24-27). In form, the first and the second pericope are connected by the key words εἰσέρχομαι (13 [2 times], 21) and πολλοί (13, 22), the second and third pericope through the key word ποιέω (altogether 9 times). In this way, essential tendencies of the section already are indicated: it is the concluding admonition to the community for Christian praxis. It has a fundamental character: all three sections are defined by antithetical contrasts (broad/narrow way or gate; good/bad fruit; doers of the will of God/doers of lawlessness; house on rocky/sandy foundation). All are concerned with the final judgment. The negative aspect, the warning of the catastrophe, predominates. The conclusion of the Sermon on the Mount corresponds to the conclusion of typical Matthean speeches, which end with a look to the judgment that the community will face.[2] Matthew has consistently carried out this structural principle, the beginnings of which are found also in Q and in the Didache.[3]

---

[41]The programmatic formulation of C. F. v. Weizsäcker of the "intelligent love of enemy" thus corresponds directly to the Golden Rule but only indirectly to Jesus' love of enemies. Cf. above p. 351.

[42]In this conviction I am close to the findings of Erikson's* fascinating reflections on the Golden Rule, which are designed from a completely different view. Erikson (213-15) demands: "Inasmuch as a nation considers itself as a collective individual, it can very well learn to see its task in maintaining mutuality" (which is for Erikson a basic principle in mediating one's own ego-existence through the other individual) "in international relationships. For the only alternative to armed conflict seems to be the effort to activate in the historical partner that which strengthens him in his historical development, just as it strengthens the one who activates it in his own development—*namely, the development toward a communal future identity*" (124f., emphasis mine).

[1]A division into four sections is possible, e.g., in Radermakers on the passage; Strecker, *Weg* 137f., n. 4; W. Nicol, "The Structure of Matthew Seven," *Neot* 11 (1977) 77-90, there 87f. and part 17. For this proposal, which divides vv. 15-23 into the two sections, 15-20 and 21-23, the correspondence of vv. 16a/20 is significant.

[2]Matthew 13:50: weeping and gnashing of teeth; 18:34f.; 24:49f.; 25:11f.,24-28,41-46 (the negative figures are mentioned last in all these parables).

[3]Bornkamm, "End-Expectation," 17, assumes on the basis of the parallels between Matthean discourse and the Didache "something of the character of a catechism." Finally one would still have to point to the source Q which concludes both in individual discourse complexes (e.g., Luke 6:47-49; 7:31-35) and as a whole (Luke 17:23-37) with the preaching of judgment (cf. Lührmann, *Redaktion*

Source critically also, the section proves to be a unit. Two sections from the Sayings Source, which the evangelist works together, constitute the basis. One is the conclusion of the Sermon on the Plain (vv. 16-19,21,24-47), the other the eschatological parenesis Luke 13:23-29 (vv. 13f.,22f.), the final logion of which, Luke 13:28f., the evangelist is not using here but will insert at the next opportunity, in Matt. 8:11f.

3.1. The Narrow and the Wide Door (7:13-14)

Literature

Denaux, A., "Der Spruch von den zwei Wegen im Rahmen des Epilogs der Bergpredigt," in *Logia* (Mem. J. Coppens), ed. J. Delobel, BETL 59, pp. 305-35 (Leuven: Uitgeverij Peeters, 1982).
Hoffmann, P. "Πάντες ἐργάται ἀδικίας: Redaktion und Tradition in Lk 13,22-30," *ZNW* 58 (1967) 188-214.
Jeremias, J., "πύλη κτλ.," *TDNT* VI 921-28.
Marguerat, *Jugement* 175-82.
Mattill, A. J., " 'The Way of Tribulation,' " *JBL* 98 (1979) 531-46.
Michaelis, W., "ὁδός κτλ.," *TDNT* V 42-114.
Zeller, *Mahnsprüche* 139-42.
Further literature** on the Sermon on the Mount at Matt. 5-7 above, pp. 209-211.

Text

13 Enter through the narrow gate.
   For the gate is wide[1]
   and the way is broad
   which leads to destruction,
   and there are many who enter through it!
14 How[2] narrow is the gate
   and how hard the way,
   which leads to life,
   and there are few who find it!

Analysis

1. *Structure.* Aside from v. 13a, the logion consists of two formally parallel parts. But there are rough edges. The images of the gate and the way stand juxtaposed without connection; the concluding sentence of v. 13 refers to the gate, the referent of the concluding sentence of v. 14 is unclear.[3] It is uncertain how gate and way belong

---

93-97). All three writings, however, stand in a common stream of tradition and are dependent on one another so that one should rather speak of a continuity of Christian parenesis.

[1]The missing of πύλη in some MSS in 13b and 14a presumably is to make the illustration more exact: a way which leads to a gate.

[2]Τί (instead of ὅτι) is, although somewhat less supported, the *lectio difficilior* (the more difficult reading). I do not think that the formulation is a Semitism (BDF §299; Black, *Muttersprache* 123f.; the comparable constructions with מָה are Hebraisms and all constructed in the LXX with a verb and not an adjective) but popular Greek (New Greek: τί καλά! = how beautiful!).

[3]Is the way or the gate or the life to be found?

together. Is it the entrance door to a certain way?[4] The order of the images would speak in favor of this view. Or is this the gate to life at the end of the way?[5] Parallel motifs would seem to support this. Or are gate and way synonyms?[6]

2. *Redaction and source.* The text has only a few words in common with Luke 13:23f.; nevertheless, it seems certain that Matthew has used Q.[7] Luke has created in 13:23-39 a strict, secondary composition which deals with the entrance into the heavenly hall for the banquet with Abraham, Isaac, and Jacob. Because he can use only the motif of the gate for this, it is conceivable that he has shortened the logion.[8] But it is also possible that the original Q saying spoke only of the narrow gate and of the fact that many want to enter, while only few can enter.[9] Then Matthew would have added the way to the gate (vv. 13c and 14b). Linguistically it cannot be proved.[10] But other deliberations speak in favor of this second proposal:

1. The motif of the two gates is relatively rare in Jewish texts;[11] but the contrast of the two ways is a topic of parenesis which can be documented in many Jewish texts.[12]

---

[4]Klostermann 69; Hoffmann (1970** 100; in the early church, e.g., Ps.-Clem. *Hom.* 7.7.3 (gate = faith/unbelief).

[5]E.g., Jeremias* 922,17ff.; in the interpretation of the early church, e.g., the *Opus imperfectum* 18 = 735 (the two gates are Christ and the devil; sins or good works lead to the devil or Christ); Maldonat 161 (the gate is the entrance into the kingdom of God; correct!).

[6]This is the interpretation of most exegetes, e.g., Michaelis* 72,16ff.; Schweizer 118 ("double parable"); Gundry 127; Guelich** 388; Marguerat, *Jugement* 177.

[7]Because Luke 13:23-29 was used continuously in Matt. 7:13f.,22f.; 8:11f.

[8]Luke also speaks of θύρα (to the festival hall). E.g., Schulz, *Q* 309-11; Zeller, *Mahnsprüche* 139 count on a shortening of a more detailed Q text by Luke.

[9]Cf. the reconstruction in Polag, *Fragmenta* 68; on the argument Hoffmann* 195f.; Denaux* 318- 23, 327-29. The order gate–way, inappropriate as far as the subject matter is concerned (cf. below, nn. 15-17), is best understandable if the motif of the way was added secondarily to the motif of the gate.

[10]Marguerat, *Jugement* 175, therefore would like to attribute the enlargement to QMt, but then he encounters the difficulty that the unprovable redaction in QMt fits excellently to the theology of the evangelist.

[11]Testament of Abraham 8, Rec. B, speaks of two gates (a large and a small gate αἱ ἀπάγουσαι εἰς τὴν ζωὴν καὶ εἰς τὴν ἀπώλειαν, presumably thinking of gates to paradise; Christian glosses are possible in this writing); the Table of Cebes 15 (= J. T. Fitzgerald and L. M. White, *The Tabula of Cebes*, Texts and Translations 24 [Chico: Scholars Press, 1983] 13f.) speaks of the narrow and difficult way which leads to the small door of true education. The passage 4 Ezra 7:6-9, mentioned by Str-B I 463 (parable of a glorious city, with a narrow entryway and only one narrow way which leads to it between the abysses); *Pesiq* 179b (path of life and gate to the life of the future world, but not two ways or two gates); *Pirqe R. El.* 15 (very late!, two ways and four gates on the way of evil) are essentially different. The contrast of two gates is quite original and possibly completely without Jewish models. Perhaps is simply a literary result that came about in Matthew by the adding of the motif of two ways.

[12]The contrast of the two ways is widespread in Greek and Jewish thought. In Greek, it has its root in the fable of Heracles at the crossroads (Prodikos in Xenophon *Mem.* 2.1.21-34) and in Hesiod, *Op.* 287-92; following Hesiod, the two ways were usually interpreted as the easy one to κακία and the difficult one to ἀρετή (so also in Philo). In the Old Testament, the motif is rooted in the opposition of the way of the righteous and of the godless, especially in Psalms and Proverbs. Early Jewish and rabbinical examples are rare. One may speak of a parenetic form of teaching in *T. Asher* 1:3–6:6 and *Did.* 1:2–5:2, parallel to 18:1–20:2; but the two texts are different. Therefore one should not speak of a *fixed* form of teaching and not at all of Jewish baptismal instruction (A. Seeberg, *Die beiden Wege und das Aposteldekret* (Leipzig: Deichert, 1906), 1-38. The material is presented distinctly by Michaelis*, especially 43-46,53-55,56-60,61f.,98-101; on the status of research cf. J. Becker, *Untersuchungen zur Entstehungsgeschichte der Testamente der zwölf Patriarchen,* AGJU 8 (1970), 365-69; W. Rordorf,

Matthew would have supplemented the word of the narrow gate, which was available to him, by the well-known parenetical topic. Exactly the same supplement can be found in the Testament of Abraham.[13]

2. The noteworthy interruption of the statements about the gate (7:13a,b,d) through a statement about the way (7:13c) is explained best if the way was added later.

3. Theologically this addition agrees with Matthew. He uses elsewhere the metaphor of the way in the ethical sense (21:32 red., cf. 22:16 trad.). The idea of the way to perfection on which the community progresses is basic to him.

4. The Semitizing *parallelismus membrorum* (parallelism of members) is a Matthean element of style.[14] Matthew speaks redactionally of the "finding" of life (indeed: ψυχή!) in 10:39; 16:25.

5. It probably can even be shown that in the Matthean community the idea of the two ways was familiar. In *Did.* 1:2–5:2 a two-ways parenesis is received which is clearly traditional and not yet influenced by Matthew. Since the Didache comes from a community influenced by Matthew, we can assume that Matthew has enlarged the Q saying of the narrow gate by a parenetic topic which was current in his own community. His redaction would then be completely "traditional"! He has enlarged the Q text, which came to him in literary form, in the style of the parenesis familiar to his community.

3. *Origin.* No assertions are possible concerning the origin of the logion of the narrow gate.

Interpretation

7:13

Πύλη is the gate of a city or a temple, in distinction from θύρα = door. One should not think of the ancient city gate with the great main gate and the more narrow side door; the two Matthean gates lead to different destinations. The image of the gate suggests various possibilities of association: the gates of the heavenly city,[15] the recall of the entry of the righteous through the gates of the temple,[16] the gates of paradise, the gates of life.[17] But it was unusual to speak of the narrow gate. Therefore the imperative of v. 13a has to be supported. The reasoning starts with the negative side. The broad way, leading to destruction, belongs to the wide gate. The idea that walking on a broad way is comfortable suggests itself, to be sure, but it is not pronounced. The broad way leads to destruction: Matthew stands here close to the Jewish usage where frequently, under the influence of Deut. 30:19 and Jer. 21:8, the way of death and the way

---

"Un chapitre d'éthique judéo-chrétienne: les deux voies," *RSR* 60 (1972) 109-28; M. J. Suggs, "The Christian Two Ways Tradition: Its Antiquity, Form and Function," in *Studies in New Testament and Early Christian Literature* (FS A. Wikgren), ed. D. Aune, NovTSup 33 (Leiden: Brill, 1972), 60-74.

[13]Testament of Abraham 11, Rec. A: The supplement of the two ways is influenced by Matthew in its formulation. On recension B cf. above n. 11.

[14]Cf. introduction 3.1.

[15]Rev. 22:14; 4 Ezra 7 (above n. 11); Isa. 26:2. Examples of the gates of heaven (especially for clouds, rain, etc.) and the gates of the throne seat of God in J. Jeremias, "θύρα," *TDNT* III 177.

[16]Especially Ps. 24:7-10; 118:19f.; on the heavenly temple *T.Levi* 5:1.

[17]*Testamant of Abraham* 8, Rec. B and *Pesiq* 179b (above n. 11). Cf. also O. Böcher, *Der johanneische Dualismus im Zusammenhang des nachbiblischen Judentums* (Gütersloh: Mohn, 1965), 82f.

of life are contrasted with each other.[18] So it is necessary to choose between two manners of life opposed to each other.

7:14

The ὁδὸς τεθλιμμένη stands opposite the broad way. This does not mean, as is frequently asserted, simply the narrow, tight way. Τεθλιμμένος can mean "narrowed," but in the sense that, e.g., there is a crowding in a city or a house when too many people are present.[19] But this does not at all fit here, because only few go on the way which leads to life. Therefore, it is better with τεθλιμμένος to think of the θλίψεις which Matthew mentions variously for the time before the eschaton (24:9 red.; 24: 21,29; cf. 13:21). Already 5:10-12,44 spoke of the persecutions which hit the community. Thus the way to life is full of afflictions.[20] If this interpretation is correct, then it is good not to overlook the possibility of a metaphorical interpretation which is contained in στένος.[21] The thought of the "distress," experienced in suffering, may be included. Thus the way to life means suffering for the sake of the faith; Matthew thinks of this and not of the special asceticism which the follower accepts.[22] Ζωή, like ἀπώλεια, is an eschatological term. The evangelist uses the verb εἰσέρχομαι, as in the sayings of the entering into the kingdom of heaven.[23]

On the basis of this, we can decide the question of the relationship of gate and way. It is not so that the gate is conceived as the entry gate to the way—the metaphorical associations which the word calls forth repudiate this view.[24] Gate and way are not two parallel, synonymous images—the manner in which Matthew intertwines both images contradicts this view. Instead, the gate is at the end of the way, for one enters through the gate into life, i.e., into the kingdom of God in the eschaton. Thus Matthew did something that is quite characteristic of him when he supplemented the illustration of the gate with the illustration of the way. He lifted out the ethical aspect of eschatology and so placed righteousness next to the kingdom of God (cf. 6:33). He took up again his model of the Christian faith as a way to perfection which is to be practiced

---

[18]Michaelis* 59,3ff.

[19]The usual interpretation (e.g., BAGD, s.v.) follows Bornhäuser** 177, but without real examples. Julius Pollux, *Onom.* 9.23, orients us concerning the meaning of θλίβομαι: Synonyms for a populous πόλις τεθλιμμένη are, e.g., φλεγμαίνουσα (swollen), ὀχλώδης (turbulent), difficult because of the crowd of people, full of noise . . . narrowness (στενοχωρία). In 9.145 he also speaks of crowds and notes: Πάντα ἐξέπλητο, ἐστενοχωρεῖτο, ἐθλίβετο (everything was filled, narrowed, crowded). The many, not the few are appropriate to τεθλιμμένος in the meaning "narrow"!

[20]So correctly Mattill*.

[21]Cf. Isa. 30:20 LXX; Job 18:11 LXX; Jer. 37:7 LXX; 1 Kings 24:14 LXX and G. Bertram, "στένος κτλ.," TDNT VII 605ff. Στενοχωρία also often has a figurative meaning.

[22]The church's interpretation often explained it ascetically: Jerome on the passage thinks of *labores* (labors) and *ieiunia* (fasting); similarly Leo the Great, *Sermo* 90.2 = BKV I/55 274; Hilarius 6,3 = 952 ("cupiditates et animi vincere et corporis frangere" (to overcome the desires of the spirit and to break those of the body). On the interpretation in regard to monasticism, cf. below n. 30.

[23]Cf. 5:20; 7:21 (entering into the kingdom of the heavens); 18:8f.; 19:16f.,29; 25:46.

[24]Cf. above, nn. 15-17.

actively by the community (5:20,48), at whose end the entry into the βασιλεία is promised (cf. 21:32). The difficult way, which with afflictions is a passage for the few to the narrow gate, is the way of righteousness as depicted in the Sermon on the Mount.

Matthew has combined this admonition with the warning against the false prophets. In 7:22 he calls attention to the fact that there will be "many" who cast out demons and do miracles in Jesus' name but do not do God's will. The many who walk on the broad way are for him obviously not only the scribes,[25] or the unbelieving majority of Israel,[26] or the "others," from which one has separated,[27] or the unbaptized, as in the Didache from whose way one takes leave in baptism,[28] but the "many" are Christians, members of the community. Thus Matthew again applies to the community a motif which up to now has been used in a different manner (*Did.* 1:2–5:2).[29] The community is on the way to the gate of life. It constantly faces the choice of the two ways. Being a Christian, being baptized, does not mean a tranquil certainty of salvation but the constant challenge of the decision between the broad way and the difficult way of the Sermon on the Mount. Therefore it is true for Matthew that many are called but only few are chosen (20:16; 22:14). The way of the Sermon on the Mount is the way to which all Christians are called, not just a minority of the perfect who have chosen for themselves a particularly difficult way.[30] Salvation depends on this way, not only on baptism or listening to grace. That is the Matthean form of "synergism." The Sermon on the Mount gives the initial impetus and the direction for action. Therefore it is grace. Matthew brought out this basic decision, which the Christian community faces again and again, at the end of almost all the discourses (cf. 13:36-43,47-50; 18:23-35; 24:37-25:46). It is in harmony with his model of the church as a *corpus permixtum* (a mixed body): Not until the final judgment will it be seen who in the eyes of God has gone the way which leads to life (13:36-43; 22:11-14).

History of influence

A focal point in the history of interpretation of vv. 13-14 is the Christological understanding of them. They lend themselves to being read in a Johannine sense. Christ is

---

[25]Bornhäuser** thinks of the broad gates of the synagogues.

[26]Frankemölle, *Jahwebund* 104, thinks, in terms of history of salvation, of the contrast between the Old Testament–Jewish order and the order of Jesus' βασιλεία.

[27]Cf., e.g., Brenz 361: On the broad way, there are "Thalmudistae, Mahumetistae" (Talmudists, Mohammedans) and unrepentant Christians; Luther, WA 32**, 500 = LW 21, 242-43, polemicizes against Turks and papists who rely on their large number. The *Liber Graduum*, 19,3 = 454 is interesting (ed. M. Kmosko, 1926[Ps 1]): the narrow way of Matt. 7:14 is distinguished from the still more constricted way to perfection!

[28]*Did.* 7:1: The parenesis of the two ways is read before the baptismal act in the worship service.

[29]Marguerat, *Jugement* 180-82.

[30]The earliest monks referred the narrow way to themselves, cf. *Apophthegmata Patrum Ammon* 11 = *PG* 65,123; Poimen 112 = *PG* 65,352.

"the gate of life: Whoever enters through me, enters into life."[31] Then a "play" could arise with the "way": the righteous are on the narrow way of suffering. But Christ, who is "the way," helps on the "way," offering healing medicines and healing the wounded, although looking like one of the wounded.[32] "He is . . . our example to bear everything patiently."[33] Thus the way becomes the way of discipleship; allegorically interpreted, Christ is the narrow gate, the devil the broad.[34]

      Such interpretations, although missing the text in a direct sense, attempt to do in their own way that which is still today the task of the interpreter and preacher: they interpret the text on the basis of the *entirety* of the biblical testimony. Thus they do nothing else but what Matthew also did with the traditional logion of the gate. Moreover, every interpreter is confronted with the question how a new interpretation is related to the text's own statement. If, e.g., the few are "not the clever or pious" "but those who are chosen by God (Mt 22:14) and who are therefore enabled to find what the many do not find,"[35] then this integration—influenced by Calvinism—of the individual text into the whole of the biblical testimony means a contradiction to the thrust of the Matthean text. Whether this contradiction is defensible has to be decided by all interpreters out of their own situation and theology. But they have to be aware and to make others aware of the fact that the scope of the text was perhaps changed; and they must not *tacitly* bend the text or consider their own interpretation as its total scope. The history of interpretation, which integrates the individual text into the entirety of the biblical testimony, points to an enduring, important task of interpreters who would enable the text to speak today, through their own words. But historical-critical exegesis invites them to a conversation with the individual text which is necessary in order that the interpreters can also question themselves critically.

3.2. Warning against False Prophets (7:15-23)

Literature

Barth, "Matthew's Understanding of the Law" 68-70, 149-54.

Betz, H. D., "Eine Episode im Jüngsten Gericht (Mt 7,21-23)," *ZTK* 78 (1981) 1-30.

Böcher, O., "Wölfe in Schafspelzen. Zum religionsgeschichtlichen Hintergrund von Mt 7,15," *TZ* 24 (1968) 405-26.

Cothenet, E., "Les prophètes chrétiens dans l'Évangile selon saint Matthieu," in Didier, *Évangile* 281-308.

Hill, D., "False Prophets and Charismatics: Structure and Interpretation in Matthew 7,15-23," *Bib* 57 (1976) 327-48.

Hoffmann, P., "Πάντες ἐργάται ἀδικίας," *ZNW* 58 (1967) 188-214.

Légasse, S., "Les faux prophètes. Matth. 7,15-20," *EtFr* 18 (1968) 205-18.

Marguerat, *Jugement* 183-203.

Mees, M., "Ausserkanonische Parallelstellen zu den Gerichtsworten Mt 7,21-23; Lk 6,46; 13,26-28 und ihre Bedeutung für die Formung der Jesusworte," *VetChr* 10 (1973) 79-102.

---

[31]Ps.-Clem. *Hom.* 3.52.2; further Clement of Alexandria, *Prot.* 10 (100,1) = BKV II/7 175. In the second passage, Christ is the way. Matt. 7:13f. was read either together with John 10:9 or with John 14:6.

[32]Makarius, *Hom.* 26.25 = BKV I/10 227.

[33]Leo the Great, *Sermo* 90.2 = BKV I/55 462.

[34]*Opus Imperfectum* 18 = 734f.

[35]Barth, *CD* I/2, 261.

Minear, P., "False Prophecy and Hypocrisy in the Gospel of Matthew," in *Neues Testament und Kirche* (FS R. Schnackenburg), ed. J. Gnilka, pp. 76-93 (Freiburg: Herder, 1974).

Otranto, G., "Matteo 7,15-16a e gli ψευδοπροφῆται nell' esegesi patristica," *VetChr* 6 (1969) 34-45.

Schneider, G., "Christusbekenntnis und christliches Handeln," in *Die Kirche des Anfangs* (FS H. Schürmann), ed. R. Schnackenburg et al., pp. 9-24 (Leipzig: St. Benno, 1977).

Simonetti, M., "Matteo 7,17-18 (= Luca 6,43) dagli Gnostici ad Agostino," *Aug.* 16 (1976) 271-90.

Further literature** on the Sermon on the Mount at Matt. 5-7 above, pp. 209-211.

Text

15 Beware of the false prophets who come to you in sheep's clothing but inwardly are ravenous wolves.

16 You will recognize them by their fruit! Or do you gather grapes from thorn bushes or figs from thistles?

17 Thus every good tree brings useful fruit, but the bad tree brings bad fruit.

18 A good tree cannot bring bad fruit, and a bad tree cannot bring useful fruit.

19 Every tree which does not bring useful fruit is cut down and thrown into the fire.

20 Therefore: You will recognize them by their fruit!

21 Not everyone who says to me "Lord, Lord!" will enter the kingdom of heaven but only the one who does the will of my Father in the heavens!

22 Many will say to me on that day: "Lord, Lord! Did we not prophesy in your name and cast out demons in your name and do many mighty deeds in your name?"

23 And then I will confess to them: "I have never known you! Go away from me, you who do what is against the law."

Analysis

1. *Structure.* The most important question for the interpretation is that of the connection of the two main sections vv. 15-20 and vv. 21-23. It seems to be loose in form. Verses 16-20 are unified. Verses 21-23 are different in form and content.

Verses 16-20 are tightly composed. Verse 16a is repeated in v. 20 (inclusion). The saying of the tree (v. 17) with its negative variation in v. 18, both in beautiful parallelism, is in the center. But between center and the frame there is in each case another little sentence: the rhetorical question of v. 16b and the threat, v. 19, that every bad tree will be thrown into the fire. Verses 16-20 are a ring composition. The introductory verse 15 is not a part of it.

Verse 21 is an unexpected introductory thematic statement, again with initial parallelism. It is bracketed with vv. 16-20 and vv. 22f. by ποιέω. It contains the transition to the eschatological perspective which was imaged before only in v. 19. It is emphasized in vv. 22-23. The future tenses—made definite by ἐν ἐκείνῃ τῇ ἡμέρᾳ—are eschatological, different from vv. 16-20. The parenesis becomes a prediction; Jesus becomes the judge. Thus vv. 16-23 are neither in form nor in the temporal perspective a unified pericope. Nevertheless, the connective words are striking (ποιέω, double κύριε vv. 21-23, and the stem προφητεύ-). All these connections were created by the evangelist in order to relate vv. 22-23 to vv. 15-21. Matthew has related these disparate pieces with each other and in this way produced a unified pericope. Its structure is to be described as follows: (1) The introductory v. 15 names the situation (false prophets). (2) The "rule for the distinction of the spirits"[1] vv. 16-20 and (3) the principle for entering into the kingdom of heaven v. 21 follow. (4) Only vv. 22-23 turn back to the prophets, unfold the principle of v. 21 in application to them, and form a bracket with v. 15.

2. *Redaction and sources.* Matthew combines two Q pieces from the Sermon on the Plain (Luke 6:43-45,46) with another Q piece (Luke 13:26f.). The Matthean redaction is intensive.

a. *Verses 15-20.* Verse 15 is completely Matthean, partly formulated in biblical language.[2] The frame, vv. 16a/20, is altered in formulation by Matthew.[3] Verse 19 is a passage from the baptismal sermon of John (Matt. 3:10), repeated by Matthew. Verses 16b-18 only partly agree with the Q pericope of the tree with the fruit and its application to the speaking of a person (Luke 6:43-45), which in the Sermon on the Plain came after the saying of the log and the splinter. The final verse 45 did not fit into the Matthean plan and therefore was omitted. Matthew will adduce this pericope once again more completely in 12:33-35. Almost all the remaining alterations are due to him. He is responsible for the front position of v. 16b = Luke 44b; thus the reader was enabled to relate "thorns" and "thistles" immediately to false prophets. The partial substitution of the adjectives καλός/σαπρός by ἀγαθός/πονηρός is probably due to him.[4] Perhaps he replaced βάτος with τρίβολος[5] and duplicated the Lukan verse 43. Everything else is uncertain.[6]

b. The Matthean thematic statement *v. 21* is the result of a redactional, new formulation of Q = Luke 6:46.[7]

c. It is difficult to make unambiguous judgments on *vv. 22-23*, since Luke also intervened greatly in the text.[8] Linguistically, there are few unambiguous Mattheisms.[9]

---

[1]Marguerat, *Jugement* 189.

[2]On the linguistic character cf. introduction 3.2. The following are Matthean: προσέχω (ἀπό), ὅστις, ἔνδυμα, πρόβατον; on ψευδοπροφήτης cf. 24:11. The image of the wolf and the sheep is modeled in the O T (Isa. 11:6; 65:25; Sir. 13:17), in Q (Matt. 10:16!), and in Greek (Aesop's fable of the wolf and lamb). The phrase λύκοι ἅρπαγες also is found in the O T (e.g., Gen. 49:27) and in Greek writings (G. Bornkamm, "λύκος," *TDNT* IV 308-11). The designation of false teachers as "wolves" is an early Christian stereotype, cf. below n. 26. Only the illustration of the wolves in sheep's clothing, a serendipitous new creation of Matthew which has become proverbial, is original.

[3]On inclusion as a Matthean technique of style, cf. introduction p. 40. Ἐπιγινώσκω instead of γινώσκω may be Matthean, cf. 11:27; 17:12; on ἄρα (γε) (v. 20) cf. introduction 3.2. The plural καρποί is Matthean.

[4]Cf. introduction 3.2 s.v. ἀγαθός, πονηρός.

[5]Τρίβολος next to ἀκάνθη Gen. 3:18; Hos. 10:8. Matthew likes LXX language.

[6]On the duplication cf. 7:13f. and introduction p. 39f. on the Matthean preference for parallelisms, ibid. 3.1. Matthew might have created the rhetorical question v. 16b, introduced with μήτι, when he rearranged v. 16b, cf. 12:23. Likewise οὕτως (cf. introduction 3.2), v. 17a, is probably a transition created by Matthew. On οὐ δύναται cf. 5:14.

[7]With Schulz, *Q* 427; Schürmann, *Lukasevangelium* I 381; Polag, *Fragmenta* 38; Schneider* 10-14, against Hahn, *The Titles of Jesus in Christology* (New York: World, 1969), 90 and 123, n. 158 (abbreviated in English). Cf. introduction 3.2 on πᾶς ὁ with participle, εἰσέρχομαι, βασιλεία, θέλημα, πατήρ (μου) and ἀλλά (?). The parallelism and the association with 5:20 also are Matthean.

[8]Cf. Hoffmann* 199-205.

[9]Linguistically, οὐδέποτε, perhaps ἐκβάλλω (cf. introduction 3.2) and ὁμολογέω (cf. 14:7) fit the redaction; πολλοί (7:13), προφητεύω (7:15), and the double κύριε (7:21) might be occasioned by the context.

Perhaps in v. 22 Matthew wanted to produce a similarity to Jer. 34:15 LXX; certainly he intensified in v. 23 the reminder of Ps. 6:9.[10] It is extremely difficult to say whether in v. 22 the Matthean version (prophesy, cast out demons, do mighty deeds) or the Lukan version (eat, drink, teach) is more original. Because the Matthean text reflects clearly the situation of the community,[11] one probably has to decide against him. The total result shows that Matthew has redacted the section very determinedly and incisively, as is rarely his manner elsewhere.

3. *Origin.* Statements are difficult for all three pieces of the tradition. With the first piece of tradition, the difficulty is its generality,[12] the second its brevity, the third the difficulty of restoring its wording. The discussion hardly contributes to the understanding of Matthean interpretation.

Interpretation

The intensive Matthean redaction, it seems to me, is understandable only if the confrontation with false prophets was a real problem in his community.[13] Who were those people?

In the second half of the 1st century and in the 2nd century the problem of the ambiguity of prophecy emerged frequently. First John (2:18-27; 4:1-6), the Gospel of Mark (9:38-40; 13:5f,21-23), the Pastoral Epistles (Tit. 1:10-16, especially v. 12), the Lukan writings (Acts 20:29f.), the Apocalypse (2:20), 2 Peter (2:1), the Didache (11:3 = 12:5), the Shepherd of Hermas (Man. 11) and the Montanists all testify to this. The ambiguity of the Spirit seems to be the problem of any charismatic movement, especially in the second and in later generations. That makes the definite identification of our false prophets difficult. The palette of proposals is therefore rich: Zealots,[14] Pharisees,[15] Essenes,[16] strict Jewish Christians,[17] Paulinists.[18] The proposal of G. Barth to see in the

---

[10]Probably Luke intensified the reminiscence of Ps. 6:9 LXX at the beginning (ἀπόστητε, πάντες) and Matthew at the end of the quotation (οἱ ἐργαζόμενοι τὴν ἀνομίαν).

[11]The counter-thesis would have to be that Luke transferred the logion into the situation of the earthly Jesus.

[12]Luke 6:45c could be a fixed phrase (cf. *T. Naph.* 2:6) and as such added secondarily. Then one cannot say whether the fruit or that which comes out of the heart referred originally to words (so Sir. 27:6 LXX; Luke 6:43-45c, Q; Matt. 12:33-35; cf. James 3:12) or to deeds (so our text in the Matthean redaction). Cf. the different possibilities of interpretation of the saying Mark 7:15, which is just as open, in Mark 7:21f; Matt. 15:19.

[13]Strecker, *Weg* 137f. n. 4 wants to understand 15-20 as a "nonspecific" warning against false prophecy; 21-23 refers "unspecifically to the community."

[14]Schlatter 252-54; Cathenet* 303f. for Jesus.

[15]Hill* 343-48: Pharisees invade the community from the outside. He points to the similar polemic in Matt. 23:25,27f. and to 12:33-35. The difficulty consists in the fact that in 21-23 the false prophets are certainly Christians so that Hill must separate these verses from 15-20 and relate them to ordinary charismatics.

[16]C. Daniel, "Faux Prophetes, Surnom des Esséniens dans le Sermon sur la Montagne," *RevQ* 7 (1969) 45-79.

[17]Guelich** 393, without reasons.

[18]J. Weiss, *Earliest Christianity* (New York: Harper & Row, 1959), vol. 2, 753, in combination with 5:17-19; Betz* 28. But a particular anti-Pauline point does not appear in our text.

false prophets Hellenistic antinomians enjoys the most agreement today.[19]

The text gives no more precise information. Matthew does not accuse the false prophets of heretical *teaching,* although there may have been such, but only bad fruit and (v. 23) ἀνομία. From this information one *can* conclude that they advocated libertine or antinomian slogans so that they represented some form of vulgar Paulinism. But it is also conceivable that they simply did not satisfy the strict standards of the Matthean interpretation of the will of God, i.e., were "imperfect." Matthew in any case does not accuse them of *teaching* ἀνομία. The Matthean community itself was strongly influenced by prophetism and possessed in Q a strongly prophetic tradition (cf. 5:12; 23:34,37). The Didache and 10:40-42 show that Matthean communities had visits from wandering prophets. Also ἔρχονται πρὸς ὑμᾶς (v. 15) is best explained by such visits. The reminiscence of the "strange exorcist" of Mark 9:38-40 also could be helpful because Matthew omits this little Markan story and renders in reverse form its theme that all those who are not against Jesus are for him (12:30, almost immediately before his second version of the text of the tree and the fruit, 12:33-35). This shows a reserve toward free charismatics, with whom Mark took a more open stance. Thus the assumption is perhaps not completely amiss that the false prophets might have been in some way "partisans of Mark."[20]

Finally, from 24:9-12[21] we learn that the false prophets, who will mislead many to lawlessness and lovelessness, are a phenomenon of the end-time. It seems probable to me that Matthew saw his own present—according to 24:14 the time of the Gentile mission—as this end-time.[22] The experience of false prophecy and the conviction that he was living in the end-time immediately before the judgment belong together for him.[23]

7:15

The warning against pseudoprophets begins without preparation. The community obviously knows who is meant. The external and the internal are in disharmony. The sheep's clothing in which they camouflage themselves is probably not the typical garment of the prophets,[24] but a metaphor: since

---

[19]"Matthew's Understanding of the Law," 159-164, previous to him similarly Bacon, *Studies* 348; in agreement: Hummel, *Auseinandersetzung* 64f.; Cothenet* 299-305.

[20]D. Marguerat, in oral communication.

[21]This text is the most important parallel to Matt. 7:15-23. Common key words: ὄνομα, πολλοί, ψευδοπροφῆται, ἀνομία.

[22]Against Schweizer 118f., who considers the time of persecutions (10:17-22) as the present, but the time of the false prophets (24:10-12) as the future, and thinks that 7:15-23 is a "proleptic" appearance of the eschatological future. I advocate the thesis that 10:17-22 is past and 24:10-12, the time of the Gentile mission, is present for the Matthean community, cf. the interpretation of 24:10-12.

[23]In distinction from Matt. 7:15-23, the warning against pseudoprophets appears in *Did.* 16 in a clearly eschatological context which is introduced by γρηγορεῖτε. In *Did.* 16:3f., Matt. 24:10-12 *and* Matt. 7:15-23 are taken up. The author of the Didache recognizes that the two passages belong together, but interprets them of the "last days."

[24]This interpretation, which was often represented in the early church, was recently again advocated by Böcher, with reference to 2 Kings 2:13; Hebr. 11:37; *I Clem* 17:1. Against this it must be argued (1) the typical prophet's garment is not a sheepskin but a pelt, be it from sheep, goats, or camels, and (2) that all passages mentioned use the word μηλωτή.

peaceful and defenseless sheep are the classical opposite to rapacious wolves,[25] their dressing in sheep's clothing means that they pretend to be peaceful and defenseless. The "ravenous" wolves who, according to widespread early Christian conviction, were false teachers,[26] were most likely commonly thought to destroy the community. Naturally it might be tempting to think that they were money-grabbers, in view of *Did.* 11:6.[27] But this would trivialize the danger which threatens the community from these people.

7:16a

Matthew gives the community a rule according to which they can recognize these apparently harmless prophets: by their fruit. "Fruit" is a metaphor which is common everywhere, but especially in the Old Testament, which may denote on the one hand the consequences of deeds,[28] on the other hand, the deed itself (as "fruit" of people).[29] In our passage, not the consequences of the activity of the false prophets in the congregations, but their deeds are meant. The preunderstanding of the readers according to 3:8,10, the stereotypical connection with the key words ποιέω[30] and πονηρός and ἀγαθός in vv. 17 and 18, as well as the Matthean understanding of the word καρπός in general (cf. especially 21:41,43) speak in favor of this view. Interpretation in terms of words, i.e., the teaching of the false prophets, is a reading of 12:33-35 into our context and is excluded by 7:21,23. The signs by which the false prophets are to be recognized are their works.[31] Ἐπιγνώσεσθε is meant gnomically, as an imperative and future, in any case not eschatologically.[32] Here and now the congregation can and should be concerned about the discerning of the spirits.

7:16b

A rhetorical question from Q makes the criterion intelligible. One does not gather grapes and figs from thorn and thistle bushes (widespread in Israel and sometimes tall). In the context, the question has the rhetorical function of

---

[25]Cf. above n. 2. Thus the reference also is not that "sheep" in Old Testament, Jewish, and Christian texts is frequently a metaphor for the people or the community so that the wolves had tried to assimilate themselves to the community sheep.

[26]Acts 20:29; *Did.* 16:3; Ign. *Phld.* 2:2; *2 Clem.* 5:2f., after Matt. 10:16. Already in the Old Testament, wolves stand alongside prophets: Ezek. 22:27f.; Zeph. 3:3f.

[27]"If he demands money, he is a false prophet."

[28]F. Hauck, "καρπός κτλ." *TDNT* III 614.

[29]E.g., Prov. 10:16 (of the godless); James 3:17 (of wisdom); Matt. 3:8.

[30]Ποιέω is to be preferred also in v. 18 on the basis of the weight of the manuscripts.

[31]Already Justin, *Apol.* 1.16.13 interprets it of works. Therefore Matthew also postponed the reference to that "which the mouth speaks" (Luke 6:45Q), which does *not* fit here, to 12:34 (see above, analysis a).

[32]*Pace* Guelich** 395. It would be illogical to speak of the future knowing of the fruit (v. 20), after the tree has already been burned in v. 19. The recognizing belongs together with the imperative προσέχετε.

moving the pseudoprophets close to the thorns and thistles and thus to devaluate them. In addition, it prepares for v. 17 (οὕτως).

7:17-18

Matthew repeats clearly the following parable of the tree and the fruit[33] in order to heighten the rhetorical effect. While it is a pure parable in the Sayings Source, Matthew suggests a metaphorical understanding: "Good" and "bad" clearly are ethically colored expressions,[34] so that the mention of the "bad" fruit is striking[35] and makes the reader think right away of deeds of people.

7:19-20

In v. 19, the metaphor is shifted. The trees which do not bring good fruit are burned. The false prophets face God's annihilating judgment. Matthew formulates it with the words of John the Baptist of 3:10 and thus emphasizes once more that the proclamation of judgment by Jesus and by John are the same.[36] With the repeated admonition to test the wolves in sheep's clothing by their works, the evangelist rounds off the first part of the text.

7:21

Verse 21 brings a new beginning. The statement that each person is judged on the basis of his or her works (v. 19) leads to a polemical statement of principle: not everyone who says "Lord, Lord!" will enter into the kingdom of heaven. This statement of principle applies not only to the false prophets. In v. 21 the perspective is broadened.[37] But now the final judgment is spoken of directly. Jesus speaks here as the judge of the world. The doubled κύριε is especially expressive and imploring.[38] "Lord" is in Matthew the address of the disciples, not of outsiders, to Jesus, but especially the address to the world judge, the Son of man.[39] Thus Matthew is thinking of the community. Not all its members will enter the kingdom of heaven. The address to the judge of the world as "Lord" is theologically correct; but nothing is decided by the correct address. As a

---

[33]There do not seem to be any direct Jewish parallels. Sir. 27:6 (the fruit prospers, depending on the care of a tree; application: thought and will of the human being), *Prov. Aesopi* 51P (in *BAGD* s.v. καρπός: the fruit is ἔλεγχος of the nature of a tree), and the Greek proverb, below n. 71, come close. Ign. *Eph.* 14:2 is influenced by Matthew.

[34]G. Harder, "πονηρός κτλ.," *TDNT* VI 550; 552; 553.

[35]Πονηρός is referred to a thing in Matthew only in our passage, otherwise always to people (demons, the devil); or the concept is an ethical abstract.

[36]Cf. above on 3:2 and 4:17; and on 13:30 and 23:33.

[37]So already Calvin I 241. Counter-theses above nn. 13 (Strecker) and 15 (Hill).

[38]Doubling is widespread in Semitic and Greek thinking, cf. Schwyzer II 60; Betz* 6 n. 24; and above at 5:33-37 n. 44.

[39]Of the 80 Matthean occurrences of κύριος, 18 are found in 24:42-25:46, among these 7 in the form of address (25:11 with duplication). The judge of the world who is addressed as κύριος is the Son of man of whose parousia 24:29-44 speaks (cf. 25:31 and Kingsbury, *Matthew* 104f.).

redactional logion of "entering into the kingdom of heaven," v. 21 recalls 5:20 where the community was confronted with the demand for higher righteousness. This is what Matthew is thinking of when he speaks of the "doing of the will of my Father" as a condition for salvation.

Is this works-righteousness? The question is to be asked still more urgently than at 5:20, because it becomes clear here that there is no certainty of salvation for the community. Although the Sermon on the Mount as a whole is for Matthew demand and not promise of salvation, he knows of grace. In our verse it is indicated by the little word πατήρ: It is the Father of the judge of the world to whom the community may say "our Father" (6:9). To do his will is not only something for which they have to be concerned but also something for which they may pray (6:10). Verse 21 also points back to the Lord's Prayer. The knowing of the will of the Father means for Matthew encouragement and aid for acting but not the certainty of entering into the kingdom of heaven.

7:22-23

The false prophets who are to be burned in the judgment like unfruitful trees are, as in later statements, the Pharisees and scribes, with whom the relationship between inside and outside is not in order,[40] a horrifying negative example which is to rattle the community. Verses 22-23 turn back to them. In retrospect, it becomes significant that Matthew had not spoken of an excommunication of the pseudoprophets in vv. 15-20 (cf. 7:1f.). This is in agreement with his understanding of community. The community is not to anticipate the divine judgment and not to separate the weeds from the wheat (13:36-43, cf. 22:11-14). Therefore, Matthew restricts himself to giving his community a "rule of recognition" and the admonition to keep to the way of righteousness. The judgment on the false prophets will be executed by the judge of the world himself. And just this is described now in vv. 22f. On that great day of judgment, many—the word recalls the broad way of 7:13—will appeal to their having prophesied in Jesus' name.[41] Many have done miracles in Jesus' name. The combination of prophecy and miracles is familiar to us not only from the Jewish tradition;[42] everywhere in early Christianity miracles stand in the service of proclamation and are signs of the coming of the kingdom of God. Matthew, who understands the disciples on the basis of the Old Testament prophets (5:12; 23:34) and for whom miracles are a part of the proclamation (10:1,7f.; 22:20-24; 17:19f.), does not turn against prophecy and miracles.[43] The judge of the world holds against the charismatics only that they do not satisfy the criterion of the works. Solemnly he testifies to them—ὁμολογέω is an

---

[40]Verse 15! Cf. the passages mentioned in n. 15.

[41]Bengel adds to ἐπροφητεύσαμεν a supplement to colleagues: "Adde: commentarios et observationes exegeticas ad libros et loca V. et N.T. scripsimus" (Add: We have written commentaries and exegetical observations on books and passages of the Old and New Testaments). Can the perfect be maintained at the last judgment?

[42]M. Hengel, *The Charismatic Leader and His Followers* (New York: Crossroad, 1981), 20-24 gives material for zealot prophets. Compare also *b. Yebam.* 112b - Str-B II 627 (Hanina ben Dosa).

[43]Cf. especially Schweizer, *Gesetz* 53-60, 65-69.

expression of legal language and stresses the irrevocability of the testimony
—that they do not belong to him. It is not a rabbinical formula of banishment
that stands behind οὐδέποτε ἔγνων;[44] rather, the judge of the world denies
fellowship with these charismatics.[45] In the final judgment, only the one with
whom the Son of man will then have fellowship will be saved (10:32f.; 25:11),
and that on the basis of his or her works (cf. 25:31-46).

Matthew designates the criterion which will be decisive in the judgment
as ἀνομία. Because the pseudoprophets belong into the end-time (24:10-12),
one may think of the idea that, according to Jewish and Christian conviction,
lawlessness will get the upper hand in the end-time.[46] As to content, lawlessness
has to be understood on the basis of the Matthean understanding of the law.
"Law" is the Old Testament will of God which Jesus has established by deed
and word, i.e., the generally valid Old Testament law which has its apex in the
love commandment. Therefore, Matthew interprets in 24:12 the fullness of
lawlessness as the growing cold of love. At the same time, he makes clear that
God's will is the Old Testament will of God. Therefore the judge of the world
speaks with the words of Ps. 66:9, just as Jesus speaks in the parallel passage
13:41 with the words of Zeph. 1:3. At the same time the biblical word imposes
on the saying of the judge of the world final authority. It is the sentence of death
which will here be passed on the false prophets, as a warning for the
community.[47]

Summary and history of influence

The criterion which in the judgment determines the "truth" of prophets or the
"genuineness" of charismatics is their practice.[48] Not only the incisive
redaction but especially v. 21, which maintains this as the basic criterion, testify
how important this is for Matthew. He demands the proof by deed for Christian
faith. God alone decides its validity, not the individual or the community.

It appears that Matthew took a unique position in early Christianity with this
criterion. The history of interpretation has again and again dealt with the relationship
between Matt. 7:21 and 1 Cor. 12:3: "No one can say 'Jesus is Lord' except by the Holy
Spirit." In my opinion, here Paul does not set up a criterion for true pneumatics but
wants to emphasize against Corinthian pneumatic exclusiveness that every one who
confesses the Lord Jesus—and every Corinthian Christian does this!—has the Holy

---

[44]Pace O. Michel, "ὁμολογέω κτλ." *TDNT* V 199-220; the only example in Str-B I 469 (from the 3rd
century) does not prove the existence of such a formula.

[45]Grotius I 265: "pro meis habui" (I have had them for my own). Schlatter 261 presents examples from
everyday life; Jewish and Greek examples in Wettstein I 244f. Betz* 5 n. 15 speaks of a "formula of
denial," cf. similarly Matt. 25:11; 26:74.

[46]Cf. *Jub.* 23:19-21; *T. Ash.* 7:5; *T. Iss.* 6:1; 1 Thess. 2:3,7f.; Berger *Gesetzesauslegung* I 23.

[47]Quite differently, Minear*: According to him 7:15-20 is directed to the (leaders of the?) community,
7:21-23 to the false prophets. The destiny of the false prophets in the judgment comforts the community
(83). The catechetical material of the Sermon on the Mount, which applies to all Christians, ends at
7:14, while 7:15-27 is a second conclusion, directed to the leaders of the community (85). From where
can he see the change of the addressees?

[48]Impressively Marguerat, *Jugement* 192: "La vérité chrétienne est éthique" (Christian truth is ethics).

Spirit. The real Pauline "criterion" stands in 1 Cor. 13: Love alone remains. Even the confession of Jesus who has come in the flesh (1 John 4:2) is an alternative to Matt. 7:21-23 only if one isolates the sections against the heretics from the texts concerning love (cf., e.g., 1 John 3:10!). Matthew naturally is closest to the Didache, which originated in his area of influence: Those who do not do the truth which they teach are pseudoprophets (*Did.* 11:10). More solid criteria are found already in the Didache: A wandering prophet who stays longer than two days in a community or asks for money is a false prophet (*Did.* 11:5). A prophet who does not go to church, chatters too much, and takes money for his prophecy is a false prophet (*Herm. Man.* 11:12f.). A true prophet is the one whose prophecy proves true (Ps.-Clem. *Hom.* 2.10) or whose prophecy agrees with that of James, the brother of the Lord (Ps.-Clem. *Hom.* 11.35). The criterion of true doctrine begins to assert itself!

There are problems in the Matthean criterion of the "fruit." On the surface it would appear that this was an "easy" criterion for deciding, which could be used by anyone, not just theologians and officeholders legitimized for the administration of the true doctrine. But the history of interpretation calls attention to the fact that difficult problems are hidden behind the "easy" criterion. The text surprisingly is one of the most used texts from the Sermon on the Mount. It was used often, because it could be applied by everyone and against everyone. In other words, the history of influence[49] shows that the "simple" Matthean criterion failed as a criterion for distinguishing.

a. The conviction is generally held that the Matthean statements on false prophets have to be applied also to teachers and preachers. Thus the text refers to the heretics.[50] But to whom? The palette of possibilities reaches from the Valentinians, Marcionites, Manicheans[51] by way of Lutherans, Calvinists,[52] Catholics,[53] enthusiasts[54] to pastors with "heart of a wolf," who exercise their office not out of love for people, "but for their own . . . living, recite written and memorized sermons to the people, baptize children, and give the sacrament," and proclaim grace to all without distinction.[55] Not any think of themselves as false prophets. Augustine formulates the

---

[49]Simonetti*, to whom I owe many examples, provides information about the history of influence. Otranto* and Mees* yield little.

[50]Origen, fragment 145 = 73; Tertullian, *Praescr. Haer.* 4 = BKV I 24 655f.

[51]Cf. below nn. 65-67.

[52]Maldonat 161: "omnes haereticos" (all heretics) but especially the Calvinists: "Sumus experti: agni nati sunt (i.e., the heretics), lupi moriuntur" (We have experienced it: they [i.e., the heretics] are born as sheep but die as wolves) (164). Lapide 180f. thinks of Luther and Zwingli. From another side, the text is interpreted of Zwingli, namely, in a letter of K. Grebel to Vadian, *QGT* Schweiz I 31. As late as Lagrange (1923!) 153 Luther receives the predicate "peau de brebis" (sheep's clothing).

[53]Examples from Luther in Loewenich, *Luther* (Munich: Kaiser, 1954), 90 n. 3; for Calvin cf. *Inst.* 3,15,6.

[54]"Until recently they were called monks; now they are the Anabaptists, the new monks. In previous ages it was the Pelagians, Ishmaelites, Esauites, and Cainites. This faith has lasted since the beginning of the world; and though these Anabaptists may be on the way out, others are on their way in. In other words, monkery must remain as long as the world stands" (Luther, WA 32**, 514 = *LW* 21, 258-59). They have to appear, for Jesus has predicted them. Thus this text even deepened the confirmation of one's own self or the confirmation of the "gospel" (cf. Luther II 260).

[55]A. H. Francke, "Predigt Von den Falschen Propheten (1968)," in *Werke in Auswahl*, ed. E. Peschke (Witten: Luther-Verlag, 1969), 312-14.

problem sharply: it is a matter of distinguishing between sheep's clothing and fruits.[56] That which is sheep's clothing for one, i.e., malicious disguise of the ravenous wolves, is fruit of faith for the other. The enumeration of the individual parts of sheep's clothing is indeed impressive: abstinence, humility, simplicity, mercy, but also biblical words,[57] the willingness for Reformation,[58] the authority of Luther, and correct investiture through the authorities of the country.[59] What is a mask and what is the fruit of the gospel? Luther opines that love is the fruit of the gospel; anything else a donkey also could do.[60] In earlier writings he appeals to the fact that the churches of the Reformation are distinguished from others by their building alone on love and the word of God while the papists rely on power.[61] But this principle could not be permanently maintained.

Thus it is not astonishing that (not yet with Luther and Zwingli but) with Calvin and in post-Reformation Protestant interpretation the fruit mainly is referred to doctrine.[62] The Enlightenment and Pietism[63] returned again to the interpretation of works, which was maintained overwhelmingly both in the early church and in Catholicism. At that time the difference was felt as typically denominational, and the Catholics rightfully warned that to interpret it in regard to doctrine would mean: "doctrina ex doctrina probare" (proving doctrine by doctrine).[64] But one must say honestly that even where the fruit was not interpreted of the teaching, the distinction of true and false prophecy was according to the criterion of orthodoxy. The Matthean criterion showed itself throughout as not objectifiable and as deeply ambiguous. The history of influence leads here to critical questioning of Matthew himself.

b. Critical questioning is necessary still in another point. It is striking that the history of interpretation was preoccupied not only with the fruit but—still more intensively—also with the trees. This was occasioned by the Gnostics, who interpreted the good and the bad tree dualistically of the divine or material nature of the person, given by God,[65] and by Marcion, who concluded from the opposition of the two trees

---

[56]"Multi enim quaedam in fructibus deputant, quae ad vestitum ovium pertinent" (For many count certain things which belong to the sheep's clothing among the fruit) (**2.24[80]).

[57]Vincent of Lérins, *Commonitorium* 1.28 = *PL* 50,672f.

[58]Lapide 180 enumerates the following sheep's clothings: (1) Freedom of conscience, (2) Scripture quotations which favor heresy, (3) "reformatio morum Ecclesiae, praesertim cleri" (reformation of the mores of the church, especially of the clergy), (4) leniency and simplicity, (5) eloquence. The Reformation in the view of its opponents!

[59]Francke (above n. 55) 310f.

[60]II 245f.

[61]Ibid. 259.

[62]Calvin I 239 (not *only* behavior. Christ did not want to subject his teaching to such an unclear judgment that it would have to be read from the life of a person); Bucer 78 ("in primis doctrina" [especially doctrine]); Bullinger on 7:166; Brenz 364 (doctrine and life); Calov 245 (the doctrine because it is the specific fruit of the "doctor" [teacher]); Calixt 144 ("ipsa dogmata quae ad normam scripturarum examinata" [those dogmas which are tested according to the norm of the scriptures]).

[63]Francke (above n. 55) 315 (professors' sayings are not fruit), 322 (especially life); Bengel on the passage ("sanctitas vitae" [sanctity of life]); Wolzogen 255 (you detect a heretic by his life); Grotius I 260 ("opera iniquitatis" [works of iniquity]).

[64]Iansen 70 ("absurdum" [absurd]) with reference to the unanimous exegesis of the early church.

[65]Gospel of Thomas 45 (*NHL* 123: the treasure *in the* heart); Apocalypse of Peter 75-76 (*NHL* 342) (of the immortal soul); Tertullian, *De Anima* 21.4 (the nature of the person is not "convertibilis" [changeable] for the Valentinians).

that there were two gods who created them.[66] The Manicheans followed the Gnostic interpretation.[67] In contrast with this, the church's interpretation made the effort to harmonize Matt. 7:16-20 with freedom of will.[68] Does the text not mean that a good person necessarily and automatically brings forth good fruit, or that a bad person cannot at all become good? This thesis was again and again gainsaid by the conversion of Paul or the adultery of David.[69] The solution finally was that the person, as long as he or she has *bona voluntas* (goodwill), is the good tree.[70]

Behind these attempts is a justified discomfort which already is to be attributed to the Gnostics and particularly Marcion. The Matthean criterion of the deed seems to neglect the Christian presupposition for deeds, namely, grace, and therefore has obviously been found wanting theologically. It practically cries out for an embedding in grace if it is not to be understood simply as a platitude in the sense of the Greek proverb "ἐκ τοῦ καρποῦ τὸ δένδρον"[71] or in the sense of the sentence by Menander "οὐδεὶς πονηρὸν πρᾶγμα χρηστὸς ὢν ποιεῖ" (No one who is good does an evil deed).[72] Thus it becomes understandable why Luther interprets the good tree as faith, from which, however, all good works then subsequently originate as fruit, almost by themselves.[73] But if in this way the Matthean text is accepted into the Reformation doctrine of justification and if works are understood in the Pauline sense as the fruit of justifying faith which is given by God, then the suspicion had to arise that the Reformation is only a new edition of old heresies.

Thus the questions to be directed to Matthew are the following: (1) Are not all "ethical" criteria for the truth of the Christian faith ambiguous to begin with and therefore useless? (2) Does not the stressing of ethical criteria in the final analysis lead to the elimination of the grace of God? Both questions are theologically fundamental and cannot be answered simply with a few sentences.

On the first question, Matthew would remind us that the ethical "criterion" is not simply a general one but the norm of the commands of Jesus

---

[66]Tertullian, *Marc.* 1.2.2: The doctrine of two gods was for Marcion the consequence from that simple saying of the Lord: If the creator of the bad tree is God, "alium deum praesumpsit esse debere in partem bonae arboris (condentem) bonos fructus" (he assumed that another god must exist instead of the good tree which brings good fruit). Tertullian himself (ibid.) interprets the tree of the *mens* (understanding) or *fides* (faith).

[67]*Kephalaia* 2 (ed. H. J. Polotsky), 17,2-9; 19,21-23,4; cf. *Die Gnosis* III, ed. A. Böhlig, BAW.AC (1980), 157.

[68]The decisive point lies with the *liberum arbitrium* (free will), cf. Origen, *In Rom.* 8.11 = *PG* 14,1191: All reasonable beings have only *one* nature which is distinguished by freedom and can become either a good or a bad tree: "bona arbor dicatur, si per arbitrii potestate elegerit bona, aut mala dicatur, si elegerit mala" (it may be called a good tree if through the power of the will it has chosen good things, or it will be called bad if it has chosen evil things).

[69]Origen, *Princ.* 1.8.2 (Latin) mentions Peter and Paul; other examples are added. Very correctly Maldonat 165 remarks that then Adam, created by God as a good tree, also could not have sinned!

[70]Augustine, *De Gratia Christi* 18f.; idem, *Ench.* 15; Strabo 111; Thomas Aquinas, *Lectura* no. 661. A classical, always repeated sentence is: "Non dixit: Arbor mala non potest fieri bona" (He did not say: A bad tree cannot become good) (*Opus imperfectum* 19 = 740).

[71]E. L. v. Leutsch and G. F. Schneidewin, *Corpus Paroemiographorum Graecorum* I (Göttingen: Vandenhoeck & Ruprecht, 1839), 252.

[72]Menander, *Sententiae*, ed. S. Jaekel (Leipzig: Teubner, 1964) 615.

[73]Loewenich, *Luther* (Munich: Kaiser, 1954), 180f.

(28:20). This norm is for him a clear point of orientation for all Christians. It remains more important that Matthew does not want to render judgments with the aid of a standard, for that would mean to anticipate the judgment of God (cf. 7:1-5). In the frame of his ecclesiology of the church as a *corpus permixtum* (mixed body), it is not primarily the issue that the community with a criterion separates weeds from the wheat before the right time, but rather that the righteousness of the genuine disciples of Jesus is greater than that of the false prophets. The criterion of works is primarily a criterion of *acting*, not of *judging*. One must not change it into a criterion by which then again (problematical) theological judgments could be rendered. The issue is that one acts personally. It is in this way that the climactic sentence, 7:21, and the following double parable of the two builders of houses, 7:24-27, have to be understood. Only in this way is it maintained that the Christian faith is the practice itself and not the basis of an (ethical!) theory of practice.

On the second question, one would have to recall everything that in Matthew points to the primacy of grace: The will of God is the will of the Father. Jesus who proclaims it is present with his community until the close of the age. The proclamation of God's will is embedded into a history of God with Jesus and so with the community. Thus the doing of God's will does not eliminate the confession of Jesus as Lord but presupposes it.[74] However, it is interpreted in a specific way. For Matthew, any separation of person and work is impossible—the tree is not burned because it is bad but because it bears bad fruit. The freedom of the human will is not eliminated by God's grace but it is directed to the right way, in good Jewish manner. God's grace therefore does not consist only in his helping us out of the water (14:28-31) but more significantly in his opening up the way on which we can go. That is the issue in the Sermon on the Mount. One must permit the question whether Matthew does not take the *grace* of God seriously after all by taking seriously the person who is called by God to *acting*.[75]

3.3. Conclusion: The Two Housebuilders (7:24-27)

Literature

Jülicher, *Gleichnisreden* II 259-68.
Marguerat, *Jugement* 203-11.
Further literature** on the Sermon on the Mount at Matt. 5-7 above, pp. 209-211.

Text

24 Every one therefore who hears these words of mine and does them,
      will become similar to a prudent person
      who built his house on the rock.

---

[74]Barth, *CD* I/2, 461: Confession of obedience.

[75]Cf. my own attempt to formulate today criteria for the truth of the interpretations of biblical texts on the level of "confession" and "praxis": "Erwägungen zur sachgemässen Interpretation neutestamentlicher Texte," *EvT* 31 (1982) 493-518. It is a little piece of the history of the influence of this Matthean text.

25 And the rain fell,
   and the rivers came,
   and the winds blew,
   and they smashed against that house,
   and it did not come to ruin,
   for it was founded on the rock.
26 And everyone who hears these words of mine and does not do them,
   will become similar to a foolish person
   who built his house on sand.
27 And the rain fell,
   and the rivers came,
   and the winds blew,
   and they dashed against that house,
   and it came to ruin,
   and its ruin was great."

Analysis

1. *Structure.* The beginning with πᾶς (vv. 24,26, cf. v. 21: οὐ πᾶς) and ποιέω connects our text with the preceding pericope. Matthew formulates symmetrically; the two halves correspond almost word for word. The double parable is narrated very artfully. After the titular-style exposition, the event follows with sparse verb sentences. Matthew mentions a threefold danger: the rain, the streams, and the wind; just as briefly the attack of the elements against the house, the result, and a final conclusion are formulated. Only the final clauses of vv. 25 and 27 are not parallel; in these nonsymmetrical sentences the decisive element is told.

2. *Redaction and source.* The double parable is from Q.[1] It is difficult to decide how far the parallelism of the two halves of the parable has been strengthened by Matthew or how far Luke has varied a Semitic parallelism which was given to him.[2] The following are redactional: the insertion of τούτους after λόγους (vv. 24,26), the connecting οὖν (v. 24), the general relative clause with ὅστις (v. 24), probably the characterization of the two builders with φρόνιμος and μωρός and the future formulation ὁμοιωθήσεται.[3] That means that here also the versions of Q which were available to Matthew and Luke probably were not completely identical.

The text which was the model for Matthew put the emphasis on the foundation of the house. The floods, which arise at rainfall in the Palestinian wadis, easily carry off the sandy soil. The houses can be destroyed by cloudbursts and winds; probably mud houses are meant. On the other hand, the text which came to Luke speaks of the flood (πλήμμυρα) of a river. A house with a good foundation, which reaches through the soil down to the natural rock, resists it. Since wind and rain as destructive powers are missing, it is more likely to think of a stone house, perhaps in a city. Thus the Matthean

[1]E. Schweizer, "Zur Sondertradition der Gleichnisse bei Matthäus," in *Matthäus und seine Gemeinde* 104f. assumes cautiously that 7:24-27 could have been influenced not only by Q but also by a parallel text in a special parable source (cf. excursus on 13:24-30). Aside from the parable introduction, there is no indication for this; the unique future tense ὁμοιωθήσεται could be redactional.

[2]On the parallelism as a Matthean principle of redaction, cf. introduction 3.1.

[3]Τούτους intensifies the key word connection to 7:28, cf. 19:1; 26:1. Φρόνιμος is indeed a Matthean favorite word but is redactional only in 10:16; the word occurs 5 times in the eschatological parables 24:45-51 and 25:1-13. Μωρός also is a favorite word, occurring 3 times in 25:1-13, perhaps redactionally in 23:17,19. On οὖν, (πᾶς) ὅστις cf. introduction 3.2. Ὁμοιόω is uncertain (cf. 25:1 in the future tense). If the thesis of the Matthean parable source is correct (cf. excursus on 13:24-30), then our passage would be the only one where it is redactional.

text is not only linguistically closer to Semitic narrative style,[4] but also closer to the rural Palestinian setting in terms of the content of the illustration.

3. *Origin.* The double parable is a unit and cannot be further dissected.[5] The illustrative content speaks in favor of the Matthean version being more original. It easily could come from Jesus. In contrast to similar Jewish texts,[6] it is striking that here the subject is not the *study* and the practice of Torah, but the *hearing* and doing of the words of Jesus.[7] The catastrophe of the storm is told and stressed graphically;[8] most likely in the original parable it was not simply a test of character but the passing in the catastrophe of the last judgment. It is in harmony with this that it is a parable which tells a unique event and not, as in the Jewish parallel texts, a parable. Then the original Jesus parable stands in close proximity to the word of Jesus in Luke 12:8f., which also is formulated positively and negatively: Every one who acknowledges me (= hears and does my words), the Son of man also will acknowledge before the angels of God (= his or her "building" will stand in the judgment).

Interpretation

Matthew concludes his Sermon on the Mount—as the Sayings Source concluded the Sermon on the Plain—with a double parable. Like the end of the holiness code (Leviticus 26), Deuteronomy (30:15-20), the final redaction of 1 Enoch (*1 Enoch* 108), and the Assumption of Moses (12:10-13), the readers are once more placed before the great alternative. As in the discourse on the community (18:23-35) and in the eschatological discourse (24:45–25:46), it is an eschatological parable which puts before the readers the two possibilities.

7:24, 26

The meaning of the parable is stated in v. 24 (26): the one who does (not) hear and do the words of Jesus. In the Matthean context, ποιέω has been the key word since 7:12 and is therefore especially emphasized in contrast to hearing.

---

[4]There are no unambiguous Semitisms, but some possible ones. Among those are the brief, paratactic sentences with the verb at the beginning (vv. 25,27; Black, *Muttersprache* 63) and the conditional participle (or the conditional relative clause) Luke 6:27,49 (Matt. 7:24,26).

[5]At the suggestion of D. Flusser, *Gleichnisse* 99f., that "my words" is a supplementary alteration of "words of the law," the wish that Jesus had spoken exactly like the rabbis is the father of the thought.

[6]Closest is the parable by Elisha ben Abuyah, *'Abot RN* 24 = Str-B I 469: A person who has learned many good works and Torah is compared with the builder of a house who builds the foundation of stone and then the wall above with bricks. Thus the foundation is not dissolved when water is standing about (then comes the negative version and a second similar parable). *'Abot* 3:17 = Str-B ibid. also is comparable where the one whose doing surpasses his or her knowing is compared with a well-rooted tree with few branches which the storm cannot blow over. Interesting is further the discussion in *b. Qidd.* 40b = Str-B I 22 between Tarphon and Akiba whether study or the practice of the law is greater. It is concluded with a mediating formulation: Study leads to deed. Further examples in Wettstein I 345f. and Montefiore, *Literature* 154-201. They all compare: Study / learning / knowledge of the law, and doing / aversion to sin / fear of God. The opposition of *hearing* and doing by Jesus is just as striking as the fact that Jesus' words stand in the place where in Jewish texts the Torah occurs; cf. Braun, *Radikalismus* II 29-32.

[7]Μου is not "put in the first place for emphasis" (thus Grundmann 243, cf. Schlatter 262; correctly BDF §284).

[8]*'Abot RN* 24 (above n. 6) formulates the parable (!): "And when many waters come and remain standing on their sides, they do not dissolve them (i.e., the stones) away from their place."

452

Through τούτους, the evangelist makes clear that he is speaking of the Sermon on the Mount. Instead of the given "is similar," Matthew says "will become similar" (ὁμοιωθήσεται), cf. 25:1. Through this future tense he indicates that it is not an inner-worldly connection of acting–destiny, but that the last judgment is meant.[9] The enduring of the work of the housebuilder who has built on the rock and the catastrophe for the one who has built on sand will become clear in the last judgment,[10] which will reveal the truth of the parable.

It tells of two builders. The word "prudent" means the one who knows what the hour of judgment means.[11] The prudent person builds the house on a rocky foundation, the foolish one on sandy soil in the valley.

7:25, 27

While the "house" does not suggest any special metaphorical associations, the storm with rain showers,[12] with rising streams that suddenly and violently flood the otherwise dry valleys, and with strong winds, make the listener think of judgment.[13] The two final clauses are asymmetrical: while v. 25 at the end once more points to the anchoring of the house on the rock, v. 27 at the end indicates the catastrophe: its ruin was great. This deviation from the scheme of the first part of the parable strikes the listener: the stress lies on this final warning.

History of influence

To understand this text it is important to realize that it is a parable and not an allegory. It can here be shown quite nicely how an allegorical interpretation of the individual elements misses the scope, even can change it into its opposite. Naturally, the rock was interpreted of Christ (cf. 1 Cor. 10:4).[14] Then the text directly appealed to hold fast to the "foundation rock of the eternal word of God" (= Christ).[15] In the Reformation, even

---

[9]In the parallel James 1:22-24 ("be doers of the word") the eschatological aspect has moved to the background (only v. 25 still mentions it). Rom. 2:13 is formulated eschatologically. Cf. also John 13:17; Sir. 19:19; not eschatological: Seneca *Ep.* 75.7 ("non est beatus, qui scit . . ., sed qui facit" (not the one who knows . . . but the one who does is happy).

[10]In the church's exegesis the storm as a rule was interpreted of historical experiences, e.g., superstition, rumors, fleshly temptations (Augustine ** 2.25[87]), flatteries, desires, the power of the devil (Hilarius 6.6 = 953), demonic thoughts (Euthymius Zigabenus 275); the eschatological interpretation appears relatively seldom (e.g., in Bengel 57f.; Maldonat 169).

[11]G. Bertram, "φρήν κτλ.," *TDNT* IX 234.

[12]Βροχή is rarely used in the LXX; but there are many occurrences in the papyri (Moulton-Milligan s.v.). In modern Greek, βροχή is the common word for "rain."

[13]Cf. Ezek. 13:11-14 (Whirlwind, flooding cloudburst which destroys the walls); Isa. 28:17; Hos. 8:7 (wind and storm); Isa. 30:30; Nah. 1:3; Ezek. 38:22.

[14]Already Origen, fragment 153 = 76, and repeatedly since then. But Christ can also be the builder of the house in the interpretation of the early church; then the house is the church, the rain the heresies or, in vv. 26f., the devil, his kingdom and truth.

[15]Quotation according to Olshausen I 256. Cf. John Chrysostom 24.2 = 341: The rock is the certainty of the teaching. Especially the exegesis of the Reformers interprets in this way; cf. Calvin I 243 (to be founded in Christ); Melanchthon 165. Bullinger 79a has a noteworthy accent: The rock is "fides . . . per dilectionem operans" (faith . . . active in love). On this basis he says (78b) that true piety is "non

this text entered the antithesis between faith and works: in contrast to building on one's own piety and one's own works, only the solid building on the foundation, Christ, offers certainty.[16] Catholic exegesis rightly objected to relating this text to faith without works, since it speaks clearly and unambiguously of the "fides bonis operibus solidata" (faith made solid by good works).[17]

The text connects with 5:19. Matthew 5:17-20 had maintained the fulfilling of God's law by Jesus and demanded the praxis of the higher righteousness by the community. Everything depends on this praxis. This does not mean that Christology is dissolved in ethics, for Jesus is the one who has fulfilled law and prophets in his mission and grants the community the possibility of going the way of righteousness. This Christological basis is maintained clearly by "my words" (cf. 28:20). But Christ cannot be used as a retreat, so that he might save in an emergency even without works, and even if it is done "as through fire" (1 Cor. 3:15), but Christ opens the way into life for those who *do* righteousness; he helps those, but only those. Christ gives his grace to the doers of the word. Any ethics of intention which is not willing to be measured by its fruit comes to ruin in view of this conclusion of the Sermon on the Mount.[18] Praxis alone is important; it is the "condition nécessaire . . . du salut" (necessary condition . . . for salvation).[19] This applies to the community for whom our parable points up the basic principle of 7:32—to be a Christian means the praxis of the commands of Jesus. *In* this practice, there is the experience of grace and prayer. This is what the Sermon on the Mount proclaims from the Beatitudes to the conclusion. Standing or falling in the judgment depends on this praxis.

3.4. Conclusion of the Sermon on the Mount (7:28-29)

Text

28 And it happened, when Jesus had finished these words, that the crowds were astonished at his teaching. 29 For he taught them as one who had authority and not like their scribes.

Analysis

The conclusion, as a part of the ringlike composition around the Sermon on the Mount,[1]

---

tantum circa theoriam & cognitionem, sed etiam (!) circa practicam & actionem versari" (not only walk by theory and knowing, but also (!) by practice and action).

[16]Luther, WA 32**, 533f. = LW 21, 281-84, with a point against monasticism. For Zwingli 248, God is the foundation. G. Neumark, in the well-known hymn *LBW* 453 "If You But Trust in God to Guide You": "For those who trust God's changeless love / Build on the rock that will not move" (German: have not built on sand). This is not what the text says.

[17]Quotation in Lapide 184. Cf. also Maldonat 169: "Arenam vocat solam fidem operibus vacuam" (faith alone which is empty of works he calls sand).

[18]Here Bornhäuser** 192 and Windisch** 50f. come to agreement ("ethics of obedience").

[19]Marguerat, *Jugement* 207.

[1]Cf. above at 4:23-25.

points back to 5:1f. (ὄχλοι, διδαχή) and 4:23,25. At the same time it contains an important key word which will play a role in the following main section, namely, ἐξουσία (cf. 9:6,8; 10:1). Matthew uses Mark 1:22 literally; the Sermon on the Mount stands in the place of the healing in the synagogue, Mark 1:23-28.[2] Verse 28a shows the first occurrence of a Matthean concluding formula which will occur at the end of all discourses, with small variations (11:1; 13:53; 19:1; 26:1).[3] The evangelist in this way distinguishes the five great discourses of his Gospel from other discourses of Jesus. Luke 7:1a makes it probable that there was a similar concluding clause in the Sayings Source at this place. How far Matthew followed Q can hardly be recognized, since Luke 7:1a is completely Lukan.[4]

The uncertainty is regrettable, for the question of the source of Matthew's inspiration is of great significance. Did he follow the Q text relatively faithfully?[5] Then one cannot build theological castles on 7:28a. Or is he influenced by Old Testament formulations? Passages such as Deut. 31:1,24; 32:44-46; but also Num. 16:31 or Jer. 33:8 LXX would be possible.[6] Does he want to recall Deuteronomy deliberately and thus to characterize the Sermon on the Mount as a new law of Moses, his book as a new Pentateuch?[7] One will have to be cautious. Literal agreements are missing, although they could have been formulated easily. Only ἀναβαίνειν εἰς τὸ ὄρος (5:1) and καταβαίνειν ἀπὸ τοῦ ὄρους (8:1) recall Exodus 19 and 34. Then perhaps (!) it is not by accident that Matthew speaks emphatically and repeatedly (7:24,26,28) of the λόγοι οὗτοι of Jesus. The decalogue was so called in Exod. 20:1. But Matthew would have had to formulate a deliberate reminder of the conclusion of Deuteronomy more clearly, especially since the situation surrounding Moses before his death would correspond at most to that of Jesus in 26:1.

Interpretation

Matthew turns back to the narrative in which he has embedded the entire Sermon on the Mount.

7:28

He brings out more clearly than in 5:1 that the crowd also heard the Sermon on the Mount. It is a speech to the disciples in the sense that the life of the disciples is to shine (5:16) in the world for mission and thus to confront the nations with the commands of Jesus which apply also to them (cf. 28:20). The crowd is

---

[2]Matthew 4:24; 5:2 recalls Mark 1:28,21.

[3]Matthew 26:1 brackets with πάντας τοὺς λόγους τούτους all five discourses. Matt. 11:1 brings the instruction to the disciples (ch. 10) to a close (διατάσσων), 13:53 the parable discourse (παραβολαί).

[4]The following expressions are Lukan in 7:1: ἐπειδή, πάντα τὰ ῥήματα, εἰς τὰς ἀκοάς (cf. Acts 17:20). Πληρόω (in the meaning "conclude") could be pre-Lukan.

[5]A possibility which, strangely enough, is hardly ever considered. It would agree with Matthew's faithfulness to the tradition. Ἐγένετο ὅτε is not Matthean. Τελέω occurs only two more times in the tradition; the evangelist might have chosen the word in order to avoid the "Christological" πληρόω. Λόγοι is given from Luke 6:47 Q; therefore the reminiscence of the decalogue (cf. below) can take place with great caution.

[6]Ἐγένετο is missing in the Deuteronomy passages and in Num. 16:31. Τελέω does not occur in any passage; Deut. always formulates with συντελέω, the other passages with παύομαι. The agreement is limited essentially to λόγοι οὗτοι.

[7]So Frankemölle, *Jahwebund* 334,370; Ogawa, *Histoire* 115f.

addressed as potential disciples; the Sermon on the Mount is not a teaching for the Christians *after* the proclamation of grace but, as the salvific command of Jesus, at the same time a missionary preaching.

7:29

The people are astonished because Jesus teaches with ἐξουσία. This authority shows first of all in his teaching; it will be shown in his deeds in what follows, and in 10:1 it is transferred to the disciples. On the basis of 28:18 it is anticipation of the universal authority which is given to the one who is exalted above heaven and earth. Thus, for the believer, there shines in the Sermon on the Mount a glimpse of the glory and power of the heavenly Lord. The church's interpretation therefore has rightly recalled the sovereign "But I say to you" of the Antitheses and the Christological sentence about the "fulfillment" of law and prophets.[8] In any case, Jesus is fundamentally distinguished by his authority from "their" scribes. By the possessive pronoun, Matthew indicates that the separation between the community of Jesus and Judaism has already taken place: the scribes are on the other side. The people who are astonished stand in the middle between "their" scribes and Jesus.

CONCLUSION: CONSIDERATIONS ON THE PRAXIS OF THE SERMON ON THE MOUNT TODAY

It is unusual to comment on the present day in a scholarly commentary. But I will do it—with fear and trembling—for two reasons: (a) For the evangelist Matthew there is no understanding of the Sermon on the Mount which is separated from praxis. Hearing and doing belong together. The criterion by which to recognize true and false prophecy—also for true and false interpretation of the tradition about Jesus—for him is praxis. An interpretation which only states what was meant would contradict the total claim of the Sermon on the Mount. (b) The observations on the history of influence were intended to be examples of what determines our own dealing with the texts and what traditions of interpretation have been repressed in our own tradition. Interpretation of the Sermon on the Mount does not occur in a vacuum, where the interpreter can take his text into consideration through the magnifying glass. Therefore, reflection on one's own standpoint is necessary; it is not an addition to the interpretation but a necessary part of the interpretation itself.

The Sermon on the Mount is today especially important on two focal points:

a. *The form of the church.* Reflection on the end of the state church has become more intensive today. The discrepancy between the institution of the state church, still intact, and the quickly disintegrating financial basis and the experience that the churches actually to a great extent have become minority churches leads to the critical question of the form of the church according to the gospel. Communities and associations like monastic orders confront the church with the Matthean question of a Christian praxis of life which is different from

---

[8]Cf. John Chrysostom 25.1 = 348: Jesus refers in his words not to another (Moses), but he is himself the one who has authority and will judge.

that of the world and which might be the light which helps people to recognize and to praise the heavenly Father (5:16).[1]

The two-kingdoms doctrine, which included a renunciation of the realization of the Sermon on the Mount *in the community,* reflects—so we assumed[2]—to a high degree the (historically conditioned) decision particularly of Lutheranism that the time for the realization of the community of those who seriously want to be Christians has not yet come. That which in the 16th century was historically understandable, and which in 18th-century Pietism led not only to a renewal but also to a burden for the church, might in the 20th century be overdue for the sake of a renewal of the church. In my opinion, the church today must, for the sake of the gospel, take conscious and proper steps in the direction of a new form of the church as a minority church which it actually has become for some time without its own will. Matthew, the advocate of a minority community that walks on the way of perfection and distinguishes itself by its practice of life (Matthew 5–7) and its fellowship of forgiveness (Matthew 18) from the world, could be of great help toward this goal.

When a church, like the Catholic church of the early and high Middle Ages, preserves the perfectionist type of the interpretation of the Sermon on the Mount from the time where it was a minority church and carries it into the time when it already had become a state church, then this can work as salt in the church. The late medieval poverty movements testify to the power of this salt. If the distinction between the perfect and the "normal" Christians, between counsels and commands, were an enduring stimulus for the "normal" Christians to start out on the way of perfection and to seek *their* form of perfection, then it could become even today "productive" and helpful for a church which wants to be on the move.

But it is different with a Protestant church[3] which has de facto been for a long time a free church. If, conscious of its tradition, it preserves its own Reformation, state-church type of interpretation of the Sermon on the Mount and refuses furthermore to make the Sermon on the Mount the vision and standard for a future shape of the *church,* then it becomes saltless salt and unable to exemplify for the world today an alternative form of community. Then it gives people little cause to praise the Father in heaven (6:16) and runs the danger of losing, in the contradiction between proclamation and its own form, also the ability for credible proclamation.

Thus I believe that the impulses of the Sermon on the Mount are to be taken very seriously today as questions about the shape of the *church,* not just for the individual Christian. This pertains to areas where the church with some justification has already made strong pronouncements, as, e.g., on marriage and

---

[1]Cf. the prophetic quote from a letter of Bonhoeffer from the year 1935: "Here (i.e., in the Sermon on the Mount) is the only source of power which can blow up the whole ghost and specter . . . . The restoration of the church certainly will come from a kind of new monasticism which has in common with the old one only the uncompromising life according to the Sermon on the Mount in following Christ" (letter to K. F. Bonhoeffer, *Gesammelte Schriften* III [Munich, 1960], 25).

[2]Cf. above, pp. 221-222.

[3]As a Protestant Christian I will forgo speaking here of the Catholic church. Genuine critique is always one which pertains to the critic too.

divorce (cf. 5:27-32).[4] But among these are also areas where the church has still definite difficulties, e.g., poverty as a manifestation of the church (6:19-34),[5] waiver of law suits (7:1; 5:38), and courage to be pious (6:2-18). It is not a matter of becoming the protagonist of legal solutions but rather of seeing that the talk of "love" can also become a pretense for a "laissez faire" attitude and for the neglect of a common church form out of a falsely understood respect for the individual. Matthew, in addition to love, also considered concrete commandments and the law as indispensable.

    b. The *peace movement* as a questioning of the shape of the church.[6] Contradictory theses are maintained. For some, the Sermon on the Mount is a "government pronouncement of the politics of Jesus."[7] The *Gesellschaft für Evangelische Theologie* stated in 1981: "We reject . . . attitudes and teachings which limit the Sermon on the Mount to the private life in order to exempt political responsibility from it" and, "Because God's peace is comprehensive, the instruction of the Sermon on the Mount tends to all areas of life."[8] The peace document of the Nederlandse Hervormde Kerk stated: "The system of deterrence forces the 'demonizing' of the opponent" and can in no way be reconciled with the commandment to love the enemy.[9] On the other hand, the political relevance of the Sermon on the Mount was energetically denied, e.g., by the then chancellor of the Federal Republic of Germany, Helmut Schmidt.[10] He received exegetical support from well-known sources. The Sermon on the Mount is the end of all politics; the fourth and fifth antitheses mean "simply and clearly the resignation of any state order; and the sixth . . ., the demand of love of enemy, also can be realized only by the individual or the small group." For the Sermon on the Mount formulates the "entrance conditions stated by God"

---

[4] I am thinking here of the discussion on the divorce of pastors in various Protestant churches, which, it is hoped, is not carried on only with pastoral considerations and administrative measures.

[5] I cannot forgo the references to the prophetic word of a man who never wanted to be a prophet and of whom this was least expected: "But still it may be asked whether it would not have been an extraordinary gain to Christianity if those who are called to be its ministers—the missionaries and pastors, had followed the Lord's rules (i.e., Paul's rule on maintenance in 1 Corinthians 9) . . . . I entertain no doubt that the time will come when the world will tolerate a life of luxury among those who are charged with the cure of souls as little as it tolerates priestly government. . . . It will no longer be thought fitting, in the higher sense of the word, for anyone to preach resignation and contentment to the poor, who is well off himself, and zealously concerned for the increase of his property . . . . The Lord's injunction that the minister of the Word is to divest himself of worldly possessions will still come to be honoured in the history of his communion" (A. Harnack, *What Is Christianity?* Lecture VI [New York: Putnam, 1901], 96f.).

[6] I deliberately do not state it as a general question of the "political relevance" of the Sermon on the Mount. It seems to me there is no question of the "political relevance" of the Sermon on the Mount which is not at the same time a question of the practice and form of the church.

[7] K. Scharf, quoted according to Reuter, *Vernunft* (above, p. 209) 62.

[8] *EK* (1981) 518. In the same place is also the sentence that the responsibility of the Christians to the state has its limit "if a state is governed contrary to the elementary directions of the Sermon on the Mount."

[9] *Kirche und Kernbewaffnung*, ed. H.-U. Kirchhoff, 4th ed. (Neukirchen-Vluyn: Neukirchener, 1983), 102.

[10] H. Schmidt, "Politik und Geist," *EK* 14 (1981) 214.

for the kingdom of God, which "means the end of history as it can be fashioned by human beings and thus is the end of all human politics."[11]

The contrasts are irreconcilable. Therefore I will attempt to formulate some perspectives which result for me from the Matthean Sermon on the Mount. First some exegetical reminders:

1. *Jesus'* ethics is one of contrast, formulated on the basis of the coming of the kingdom of God, which is different from the world. To live on the basis of this ethics means to display in the world a sign of the—wholly other—kingdom of God.

2. Jesus' ethics of the kingdom of God does not mean that the world can be left to itself but involves a fundamental questioning of the world.

3. Because *Matthew* was aware of this wider horizon, he has unfolded his Sermon on the Mount not merely as an "internal" discipleship ethics of the community, which outsiders would not have to be concerned with.

4. Proclamation according to Matthew takes place primarily by the fact that the church practices the ethics of the Sermon on the Mount (cf. 5:16).

5. The individual commandments of the Sermon on the Mount do not pertain only to "internal issues" of the Christian community but tend—clearly most of all in the fourth to sixth antitheses and in Matt. 6:19-34—to an actively lived relationship of the community to the world.

The history of influence of the Sermon on the Mount in the churches of the Reformation and of the Anabaptists demonstrated two very different models of how this relationship to the world could be lived. Both had their weaknesses. The Anabaptist churches were inclined, for the sake of the purity of the gospel, to limit the Sermon on the Mount to the Christian's inner realm and to leave secular responsibility to others. The distinction of the Reformation between Christians and humans in the world exhibited the danger that the Christian in the world could only internalize the contrast commandments of the Sermon on the Mount. But communities and churches are called by the Sermon on the Mount to demonstrate in *all* secular realms obedience to the will of the Father. In distinction from the Anabaptist churches of the 16th and 17th centuries, they (still!) have this opportunity in the political realm.

If the church today, in certain aspects of the world, e.g., in politics, would abandon the duty to actualize the will of the Father and to practice the entrance conditions into the kingdom of God which are valid for the whole world, then it would become unfaithful to its commission of proclamation. It would no longer be the church. But the question of *how* this can be done in the political realm remains open. The church is not alone responsible for its commission, but only in shared responsibility and in rational communication with non-Christians. Action, which occurs *directly* out of obedience of the Christian *community* toward the entrance commandments of the kingdom of God, and a policy of peace, for which *Christians and non-Christians together* are rationally responsible, have a different character. Both are necessary, because the kingdom of God concerns the entire world. Political action which is executed with others will be more rational and will agree with the will of the

---

[11]M. Hengel, "Das Ende aller Politik," *EK* 14 (1981) 686-90; idem, "Die Stadt auf dem Berge," ibid. 15 (1982) 19-22. Quotations from 689,688.

Father in a more indirect way than the direct obedience which the church can render and permit in its own body.[12]

Matthew—without wanting to do so—has given a very noteworthy indication for a possible translation of the Sermon on the Mount into rationally communicable action, namely, the Golden Rule (7:12). He projects it on the basis of love as an incipient, initiative Christian approach to the neighbor. It contains a premise, namely, that the fellow human being is not a monster but is able to respond to love. To that extent, even the Golden Rule cannot be argued in a purely rational way but rests on presuppositions which correspond to faith. Nevertheless, its wide dissemination shows that there is a high measure of rationality and a great potential for consensus in it. Thus it could be a guideline for political action of Christians in communication with non-Christians. Only when somebody like a "Manichean" is of the opinion that the enemy is a complete embodiment of evil is it senseless "to carry the Golden Rule out of the houses of God into the parliaments and foreign offices."[13] But such Manicheism as a principal thesis can just as little be proved as the Christian counter-thesis and, in addition, it leads into complete hopelessness. Against any kind of Manicheism, even that of a political nature, the Christian faith, because of Jesus, is called to opposition.

---

[12]Thus I believe that there must be two kinds of signs of the kingdom of God, namely, direct signs of peace and renunciation of the use of power, which churches and Christians cannot demand of others but can only practice themselves. In what follows however, I am not speaking of this particular matter but of the fact that the church and Christians have to attempt to fashion politics in a mediated way, in rational argumentation, but under conscious reference to premises and guidelines of the Sermon on the Mount.

[13]Lapide, *Bergpredigt* (above p. 209) 144.

DATE DUE

NOV 28 2017

Printed in the United States
1464200002B/57-94

9 780800 696009